AFTER ALL IS SAID AND DONE

First published in the United States of America in 2022
by Anthology Editions

87 Guernsey Street
Brooklyn, NY 11222

anthologyeditions.com

Editors: Mark Iosifescu, Mark A. Rodriguez
Creative Directors: Jesse Pollock, Keith Abrahamsson
Art Directors: Bryan Cipolla, Bailey Elder, Mark A. Rodriguez
Cover Design: Bryan Cipolla
Interior Design: Bryan Cipolla, Bailey Elder
Design Assistance: Alex Tults

First Edition
Third Printing
ARC 082
Printed in China

ISBN: 978-1-944860-50-9
Library of Congress Control Number: 2021949834

AFTER ALL IS SAID AND DONE

TAPING THE GRATEFUL DEAD 1965–1995

Mark A. Rodriguez

Table of Contents

Photo: Jeff McLane

Foreword

By Trixie Garcia

Dennis McNally, the accomplished author, band biographer and former publicist for the Grateful Dead, introduced me to Mark Rodriguez sometime around 2014. At that time, Mark was interested in learning more about my dad's explorations of digital art. No one had ever expressed interest in that very specific niche of Jerry's life. He died in 1995, very early in the history of digital art software—I recall our family spending hours exploring MacPaint and printing out our images when that was still just a two-tone experience. Every advancement of the technology warranted an exploration, which was always lots of fun. Jerry had a special interest in technology that I can only guess stemmed from his appreciation of science fiction; he had grown up with the kind of fifties futurism that predicted such advancements would change all our lives.

Mark's angle was different, and the fact that his research evolved into artwork does not surprise me. A couple of years after we met, he shared with me an image of a large collection of Grateful Dead tapes in an art gallery. It was awesome: the fine art world is so finicky sometimes, and the Grateful Dead were so misunderstood by the mainstream, that seeing that wall of tapes in a gallery made my life experience shine in a new light.

This specific body of work from Mark's studio practice memorialized the natural inclination of Grateful Dead fans to collect, which was what led the band to make the groundbreaking decision to allow taping at shows. This accommodation nurtured the development of another facet of the phenomenon that emerged from the Grateful Dead ecosystem, one that made the mystique around the band that much more magical. This was what became known as the tapers section, which developed its own culture of recording and trading cassettes of live shows. Now, even though we've gone mostly digital with our music sharing, this phenomenon has persisted, even grown: nostalgia for the physical item has increased, and here we are in 2021 experiencing a resurgence in actual vinyl record sales. Mark's "Dead Tape Collector" project plays to this aspect of the culture surrounding the Grateful Dead, but he also twists it ever so slightly to make an earnest proposition for fine art.

The tapers section of the audience was its own world. It had its own rules, and I remember it was certainly no place for kids. The tapers had always been different from the rest of the fans in that they had taken on the responsibility of capturing the magic of the Grateful Dead concert experience; they were almost members of the crew, with everything meticulously laid out and guarded while the rest of the fans were off socializing and dancing. They had their own style, typically wearing a tidier outfit than the other fans, as there was no room for fringe or ornamentation while going about the serious business of capturing the exquisitely unexplainable—not to mention the strong correlation of obsessive personality types being drawn to this chance for control within the concert. When the high-end recording equipment became accessible enough, the crowds of tapers grew. Eventually, the issue of audience members vying for the sonic sweet spot right by the sound booth became so undeniable that the tapers section was born: an invisible rope was ceremoniously draped around the section, and our guardians of sound were knighted.

The band decided that they'd relinquish ownership of the music once it was played, and the tapers were given the privilege of recording as long as they did so in the spirit of sharing. They would set up in their predetermined area, the lights would dim, and they'd lean into their little box of knobs and perform their own micro–sound checks. Throughout the show, their little lights would dance in unison with the rest of the fans, and then, the treasure captured, everything would get packed squarely away and carried off to join the taped documents of previous journeys. Over time, tape exchange became cultural currency. A social currency, even, for those types who didn't otherwise experience the social scene at the show because they were too busy watching the lights. Tapes would be shared and worlds would be expanded, minds opened by the gift of revelry captured on a cassette.

These recordings are all slightly different, just like the individuals who arranged the microphones, inserted the tapes, and pressed the buttons. And the actual shows were just the beginning: Imagine all the journeys traveled and locales this mass of tapes must have reached, from Mount Everest to New Guinea, probably even the moon by now, and soon Mars! The life of these recordings has just begun!

The participatory and communal nature of the Grateful Dead scene has unspooled a magnetic ribbon of memories across the globe and beyond. This book is a piece of that story.

Photos: Gillian Garcia

Hippie Eternal Return: Mark A. Rodriguez, Conceptual Art, and the Recorded Legacy of the Grateful Dead

By Stuart Krimko

Like many Deadheads confronting the passage of time and the inevitable material reckonings that accompany it, I recently found myself in the basement of my childhood home on Long Island, wondering what to do with the tapes that had been stored there since I moved to Los Angeles over a decade ago. The house had been sold, and decisions had to be made about whether to keep or discard its contents. A Deadhead in this position, by now an archetypal one, is faced with many questions: about nostalgia and age, about consumer culture and the ambivalent (some would say contradictory) attitude the Dead universe takes toward it, about community and self-identity, and about the anthropological fact of bootleg tape as charged object. Tapes are records of the rituals and texts of the faith, and as we collect them, they—as well as the collections in which they are housed—become the palimpsests in which we can trace the band's progress as well as our own.

There is no way to answer such questions or address their complexity in any less multifaceted means than art; certainly this is the conclusion Mark A. Rodriguez reaches with the provocative series of sculptures that began in 2010, as initial steps toward the making of his piece *1st Gen*, and is still going strong, eleven years and nine *Gens* (and counting) later. Through sheer persistence and long-term vision, the project has the potential to unfold as a lifelong performative artwork. Already it has taken its place within not only the constellation of truly remarkable Grateful Dead–related artifacts but a lineage of conceptualism that is a defining feature of postwar American art. What makes the sculptures special, though, are their democratic appeal and their tangibility: every one of the thousands of tapes that make up any given *Gen*, with its unique J-card and its eccentricities of notation and Dead iconography, is a small objet d'art.

A little over a decade ago, Rodriguez was struck with the Sisyphean impulse, perhaps familiar to many completist Deadheads, to acquire a copy of a tape of every show the band ever played. Since he was already an active artist with a conceptual bent, it wouldn't be a mischaracterization to call the idea itself an artistic proposition. As a Deadhead himself, however, he was also interested in listening to the music—though it wasn't just that. Nor was it merely the desire to revel in the compelling visual and physical qualities of such a vast collection, which he sensed would appeal also to audiences that weren't necessarily into the Dead. The current broader renaissance of all things Dead-related—initiated by the fiftieth-anniversary extravaganzas of the "Fare Thee Well" shows in Santa Clara and Chicago, as well as the subsequent formation of Dead and Company—had only just begun to flower at the moment when Rodriguez publicly exhibited *1st Gen* (2010–2016), the initial work in the series, in a 2016 exhibition at the gallery Park View in Los Angeles.

For Rodriguez there was a deeper motivation, an intuition that the labor required to amass such a collection, with all the social interactions and ad hoc cultural research it would entail, might shed light on his work as a whole, and constitute a contribution to a legacy of artmaking in which objects, even utterly transfixing ones, aren't the whole story. The author of sly, prickly, and impeccably constructed objects that look like preexisting readymades but are produced entirely in his studio—artworks that resemble things like tables, painted roadside attraction boards, business trophies, napkin holders, and jigsaw puzzles, to name a few—Rodriguez is interested in both beauty and provocation, but also in a rare kind of attention to detail that is oriented toward objects without being totally subsumed by them.

When Rodriguez began the series, there was no denying that cassette tapes had become obsolete; even Dead tapes, those

formerly prized objects traded among fervent and committed aficionados, had been replaced by digital files easily streamed or downloaded from the vast online library known as the Internet Archive. Craigslist and other message boards were filled with offers from Deadheads looking to purge their collections and find welcoming new homes for them. If the tapes once carried a kind of cultural capital within the scene, they had largely been reduced to relics, even as interest in the band began to grow among younger listeners. Making something out of or with them would restore value to them. But what kind of value? As the tapes became components in an artwork that was designed to be seen rather than heard, the music on them would become more or less inaccessible, except perhaps to a collector—an *art* collector rather than a *tape* collector—who acquired it.

Part of the origin of the *Gen* works, therefore, was a reckoning with the notion that the value of the tapes would necessarily be transformed. As art, they would become commodified, to use something of a dirty word, in a different system of ideas and a different system of monetary exchange. It's long been assumed that the "contract" between the Grateful Dead and Deadheads stipulated that the tapes could be freely made and traded as long as the tapers and traders weren't reaping economic benefit from them. But there is no official version of this document; inasmuch as it exists, it's based on comments made in passing by those associated with the band. In truth, the agreement was a tacit one, a cultural convention that lent its own character to the Dead's contrarian mystique and the intimate bond between the musicians and their fans. With all this in mind, Rodriguez authored a situation in which his *Gen* sculptures honor the history and contrarian ethos of the Dead precisely by defying the intentions that led to the creation and circulation of the tapes in the first place—breaking the "contract," in other words, and inserting the tapes into an economic system for which they weren't originally designed.

Debates surrounding authorship, appropriation, and proprietary value make frequent appearances in conversations about modern and contemporary art. Kerfuffles (and lawsuits) related to the artist Richard Prince's use of data and information "borrowed" from Instagram users represent one recent example; so do sculptures by Rodriguez's Los Angeles–based colleague Kathryn Andrews, which incorporate both certified film props and highly finished forms in arrangements that make it hard to tell what is made by the artist and what she acquires from prop houses and Hollywood auctions. While the *Gen* works are, at least nominally, connected to this lineage of readymades and covert conceptual "borrowings," such considerations don't reveal the true value of Rodriguez's Grateful Dead–related works. Nor, frankly, does too tight a focus on the inarguable historiographic interest that the *Gen* sculptures hold, as records of a remarkable body of American popular music and the community that has grown up around it.

Rather, it is only when fully considering the laborious processes the project has necessitated that the full scope of the artist's intentions becomes clear. *1st Gen*, for instance, consists of 2,976 tapes sourced from Deadheads throughout the country and installed in custom mahogany cases, made by Rodriguez himself, that are designed to resemble the Napa brand wine crates often used by cassette collectors to house and display their treasures. It is not, strictly speaking, an exhaustive collection of every show the band played, but it comes close; in so doing, it sets up an expectation that it never quite fulfills.

Another part of *1st Gen*'s raison d'être is the role it played in seeding *2nd Gen* (2010–2017), a collection of 3,000 tapes that is made up largely of copies dubbed from the "originals" that constitute *1st Gen*. In other words, before releasing *1st Gen* into the world, Rodriguez spent almost a year copying approximately 1,700 tapes (that's 106 days' worth of music) to ensure that he would have the foundation for the next work in the series, which also included an additional 24 tapes he had found in the meantime. Tapes continued (and continue) to make their way to his studio; *3rd Gen* (2010–2018) consists of doubles that were left over after assembling *1st Gen* and *2nd Gen*, dubs of a large part from *2nd Gen*, and 16 tapes that hadn't appeared in either of the two previous editions, so that there now totaled 3,016.

As the project has evolved, there are many cases in which, to account for a given show, Rodriguez has had the option of using *either* a dubbed tape or an "original" made by someone else, sometime in the past. Dubbing tapes requires him to produce his own J-cards, an activity that has forced him to absorb, replicate, and reinvent the indelible syntax of Dead iconography,

1st Gen, 2010–2016, 2976 Dead tapes, 95 1/4 x 118 1/2 x 3 1/2 inches.

2nd Gen, 2010–2017, 3000 Dead tapes, 92 x 122 x 3 1/2 inches.

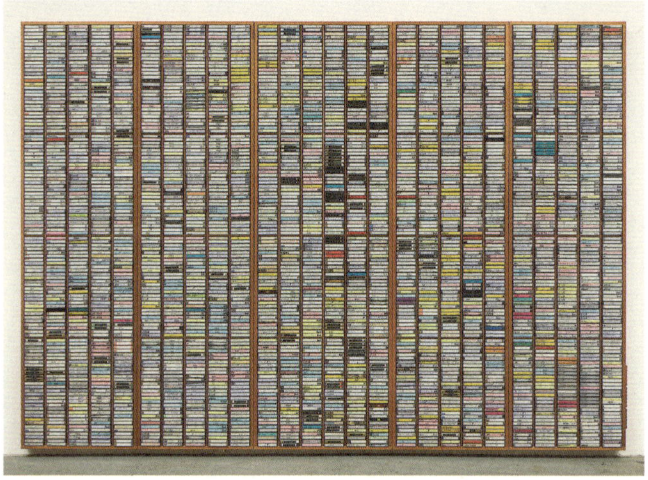

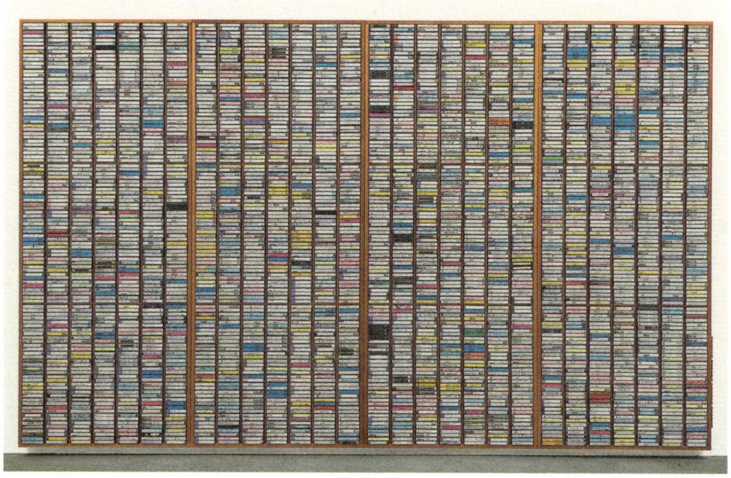

Left to right:
3rd Gen, 2010–2018, 3016 Dead tapes, 89 1/16 x 129 1/2 x 3 1/2 inches
4th Gen, 2010–2018, 3024 Dead tapes, 82 7/8 x 137 3/4 x 3 1/2 inches
5th Gen, 2010–2019, 3038 Dead tapes, 75 5/16 x 153 3/8 x 3 1/2 inches
6th Gen, 2010–2019, 3050 Dead tapes, 93 3/8 x 124 7/8 x 3 1/2 inches
7th Gen, 2010–2020, 3060 Dead tapes, 80 1/2 x 148 1/8 x 3 1/2 inches
8th Gen, 2010–2020, 3068 Dead tapes, 90 3/8 x 128 1/2 x 3 1/2 inches

Photos: Jeff McLane

setlist notation, and personal eccentricity that, as the photographs and scans in this book attest to, gives Dead tapes and the *Gen* project a large measure of their character. An indispensable part of this story are the designers and printers of premade J-cards—they include outfits like Smoking Gun Tape Covers, Tapestry Tape Covers, John Battaglia, T.A.B., Marbelizin' Mike a.k.a. Marbleized Mike, Wiseguy Productions, Dan Shramo and Purple Moon Design, among countless other underground one-time contributors to the genre—whose products were distributed in parking lots and flea markets and advertised in the back of magazines like *Relix*, *Unbroken Chain*, and *Dupree's Diamond News*.

This process proceeds apace; at the time of this writing, *9th Gen*, with 3,072 tapes, is nearing completion, and *10th Gen*, with 3,074, is underway. As each *Gen* leads to the next, and as he continues to receive collections of tapes from Deadheads offloading collections, Rodriguez affords himself more and more opportunities to juxtapose his own J-cards with those of the many other Heads who came before him. This freedom in turn allows him to choreograph particular color combinations and textural compositions for which the raw materials are fragments of Dead symbols, DIY graphic design, and variations in handwriting. Moves of this sort have visual impacts large and small—the final look of each *Gen* depends, after all, on the outward-facing spines of the tapes' J-cards—so this interplay becomes an area of the project in which Rodriguez can exert a kind of painterly control over its aesthetic presentation. Setting their myriad sociocultural references and pleasures aside, these works are purely visual tours de force in which teeming arrays of tape spines give off a prismatic, pixelated glow that calls to mind, if unexpectedly, the stained glass windows designed by the German artists Gerhard Richter and Sigmar Polke, projects which were inaugurated between 2007 and 2010 at the Cologne Cathedral and the Grossmünster church in Zurich, respectively.

As tempting as it can be to lose oneself in the physical manifestation of Rodriguez's project, its conceptual and, most of all, performative ramifications account for its true sublimity. Especially as it enters its second decade as a prominent fixture of his daily life, the sustained effort needed to acquire and catalog existing tapes, dub and make J-cards for new ones (including the many hours of mostly pleasurable but at times maddening listening that this entails), and construct the meticulous mahogany cabinets that hold them is truly devotional in nature. This is a concentrated expression of what Rodriguez himself has called the "hippie eternal return": a compulsion to return to the source—the source of the music, the source of art, the source of inspiration—over and over again, and to

cultivate a structure in which this perennial longing can be acknowledged throughout life's seasons. It is a compulsion that lies at the core of what has made Dead shows such enduring sites of communion for half a century, and that continues to make the recordings of them such vital, living documents. The whole point of listening to a tape from 1968 or 1978 or 1988 is to go back to the present as it arose during that show, at that moment, and to immerse yourself in the unrepeatable energy that filled the room. Similarly, each stage of Rodriguez's process brings together disparate moments in time: the moments of the shows themselves, the moments in the past when the tapes entered their original collections, whether by trade or other means, and the moments he spends copying them and repurposing them for an entirely new context. That he will likely never be able to put together an entirely "complete" collection that documents every show the Dead played is beside the point—or rather is the point, inasmuch as it's the attempt in the face of the impossible that really matters.

Here, then, is conceptual art at its most personal. Rodriguez gets his hands dirty, so to speak, with material that matters deeply to him, dedicating a large portion of his waking hours and his studio space to grappling with the expansive archival system he has created. He is fueled by his love of the music and the scene, as well as his commitment to a way of artmaking that celebrates process and blurs the boundary between art and life. This approach doesn't always result in physical traces; such nontraditional, endurance-based practices often leave behind nothing but a few photographs or written accounts. Rodriguez, however, exemplifies a romantic tendency within this larger framework of conceptualism that does take the making of objects to be of prime importance, one in which artists are willing to subsume their lives in the crafting of something that completely absorbs their efforts and transcends them at the same time. The making of such objects amounts to a private performance that goes on in the studio for years. For artists who work this way, time is the primary material.

Given its inherently radical premise, it should come as no surprise that, like the *Gen* sculptures, several of the most important contributions to this lineage have connections to both California and the sixties-era counterculture. Jay DeFeo's singular painting-as-sculpture *The Rose*, made in her own apartment between 1958 and 1966, is a monumental flowering of the ideas and energies that coursed through San Francisco during the Beat years. It dominated the artist's home as it dominated her psychic life. Her colleague Bruce Conner, who made a film (an artwork in its own right) about the inadvertent "completion" of the ten-foot-tall work and the complications of removing it from her walk-up apartment (which included having to cut away an entire bay window), spoke about watching *The Rose* leave the domestic "temple" where it had been made and wondering whether "Jay was going to go out the window herself," since the work was "the only kind of identity she had with any kind of exterior reality."*

The Rose represents one extreme of the art-as-life phenomenon. The almost macabre single-mindedness of its creator illuminates Rodriguez's work by contrast, however, since his is the manifestation of a need to open himself to the world and the endless web of social connections the work generates. As it materializes, each individual *Gen* is a stop along the way, but the way itself is filled with visits to Deadheads' garages to pick up tapes, correspondence with denizens of the Dead universe inside and outside of official institutions, and participation in the ongoing act of retelling, reinterpreting, and preserving the legend of the Grateful Dead for present and future generations. The work gives as much life as it takes, something that it shares with another, less-known example of large-scale, long-term quasi-conceptual artmaking.

Jay DeFeo working on *The Rose*, then known as *Deathrose*, in 1960. Photo: Burt Glinn © Burt Glinn/Magnum Photos

* Bruce Conner in "Jay DeFeo's *The Rose*: The Enormous Painting That Was 'Almost Alive,'" available at www.sfmoma.org/watch/jay-defeos-the-rose-the-enormous-painting-that-was-almost-alive/. Accessed January 19, 2021.

Stephen Kaltenbach in his studio with *Portrait of My Father* in progress.

Stephen Kaltenbach's *Portrait of My Father* (1972–1979) is, like *The Rose*, a big painting that took a long time to make. It depicts the artist's father as he approaches death, looking beatific; his upturned face, framed by his white hair and beard, fills the roughly ten-by-fourteen-foot canvas like a landscape of overwhelming humanity. The painting's larger-than-life photorealism is offset by what seems at first to be a barely visible network of colorful patterning. Upon closer inspection, it becomes clear that this abstraction is woven throughout the entire image, making its spectral intensity all the more otherworldly. Kaltenbach approached the project not as a painter per se but as a conceptual artist attempting to work against the grain of what he understood to be his own tendencies, as well as those of the prevailing avant-gardes in New York and other international centers. Moved by key moments in his own life—his father's decline due to a series of strokes, his formative experiences with psychedelics—he decided to make a totalizing picture that was as uncool as it was spiritually heartfelt and technically ambitious. A rustic and rather primitive barn near Davis, California, would serve as the site for its creation, a decision born of necessity and one that demanded its own ways of living and seasonal schedules over the course of seven years.* The painting is a meditation on, and organic outgrowth of, life cycles of many kinds. For Kaltenbach, like Rodriguez, art serves as a medium through which to capture the passage of time and the transitions between one generation and the next.

* John Fitz Gibbon, "Art in Heaven: Son, Host, Father, Guest," in *Steven Kaltenbach: Portrait of My Father*, E. B. Crocker Art Gallery, Sacramento, California, 1979.

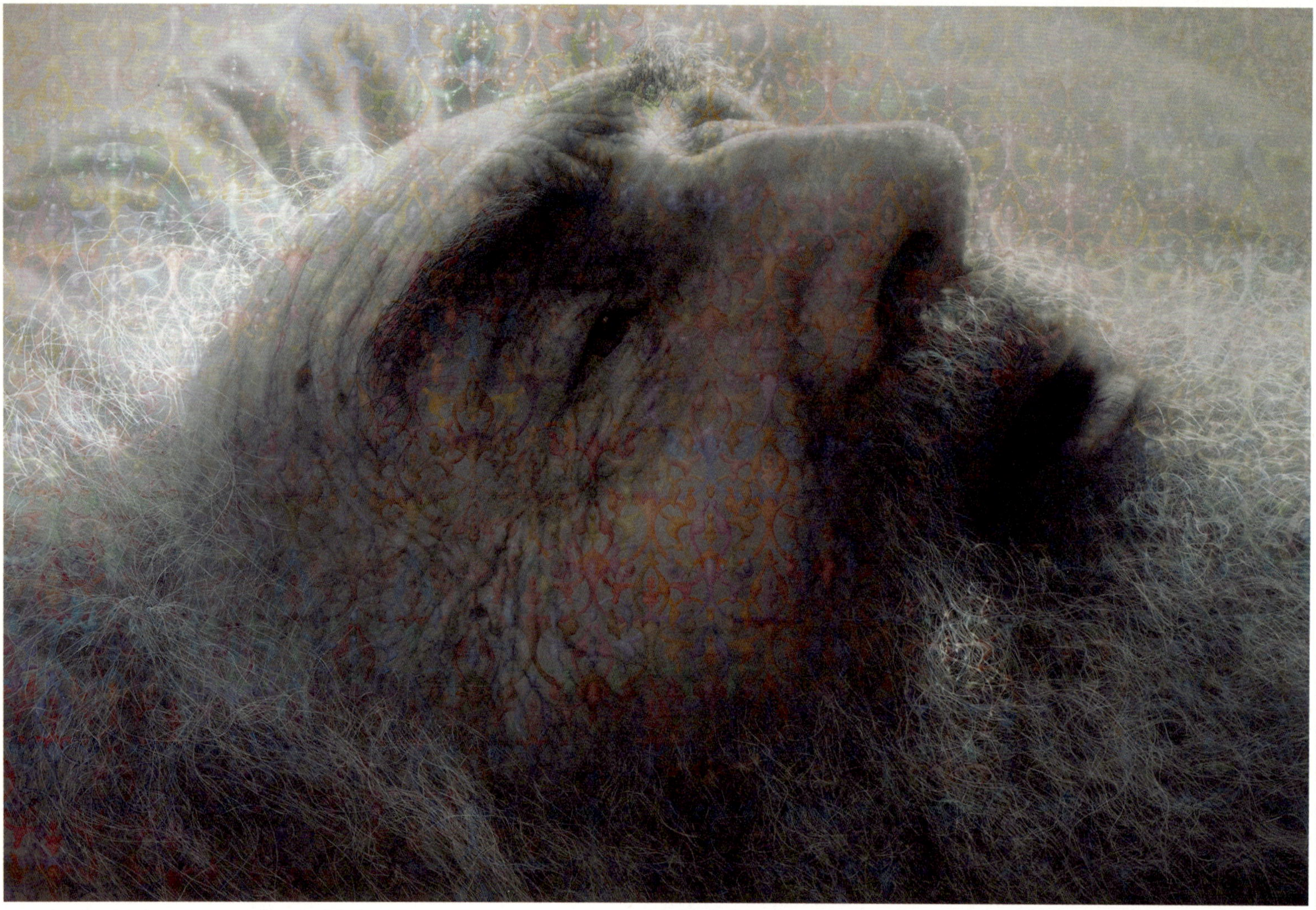

Stephen Kaltenbach, *Portrait of My Father*, 1972-1979, acrylic on canvas, 114 x 170 3/4 inches

In Rodriguez's case, of course, this is a literal proposition that lies implicit in his chosen medium: tapes degrade, tapes beget tapes, tapes are a way of extending the life of a community. But collective existence is also subject to the pressures of mortality. What the *Gen* sculptures "depict," if that word can be used, is the continuing efforts of the Grateful Dead community to remember and renew itself. As with all things related to the Dead, no such depiction would be complete without an acknowledgment, however tacit, of the pathos that accompanies all life as it unfolds. The specter of death is never too far off; the improvisatory dance of living often includes missed steps and broken ankles; saying goodbye to old friends becomes more common than saying hello to new ones. Rodriguez has addressed this condition by devising an artwork that can keep going, at least hypothetically, as long as he does. Which begs a question familiar to Deadheads, at least since Jerry Garcia died in 1995: Could it continue without him?

Perhaps it could. By design, the mission Rodriguez has set out for himself in *Gen* can never be fully completed. Paradoxically, this means that it is always successful: possibility is always there in the form of those few tapes he hasn't yet found, and in the fact that he is still receiving new "old" tapes from collectors like me who don't know what to do with them anymore. (Full disclosure: the tapes from my parents' basement made their way to Rodriguez's studio and are now sitting in cardboard boxes, patiently awaiting their rebirth as art.) Even when the originals run out, traces of the sounds that first made their way through ballrooms, concert halls, arenas, and stadiums will still be stored inside the dubbed versions that Rodriguez can reproduce ad infinitum. So it was, or is, with the Dead and their rhizomatic offshoots, which now include contributions from creative people like Rodriguez who are reinterpreting the "core texts" and the ideas and energy behind them in unexpected, unintended, and sometimes heterodox ways. Any way you look at it, there will always be a next show. And it's there that we lose ourselves, in another time's forgotten space, as past and future dissolve, once again, into the ever-present now.

TAPE COLLECTOR

Scanning the Trader Network

GRATEFUL DEAD
2-25-66
Ivar Theater
LA, CA
SOURCE
GEN:

Stealin'
Hey Little One
Hog For You
Don't Have to Ask
Cold Rain + Snow
Lied + Cheated
Viola Lee Blues
Big Boss Man
Sitting on Top
Of The World
Dancin'
Rider
Other 1
Cryptical Envelopement
Other 1
Cosmic Charlie
NFA
at Trouper's Hall
3/25/66
SET
SOUND BOARD
AUDIENCE

NUTHIN' LEFT TO DO BUT SMILE, SMILE, SMILE
7-3-66
Viola Lee
Big Boss Man
SOTOTW
Dancin
Rider
He was a Friend
3-25-66
stealin
Jam
Hey Little One
I'm a Hog for you baby
You don't have to ask
cold rain & snow
next time you see me
5-8-77 Cornell II
Stephen - NFA - Stephen
morning dew

Grateful Dead
Commons, SF State College
10-2-66
Acid test

10-2-66
Long Strange Trip
1-29-66
San Fransisco State college Acid test at the Commons
San Fransisco Sound city acid test
only Jerry & Pigpen
Grateful Dead 10-2-66/1-29-66 SF Acid Tests

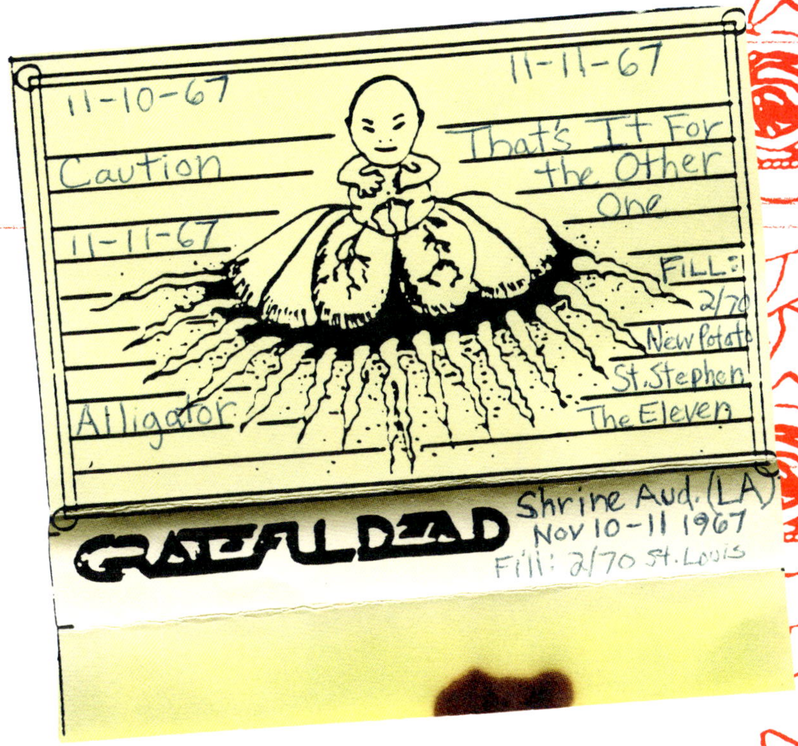
11-10-67
Caution
11-11-67
Alligator
11-11-67
That's It For the Other One
FILL: 2/70
New Potato
St. Stephen
The Eleven
GRATEFUL DEAD
Shrine Aud. (LA)
Nov 10-11 1967
Fill: 2/70 St. Louis

Eureka, CA 1·20·68
Seattle, WA 1·22·68
SOURCE
GEN.

DARK STAR
CRYPTICAL
OTHER ONE
CRYPTICAL
NEW POTATOE CABOOSE
ST. STEPHEN
THE ELEVEN
DEATH DON'T HAVE NO MERCY
ALLIGATOR
DRUMZ
CAUTION JAM
FILLMORE WEST 8-22-68

Audience
Soundboard
Radio
SB A
Sweetness Scale
1 2 3 4 5 6 7 8 9 10
Grateful Dead
FILLMORE WEST
2/28/69
A
Criptical
Drumz/OtherOne
Criptical
DarkStar
StStephen
TheEleven
SB/ A
B
TheEleven
DeathDontHNM
filler:CreamPuffWar
SomethingOnYourMind

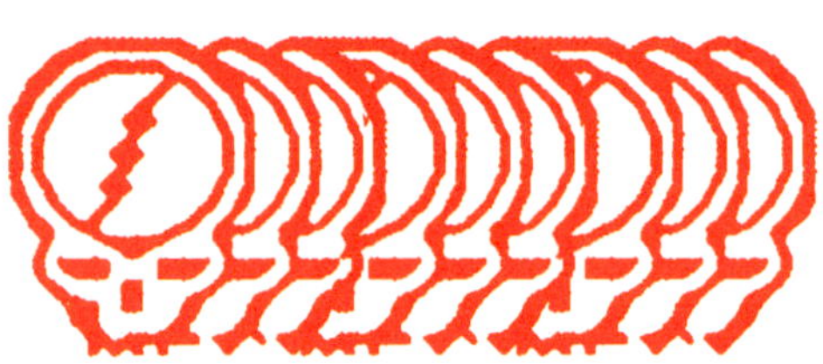

THE GRATEFUL DEAD
LOCATION Fillmore West, SF
DATE 3/1/69
SIDE A
That's It For The Other One
Crypticel Envelopment
New Potatoe Caboose
Doin' That Rag
Cosmic Charlie
SIDE B
Dupree's Diamond Blues
Mountains Of The Moon
Dark Star
St. Stephen
The Eleven
DARK STAR
CRASHES POURING ITS LIGHT INTO ASHES
TDK
3:27:69 Merced California
SA90
SA 90
TDK

GRATEFUL DEAD
Avalon Ballroom set II - 4-5-69
Crypical
Drumz
The other One
Cryptical
The Eleven
It's a Sin
Alligator
Drumz/Feedback
Feedback
Bid you Good Night

STUDENT PEACE ASSOCIATION presents the
GRATEFUL DEAD
UNIVERSITY AUDITORIUM
APRIL 11 8:00 P.M.
$2 & $3
Tickets Available:
S.U. 106, Discount Records, Mars-Hall, Mead Book Sto
Park Music, Arizona Enterprises and Rubitoms
the Grateful Dead
4/11/69
University Auditorium
University of Arizona
Tuscon, Arizona
It's a Sin
Hard to Handle
Dark Star>
St. Stephen>
The Eleven>
Turn on your Lovelight
4·11·69 dark star
dubbed by Dwight Holmes, November 15, 1997

Generation
on off Noise Reduction
Audience
Board
Radio
Grateful Dead WINTERLAND 5/3/69 A
Side A.
Criptical
Drumz
OtherI
Criptical
DoinThatRag
Me&Uncle
Side B.
SB A-
6/11/72
OSAKA
THPPFT!

Dead
W. Hollywood, FL.
5-24-69 II
Lovelight
Doin That Rag →
He was a Friend of Mine →
China Cat →
The Eleven →
Death Don't have no Mercy →
Alligator →
Drums →
St. Stephen →
FeedBack
W.B.Y.G.

Lovelight
Doin' that Rag
He was a friend of Mine
China cat
The 11
Death don't have no mercy
Alligator
Drums
St. Stephen
Feedback
Bid You Goodnight
Grateful Dead
5·24·69
SET
AUDIENCE
BOARD
DOLBY
Big Rock Pow Wow
Hollywood, FL.

Garcia's Legacy
6-14-69 Monterey CA
SBD

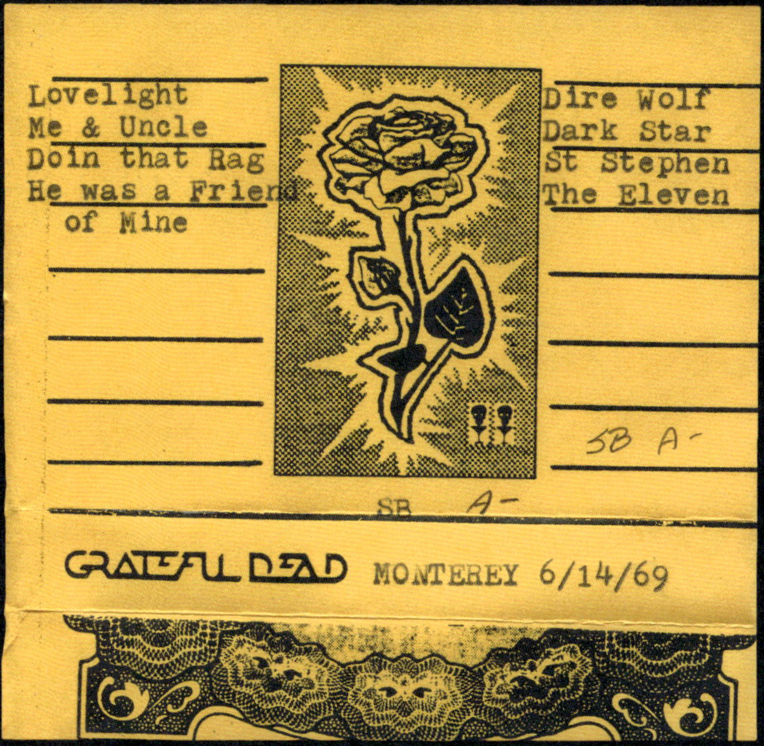
Lovelight
Me & Uncle
Doin that Rag
He was a Friend of Mine
Dire Wolf
Dark Star
St Stephen
The Eleven
SB A-
SB A-
GRATEFUL DEAD MONTEREY 6/14/69

Quality:Good/Very Good
Side A: Missing most of Dark Star,no words.
Side B Missing:Doin That Rag>China Cat>
Mama Tried>High Time,Mountains,Green Green
Grass,Slewfoot.
Side B Filler: 11/10/67 Shrine Aud.
Los Angeles,Ca

Hurts Me Too
Morning Dew
Schoolgirl*
BIODTL*
Baby Blue*
*could be from 4/6/69 Avalon Ballroom,S.F.,Ca

KNOW OUR LOVE
California
MT.SU JRY
WILL NOT FADE AWAY
9-1-69 Prairieville, LA CD New Orleans Pop Festival

AM Dew
Mama Tried
Next Time
Good Lovin
China Cat>
I Know You Rider
Dark Star>
INSPIRATION MOVE ME BRIGHTLY...
Dark Star>
Cryptical>
Drums>
Other One>
Cryptical>
Lovelight (cut)
DEAD 11/7/69
Fillmore West
San Francisco,Ca
GENERATION ___
SBD ___ AUD ___
RAD ___ DAT ___
H. CANTEY

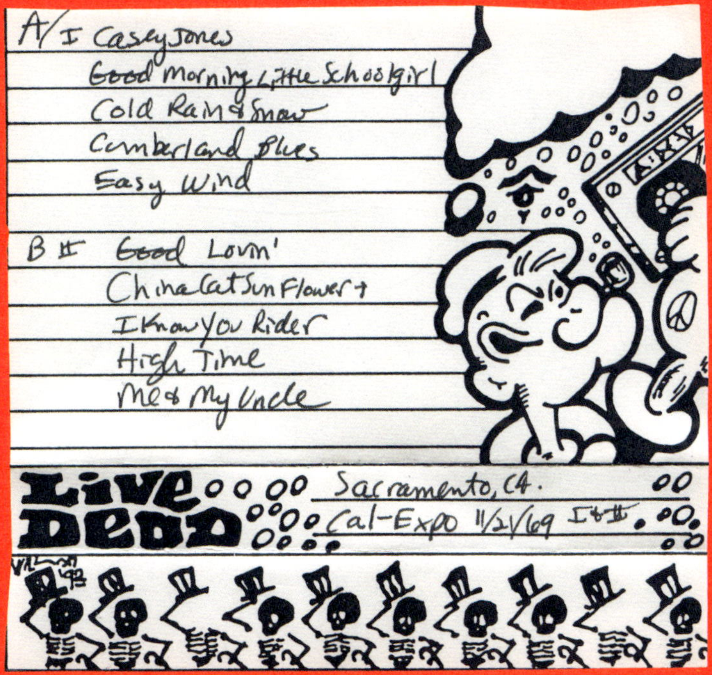
A/ I Casey Jones
Good Morning Little Schoolgirl
Cold Rain & Snow
Cumberland Blues
Easy Wind
B II Good Lovin'
China Cat Sun Flower +
I Know You Rider
High Time
Me & My Uncle
LIVE DEAD
Sacramento, CA.
Cal-Expo 11/21/69 I & II

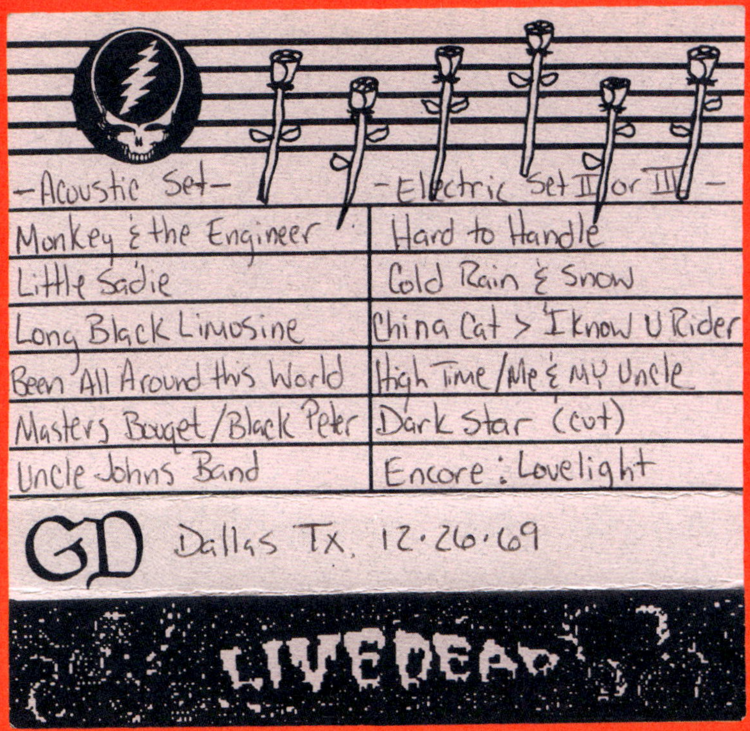
-Acoustic Set-
-Electric Set II or III-
Monkey & the Engineer
Little Sadie
Long Black Limousine
Been All Around this World
Masters Bouget / Black Peter
Uncle Johns Band
Hard to Handle
Cold Rain & Snow
China Cat > I Know U Rider
High Time / Me & My Uncle
Dark Star (cut)
Encore: Lovelight
GD Dallas Tx. 12·26·69
LIVEDEAD

GOOD LOVIN
COLD RAIN + SNOW
HARD TO HANDLE
MASON'S CHILDREN
LOVE LIGHT
THE OTHER ONE
CRYPTICAL
NEW POTATO CABOOSE
BORN CROSS EYED
ALLIGATOR
JAM
A
MIAMI POP
12/28/69
CAROUSEL BALLROOM
2/14/68
Noise Reduction
YES NO
SET...
Board... Radio... Audience...
A. Fitch 88

A
PSYCHEDELIC
BEYOND
BELIEF
B
CHINA → RIDER
ME + MY UNCLE
DIREWOLF
HARD TO HANDLE *
CASEY JONES
MASON'S CHILDREN
BLACK PETER
GOOD LOVIN *
COLD RAIN + SNOW
LOVELIGHT
KING BEE
* PIGPEN
QUESTION REALITY
The Grateful Dead comes alive
1/10/70
SHAKE YER BONES
GOLDEN HALL, COMMUNITY CONCOURSE

CHINA CAT
I KYR
ME + UNCLE
DIRE WOLF
HARD TO HANDLE
CASEY JONES
MASON'S CHILDREN
BLACK PETER
GOOD LOVIN'
DRUMS
COLD RAIN + SNOW
LOVE LITE
FILL: MONTEREY POP FESTIVAL 6.18.67
VIOLA LEE BLUES
OLD DEAD
COMMUNITY CONCOURSE
SAN DIEGO, CA
1.10.70
X Soundboard (?)
Audience
Radio
Generation
Ø Noise Reduction

TAPESTRY
Tape Covers
P.O. Box 05487
Milwaukee, Wisconsin
53205-0487
Quantity Price Postage
10 1.50 .50
40 5.00 1.00
75 7.50 1.50
150 12.50 2.50

2/14/70 Fillmore East Set 1 SBD

Casey Jones	Katie Mae
Mama Tried	Filler 10-2-80
Hard To Handle	Iko Iko
Monkey + Engineer	The Race Is On
Dark Hallow	To Lay Me Down
All Around World	Cassidy
Wake Up Lil Susie	Jack A Roe
Black Peter	On The Road Again
Uncle John	Bird song
	Ripple

Fillmore East SBD
2-14-70 Set 1

Grateful Dead

Noise Reduction: NO ***Source:*** sbd.

A	B
Cold Rain & Snow	St. Stephen>
Beat It On Down The Line	Not Fade Away
Good Lovin'	Casey Jones
Mama Tried	**fill: 4/2/73**
Black Peter	**Music Hall, Boston, MA**
Hard To Handle	Here Comes Sunshine> Space> Bobby McGee/

2/13/70 early
Fillmore East
N.Y., NY

Set #: all
90 ***min.***

master sbd. reel>DAT>Sonic Solutions workstation>
CD>DAT>Nakamichi ZX-7 3 head cass

Noise Reduction: NO ***Source:*** sbd.

A	B
Dark Star>	Lovelight
St. Stephen/>	**fill: 6/26/74**
	Civic Center, Providence, RI
	W.R.S. Prelude>
	W.R.S. Pt. 1>
	Let It Grow
/The Eleven>	

2/14/70 early
Fillmore East
N.Y., NY

Set #: all
90 ***min.***

master sbd. reel>DAT>Sonic Solutions workstation>
CD>DAT>Nakamichi ZX-7 3 head cass

SBD AUD FM GEN
Fillmore East
Casey Jones
Mama Tried
Hard To Handle
~Acoustic~
Monkey + the Engineer
Dark Hollow
All Around this World
Wake up lil Susie
Black Peter
UJB
Katie Mae
Electric
Set II
Dancin →
China Cat →
Rider
High Time
Dire Wolf
Alligator →
Drumz /
*Bears Choice!

SBD AUD FM GEN
Harper College
Binchamptonny 3.2.70 II
St. Stephen>
Cryptical>
Drumz>
Other One>
Cryptical
Cosmic Charlie
Casey Jones
Good Lovin>
Drumz>
Good Lovin
Cold Rain & Snow
It's a Man's World
Dancin in the Streets

Operator
Dancin
St. Stephen→
NFA→
Good Lovin
Drumz
Good Lovin
We Bid You Goodnite
-(B)- 9.20.70
Casey Jones
China Cat→Rider
Anderson TH 11-23-70
Mama Tried
Truckin→Drumz
Other One
U.J. Band
DEAD
Fillmore East DAT
9.18.70 · 9.20.70 · 11.23.70
Side B Dead Zone
NOISE REDUCTION YES NO Dolby "C"
BOARD RADIO AUDIENCE

GRATEFUL DEAD 9/20/70 Set I
Uncle John's Band
Deep Elem Blues
Friend Of The Devil
Big Railroad Blues
Dark Hollow
Ripple
To Lay Me Down
Truckin'
Rosalie McFall
Cumberland Blues
New Speedway Boogie
Brokedown Palace
-x-x-x- Electric -x-x-x-
Casey Jones
China Cat Sunflower->
I Know You Rider
Sitting On Top Of The World
GRATEFUL DEAD 9/20/70
Fillmore East - NYC, NY Set I
S DOW: Sun, Source: J.Anderson (517-546-5106), Comments: First set acoustic with David Grisman and David Nelson on mandolin Other artist(s): GD: NRPS

FILLMORE EAST, NEW YORK, NY, 20 SEP 1970, SET 1 1st generation soundboard
SIDE A:
Uncle John's Band
Deel Elem Blues
Friend Of The Devil
Big Railroad Blues
Dark Hollow
Ripple
To Lay Me Down
Truckin'
Rosalie McFall
entire acoustic set features David Grisman and David Nelson on mandolin
SIDE B:
Cumberland Blues
New Speedway Boogie
Brokedown Palace
(from the electric set, out of order (should be between Easy Wind and Not Fade Away, and from a higher-generation source ...)
Sugar Magnolia
Attics Of My Life
Mama Tried
NO DOLBY NOISE REDUCTION
The Grateful Dead
The Fillmore East
New York, New York
20 SEP 1970
TAPE ONE
Dubbed 20 Jan 1995
BY CARL "CARL THE DRUMMER" MINK
this label printed on recycled paper

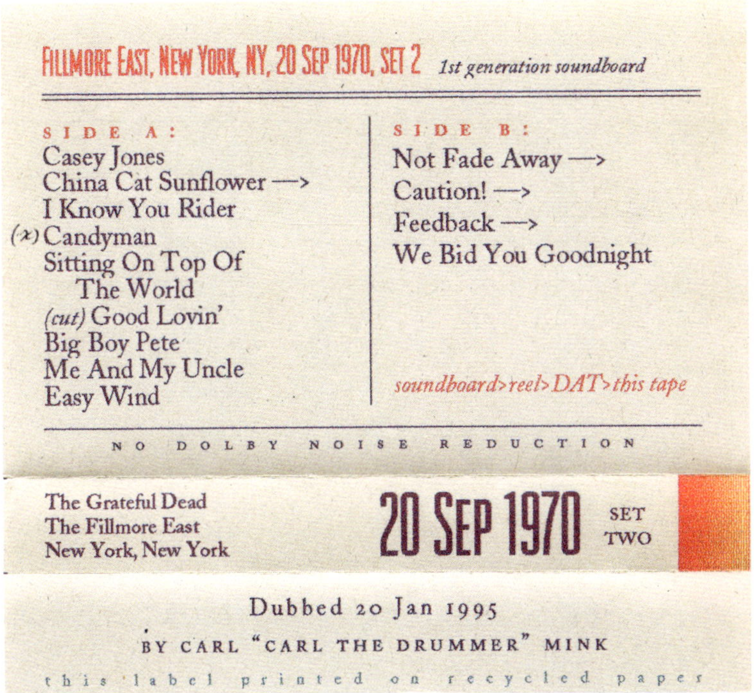
FILLMORE EAST, NEW YORK, NY, 20 SEP 1970, SET 2 1st generation soundboard
SIDE A:
Casey Jones
China Cat Sunflower —>
I Know You Rider
(x) Candyman
Sitting On Top Of The World
(cut) Good Lovin'
Big Boy Pete
Me And My Uncle
Easy Wind
SIDE B:
Not Fade Away —>
Caution! —>
Feedback —>
We Bid You Goodnight
soundboard>reel>DAT>this tape
NO DOLBY NOISE REDUCTION
The Grateful Dead
The Fillmore East
New York, New York
20 SEP 1970
SET TWO
Dubbed 20 Jan 1995
BY CARL "CARL THE DRUMMER" MINK
this label printed on recycled paper

LIVE
11/16/70 Fillmore East NYC
DEAD
source:
gen:

AND WHY DO THEY KEEP FOLLOWING ME?
Cold Rain
Mama Tried
Frozen Logger
Eazy Wind
* Til The Morning Comes
Truckin'
FOTD.
Me & My Uncle
Candy man
Big RR. Blues
Mingle wood
Black Peter
BIODTL
Morning Dew
Casey Jones
El Monte CA.
- Set I -
GD
12·26·70
THE BUS CAME BY AND I GOT ON THAT'S WHEN IT ALL BEGAN

GRATEFUL DEAD 2-19-71 I Port-chester NY
A DATE 2-19-71 I
N.R.
B DATE soundboard
N.R.
Truckin'
Loser
Cumberland
Hurts Me Too
Bertha
Playin'
Dark Hollow
Smokestack
China Cat >
Rider
GRATEFUL DEAD 2-19-71 II Port-chester NY
I NEED A MIRACLE
A DATE 2-19-71 II
N.R.
B DATE soundboard
N.R.
6SET >
JB Goode
Bird Song ✱
Easy Wind
Deal ✱
KC Jones
✱ Debut
Cryptical >
Drumz >
The Other one >
Wharf Rat
Good Lovin'

02-21-71 - 1st Set
Capital Theater-Portchester, NY
Cold Rain And Snow
Me and My Bobby Mgee
Loser
Easy Wind
Playin' in the Band
Bertha
Me and My Uncle
Ripple
Things Won't Be the Same
Sugar Magnolia
Quasar
Johnny B. Good
China Cat Sunflower
I Know You Rider
Generation: Unknown
Capital Theater-Portchester, NY
Grateful Dead
02-21-71 - 1st Set
Jonathan Harris 59 Huntington st., Newbrunswick, NJ 08901
(908)937-6649 ramrose@eden.rutgers.edu

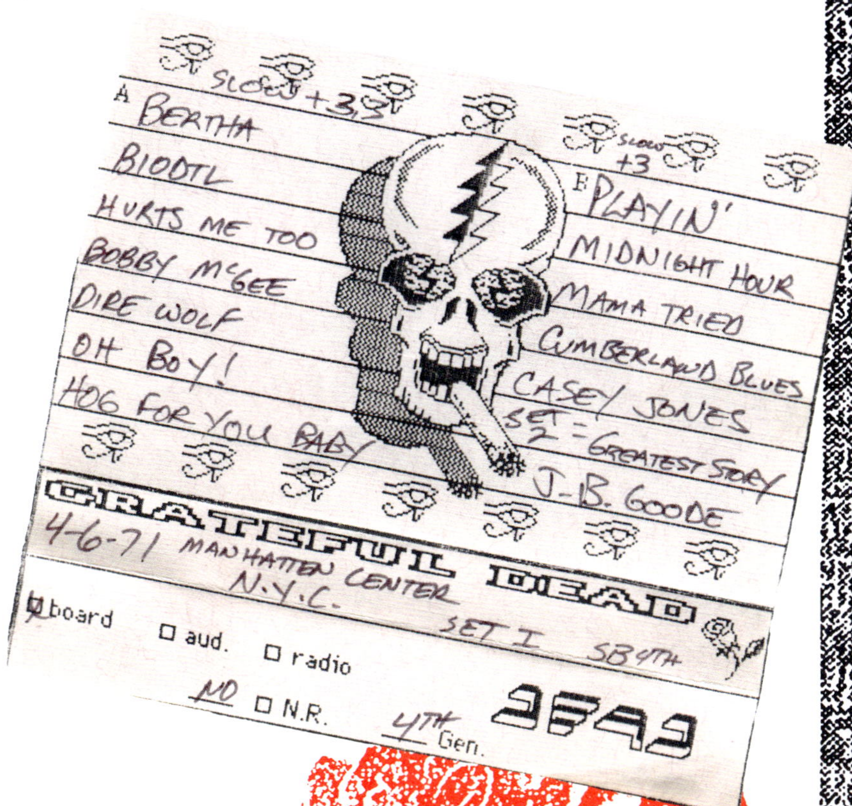
SLOW +3.5
A BERTHA
BIODTL
HURTS ME TOO
BOBBY McGEE
DIRE WOLF
OH BOY!
HOG FOR YOU BABY
SLOW +3
B PLAYIN'
MIDNIGHT HOUR
MAMA TRIED
CUMBERLAND BLUES
CASEY JONES
SET 2 = GREATEST STORY
J.B. GOODE
GRATEFUL DEAD
4-6-71 MANHATTEN CENTER
N.Y.C.
SET I SB 4TH
board
aud.
radio
NO N.R.
4TH Gen.

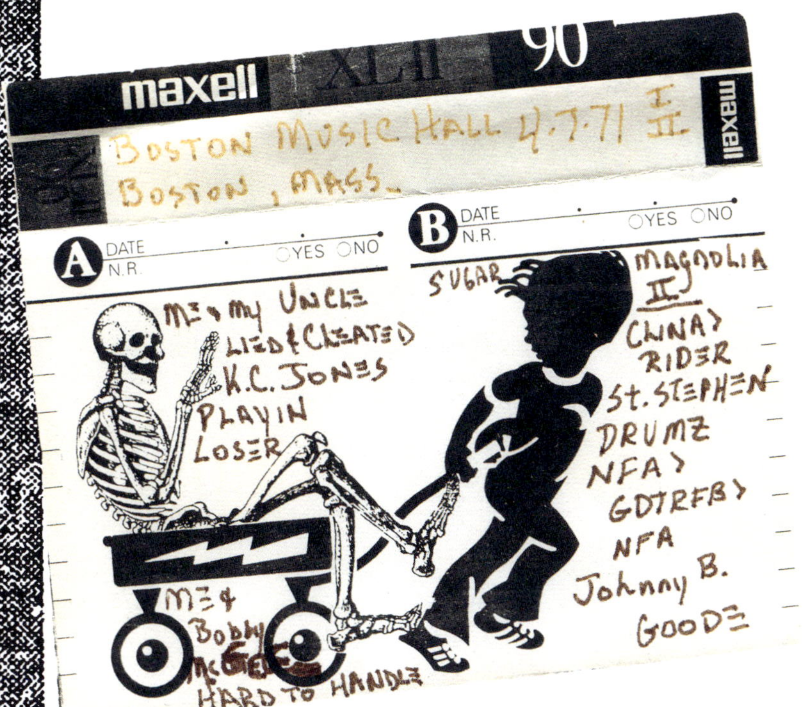
maxell
XLII
90
BOSTON MUSIC HALL 4.7.71 I II
BOSTON, MASS.
A DATE N.R. YES NO
ME & MY UNCLE
LIED & CHEATED
K.C. JONES
PLAYIN
LOSER
ME & BOBBY McGEE
HARD TO HANDLE
B DATE N.R. YES NO
SUGAR MAGNOLIA II
CHINA >
RIDER
St. STEPHEN
DRUMZ
NFA >
GDTRFB >
NFA
Johnny B. GOODE

Grateful
Dead
TRUCKIN'
BERTHA
NEXT TIME
PLAYIN'
LOSER
BEAT IT ON DOWN
2ND THAT EMOTION
SUGAR MAGNOLIA
CHINACAT
I KNOW YOU RIDER
CASEY JONES
FILLER ?
SB BOSTON MUSIC HALL
BOSTON MASS
Live Dead - 4.8.71
I Set

Grateful
Dead
DARK STAR
St. STEPHEN
NOT FADE AWAY
GOIN' DOWN THE ROAD
NOT FADE AWAY
SING ME BACK HOME
CUMBERLAND BLUES
GREATEST STORY
J. B. GOODE
GOOD LOVIN'
DRUMZ
GOOD LOVIN'
FILLER ?
SB BOSTON MUSIC HALL
BOSTON, MASS.
Live Dead - 4.8.71
II Set

A
Cold Rain & Snow
Me & My Uncle
Bertha
Me & Bobby McGee
Things Won't Be the Same
China Cat Sunflower >
I Know You Rider
Casey Jones
B
Sugar Magnolia
Second That Emotion
Truckin'
Hard to Handle
Loser
Playin' in the Band
* Deal
DEAD: State University of New York
Cortland, NY
4/18/71
Soundboard
Audience

(A) BIG BOSS MAN
LOSER
PLAYIN'
HARD TO HANDLE
DARK....
(B) ... STAR
WHARF RAT
K C JONES
SET II
SUGAR MAGNOLIA *
HURTS ME TOO *
BFODTL *
*w/ DUANE ALLMAN
Grateful Dead
4/26/71 SET I
FILLMORE EAST
SBD/5
Grateful Dead

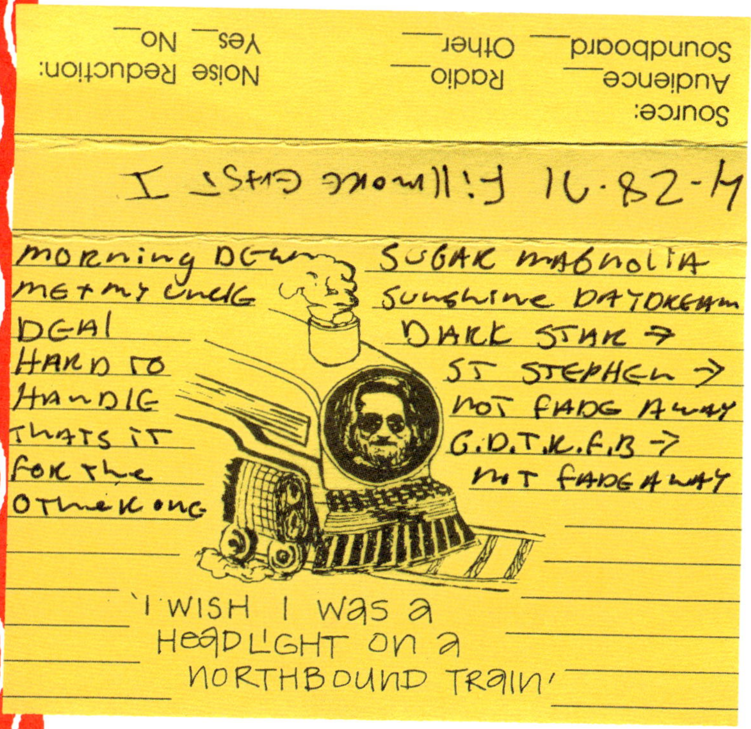
Source:
Audience___ Radio___
Soundboard___ Other___
Noise Reduction:
Yes___ No___
4-28-71 Fillmore East I
Morning Dew
Me + My Uncle
Deal
Hard To Handle
That's It For The Other One
Sugar Magnolia
Sunshine Daydream
Dark Star →
St Stephen →
Not Fade Away
G.D.T.R.F.B →
Not Fade Away
'I wish I was a headlight on a northbound train'

Fillmore East NYC 4-28-71 II SBD

Fillmore East 4/29/71
Truckin, Bertha, Hurts Me Too, Cumberland Blues, Uncle Bird Song
Playin in the Band, Loser, Dark Hollow, Hard To Handle Ripple
TAPE ONE
GRATEFUL DEAD
FILLMORE EAST

Bobby McGee
Casey Jones
Morning Dew
Minglewood
Magnolia
Black Peter
DEW
IN THE
U★S★A
Beat It On Down the Line
2nd that Emotion
Alligator
Drums
GDTRFB
Cold Rain & Snow
Fillmore East 4/29/71
TAPE TWO
GRATEFUL DEAD
FILLMORE EAST

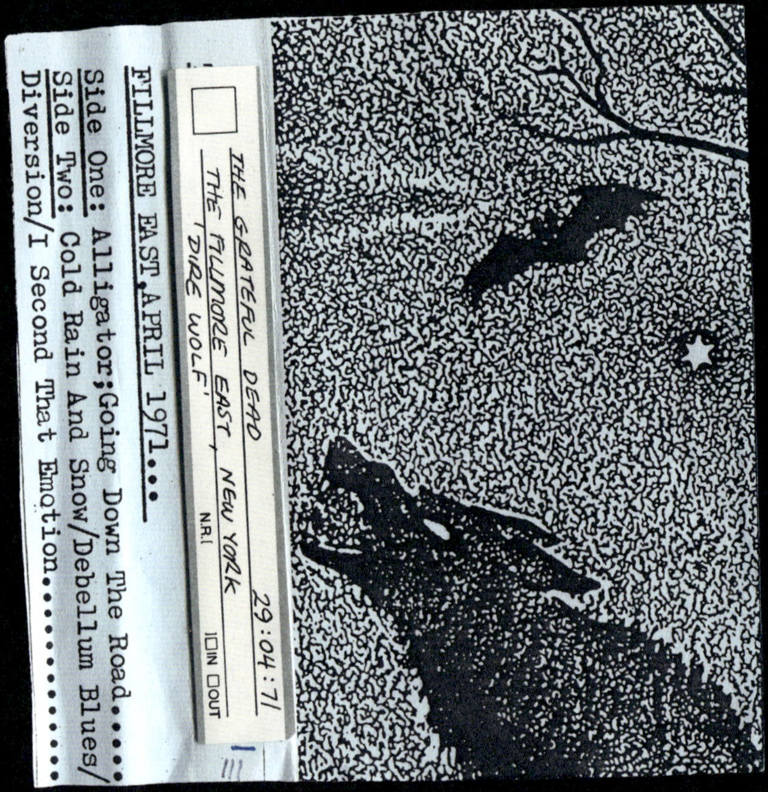
THE GRATEFUL DEAD
THE FILLMORE EAST, NEW YORK
'DIRE WOLF'
29:04:71
FILLMORE EAST,APRIL 1971...
Side One: Alligator;Going Down The Road.....
Side Two: Cold Rain And Snow/Debellum Blues/
Diversion/I Second That Emotion.........

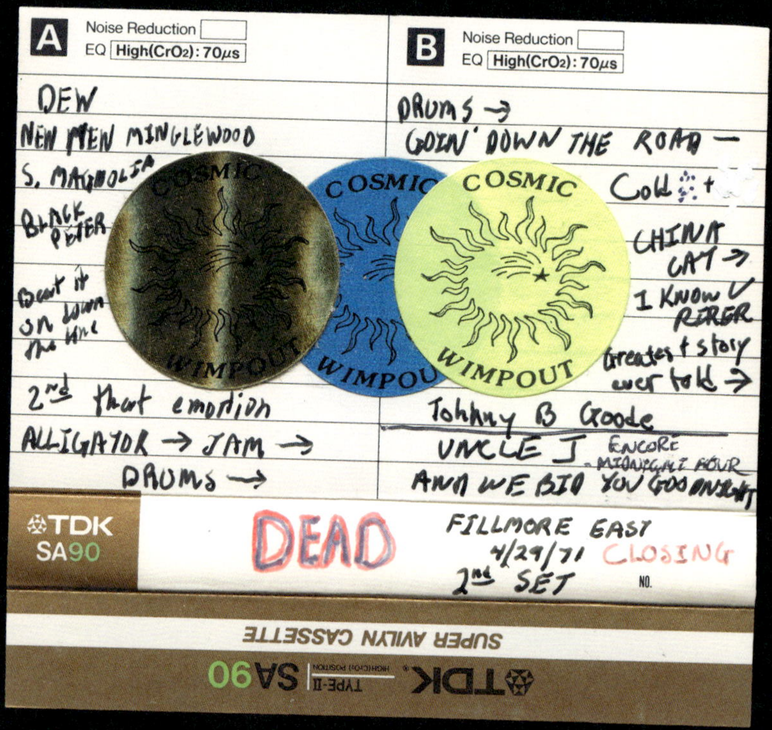
A Noise Reduction
EQ High(CrO2): 70μs
DEW
NEW NEW MINGLEWOOD
S. MAGNOLIA
BLACK PETER
Beat it on down the line
2nd that emotion
ALLIGATOR → JAM →
DRUMS →
B Noise Reduction
EQ High(CrO2): 70μs
DRUMS →
GOIN' DOWN THE ROAD —
CHINA CAT →
I KNOW RIDER
Greatest story ever told →
Johnny B Goode
UNCLE J
ENCORE MIDNIGHT HOUR
AND WE BID YOU GOODNIGHT
COSMIC WIMPOUT
COSMIC WIMPOUT
COSMIC WIMPOUT
TDK SA90
DEAD
FILLMORE EAST 4/29/71 CLOSING
2nd SET
SUPER AVILYN CASSETTE
TDK SA90

BEAT IT ON DOWN THE LINE
SECOND THAT EMOTION
ALLIGATOR →
DRUMS →
CAUTION (DON'T STEP ON THE TRACKS) JAM →
GD TRBB →
COLD RAIN + SNOW
CHINA CAT SUNFLOWER →
I KNOW YOU RIDER
GREATEST STORY →
JOHNNY B. GOODE
UNCLE JOHN'S BAND
MIDNIGHT HOUR →
WE BID YOU GOODNITE
Filler: KAISER CAL. 11-21-85
WALKIN the Dog
She Belongs to Me
GRATEFUL DEAD Set: II/ENCORE
Locale: FILLMORE EAST. NYC
Date: 4.29.1971

FILLMORE WEST 7/2/71

A
B
Bertha
Me & Bobby McGee
Next Time You See Me
Big RxR Blues
The Rub
Deal #1
Promised Land
Good Love
Sugar Magnolia
Sing Me Back Home
Big Boss Man
The Other One
There was Cowboy Neal at the wheel.
AUD.
FM
SDB
Grateful Dead
Fillmore West, S.F., Calif.
close of the Fillmore
07/02/71 - 1
NR.
ON
OFF
Gen.
?

LIVE
Bertha
Me and Bobby McGee
Things won't be the same
China cat sunflower
I Know you Rider
Playin' in the Band
Loser
Ain't it Crazy
Me and My Uncle
Big Railroad Blues - Cut
Sing me back home
Mama Tried
Big Boss Man
Casey Jones
Johnny B. Goode
Sugar Magnolia
Sunshine Daydream
Uncle John's Band
Other One - cut
GRATEFUL DEAD AT: FILLMORE West
7-2-71
R.I.P.

Bertha
Playin
Loser
Mr. Charlie
Cumberland
Brokendown
Bobby McGee
hard 2 Handle
KC Jones
8-5-71
Hollywood Palladium
8-6-71 Set 1

St. Stephen>
Truckin>
Drumz>
Other1>
Uncle>
Other1>
Deal
Suger Magnolia
Morning Dew
Lovelight
Hollywood Palladium
8-6-71 Set 2

Grateful Dead
TAFT AUDITORIUM
CINN. OHIO 10-30-71
Gen
SBD
Aud
FM
NR

A
Bobby McGee
cryptical
drumz
other one
cryptical
Comes a time
B
Sugar mag
BE women
NFA
GDTRFB
NFA
Fill - 3-14-83 studio - Help on the Way
Slipknot
10-20-68
The Eleven
Grateful Dead 11-6-71 II
Harding Theater SF, CA
SOURCE:
GENERATION:
DATE:

Harding Theatre, San Francisco, CA
DARK STAR
DRUMZ
Other One
Me and My Uncle
Other One
Playin' in the Band
Not Fade Away
GDTRFB
Not Fade Away
encore
Uncle John's Band
Comes a Time
Saturday Nite
GRATEFUL DEAD
HARDING THEATRE
SAN FRANCISCO
11•7•71

A
12/1/71 BOSTON MUSIC HALL
B
Noise Reduction
Equalizer High(CrO2): 70µs
SUGAR MAGNOLIA
DEAL
EL PASO
BROKEDOWN PALACE
UNCLE JOHN'S BAND
NOT FADE AWAY
LOVELIGHT
GOIN' DOWN THE ROAD
NOT FADE AWAY
JOHNNY B. GOODE
WE BID YOU GOODNIGHT
119 on tape counter
(from end of tape)
TDK
BOSTON MUSIC HALL 12/1/71
SA-C90

THE GRATEFUL DEAD. "SUGAREE." FELT FORUM
05:12:71
RECORDED LIVE IN ANYTOWN......
Side One: Sugaree/So Long/Ramblin' Rose/You Win Again.....
Side Two: Truckin'/It Hurts Me Too/Big Railroad Blues.......
109

THE GRATEFUL DEAD. "DARK STAR."
RECORDED LIVE IN ANYTOWN.....
Side One: Me And Bobby McGee/Bertha/Big Boss Man.....
Side Two: Dark Star;Me And My Uncle.........
190

Set I
TRUCKIN
EL PASO
SUGAREE
BIG RXR
MR. CHARLIE
ME + MY UNCLE
BIODTL
LOSER
RUN RUDOLPH
JACK STRAW
BLACK PETER
PLAYIN
LIED + CHEATED
K.C. JONES
TENN. JED
HILL AUD. ANN ARBOR MICH. 12-14-71 I
GOOD OL' GRATEFUL DEAD

AN EVENING WITH
THE GRATEFUL DEAD
BERTHA
ME + BOBBY McGEE
CHINA CAT → RIDER
BIODTL
HURTS ME TOO
CUMBERLAND
JACK STRAW
YOU WIN AGAIN
RUN RUDOLPH, RUN
PLAYIN
B.E. WOMEN
MEXICALI
BIG RXR
BROKE DOWN
EL PASO
K.C. JONES
HILL AUD. ANN ARBOR-MICH. 12-15-71 Set I
Grateful Dead

Grateful Dead
12-15-71
Hill Auditorium
Ann Arbor, MI
Quality A-
Source ?
Gen ?
Bertha
Me + Bobby McGee
Mr. Charlie
China → Rider
B.I.O.D.T.L.
Hurts Me Too
Cumberland
Jack Straw
You Win Again
Run Rudolph Run *
Playin'
B.E. Women
Mexicali
Big RxR Blues
Brokedown
El Paso
Casey Jones
* Final "Run Rudolph Run"

A
B
Academy of Music 3/25/72
Noise Reduction
Equalizer
How Sweet it Is
Last Train to Jacksonville
You Lied, You Cheated
Brown-Eyed Women
Smokestack Lightnin
Sittin on top of the World
Sugaree
Looks Like Rain
Bertha
Mr. Charlie
Playin in the Band
Turn on Your Lovelight
NO.
Grateful Dead
Academy of Music
New York, New York 3/25/72
TDK
SA-C90

Bertha
me+my uncle
mr.Charlie
U win again
Black-throated wind
chinatown shuffle
Bobby McGee
cumberland
Playin
Playin
El Paso
B.I.O.D.T.L
Casey Jones
Set II
Truckin
Dark Star
Set (1)
Tivoli The Copenhagen
Denmark 4.14.72
NOISE REDUCTION
IN OUT
SBD AUD RAD.
SOUND QUALITY
SBD GOOD AUD FAIR

Dark Star
Sugar mag
Good Lovin
Caution
Caution
Good Lovin
NFA
GDTRFB
NFA
enc. 1 more Sat
fill: 7.3.84
Dont need love
Set (2)
Tivoli The Copenhagen Denmark
4.14.72 II
NOISE REDUCTION
IN OUT
SBD AUD RAD.
SOUND QUALITY
SBD GOOD AUD FAIR

off DAT
Digital Audio Tape

The Grateful Dead LIVE Set I
5/11/72 Civic Hall, Rotterdam, The Netherlands

Playin In the Band*
Sugaree
Mr. Charlie
Black Throated Wind
Deal
Chinatown Shuffle
Mexicali Blues
China Cat->
I Know You Rider (cut)

Hurts Me Too
BIODTL
Brown Eyed Women
Jack Straw
Big RxR Blues
Good Lovin
Casey Jones

off DAT
Digital Audio Tape

The Grateful Dead LIVE Set II
5/11/72 Civic Hall, Rotterdam, The Netherlands

Morning Dew
Me & My Uncle
Two Souls
El Paso
Tennessee Jed
Next Time You See Me

Dark Star->
Drums->
Dark Star->

off DAT
Digital Audio Tape

The Grateful Dead LIVE Set II, 2
5/11/72 Civic Hall, Rotterdam, The Netherlands

Sugar Magnolia->
Caution->
Who Do You Loce->
Caution->
Truckin->
Uncle John's Band

Filler:
Blues Traveler 8/15/91
The Wetlands, NYC, NY
off DSBD

Mulling it Over
Slow Change
Warmer Days
Love & Greed
Sweet Talking Hippie

Me & My Uncle
Mr. Charlie
Sugaree
Black thr. Wind
No Help at all
China Cat > Rider
BIODTL
Hurts Me too
Ten. Jed
Playin' in the Band
Promise Land
grateful dead
Luxemburg 5.16.72
sbd o aud o fm o

MARBLEIZED MIKE
3435 OAKTON DR.
HOPKINS, MN 55305

MISSING: PROMISED LAND
BROWN EYED WOMEN
MEXICALI BLUES
TRUCKIN'
DRUMS
OTHER ONE
...OTHER ONE
STELLA BLUE
EL PASO
RAMBLE ON
N.F.A.
G.D.T.R.
BO DIDDLEY
N.F.A./
GRATEFUL DEAD
8-22-72 SET II SB
BERKELEY COMMUNITY THEATRE
AZIM = 2
SOURCE: TSALIKES
GENERATION
AUDIENCE
RADIO
SOUNDBOARD X
OTHER
NOISE REDUCTION: YES C
NO

GRATEFUL DEAD
GRATEFUL DEAD
SOURCE:
GENERATION:
DATE:
9-21-72 I Philly, PA
Spectrum
A
Promised
Bird Song
El Paso
China> Rider
BT Wind
Big RxR Blues
Jack Straw
Loser
B
Big River
RU Rose
Cumberland
Playin
II He's Gone>
Truckin.....

Dead
11-19-72 #1
HOFFHIENZ PAVILLION
Houston TX
Mstr Reel >
Soundboard
Audience
GEN
FM
Let your mind wander...

Dead
11-19-72 #2
HOFFHIENZ PAVILLION
HOUSTON TX
Mstr Reel 7
Soundboard
Audience
GEN
FM
Let your mind wander...

Going Down The Road
A
PROMISED LAND
ROW JIMMY
BLACK THROATED WIND
DEAL
ME + MY UNCLE
SUGAREE
LOOKS LIKE RAIN
BEER BARREL POLKA
MEXICALI BLUES
B
LOOSE LUCY
BROWN EYED WOMEN
EL PASO
HERE COMES THE SUNSHINE
PLAYIN
Feeling Bad
Grateful Dead
MAPLES PAVILLION
PALO ALTO, CA.
STANFORD UNIV.
2·9·73
I
Source:
Gen.
NR
A
CHINA ~
RIDER
JACK STRAW
THEY LOVE EACH OTHER
BOX OF RAIN
US BLUES
SUGAR MAGNOLIA
SUNSHINE DAYDREAM
B
TRUCKIN
EYES
CHINA DOLL
BIG RIVER
RAMBLE ON ROSE
FIRST LIVE
Grateful Dead
MAPLES PAVILLION
PALO ALTO, CA.
STANFORD UNIV.
2·9·73
II
Gen.
NR
Source:
CHINA CAT
KNOW YOU RIDER
THEY LOVE
EACH OTHER
BOX O RAIN
US BLUES
SUGAR MAG'S
TRUCKN
EYES
CHINA DOLL
BIG RIVER
RAMBLE ON ROSE
STANFORD U. PALO ALTO
2-9-73

LIVE STANFORD 2-9-73 II DEAD
Soundboard
Audience
Generation
A
CHINA CAT 7
RIDER
JACK STRAW
THEY LOVE
EACH OTHER
BOX OF RAIN
(1st) U.S. BLUES
SUGAR MAGS
B
TRUCKIN'
EYES 7
STRONGER
THAN DIRT
CHINA DOLL
BIG RIVER
RAMBLE ON ROSE

LIVE! MADISON WI 2-15-73
A
AUD
FM
SBD
PHOTO BY T.A.B.
© 1988
B
AUD
FM
SBD

Playin In THE Band→
JAM...
Promised Land
Bertha
GReatest Story
Loser
Big River
Dont Ease Me In
Me & My Uncle
Dark Star→
Truckin→
Morning Dew
Grateful Dead
Nassau Coliseum
Uniondale NY
II
3·16·73 "Swell Dance Concert"
Source AUD /Low
Generation Low
Sbd
Aud
FM

Big River
Stella Blue
Me + My Uncle
He's Gone
Truckin'
Spanish Jam
Dark Star
Sing Me
Sugar Mag
S.S. DD
E. J.B. Goode
DEAD
DEAD
Spectrum 3/24/73 2

WRS →
Dark Star →
Eyes →
Warf Rat...
Sugar Magnolia
Casey Jones
Casey Jones
Throwing Stones
Sat. Nite

GRATEFUL DEAD:
RFK STADIUM
BOARD
FM
AUDIENCE

Source:
Audience___ Radio___ Noise Reduction:
Soundboard___ Other___ Yes___ No___
6-22-73
"IF YOU GET CONFUSED
LISTEN TO THE MUSIC PLAY"

HALL: RFK STADIUM
DATE: 6-10-73
The Grateful Dead Live
SET: #1
DEAD
6-10-73 RFK/D.C. SB #1
A
B
DEW
BIODTL
RAMBLE ON
JACK STRAW
WAVE THAT FLAG
L.L. RAIN
BOX OF RAIN
TLEO
TLEO
RACE IS ON
ROW JIMMY
(MISSING MEET MY UNCLE)
BIRDSONG
PLAYIN

Source:
Audience___ Radio___ Noise Reduction:
Soundboard___ Other___ Yes___ No___
Live at 6.22.73
PLAYIN
JAM
SET II
H.C. Sunshine
Promised Land
B.E. Woman
El Paso
BLACK PETER
GREATEST STORY
BIG RXR BLUES
NASSAU 5.16.73
SUGAR MAGNOLIA
JUST A TIGGER IN A TRANCE

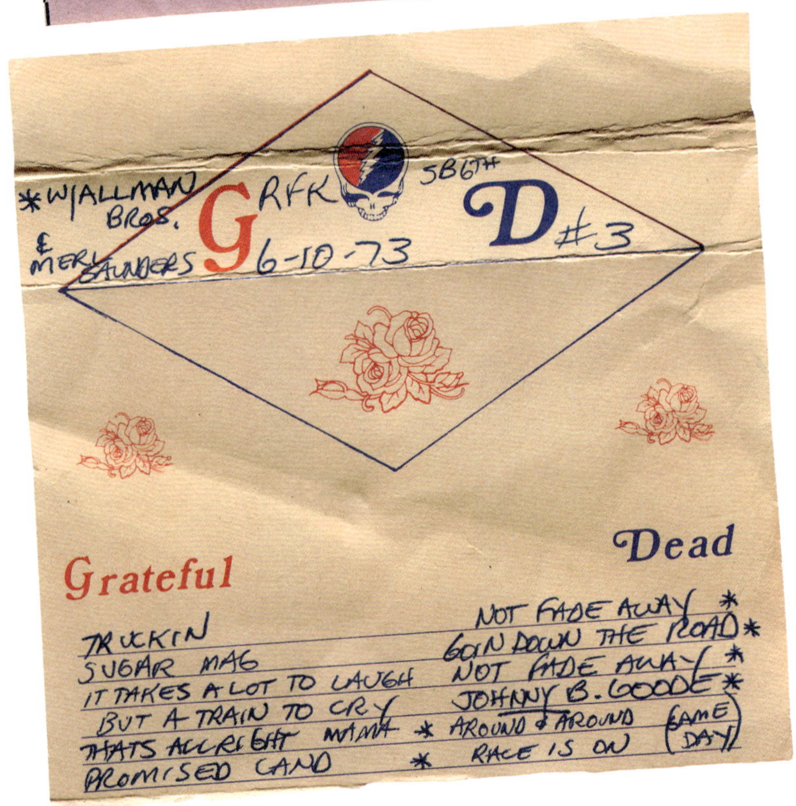

*W/ALLMAN BROS. & MERL SAUNDERS
G RFK
D #3
6-10-73
Grateful
Dead
TRUCKIN
SUGAR MAG
IT TAKES A LOT TO LAUGH BUT A TRAIN TO CRY
THATS ALLRIGHT MAMA *
PROMISED LAND *
NOT FADE AWAY *
GOIN DOWN THE ROAD *
NOT FADE AWAY *
JOHNNY B. GOODE *
AROUND & AROUND
RACE IS ON *
(SAME DAY)

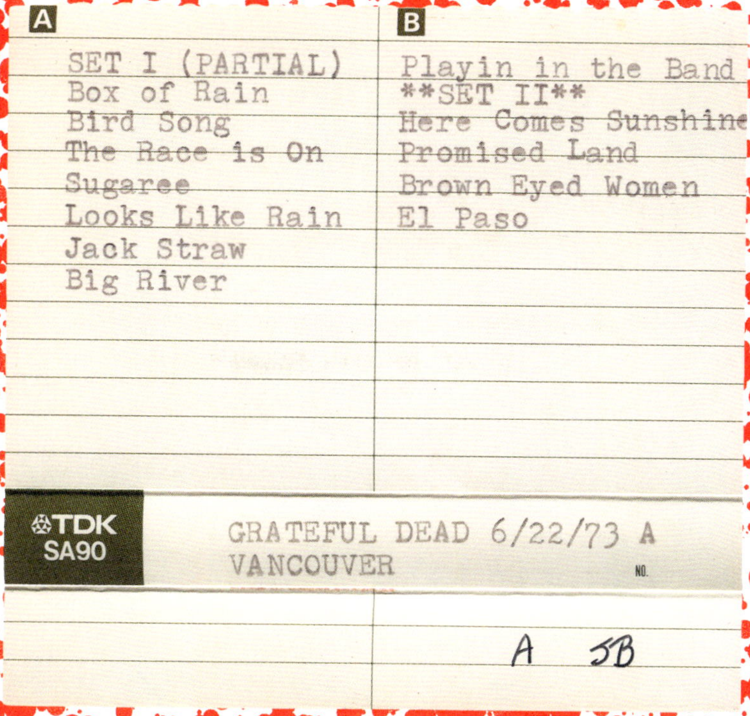
A
SET I (PARTIAL)
Box of Rain
Bird Song
The Race is On
Sugaree
Looks Like Rain
Jack Straw
Big River
B
Playin in the Band
SET II
Here Comes Sunshine
Promised Land
Brown Eyed Women
El Paso
TDK SA90
GRATEFUL DEAD 6/22/73 A
VANCOUVER
NO.
A SB

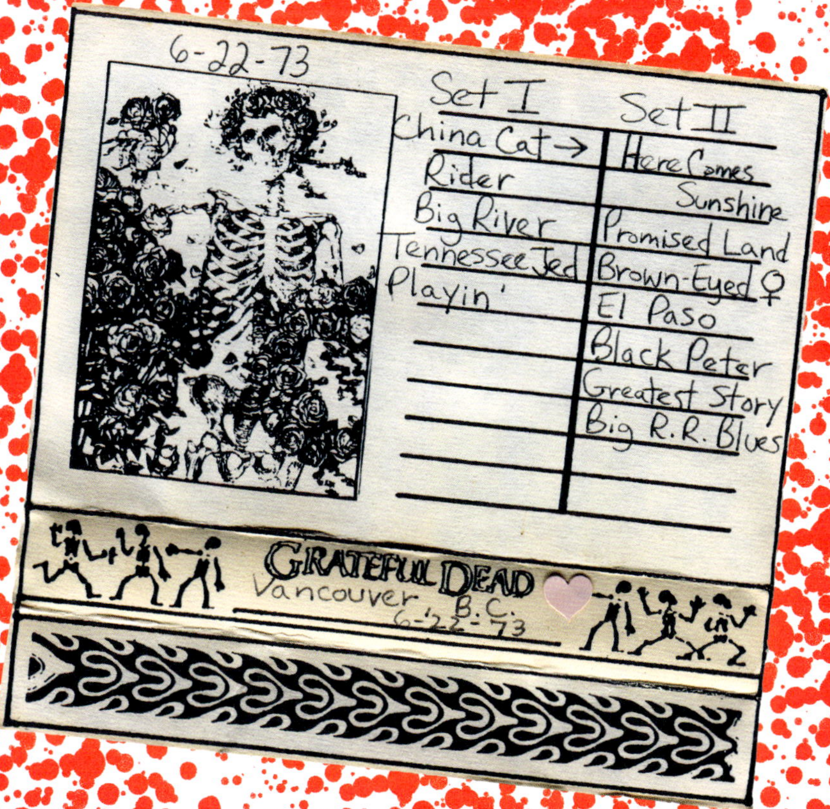
6-22-73
Set I
China Cat →
Rider
Big River
Tennessee Jed
Playin'
Set II
Here Comes Sunshine
Promised Land
Brown-Eyed ♀
El Paso
Black Peter
Greatest Story
Big R.R. Blues
GRATEFUL DEAD
Vancouver B.C.
6-22-73

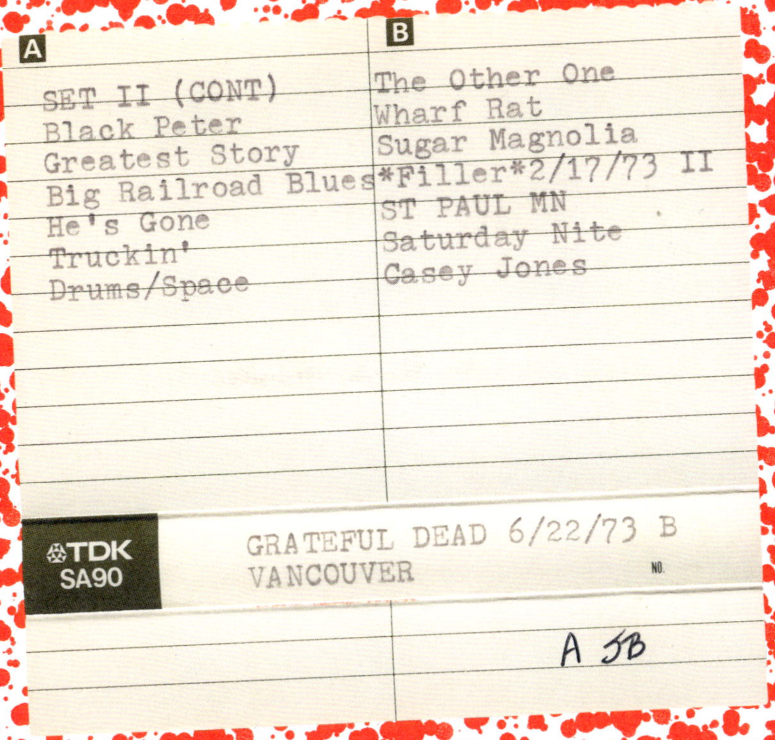
A
SET II (CONT)
Black Peter
Greatest Story
Big Railroad Blues
He's Gone
Truckin'
Drums/Space
B
The Other One
Wharf Rat
Sugar Magnolia
*Filler*2/17/73 II
ST PAUL MN
Saturday Nite
Casey Jones
TDK SA90
GRATEFUL DEAD 6/22/73 B
VANCOUVER
NO.
A SB

LIVE DEAD
Watkins Glen Soundcheck
7-26-73
Source: Stella Blue Club
Quality:
~JAM
Wharf Rat
Around n' Around
Big River
~Tennessee Jed
Mississippi ½ Step
JAM
Dark Star
Remember! This is only A Test!

Encore One:
Sing Me Back Home(cut)
Encore Two:
Not Fade Away
Mountain Jam
Johnny Be Goode
Encore Two with Allman Brothers Band and The Band
Filler: 07/27/73 Aud
Watkins Glen Sound Check
Jam→
Wharf Rat
Me and My Uncle
Jam is cut when taper is busted by a roadie. Aud picks up again at the start of Wharf Rat. The missing portion is supplied by SBD>D>C>seed
Grateful Dead
GRAND PRIX RACECOURSE
WATKINS GLEN, NY
07-28-73
ENCORES
Watkins Glen 25th Anniversary Tree This tape is ____ gen from seed.
encore seed gens:
Encore One - aud master cassette→cassette2 Encore Two - unknown sbd
07/27/73 - aud master cassette→reel→cassette

JERRY'S BIRTHDAY
DARK STAR →
EL PASO →
EYES OF THE WORLD →
EYES
DEW
SUGAR MAG'S
GDTRFB
1 MO
SATURDAY NIGHT
THE DEAD
Roosevelt University II
New Jersey 8·1·73
[ ] SOUNDBOARD
[ ] FM RADIO
[ ] AUDIENCE
SET:____ GEN:____
NR [ ]ON . [ ]OFF
COSMIC CHARLIE

SING YOUR* BLUES AWAY
WRS PRELUDE*
WRS P+ I* LET IT
GROW* ROW JIMMY
BIG RIVER·DEAL
B.I.O.D.T.L.
DARK STAR
MORNING
DEW
SUGAR MAG
DEAD
COLLEGE OF WILLIAM & MARY
WILLIAMSBURG.VA. 9·11·73
6 GEN
SBD
FM
AUDIENCE
NOISE REDUCTION

Spectrum
BIG RAILROAD BLUES
ME & MY UNCLE
BROWN EYED ♀
B.I.O.D.T.L.
SUGAREE
BIG RIVER
HERE COMES SUNSHINE
EL PASO
LOOSE LUCY
JACK STRAW
BLACK PETER
PLAYIN' IN BAND
The Spectrum 9.21.73 I
Soundboard
Audience
Radio
Generation
Noise Reduction

TAPESTRY
Tape Covers
P.O. Box 05487
Milwaukee, Wisconsin
53205-0487
Quantity Price Postage
10 1.50 .50
40 5.00 1.00
75 7.50 1.50
150 12.50 2.50

Grateful Dead
10-21-73
TDK SA-X90
Here comes Sunshine
On down the Line
The Loser
Black-Throated Wind
They love each other
Cumberland Blues
You aint Women Enough
Playin'
Mississippi half-Step
Big River
Playin' II
OMAHA - Oct. 21
1973
A
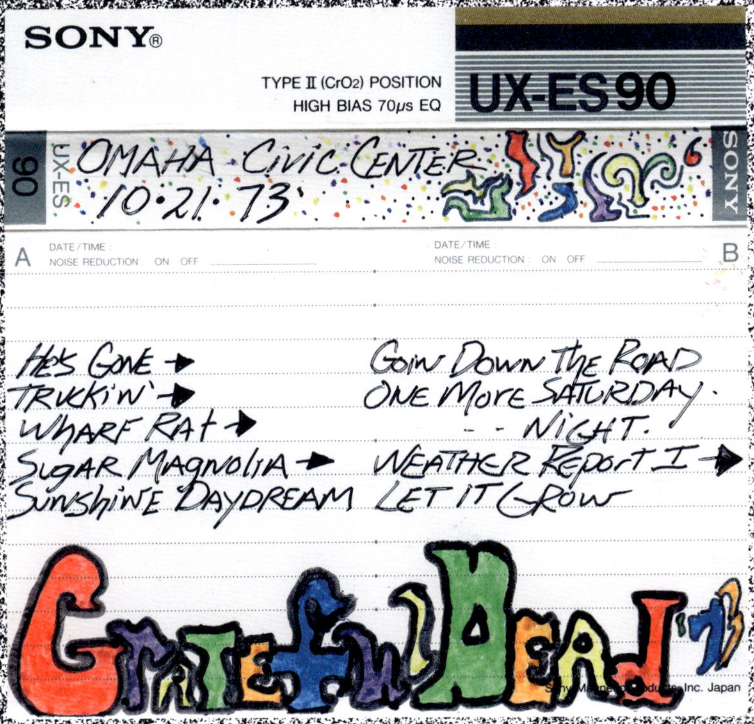
SONY
TYPE II (CrO2) POSITION
HIGH BIAS 70μs EQ
UX-ES 90
OMAHA CIVIC CENTER
10.21.73
A
B
DATE / TIME
NOISE REDUCTION ON OFF
HE'S GONE
TRUCKIN'
WHARF RAT
SUGAR MAGNOLIA
SUNSHINE DAYDREAM
GOIN' DOWN THE ROAD
ONE MORE SATURDAY NIGHT
WEATHER REPORT I
LET IT GROW
GRATEFUL DEAD '73

LIVE DEAD
Winterland 11-11-73
San Francisco, Cal Set II
Source:
Quality:
Loose Lucy
Weather Report Suite
Mississippi ½ Step
Big River
Dark Star
DARK Star (cont)
Eyes of the World
China Doll

DARK STAR
Eyes of the WORLD
CHINA DOLL
Weather Report I+II
MISSISSIPPI 1/2 Step
BIG RIVER
Loose Lucy
Black Throated Wind
DEAD ZONE
WINTERLAND, SF
11•11•73

WHARF RAT
1/2 STEP
PLAYIN
HE'S GONE
TRUCKIN
STELLA BLUE
SUGAR MAG
12-2-73
BOSTON MUSIC HALL
II
SBD AUD FM DAT CD DOLBY
QUALITY: GREAT GOOD OK POOR

Cumberland
Must've been
Big River
Bertha
WRS Prelude →
WRS Part I →
Let it grow →
Jimmy
Ship
Promised
QUALITY
Dark Star →
Morning Dew
Baby Blue
SOURCE
Live Dead
Winterland
2·24·74

A
B
Passenger
Deal
Brent's
1st
Show
DEAD
SBD
AUD
FM

1/2 step
Mexicali
B RxR Blues
BT wind
Scarlet
BIODTL
Loose Lucy
Money money
China cat → rider
promised land
Bertha
SBD 5th
GSET
Fill - 6-28-74 Boston jam
Portland Coliseum, OR
5-19-74 I
DEAD
The Phil Zone

live dead - Louisville, Ky
6-18-74
Promised Land
Must've Been The Roses
Black Throated Wind
Ramble on Rose
Beat it on Down The Line
Loser
Mexicali Blues
Row Jimmy
Eyes of The World
China Doll
Around + Around
Loose Lucy
El Paso →
Big River

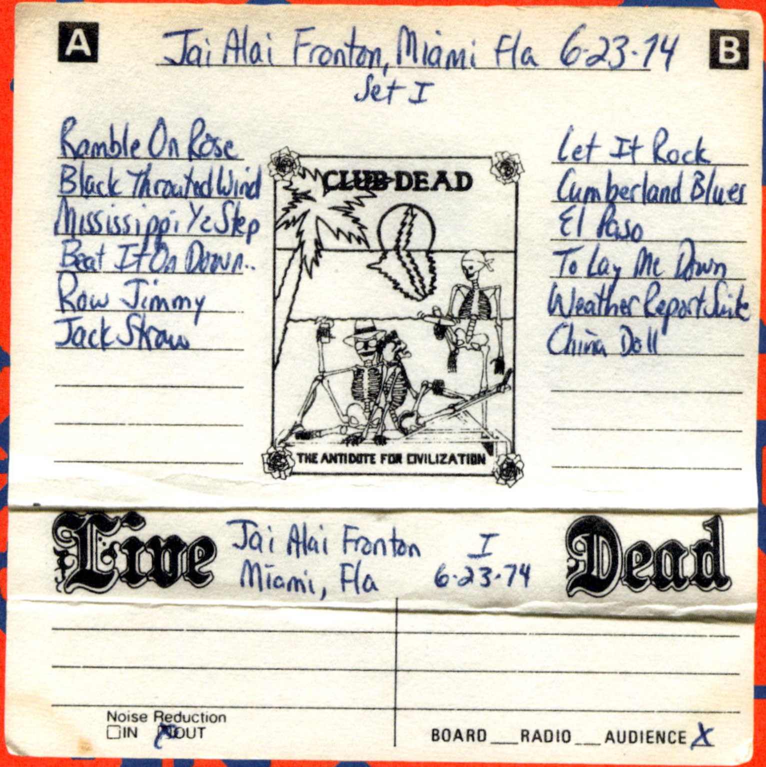
A
Jai Alai Fronton, Miami Fla 6-23-74
B
Set I
Ramble On Rose
Black Throated Wind
Mississippi ½ Step
Beat It On Down..
Row Jimmy
Jack Straw
CLUB DEAD
THE ANTIDOTE FOR CIVILIZATION
Let It Rock
Cumberland Blues
El Paso
To Lay Me Down
Weather Report Suite
China Doll
Live
Jai Alai Fronton
Miami, Fla
I
6-23-74
Dead
Noise Reduction
IN
OUT
BOARD __ RADIO __ AUDIENCE X

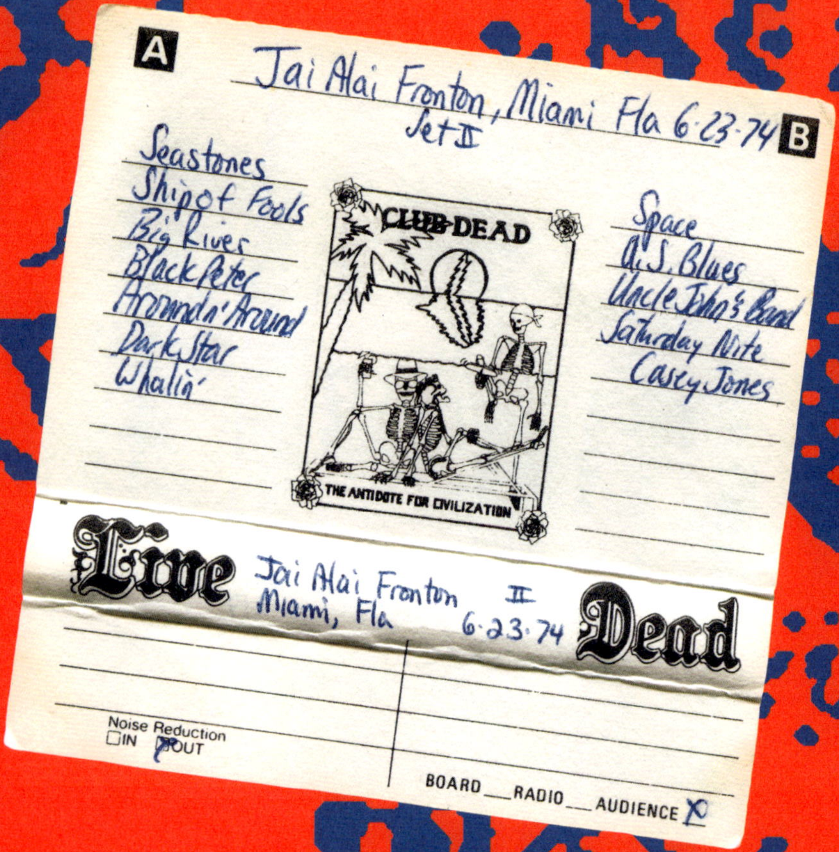
A
Jai Alai Fronton, Miami Fla 6-23-74
B
Set II
Seastones
Ship of Fools
Big River
Black Peter
Around n' Around
Dark Star
Whalin'
CLUB DEAD
THE ANTIDOTE FOR CIVILIZATION
Space
U.S. Blues
Uncle John's Band
Saturday Nite
Casey Jones
Live
Jai Alai Fronton
Miami, Fla
II
6-23-74
Dead
Noise Reduction
IN
OUT
BOARD __ RADIO __ AUDIENCE X

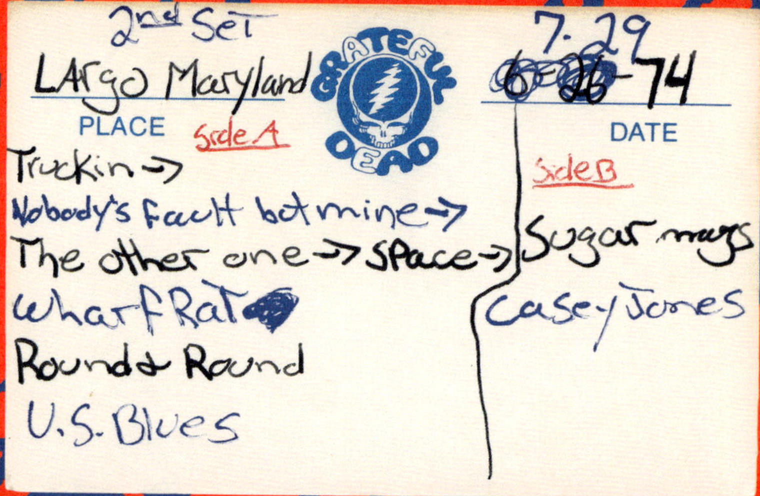
2nd Set
Largo Maryland
PLACE
Side A
GRATEFUL DEAD
7-29
-74
DATE
Side B
Truckin →
Nobody's Fault but mine →
The other one → Space →
Wharf Rat
Round & Round
U.S. Blues
Sugar mags
Casey Jones

Scarlet, Me & My Uncle
B.E. Women, BIODTL,
1/2 Step → Roses
Mexicali, Row Jimmy
Jack Straw, China →
Rider, Round n' Round
from Set 2
Bertha, Big River
Grateful Dead
7-31-74-Set 1
Hartford, CT.
Custom Tape Covers by Jay Michels
249 Pennsylvania Ave. - E. Liverpool, OH. 43920
(216) 385-5127

A: Playin
Seastones
B: Seastones
Eyes of the World
Space
London, England
9/11/74 II
Alexander Palace

SCARLET
BIG RIVER
RAMBLE
ME
HE'S GONE
OTHER ONE
SPANISH JAM
MLB JAM
OTHER ONE
STELLA
SUGAR MAGS
E: CASEY
Winterland 10·17·74 II
Soundboard
Audience
Radio
Generation
Noise Reduction

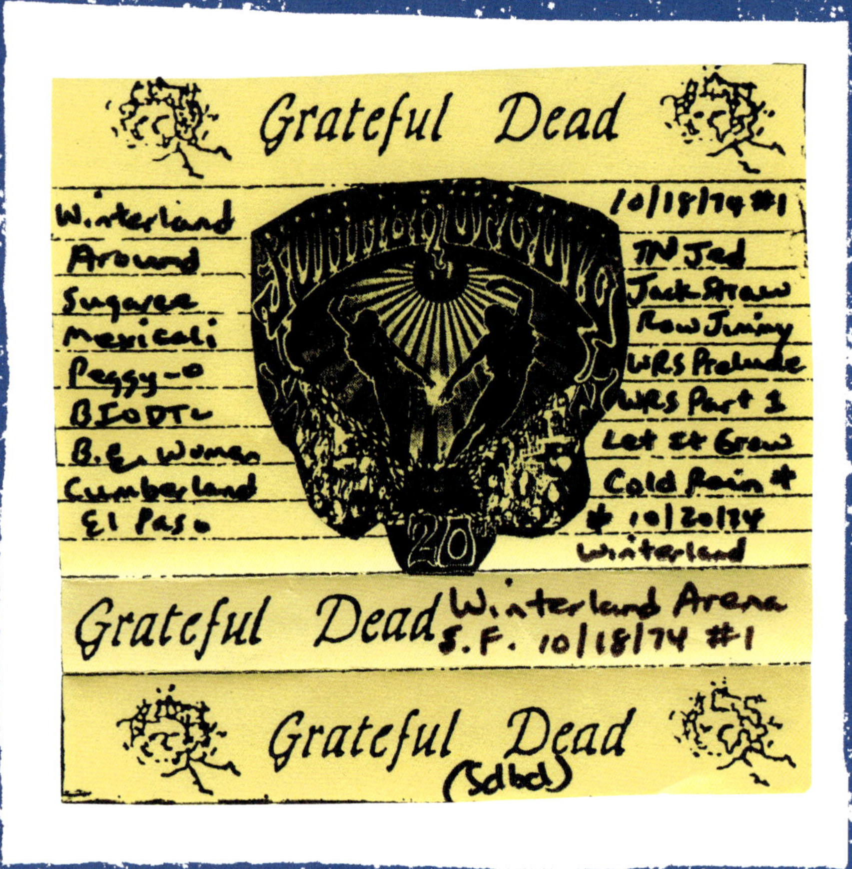
Grateful Dead
Winterland
Around
Sugaree
Mexicali
Peggy-O
BIODTL
B.E. Women
Cumberland
El Paso
10/18/74 #1
TN Jed
Jack Straw
Row Jimmy
WRS Prelude
WRS Part 1
Let It Grow
Cold Rain *
* 10/20/74
Winterland
Grateful Dead Winterland Arena
S.F. 10/18/74 #1
Grateful Dead
(sdbd)

Grateful Dead
Winterland
Set II
Phil + Ned
Dark Star
Drums
Dark Star →
10/18/74 #2
→ Dark Star
A.M. Dew
Set III
Promised Land
Bertha
Gr. Story
Grateful Dead Winterland Arena
S.F. 10/18/74 #2
Grateful Dead
(sdbd)

Grateful Dead
10/18/74 #3
NFA
GDTRFB
Sat. Night
E) U.S. Blues
Help *
Slipknot *
Music *
* G.G. Park
9/28/75
Chico, CA
11/1/68
Dark Star
Cryptical
Other One
Cryptical
N.F. Caboose
Bid You Goodnight
Grateful Dead A) 10/18/74 #3
B) 11/1/68
Grateful Dead

Grateful Dead
WINTERLAND, 10-19-74

A
B
½ Step
Me + My Uncle
Friend of the Devil
BIODTL
Must Have Been The Roses
El Paso
Loose Lucy
Black Throated Wind
Scarlet Begonias
To Lay Me Down
Mama Tried
Eyes of The World
China Doll
BY ELISE
Live
Winterland Arena
10·19·74 I
Dead
TAPE GENERATION
NOISE REDUCTION IN OUT
A GOLDEN ROAD PRODUCTION
BOARD
MONO STEREO
RADIO AUDIENCE

TAPE 1-10/20/74/track list
1.Cold Rain and Snow/Mama Tried/Deal/Beat It On Down The Line/Loser/Jackstraw/
Tennessee Jed/El Paso
2.Brokedown Palace/Chinese Sunflower/I Know You Rider/Around + Around
GRATEFUL DEAD : 10/20/74
GRATEFUL DEAD

TAPE 2-10/20/74/track list
1.Seastones/Space/Playing In The Band/Percussion/Not Fade Away/Drums
2.Drums/The Other One/Wharf Rat/Playing In The Band/Good Lovin/It Must Have Been
The Roses
GRATEFUL DEAD : 10/20/74
GRATEFUL DEAD

A
B
Last Wall of Sound
Set II
Set III
Drumzz
NFA
Drumz
Other One
Wharf Rat
Playin
w/ Hart on II
Good Lovin
MHBTR
Promised
Eyes
Slipknot
Stella
miss Sug. Mag
Winterland
CA 10-20-74 II/III
GRATEFUL DEAD The motif of a cycle of folk tales which begin with the hero's coming upon a group of people ill-treating or refusing to bury the corpse of a man who had died without paying his debts. He gives his last penny, either to pay the man's debts or to give him a decent burial. Within a few hours he meets with a traveling companion who aids him in some impossible task, gets him a fortune, saves his life, etc. The story ends with the companion's disclosing himself as the man whose corpse the other had befriended.

©1992
SBD AUD FM GEN
P.O. BOX No. 2151
Baltimore, MD 21203-2151
G.A.M.H., S.F., CA. 8-13-75
Set I
Help on the Way →
Slipknot →
Franklins Tower
*Music
Must Have Been the Roses
Eyes
King Solomons Marbles
(Stronger Than Dirt)
Set II
Around 'n' Round
Sugaree
Big River
Crazy Fingers
Drumz

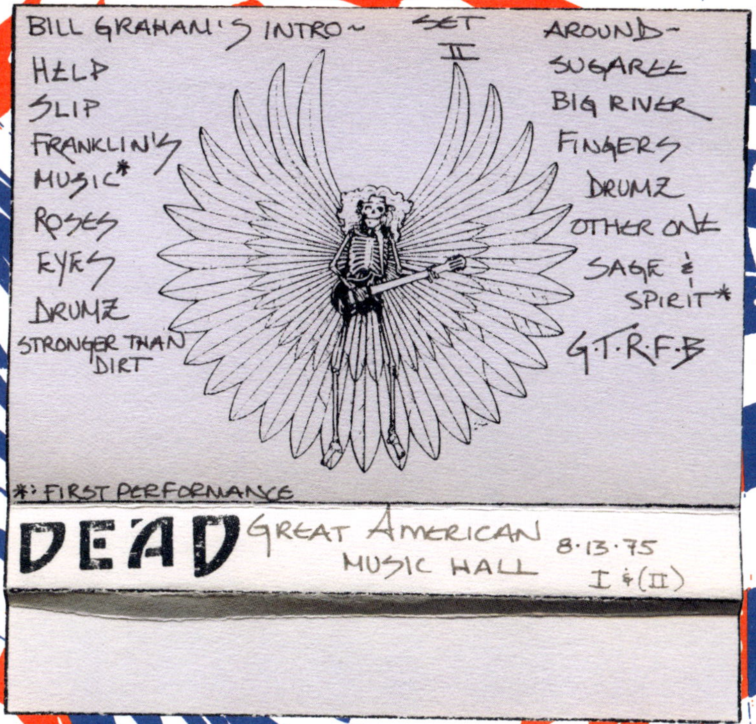
BILL GRAHAM'S INTRO ~
HELP
SLIP
FRANKLIN'S
MUSIC*
ROSES
EYES
DRUMZ
STRONGER THAN DIRT
SET II
AROUND ~
SUGAREE
BIG RIVER
FINGERS
DRUMZ
OTHER ONE
SAGE & SPIRIT*
G.T.R.F.B
*: FIRST PERFORMANCE
DEAD
GREAT AMERICAN MUSIC HALL
8.13.75
I & (II)

the DEAD
Golden Gate Park
San Fransisco Ca
5 28 75
Help On the Way
Slipknot
Music Never Stopped
Beat It On Down
Franklins Tower
Big River
Must of Been Roses
Truckin
King Solomon's Marbles
Stronger Than Dirt
Not Fade Away
Going Down The Road
One More Saturday

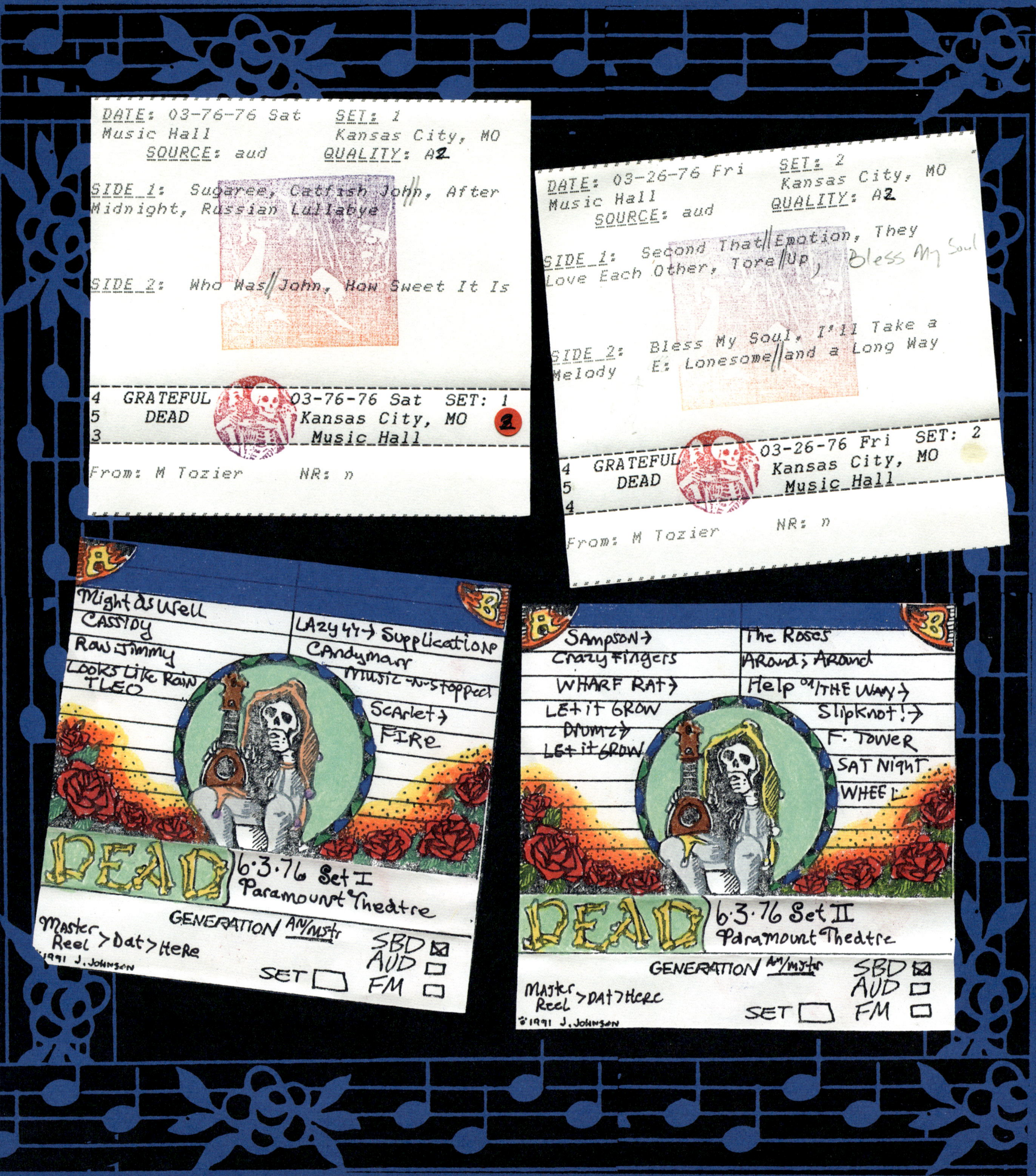

DATE: 03-76-76 Sat
SET: 1
Music Hall
Kansas City, MO
SOURCE: aud
QUALITY: A2
SIDE 1: Sugaree, Catfish John, After Midnight, Russian Lullabye
SIDE 2: Who Was John, How Sweet It Is
4 GRATEFUL
5 DEAD
3
03-76-76 Sat SET: 1
Kansas City, MO
Music Hall
From: M Tozier
NR: n
DATE: 03-26-76 Fri
SET: 2
Music Hall
Kansas City, MO
SOURCE: aud
QUALITY: A2
SIDE 1: Second That Emotion, They Love Each Other, Tore Up, Bless My Soul
SIDE 2: Bless My Soul, I'll Take a Melody E: Lonesome and a Long Way
4 GRATEFUL
5 DEAD
4
03-26-76 Fri SET: 2
Kansas City, MO
Music Hall
From: M Tozier
NR: n
A
B
Might as Well
Cassidy
Row Jimmy
Looks Like Rain
TLEO
Lazy 44 → Supplication
Candyman
Music -n- stopped
Scarlet →
Fire
DEAD
6·3·76 Set I
Paramount Theatre
GENERATION AM/mstr
Master Reel > Dat > Here
SBD
AUD
FM
SET
©1991 J. Johnson
A
B
Sampson →
Crazy Fingers
Wharf Rat →
Let it Grow
Drumz →
Let it Grow
The Roses
Around, Around
Help on The Way →
Slipknot! →
F. Tower
Sat Night
Wheel
DEAD
6·3·76 Set II
Paramount Theatre
GENERATION AM/mstr
Master Reel > Dat > Here
SBD
AUD
FM
SET
©1991 J. Johnson

A SAMSON AND DELILAH
ROW JIMMY
MUSIC NEVER STOPPED
BROWN-EYED WOMEN
BIG RIVER
MISSION IN THE RAIN
LOOKS LIKE RAIN...
B FRIEND OF THE DEVIL
LAZY LIGHTNING
→ SUPPLICATION
PROMISED LAND
CASSIDY
TENNESSEE JED
Fill JOB
That's what Love will make you Do
Grateful Dead
THE MUSIC HALL BOSTON, MA.
6-12-76 SET I
Noise Reduction IN OUT
BOARD RADIO AUDIENCE
A
B
CASSIDY
TENNESSEE JED →
WEATHER REPORT SUITE
→ WHARF RAT →
COMES A TIME ...
(BILLY'S BIRTHDAY!)
... COMES A TIME
→ DANCIN' IN THE STREETS
AROUND & AROUND
SUGAR MAGNOLIA
→ U.S. BLUES
→ SUNSHINE DAYDREAM
9-17-82 PORTLAND
Touch of Grey / Man Smart Woman Smarter
Grateful Dead
BOSTON MUSIC HALL 6-12-76 SET II
Noise Reduction IN OUT
BOARD RADIO AUDIENCE
grateful dead
BOSTON MUSIC HALL
6/12/76
A.SAMSON&DELILAH/ROW JIMMY ROW/THE
MUSIC NEVER STOPPED/BROWN EYED WOMEN/
BIG RIVER/MISSION IN THE RAIN/
B.LOOKS LIKE RAIN/FRIEND OF THE DEVIL/
LAZY LIGHTNING/SUPPLICATION/HIGH TIME/
PROMISED LAND*************************
A
B
CASSIDY
Tenn. Jed
Let it Grow
Drumz
Let It Grow
Wharf Rat
*Comes A Time
Dancin
Around
Sugar Mag
U.S. Blues
Sunshine Daydream
Filler: 7-18-76
& last one San Fran 10-19-74
Summer Tour
Boston Music Hall 6-12-76 Set II
SBD
AUD
Let There Be Songs To Phil The Air

HELP
SLIP
FRANKLIN
MUSIC
B.E. WOMEN
CASSIDY
TLEO
L.L. RAIN
TENNESSEE JED
PLAYIN'
DEAD PASSAIC 6-19-76 I
PRODUCED BY THE GRATEFUL DEAD

A
MIGHT AS WELL
SAMPSON + DELILAH
HIGH TIME
WEATHER REPORT
DANCIN' IN THE STREETS
B
COSMIC CHARLIE
ROUND AND ROUND
GDTRFB
ONE MORE SAT NIGHT
CASEY JONES
DEAD
CAPITOL THEATRE PASSAIC, NJ SET II 6-19-76
Source
Gen.

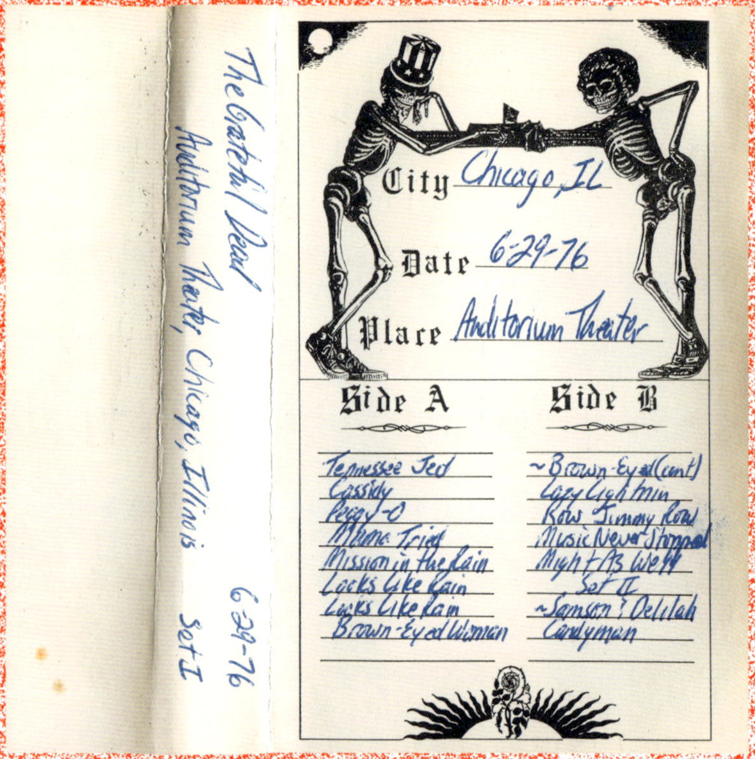
The Grateful Dead
Auditorium Theater, Chicago, Illinois
6-29-76
Set I
City Chicago, IL
Date 6-29-76
Place Auditorium Theater
Side A
Tennessee Jed
Cassidy
Peggy-O
Mama Tried
Mission in the Rain
Looks Like Rain
Looks Like Rain
Brown-Eyed Woman
Side B
~Brown-Eyed (cont)
Lazy Lightnin
Row Jimmy Row
Music Never Stopped
Might As Well
Set II
~Samson & Delilah
Candyman

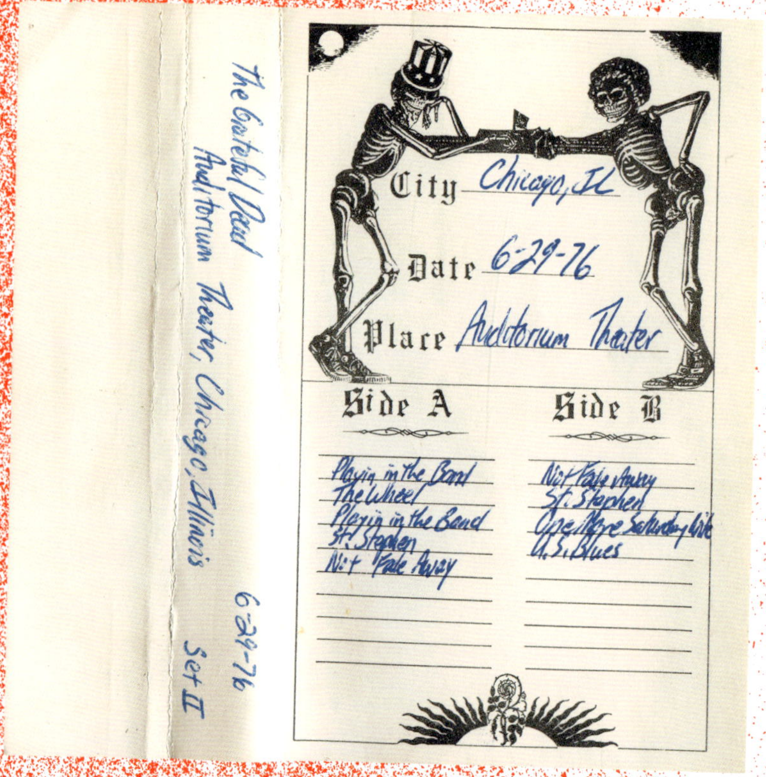
The Grateful Dead
Auditorium Theater, Chicago, Illinois
6-29-76
Set II
City Chicago, IL
Date 6-29-76
Place Auditorium Theater
Side A
Playin in the Band
The Wheel
Playin in the Band
St. Stephen
Not Fade Away
Side B
Not Fade Away
St. Stephen
One More Saturday Nite
U.S. Blues

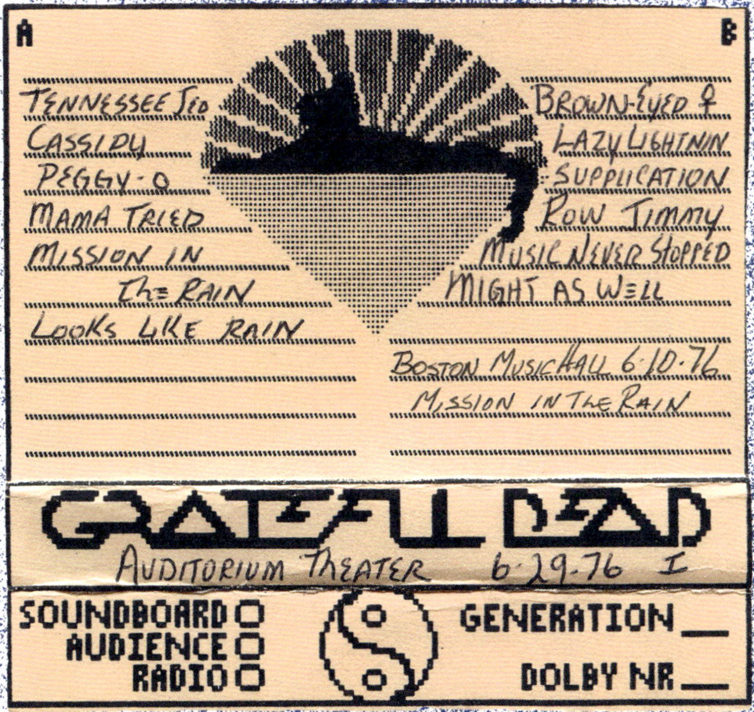
A
B
Tennessee Jed
Cassidy
Peggy-O
Mama Tried
Mission in The Rain
Looks Like Rain
Brown-Eyed Women
Lazy Lightnin
Supplication
Row Jimmy
Music Never Stopped
Might as Well
Boston Music Hall 6-10-76
Mission in The Rain
GRATEFUL DEAD
Auditorium Theater 6-29-76 I
SOUNDBOARD
AUDIENCE
RADIO
GENERATION
DOLBY NR

Might as Well
Sampson & Delilah
Candyman
Lazy Lightning
Let It Grow
Wharf Rat
Wharf Rat
Other One →
St. Stephen →
Not Fade Away →
St. Stephen →
Wheel →
Other One
Stella Blue
Electric Dead
Orpheum Theater 7/18/76
San Francisco
[ ] SOUNDBOARD
[ ] FM RADIO
[ ] AUDIENCE
SET:
GEN:
NR [ ]ON [ ]OFF

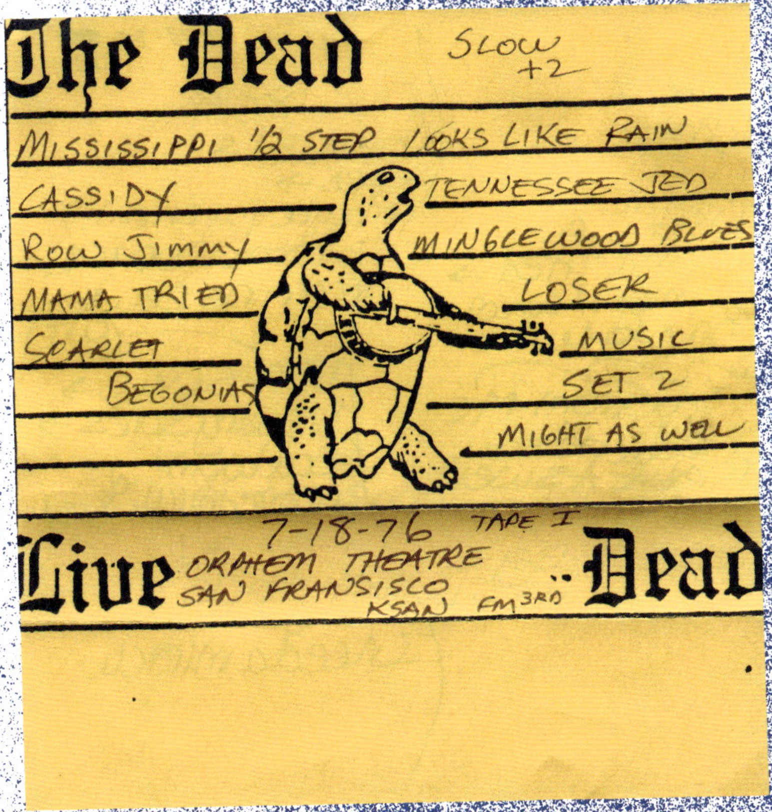
The Dead
Slow +2
Mississippi 1/2 Step
Looks Like Rain
Cassidy
Tennessee Jed
Row Jimmy
Minglewood Blues
Mama Tried
Loser
Scarlet Begonias
Music
Set 2
Might as Well
Live Dead
7-18-76 Tape I
Orpheum Theatre
San Fransisco
KSAN FM 3rd

Slow +2
Grateful Dead
Samson & Delilah
Candy Man
Lazy Lightning
Supplication
Lazy Lightning
Let It Grow
Drumz
Let It Grow
Wharf....
Wharfrat
Other One
St. Stephen
Not Fade Away
St. Stephen
Wheel
Other....
Live Dead
7-18-76 Tape II
Orpheum Theatre
San Fransisco
KSAN FM 3rd

UNCLE JON'S WOODSHOP
SPECIALIZING IN CUSTOM
AUDIO AND VIDEO CASES
TAPE SIZES
TP-125 $40.00
TP-255 $79.00
CD SIZES
CD-100 $49.00
CD-200 $84.00
DAT SIZES
DAT-102 $35.00
DAT-170 $49.00
VIDEO SIZES
V-35 $39.00
V-55 $59.00
Prices INCLUDE S & H
CD-100
TP-255
All cases are hand made with the finest American oak ply. Wall mountable. Solid oak & custom size cases also available.
Your choice of finish: Dark, Medium or Natural.
Superior Quality. Reasonable Prices.
Quantity Discounts. Satisfaction Guaranteed!!
Visa/MC accepted.
2-3 week delivery. Shipped UPS ground.
For more information or to order, call . . .
SEND CHECK OR M.O. TO: UNCLE JON'S P.O. BOX 18353, ERLANGER, KY 41018
1-800-497-0791
Uncle Jon's Woodshop
SPECIALIZING IN CUSTOM
ANALOGUE, CD & DAT CASES
TAPE & CD SIZES
TP-125 $55.00
TP-255 $95.00
CD-150 $79.00
CD-250 $115.00
DAT SIZES
DAT-102 $49.00
DAT-170 $69.00
DAT-272 $95.00
DAT-340 $125.00
PRICES INCLUDE S & H
All Cases are hand made with the finest American Oak Ply. Wall mountable. Solid Oak & other size cases also available.
Your choice of lacquer finish: Brown Oak, Golden Oak or Natural.
Superior Quality. Reasonable Prices.
Convenient no-slot storage.
Satisfaction Guaranteed!! Visa/MC accepted.
Video & Portable cases also available.
2-4 week delivery.
ORDERS: 1-800-497-0791
E-MAIL: UJW@AOL.COM
TEL/FAX: 606-341-4720
SEND CHECK OR M.O. TO: Uncle Jon's P.O. BOX 175975 COVINGTON, KY 41017

UNCLE JON'S WOODSHOP
SPECIALIZING IN CUSTOM
AUDIO AND VIDEO CASES
TAPE SIZES
TP-125 $40.00
TP-255 $79.00
DAT SIZES
DAT-102 $35.00
DAT-170 $49.00
CD SIZES
CD-100 $49.00
CD-200 $84.00
VIDEO SIZES
V-35 $39.00
V-55 $59.00
Prices INCLUDE S & H
CD-100
TP-255
All cases are hand made with the finest American oak ply. Wall mountable. Solid oak & custom size cases also available.
Your choice of finish: Dark, Medium or Natural.
Superior Quality. Reasonable Prices.
Quantity Discounts. Satisfaction Guaranteed!!
Visa/MC accepted.
2-3 week delivery. Shipped UPS ground.
For more information or to order, call
SEND CHECK OR M.O. TO: UNCLE JON'S P.O. BOX 18353, ERLANGER, KY 41018
1-800-497-0791

A Recording Date: 4/2/82
Noise Reduction Yes No B
GRATEFUlDEAD
Orpheum Theater
SanFrancisco 7/18/76
Kazar Stadium
SanFrancisco 3/23/75
Cassidy
CrazyFingers
LetItGrow
MightAsWell
BluesForAllah
StrongerThanDirt
RiverMusic
MilkintheTurkey
BluesForAllah
GRATEFUlDEAD 7/18/76 3/23/75
maxell UD XLII

DEAD Oakland, California 10.9.76
St. Stephen →
Not Fade Away →
St. Stephen
Help on the Way
Sampson →
Slipknot →
Franklins Tower
Franklins Tower
One More Saturday Night (Encore)
US Blues
5.15.70 - Fillmore East
Lovelight
Cold Jordan
10.21.88 - Dallas
Dupree's
Jack Straw
Wang Dang Doodle

Cal. 2-26-77 Set I
*Terrapin Station
Minglewood
T.L.E.O.
*Estimated Prophet
Sugaree
Mama Tried
*1st Live
Deal
Playin →
Wheel →
Playin
Set II
Samson
Tenn. Jed

A
• LADY w/ Fan >
• TERRAPIN Station
MINGLEWOOD BLUEZ
They love each other
• Estimated Prophet
SUGAREE
B
MAMA TRIED
DEAL
Playin in the Band >
The Wheel >
Playin in the Band
• = First
GRATEFUL DEAD
Swing AUDITORIUM
2-26-77
San Bernardino, Ca.
SET I
SOURCE
SBD
RAD
AUD
DOLBY
ON
OFF
QUALITY
1 2 3 4
A
SAMSON & DELILAH
TENNESSEE JED
Music Never Stopped
Help on the Way >
Slipnot >
Franklins Tower
B
> Franklins Tower
Promised Land
Eyes of the World >
Dancin in the Sts >
Around & Around
GRATEFUL DEAD
Swing AUDITORIUM
2-26-77
San Bernardino, Ca
SET II
SOURCE
SBD
RAD
AUD
DOLBY
ON
OFF
QUALITY
1 2 3 4
SBD It's A RAINBOW FULL OF SOUND
IT'S LIVE IT'S DEAD
Swing Auditorium
San Bernardino Ca.
2-26-77 II
A set II
Samson
Tenn. Jed
Music
Help! →
Slip Knot →
Franklins Tower
Promised Land
st. stephen tease
B
Eyes of the world
Phil Zone →
Dancin
Around
U.S. Blues
Filler: I
1st Terrapin St.
1st Estimated prophet
very best
Help → Slip → Frank
& Eyes → Dancin
My Favorite #1 Show of
Old School Dead

Terrapin+
Minglewood
T.L.E.O
Estimated+
Sugaree
+=1st Time
Mama Tried
Deal →
Playin' →
Wheel →
Playin'
Swing Aud.
San Bernadino CA.
2-26-77 -Set I-
LIVE
SET I
NOISE REDUCTION — IN — OUT
SOURCE — RADIO — AUDIENCE — BOARD

SamSon
Ten. Jed
Music
Eyes
Dancin' Around & Around
Help on the Way →
Slipknot →
Franklins
Promised Land
Phillin' Fine
San Bernadino CA.
Swing Aud.
2-26-77 II
SET II
N.R. — IN — OUT
SOURCE:

Cornell 5-8-77 I Barton Hall

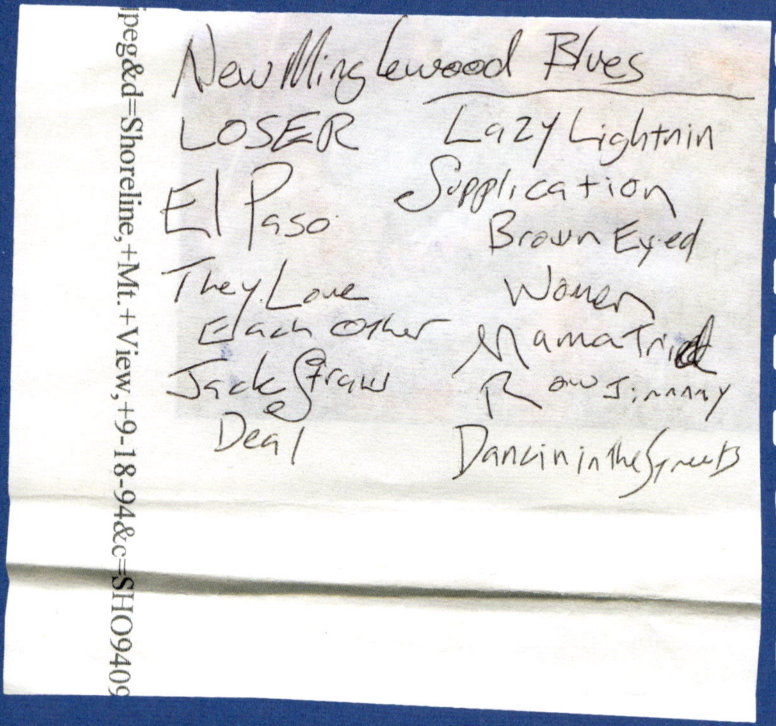
New Minglewood Blues
LOSER
El Paso
They Love Each Other
Jack Straw
Deal
Lazy Lightnin
Supplication
Brown Eyed Women
Mama Tried
Row Jimmy
Dancin in the Streets
jpeg&d=Shoreline,+Mt.+View,+9-18-94&c=SHO9409

5-8-77 Cornell

...jerry.021.jpeg&d=Seattle,+5-25-95&c=SEA95052
Scarlet Begonias
→ Fire On The Mountain
Estimated Prophet
Saint Stephen
→ Not Fade Away →
Saint Stephen
→ Morning Dew
∴ 1 More Saturday Nite

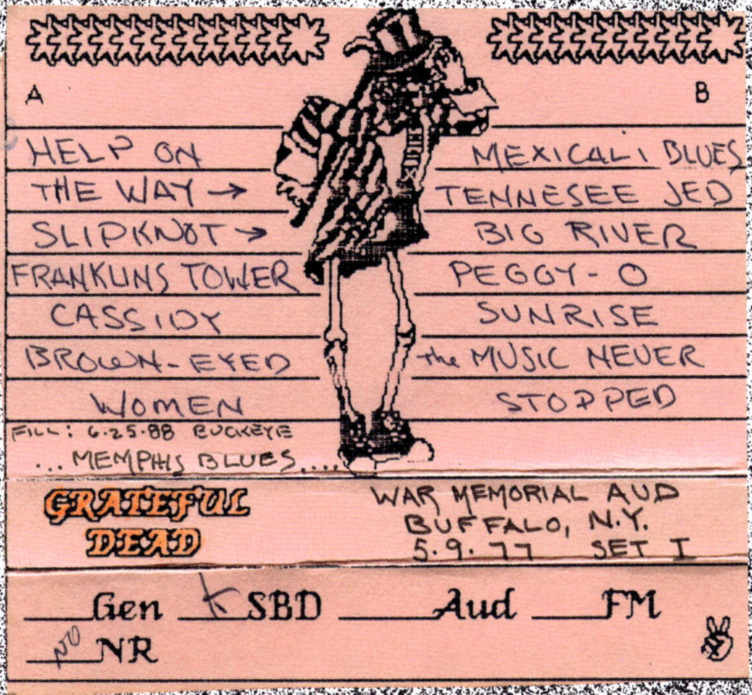
A
HELP ON THE WAY →
SLIPKNOT →
FRANKLINS TOWER
CASSIDY
BROWN-EYED WOMEN
FILL: 6-25-88 BUCKEYE
.. MEMPHIS BLUES....
B
MEXICALI BLUES
TENNESEE JED
BIG RIVER
PEGGY-O
SUNRISE
the MUSIC NEVER STOPPED
GRATEFUL DEAD
WAR MEMORIAL AUD
BUFFALO, N.Y.
5-9-77 SET I
Gen SBD Aud FM
NR

A
B
LOONEY TUNES
TH-TH-TH-TH-
THIS IS THE TAPE, FOLKS!
BERTHA →
GOOD LOVIN'
SHIP OF FOOLS
ESTIMATED →
OTHER ONE →
DRUMS →
NOT FADE
NOT FADE →
COMES A TIME →
SUGAR MAGNOLIA
E: UNCLE JOHN'S
from 4-27-85:
MUSIC NEVER STOPPED
MERRY MELODIES
BUFFALO, NY
5-9-77 SET II

A
CHICAGO - '77
B
Music Never Stopped
Ramble On Rose
Cassidy
brown-eyed women
New Minglewood
Friend o' tho' Devil
El Paso
Jack-a-roe
Looks Like Rain
Scarlet → Fire
Live CHICAGO, ILL. Dead
5·13·77 1st SET
NOISE REDUCTION: YES NO
BOARD X RADIO AUDIENCE

A Dead
Estimated →
Eyes
Sampson + Delilah
Ship of Fools
St. Stephen →
Aiko-Aiko →
Not Fade Away
Sugar Magnolia
Uncle J's Band
Morning Dew
Grateful Dead
St. Louis II
5·15·77
Source: Gen.

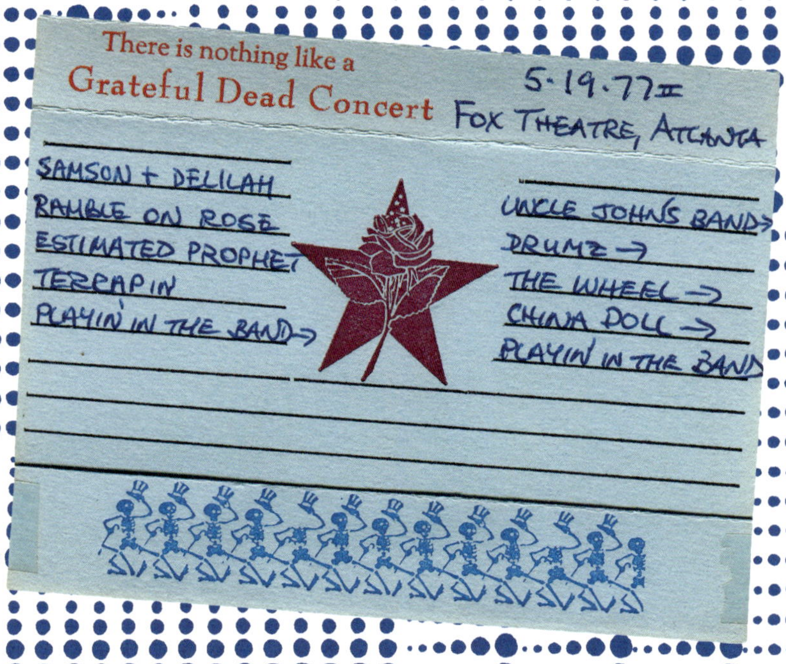
There is nothing like a
Grateful Dead Concert
5·19·77 II
FOX THEATRE, ATLANTA
SAMSON + DELILAH
RAMBLE ON ROSE
ESTIMATED PROPHET
TERRAPIN
PLAYIN' IN THE BAND →
UNCLE JOHN'S BAND →
DRUMZ →
THE WHEEL →
CHINA DOLL →
PLAYIN' IN THE BAND

Grateful Dead
LIVE DEAD
Fox Theatre, Atlanta Ga.
5-19-77 Set I
Source:
Quality:
Promised Land
Sugaree
El Paso
Peggy-O
Looks Like Rain
Row Jimmy
Passenger
Loser
Dancin in the Streets
11-11-85 Brendan Byrne
Walkin the Dog

Grateful Dead Forum 6.4.77 I
SOURCE: DAT → CD → A
GENERATION: 2nd
DATE:
THE GRATEFUL DEAD
A
Promised Land
Tennessee Jed
El Paso
Peggy-O
Jack Straw
F.O.T.D.
Lazy Lightning
Supplication
B
Candyman
Minglewood
B.E. Women
Music Never stopped
II
Samson
Ship of Fools
Cover: deadhead@mhv.net
http://www.geocities.com/SunsetStrip/Towers/6128

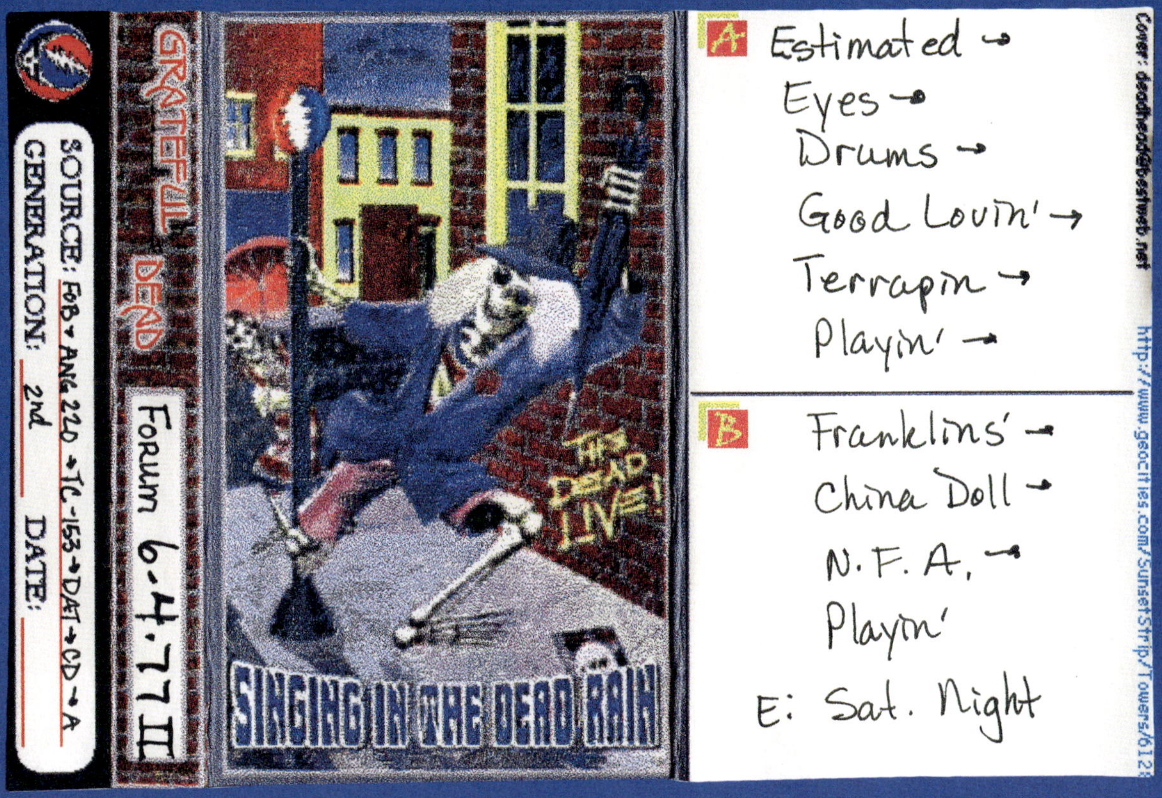
GRATEFUL DEAD
Forum 6.4.77 II
SOURCE: FOB • AKG 22D → TC-153 → DAT → CD → A
GENERATION: 2nd
DATE:
THE DEAD LIVE!
SINGING IN THE DEAD RAIN
A
Estimated →
Eyes →
Drums →
Good Lovin' →
Terrapin →
Playin' →
B
Franklins' →
China Doll →
N.F.A. →
Playin'
E: Sat. Night
Cover: deadhead@bestweb.net
http://www.geocities.com/SunsetStrip/Towers/6128

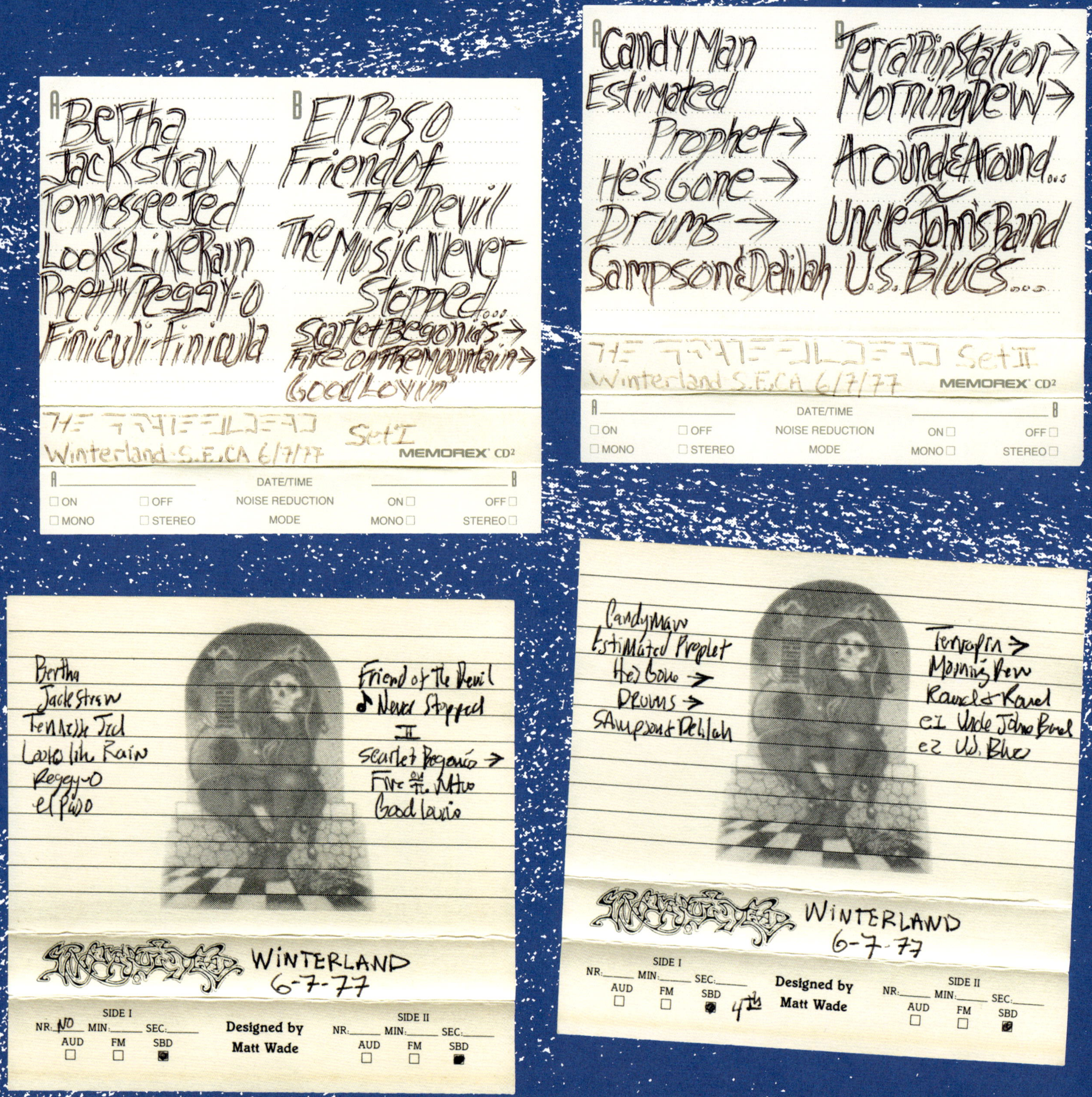
A
Bertha
Jack Straw
Tennessee Jed
Looks Like Rain
Pretty Peggy-O
Finiculi-Finicula
B
El Paso
Friend of The Devil
The Music Never Stopped...
Scarlet Begonias →
Fire on the Mountain →
Good Lovin'
THE GRATEFUL DEAD Set I
Winterland S.F., CA 6/7/77
MEMOREX CD2
A
DATE/TIME
B
ON
OFF
NOISE REDUCTION
ON
OFF
MONO
STEREO
MODE
MONO
STEREO
A
Candy Man
Estimated Prophet →
He's Gone →
Drums →
Sampson & Delilah
B
Terrapin Station →
Morning Dew →
Around & Around...
Uncle John's Band
U.S. Blues...
THE GRATEFUL DEAD Set II
Winterland S.F., CA 6/7/77
MEMOREX CD2
A
DATE/TIME
B
ON
OFF
NOISE REDUCTION
ON
OFF
MONO
STEREO
MODE
MONO
STEREO
Bertha
Jack Straw
Tennessee Jed
Looks like Rain
Peggy-O
el Paso
Friend of The Devil
♪ Never Stopped
II
Scarlet Begonias →
Fire on the Mtn
Good lovin
WINTERLAND
6-7-77
SIDE I
NR: NO
MIN:
SEC:
AUD
FM
SBD
Designed by
Matt Wade
SIDE II
NR:
MIN:
SEC:
AUD
FM
SBD
Candyman
Estimated Prophet
He's Gone →
Drums →
Sampson & Delilah
Terrapin →
Morning Dew
Round & Round
e1 Uncle John's Band
e2 U.S. Blues
WINTERLAND
6-7-77
SIDE I
NR:
MIN:
SEC:
AUD
FM
SBD
4th
Designed by
Matt Wade
SIDE II
NR:
MIN:
SEC:
AUD
FM
SBD

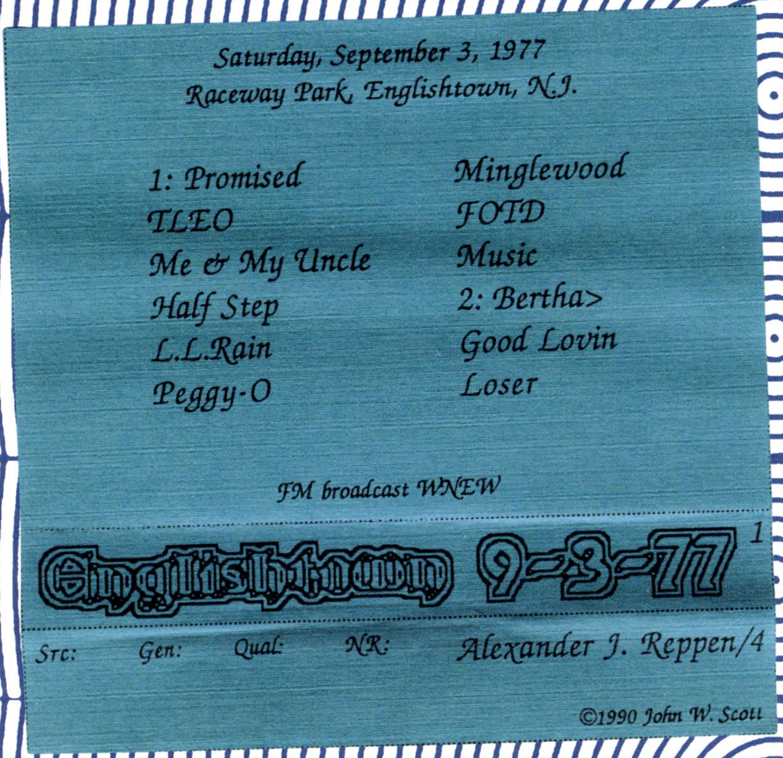
Saturday, September 3, 1977
Raceway Park, Englishtown, N.J.
1: Promised
TLEO
Me & My Uncle
Half Step
L.L.Rain
Peggy-O
Minglewood
FOTD
Music
2: Bertha>
Good Lovin
Loser
FM broadcast WNEW
Englishtown 9-3-77 1
Src:
Gen:
Qual:
NR:
Alexander J. Reppen/4
©1990 John W. Scott

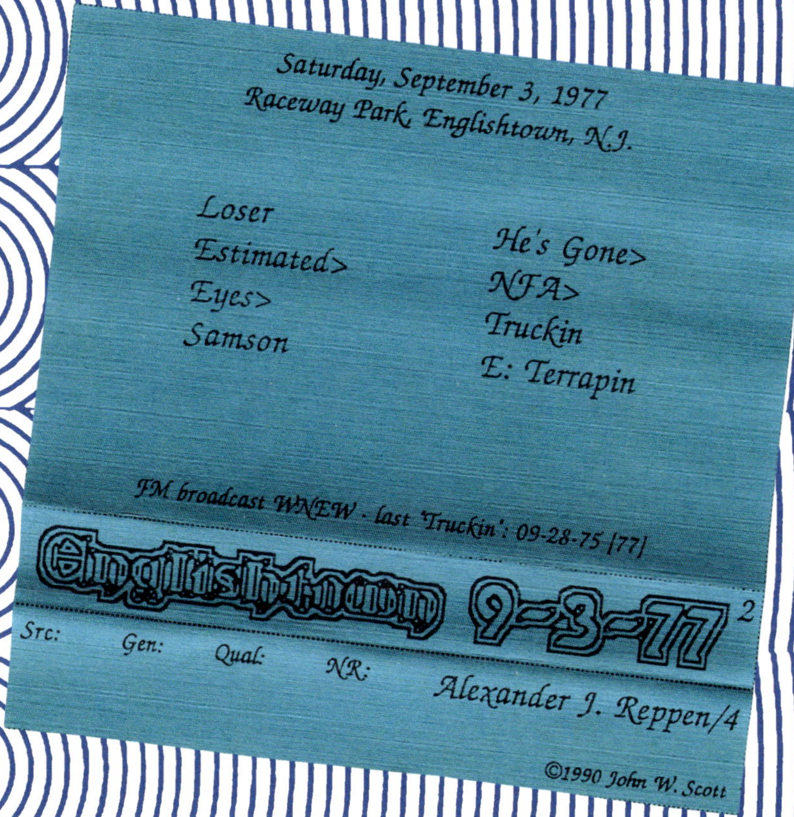
Saturday, September 3, 1977
Raceway Park, Englishtown, N.J.
Loser
Estimated>
Eyes>
Samson
He's Gone>
NFA>
Truckin
E: Terrapin
FM broadcast WNEW - last 'Truckin': 09-28-75 [77]
Englishtown 9-3-77 2
Src:
Gen:
Qual:
NR:
Alexander J. Reppen/4
©1990 John W. Scott

10-16-77:
SCARLet
FIRE
ESTIMATED
LOOSE LUCY:
Portland 5-19-74
Johny Cash's Big River
U.S. BLUES
8 years
LA BAMBA>
GOOD LOVIN'
HEY POCKY WAY
Cornell 77
Scarlet
FIRE
ESTIMATED
EYES
Grateful
BATON ROUGE
10-16-77
Dead

Broome County Coliseum
Binghampton, NY
11-6-77 Set #1
Mississippi ½ Step
Jack Straw
Tennessee Jed
Mexicali Blues
Me and My Uncle
Minglewood Blues
Dupree's Diamond Blues
Passenger
Dire Wolf
Music Never Stopped
Set II
~Samson & Delilah
Sunrise
GRATEFUL DEAD
Broome County Coliseum Set I
Binghampton, N.Y. 11-6-77
12 cards/$1.50
Wiseguy Productions – C
PO Box 6384
Evanston, Illinois 60204

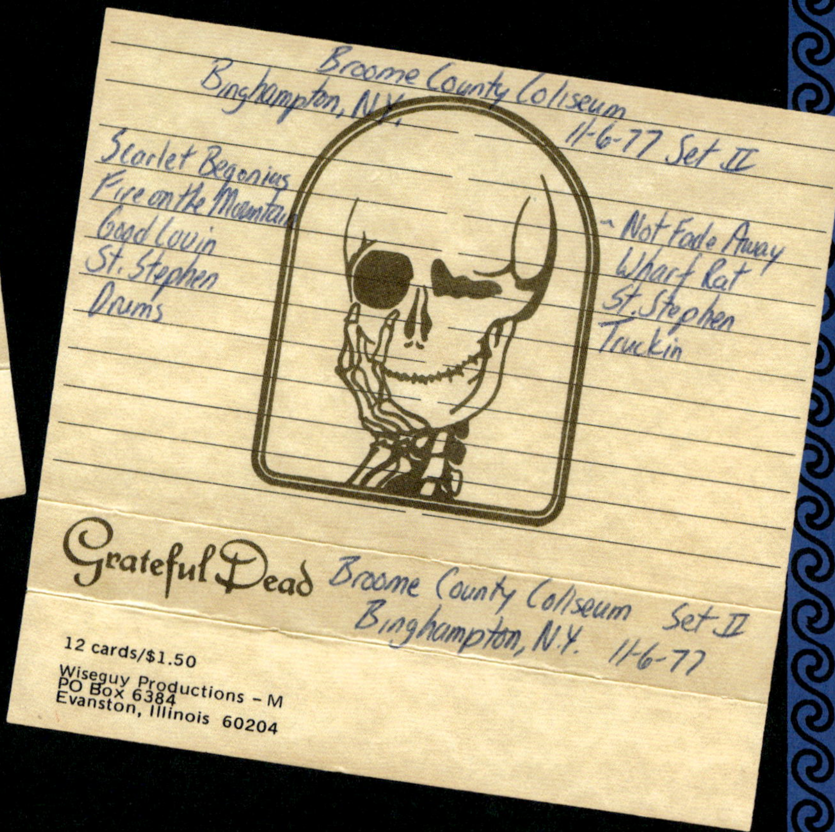
Broome County Coliseum
Binghampton, N.Y.
11-6-77 Set II
Scarlet Begonias
Fire on the Mountain
Good Lovin
St. Stephen
Drums
~Not Fade Away
Wharf Rat
St. Stephen
Truckin
Grateful Dead
Broome County Coliseum Set II
Binghampton, N.Y. 11-6-77
12 cards/$1.50
Wiseguy Productions – M
PO Box 6384
Evanston, Illinois 60204

GRATEFUL DEAD
Grateful Dead
SAN DIEGO
1-7-78 2
BOARD ■ RADIO □ AUDIENCE [ ]

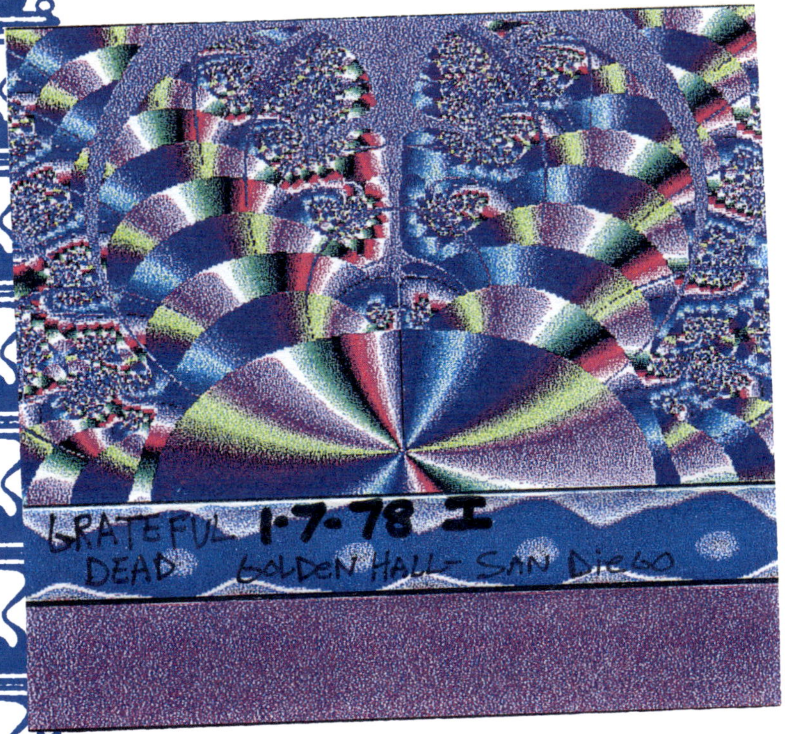
GRATEFUL DEAD
1-7-78 I
GOLDEN HALL- SAN DIEGO

GRATEFUL DEAD
1-7-78 II
GOLDEN HALL -SAN DIEGO

SHRINE 1.1.78
SBD
AUD
FM
Gen
HAIGHT

MAGNOLIA COVERS
4120 Maine St. #1
Lake Worth, FL 33461

LIVE!
A
AUD FM SBD
Grateful Dead 4-8-78 Tape II
Veteran's Memorial Coliseum
PHOTO BY T.A.B.
© 1988
B
AUD FM SBD

DEAD
SBD
AUD
FM

WILLIAMSBURG VA
4/15/78 SET II SBD
BERTHA
GOOD LOVIN'
CANDYMAN
SUNRISE
PLAYIN'
DRUMS
DRUMS
NOT FADE AWAY
MORNING DEW
ROUND & ROUND

Bertha >
Good Lovin' >
Candy Man
Sunrise >
Playin' in the Band >
Drumz
Drumz >
Not Fade Away >
Morning Dew
Around & Around
-Encore-
One more Sat. Night
DEAD Williamsburg Va. 4.15.78 -set II-
SBD AUD FM GEN

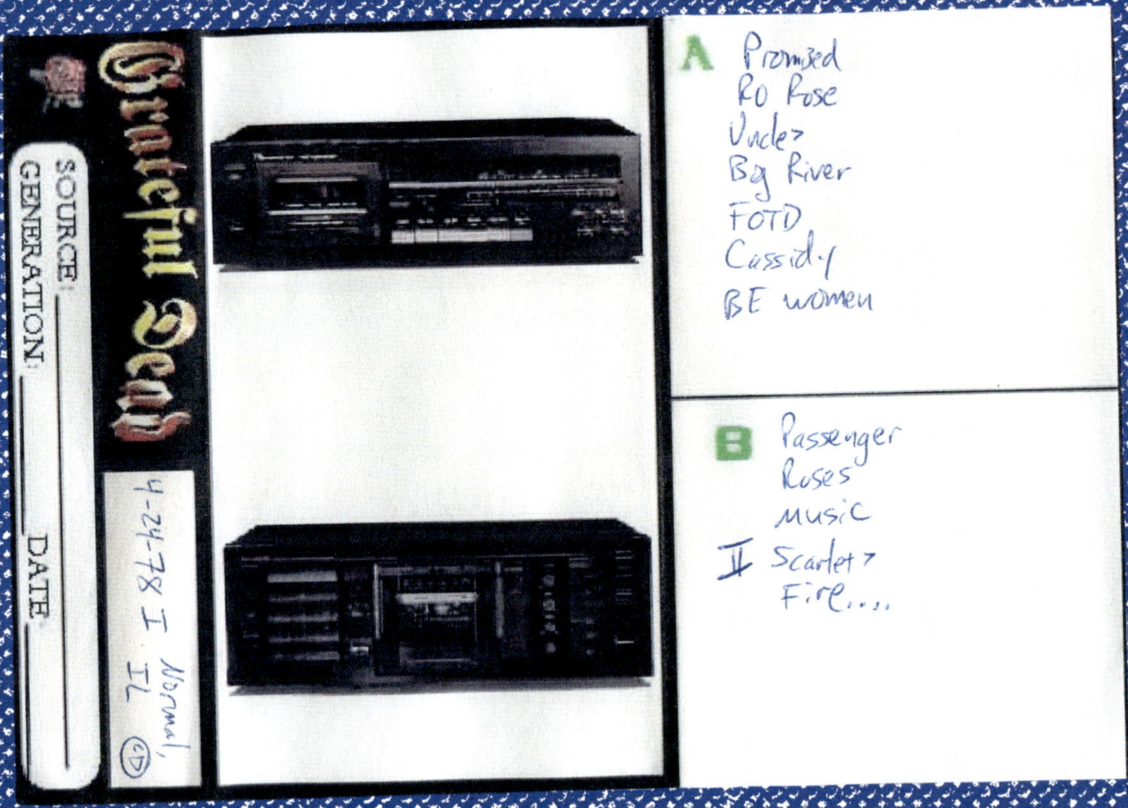

Grateful Dead
SOURCE
GENERATION
DATE
4-24-78 I IL Normal,
A
Promised
Ro Rose
Uncle>
Big River
FOTD
Cassidy
BE women
B
Passenger
Roses
Music
II Scarlet>
Fire....

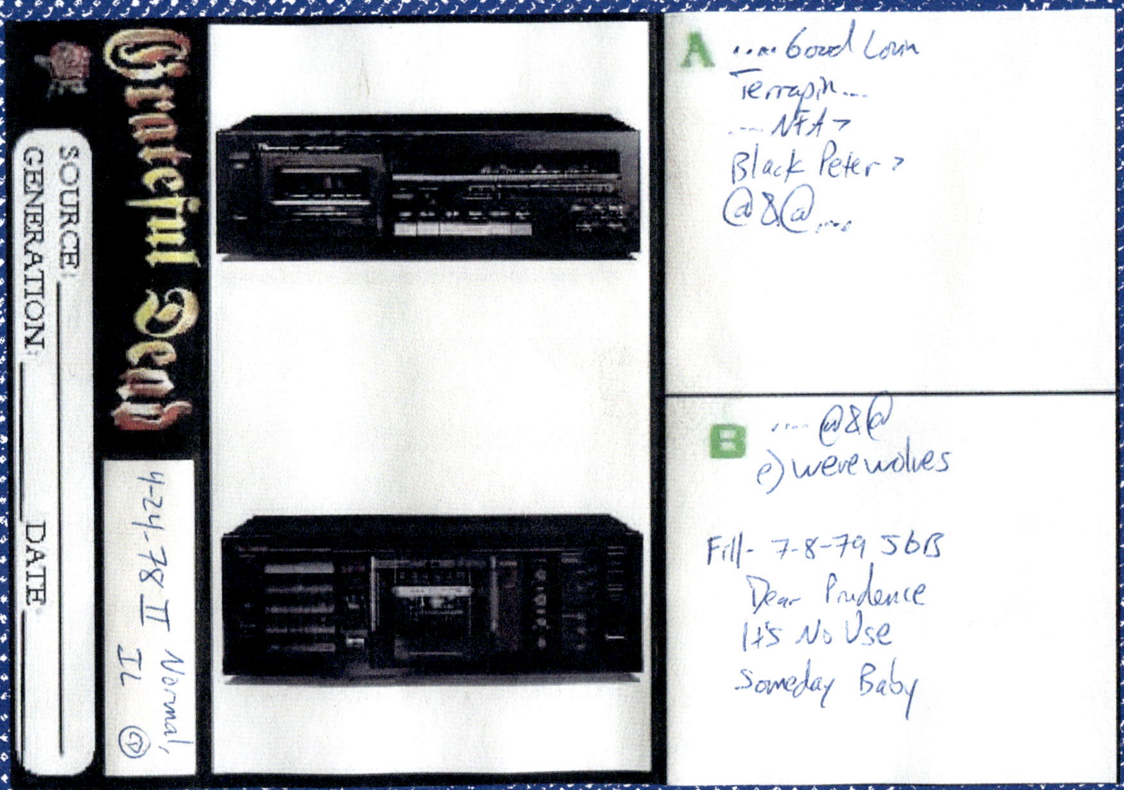

Grateful Dead
SOURCE
GENERATION
DATE
4-24-78 II IL Normal,
A
....Good Lovin
Terrapin...
...NFA>
Black Peter>
@&@....
B
....@&@
e) werewolves
Fill- 7-8-79 SbB
Dear Prudence
It's No Use
Someday Baby

©1992
P.O. BOX No. 2151
Baltimore, MD 21203-2151
SBD AUD FM GEN
7-8-78
Red Rocks
set II (cont)
Estimated ->
Other One ->
Eyes ->
Drumz
Space Jam
Wharf Rat ->
Franklin ->
Sugar Mag
E Werewolves
Maybe You Had Too Much Too Fast
A
B
Grateful Dead
SOURCE:
GEN:
NR:
SBD
FM
AUD
Bertha
Good Lovin'
Dire Wolf
El Paso
Must Have Been the Roses
Minglewood
-Filler-
B. Eyed Women
Ramble on Rose
Promised Land
Deal
-Set II-
Samson & Delilah
Ship of Fools
-Filler-
Cassidy
GD
Red Rocks Co.
7-8-78
I
II
SBD AUD FM NR
-Set II cont.-
Estimated
The Other One
Eyes of the World
Drumz (cut)
-Encore-
Werewolves of London
Warf Rat
Franklins Tower
Sugar Magnolia
Terrapin
One More Saturday Night
GD
Red Rocks Co.
7-8-78
I
II
SBD AUD FM NR

Grateful Dead
CAIRO, EGYPT (#1)
SEPTEMBER 16, 1978
GRATEFUL DEAD

HOMMZA EL DIN
JAM
NOT FADE
ME AND MY UNCLE
THEY ♡
EACHOTHER
THEY ♡ EACHOTHER
MINGLE WOOD
PEGGY-O
BEAT IT ON
DEAL
GRATEFUL DEAD
CAIRO, EGYPT
9/16/78

GRATEFUL DEAD
Cairo Egypt
S 16 1978 1
Gizeh Theater Cairo Egypt 1978

GRATEFUL DEAD
Cairo Egypt
S 16 1978 2
bertha
good lovin
candyman
looks like rain
row jimmy
el paso
ramble on rose
new minglewood
deal
percussion
fire on mountain
iko iko
i need a miracle
its all over now
sunrise
shakedown st
truckin
stella blue
around & around
one more saturday

WINTERLAND, S.F. CA!
10-17-78 Set II
Scarlet
Fire
Estimated
Eyes
(cut)
Eyes
Drums
Space
World to
Give
Around
U.S. Blues
Live
WINTERLAND S.F. CA. 10-17-78 II
Dead
2ND Live "WORD" OUT OF 3
Noise Reduction IN OUT
BOARD X RADIO __ AUDIENCE __

Date: 11-17-78 Set:
Loyola University Bob Weir & Friends
Source: Aud Quality: B
Side A:
Winnin' Boy Blues; Tom Dooley; This Time Forever; Casey Raod; Knockin' on Heaven's Door; Big Boy Pete; Jack A Roe; Dark Hollow; Oh Boy
Side B:
Jerry Garcia Band 2-11-81: Mississippi Moon; Tore Up -> Tangled Up in Blue Dead - Oakland Aud: Bird Song; On the Road Again
GRATEFUL DEAD
11-17-78 Set:
Bob Weir & Friends
Loyola University

Jack Straw
Sugaree
Me & My Uncle ->
Big River
Stagger Lee
Passenger
Candyman ->
-> Candyman
Minglewood
From the ♡ of Me
Loser
Promised land
Set II. Miracle -> Good Lovin
LIVE DEAD
Capitol Theatre NJ 11-24-78 SET I

I need a Miracle
-> Good Lovin
Friend of the Devil
Estimated
Prophet ->
Shakedown Street
-> Shakedown Street
-> Drums
-> Rollin Aragee(?)
-> Fire on the Mt
-> Sugar Magnolia
Live Dead
11-24-78 Set II
SBD
AUD
FM
DAT

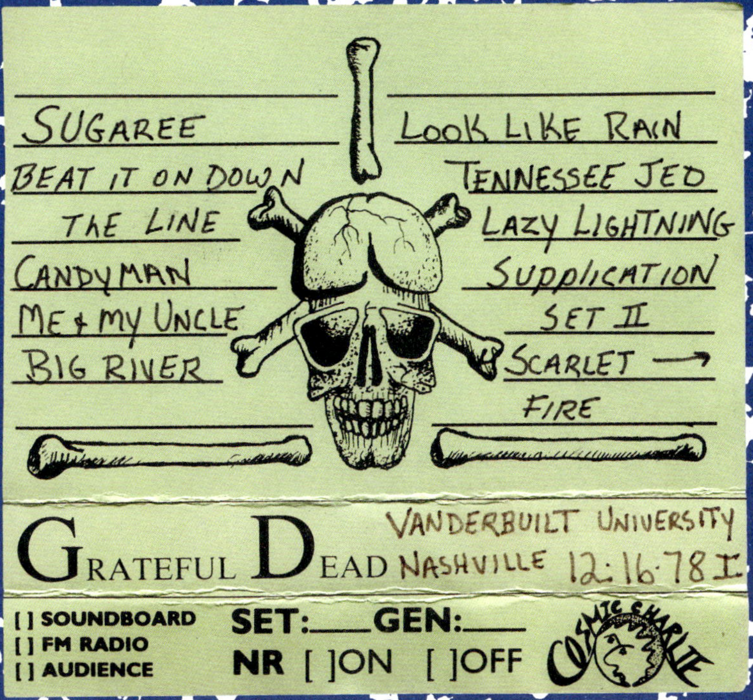
SUGAREE
BEAT IT ON DOWN THE LINE
CANDYMAN
ME & MY UNCLE
BIG RIVER
LOOK LIKE RAIN
TENNESSEE JED
LAZY LIGHTNING
SUPPLICATION
SET II
SCARLET →
FIRE
GRATEFUL DEAD
VANDERBUILT UNIVERSITY NASHVILLE 12·16·78 I
[ ] SOUNDBOARD
[ ] FM RADIO
[ ] AUDIENCE
SET:___ GEN:___
NR [ ]ON [ ]OFF
COSMIC CHARLIE

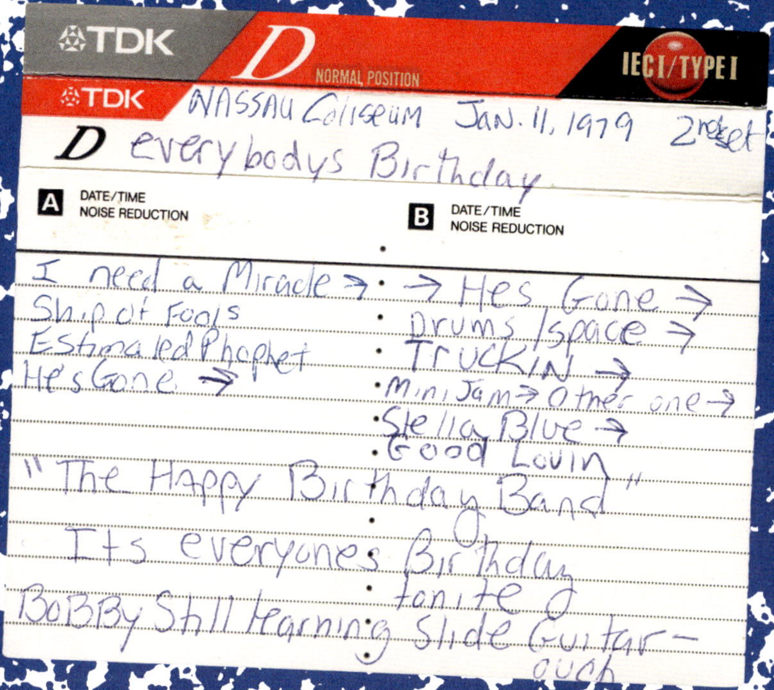
TDK D NORMAL POSITION IECI/TYPE I
TDK
NASSAU Coliseum Jan. 11, 1979 2nd set
D everybodys Birthday
A DATE/TIME NOISE REDUCTION
B DATE/TIME NOISE REDUCTION
I need a Miracle →
Ship of Fools
Estimated Prophet
He's Gone →
→ Hes Gone →
Drums/Space →
Truckin →
Mini Jam → other one →
Stella Blue →
Good Lovin
"The Happy Birthday Band"
Its everyones Birthday tonite
BoBBy Still learning Slide Guitar — ouch

SCARLET
FIRE
Estimated
Eyes
The Other One
Warf Rat
I need a miracle
Casey Jones
China Cat
I know you Rider
MDCCLXXVI
LIVE INDIANAPOLIS 2·3·79 DEAD
NOISE REDUCTION: B C
QUALITY: 1 2 3 4 5 6 7 8 9 10
GENERATION:

ARKIN MY IMAGINATION
GREATEST STORY
DONT EASE ME IN
MAMA TRIED
MEXACALLI BLUES
FOTD
PASSENGER
HIGH TIME
LOOKS LIKE RAIN
JACK-A-ROE
LAZY LIGHTNING
SUPPLICATION
MIGHT AS WELL
MIRACLE
BERTHA
GOOD LOVIN
Live Dead
Oakland Collesium 2·17·79 — Keith/Donna's Last…
[ ] SOUNDBOARD
[ ] FM RADIO
[ ] AUDIENCE
SET:___ GEN:___
NR [ ]ON [ ]OFF
COSMIC CHARLIE

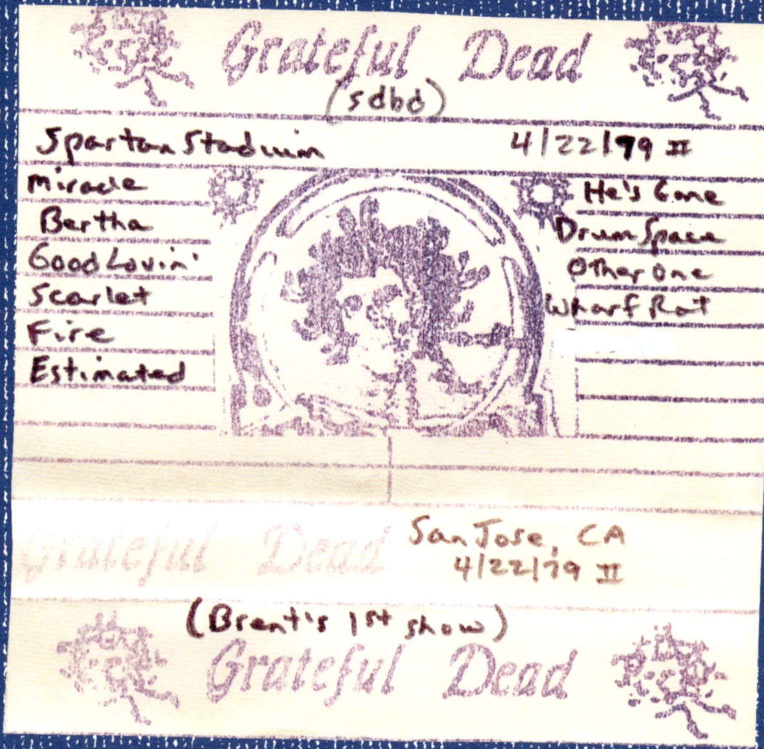
Grateful Dead
(sdbd)
Spartan Stadium
4/22/79 II
Miracle
Bertha
Good Lovin'
Scarlet
Fire
Estimated
He's Gone
Drum Space
Other One
Wharf Rat
Grateful Dead
San Jose, CA
4/22/79 II
(Brent's 1st show)
Grateful Dead

4-22-79 II
SPARTAN STADIUM
SAN JOSE
Dead

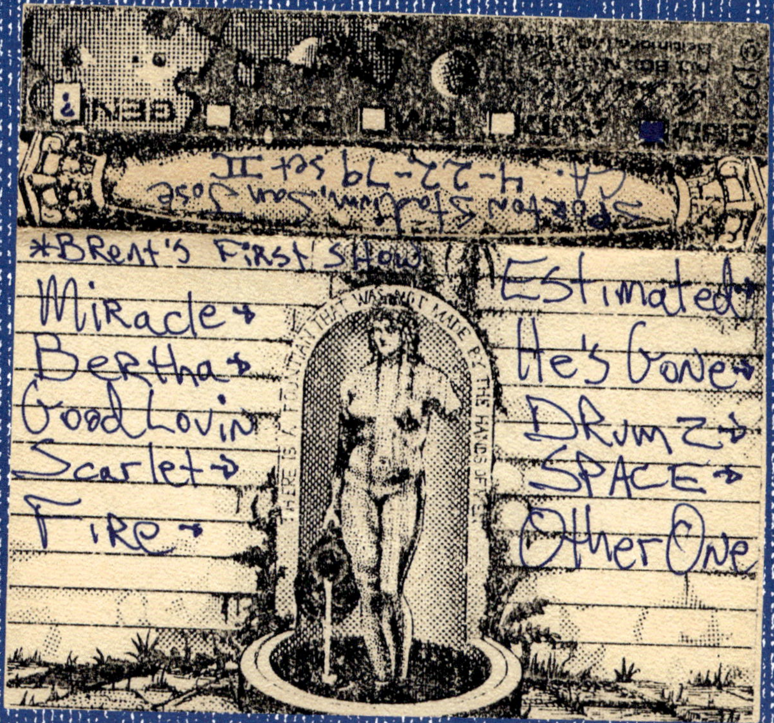
*Brent's First Show
Miracle
Bertha
Good Lovin
Scarlet
Fire
Estimated
He's Gone
Drumz
SPACE
Other One

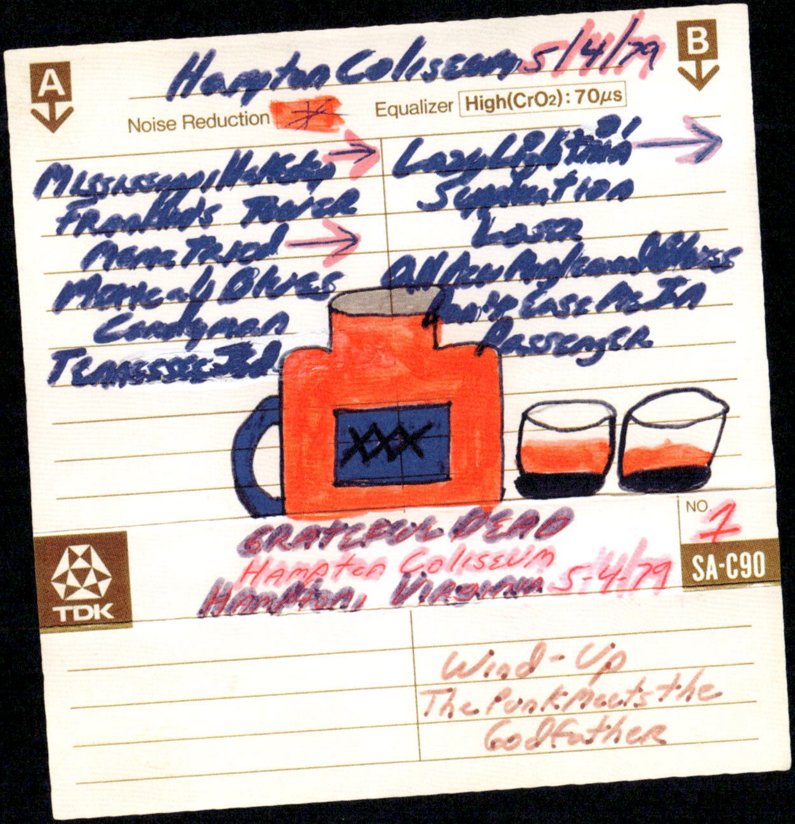

Hampton Coliseum 5/4/79
Noise Reduction
Equalizer High(CrO2): 70μs
Mama Tried
Candyman
Loser
Passenger
GRATEFUL DEAD
Hampton Coliseum
Hampton, Virginia 5-4-79
NO. 7
SA-C90
TDK
Wind-Up
The Punk Meets the Godfather

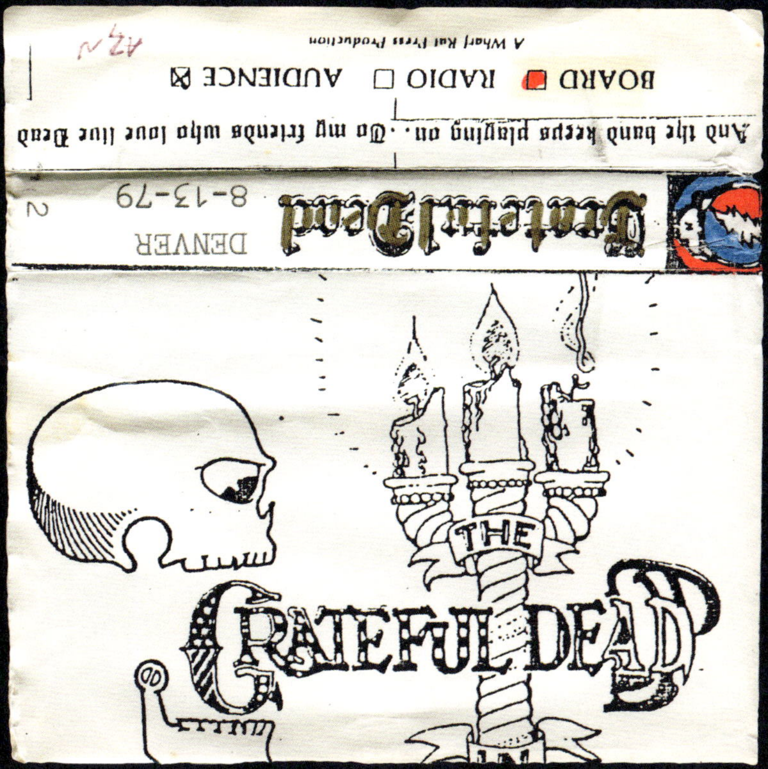

A Wharf Rat Press Production
BOARD
RADIO
AUDIENCE
And the band keeps playing on.. To my friends who love the Dead
Grateful Dead
DENVER
8-13-79
THE
GRATEFUL DEAD

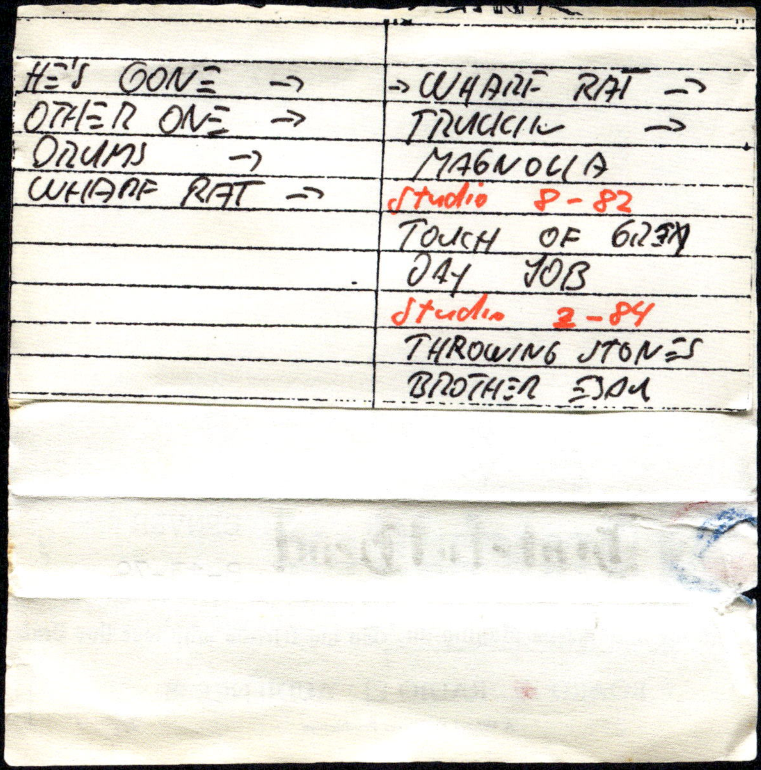

HE'S GONE →
OTHER ONE →
DRUMS →
WHARF RAT →
→ WHARF RAT →
TRUCKIN →
MAGNOLIA
Studio 8-82
TOUCH OF GREY
DAY JOB
Studio 2-84
THROWING STONES
BROTHER ESAU

Grateful Dead 9-1-79 I Rochester, NY
SOURCE:
GENERATION:
DATE
Upstate Jam 9/1/79
Noise Reduction
Equalizer High(CrO2): 70µs
Good Lovin'
ENCORE
Another Saturday Night
GRATEFUL DEAD
Rochester, New York 9/1/79
TDK
SA-C90
CASEY JONES
Bob Weir, Jerry Garcia
TRUCKIN
GRATEFUL DEAD
JACK STRAW
CANDYMAN
ME AND MY UNCLE →
BIG RIVER
BROWN-EYED WOMEN
EASY TO LOVE YOU
MINGLEWOOD BLUES
STAGGER LEE
LOST SAILOR →
SAINT OF CIRCUMSTANCE →
DEAL
II
DANCIN' IN THE STREETS →
FRANKLIN'S TOWER
DEAD
CAPE COD COLISEUM
SOUTH YARMOUTH, MA.
10-27-79
I...II

A
B
PHILADELPHIA, PA 11/6/79
ALABAMA GETAWAY
PROMISED LAND
TENN. JED
ME + MY UNCLE
MEXICALI BLUES
CANDYMAN
EASY TO LOVE YOU
LOOKS LIKE RAIN
JACK-A-ROE
JACK STRAW
DEAL
10/25/85 FLA.
ESTIMATED
Live PHILADELPHIA 11/6/79 Dead
NOISE REDUCTION: YES__ NO X
BOARD__ RADIO__ AUDIENCE X

11/9/79 II
Dancin in the Streets ->
Franklins Tower
-> Estimated Prophet
-> He's Gone
Drums ->
Wharf Rat ->
I Need a Miracle ->
Bertha ->
Good Lovin' (x)
Live Dead !
11-9-79
Set II
War Memorial – Buffalo.Ny.
3rd Gen - Soundboard

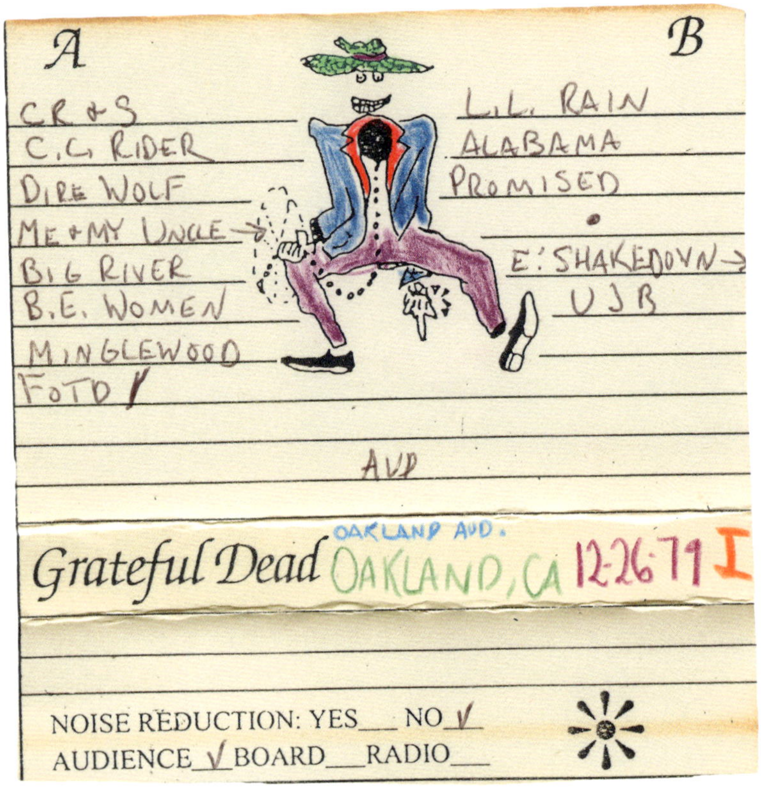
A
B
CR & S
C.C. RIDER
DIRE WOLF
ME & MY UNCLE →
BIG RIVER
B.E. WOMEN
MINGLEWOOD
FOTD
L.L. RAIN
ALABAMA
PROMISED
E: SHAKEDOWN →
UJB
AUD
OAKLAND AUD.
Grateful Dead OAKLAND, CA 12-26-79 I
NOISE REDUCTION: YES___ NO ✓
AUDIENCE ✓ BOARD___ RADIO___

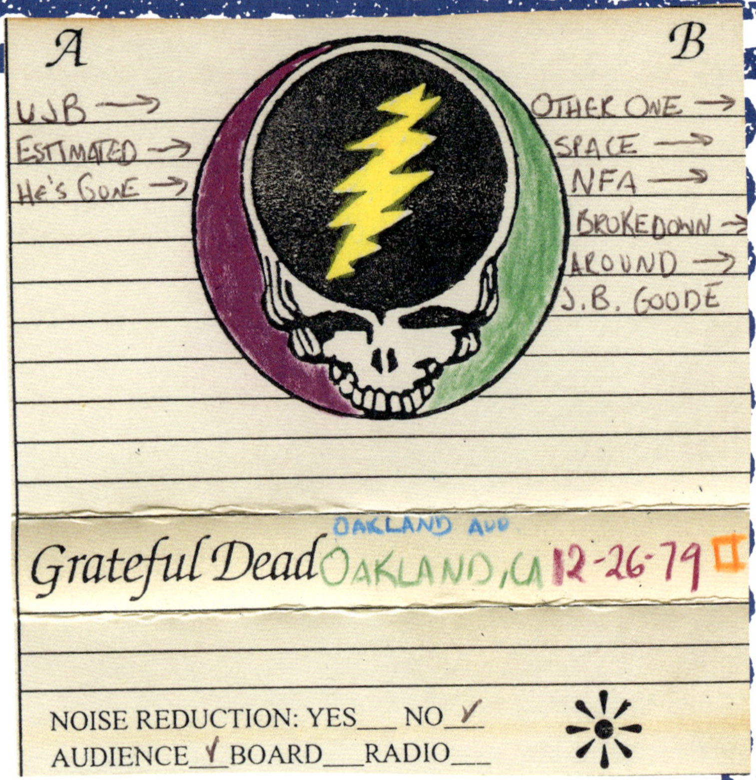
A
B
UJB →
ESTIMATED →
He's Gone →
OTHER ONE →
SPACE →
NFA →
BROKEDOWN →
AROUND →
J.B. GOODE
OAKLAND AUD
Grateful Dead OAKLAND, CA 12-26-79 II
NOISE REDUCTION: YES___ NO ✓
AUDIENCE ✓ BOARD___ RADIO___

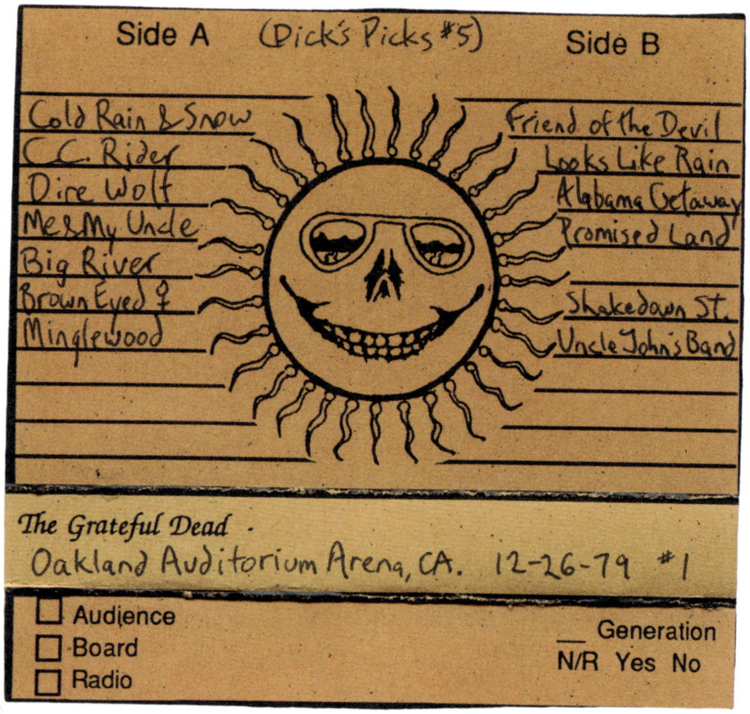
Side A (Dick's Picks #5) Side B
Cold Rain & Snow
C.C. Rider
Dire Wolf
Me & My Uncle
Big River
Brown Eyed W
Minglewood
Friend of the Devil
Looks Like Rain
Alabama Getaway
Promised Land
Shakedown St.
Uncle John's Band
The Grateful Dead
Oakland Auditorium Arena, CA. 12-26-79 #1
Audience
Board
Radio
__ Generation
N/R Yes No

Side A (Dick's Picks #5) Side B
Uncle John's Band
Estimated Prophet
Jam
He's Gone
Other One
Drums, Space
Not Fade Away
Brokedown Palace
Around & Around
Johnny B. Goode
The Grateful Dead
Oakland Auditorium Arena, CA. 12-26-79 #2
Audience
Board
Radio
__ Generation
N/R Yes No

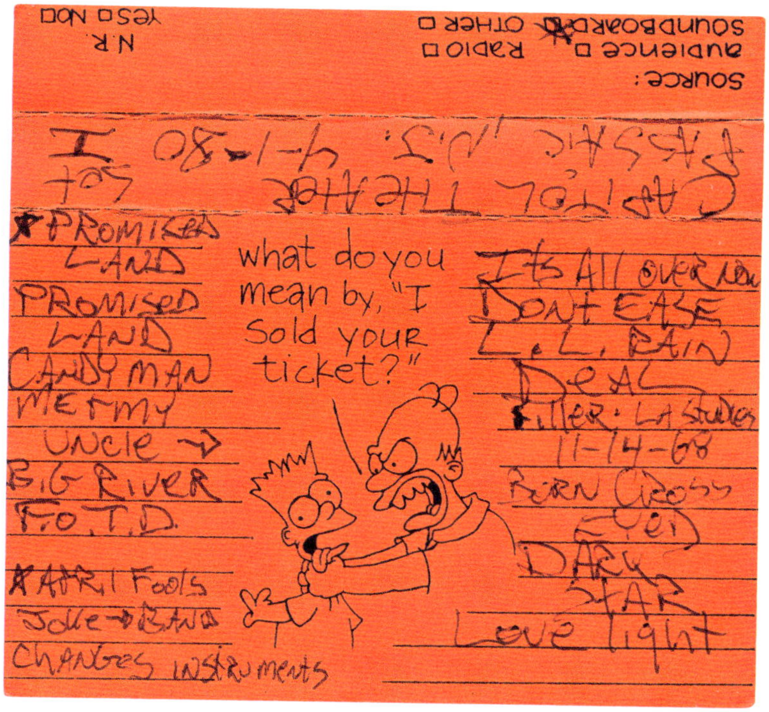
SOURCE:
audience □ Radio □ N.R.
soundboard ✱ other □ yes □ no □

PASSAIC, N.J. 4-1-80
CAPITOL THEATRE

I set

✱PROMISED LAND
PROMISED LAND
CANDYMAN
MET MY UNCLE →
BIG RIVER
F.O.T.D.

✱APRIL Fools Joke → BAND CHANGES INSTRUMENTS

what do you mean by, "I sold your ticket?"

It's All Over Now
Don't Ease
L.L. RAIN
DEAL
Filler: LA Studios 11-14-68
BORN CROSS EYED
DARK STAR
Love light

APRIL FOOLS
BRENT & JERRY - DRUMZ
BOBBY - KEYBOARD - VOCALS
Bill - BASS phil - lEAD
MICKEY - Rhythm - VOCAL

Boston Garden

SIDE 1 TITLE: 5.12	SIDE 2 80 TITLE: 2nd Set
Ship of Fools	St. Of Circum-
Estimated Profet	stance
He's Gone	Wharf Rat
JAM	Sugar Magnolia
Drumz	
Space	E. U.S. Blues
SUN SHINEY DAYDREAM ↗	Feel Like A Stranger
	UnCle John's Band

DEAD IN BOSTON 80★

LENGTH 30 □ BIAS ____ NOISE REDUCTION

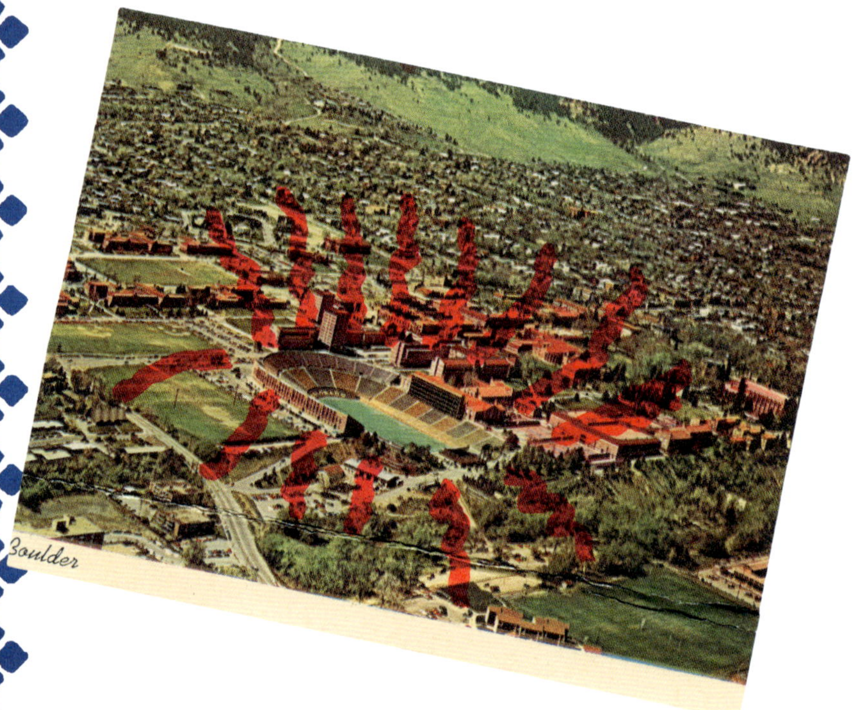

A] Uncle John's Band →
Playing in the Band →
Uncle John's Band
Me & My Uncle
Mexicali Shoes
Tennessee Jed
Sampson & Delilah

B] Easy to love You
Althea →
Looks Like Rain
Deal
Feel like a Stranger
Ship of Fools

DEAD
Folsom Field, Boulder, Co
June 8, 1980 1st SET

162—Aerial view of the UNIVERSITY OF COLORADO
campus at BOULDER, COLORADO.
Color by Lew Dakan
CURTEICHCOLOR® 3-D NATU

A] Estimated Prophet
Eyes of the World
Folsom Space
Drumz

B] Saint of Circumstance
Black Peter
Sugar Magnolia
Alabama Getaway
Brokedown Palace

Grateful DEAD
Folsom Field, Boulder, Colorado
June 8, 1980 SET 2
Sunday

erial view of the UNIVERSITY OF COLORADO
s at BOULDER, COLORADO.
Color by Lew Dakan
CURTEICHCOLOR® 3-D NATURAL COLOR REPR

Source:
Audience X Radio —
Soundboard — Other —
Generation —
Noise Reduction YES— NO—
Jack Straw
Franklin's Tower
Mama Tried
Mexicalli Blues
Friend of the Devil
Easy to Love You
Let it Grow
Althea
Lost Sailor
St. of Circumstance
Deal
Brook '85 → Touch of Grey

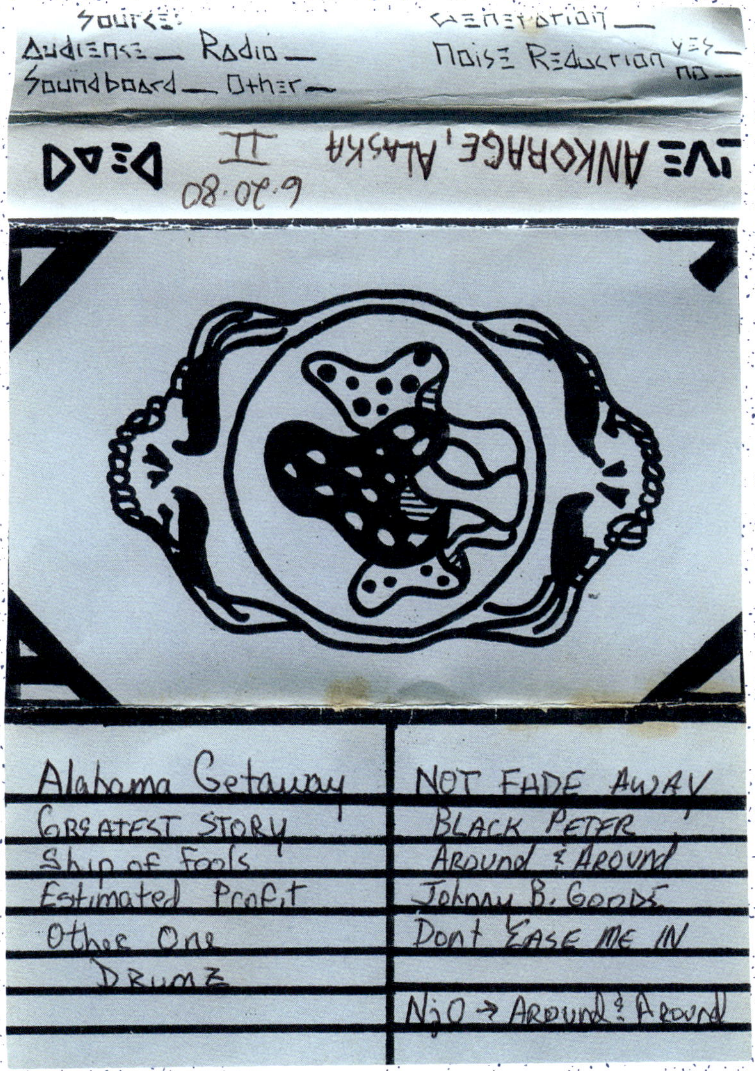
Source:
Audience — Radio —
Soundboard — Other —
Generation —
Noise Reduction YES— NO—
Alabama Getaway
Greatest Story
Ship of Fools
Estimated Profit
Other One
Drumz
Not Fade Away
Black Peter
Around & Around
Johnny B. Goode
Dont Ease Me In
NjO → Around & Around

Grateful
Dead
Start Set 1
Loser
Lazy lightning
Supplication
Far From Me
Ramble on Rose
Feel like A Stranger
Sugaree →
Sugaree
New Minglewood
Candyman
Me & my Uncle
Big River
Berkeley 11-23-84
Gloria
Why Don't we Do it in the Road
GRATEFUL DEAD
Anchorage, Alaska
Anchorage High School 6-21-80
Gen
SBD
Aud
FM
NR

Grateful Dead 8-30-80 Set 2
Scarlet Begonias->
Fire On The Mountain
m: CC Rider->
m: Ramble On Rose
Estimated Prophet->
Eyes Of The World->
Drums->
Not Fade Away->
Black Peter->
Sugar Magnolia
E: One More Saturday Night
GRATEFUL DEAD
The Spectrum - Philadelphia, PA
8-30-80
Set 2
Rating: A, Source: S:C, Gen.: ?, NR: None, DOW: Sat, from Drew Berry, Comments: Set 1: SB/? Set 2 is from a different source: FOB/6, taped with a JVC-KD2 w/ Nak 300 mics, from 10th row center. CC Rider and Ramble on Rose are missing.

LIVE! - Rochester, NY 9/2/80 I
A
Source SB
PHOTO BY T.A.B.
©1987
B
Source
SB

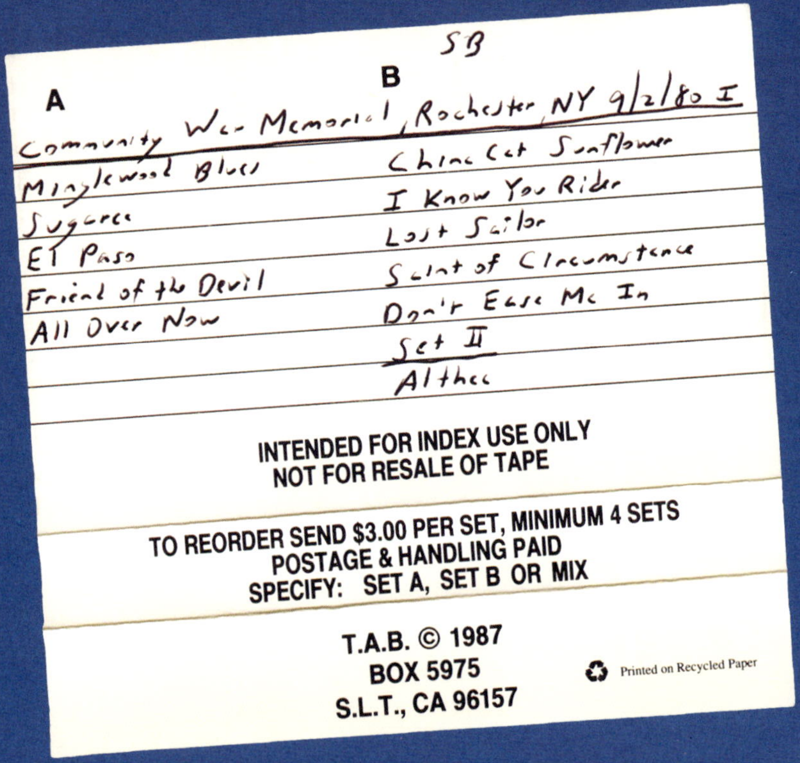
SB
A
B
Community War Memorial, Rochester NY 9/2/80 I
Minglewood Blues
Sugaree
El Paso
Friend of the Devil
All Over Now
China Cat Sunflower
I Know You Rider
Lost Sailor
Saint of Circumstance
Don't Ease Me In
Set II
Althea
INTENDED FOR INDEX USE ONLY
NOT FOR RESALE OF TAPE
TO REORDER SEND $3.00 PER SET, MINIMUM 4 SETS
POSTAGE & HANDLING PAID
SPECIFY: SET A, SET B OR MIX
T.A.B. © 1987
BOX 5975
S.L.T., CA 96157
Printed on Recycled Paper

SIDE A
ALABAMA
GetAWAY
Greatest
Story
SugAree
ME & MY Uncle
Mexicali
TENN. JED
B
Feel
like A
STRANGER
F.O.T.D.
FAR From
me
Rooster
State Fair Grounds
Lewiston, ME
GD 9-6-80 GD Set I

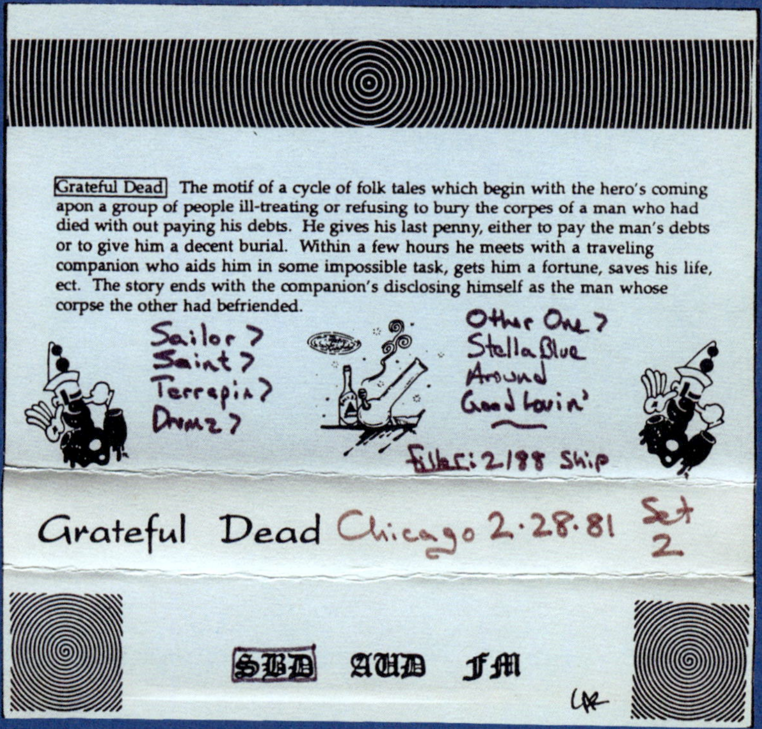
Grateful Dead The motif of a cycle of folk tales which begin with the hero's coming apon a group of people ill-treating or refusing to bury the corpes of a man who had died with out paying his debts. He gives his last penny, either to pay the man's debts or to give him a decent burial. Within a few hours he meets with a traveling companion who aids him in some impossible task, gets him a fortune, saves his life, ect. The story ends with the companion's disclosing himself as the man whose corpse the other had befriended.
Sailor ?
Saint ?
Terrepin ?
Drums ?
Other One ?
Stella Blue
Around
Good lovin'
Filler: 2/88 Ship
Grateful Dead Chicago 2·28·81 Set 2
SBD AUD FM

A SPAIN
Scarlet
Fire
Sailor
Saint
B 10-19-81 II
Drumz/Space
other one
Stella Blue
Sugar Mag
Don't Ease
THE "FURTHUR" ADVENTURES!
BARCELONA, SPAIN
10-19-81
SET II
SBD
AUD
UNCLE SAM

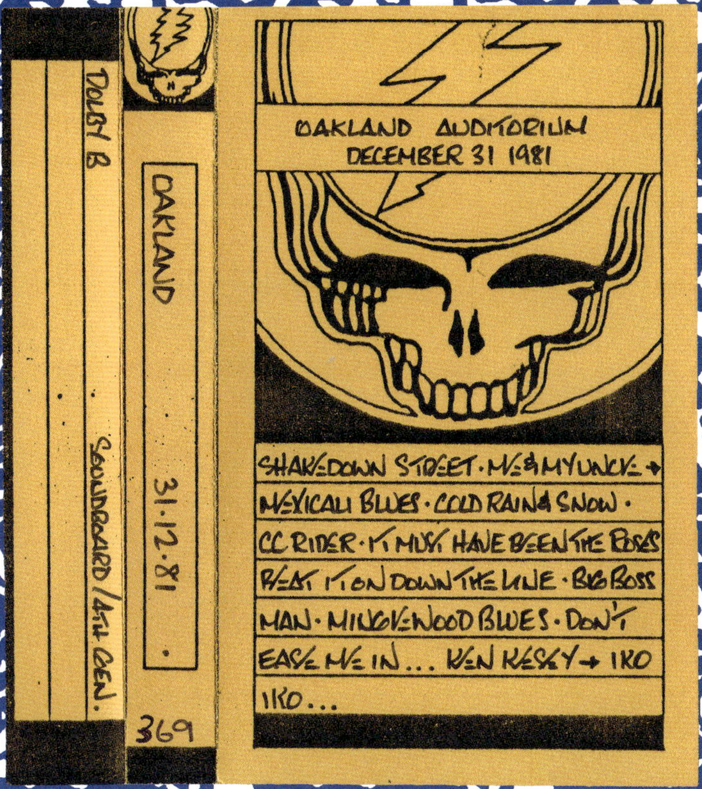
DOLBY B
OAKLAND
31.12.81
SOUNDBOARD/4th GEN.
369
OAKLAND AUDITORIUM
DECEMBER 31 1981
SHAKEDOWN STREET · ME & MY UNCLE →
MEXICALI BLUES · COLD RAIN & SNOW ·
CC RIDER · IT MUST HAVE BEEN THE ROSES
BEAT IT ON DOWN THE LINE · BIG BOSS
MAN · MINGLEWOOD BLUES · DON'T
EASE ME IN ... KEN KESEY → IKO
IKO ...

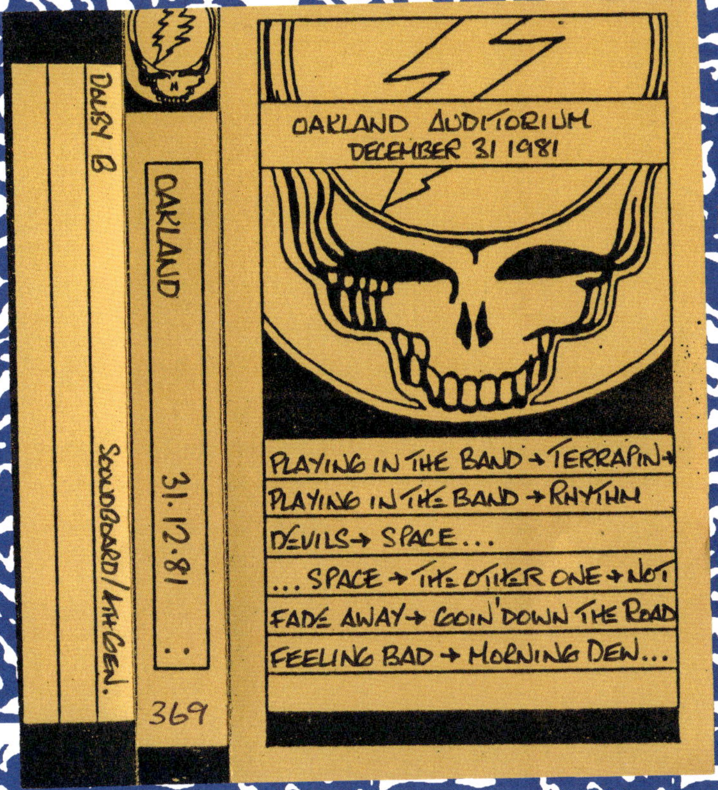
DOLBY B
OAKLAND
31.12.81
SOUNDBOARD/4th GEN.
369
OAKLAND AUDITORIUM
DECEMBER 31 1981
PLAYING IN THE BAND → TERRAPIN →
PLAYING IN THE BAND → RHYTHM
DEVILS → SPACE ...
... SPACE → THE OTHER ONE → NOT
FADE AWAY → GOIN' DOWN THE ROAD
FEELING BAD → MORNING DEW ...

Jack Straw
TLEO
On The Road Again
Peggy O
Cassidy
Roses>
Little Red Rooster
Cumberland Blues>
Woman Smarter>
Might As Well
E:Brokedown Palace
DEAD
4/19/82
#1
Civic Center
Baltimore,Md
GENERATION
N.R. IN☐ OUT☐
BOARD
RADIO
AUD.
H. Cantey

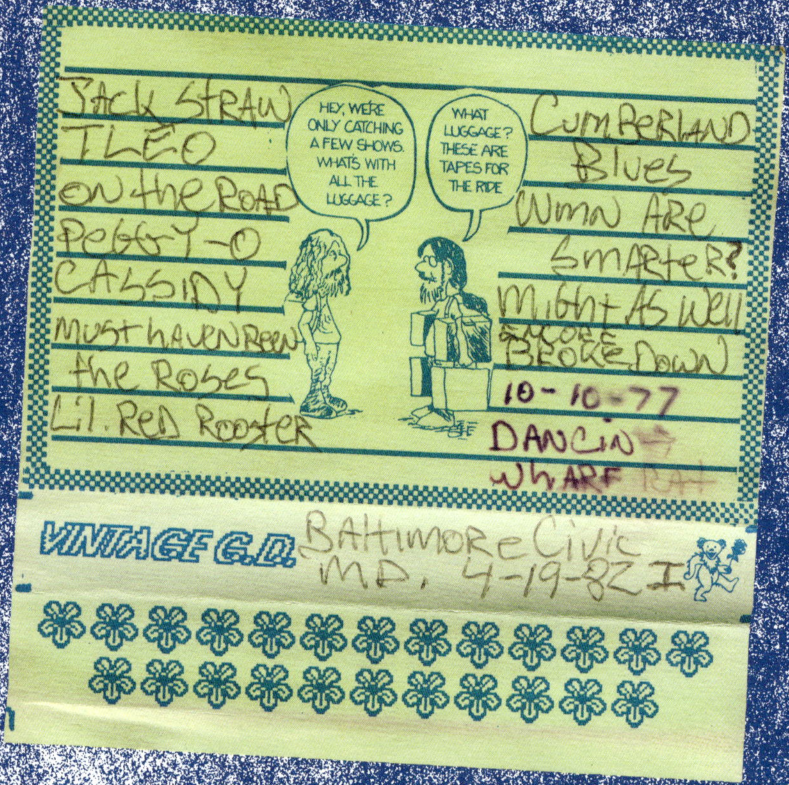

Jack Straw
TLEO
On the Road
Peggy-O
Cassidy
Must have been the Roses
Lil. Red Rooster
HEY, WERE ONLY CATCHING A FEW SHOWS. WHATS WITH ALL THE LUGGAGE?
WHAT LUGGAGE? THESE ARE TAPES FOR THE RIDE
Cumberland Blues
Womn Are Smarter?
Might As Well
Encore Broke Down
10-10-77
DANCIN
VINTAGE G.D.
Baltimore Civic
MD. 4-19-82 I

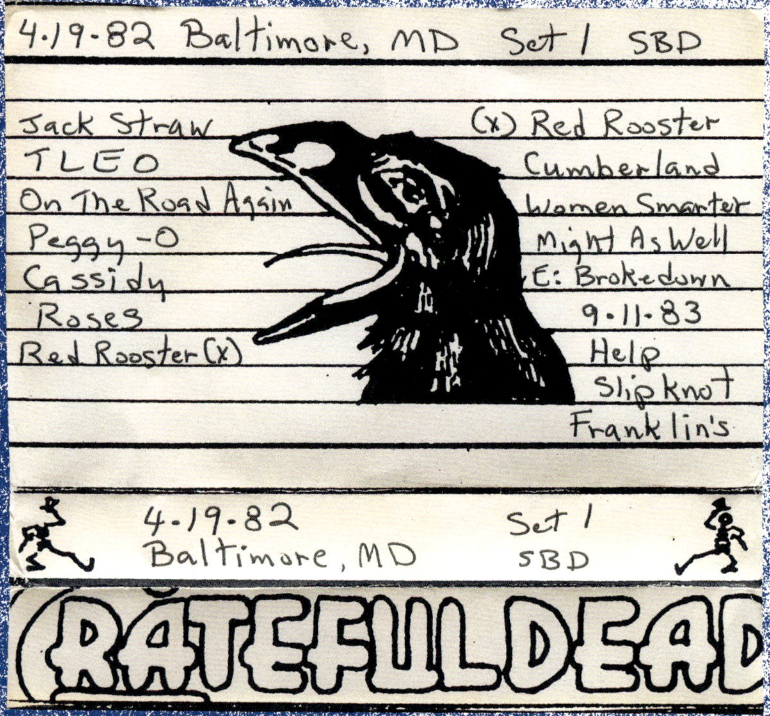

4-19-82 Baltimore, MD Set 1 SBD
Jack Straw
TLEO
On The Road Again
Peggy-O
Cassidy
Roses
Red Rooster (x)
(x) Red Rooster
Cumberland
Women Smarter
Might As Well
E: Brokedown
9-11-83
Help
Slip knot
Franklin's
4-19-82
Baltimore, MD
Set 1
SBD
GRATEFUL DEAD

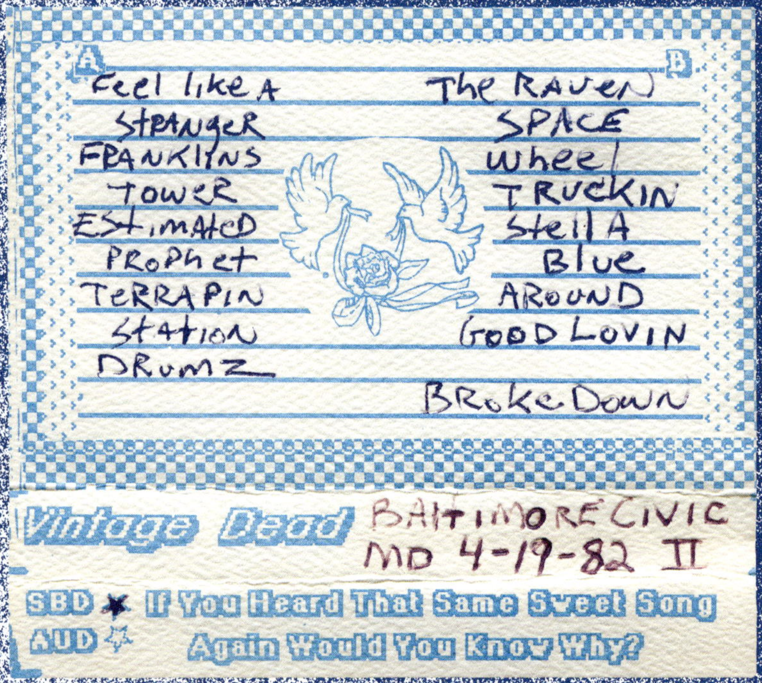

A
B
Feel like A Stranger
Franklins
Tower
Estimated
Prophet
Terrapin
Station
Drumz
The Raven
Space
Wheel
Truckin
Stella
Blue
Around
Good Lovin
Broke Down
Vintage Dead
Baltimore Civic
MD 4-19-82 II
SBD ✶ If You Heard That Same Sweet Song
AUD ☆ Again Would You Know Why?

EDgAR Allen Poe's
BIRTHDAY AND PlACE

Alabama Getaway
Greatest Story
Althea
Red Rooster
Tennessee Jed
Truckin>
INSPIRATION MOVE ME BRIGHTLY
Drums**>
GDTRFB>
NFA
Set # 2
Walkin Blues*>
A Mind To Give Up Living*
Lovelight*>
Johnny B. Goode*
DEAD 5 28 82 (A) #1 (B) #2 Moscone Convention Center San Francisco, Ca
GENERATION
SBD
AUD
RAD
DAT
H. CANTEY

Grateful Dead / Live:
A. SAMSON & DELILAH
FRANKLIN'S TOWER
WOMEN ARE SMARTER
SHIP OF FOOLS
CRAZY FINGERS
DRUM'S
B. SPACE
NOT FADE AWAY
OTHER ONE
WHARF RAT
SUGAR MAGNOLIA
SATISFACTION
BROKE DOWN PALACE
Grateful Dead LIVE 7/18/82 II
VENTURA, CALIF

A
B
SHAKEDOWN
SAMPSON & DELILAH
TO LAY ME DOWN
LET IT GROW
DRUMZ
SPACE
HE'S GONE
OTHER ONE
STELLA BLUE
GRATEFUL DEAD
STARLIGHT THEATER
8·3·82 II
SOUNDBOARD
AUDIENCE
RADIO
GENERATION
DOLBY NR

STRANGER
FOTD
C.C. RIDER
B.E.
WOMEN
MAMA
TRIED→
mexicali
ROW
Jimmy→
L.L.
RAIN
STAGGER lee
PROMISED LAND
Set II
Never Trust A Women
Set II
KIEL ARENA SET I
St. Louis, MO 8-4-82
NOISE REDUCTION
IN OUT
SBD AUD RAD.
SOUND QUALITY
SBD
GOOD
AUD
FAIR

BERTHA
MINGLEWOOD
TENNESEE JED
ME & MY UNCLE →
BIG RIVER
ALTHEA
ALL OVER NOW
CHINA CAT →
I.K.Y.R.
II
DAY JOB
WOMEN R SMARTER
WEST L.A.
FIRST "DAY JOB" + "WEST L.A."
GRATEFUL DEAD LIVE
noise reduction
in out
SBD
Audience
Radio
GR Production

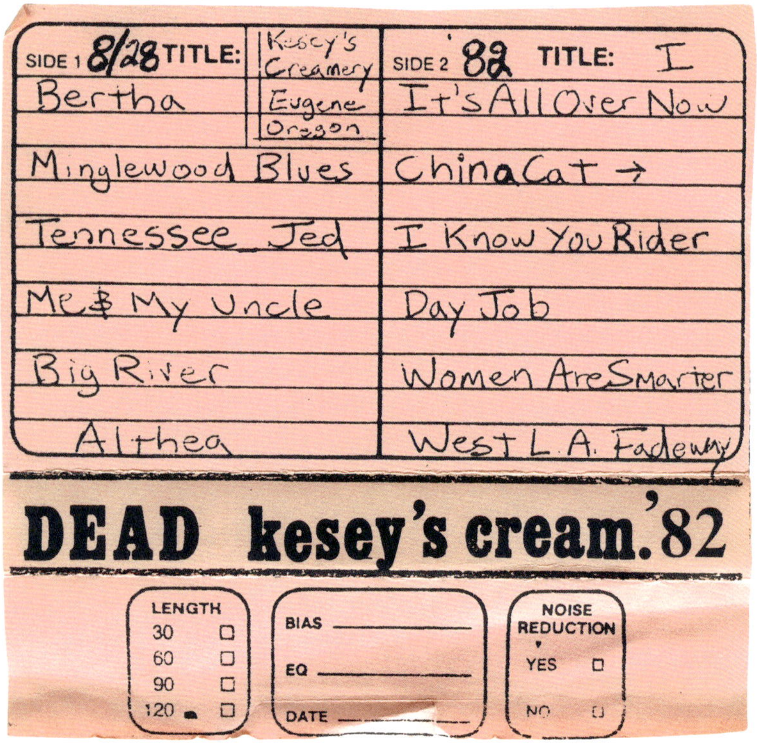
SIDE 1 8/28 TITLE: Kesey's Creamery Eugene Oregon
SIDE 2 '82 TITLE: I
Bertha
Minglewood Blues
Tennessee Jed
Me & My Uncle
Big River
Althea
It's All Over Now
China Cat →
I Know You Rider
Day Job
Women Are Smarter
West L.A. Fadeaway
DEAD kesey's cream.'82
LENGTH 30 60 90 120
BIAS
EQ
DATE
NOISE REDUCTION
YES
NO

Day Job>
Woman Smarter
West L.A.
Far From Me>
Playin>
Drums>
The Wheel>
Other One>
Truckin>
Black Peter>
Playin>
Saturday Night
Dead
Oregon Country Fair Site
Veneta, OR
8/28/82
#2
GEN.
SBD
AUD
RAD
N.R.
off
on
H. Cantey

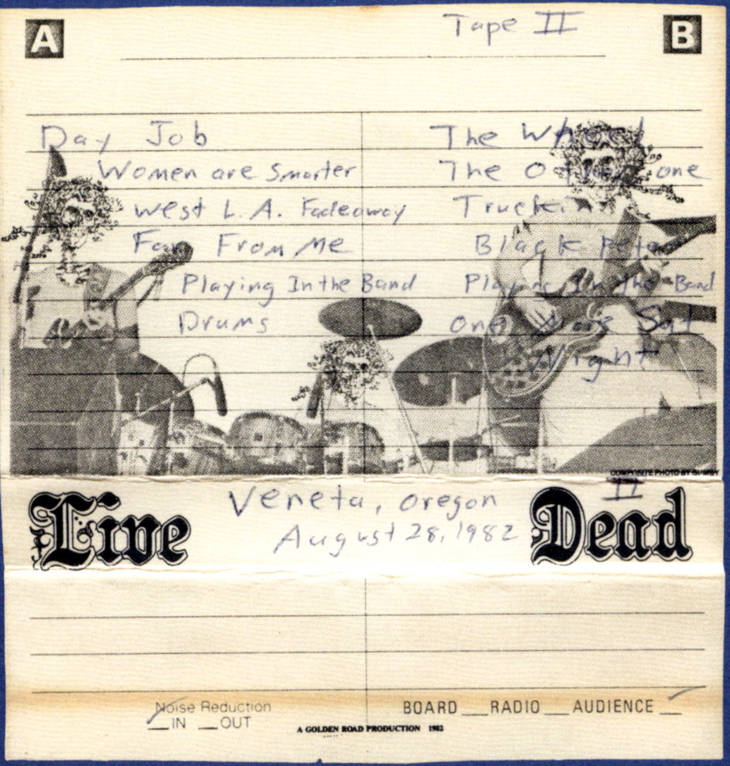
Tape II
A
B
Day Job
Women are Smarter
West L.A. Fadeaway
Far From Me
Playing In the Band
Drums
The Wheel
Truckin
Black Peter
Live
Dead
II
Veneta, Oregon
August 28, 1982
Noise Reduction
IN OUT
BOARD RADIO AUDIENCE
A GOLDEN ROAD PRODUCTION 1982

SOURCE:
AUDIENCE
SOUNDBOARD
RADIO
OTHER
YES
NO
LIVE AT
U. of VA. 9-14-82
Charlottesville Set I
UNIVERSITY OF VA, Sept 14, 1982 I
JACK STRAW
PEGGY-O
C.C. RIDER
BIG RXR BLUES
EL PASO
BIRD SONG
LAZY LIGHTNING
SUPPLICATION
DEAL
Set II
CHINA CAT
(cut)
Ain't no time to hate

DOLBY B/C
RECORD DATE
AUD
FM
SBD
GRATEFUL DEAD
CUMBERLAND CTY. C.C.
PORTLAND, ME.
9-17-82
II
HIGH TIME
ESTIMATED
PROPHET
EYES OF THE WORLD
DRUMS
SPACE...
...SPACE
SPANISH JAM
GDTRFB
MORNING DEW
SUGAR MAGNOLIA
U.S. BLUES

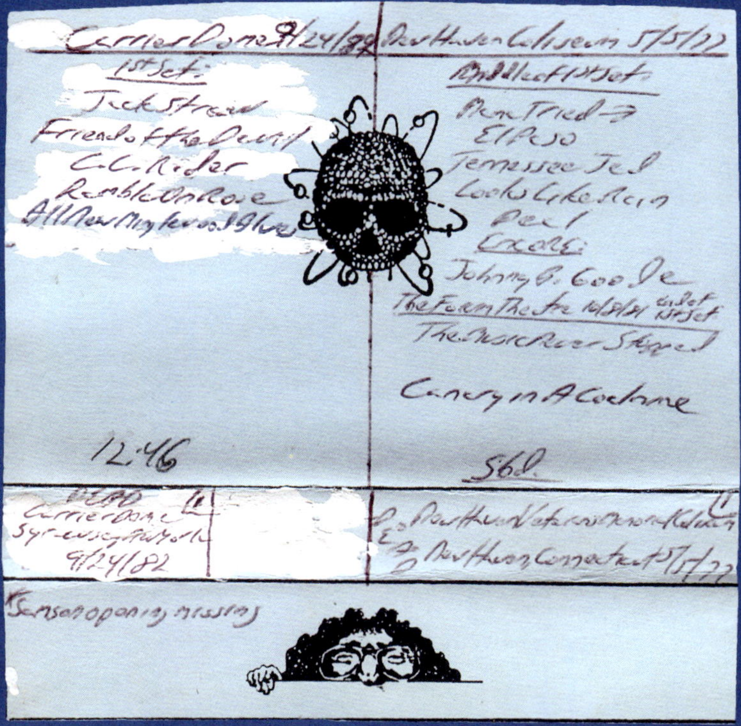
Carrier Dome 9/24/82
New Haven Coliseum 5/5/77
1st Set:
Jack Straw
Friend of the Devil
C.C. Rider
Ramble On Rose
El Paso
Tennessee Jed
Looks Like Rain
Deal
Johnny B. Goode
Canary in A Coalmine
12:46
SBD
Carrier Dome
Syracuse, New York
9/24/82

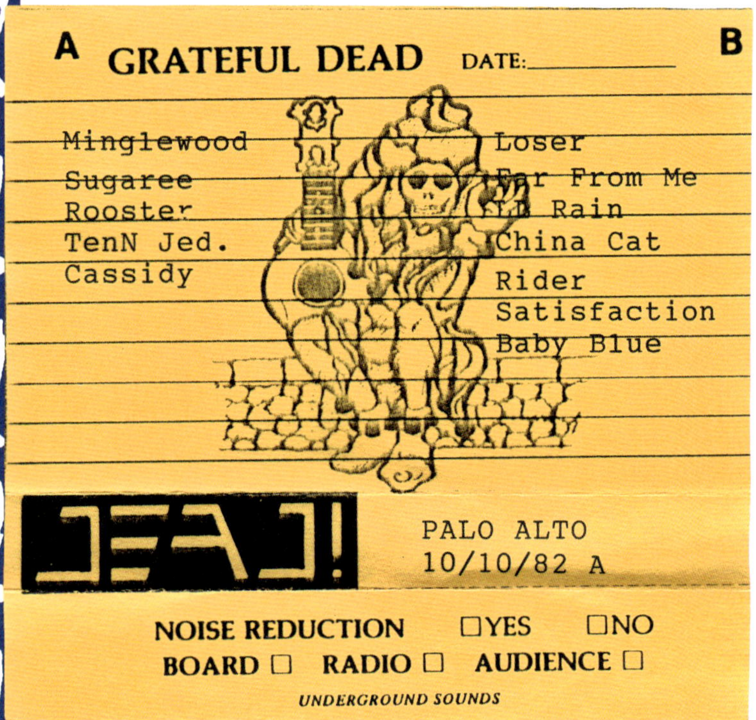
A
GRATEFUL DEAD
DATE:
B
Minglewood
Sugaree
Rooster
TenN Jed.
Cassidy
Loser
Far From Me
Rain
China Cat
Rider
Satisfaction
Baby Blue
DEAD!
PALO ALTO
10/10/82 A
NOISE REDUCTION ☐YES ☐NO
BOARD ☐ RADIO ☐ AUDIENCE ☐
UNDERGROUND SOUNDS

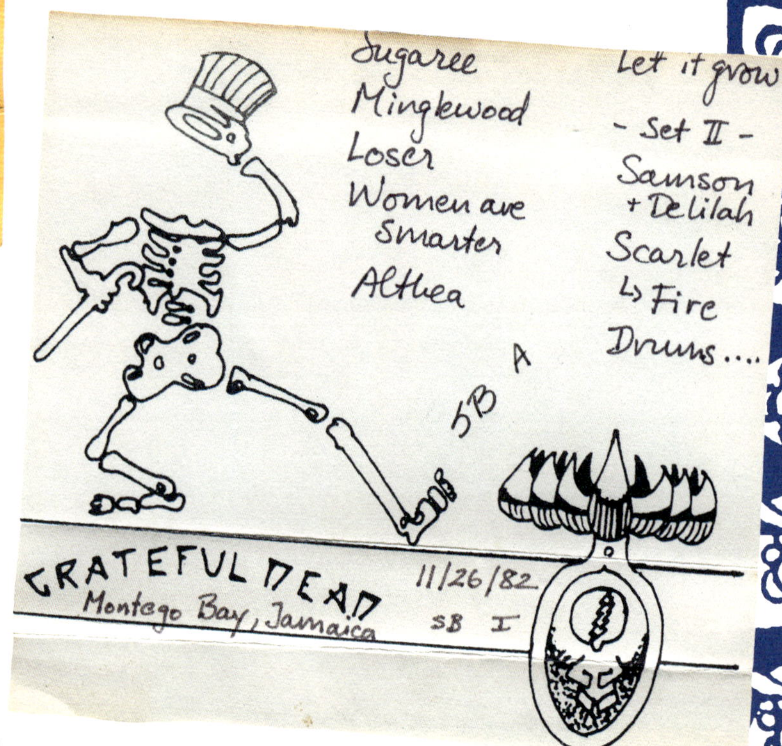
Sugaree
Minglewood
Loser
Women are Smarter
Althea
Let it grow
- Set II -
Samson + Delilah
Scarlet
↳ Fire
Drums....
SB A
GRATEFUL DEAD
Montego Bay, Jamaica
11/26/82
SB I

Touch
Brother Esau
Might As Well
Playin
Drumz →
Women R Smarter
China Doll
Playin
Sugar Mags
6.19.80
LL Rain
DEAD
WARFIELD THEATRE
S.F. 3.30.83
SET II
PRODUCED BY THE GRATEFUL DEAD

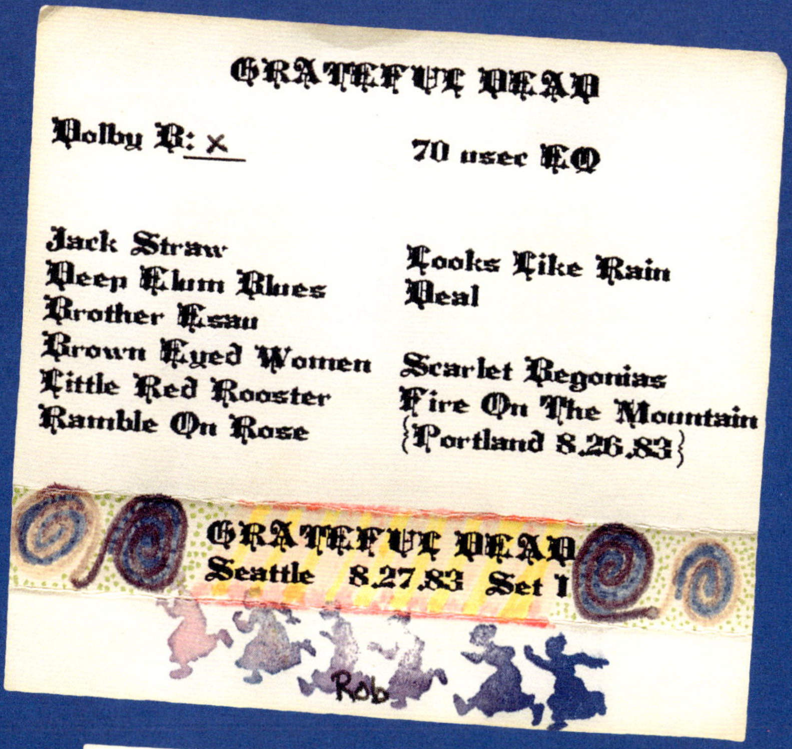
GRATEFUL DEAD
Dolby B: x
70 usec EQ
Jack Straw
Deep Elum Blues
Brother Esau
Brown Eyed Women
Little Red Rooster
Ramble On Rose
Looks Like Rain
Deal
Scarlet Begonias
Fire On The Mountain
(Portland 8.26.83)
GRATEFUL DEAD
Seattle 8.27.83 Set 1
Rob

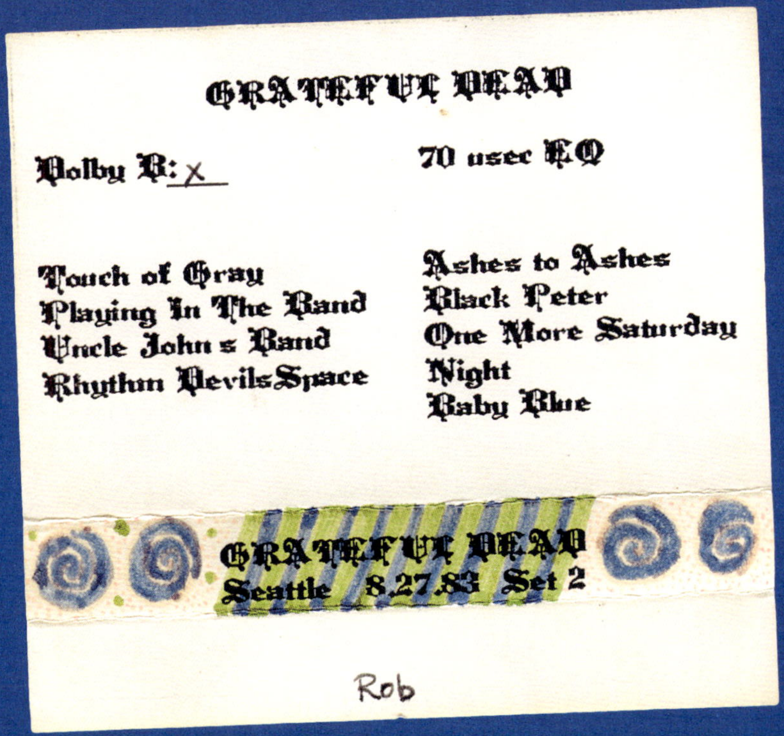
GRATEFUL DEAD
Dolby B: x
70 usec EQ
Touch of Gray
Playing In The Band
Uncle John s Band
Rhythm DevilsSpace
Ashes to Ashes
Black Peter
One More Saturday
Night
Baby Blue
GRATEFUL DEAD
Seattle 8.27.83 Set 2
Rob

A
B
WANG DANG
DOODLE →
JACK STRAW
THEY LOVE
EACH OTHER
MAMA TRIED
→ BIG RIVER
BROWN-EYED
WOMEN
MINGLEWOOD
BIG RR BLUES
LOOKS LIKE
RAIN →
DEAL →
SUGAR
MAGNOLIA
E: BABY
BLUE
Grateful Dead
THE PAVILLION
BOISE, IDAHO 9-2-83 I
Noise Reduction
IN OUT
BOARD RADIO AUDIENCE

CHINA CAT
RIDER
MIRACLE
BERTHA
JAM
China Doll
Drumz
St. Stephen
Throwing
Stones
Touch
6.19.80
MAMA TRIED
MEXICALI BLUES
CANDYMAN
Grateful
M.S.G. 10.11.83
II
Dead
BOARD
RADIO
AUDIENCE
NOISE REDUCTION
YES
NO

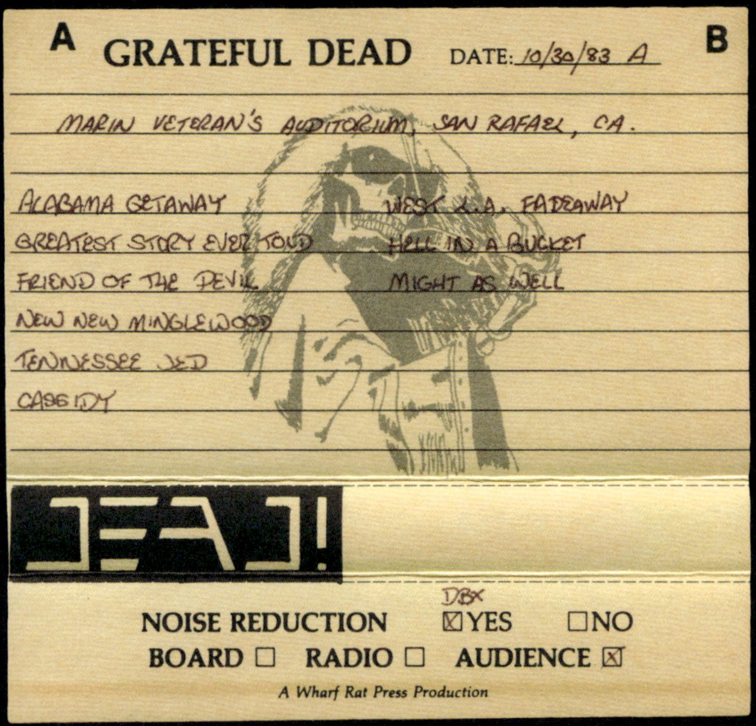
A
GRATEFUL DEAD
DATE: 10/30/83 A
B
MARIN VETERAN'S AUDITORIUM, SAN RAFAEL, CA.
ALABAMA GETAWAY
GREATEST STORY EVER TOLD
FRIEND OF THE DEVIL
NEW NEW MINGLEWOOD
TENNESSEE JED
CASSIDY
WEST L.A. FADEAWAY
HELL IN A BUCKET
MIGHT AS WELL
DEAD!
NOISE REDUCTION DBX YES NO
BOARD RADIO AUDIENCE
A Wharf Rat Press Production

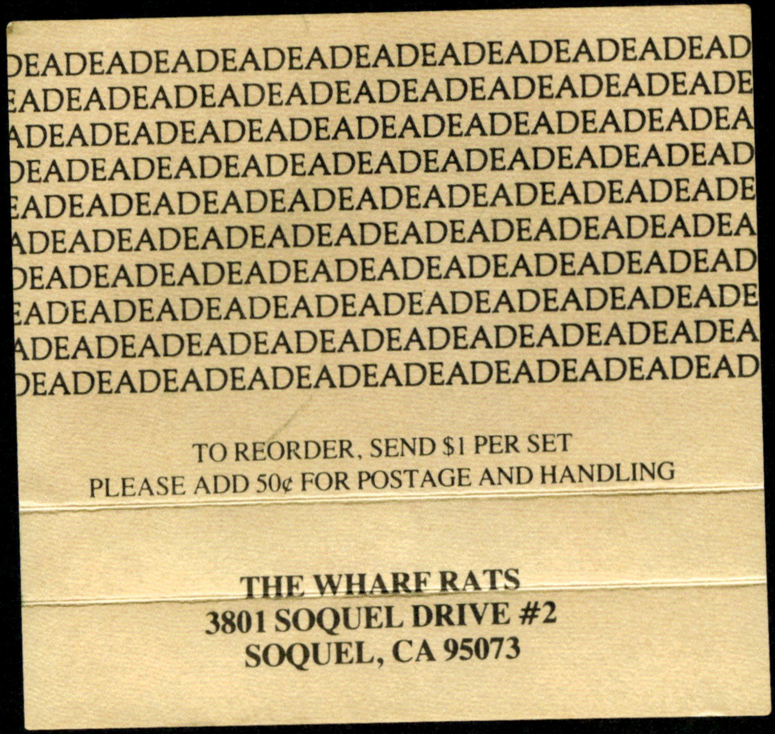
DEADEADEADEADEADEADEADEADEADEADEAD
TO REORDER, SEND $1 PER SET
PLEASE ADD 50¢ FOR POSTAGE AND HANDLING
THE WHARF RATS
3801 SOQUEL DRIVE #2
SOQUEL, CA 95073

GRATEFUL DEAD
70 usec EQ
Dolby B: X
Estimated Prophet
Eyes Of The World
Rhythm Devils
St. Stephen
Ashes To Ashes
Not Fade Away
Revolution
GRATEFUL DEAD
10.31.83
San Rafael
Set 2
Rob

Side 1
Side 2
Minglewood
Candyman
Brother Esau
Tennessee Jed
Hell in A Bucket
(Static)
Don't Ease me In
Band ?- Danko
Shape em In
Interview
New Year
Soundboard Audience Radio
LiveDead
San Francisco, CA Civic
12/31/83 SET I

3/31/84 Set #2
A
B
San Rafael,Ca
Scarlet Begonias>
Fire On The Mountain
Woman Smarter
He's Gone>
Drums>
Drums>Space>
Blues For Allah
Jam>
Throwin Stones
NFA(cut)
BEARKENSTOCKS
LIVE
3-31-84 #2 Vets Aud
San Rafael,Ca
DEAD
"DANCIN IN THE STREETS"

DEAD at Irvine 4-7-84 #2 | STEELY DAN "AJA"

maxell XLII 90
POSITION IEC TYPE II HIGH[CrO2]
GRATEFUL DEAD / ROCHESTER 4-16-84
SET II
A DATE N.R. YES NO
HELL IN A BUCKET
SHIP OF FOOLS
FAR FROM ME
HE'S GONE
JAM
DRUMS
B DATE N.R. YES NO
SPACE
THE OTHER ONE
STELLA BLUE
AROUND + AROUND
JOHNNY B. GOODE
DAY JOB

6·13·84 Red Rocks, CO Set 2 SB

China Cat >
Rider
Women Smarter
Ship of Fools
Let It Grow
Drumz

Space
Wheel
Miracle
Stella Blue
Sugar Mag.
Baby Blue

6·13·84
Red Rocks, CO
Set 2
SBD

Grateful Dead

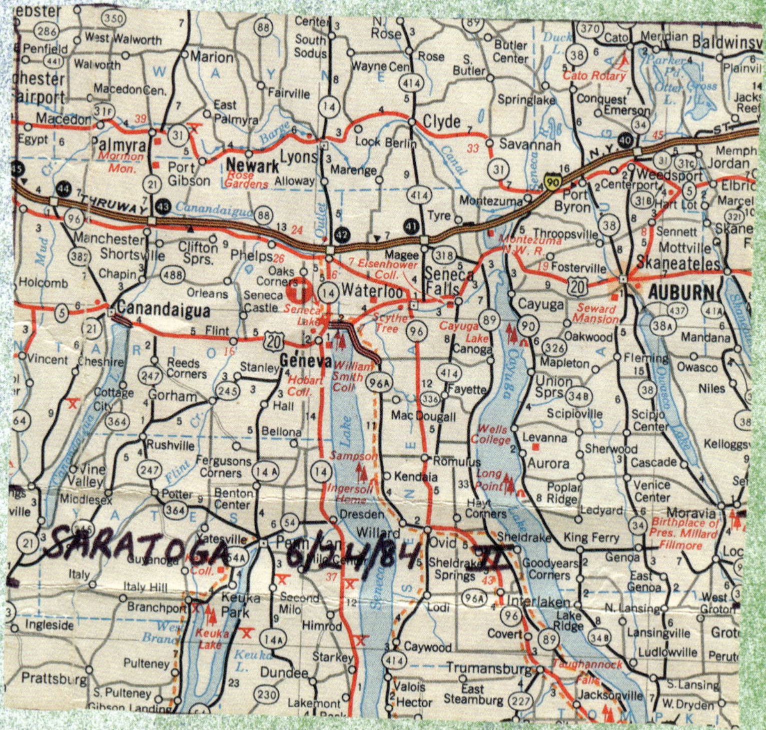

Casey Jones
Stranger
Althea
Cassidy
Tennessee Jed
L.L.Rain

L.L.Rain (con)>
Might As Well

From Set #2
Good Lovin' (cut)
E)Day Job

Merriweather Post Pavillion
columbia,Md 6/26/84 #1

Generation ______ Quality Excellent ☐
Source ______ Good ☒
Noise Reduction ______ Fair ☐

LJ's Tape Covers • 18883 Auburn Lane • Noblesville, IN 46060

China Cat>
IKnow You Rider
Woman Are Smarter>
He's Gone>
Drums>

Space>
Don't Need Love>
Truckin'>
Wang Dang Doodle>
Stella Blue>
Around>

Merriweather Post Pavillion
Columbia,Md 6/26/84 #2

Generation ______ Quality Excellent ☐
Source ______ Good ☒
Noise Reduction ______ Fair ☐

LJ's Tape Covers • 18883 Auburn Lane • Noblesville, IN 46060

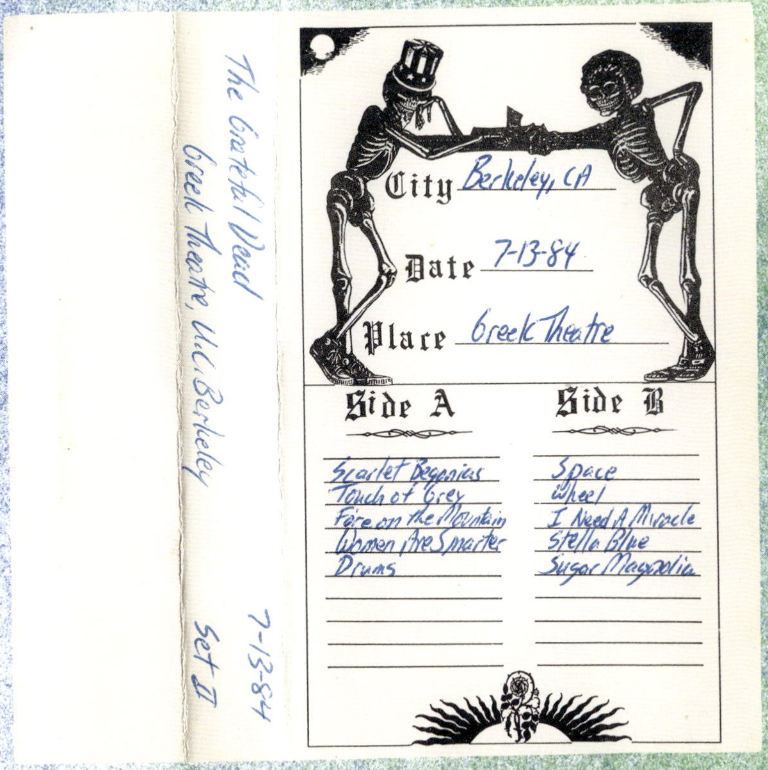
The Grateful Dead
Greek Theatre U.C. Berkeley
7-13-84
Set I
City Berkeley, CA
Date 7-13-84
Place Greek Theatre
Side A
Scarlet Begonias
Touch of Grey
Fire on the Mountain
Women Are Smarter
Drums
Side B
Space
Wheel
I Need A Miracle
Stella Blue
Sugar Magnolia

The Grateful Dead
Greek Theatre, U.C. Berkeley
7-13-84
Set I III
City Berkeley, CA
Date 7-13-84
Place Greek Theatre
Side A
Bertha
Greatest Story
Dire Wolf
C.C. Rider
Loser
Cassidy
Side B
Du Pree's Diamond Blues
Hell In A Bucket
Might As Well
Set III
~ Dark Star

ΓΡΑΤΕΦΥΛ
ΔΕΑΔ
Bertha
Greatest Story
Dire Wolf
C.C. Rider
Loser
Cassady
Duprees Blues
Hell in Bucket
Might as well
Encore
Dark Star
1st since 12-81
Last till 10-89
GREEK DEAD
Berkley, CAL.
7-13-84 Set I
SOURCE:
DIGITAL ANALOG
BOARD RADIO AUDIENCE
MONO STEREO
DOLBY OFF ON
TYPE
GENERATION

Dancin' in the Streets
Bird Song
Minglewood Blues
Cumberland Blues
Brother Esau
Ramble on Rose
Hell in A Bucket
-Filler-
Estimated Prophet
Eyes of the World
Greek Theater
Berkley, CA. 7-15-84
I

COLD RAIN
LOST SAILOR
SAINT OF
CIRCUMSTANCE
DON'T NEED LOVE
UNCLE JOHN'S
DRUM2
N2O
SPACE
PLAYIN
UNCLE JOHN'S
MORNING DEW
GRATEFUL DEAD
AUGUSTA, ME
10/12/84

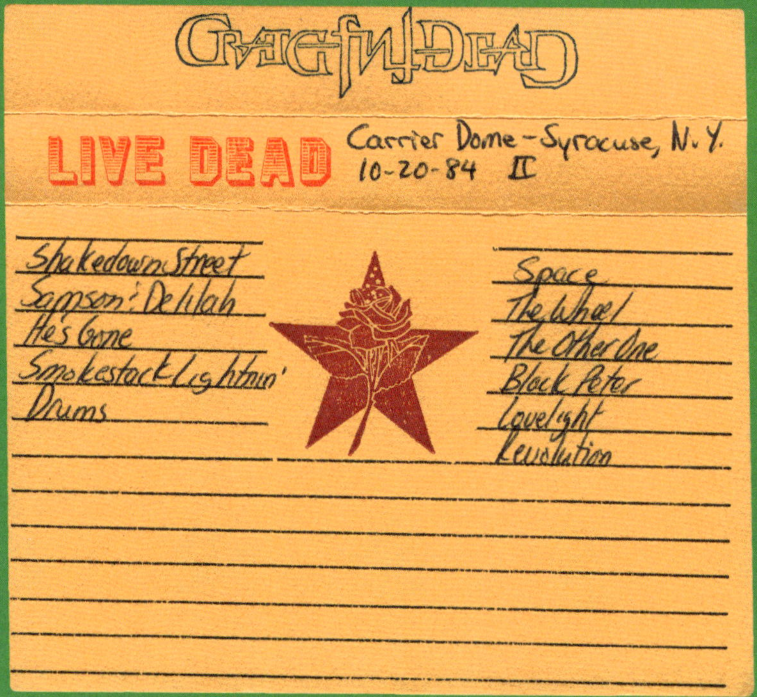
GratefulDead
LIVE DEAD
Carrier Dome - Syracuse, N.Y.
10-20-84 II
Shakedown Street
Samson & Delilah
He's Gone
Smokestack Lightnin'
Drums
Space
The Wheel
The Other One
Black Peter
Lovelight
Revolution

A DATE
Pocky Way
Scarlet
Fire
Truckin'
B DATE
Drums
Space
IWTYH
Other 1
Wharf
Rat
(Rest on I)
GRATEFUL DEAD
DATE; II
Spectrum
10/20/84
LIVE
NOISE REDUCTION YES NO
SOUND BOARD

PLAYIN IN THE BAND
SAME THING
ALL OVER NOW
MORNING DEW
DOWN ON THE BOTTOM
FEEL LIKE A STRANGER
CUMBERLAND BLUES
GLORIA
DEAR MR FANTASY
DEAD
BERKELEY COMMUNITY THEATER NOV 3 84
VARIOUS 9/1

COLD RAIN: SNOW
BOTTOM >
SUPERSTITIOUS,
FOTD
SUPPLICATION
JAM >
ESAU
TENNESSE JED
W/MATT KELLY
MINGLEWOOD
DONT EASE
FILLER: VENETA
8/27/72
ME & MY UNCLE
DEAL
BLACK THROATED WIND.
GRATEFUL DEAD
NASSAU COLISEUM
3·29·85 I 2nd GEN AUD 90
SOURCE: AUD
GEN: 2
NOISE RED: B

Nassau Coliseum - Uniondale Long Island
03-28-85
Scarlet Begonias
Fire On The Mountain
Looks Like Rain
Jam
Drumz
Drumz
Space
Gimme Some Lovin
The Other One
Black Peter
Sugar Magnolia
Generation:
Grateful Dead
Nassau Coliseum - Uniondale Long Island
03-28-85
Jonathan Harris 59 Huntington st., Newbrunswick, NJ 08901
(908)937-6649 ramrose@eden.rutgers.edu

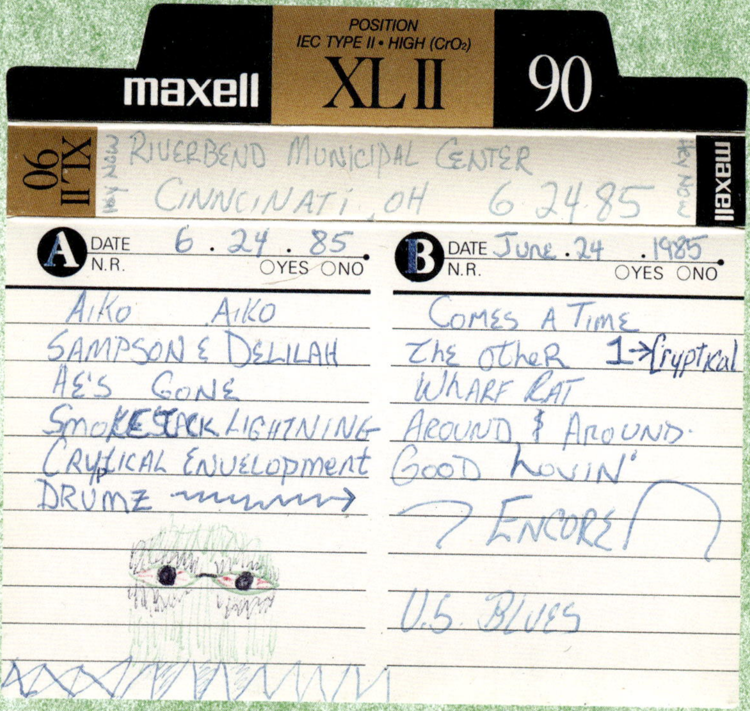
POSITION
IEC TYPE II • HIGH (CrO2)
maxell
XL II
90
RIVERBEND MUNICIPAL CENTER
CINNCINATI, OH 6.24.85
A DATE 6.24.85
N.R. YES NO
AIKO AIKO
SAMPSON & DELILAH
HE'S GONE
SMOKESTACK LIGHTNING
CRYTICAL ENVELOPMENT
DRUMZ
B DATE June 24 1985
N.R. YES NO
COMES A TIME
THE OTHER 1→Cryptical
WHARF RAT
AROUND & AROUND
GOOD LOVIN'
ENCORE
U.S. BLUES

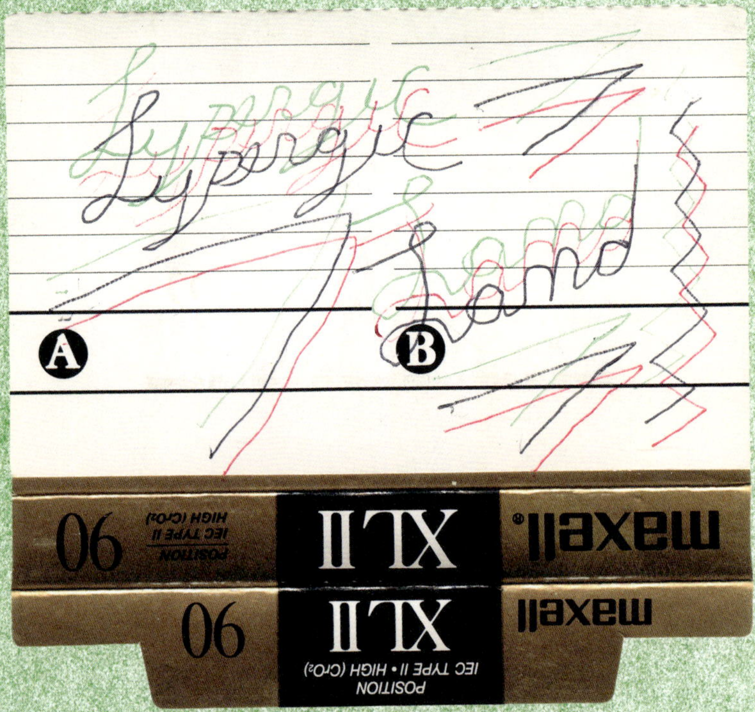
A
B
XL II
90

A GRATEFUL DEAD DATE B
Day Tripper
West L.A. Fadeaway
C.C. Rider
Dire Wolf
Beat it on Down
Row Jimmy
COSMIC CHARLIE CAMPAIGN
Me & My Uncle
Big River
Big Railroad Blues
Jack Straw
Might As Well
Unbroken Chain
Loose Lucy
Estimated Prophet
Deal
DEAD!
Blossom Music 6-25-85 #1
Center; Cuyahoga Falls, Ohio
NOISE REDUCTION YES NO
BOARD RADIO AUDIENCE

A GRATEFUL DEAD DATE B
Gimme Some Lovin'
China Cat Sunflower
I Know You Rider
Playin' in the Band
Drums
COSMIC CHARLIE CAMPAIGN
Space
The Wheel
Playin' in the Band
China Doll
Sugar Magnolia
Touch of Grey
DEAD!
Blossom Music 6-25-85 #2
Center; Cuyahoga Falls, Ohio
NOISE REDUCTION YES NO
BOARD RADIO AUDIENCE

Day Tripper
West L.A. Fadeaway
C.C. Rider
Dire Wolf
Beat it on down the line
Row Jimmy
Me and My Uncle →
Big River
Jackstraw →
Might as Well
LIVE DEAD
CUYAHOGA FALLS, OH
6·25·85 I

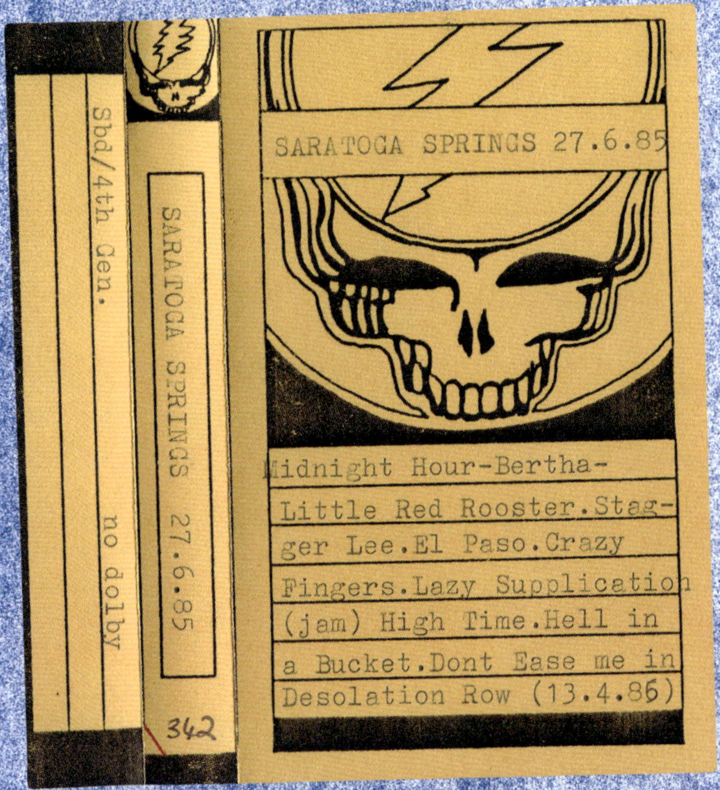
Sbd/4th Gen.
no dolby
SARATOGA SPRINGS 27.6.85
342
SARATOGA SPRINGS 27.6.85
Midnight Hour-Bertha-
Little Red Rooster.Stag-
ger Lee.El Paso.Crazy
Fingers.Lazy Supplication
(jam) High Time.Hell in
a Bucket.Dont Ease me in
Desolation Row (13.4.86)

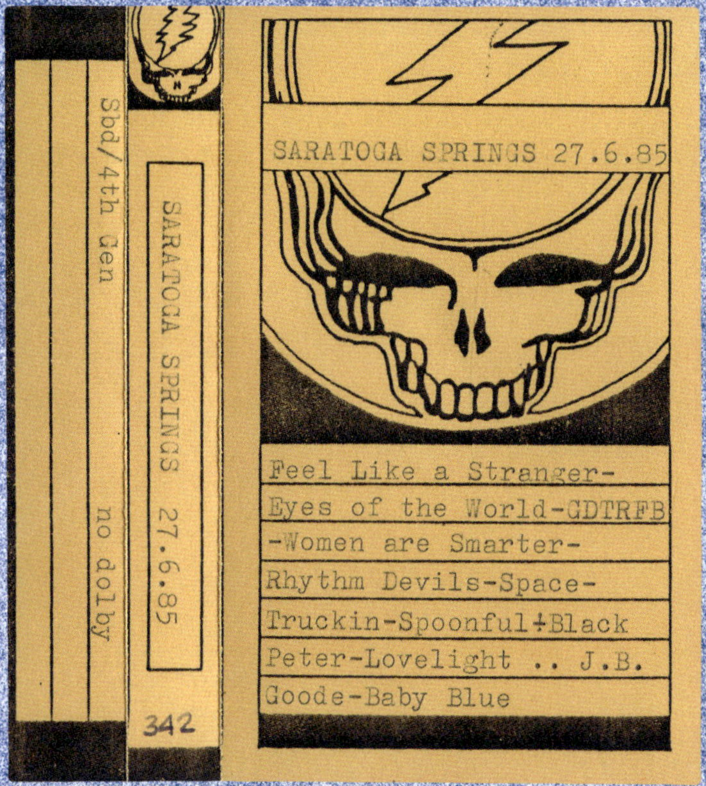
Sbd/4th Gen
no dolby
SARATOGA SPRINGS 27.6.85
342
SARATOGA SPRINGS 27.6.85
Feel Like a Stranger-
Eyes of the World-CDTRFB
-Women are Smarter-
Rhythm Devils-Space-
Truckin-Spoonful+Black
Peter-Lovelight .. J.B.
Goode-Baby Blue

THE MUSIC NEVER STOPPED
TOM THUMB BLUES
ESTIMATED PROPHET
TERRAPIN
DRUMZ
SPACE
I NEED A MIRACLE
MORNING DEW
THROWIN STONES
NOT FADE
GRATEFUL
DEAD
HERSHEY, PA.
6/28/85
II

GRATEFUL DEAD at Merriweather, MD. 7-1-85
#1
A
Dancing in the Streets
Dupree's ◇ Blues
Walking Blues
Jack-A-Roe
Brother Esau
Stagger Lee
B
Let it Grow
Day Job
Satisfaction
Baby Blue
Willy & the Hand Jive
Hell in A Bucket
Cold Rain and Snow
GRATEFUL DEAD at Merriweather, MD. 7-1-85
#2
A
Scarlet Begonias
Fire On the Mountain
Playing in the Band
Uncle John's Band
Drums...
B
Space...
Dear Mr. Fantasy
Going Down the Road
Good Lovin'
Sugaree (New Year's '86)

Women R Smarter
Crazy Fingers
Lost Sailor
St. of Circ.
Terrapin →
Drumz
Space →
Warf Rat
Throwing Stones
Love Light
Revolution
Brokendown
Palace
Grateful Dead
Civic Center 7.2.85
Pittsburgh, PA.- set II

DEAD Ventura County fairgrounds, CA.
7-13-1985 II
One More Sat. Night
Fire On The Mountain
Walkin' Blues
Duprees Diamond
/Blues
Mama Tried →
Big River
Bird Song
Music Never
/Stopped
e) U.S. Blues
Saint Stephen →
Not Fade Away →
Saint Stephen
Help On The Way (CUT)
THERE IS A FOUNTAIN THAT WAS NOT MADE BY THE HANDS OF MEN

DEAD Ventura County Fairgrounds, CA.
7-13-1985 II
Touch Of Grey
Women Are Smarter
Lady With A Fan →
Terrapin Station →
Drums →
Space...
...Space →
The Wheel
Cryptical Envelopment
→ Other One →
Comes A Time →
Around & Around
Sugar Magnolia
Sunshine Daydream

Set II
9-7-85
Shakedown Street
CRAZY FINGERS
Sampson & Delilah
Uncle John's BAND
Playin' in the Band
Jam....
Drums / SPACE
DEAR MR. FANTASY
Hey Jude (Refrain)
Dear Mr. Fantasy
Truckin'
Comes a Time
Lovelight
9-7-85
Red Rocks
Morrison, Colo
NOISE REDUCTION YES NO
BOARD RADIO AUDIENCE

A
B
SCARLET BEGONIAS
FIRE ON THE MTN
SAMSON & DELILAH
SMOKE STAK LIGHTNING
STANDING ON THE
MOON (3-30-90)
DANCIN →
WHARF RAT
DANCIN (REPRISE)
FRIEND OF THE DEVIL
(6-16-90)
GRATEFUL DEAD
CHULA VISTA 9-15-85
VARIOUS 77-90
Date: 11-01-85 Set: 1
Richmond Colliseum Richmond, VA
Source: aud Quality: A-
Side A:
Dancin' In The Streets; Cold Rain and Sn
ow; Little Red Rooster; Me and My Uncle
; Big River;
Side B:
Brown Eyed Women; Jack Straw; Don't Ease
Me In 2ND SET: S
he Belongs to Me -> Gloria ENCORE: Day
Job
1 GRATEFUL 11-01-85 Set: 1
7 DEAD Richmond, VA
6 Richmond Colliseum

St. of Circumstance
Gimme Some Lovin
He's Gone
Spoonful
Comes A Time
Lost Sailor
Drums
Space
She Belongs to Me
Gloria
GRATEFUL DEAD
Richmond Coliseum
Richmond, Virginia
Set II
11/1/85
Source
SBD
Gen.
4TH

Sampson + Delilah
Nightime
He's Gone
Spoonfull
Comes A Time
Lost Sailor
Drums
St of Circumstance
Gimme Some Lovin
She Belongs to Me
Gloria
Day Job
FALL TOUR
Richmond VA
Nov/1/85
Richmond, Colleseium
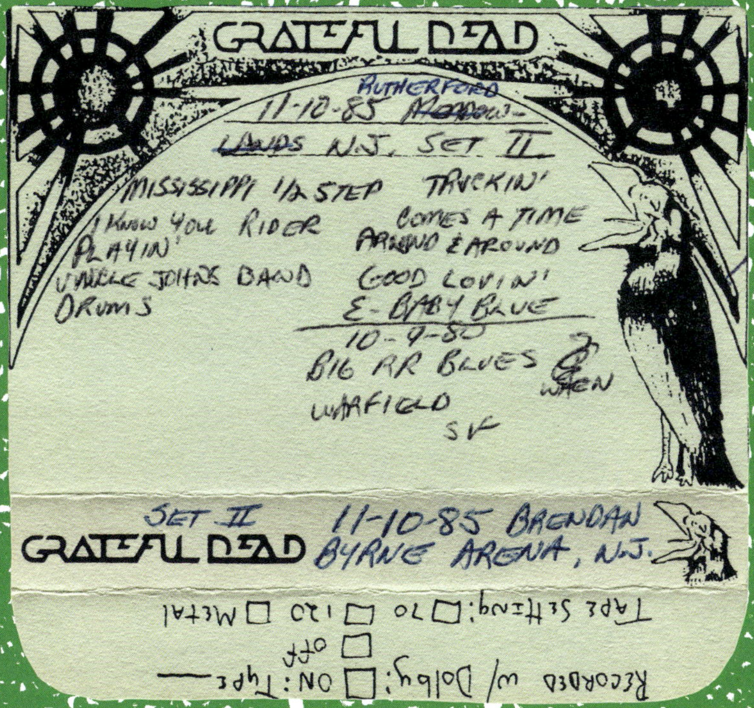
GRATEFUL DEAD
Rutherford
11-10-85 Meadowlands N.J. Set II
Mississippi 1/2 Step
I Know You Rider
Playin'
Uncle John's Band
Drums
Truckin'
Comes A Time
Around & Around
Good Lovin'
E-Baby Blue
10-9-80
Big RR Blues
Warfield
SF
Set II
11-10-85 Brendan Byrne Arena, N.J.
GRATEFUL DEAD
Tape Setting: ☐ 70 ☐ 120 ☐ Metal
Recorded w/ Dolby: ☐ ON: Tape
☐ off

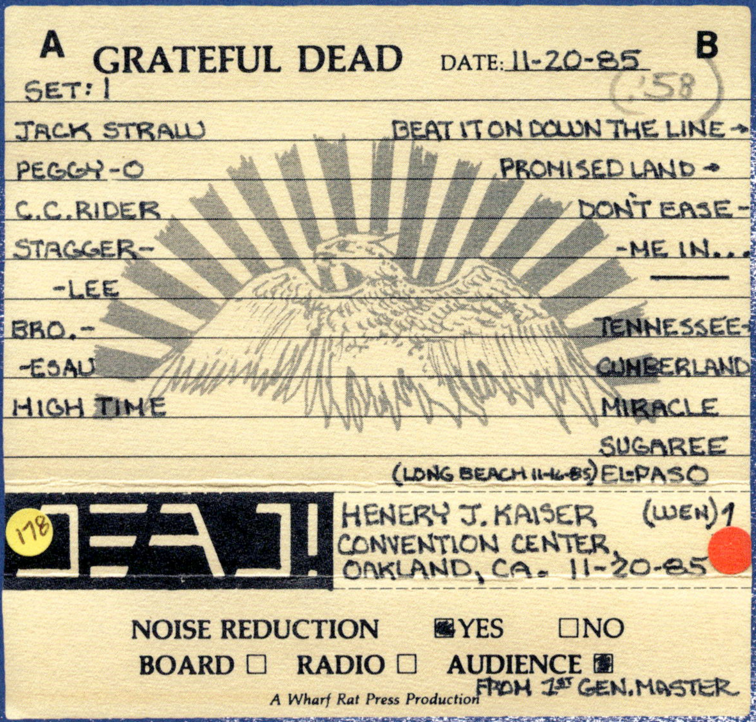

A GRATEFUL DEAD DATE: 11-20-85 B

SET: 1 (:58)

JACK STRAW — BEAT IT ON DOWN THE LINE →
PEGGY-O — PROMISED LAND →
C.C. RIDER — DON'T EASE-
STAGGER- — -ME IN..
-LEE
BRO.- — TENNESSEE-
-ESAU — CUMBERLAND
HIGH TIME — MIRACLE
SUGAREE
(LONG BEACH 11-16-85) EL PASO

178 DEAD! HENRY J. KAISER (WEN) 1
CONVENTION CENTER,
OAKLAND, CA. 11-20-85

NOISE REDUCTION ■ YES □ NO
BOARD □ RADIO □ AUDIENCE ■
FROM 1st GEN. MASTER

A Wharf Rat Press Production

A GRATEFUL DEAD DATE: 11-20-85 B

SET: 2

AIKO-AIKO → — DRUMS / SPACE →
LOST SAILOR → — STELLA BLUE →
ST. OF CIRCUMSTANCE → — SUGAR-
TERRAPIN- — -MAGNOLIA
-STATION → — ENCORE
JAM → — U.S.-
I DONT- — -BLUES
-NEED LOVE →
(1:20)

179 DEAD! HENRY J. KAISER (WEN) 2
CONVENTION CENTER,
OAKLAND, CA. 11-20-85

NOISE REDUCTION ■ YES □ NO
BOARD □ RADIO □ AUDIENCE ■
FROM 1st GEN. MASTER

A Wharf Rat Press Production

A GRATEFUL DEAD DATE: 3·21·86 B

UNCLE JOHNS — SPACE
TERRAPIN — MIRACLE
STELLA BLUE
PLAYIN — SUGAR MAGNOLIA
DAYDREAM
DRUMZ — BABY BLUE

DEAD! 3·21·86 II
COLISEUM, HAMPTON, VA

NOISE REDUCTION □ YES ■ NO
BOARD □ RADIO □ AUDIENCE □

A Wharf Rat Press Production

EX-QUALITY — PHILLY SPECTRUM
GRATEFUL DEAD: MARCH 25, 1986 II
BOARD □ FM □ AUDIENCE ☑ NR YES

AIKO
MINGLEWOOD
PEGGY-O
Desolation Row
1/2 STEP
SUPPLICATION
Let it Grow
Fill: DALLAS, TX. 10-21-88
DUPREES
JACK STRAW
WANG DANG
1st since 3-86
LIVE
IRVINE MEADOWS, CAL. 4-13-86 Set I
SOURCE: SBD
GENERATION:
QUALITY: A
*FINAL SUPPLICATION TILL "90

SOURCE:
AUDIENCE
SOUNDBOARD
RADIO
OTHER
N.R.
YES NO
A-
LIVE DEAD
IRVINE MEADOWS CAL. 4-13-86 Set II
CHINA CAT RIDER
LOOKS LIKE RAIN
LADY W/A FAN
DON'T NEED LOVE
DRUMZ
SPACE → MIRACLE
BLACK PETER
THROWIN STONES
LOVELIGHT
BOX OF RAIN
"IT LOOKS LIKE RAIN AND IT FEELS LIKE RAIN"

maxell
POSITION IEC TYPE II • HIGH (CrO2)
XL II
4/19/86 BERKELEY COMMUNITY THEATRE: SB/4
BERKELEY, CALIFORNIA—Set Two—
FOR RENT

A
GLORIA
GIMME SOME LOVIN'
PLAYING IN THE BAND
JAM →
DRUMS
SPACE
B
CHINA CAT SUNFLOWER
I KNOW YOU RIDER
I NEED A MIRACLE
WHARF RAT
ROUND & ROUND
GOOD LOVIN'
Live
CALIFORNIA EXPOSITION
5/4/86
Dead

Taping the Tour?
HIGH BIAS
MAXELL US II 90
THE CHROME/HIGH BIAS TAPE IDEAL FOR RECORDING LIVE!
99¢
MAXELL XL II 90
AMERICA'S MOST POPULAR HIGH BIAS CASSETTE. FOR HIGH QUALITY RECORDINGS!
1.49
TDK SA•90 High Bias..........1.49
Maxell XLIIS•90 High Bias......1.99
Maxell GXT•120 VHS..........1.99
TDK DAR•90 DAT..........6.49
TDK DAR•120 DAT..........6.79
The Advantage Company
5195 Main Street Williamsville, NY 14221
Minimum 10 Tape order. We accept M.C. Visa, Discover or C.O.D.
800-394-2347
Berkeley '77
would sound great on one of our tapes.
TDK
TDK SA-90
90 Minutes of Taping High Bias Sound
$1.49
SA-60 1.49 VHS•T120HS 1.89
SA-100 1.89 DAT•DAR-90 6.49
SAX-90 1.99 DAT•DAR-120 6.49
SAX-100 2.29 DAT•DAR-180 9.99
LIFETIME WARRANTY on all tapes
We carry EVERY tape TDK makes, give me Jack "Straw" a call!
Minimum 10 Tape Order Please
C.O.D. Visa, M.C. & Discover
1•800•835•7290
The Stereo Advantage 5195 Main Street Williamsville, NY 14221
DAT TAPES
120 Minute/180 Minute Maxell
$6.99/$8.99 ea.
Buy 10 get one free!
CASSETTE HOUSE
180 Minute Maxell
$5.99 ea.
DDS computer grade, exceeds audio DAT specs
Used 1x - Over 100,000 sold!
800-321-5738
M/CARD-VISA-AMEX - MONEY-BACK GUARANTEE
Internet Surfers: Visit our WEB page
http://www.edge.net/ch/index.html
CASSETTE HOUSE
TERRAPIN AT GRATEFUL PRICES
MAXELL XLII90
MAXELL XLIIS90
MAXELL XLIIS100
TDK SA90
Video tapes also available on request
All prices include tax, shipping &
Call 1-800-677-8650 for ordering information.
Minimum order 10 tapes.
VISA/MC accepted
NOW! YOU CAN CHOOSE!
TDK PRO SA BULK
CUSTOM LOADED HIGH BIAS (TYPE II) CASSETTES
MAXELL XLII BULK
CUSTOM LOADED CHROME HIGH BIAS (TYPE II) CASSETTES
PREMIUM ROUNDED-EDGE ALL CLEAR NORELCO BOXES
CALL FOR FREE FULL LINE A/V CATALOG
NOW RECORDING SYSTEMS, INC.
32 WEST 39TH STREET, 9TH FLOOR, NEW YORK, NY 10018
Telephone: 212-768-7800 • 800-859-3579
FREE SAMPLE CASSETTE — ASK FOR ED STERN
DIGITAL AUDIO TAPE PRICES
Maxell (DDS) 90m $5.00
KAO (DDS) 60m $5.35
KAO (DDS) 90m $6.00
Sony (DDS) 60m $6.75
Sony (DDS) 90m $7.35
AUDIO CASSETTE PRICES
Maxell XLII 90 $1.60
Maxell XLII 100 $2.00
Maxell XLIIS 90 $2.05
Maxell XLIIS 100 $2.30
Maxell MXS 90 $3.00
CONSIDERING GOING DAT? GIVE US A CALL!
We have great prices on DAT machines!
SIDE A
Checks/Money Orders 7 to 10 days delivery
Tapes shipped UPS
Under 50 Tapes ($4.50 Shipping Charge)
TERRAPIN TAPES
We have microphones, cables and other audio essentials!
SIDE B
Amex/VISA/MC/Discover
1 week delivery
Tapes shipped UPS
50 or More Tapes (FREE Shipping)
336 FEDERAL ROAD BROOKFIELD, CT 06804 800-677-8650
TAPE WORLD
OUR 17TH YEAR
MAXELL SONY FUJI TDK

AT GRATEFUL PRICES!
DAT Tapes Now Available!
TDK DAR•120 DAT..........6.79
The Advantage Company
5195 Main Street
Williamsville, NY 14221
Minimum 10 Tape order.
We accept M.C., Visa, Discover or C.O.D.
800•394•2347
CALL FOR FREE FULL LINE A/V CATALOG
NOW RECORDING SYSTEMS
32 WEST 39TH STREET, 9TH FLOOR, NEW Y
MASTER DISTRIBUTORS OF:
AND MUCH, MUCH, MORE...
FREE SAMPLE CASSETTE — ASK FOR ED ST
Terrapin Tapes
PO Box 1408
Greenwich, CT 06836
Berkeley
would sound great on one of our tapes.
TDK
TDK SA-90
90 Minutes of Taping
High Bias Sound
$1.49
SA-60 1.49 VHS-T120HS 1.89
SA-100 1.89 DAT-DAR-90 6.49
SAX-90 1.99 DAT-DAR-120 6.49
SAX-100 2.29 DAT-DAR-180 9.99
LIFETIME WARRANTY on all tapes
We carry EVERY tape TDK makes, give me Jack 'Straw' a call!
Minimum 10 Tape Order Please
C.O.D. Visa, M.C. & Discover
FREE POSITIVE ENERGY
1•800•835•7290
The Stereo Advantage
5195 Main Street
Williamsville, NY 14221
DEADHEADS
DEADHEADS
Terrapin Tapes
AT GRATEFUL PRICES!
NEW LOWER PRICES!
Maxell XLII 90....$1.60
Maxell XLIIS 90....$2.05
Maxell XLII 100....$2.00
Maxell XLIIS 100....$2.30
DAT Tapes Now Available!
SIDE A
Checks/Money Orders
Minimum 10 tapes
Tapes shipped UPS
7 to 10 days delivery
Under 50 Tapes - $3.50 shipping charge
50 or More Tapes - FREE SHIPPING!
SIDE B
VISA/MC/Discover
Minimum 20 tapes
Tapes shipped UPS
Guaranteed 1 week delivery
Terrapin Tapes
PO Box 1408
Greenwich, CT 06836
800-677-8650
MAXELL
MAXELL
MAXELL
TDK SA90
Video tape
All prices inclu
Call 1-800-67
for ordering info
Minimum order
VISA/MC
ing the Tour?
MAXELL XLII 90
AMERICA'S MOST POPULAR HIGH BIAS CASSETTE, FOR HIGH QUALITY RECORDINGS!
1.49
99¢
TDK SA•90 High Bias..........1.49
Maxell XLIIS•90 High Bias......1.99
Maxell GXT•120 VHS.............1.99
TDK DAR•90 DAT..........6.49
TDK DAR•120 DAT..........6.79
The Advantage Company
Minimum 10 Tape order.
We accept M.C., Visa, Discover or C.O.D.
800•394•2347
MAXELL SONY FUJI OUR 17TH YEAR
TAPE WORLD
DAT TAPES
120 Minute/180 Minute Maxell
$6.99/$8.99 ea.
Buy 10 get one free!
$5.99 and $7.99 apiece @ 50 qty.
Computer grade, exceeds audio DAT specs! Lower error counts, higher reliability, last up to 3 times longer. Used once. THOUSANDS SOLD!
800-321-5738
M/CARD-VISA
Money Back Guarantee
CASSETTE HOUSE
NOW! YOU C
TOM LOADED HIGH
UNBOXED • MAGNETIC MEDIA
C-20 $0.37
C-30 $0.44
C-40 $0.49
LOADED CHROME
C-20 $0.37
C-30 $0.42
C-40 $0.52
TERRAPIN TAPES
AT GRATEFUL PRICES
MAXELL XLII90
MAXELL XLIIS90..........$1.85
MAXELL XLIIS100..........$2.15
TDK SA90..........$2.20
..........$1.75
Video tapes also available on request.
All prices include tax, shipping & handling!
Call 1-800-677-8650
for ordering information.
Minimum order 10 tapes.
or pay by Money Order:
Terrapin Tapes
P.O. Box 1408
Greenwich, CT 06836
Sorry, no personal checks.
Berkeley
would sound great on one
TDK
TDK SA-90
90 Minutes of Taping
High Bias Sound
SA-60 1.49 VHS-T120HS
SA-100 1.89 DAT-DAR-90
SAX-90 1.99 DAT-DAR-120
SAX-100 2.29 DAT-DAR-180
LIFETIME WARRANTY

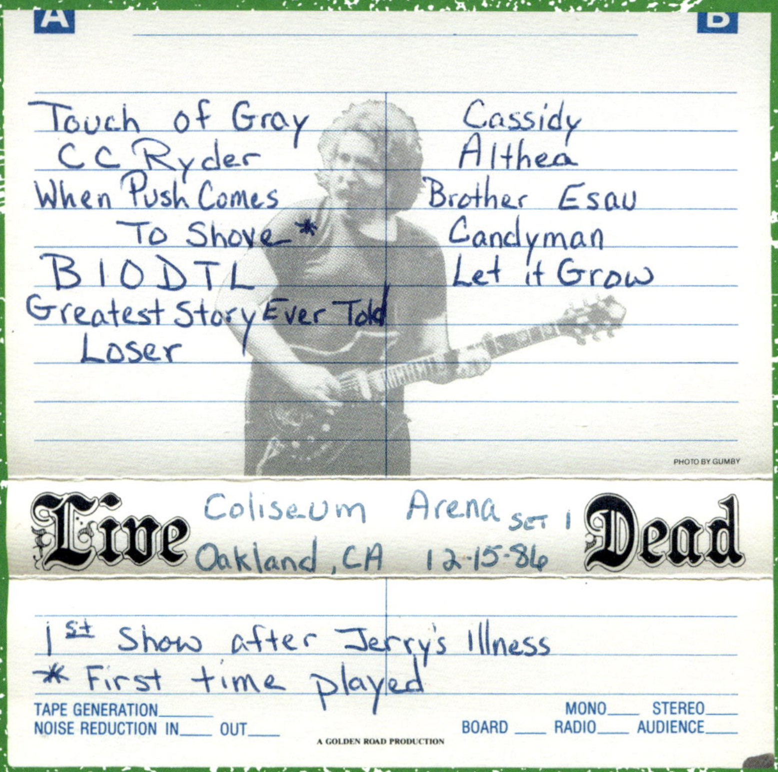
A
B
Touch of Gray
C C Ryder
When Push Comes
To Shove *
B I O D T L
Greatest Story Ever Told
Loser
Cassidy
Althea
Brother Esau
Candyman
Let it Grow
PHOTO BY GUMBY
Live
Coliseum Arena
Oakland, CA 12-15-86
Set 1
Dead
1st Show after Jerry's Illness
* First time played
TAPE GENERATION
NOISE REDUCTION IN OUT
A GOLDEN ROAD PRODUCTION
BOARD
MONO
RADIO
STEREO
AUDIENCE

A
B
Aiko Aiko
Looks Like Rain
Muddy River *
Playin' In The Band
Terripan Station
Drums
Space
Truckin'
Wharf Rat
Jam
Playin' In The Band
Good Lovin'
(Encore)
Johnny B. Goode
PHOTO BY GUMBY
Live
Coliseum Arena
Oakland, CA 12-15-86
Set II
Dead
* First time played
TAPE GENERATION
NOISE REDUCTION IN OUT
A GOLDEN ROAD PRODUCTION
BOARD X
MONO
RADIO
STEREO
AUDIENCE

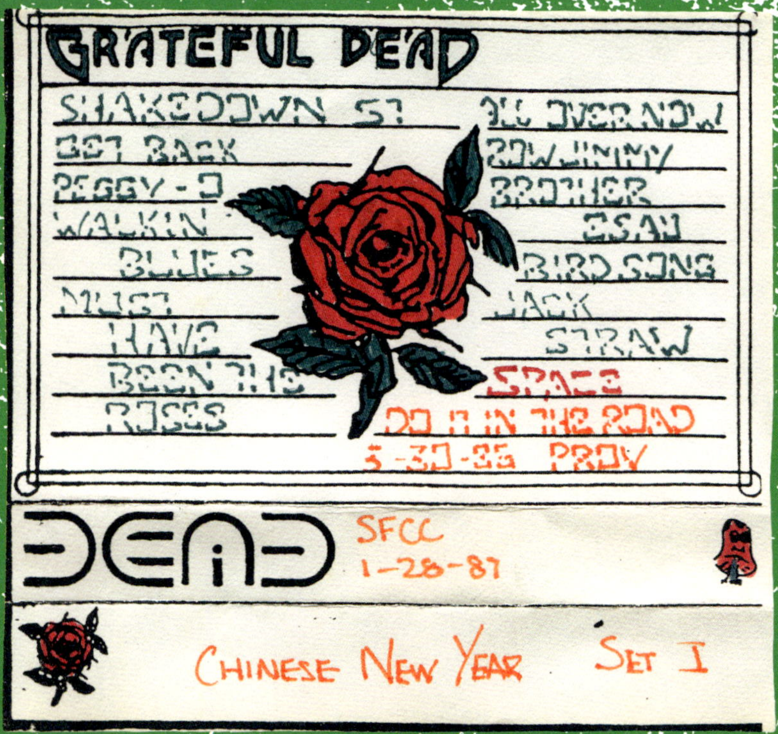
GRATEFUL DEAD
SHAKEDOWN ST
GET BACK
PEGGY-O
WALKIN' BLUES
MUST HAVE BEEN THE ROSES
ALL OVER NOW
ROW JIMMY
BROTHER ESAU
BIRD SONG
JACK STRAW
SPACE
DO IT IN THE ROAD
5-30-85 PROV
DEAD
SFCC
1-28-87
CHINESE NEW YEAR
SET I

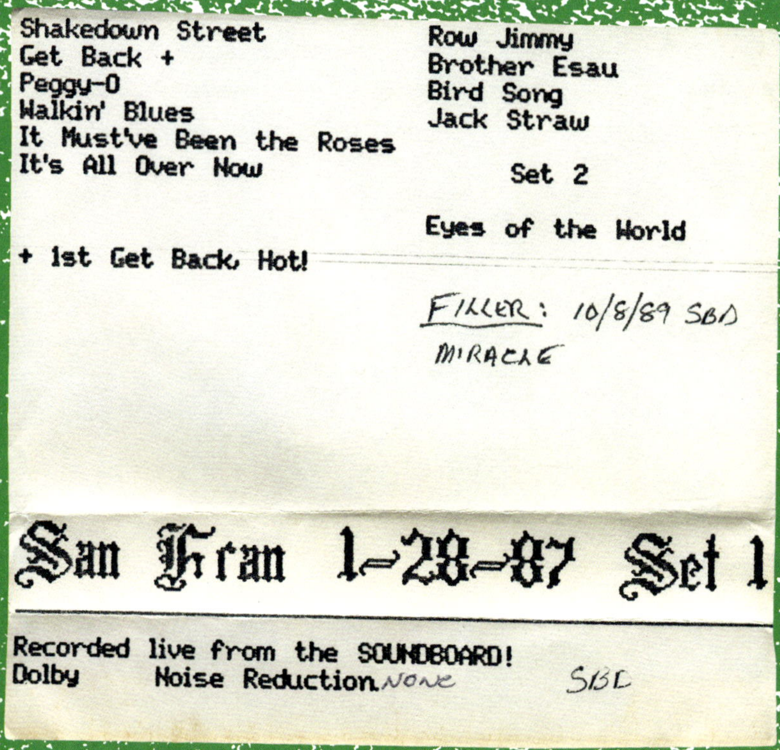
Shakedown Street
Get Back +
Peggy-O
Walkin' Blues
It Must've Been the Roses
It's All Over Now
Row Jimmy
Brother Esau
Bird Song
Jack Straw
Set 2
Eyes of the World
+ 1st Get Back, Hot!
FILLER: 10/8/89 SBD
MIRACLE
San Fran 1-28-87 Set 1
Recorded live from the SOUNDBOARD!
Dolby Noise Reduction NONE
SBD

GRATEFUL DEAD
Touch of Grey
Minglewood
Candyman
Me & Uncle
Mexicalli
Push/Shove
BIODTLine
Promised
Land
NOT F Away
Brokedown
Palace
GRATEFUL DEAD
SAN FRANCISCO
1/30/87 A
AUD A

GRATEFUL DEAD
Worcester 4-2-87
Cold Rain & Snow
New Minglewood Blues
Dupree's Diamond Blues
Far From Me
Me & My Uncle
Mexicali Blues
Push Comes To Shove
Beat it on down the Line
Birdsong
Music Never Stopped

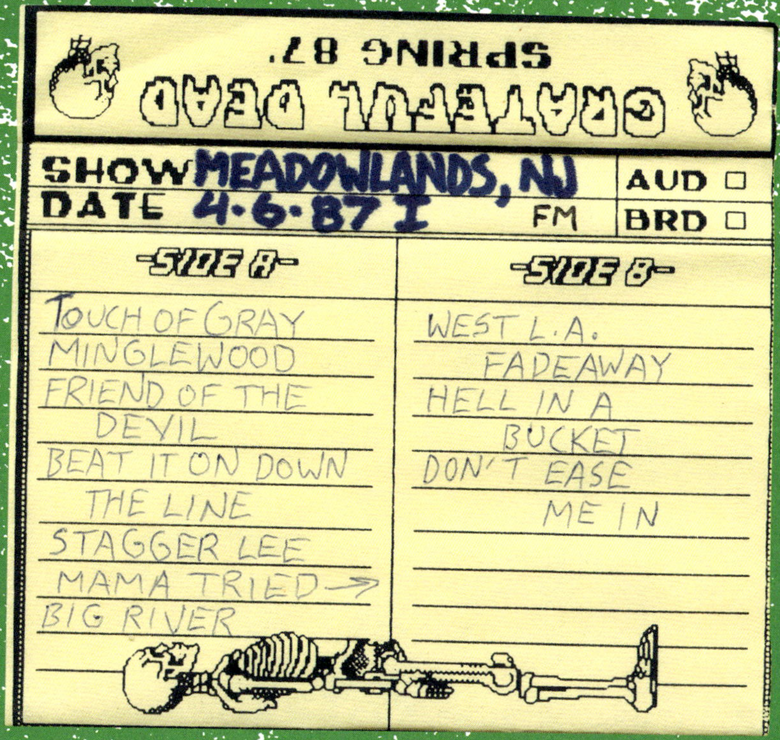
SPRING 87
GRATEFUL DEAD
SHOW MEADOWLANDS, NJ
DATE 4·6·87 I
AUD
FM
BRD
SIDE A
TOUCH OF GRAY
MINGLEWOOD
FRIEND OF THE DEVIL
BEAT IT ON DOWN THE LINE
STAGGER LEE
MAMA TRIED
BIG RIVER
SIDE B
WEST L.A. FADEAWAY
HELL IN A BUCKET
DON'T EASE ME IN

JDS

DANCIN IN THE STREETS
JACK STRAW
FRANKLIN'S TOWER

FEEL LIKE A STRANGER
CUMBERLAND BLUES
TONS OF STEEL
ST. OF CIRCUMSTANCE
DRUMS
SPACE
SPACE
TERRAPIN STATION
THE OTHER ONE
STELLA BLUE
SUGAR MAGNOLIA
BLACK MUDDY RIVER

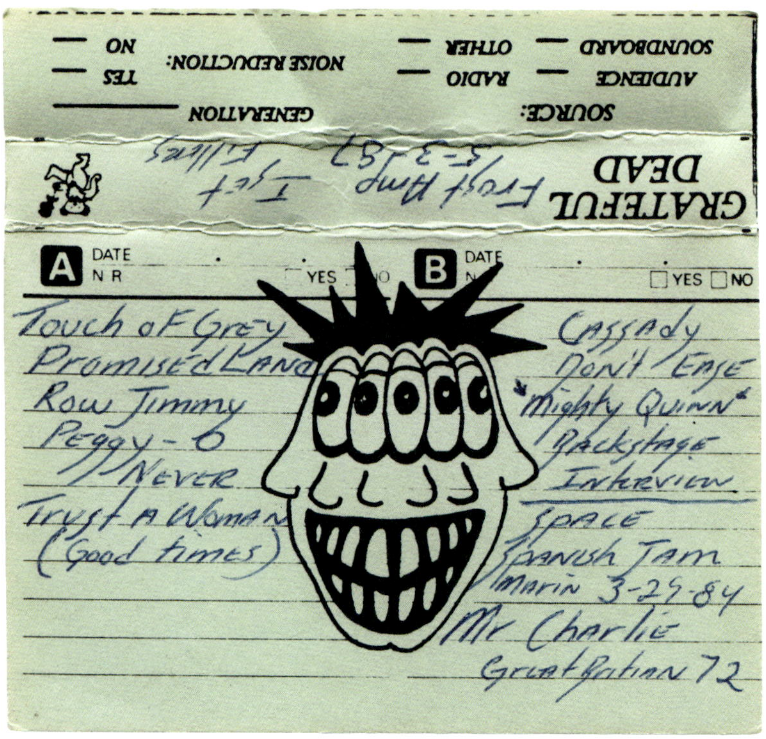
GRATEFUL DEAD
SOURCE:
GENERATION
SOUNDBOARD
AUDIENCE
OTHER
RADIO
NOISE REDUCTION:
YES
NO
A
B
Touch of Grey
Promised Land
Row Jimmy
Peggy-O
Never Trust A Woman (Good times)
Cassady
Don't Ease
"Mighty Quinn"
Backstage Interview
Space
Spanish Jam
Mr Charlie

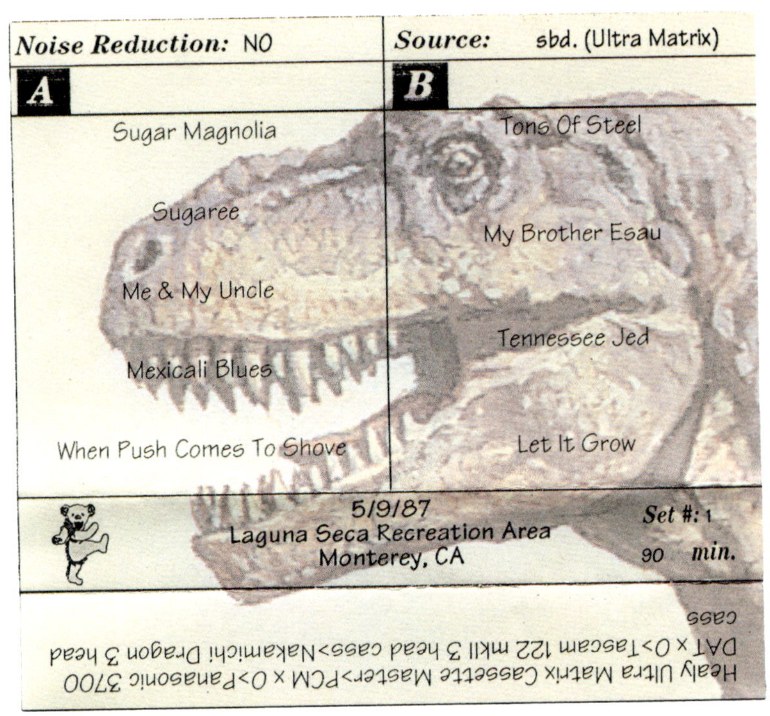
Noise Reduction: NO
Source: sbd. (Ultra Matrix)
A
Sugar Magnolia
Sugaree
Me & My Uncle
Mexicali Blues
When Push Comes To Shove
B
Tons Of Steel
My Brother Esau
Tennessee Jed
Let It Grow
5/9/87
Laguna Seca Recreation Area
Monterey, CA
Set #: 1
90 min.
Healy Ultra Matrix Cassette Master>PCM x O>Panasonic 3700 DAT x O>Tascam 122 mkII 3 head cass>Nakamichi Dragon 3 head cass

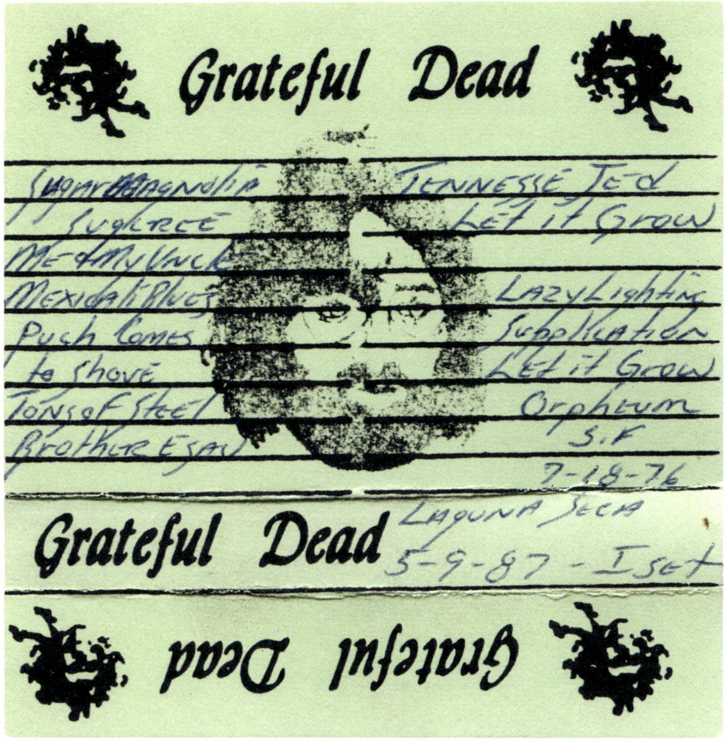

Grateful Dead
Tennessee Jed
Let it Grow
Lazy Lightning
Supplication
Let it Grow
Orpheum
S.F
7-18-76
Grateful Dead
Laguna Seca
5-9-87 - I set
Grateful Dead

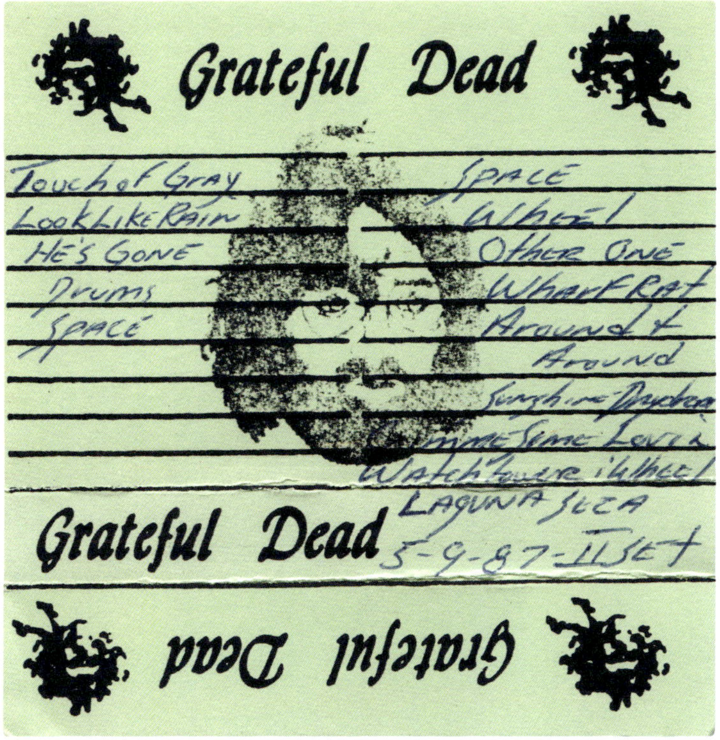

Grateful Dead
Touch of Gray
Look Like Rain
He's Gone
Drums
Space
Space
Wheel
Other One
Wharf Rat
Around + Around
Grateful Dead
Laguna Seca
5-9-87 - II Set
Grateful Dead

BERKELEY, CA.
GREEK THEATRE
6-21-87 II
(Sunday)
SIDE A

WOMEN ARE SMARTER >
CRAZY FINGERS >
SAINT OF CIRCUMSTANCE >
CHINA DOLL >
PLAYING IN THE BAND >
DRUMS >
SIDE B

SPACE >
MASTERPIECE >
BLACK PETER >
THROWING STONES >
NOT FADE AWAY
QUALITY: A (SB-FM)
SOURCE: Dawn Izzo
GRATEFUL DEAD
BERKELEY 6-21-87 II
SBD FM AUD B
SBD FM AUD A

TORONTO 6-30-87 I
GRATEFUL DEAD
LIVE DEAD
TORONTO, CANADA
KINGSWOOD MUSIC THEATRE
6-30-87 I
(Tuesday)
SIDE A

TOUCH OF GREY >
GREATEST STORY EVER TOLD
LOSER
NEW MINGLEWOOD BLUES
CANDYMAN
FAR FROM ME
SIDE B

MAMA TRIED >
BIG RIVER
RAMBLE ON ROSE
MASTERPIECE
DON'T EASE ME IN
(Break)
SCARLET BEGONIAS >
FIRE ON THE MOUNTAIN
QUALITY: A+ (SB-FM)
SOURCE: Steve Symonanis

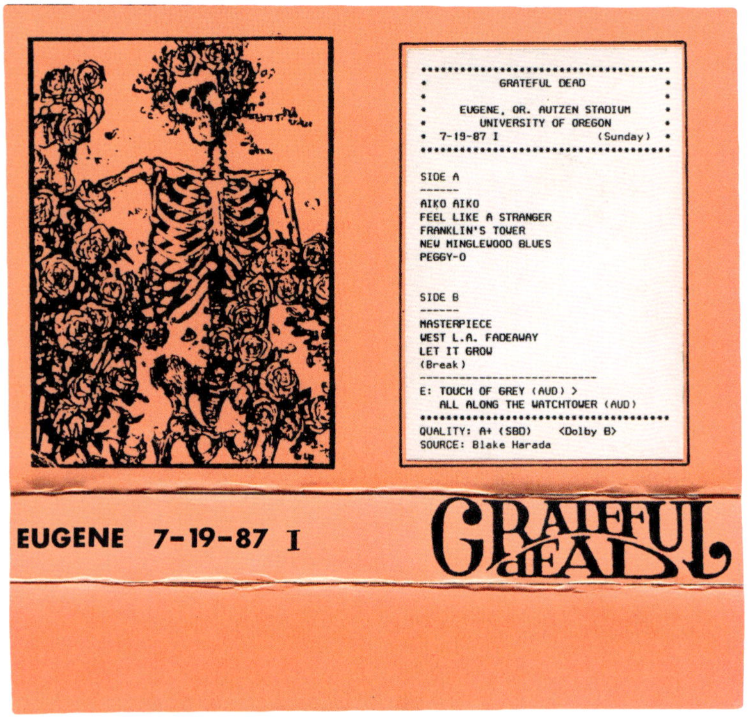
GRATEFUL DEAD
EUGENE, OR. AUTZEN STADIUM
UNIVERSITY OF OREGON
7-19-87 I (Sunday)
SIDE A
AIKO AIKO
FEEL LIKE A STRANGER
FRANKLIN'S TOWER
NEW MINGLEWOOD BLUES
PEGGY-O
SIDE B
MASTERPIECE
WEST L.A. FADEAWAY
LET IT GROW
(Break)
E: TOUCH OF GREY (AUD) >
ALL ALONG THE WATCHTOWER (AUD)
QUALITY: A+ (SBD) <Dolby B>
SOURCE: Blake Harada
EUGENE 7-19-87 I
GRATEFUL DEAD

GRATEFUL DEAD
EUGENE, OR. AUTZEN STADIUM
UNIVERSITY OF OREGON
7-19-87 II (Sunday)
SIDE A
GIMME SOME LOVIN'
PLAYING IN THE BAND >
HE'S GONE >
SPOONFUL >
DRUMS >
SPACE >
SIDE B
SPACE >
THE WHEEL >
TRUCKIN >
WHARF RAT >
LOVELIGHT
QUALITY: A+ (SBD) <Dolby B?>
SOURCE: Blake Harada
EUGENE 7-19-87 II
GRATEFUL DEAD

GRATEFUL DEAD
RED ROCKS 8/12/87 A
AUD A-
GRATEFUL DEAD
Hell in a Bkt
Sugaree
Good Times
Cumberland
Mexicalli
FOTD
Essau
Birdsong
Music Stoppe
FILL 8/22 87
Birdsong
Schoolgirl
Midnite Hour
C SANTANA

SCARLET →
FIRE →
L.L. RAIN
EYES →
DRUMS →
SPACE →
MIRACLE →
BERTHA →
MORNING DEW →
SAT. NIGHT
E: BABY BLUE
grateful dead
8.15.87
TOWN PARK
TELLURIDE, CO.
SET II
sunshine daydream

Grateful Dead
#1
GRATEFUL DEAD - Mountain Aire 8-23-87

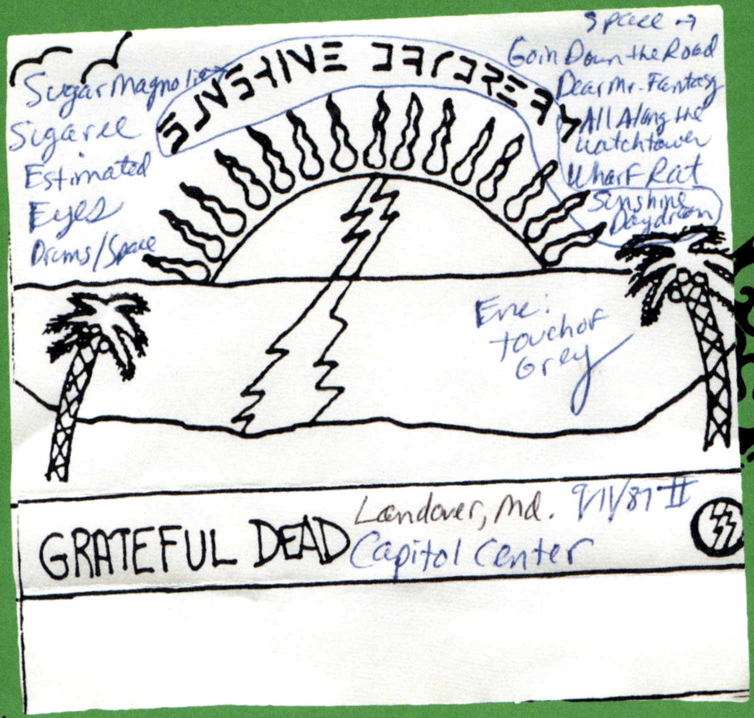
Sugar Magnolia
Sigaree
Estimated
Eyes
Drums/Space
Space →
Goin Down the Road
Dear Mr. Fantasy
All Along the Watchtower
Wharf Rat
Sunshine Daydream
Enc: Touch of Grey
GRATEFUL DEAD
Landover, Md. 9/11/87 II
Capitol Center

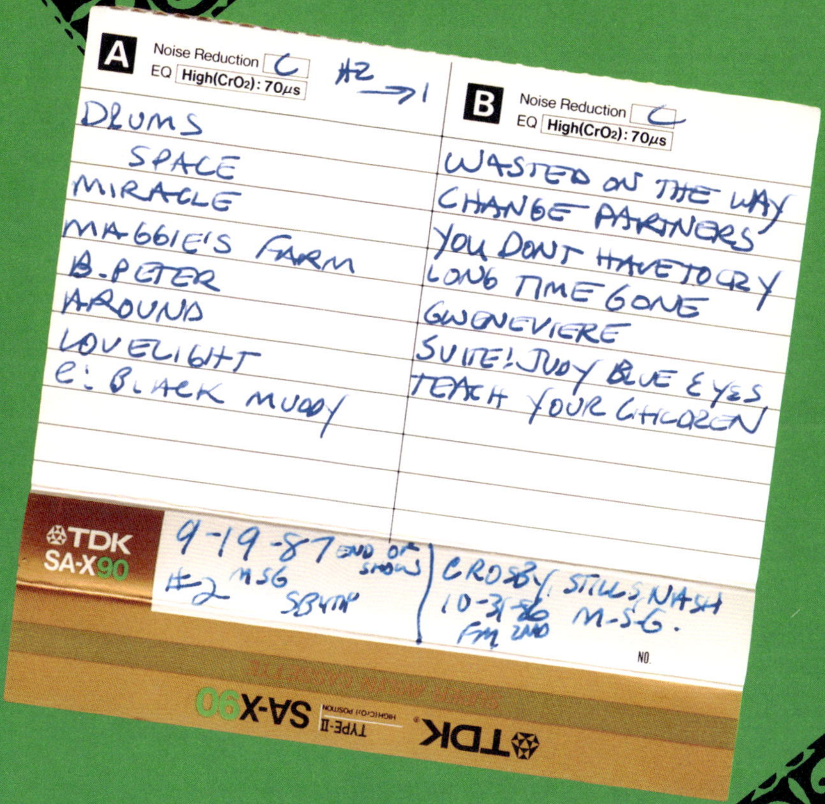
A
Noise Reduction C
EQ High(CrO2): 70µs
#2 → 1
DRUMS
SPACE
MIRACLE
MAGGIE'S FARM
B.PETER
AROUND
LOVELIGHT
E: BLACK MUDDY
B
Noise Reduction C
EQ High(CrO2): 70µs
WASTED ON THE WAY
CHANGE PARTNERS
YOU DONT HAVE TO CRY
LONG TIME GONE
GWENEVIERE
SUITE: JUDY BLUE EYES
TEACH YOUR CHILDREN
TDK
SA-X90
9-19-87 END OF SHOW
#2 MSG
SBD
CROSBY, STILLS, NASH
10-31-86 M-S-G.
FM 2ND
TDK
SA-X90
TYPE II

Side A NYC 9/19/87 CONCL.
DRUMS
Miracle
MAGGIE'S FARM
BLACK Peter
Arounds Around
LOVELIGHT
ENCORE: BLACK MUDDY RIVER

Side B
CSN MSG NYC 10/31/86
FM Simulcast 2ND GEN.
DOLBY C
WASTED ON the WAY
CHANGE PARTNERS
YOU DON'T HAVE to CRY
LONG TIME GONE
GUINEVIERE
SUITE JUDY BLUE EYES
TEACH YOUR CHILDREN

Master: DAN Healy's DAT
COPY: 1st GEN SONY DTC 1000 ES + SONY D120 → (DAT DECK)
PB: 1st GEN ON SONY DTC 1000 ES
Rec: 2ND Gen. ON Technics RS 1506 US OPEN REEL 7½ IPS + DOLBY
PB: 2ND GEN ON TEAC A 3300 S OPEN REEL
Rec: 3rd Gen ON TECHNICS RS 1506 US 7½ IPS NO DOLBY MAXELL XL I 35-90
PB: 3rd Gen. ON TEAC X 300R OPEN REEL
Rec: 4th GEN ON NAK BX300 TDK SA-X DOLBY C

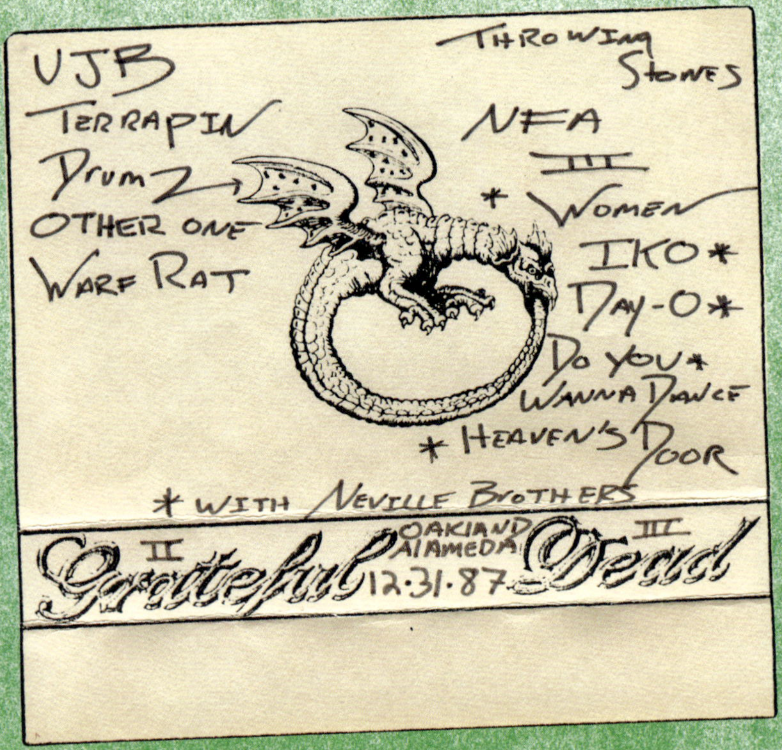

HAMPTON

GRATEFUL DEAD

3/27/88 A

AUD B+

GRATEFUL DEAD

Aiko	Let it Grow
Red Rooster	6/28/85 FIL
Stagerlee	Cold Rain
Thin Man	Promised Ld
Cumberland	Ramble On
Me & Uncle	Birdsong
Lay Me Down	Comes a Tim

Civic Center 4/4/88 # 2

Hartford,CT

Good Quality

A)Bucket›
Sugaree
Stir It Up
Minglewood
Peggy-O

B)Mexicali›
Big River
Row Jimmy
Memphis Blues
Might As Well

Side A Filler:3/30/88
Meadowlands Arena
East Rutherford,NJ
Gretest Story
Hey Pocky Way
Good Quality

Side B Filler:
6/30/88 #1
Silver Stadium
Rochester,NY
Cold Rain&Snow
Good Quality

CLUB DEAD
SCARLET BEGONIAS
FIRE ON THE MOUNTAIN
WALKIN' BLUES
CANDY MAN
LOUIE - LOUIE
CUMBERLAND BLUES
...... MEMPHIS BLUES AGAIN
DEAL
SET 1 DB IN OUT ✓
REC. TYPE A. AUD / B. SOUNDBD
ROSEMONT HORIZON
THE ANTIDOTE FOR CIVILIZATION

CLUB DEAD
HELL IN A BUCKET
CRAZY FINGERS
LOOKS LIKE RAIN
TERRAPIN
DRUMS
SPACE
THE OTHER ONE
I NEED A MIRACLE
DEAR MR. FANTASY
HEY JUDE
LOVELIGHT
* KNOCKIN ON HEAVENS DOOR
FILLER: 4.13.88
SET 2 DB IN OUT ✓
REC. TYPE 3RD GEN SOUNDBOARD
4.15.88.
THE ANTIDOTE FOR CIVILIZATION

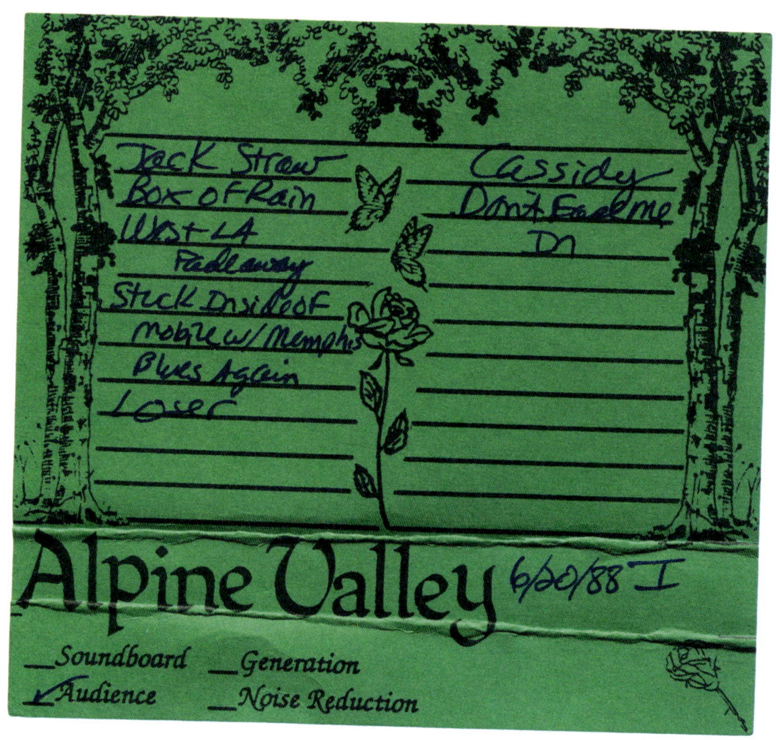
Jack Straw
Box of Rain
West LA Fadeaway
Stuck Inside of Mobile w/Memphis Blues Again
Loser
Cassidy
Don't Ease me In
Alpine Valley 6/20/88 I
Soundboard
✓ Audience
Generation
Noise Reduction

Saratoga Performing Arts Center 6/28/88 #1
Saratoga, NY

A) Scarlet Begonias>
Fire On The Mt.
Estimated>
Crazy Fingers>
Drums>

B) Drums>Space>
Take You Home>
GDTRFB>
Miracle>
Stella Blue>
NFA

grateful dead

Green Onions
China Rider
Sampson
Believe It Or Not
Truckin'
He's gone
Drums

Space
The Other One
Wharf Rat
Throwing Stones
Love Light

Live

GRATEFUL DEAD LIVE Silver Stadium Rochester NY 6/30/88 2

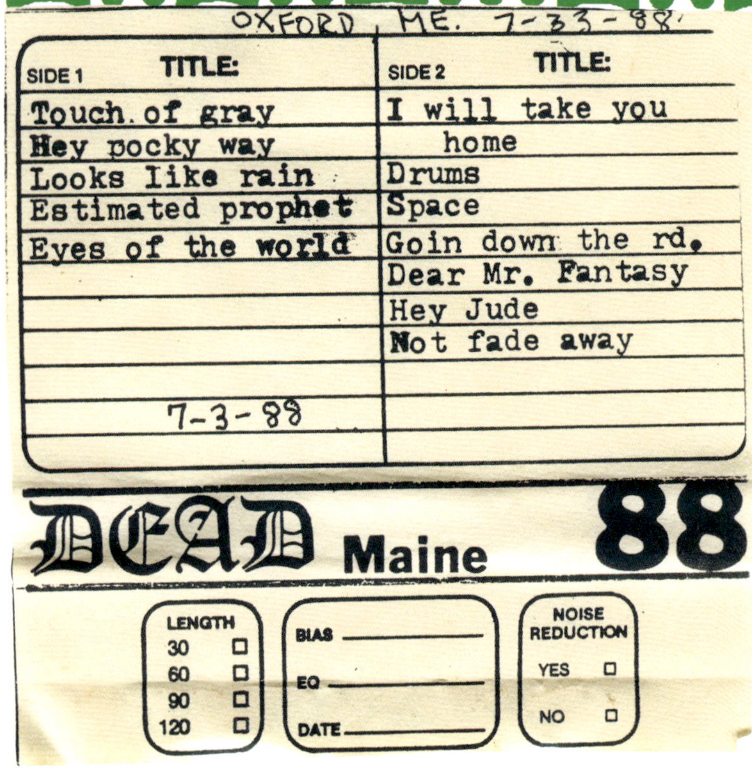
OXFORD, ME. 7-33-88

SIDE 1 TITLE:	SIDE 2 TITLE:
Touch of gray	I will take you home
Hey pocky way	Drums
Looks like rain	Space
Estimated prophet	Goin down the rd.
Eyes of the world	Dear Mr. Fantasy
	Hey Jude
	Not fade away
7-3-88	

DEAD Maine 88

LENGTH 30 60 90 120 — BIAS — EQ — DATE — NOISE REDUCTION YES NO

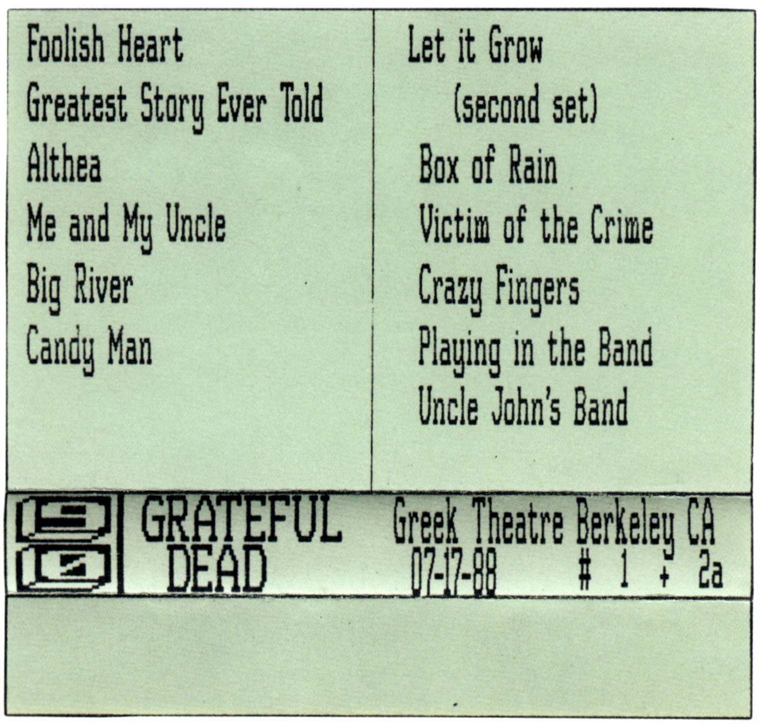
Foolish Heart
Greatest Story Ever Told
Althea
Me and My Uncle
Big River
Candy Man

Let it Grow
(second set)
Box of Rain
Victim of the Crime
Crazy Fingers
Playing in the Band
Uncle John's Band

GRATEFUL DEAD — Greek Theatre Berkeley CA 07-17-88 # 1 + 2a

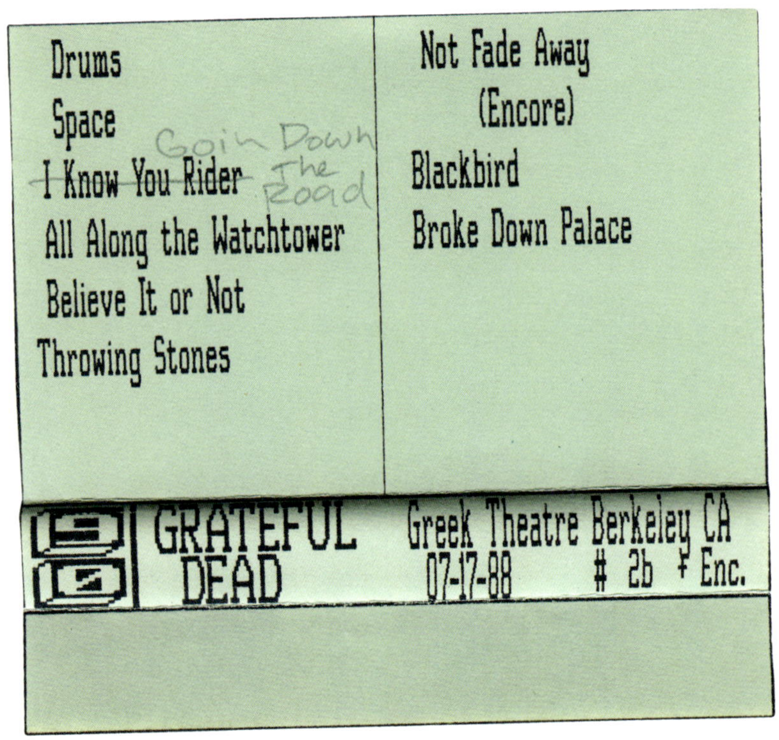
Drums
Space
~~I Know You Rider~~ Goin Down The Road
All Along the Watchtower
Believe It or Not
Throwing Stones

Not Fade Away
(Encore)
Blackbird
Broke Down Palace

GRATEFUL DEAD — Greek Theatre Berkeley CA 07-17-88 # 2b + Enc.

Let The Good Times
/Roll →
Feel Like A Stranger
Loser
Minglewood Blues
Row Jimmy
Stuck Inside A Mobile
When Push Comes
/To Shove
Music Never
/Stopped
Don't Ease Me In
e) U.S. Blues
Knockin' On Heavens
/Door
Laguna Seca Raceway
Monterey, CA. 7·30·1988
I LIVE DEAD
Soundboard
Audience
Radio
Generation
Noise Reduction

Victim Or The Crime
Touch Of Grey
Estimated Prophet →
Eyes Of The World →
Drums
Space →
Smokestack Lightnin' →
Goin Down The Road
/Feelin' Bad →
Warf Rat →
Throwing Stones →
One More Saturday
/Night
Laguna Seca Raceway
Monterey, CA. 7·30·1988
(ENCORE) On 1ST Tape
LIVE II DEAD
Soundboard
Audience
Radio
Generation
Noise Reduction

Hell In A Bucket →
Foolish Heart
Women Are Smarter
Terrapin Station →
I Will Take
/You Home →
Drums
Space →
The Other One
I Need
/A Miracle →
Morning Dew
e) Midnight Hour
LIVE DEAD II
Laguna Seca Raceway
Monterey, CA. 7·31·1988
Soundboard
Audience
Radio
Generation
Noise Reduction

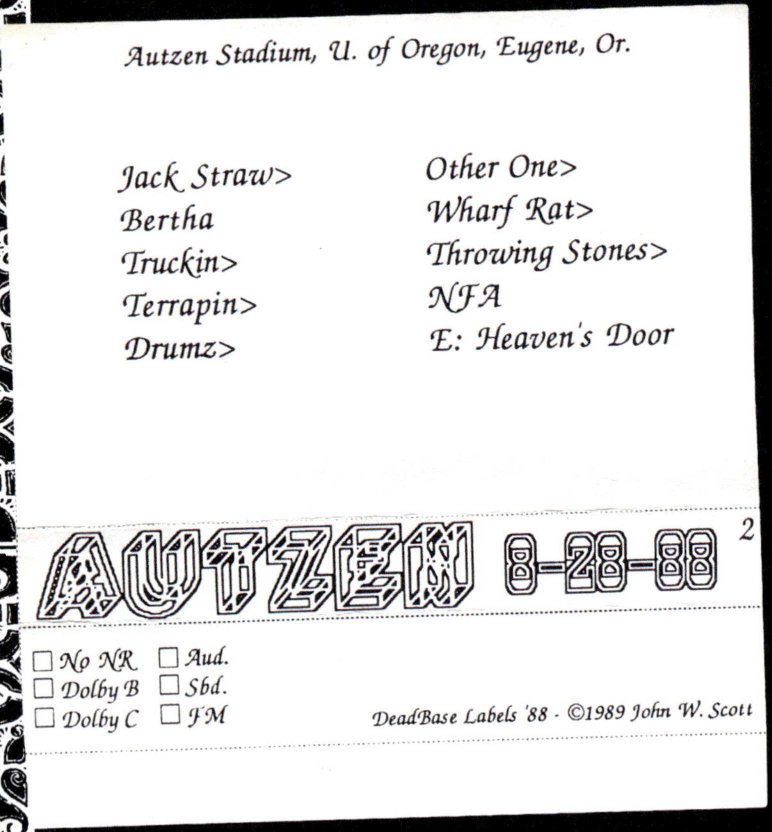
Autzen Stadium, U. of Oregon, Eugene, Or.
Jack Straw>
Bertha
Truckin>
Terrapin>
Drumz>
Other One>
Wharf Rat>
Throwing Stones>
NFA
E: Heaven's Door
AUTZEN 8-28-88
2
No NR
Dolby B
Dolby C
Aud.
Sbd.
FM
DeadBase Labels '88 - ©1989 John W. Scott

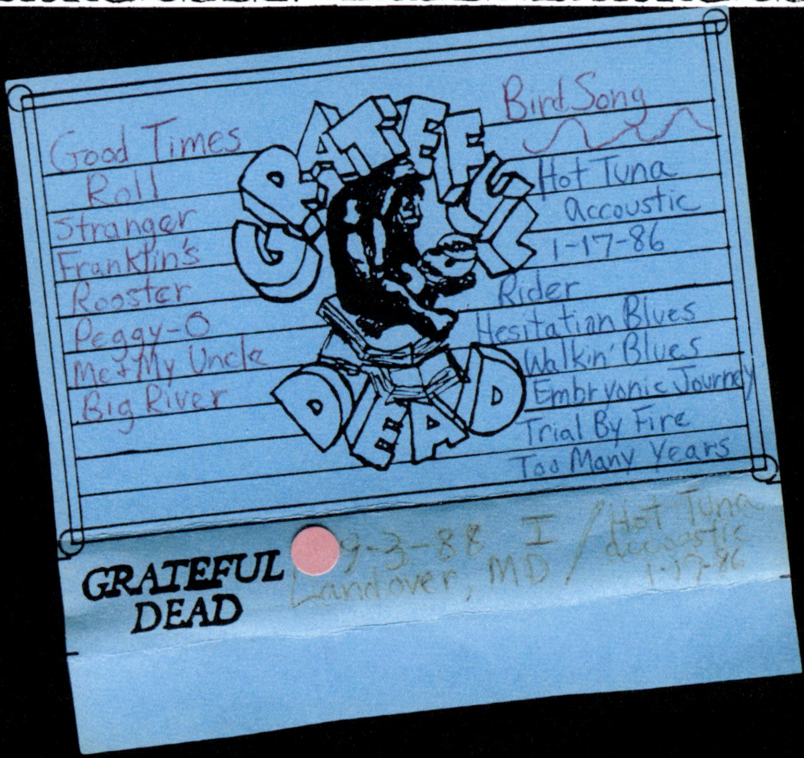
Good Times
Roll
Stranger
Franklin's
Rooster
Peggy-O
Me+My Uncle
Big River
GRATEFUL DEAD
Bird Song
Hot Tuna
Accoustic
1-17-86
Rider
Hesitation Blues
Walkin' Blues
Embryonic Journey
Trial By Fire
Too Many Years
GRATEFUL DEAD
9-3-88 I
Landover, MD
Hot Tuna accoustic 1-17-86

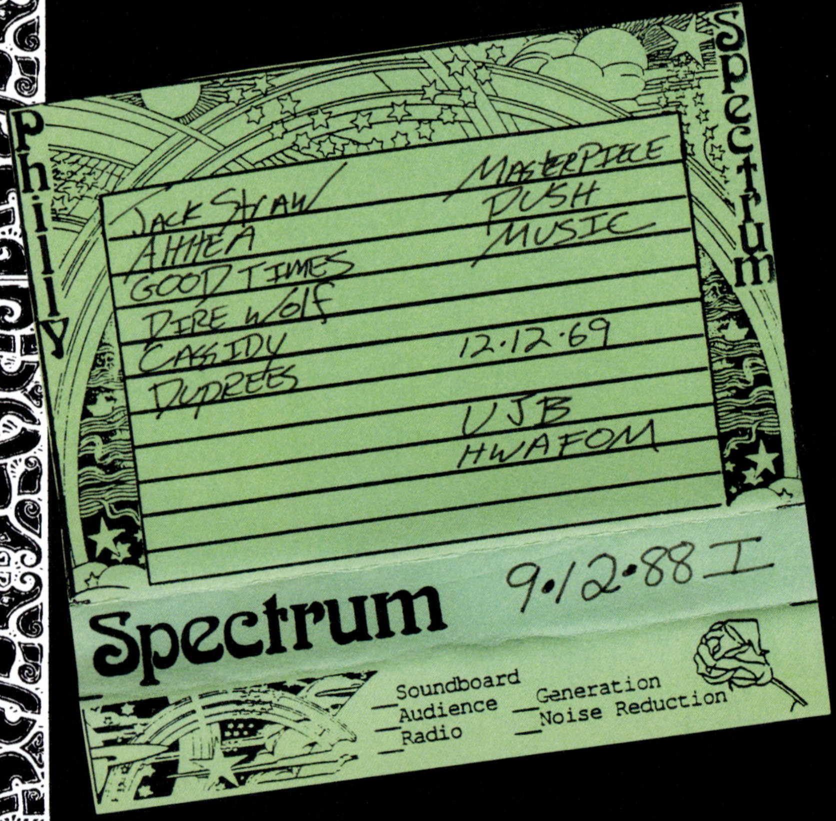
Philly
Spectrum
JACK STRAW
AHHEA
GOOD TIMES
DIRE WOLF
CASSIDY
DUPREES
MasterPiece
PUSH
MUSIC
12.12.69
UJB
HWAFOM
9.12.88 I
Spectrum
Soundboard
Audience
Radio
Generation
Noise Reduction

China Cat
Rider
Tom Thumb
Prophet
Eyes
Drumz/Space
Miracle
Mr Fantasy
Hey Jude
Lovelight
E*Broke Palace
GARCIA 11/20/91
Cats/Money Honey
Waiting for Mirac
NH
DEAD
NEW YORK
9/22/88 II
SBD
FM
AUD
AUD B+

Bertha
Playin in the Band
TERRAPIN STATION
Drums .. Space
The Wheel
All Along the Watchtower
Black Peter
Sugar Magnolia
Enc. U.S. Blues
5/15/86 BCT Wavy Gravy 50th B-Day
Mountain View, CA. 9/30/88 II
Shoreline Amphitheater

Crazy Fingers
Samson & Delilah
Jam
Estimated Prophet
Eyes of the World
Drums
Space
Gimme Some Lovin
Stella Blue
Throwing Stones
Not Fade Away
Enc. Knockin on Heavens Door
Mountain View, CA. 10/2/88
Shoreline Amphitheatre II

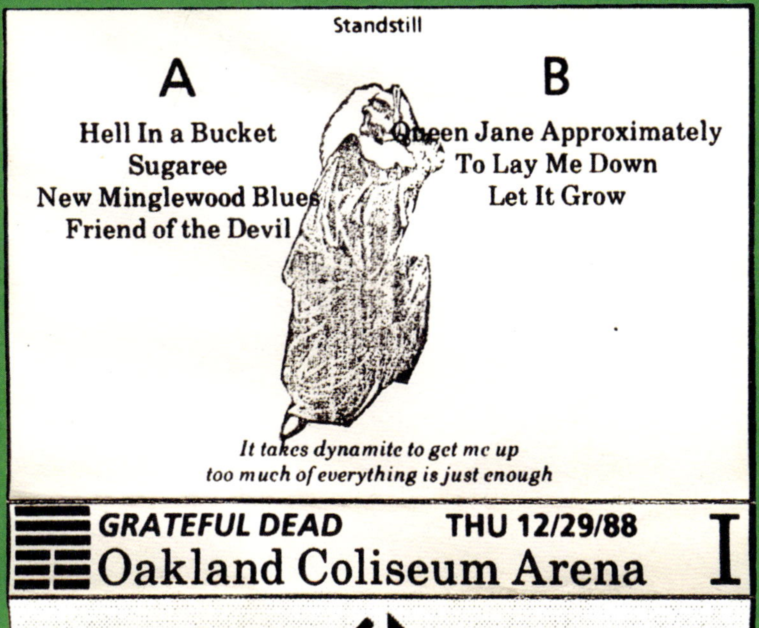
Standstill
A
Hell In a Bucket
Sugaree
New Minglewood Blues
Friend of the Devil
B
Queen Jane Approximately
To Lay Me Down
Let It Grow
It takes dynamite to get me up
too much of everything is just enough
GRATEFUL DEAD THU 12/29/88
Oakland Coliseum Arena I

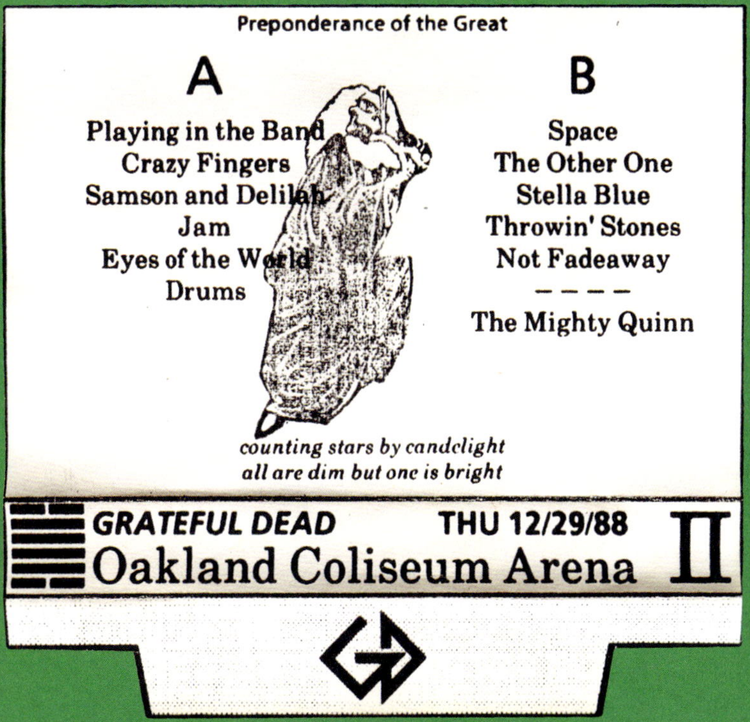
Preponderance of the Great
A
Playing in the Band
Crazy Fingers
Samson and Delilah
Jam
Eyes of the World
Drums
B
Space
The Other One
Stella Blue
Throwin' Stones
Not Fadeaway
– – – –
The Mighty Quinn
counting stars by candlelight
all are dim but one is bright
GRATEFUL DEAD THU 12/29/88
Oakland Coliseum Arena II

Cold Rain And Snow
Hell In A Bucket
Row Jimmy
BIODTL⇨
The Promised Land
West L.A. Fadeaway
How Long Blues *
Gimme Some Lovin' *
* w/ Spencer Davis
Filler: JGB
3/18/78
Soundboard
THE FORUM
02-12-89 - 1st SET
Great Western Forum, Los Angeles, CA
GRATEFUL DEAD

A
PITTSBORG PA
4.2.89 II
B
SHAKEDOWN
WOMEN
FOOLISH HEART
DRUMS
SPACE
WHEEL
DEAR MR. FANTASY
HEY JUDE
ROUND N ROUND
GOIN' DOWN THE ROAD
Lovelight
BABY BLUE
Live
PITTSBURGH, PA
4-2-89
SET II
Dead
NOISE REDUCTION: YES NO
BOARD RADIO AUDIENCE

A
PITTSBURGH, PA
4/3/89 I
B
GREATEST STORY...
BERTHA →
WALKING BLUES
JACK A ROE
EL PASO
BUILT TO LAST
VICTIM OR THE CRIME
TOM THUMB BLUES
DON'T EASE
Live
PITTSBURGH, PA
SET I
4/3/89
Dead
NOISE REDUCTION: YES NO X
BOARD X RADIO AUDIENCE

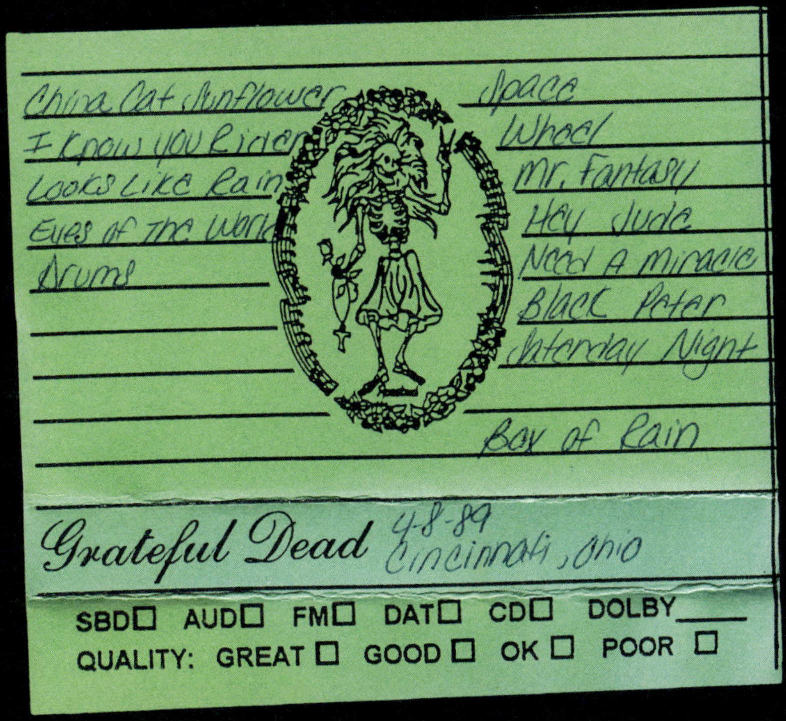
China Cat Sunflower
I Know You Rider
Looks Like Rain
Eyes of the World
Drums
Space
Wheel
Mr. Fantasy
Hey Jude
Need A Miracle
Black Peter
Saturday Night
Box of Rain
Grateful Dead 4-8-89 Cincinnati, Ohio
SBD☐ AUD☐ FM☐ DAT☐ CD☐ DOLBY____
QUALITY: GREAT ☐ GOOD ☐ OK ☐ POOR ☐

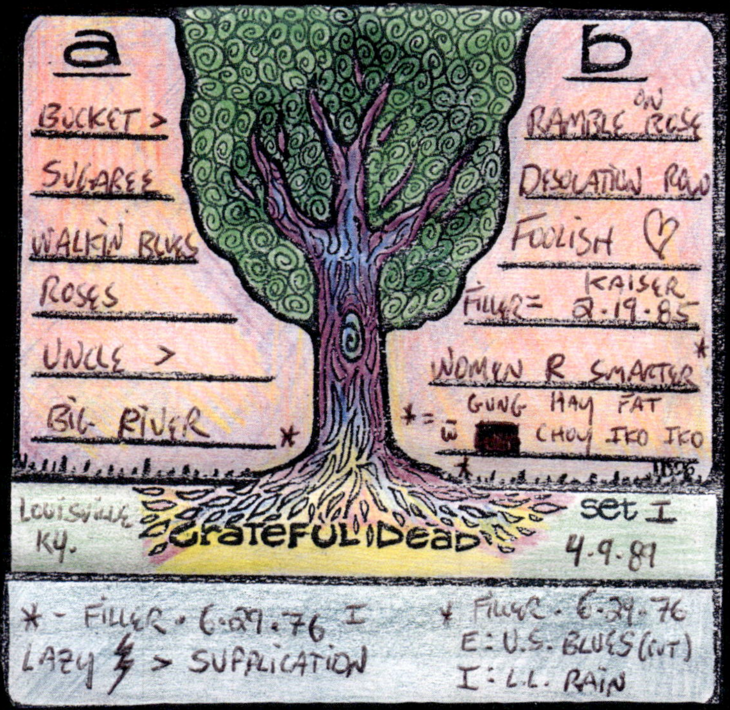
a
BUCKET >
SUGAREE
WALKIN' BLUES
ROSES
UNCLE >
BIG RIVER *
b
ON
RAMBLE ROSE
DESOLATION ROW
FOOLISH ♡
KAISER
FILLER = 2.19.85
WOMEN R SMARTER *
*= GUNG HAY FAT CHOY IKO IKO
LOUISVILLE KY.
Grateful Dead
set I
4.9.89
* - FILLER · 6.29.76 I
LAZY ⚡ > SUPPLICATION
* FILLER · 6.29.76
E: U.S. BLUES (INT)
I: L.L. RAIN

FREEDOM HALL
Louisville, Kentucky 4-9-89 II
Audience Tape
set II
Louie-Louie>
Women Smarter>
Ship Of Fools>
Estimated Prophet>
Uncle Johns Band>
Drums>
Space>
The Other One>
Stella Blue>
Sugar Magnolia
encore
Heavens Door

Source ____ Audience ☐ Soundboard ☒
Generation ____ FM ☐
LIVE Rosemont 4/2/89 DEAD
Steal Your Speaker

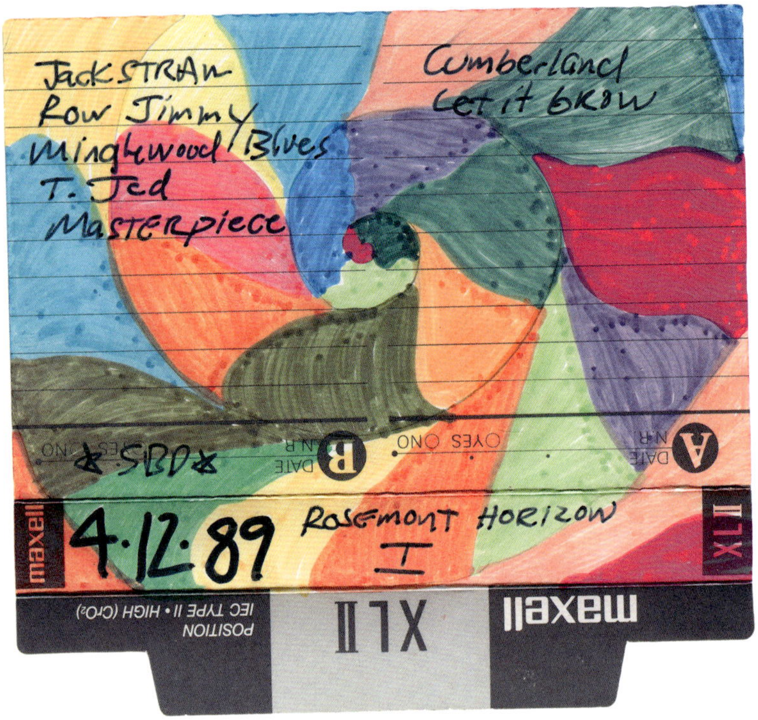
Jack Straw
Row Jimmy
Minglewood Blues
T. Jed
Masterpiece
Cumberland
Let it Grow
SBD
4.12.89 Rosemont Horizon
I
maxell
XL II
POSITION
IEC TYPE II • HIGH (CrO2)

Touch of Grey
Truckin
Smokestack
Spoonful
Smokestack
He's Gone
Drumz
Space
Will Take U Home
All Along The Watchtower
Wharf Rat
Lovelight
Muddy River
SBD
4.12.89 Rosemont Horizon
II
maxell
XL II
90
POSITION
IEC TYPE II • HIGH (CrO2)

maxell UDS-II 60
POSITION·IEC TYPE II·HIGH[CrO2]
Rosemont Horizon
4.13.89
Rosemont Horizon
Chicago Ill. 4.13.89
Iko-Iko
Greatest Story
All over now
To lay me Down
Cassidy
Peggy-O
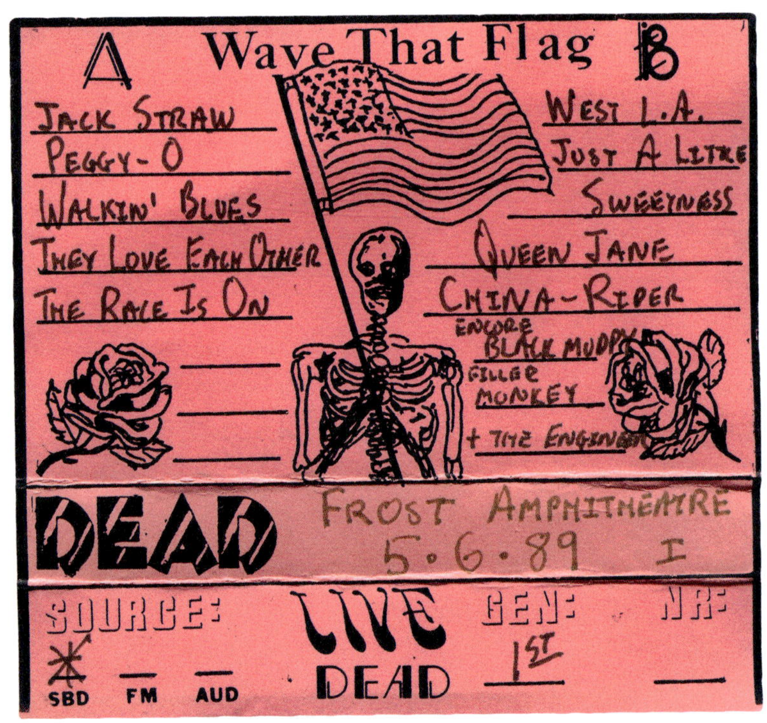
A Wave That Flag B
Jack Straw
Peggy-O
Walkin' Blues
They Love Each Other
The Race Is On
West L.A.
Just A Little
Sweetness
Queen Jane
China-Rider
Encore
Black Muddy
Fillee
Monkey
+ The Engineer
DEAD
Frost Amphitheatre
5.6.89 I
SOURCE:
SBD FM AUD
LIVE DEAD
GEN:
1st
NR:

FROST 5·7·89 #1
Aiko-Aiko
Little Red Rooster
Bertha
Me & My Uncle →
Mexicali Blues
Built to Last
Picasso Moon
Birdsong
Encore:
Knockin' On Heaven's Door

FROST 5·7·89 #2
Foolish Heart
Victim of the Crime
Crazy Fingers
Women Are Smarter
He's Gone
Spoonless
Drumz
Space →
The Other One
Black Peter
Lovelight

maxell XLII 90
POSITION • IEC TYPE II • HIGH (CrO2)
FROST → STANFORD 5·7·89
A
DATE
N.R.
YES NO
AIKO
LIL RED ROOSTER
BERTHA
ME & MY UNCLE
MEXICALI
BUILT TO LAST
B
DATE
N.R.
YES NO
PICASSO MOON
BIRD SONG
5·6·89
ENCORE
KNOCKIN' ON
HEAVENS
DOOR

GRATEFUL DEAD
SUMMER SOLSTICE -89
TOUCH OF GREY
MINGLEWOOD BLUES
RAMBLE ON ROSE
BOX OF RAIN
DIRE WOLF
WHEN I PAINT MY
MASTERPIECE
ROW JIMMY ROW
CASSIDY
DEAL
TURN ON YOUR
LOVELIGHT
BROKEDOWN
PALACE
DEAD
SHORELINE AMP., MTN. VIEW, CA
6-21-89 * 1ST SET

Mountain View Summer Solstice - CA
06-21-89 - 1st Se
Jazzy Jam (HiDeaway)
Touch Of Grey
Minglewood Blues
Ramble On Rose
Box Of Rain
Dire Wolf
Paint My Masterpiece
Row Jimmt Row
Cassidy
Dealon
UNDO 2
Deadheads Against Discrimination
Generation:
Mountain View Summer Solstice - CA
Grateful Dead
06-21-89 - 1st Set
Jonathan Harris 59 Huntington st., Newbrunswick, NJ 08901
(908)937-6649 ramrose@eden.rutgers.edu

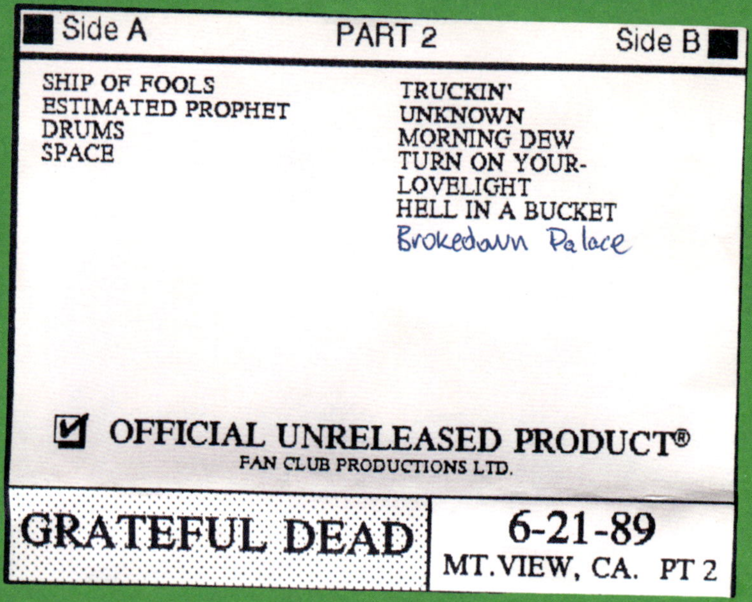
Side A
PART 2
Side B
SHIP OF FOOLS
ESTIMATED PROPHET
DRUMS
SPACE
TRUCKIN'
UNKNOWN
MORNING DEW
TURN ON YOUR-
LOVELIGHT
HELL IN A BUCKET
Brokedown Palace
OFFICIAL UNRELEASED PRODUCT®
FAN CLUB PRODUCTIONS LTD.
GRATEFUL DEAD
6-21-89
MT.VIEW, CA. PT 2

Touch of Grey
Women R Smart
Ship of Fools
Playin (Reprise)
Terrapin
Drumz
Space
I Will Take
You Home
Watchtower
Dew
NFA
Rich Stadium
Buffalo, NY
7.4.89 II
1st show I saw on summer Tour

Bertha
Greatest Story
Cold Rain + Snow
Walkin' Blues
Row Jimmy
Mastepiece
Stagger
LL Rain
Deal
E: US Blues
7/4/89 Buffalo II

PHILADELPHIA PENNSYLVANIA
JFK 7·7·89 II
Box of Rain
Scarlet →
Fire
Estimated Margin
Standing on the Moon
Lovelight
Space
Other One
Wharf Rat
E: Knockin on Heavens Door

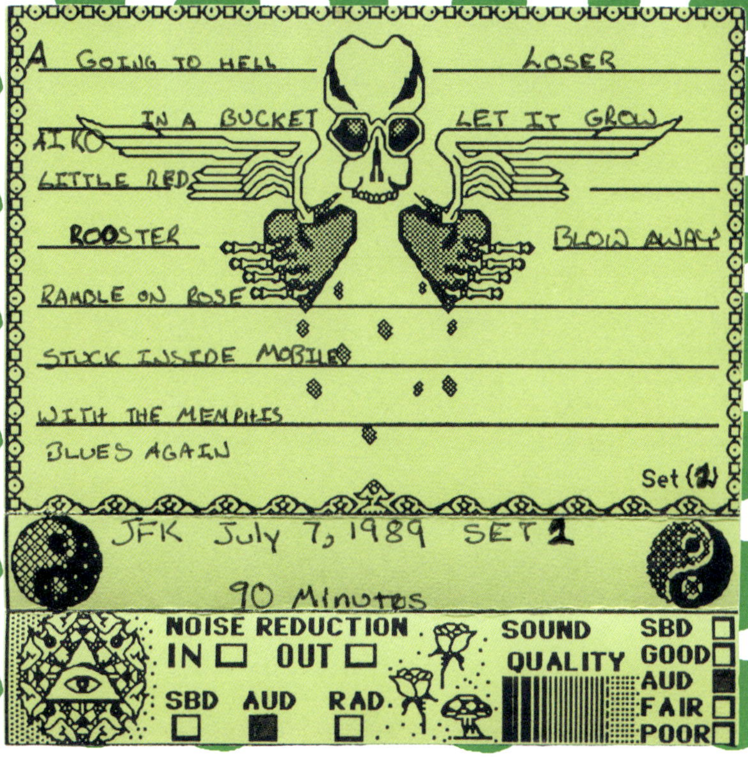

A Going to Hell
In a Bucket
Aiko
Little Red
Rooster
Ramble on Rose
Stuck Inside Mobile
With the Memphis
Blues Again
Loser
Let It Grow
Blow Away
Set (1)
JFK July 7, 1989 SET 1
90 Minutes
NOISE REDUCTION
IN
OUT
SBD
AUD
RAD.
SOUND QUALITY
SBD
GOOD
AUD
FAIR
POOR

Box of Rain
Scarlet Begonias
Fire on the
Mountain
Estimated Prophet
Standing on
The Moon
Space
The Other One
Wharf Rat
Turn on Your
Love Light
Knockin' on
Heaven's Door
Set (2)
JFK July 7, 1989 SET 2
NOISE REDUCTION
IN
OUT
SBD
AUD
RAD.
SOUND QUALITY
SBD
GOOD
AUD
FAIR
POOR

China Cat →
Rider
Sampson & Delilah
Built to Last
Truckin
Drumz
Space
Gimme Some Lovin
GDTRFB
Throwin Stones
Not Fade Away
Giants Stadium, Jersey 7·9·89 II
Meadowlandsmania

ALPINE VALLEY
CHINA CAT →
RIDER
PLAYIN →
UNCLE JOHNS
BAND
STANDING ON
THE MOON
DRUMZ
SPACE →
WHEEL
Gimme Lovin
GDTRFB
NFA
AND I BID U Goodnite
Johnny B Goode
ALPINE VALLEY, WISC 7·17·89 set II
PEAKININTHEVALLEY

Grateful Dead
SOURCE:
GEN:
NR:
Dead
BELIEVE IT IF YOU NEED IT

?SPACE YOUR FACE?
A
AIKO AIKO
LOOKS LIKE RAIN
TERRAPIN
DRUMZ
SPACE
B
CRAZY FINGERS
MIRACLE
STELLA BLUE
THROWIN STONES
LOVELIGHT
GRATEFUL DEAD
Greek Theater 8·18·89 II
SOUNDBOARD
AUDIENCE
RADIO
GENERATION
DOLBY NR

IT LEFT A SMOKING CRATER ON MY MIND...
Let The Good Times Roll
Jack Straw
We Can Run
Tennessee Jed
All Over Now
Loser
Memphis Blues
Box Of Rain
4·16·89
Brent Mydland
solo
GRATEFUL DEAD 8·19·89
Greek Theathre, Berkeley, Ca I
SBD
AUD
FM
GEN

SET I
GOOD TIMES ROLL
JACK STRAW
WE CAN RUN
TENNESSEE JED
ALL OVER NOW
LOSER
STUCK IN MOBILE
BOX OF RAIN
FILLER 7-2-88 I
VICTIM OR CRIME
FOOLISH HEART
Greek Theater 8-19-89 I
Soundboard
Generation
Audience
Noise Reduction
X Radio

SET II
CHINA CAT →
I KNOW YOU RIDER
PLAYIN IN BAND →
UNCLE JOHNS BAND →
PLAYING IN THE BAND
DRUMS →
SPACE →
THE OTHER ONE! →
WHARF RAT →
NOT FADE AWAY
ENCORE –
FOOLISH HEART
Greek Theater 8-19-89 II
Soundboard
Generation
Audience
Noise Reduction
X Radio

Audience
Board
Radio
Generation
on Noise
off Reduction
Grateful Dead SHORELINE 9/30/89 A
Side A.
Bertha
GrtstStory
WestLA
QueenJane
RowJimmy
Side B.
SB B
LetItGrow
WEIR/WASSERMAN
GOLDEN GATE PK 9/30/89
Victim
ez2Slip
Stones

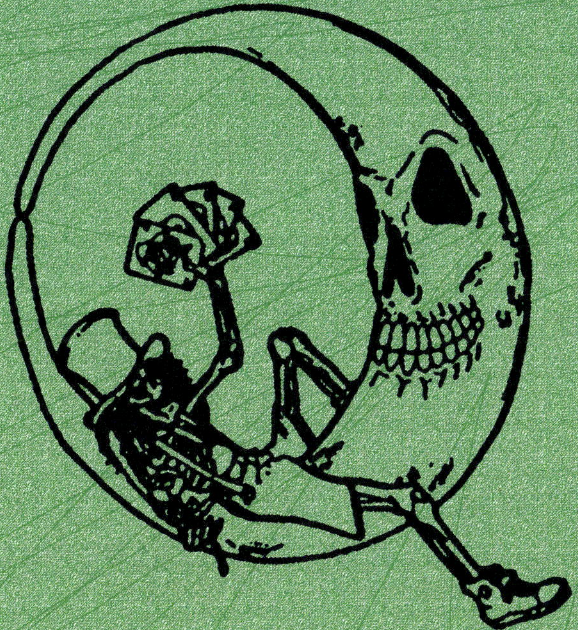

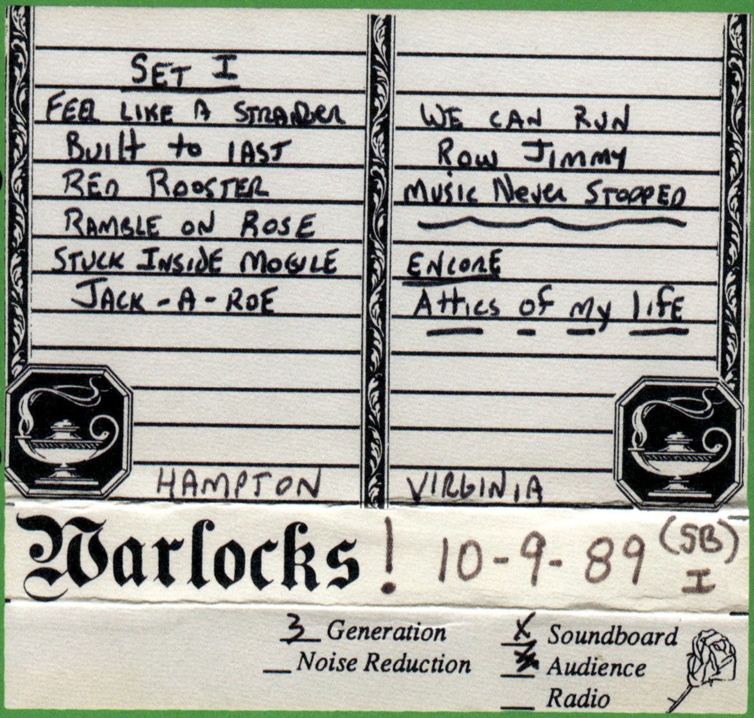
SET I
FEEL LIKE A STRANGER
Built to LAST
RED ROOSTER
RAMBLE ON ROSE
STUCK INSIDE MOBILE
JACK-A-ROE
WE CAN RUN
Row JIMMY
MUSIC NEVER STOPPED
ENCORE
Attics of my life
HAMPTON
VIRGINIA
Warlocks! 10-9-89 (SB) I
3 Generation
Noise Reduction
X Soundboard
Audience
Radio

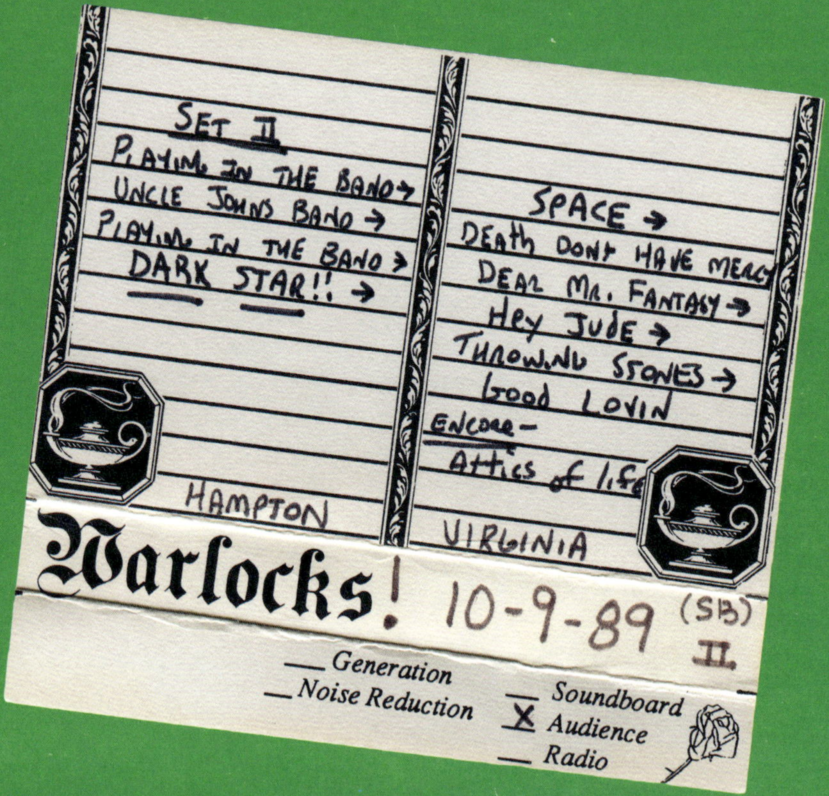
SET II
PLAYING IN THE BAND →
UNCLE JOHNS BAND →
PLAYING IN THE BAND →
DARK STAR!! →
SPACE →
DEATH DONT HAVE MERCY
DEAR MR. FANTASY →
Hey JUDE →
THROWING STONES →
Good LOVIN
ENCORE -
Attics of life
HAMPTON
VIRGINIA
Warlocks! 10-9-89 (SB) II
Generation
Noise Reduction
Soundboard
X Audience
Radio

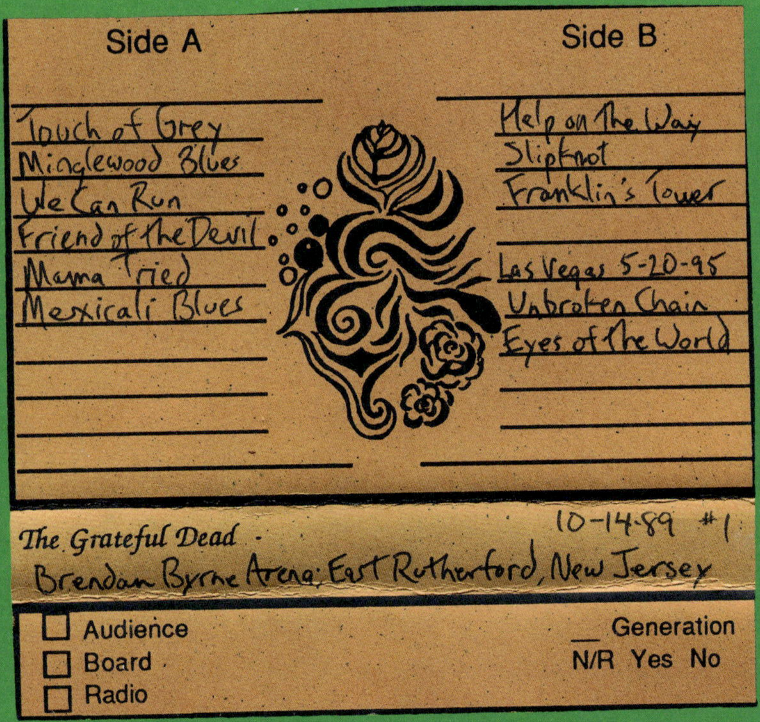
Side A
Side B
Touch of Grey
Minglewood Blues
We Can Run
Friend of the Devil
Mama Tried
Mexicali Blues
Help on The Way
Slipknot
Franklin's Tower
Las Vegas 5-20-95
Unbroken Chain
Eyes of The World
The Grateful Dead
10-14-89 #1
Brendan Byrne Arena, East Rutherford, New Jersey
Audience
Board
Radio
Generation
N/R Yes No

10·16·89
MEADOWLANDS ARENA
NEW JERSEY
II
DARK STAR
PLAYIN
UNCLE JOHN'S
DRUMS
SPACE
I WILL TAKE YOU HOME
MIRACLE
DARK★
ATTICS OF MY LIFE
PLAYIN
WE BID YOU GOODNIGHT

LIVE
DEAD
MEADOWLANDS 10-16-89 II
A
DARK STAR
PLAYIN'
UNCLE JOHNS
PLAYIN'
DRUMZ
B
SPACE
TAKE YOU HOME
MIRACLE
DARK STAR
ATTICS
PLAYIN'
E BID U GOODNITE

BILL GRAHAM PRESENTS
Grateful Dead
OAKLAND COLISEUM ARENA
SATURDAY, DECEMBER 30, 1989-7:00 P.M.
NO REFUND - NO EXCHANGE
NO CANS, BOTTLES, ALCOHOL,
FLASH CAMERAS OR
VIDEO EQUIPMENT OF ANY KIND
TKT. NO. 9123
GENERAL ADM. $20.00
NO REFUND - NO EXCHANGE
12-30-89 #2
GRATEFUL DEAD - Oakland Coliseum

A side
DATE 3/22/90 set one
Hamilton, Ontario
side B
Stranger
West LA
Easy to Love You
B.I.O.D.T.L.
Roses
The Last Time
Picasso Moon
Don't Ease Me In
encore
Baby Blue
B+
recorded
Live 3-22-90
NOISE REDUCTION
SOUNDBOARD
YES
NO
AUD B+

A
B
Cold Rain & Snow
Feel Like A Stranger
Good Times Blues
Mama Tried
Big River
LOOSE LUCY*
*(1st in 16 yrs)
Memphis Blues
Row Jimmy
Let It Grow
3.15.90 I
Black Throated Wind*
Birdsong
DEAD
3-14-90/3-15-90 I
Capital Center, MD
NOISE REDUCTION YES NO
SOUNDBOARD RADIO AUDIENCE
GENERATION ___ SET ___

SIDE A
DATE of SHOW: 3/22/90
set two
SIDE B
LIVE
Scarlet Begonias →
Fire on the Mtn →
Samson
Believe it or not
Truckin →
Drums...
Hamilton Ontario
...Space
Other One
Hey Jude
Mr. Fantasy
Hey Jude
Sugar Magnolia
THE GRATEFUL DEAD
DATE: 3-22-90 II
NOISE REDUCTION YES NO
SOUNDBOARD
AUD B+

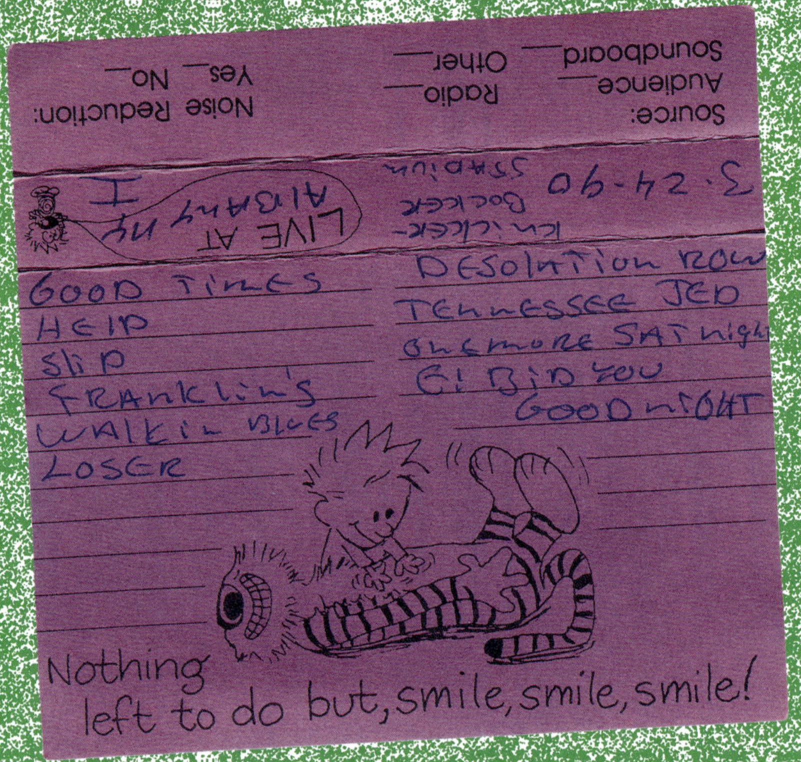
3-24-90
LIVE AT ALBANY NY
I
GOOD TIMES
HELP
SLIP
FRANKLIN'S
WALKIN BLUES
LOSER
DESOLATION ROW
TENNESSEE JED
ONEMORE SAT NIGHT
WE BID YOU GOODNIGHT
Nothing left to do but, smile, smile, smile!

LTGTR →
HELP ON THE WAY →
SLIPKNOT →
FRANKLIN'S
TOWER
WALKIN' BLUES
LOSER, DESOLATION ROW
TENNESSEE JED
ONE MORE
SATURDAY
NIGHT
~9-16-72~
DARK STAR
Live Dead
KNICKERBOCKER ALBANY, N.Y.
3-24-90 I
board radio audience

PLAYING IN THE BAND →
UNCLE JOHN'S BAND →
TERRAPIN STATION →
MINDLEFT
BODY JAM →
DRUMS....
...SPACE →
THE WHEEL →
ALL ALONG THE WATCHTOWER
→ STELLA BLUE
→ NFA
WE BID YOU GOODNIGHT
Live Dead
KNICKERBOCKER ARENA ALBANY, N.Y.
3-24-90 II
board radio audience

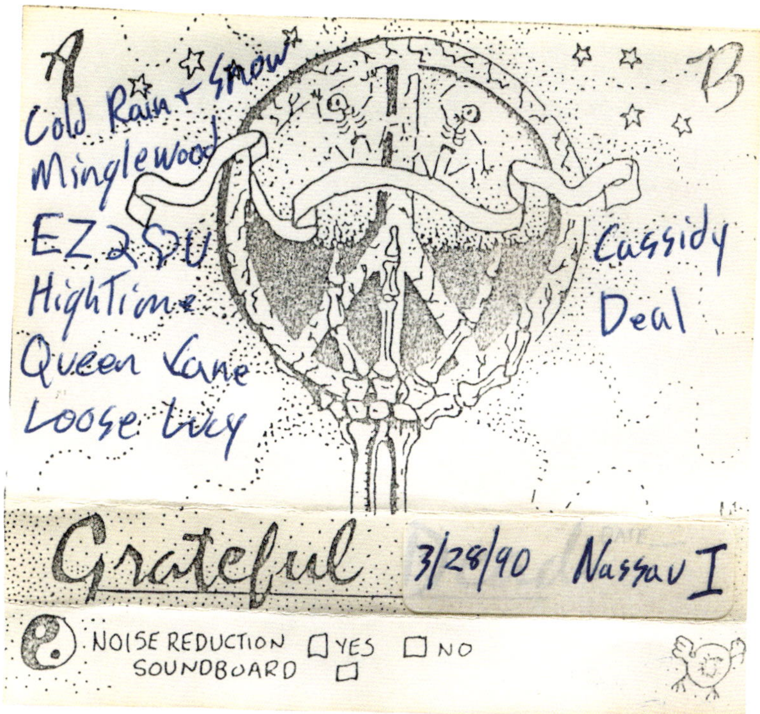

Nassau Veterans Memorial Coliseum
"Help~Slip~Franklins" appears on "Without a Net"

Nassau Veterans Memorial Coliseum
"Help~Slip~Franklins" appears on "Without a Net"

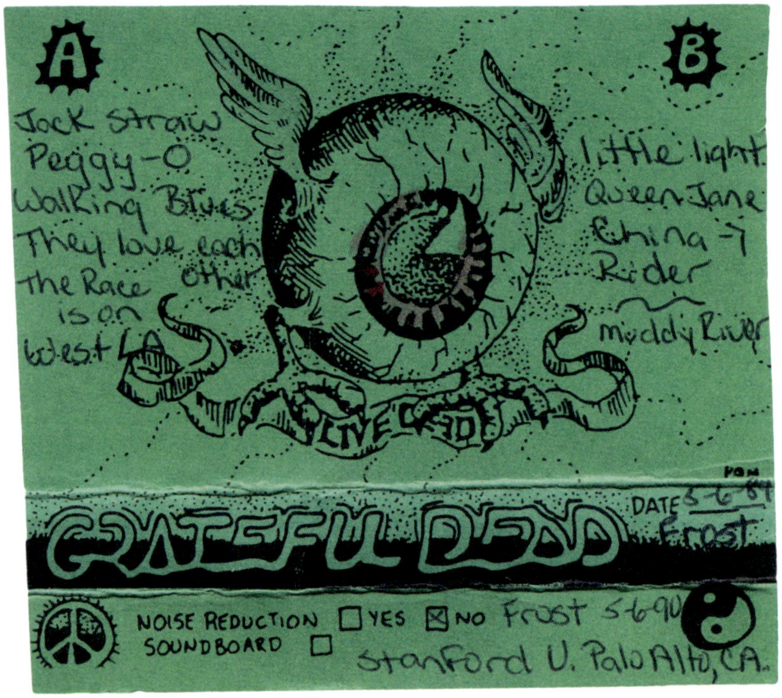
A
B
Jack Straw
Peggy-O
Walking Blues
They love each other
The Race is on
West L.A.
Little light
Queen Jane
China -> Rider
Muddy River
LIVE DEAD
GRATEFUL DEAD
DATE 5-6-89
Frost
NOISE REDUCTION ☐ YES ☒ NO Frost 5-6-90
SOUNDBOARD ☐ Stanford U. Palo Alto, CA.

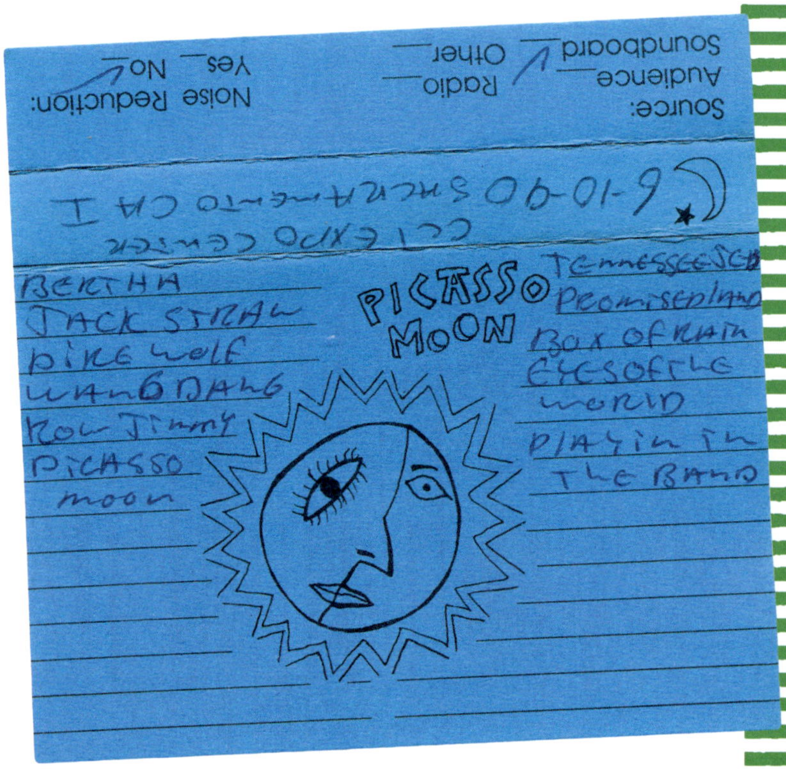
Source:
Soundboard
Audience
Radio
Other
Noise Reduction:
Yes
No
BERTHA
JACK STRAW
BIKE WOLF
WANG DANG
ROW JIMMY
PICASSO MOON
PICASSO MOON
TENNESSEE JED
PROMISED LAND
BOX OF RAIN
EYES OF THE WORLD
PLAYIN IN THE BAND

DEAD
CARDINAL STADIUM
Louisville, KY. 7-6-90 II
CHINA CAT ->
RIDER
Wman R Smtr
S.O.T.M.
Hes Gone ->
Other One
Jane
DRUMZ/SPACE
TRUCKIN
WHARF RAT
GDTRFB
AROUND N ROUND

Dan Shramo
2665 Camden Rd.
Columbus, OH 43221

SBD
AUD
RADIO
IF ITS THE END OR BEGINNING I CANT FIGURE OUT
GEN
Quality A++
Always Live Always Dead
Three Rivers Stadium Pittsburg, PA. 7-8-90 II
A. 7-8-90 II
GRATEFUL DEAD
II (cont.)
B
Samson
Eyes
Estimated
Terrapin Station
Jam
Drumz
Space
Space
Miracle
Wang Dang Doodle
Black Peter
Throwing Stones
Lovelight
Knockin on Heavens Door
Inspiration
Filler From Set I Jack-a-Roe

Been There, Saw It!
& It was fuckin' Great!!

GRATEFUL DEAD 7·12·90
I
Grateful Dead

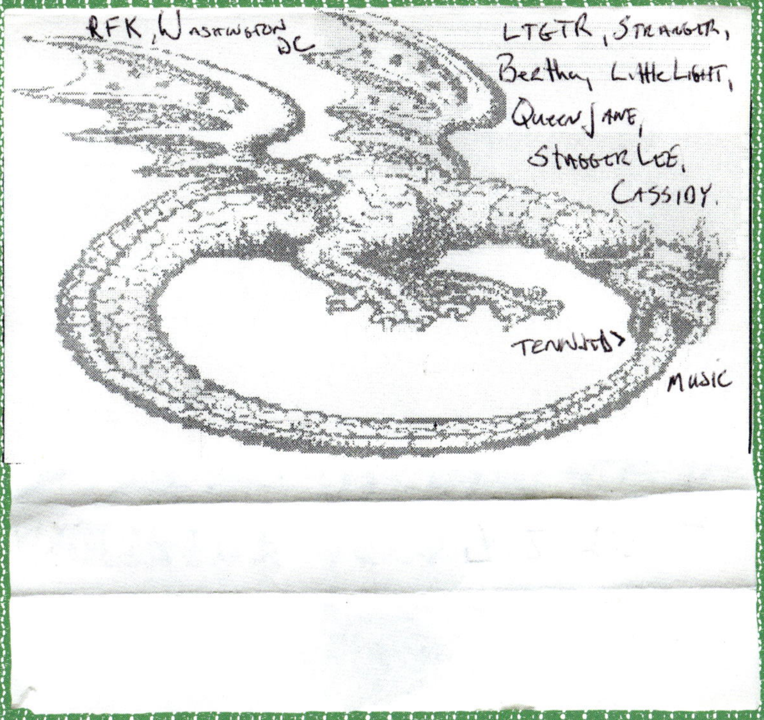
RFK, Washington DC
LTGTR, Stranger, Bertha, Little Light, Queen Jane, Stagger Lee, Cassidy.
Terrapin >
Music

R.F.K. STADIUM
W.D.C. 7-12-90 II
Box of Rain
Victim
Foolish ♡
DARK ☆
~JAM~
☆ STAR
DRUMS
SPACE
watchtower
DEAR MR
FANTASY
Hey JUDE
(REPRISE)
Touch
(cut)

Help
1/2 Step
Blow Away
Mama Tried
Mexicali
Loose Lucy
All Over Now
High Time
Let it
Grow
Don't Ease
E: Brokedown
Buffalo 7-16-90 I
SOUND BOARD —
AUDIENCE X

Set I
Bucket
1/2 Step
Blow Away
MAMA
Tried
mexicali
Loose
Lucy
All over
Now
HIGH Time
Let it
Grow
Don't EASE
6-26-90
EYES
Rich STADIUM
BUFFALO, NY 7-16-90 Set I
SOURCE: AT
MONO
STEREO
DIGITAL
ANALOG
DOLBY
TYPE
BOARD
RADIO
AUDIENCE
GENERATION ?

Recording date
Live Dead
DOLBY
B
HELP ON the WAY
SlipKnot
FRANKlins
Tower
New Minglewood
*EASY to Love You
PeGGY-O
* Last live PERFORMANCE
MASTER ☮
B.E. WOMEN
CASSIDY
DEAL
☆set II☆
China Cat
Rider
Deer
Creek IN 7-18-90 I
SBD ☆ 3RD B+ 2ND
AUD 3RD Gen.

A
B
CHINA CAT >
RIDER
LOOKS LIKE
RAIN
TERRAPIN
DRUMZ
SPACE
OTHER ONE
MORNING
DEW
—E—
THE WEIGHT
GRATEFUL DEAD
DEER CREEK, IN
7·18·90 II
SOUNDBOARD
AUDIENCE
RADIO
GENERATION
DOLBY NR

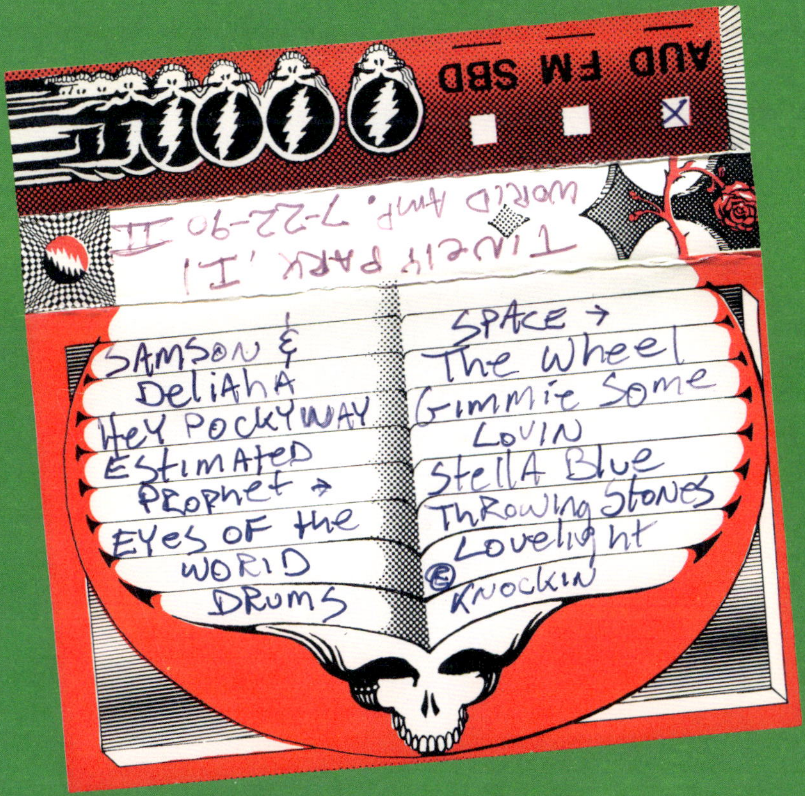
AUD FM SBD
TINELY PARK, I.L.
WORLD AMP. 7-22-90 II
SAMSON &
DELIAHA
HEY POCKYWAY
ESTIMATED
PROPHET >
EYES OF THE
WORLD
DRUMS
SPACE >
The Wheel
Gimmie Some
Lovin
Stella Blue
Throwing Stones
Lovelight
© Knockin

GRATEFUL DEAD
Cold Rain & Snow
Picasso Moon
Good Times
Stagger Lee
Cassidy
Truckin >
Smokestack
Lightning
—Encore Set II—
The Weight
—Filler—
Foxboro / Shakedown
Ma. 7.14.90 Walkin Blues
Grateful
Dead
World Ampitheater
Tinley Park IL. 7.23.90
I
AUD
SBD
FM

Victim or the Crime
Foolish Heart
Women are
Smarter
Terrapin
Drumz
Space
Watchtower
Standing on the
Moon
Around &
Around
Good Lovin'
•Brents Last Show on Earth•
DEAD
World Ampitheater
Tinley Park IL. 7.23.90
II
SBD
AUD
FM
Gen-6th

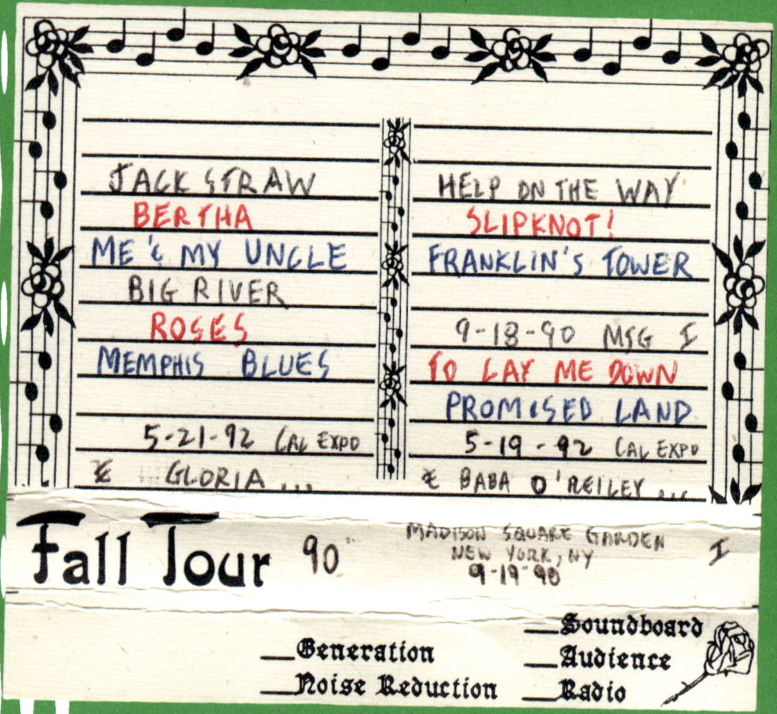
JACK STRAW
BERTHA
ME & MY UNCLE
BIG RIVER
ROSES
MEMPHIS BLUES
5-21-92 CAL EXPO
& GLORIA ...
HELP ON THE WAY
SLIPKNOT!
FRANKLIN'S TOWER
9-18-90 MSG I
TO LAY ME DOWN
PROMISED LAND
5-19-92 CAL EXPO
& BABA O'REILEY ...
Fall Tour 90
MADISON SQUARE GARDEN NEW YORK, NY 9-19-90 I
Generation
Noise Reduction
Soundboard
Audience
Radio

SIDE 1 Set II 9/20/90 SIDE 2
Truckin' →
China Cat →
Rider →
Women Are Smarter →
Drums →
Space →
Dark Star →
Playin' (reprise)
Dark Star →
Throwin' Stones →
Touch of Grey (cut)
AUDIENCE SOUNDBOARD RADIO
Madison Square Garden
9-20-90 II

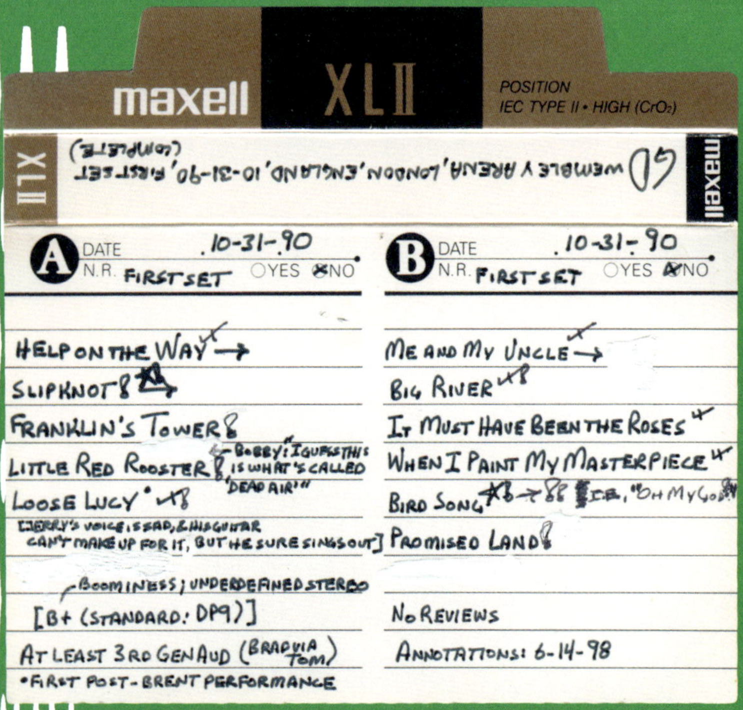
maxell XL II
POSITION IEC TYPE II • HIGH (CrO2)
GD WEMBLEY ARENA, LONDON, ENGLAND, 10-31-90, FIRST SET (COMPLETE)
A DATE 10-31-90 N.R. FIRST SET YES NO
B DATE 10-31-90 N.R. FIRST SET YES NO
HELP ON THE WAY →
SLIPKNOT!
FRANKLIN'S TOWER
LITTLE RED ROOSTER — BOBBY: "I GUESS THIS IS WHAT'S CALLED 'DEAD AIR'"
LOOSE LUCY
[JERRY'S VOICE IS BAD, & HIS GUITAR CAN'T MAKE UP FOR IT, BUT HE SURE SINGS OUT]
ME AND MY UNCLE →
BIG RIVER
IT MUST HAVE BEEN THE ROSES
WHEN I PAINT MY MASTERPIECE
BIRD SONG
PROMISED LAND
BOOMINESS; UNDERDEFINED STEREO
[B+ (STANDARD: DP9)]
AT LEAST 3RD GEN AUD (BRAD VIA TOM)
•FIRST POST-BRENT PERFORMANCE
NO REVIEWS
ANNOTATIONS: 6-14-98

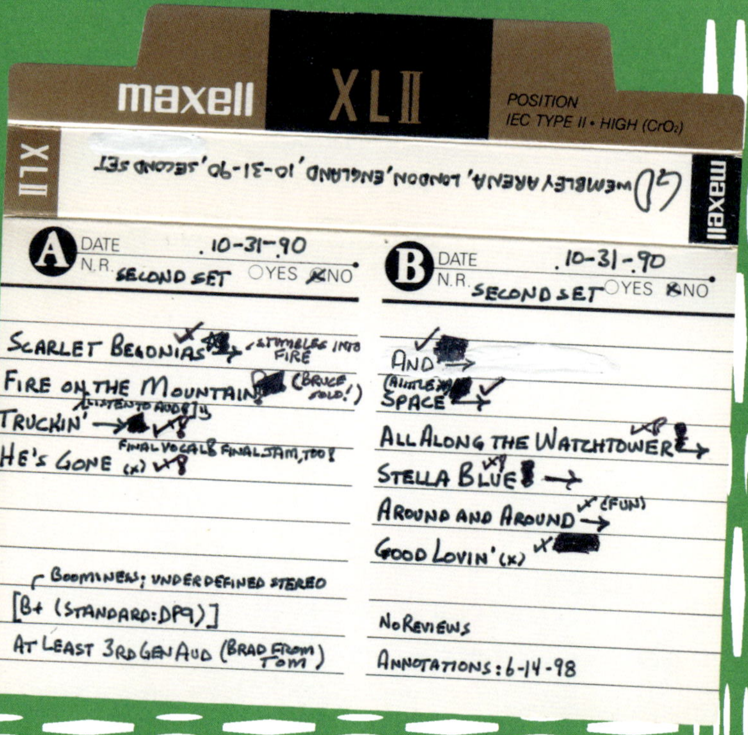
maxell XL II
POSITION IEC TYPE II • HIGH (CrO2)
GD WEMBLEY ARENA, LONDON, ENGLAND, 10-31-90, SECOND SET
A DATE 10-31-90 N.R. SECOND SET YES NO
B DATE 10-31-90 N.R. SECOND SET YES NO
SCARLET BEGONIAS → STUMBLES INTO FIRE
FIRE ON THE MOUNTAIN (BRUCE SOLO!)
TRUCKIN' →
HE'S GONE (X) FINAL VOCALS & FINAL JAM, TOO!
AND
SPACE →
ALL ALONG THE WATCHTOWER →
STELLA BLUE →
AROUND AND AROUND → (FUN)
GOOD LOVIN' (X)
BOOMINESS; UNDERDEFINED STEREO
[B+ (STANDARD: DP9)]
AT LEAST 3RD GEN AUD (BRAD FROM TOM)
NO REVIEWS
ANNOTATIONS: 6-14-98

A
B
BUCKET
BERTHA
ROOSTER
JACK-A-ROE
MAGGIES FARM
BLACK-THROATED WIND
BIRDSONG
OLD VALLEY ROAD
&
BROKEDOWN PALACE
GRATEFUL DEAD
COMPTON TERRACE 12-9-90 I
SOUNDBOARD
AUDIENCE
RADIO
GENERATION
DOLBY NR

THE GRATEFUL DEAD
27 Dec 90
Oakland Coliseum
A.
Jack Straw
Sugaree
Minglewood
Must've Been the Roses
Queen Jane
B
Loose Lucy
Cassidy
Don't Ease Me In

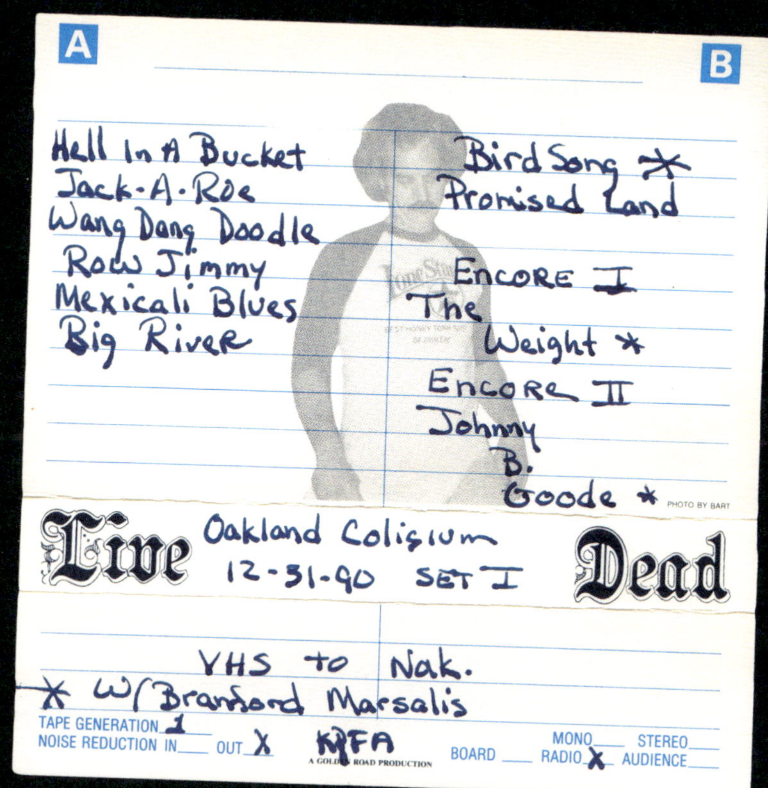
A
B
Hell In A Bucket
Jack-A-Roe
Wang Dang Doodle
Row Jimmy
Mexicali Blues
Big River
Bird Song *
Promised Land
Encore I
The Weight *
Encore II
Johnny B. Goode *
PHOTO BY BART
Live
Oakland Coligium
12-31-90 SET I
Dead
VHS to Nak.
* W/ Branford Marsalis
TAPE GENERATION 1
NOISE REDUCTION IN OUT X
KPFA
A GOLDEN ROAD PRODUCTION
BOARD
MONO
STEREO
RADIO X
AUDIENCE

TAPESTRY Tape Covers
P.O. Box 575
Lansing, IL 60438
Cover Your Tape Collection with Tapestry's Beautiful, Hi-Quality Cassette Inserts
• An Amazing Variety of Designs for the Dead and JGB
• Featuring a Rainbow of Colors and Unique paper textures
(choose from Vivid Brights, Pastels, Parchment and others)
• Printed on Heavy Cardstock Paper
• Cut to fit, marked for easy folding
Also Specialty Designs for Spring, Summer, Fall Tour, Europe '90, MSG, Nassau, Meadowlands, Spectrum, Omni, Deer Creek, Alpine, Greek, Frost, Shoreline, Oakland Coliseum, New Years, Winterland, Fillmore, Warlocks, Acoustic
Qty. Price Postage Total
10 2.50 .50 $3.00
40 6.00 1.00 $7.00
75 8.50 1.50 $10.00
150 15.00 3.00 $18.00
SMOKING GUN TAPE COVERS
INTRODUCING XXX ANNIVERSARY FULL COLOR! COVERS 6/$2.00
80 lb. CARD STOCK
5 Different Sets of Colors & Designs
$1.00 per Set of 6 Labels
S&H= $1. every 10 sets
Wholesale Inquires Welcome
Send Check, American M.O. To:
Michael P. Cohen
P.O. BOX No. 2151
Baltimore, MD 21203-2151
COVERS sets of 9/$1.00
TAPE COVERS
VARIETY OF COLORS & DESIGNS
40.....$8.00
100...$15.00
250..$25.00
LJ'S TAPE COVERS
301 Blake Dr. Suite 1
Fort Wayne, IN 46804
Wholesale Inquiries Welcome!

SMOKING GUN
TAPE COVERS
INTRODUCING
XXX ANNIVERSARY
FULL COLOR!
COVERS 6/$2.00
80 lb. CARD STOCK
5 Different Sets of Colors & Designs
$1.00 per Set of 6 Labels
S&H= $1. every 10 sets
Wholesale Inquires Welcome
Send Check, American M.O. To:
Michael P. Cohen
P.O. BOX No. 2151
Baltimore, MD 21203-2151
NEW 2 COLOR
COVERS sets of 9/$1.00
TAPE COVERS
VARIETY OF COLORS & DESIGNS
40.....$8.00
100...$15.00
250..$25.00
LJ'S TAPE COVERS
301 Blake Dr. Suite 1
Fort Wayne, IN 46804
Wholesale Inquiries Welcome!
TAPESTRY
Tape Covers
P.O. Box 575
Lansing, IL 60438

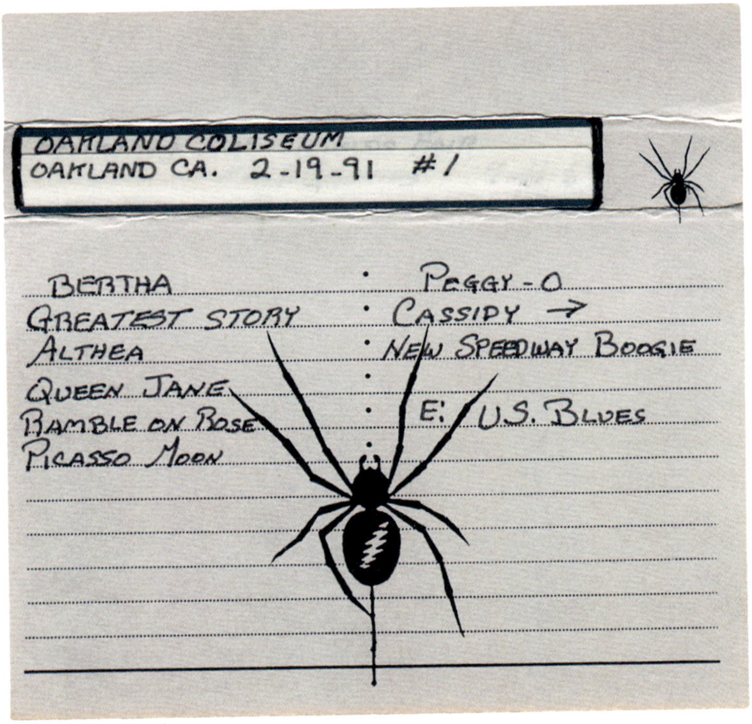
OAKLAND COLISEUM
OAKLAND CA. 2-19-91 #1
BERTHA
GREATEST STORY
ALTHEA
QUEEN JANE
RAMBLE ON ROSE
PICASSO MOON
PEGGY-O
CASSIDY →
NEW SPEEDWAY BOOGIE
E: U.S. BLUES

PEACE, LOVE, AND MUSIC!
PEACE MAN
A
Hell in A Bucket
Sugaree
Walkin Blues
Peggy-O
Queen Jane
B
First
Rubin and Cherise
Let it Grow
U.S. Blues
9-10-91 MSG
Miracle
GARCIA - GRISMAN
ARABIA

LIVE
3-20-91 II
DEAD

A
Help on the Way>
Slipknot>
Franklin's Tower
Wang Dang Doodle
Jack-a-Roe
BIODTL
Brown-Eyed Women
B
Desolation Row
Deal
Fare Thee Well
LIVE
Knickerbocker Arena
3/24/91 #1 Albany, NY
DEAD
for this is all a dream
we dreamed...

A
B
Samson & Delilah
China Cat>
Know You Rider
Looks Like Rain
>He's Gone>
Drums>
Drums>Space>
The Wheel>
I Need A Miracle>
SOTM>
Good Lovin
E: U.S. Blues
LIVE
Knickerbocker Arena
Albany, NY
3/24/91 #2
DEAD
NOTHIN' LEFT TO DO...
BUT SMILE, SMILE, SMILE

A
B
Set I 4-4-91
Let the Good
Times Roll
Stranger
They Love
Each other
Walkin Blues
Ramble on Rose
Memphis Blues
Omni The.
High
Time
Promised Land
Set II
Help on
the Way>
Slipknot>
Franklins
Tower
ATLANTA, GA. Set I/
OMNI The. 4-4-91 II
AUD. 1st Gen.

Warning: This tape contains long improvisations; brace yourself!
Grateful
4.4.91 Omni
ATLANTA I
SBD/2
Dead!
Soundboard
Audience
GEN
FM
Let your mind wander...

Grateful Dead!
4.4.91 Omni
ATLANTA II
SBD/2
Warning: This tape contains long
improvizations and tasty jams.
Don't fight it, let your mind wander!
Soundboard
Audience
GEN
FM

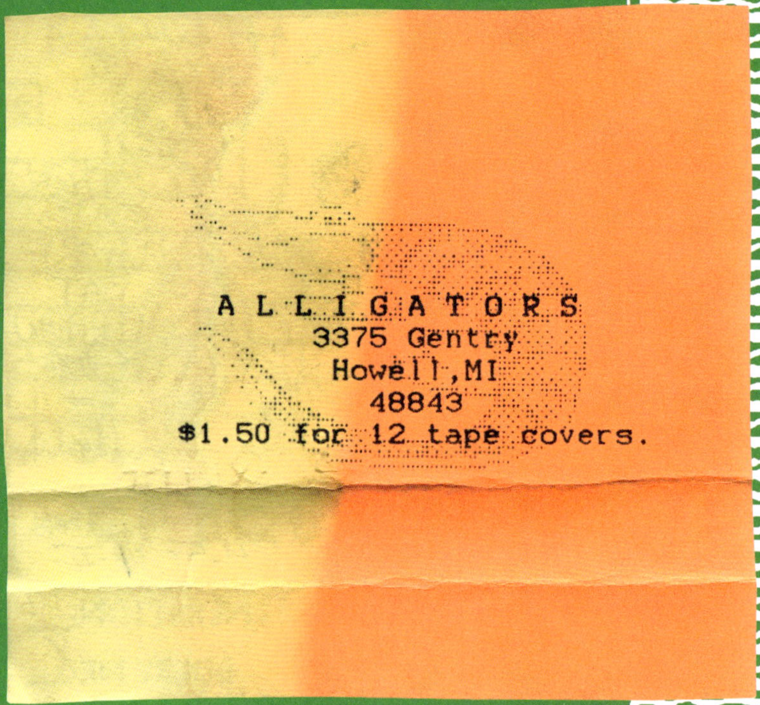

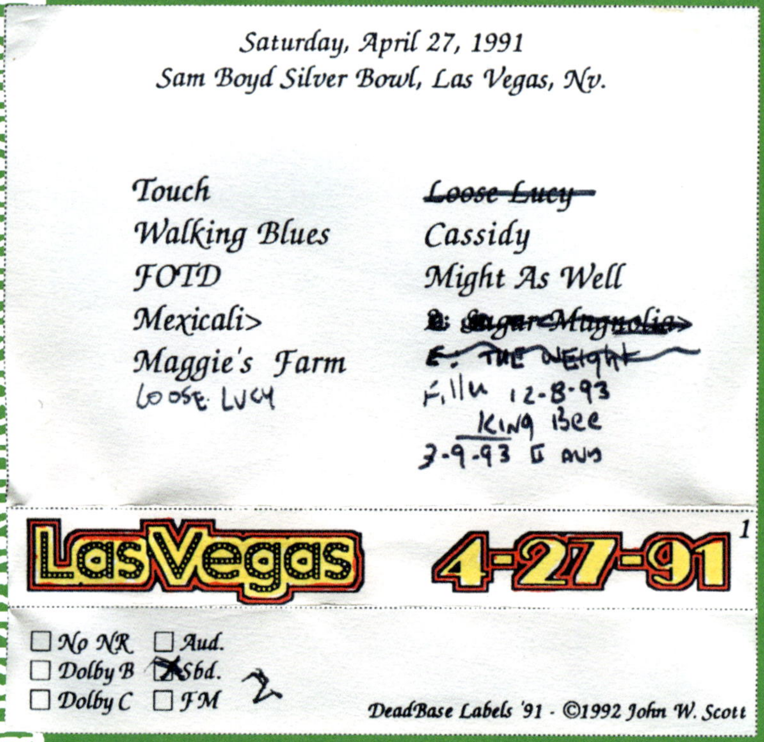

Saturday, April 27, 1991
Sam Boyd Silver Bowl, Las Vegas, Nv.

Touch	~~Loose Lucy~~
Walking Blues	Cassidy
FOTD	Might As Well
Mexicali>	~~Sugar Magnolia>~~
Maggie's Farm	~~E: The Weight~~
Loose Lucy	Fill 12-8-93
	King Bee
	3-9-93 II

Las Vegas 4-27-91 1

☐ No NR ☐ Aud.
☐ Dolby B ☒ Sbd.
☐ Dolby C ☐ FM

DeadBase Labels '91 · ©1992 John W. Scott

Saturday, April 27, 1991
Sam Boyd Silver Bowl, Las Vegas, Nv.

Sugar Magnolia>	Drumz>
Scarlet>	Miracle>
Fire	Black Peter>
Playin>	Saturday Night
Uncle John>	E: The Weight

piano jam tuning before 'Sugar Magnolia'

Las Vegas 4-27-91 2

☐ No NR ☐ Aud.
☐ Dolby B ☐ Sbd.
☐ Dolby C ☐ FM

DeadBase Labels '91 · ©1992 John W. Scott

Live CAL EXPO.
Dead SACREMENTO, CA. 5/3/91
Set I
Aud./Sbd.
Last Minute Productions

Set II (Cont.)
ESTIMATED ->
UNCLE JOHNS BAND ->
DRUMZ ->
SPACE ->
SPACE (CONT.)
The Wheel
WATCHTOWER
Stella Blue
Love Light
Box of Rain
GRATEFUL DEAD
DEER CREEK IN. 6-6-91 II

GRATEFUL DEAD
Grateful Dead live in...
Buckeye Lake - OH 6/9/91
I
Buckeye Lake Music Center
A
Picasso Moon
Sugaree
New Minglewood Bls.
Ramble on Rose
Masterpiece
B
Reuben & Cherise
Let it Grow
≈
6/8/90 Cal Expo
Uncle John's ->
China -> Rider
Soundboard - 4th Gen - No NR
Summerfield

GRATEFUL DEAD
Grateful Dead live in...
Buckeye Lake - OH 6/9/91
II
Buckeye Lake Music Center
A
Samson & Delilah
Crazy Fingers
Playin' in the Band ->
He's Gone ->
Drumz ->
B
Space ->
The Other One ->
Wharf Rat ->
Around & Around
E: Knockin'
4th SBD - No NR
Summerfield ≈ ad503@Freenet.carleton.ca

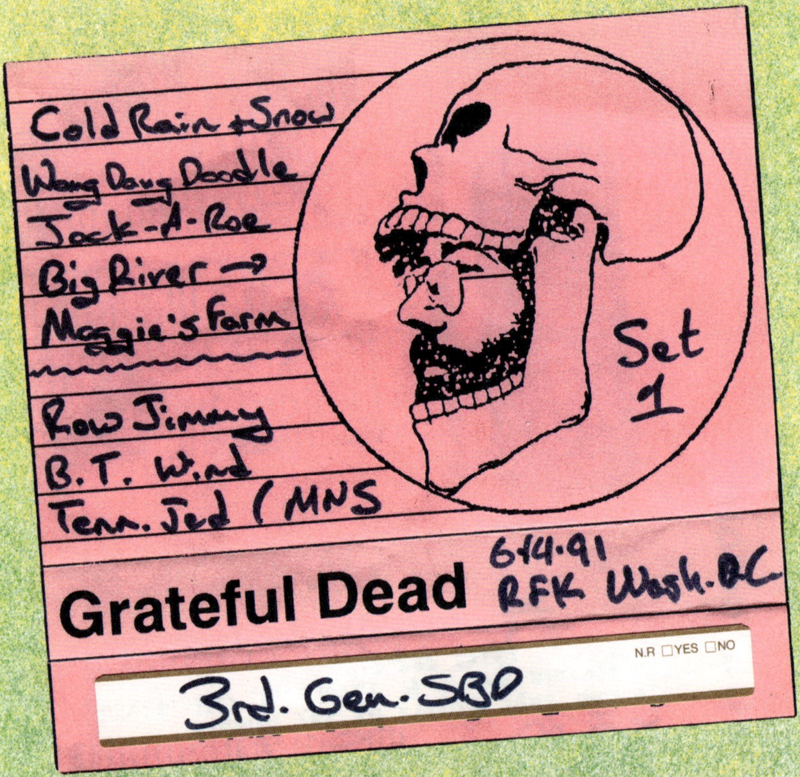
Cold Rain + Snow
Wang Dang Doodle
Jack-A-Roe
Big River →
Maggie's Farm
Row Jimmy
B.T. Wind
Tenn. Jed / MNS
Set 1
Grateful Dead
6.14.91
RFK Wash. D.C
3rd. Gen. SBD
N.R YES NO

* Shipping / Handling info.
$1.00 .... 1 - 10 sheets
$2.00 .... 11 - 20 sheets
$2.75 .... 21 - 50 sheets
Wholesale Inquiries Invited
read colors
BACK

Help → Slip →
Franklin's
Estimated →
Dark Star →
→ Space →
Stella Blue →
Lovelight
Set 2
Grateful Dead
6.14.91
RFK, Wash. D.C
3rd. Gen. SBD
N.R YES NO

Style #6

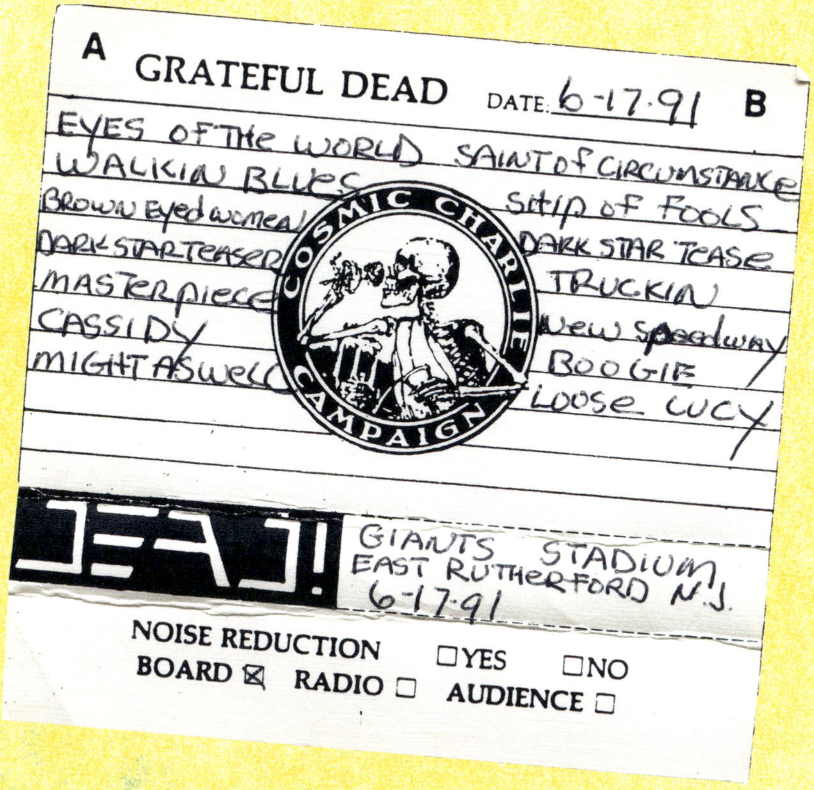
A GRATEFUL DEAD DATE: 6-17-91 B
EYES OF THE WORLD
WALKIN BLUES
BROWN EYED WOMEN
DARK STAR TEASE
MASTERPIECE
CASSIDY
MIGHT AS WELL
SAINT OF CIRCUMSTANCE
SHIP OF FOOLS
DARK STAR TEASE
TRUCKIN
NEW SPEEDWAY
BOOGIE
LOOSE LUCY
COSMIC CHARLIE CAMPAIGN
GIANTS STADIUM EAST RUTHERFORD N.J. 6-17-91
NOISE REDUCTION YES NO
BOARD RADIO AUDIENCE

Feel Like A Stranger
T.L.E.O
Minglewood
Dire Wolf
Queen Jane
Ramble On Rose
Promised Land
Set II
Victim
Jam
Scarlet
Fire
The New Pine Knob Mich. 6-19-91 Set I/II

6-19-91 Set II
Women Are Smarter
Drumz
Space
Stella Blue
The Other One
J.B. Goode
E Quinn
Greensboro 4-1-91
Dark Star Space
Star Playin Reprise
Grateful Dead
Pine Knob, Mich 6-19-91 Set II

Dead
Sandstone The Set I
Kansas, Kansas 6-24-91
Set I
Help
Slip
Frank
C.C. Rider
Me & My Uncle
Big River
Althea
Promised Land
Charlotte NC 6-18-92
Dew!
Satisfaction

Last Minute Productions
Aud./Sbd.
Set II

JACK STRAW
SUGAREE - WALKIN
CANDYMAN
MEMPHIS BLUES
GOOD LOVIN
BABY BLUE
SANDSTONE THE.
KASAS 6-25-91 I
SOURCE:
MONO
STEREO
DIGITAL
ANALOG
DOLBY
OFF
ON
TYPE
BOARD
RADIO
AUDIENCE
GENERATION 4

Shoreline, Mountain View
CAL. 8-16-91 SET I
SBD
AUD
RADIO
A. Set I
JACK STRAW
BERTHA
All OVER NOW
RAMBLE ON ROSE
DESOLATION ROW
B. Set I (cont)
DARK STAR
PROMISED LAND
BLOW AWAY
SAILOR →
SAINT →

Set 1
Help > Slip >
Franklin's
B.E. Women
Queen Jane
Tenn. Jed
Music
Filler
8.18.91
Grateful Dead Shoreline 8.17.91
2nd DAT
SBD AUD FM

Set 2
♀ are Smarter
Ship of Fools
Smokestack >
He's Gone >
Jam >
Drums >
Space >
Dark Star
Jam >
Morning Dew
Sat. Night
E) Baby Blue
Grateful Dead Shoreline 8.17.91
2nd DAT
SBD AUD FM

SHORELINE 8/18/91 I
I
HELL IN A BUCKET
JACK-A-ROE
C.C. RIDER →
TRAIN TO CRY
BEAT IT DOWN
— THE LINE
WEST. L.A.
FADEAWAY
MASTERPIECE
STAGGER LEE
JOHNNY B. GOODE
ENCORE
BROKEDOWN PALACE
SHORELINE
Soundboard
Generation
Audience
Noise Reduction
Radio

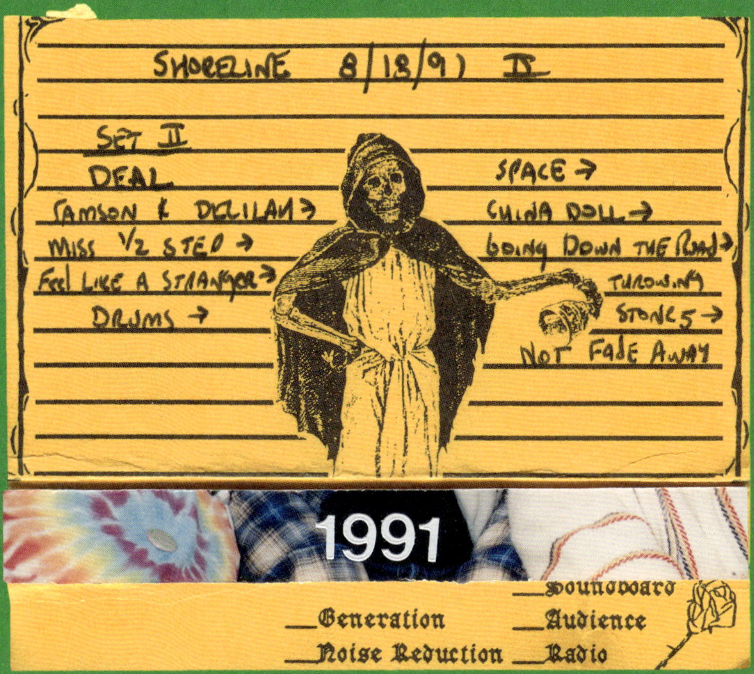
SHORELINE 8/18/91 II
SET II
DEAL
SAMSON & DELILAH →
MISS 1/2 STEP →
FEEL LIKE A STRANGER →
DRUMS →
SPACE →
CHINA DOLL →
GOING DOWN THE ROAD →
THROWING
STONES →
NOT FADE AWAY
1991
Soundboard
Generation
Audience
Noise Reduction
Radio

DEAD
Richfield Col.
OHIO 9-5-91 Set I
Set I
MISS. 1/2
Step
Lil, Red
Rooster
Stagger
Lee
Queen Jane
Ramble on
Rose
Cassady
Don't
Ease
Set II (cont)
Sunshine
Daydream
Ⓔ U.S. Blues
Filler: Giants 6-17-91
B.E. Women
Star tease
Master ☮
Loose Lucy

Dan Shramo
2665 Camden Rd.
Columbus, OH 43221

DEAD
Richfield Col.
OHIO 9-6-91 II
Set II
Victim
Crazy
Fingers
Playin
Jam
Terrapin
Drumz
Bong
Space
Dark ★
Jam
Watch-
tower
Stella
Blue
Around N
Round
DS

Dan Shramo
2665 Camden Rd.
Columbus, OH 43221
my 50th
show
Did Bongs
During
Drumz - Space
The Deads
2000 th
show ?

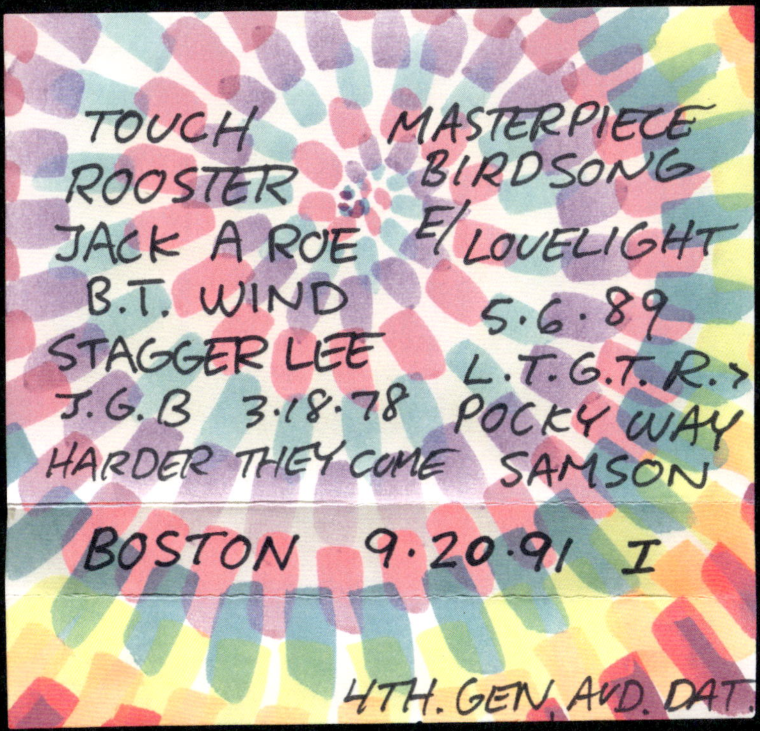
TOUCH
ROOSTER
JACK A ROE
B.T. WIND
STAGGER LEE
J.G.B 3.18.78
HARDER THEY COME
MASTERPIECE
BIRDSONG
E/ LOVELIGHT
5.6.89
L.T.G.T.R.>
POCKY WAY
SAMSON
BOSTON 9.20.91 I
4TH. GEN. AUD. DAT

HELP>
SLIP>
FIRE
ESTIMATED>
TRUCKIN
DRUMS>
SPACE>
WATCHTOWER
DEW
4TH GEN AUD DAT
BOSTON 9.20.91 II
4TH GEN. AUD. DAT

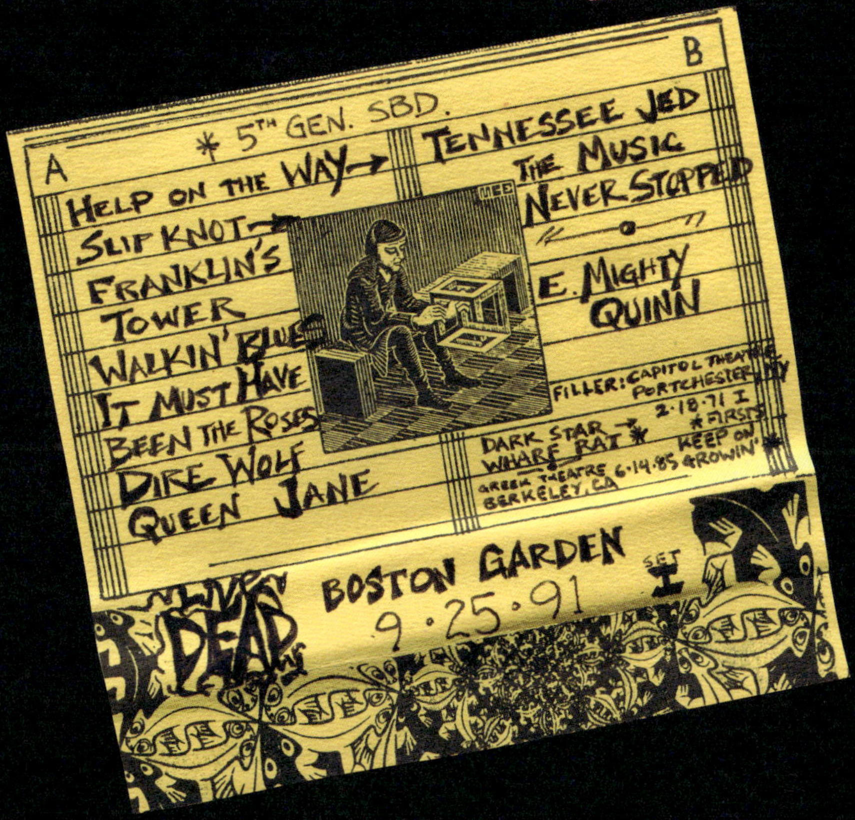
A
B
* 5TH GEN. SBD.
HELP ON THE WAY→
SLIP KNOT→
FRANKLIN'S
TOWER
WALKIN' BLUES
IT MUST HAVE
BEEN THE ROSES
DIRE WOLF
QUEEN JANE
TENNESSEE JED
THE MUSIC
NEVER STOPPED
E. MIGHTY
QUINN
FILLER: CAPITOL THEATRE
PORTCHESTER, NY
2.18.71 I
* FIRST
DARK STAR →
WHARF RAT *
KEEP ON
GROWIN'
GREEK THEATRE 6.14.85
BERKELEY, CA
BOSTON GARDEN
9.25.91
SET
I
DEAD

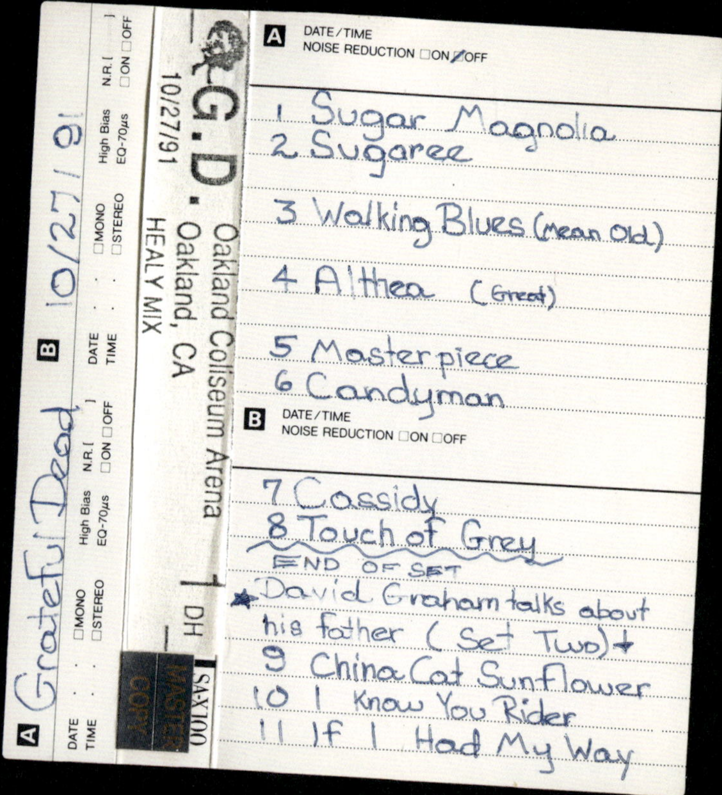
Grateful Dead 10/27/91
G.D. 10/27/91
Oakland Coliseum Arena
Oakland, CA
HEALY MIX
1 DH
DATE/TIME
NOISE REDUCTION ON OFF
1 Sugar Magnolia
2 Sugaree
3 Walking Blues (mean Old)
4 Althea (Great)
5 Masterpiece
6 Candyman
7 Cassidy
8 Touch of Grey
END OF SET
David Graham talks about his father (Set Two)
9 China Cat Sunflower
10 I Know You Rider
11 If I Had My Way
MASTER
COPY
SA-X100

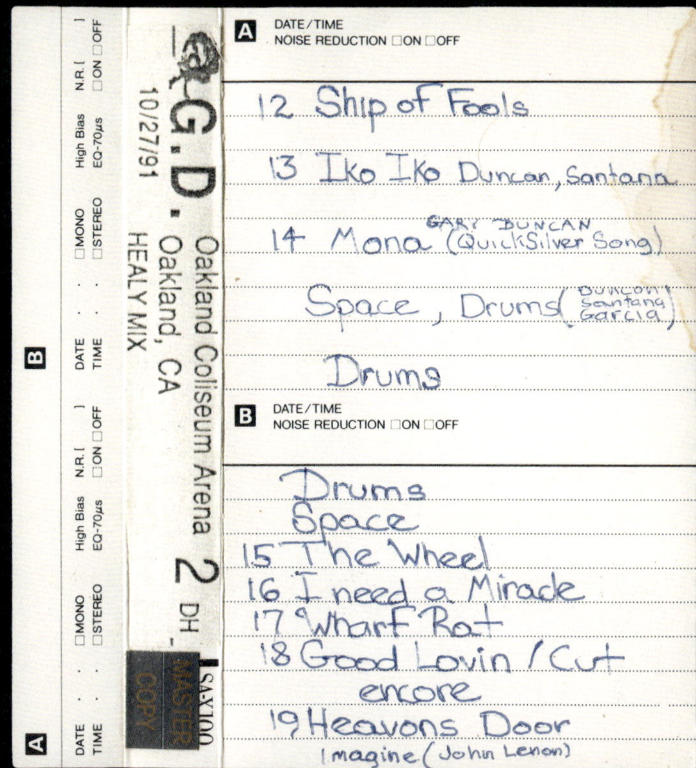
G.D. 10/27/91
Oakland Coliseum Arena
Oakland, CA
HEALY MIX
2 DH
DATE/TIME
NOISE REDUCTION ON OFF
12 Ship of Fools
13 Iko Iko Duncan, Santana
14 Mona GARY DUNCAN (QuickSilver Song)
Space, Drums (Duncan Santana Garcia)
Drums
Drums
Space
15 The Wheel
16 I need a Miracle
17 Wharf Rat
18 Good Lovin / Cut
encore
19 Heavens Door
Imagine (John Lenon)
MASTER
COPY
SA-X100

a
b
HELP ON THE WAY
SLIPKNOT
FRANKLINS TOWER
LITTLE RED ROOSTER
LOSER
TOM THUMBS BLUES
LET IT GROW
SET II
SCARLET BEGONIAS
FIRE ON THE MOUNTAIN
GRATEFUL DEAD
OAK COLISEUM OAK. CA. 10-31-91
SET I

Oakland Coliseum Arena - 10/31/91 - I

Help On The Way >	Let It Grow
Slipknot >	(Break)
Franklin's Tower	
Red Rooster	(set II...)
Loser	Drums > Space
Tom Thumb Blues	

Grateful Dead

Oakland Coliseum Arena
Halloween
Thursday October 31, 1991

I

☒ Aud Gen. 1 N.R.
☐ SBD Mics. Bias/Eq.
☐ FM Deck

Sunday, November 3, 1991
Polo Field, Golden Gate Park, San Francisco, Ca.

Bucket	Truckin>
China Cat>	Other One>
I Know You Rider	Wharf Rat>
Wang Dang Doodle*	Sunshine Daydream
Born On The Bayou**	E: Forever Young***
Green River**	Touch
Bad Moon Rising**	
Proud Mary**	

*with John Popper on harmonica **with John Fogerty on guitar and vocals
***with Neil Young on vocals - without Bruce Hornsby
"A benefit for Laughter, Love, and Music" - memorial for Bill Graham

Golden Gate Park 11-3-91

☐ No NR ☐ Aud.
☐ Dolby B ☐ Sbd.
☐ Dolby C ☒ FM 1/2

DeadBase Labels '91 - ©1992 John W. Scott

ONE MORE SAT →	CASSADY
J. STRAW	DEAL
PEGGY-O	(E)
MINGLEWOOD	U.S. BLUES
DIRE WOLF	12-27-91
QUEEN JANE	SUG MAG →
LOSER	SUGAREE
	CANDYMAN

GRATEFUL DEAD

OAKLAND COLISEUM
OAKLAND, CA 12-28-91 I

NO FM AUD SBD

GRATEFUL
DEAD
NEW YEARS EVE
1991
hell in a bucket
candyman
beat it..
musta been roses
blackthroated wind
west la fadeaway
masterpiece
help on the way
slipknot
franklins tower
not fade away
eyes of world
estimated prophet
drums/space
other one
wharf rat
sugar magnolia
knockin on...

EVE
GRATEFUL
DEAD
NEW YEARS EVE
1991
LIVE OFF THE RADIO

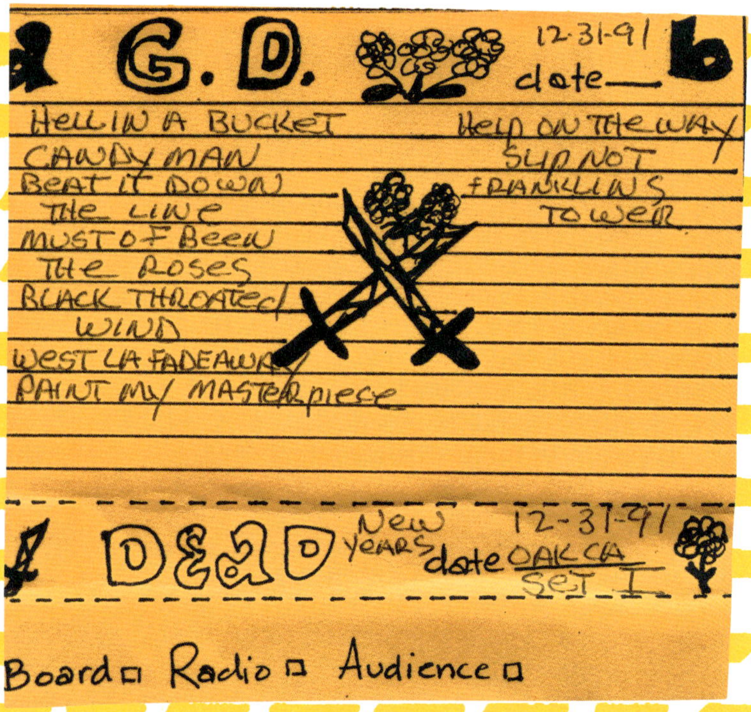
G.D.
12-31-91
date
b
HELL IN A BUCKET
CANDY MAN
BEAT IT DOWN
THE LINE
MUST OF BEEN
THE ROSES
BLACK THROATED
WIND
WEST LA FADEAWAY
PAINT MY MASTERPIECE
HELP ON THE WAY
SLIP NOT
FRANKLINS
TOWER
DEAD
New
Years
date
12-31-91
OAK CA
SET I
Board
Radio
Audience

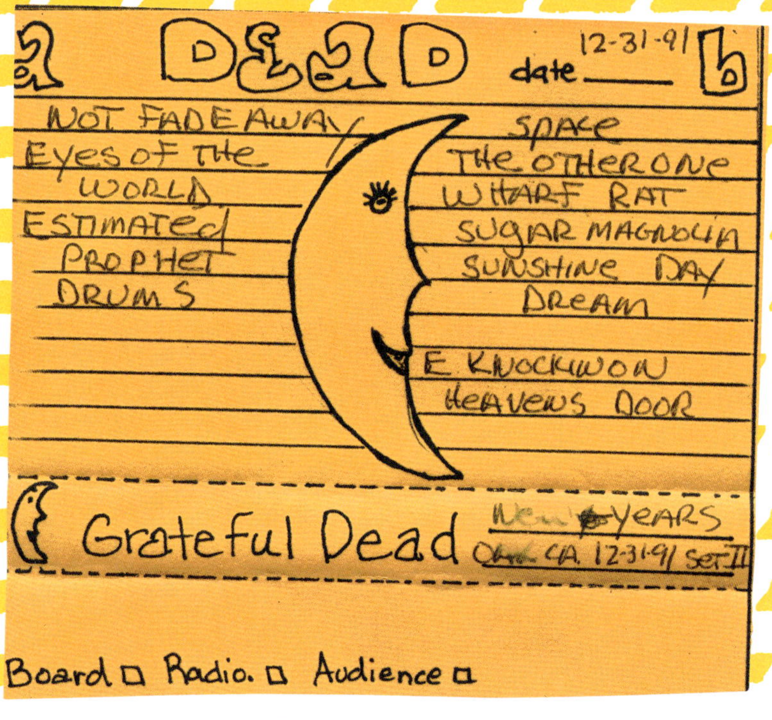
DEAD
date
12-31-91
b
NOT FADE AWAY
EYES OF THE
WORLD
ESTIMATED
PROPHET
DRUMS
SPACE
THE OTHER ONE
WHARF RAT
SUGAR MAGNOLIA
SUNSHINE DAY
DREAM
E KNOCKIN ON
HEAVENS DOOR
Grateful Dead
New Years
CA 12-31-91 SET II
Board
Radio.
Audience

LIVE LANDOVER, MD 3-9-92 II
SOURCE: AUD
GENERATION ↑10
QUALITY: A-/B+
Victim
AIKO~
AIKO
CORINNA→
JAM→
DARK★
STAR
JAM
DRUMZ→
SPACE
→
MIRACLE
MORNING
DEW
©
SATISFACTION
1st SINCE
7-7-86

Audience
Board
Radio
Generation
on Noise
off Reduction
Grateful Dead SACRAMENTO 5/12/92 A
Side A.
Touch
WangDang
RowJimmy
Me&Uncle
MaggiesFarm
SB A
Side B.
Birdsong
E*Gloria
5/19/92

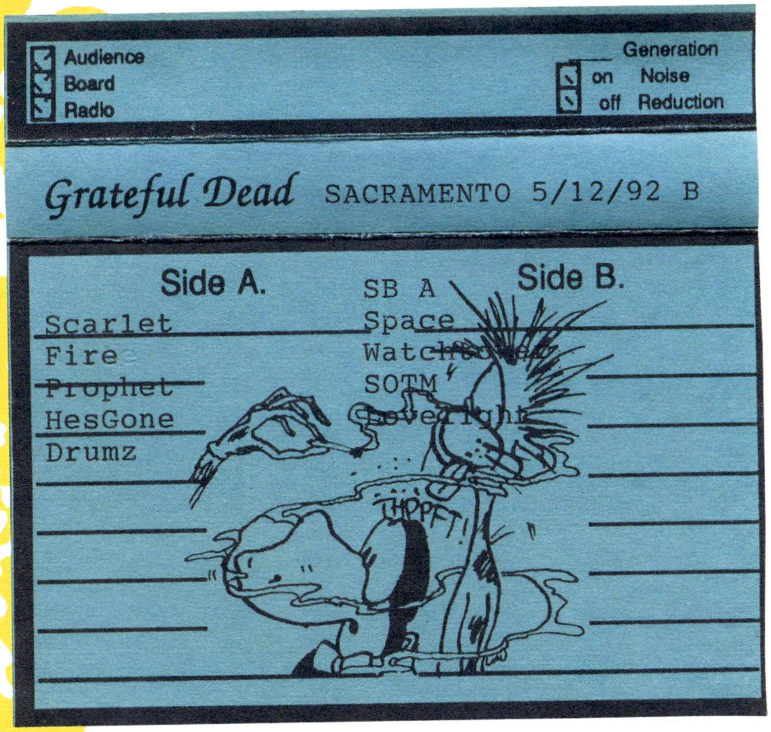
Audience
Board
Radio
Generation
on Noise
off Reduction
Grateful Dead SACRAMENTO 5/12/92 B
Side A.
Scarlet
Fire
Prophet
HesGone
Drumz
SB A
Side B.
Space
SOTM
THOPFT!

A
VICTIM OR THE
CRIME
AIKO
SPOONFUL
NEW SPEEDWAY
BOOGIE
DRUMS
SPACE
B
SPACE
THROWING
STONES
ATTICS OF
MY LIFE
NOT FADE
AWAY
BABA O REILLY
TOMORROW
NEVER KNOWS
Grateful Dead
SHORELINE AMP.
MTN VIEW CA.
5-25-92 SET II
SOUNDBOARD
AUDIENCE
RADIO
GENERATION
DOLBY NR

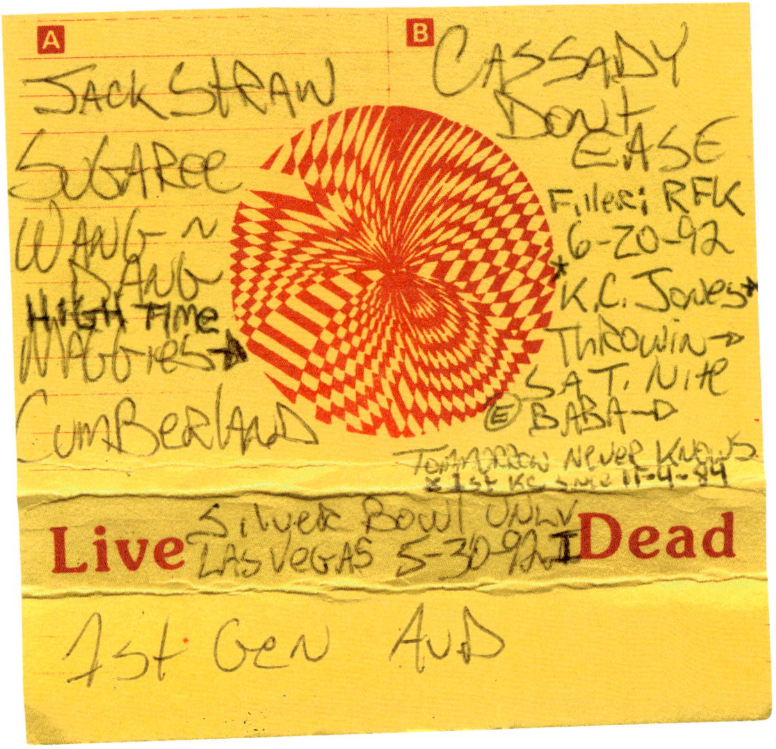
A
JACK STRAW
SUGAREE
WANG ~ DANG
HIGH TIME
MAGGIES →
CUMBERLAND
B
CASSADY
DON'T EASE
Filler: RFK 6-20-92
K.C. Jones
Throwin →
SAT. Nite
E BABA →
Tomorrow Never Knows
Live
Silver Bowl UNLV
Las Vegas 5-30-92 I
Dead
1st Gen AUD

FEEL LIKE A STRANGER
LOSER
LITTLE RED ROOSTER
SO MANY ROADS
TOM THUMB BLUES
BLACK THROATED WIND!
DON'T EASE ...
LIVE
JUNE 8 1992
RICHFEILD, OHIO
DEAD
SET I

BOAR
AUDIENCE
RADIO
4 GENERATION
on off NOISE REDUCTION
GRATEFUL
BUFFALO, NY. 6-6-92 II
DEAD
a. Aiko~Aiko →
Estimated →
SAME THING ↓
He's Gone →
Jam –
Drumz
B. SPACE →
SPANISH JAM →
Other One →
wheel
Throwin Stones →
E SAT. Night
BABA → Tommorow Never Knows

MARBELIZIN' MIKE
18 MARBURY RD,
SEVERNA PARK, MD, 21146

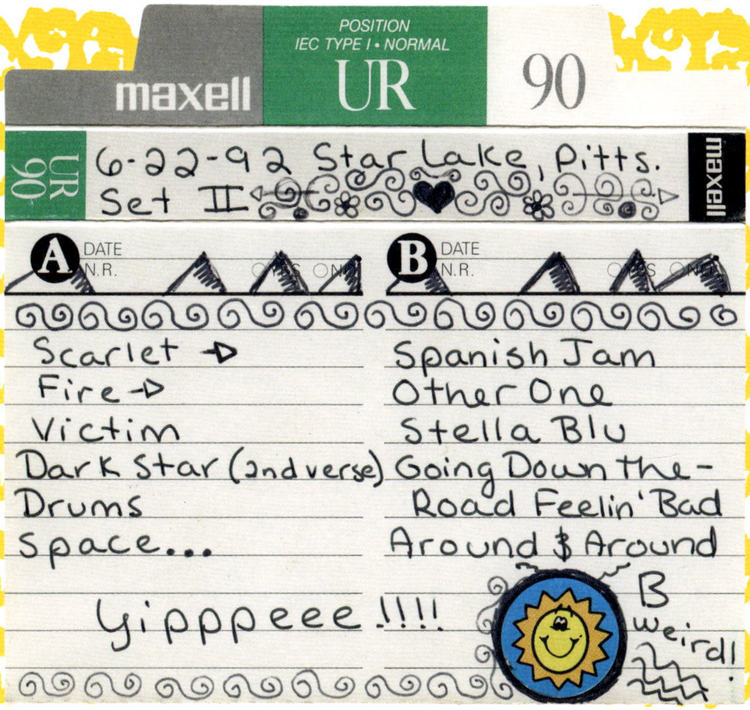
maxell
POSITION
IEC TYPE I • NORMAL
UR
90
UR 90
maxell
6-22-92 Star Lake, Pitts.
Set II
A DATE N.R.
B DATE N.R.
Scarlet →
Fire →
Victim
Dark Star (2nd verse)
Drums
Space...
Spanish Jam
Other One
Stella Blu
Going Down the-
Road Feelin' Bad
Around $ Around
Yipppeee!!!!
B
weird!

Truckin
Spoonful
So Many Road
Wave to the
Wind
Corina
Drums
Space
Last Time
SOT Moon
Sugar Mag
E*Broke
Palace
AUD/2 A
PITTSBURGH 6/23/92 B
C
B
ON
FM
AUD
SBD

China Cat SunFlower →
I Know You
Rider
Estimated
Prophet
Long Way →
Home
Drumz
...Space →
This Could Be the
Last Time →
China Doll →
Around & Around
Enc.
Casey Jones
6/25/92
Noblesville, Ind.
Deer Creek
6/28/92
II
Grateful Dead
© Thunderase, Inc.

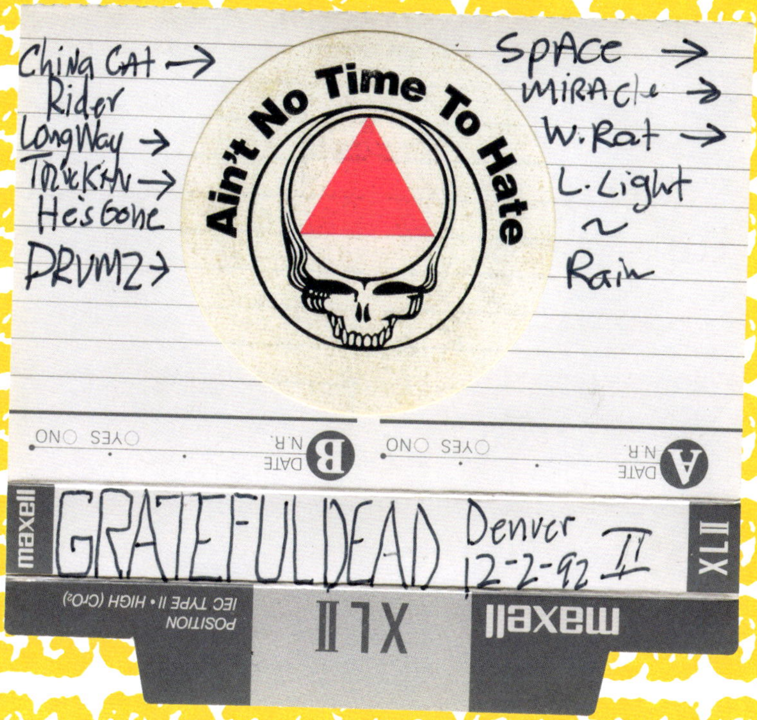
China Cat →
Rider
Long Way →
Truckin →
He's Gone
DRUMZ →
SPACE →
Miracle →
W. Rat →
L. Light
~
Rain
Ain't No Time To Hate
A DATE N.R.
B DATE N.R.
YES NO
maxell
GRATEFUL DEAD
Denver
12-2-92
II
XLII
POSITION
IEC TYPE II • HIGH (CrO2)
XL II
maxell

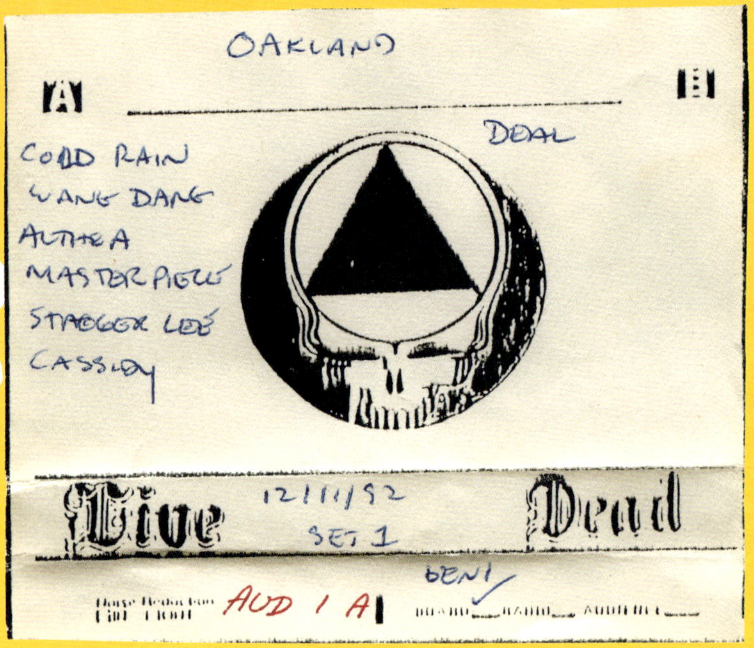
OAKLAND
A
B
COLD RAIN
WANG DANG
ALTHEA
MASTERPIECE
STAGGER LEE
CASSIDY
DEAL
Live
12/11/92
SET 1
Dead
AUD 1 A

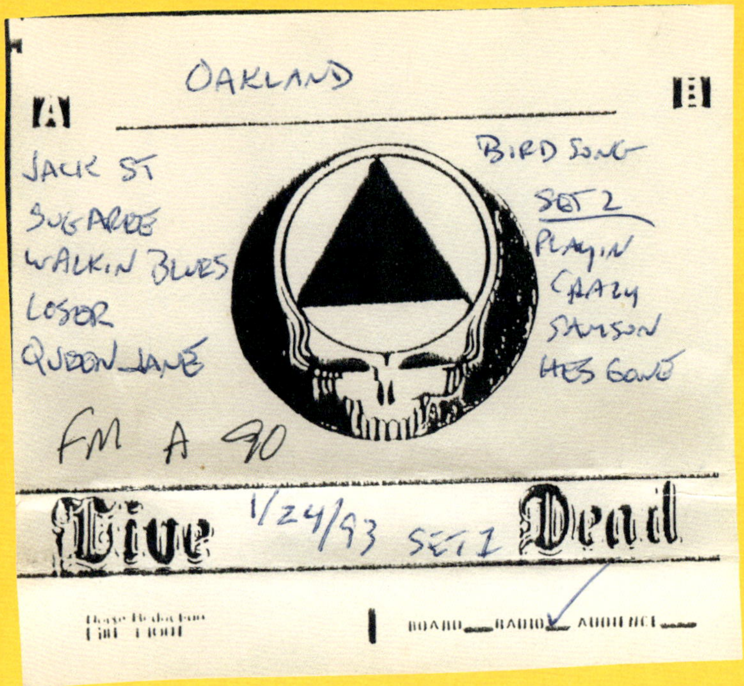
OAKLAND
A
B
JACK ST
SUGAREE
WALKIN BLUES
LOSER
QUEEN JANE
BIRD SONG
SET 2
PLAYIN
CRAZY
SAMSON
HES GONE
FM A 90
Live
1/24/93 SET 1
Dead

Picasso Moon
Row Jimmy
Wang Dang Doodle
Brown-Eyed Women
Desolation Row
Ramble On
Promised Land
ONCE IN AWHILE YOU CAN GET SHOWN THE LIGHT...
...IN THE STRANGEST OF PLACES IF YOU LOOK AT IT RIGHT
DEAD
1/26/93 #1
Oakland Coliseum
Oakland,Ca
NOISE REDUCTION
GEN.
SBD.
RAD.
AUD.

Here Comes Sunshine
Wang Dang
Me & My Uncle
Mexicali Blues
Broken Arrow
Row Jimmy
Eternity
Liberty
dead
Rosemont 3·9·93 I
aud o fm o sbd o

goin' where the water tastes like wine...
DEAD
ROSEMONT HORIZION SET I
CHICAGO. ILL. 3·11·93
Soundboard__ Audience X FM__
Gen. 1ST Grade A

GRATEFUL DEAD
GD
THE Omni ~ AtLanta, GA #2
3-20-93
GEN 2nd
SOURCE NAK 300's → D5
TAPERS SECTION

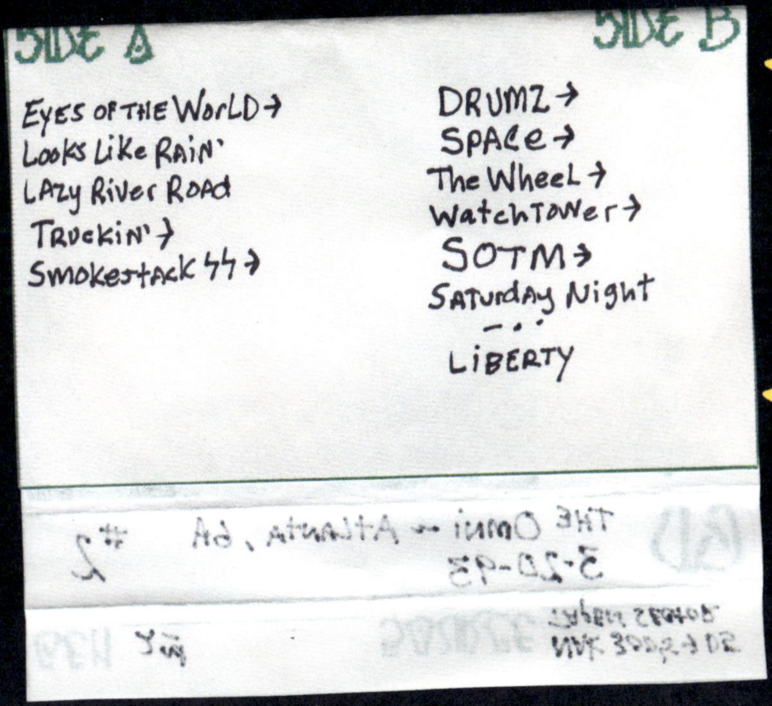
SIDE A
Eyes of THE WorLD →
Looks Like Rain'
Lazy River Road
Truckin' →
Smokestack ll →
SIDE B
DRUMZ →
SPACE →
The Wheel →
WatchTower →
SOTM →
Saturday Night
- • -
LIBERTY

A Jack Straw
Stagger Lee
Wang Dang Doodle
Must Have Been
/The Roses
Memphis Blues
Tennesee Jed
1st/Gen. DAT
B Let It Grow
GD
Dean E. Smith Centre
U.N.C.-Chapel Hill, NC. 3-24-93
☒ I
☐ II
☐ SBD ☒ AUD ☐ FM

Here Comes
/Sunshine
Playin'
Box Of Rain
Crazy Fingers →
Drums →
Space
Spanish Jam →
Goin' Down The Road
Throwing Stones →
Not Fade Away
C) L.S.D.
GD
Dean E. Smith Centre
U.N.C.-Chapel Hill, NC. 3-24-93
☐ I
☒ II
☒ SBD ☒ AUD ☐ FM ☐ NR

Bucket
Bertha
Same Thing
Peggy-O
Queen Jane
Broken Arrow
Loose Lucy
Cassidy
Casey Jones
Knickerbocker Arena
Albany, N.Y.
3-27-93
#1
© 1991 TSI Visuals

Box #55
To reorder please send a chec
or money order payable to :
TSI Visuals
506 Bethlehem Pike
Fort Washington, PA 19034
Specify Style No. 3
$1.50 per pack of 10 (includes pos
PA residents add 6% sales tax
Excellent Quality.
Side B Filler:3/22/93 #1
The Omni,Atlanta,Ga
Help>Slipknot>Franklin's
Excellent Quality

Eyes>
Estimated>
Comes A Time>
CORRINA>
DRums
Space>
Wheel>
Watchtower>
Days Between>
Sat. Night
E: I Fought
The Law
KnickerBocker Arena 3-27-93 #2
Albany, N.Y.
© 1991 TSI Visuals
Excellent Quality
To reorder please send a check
or money order payable to :
TSI Visuals
506 Bethlehem Pike
Fort Washington, PA 19034
Specify Style No. 2
$1.50 per pack of 10 (includes postage)
PA residents add 6% sales tax
Audience
Board
Radio
Generation
on Noise
off Reduction
Grateful Dead
ALBANY 3/29/93 B
Side A.
HCSunshine
LLRain
Box
HesGone
Drumz
AUD/2 A-
Side B.
Space
play
dead,
man
Eyes,Samson,Broken Arrow,Prophet,Drumz*
B)Space,OtherOne,Attics,Stones,NFA,E*Libery
AUD/2 A-
UNIONDALE
4/4/93 B
© 1991 TSI Visuals

LIVE
Nasau Coliseum
4·4·1993 II
DEAD
1ST GEN. Master
AUDIENCE
SOUNDBOARD
RADIO

Jack Straw
Loser
It's All Over Now
Tom Thumbs Blues
Bird Song
Music Never
Stopped
Todd Rundgren
Warfield, S.F.
1·16·1993
1ST GEN. DAT
LIVE
Shoreline Amph.
Mtn. View, CA.
I
5·23·1993
DEAD
1ST GEN. DAT
AUDIENCE
SOUNDBOARD
RADIO

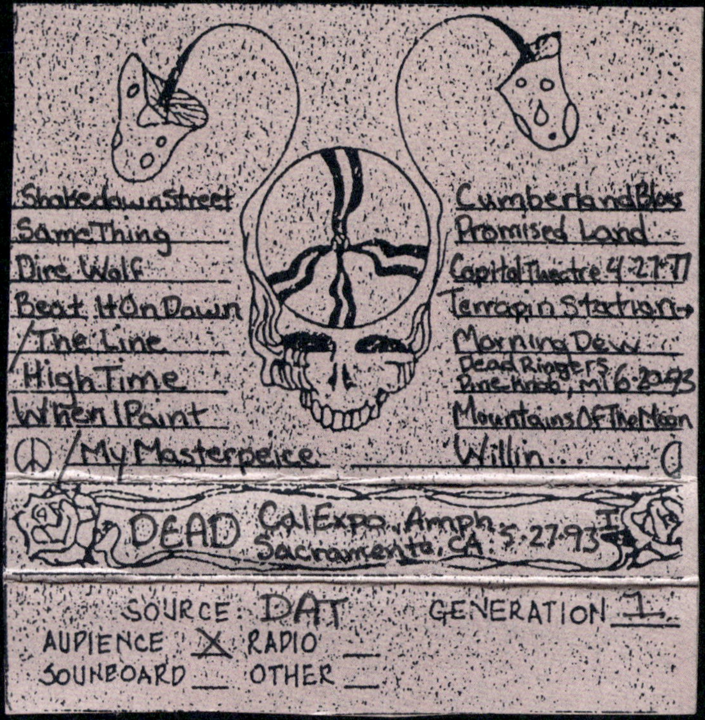

Shakedown Street
Same Thing
Dire Wolf
Beat It On Down
The Line
High Time
When I Paint
My Masterpeice
Cumberland Blues
Promised Land
Capitol Theatre 4·27·77
Terrapin Station
Morning Dew
Dead Ringers
Pine Knob, MI 6·20·93
Mountains Of The Moon
Willin
DEAD
Cal Expo. Amph.
Sacramento, CA
5·27·93
I
SOURCE DAT
GENERATION 1
AUDIENCE X
RADIO
SOUNBOARD
OTHER

Picasso Moon →
Fire On The Mountain →
Wave To The Wind →
Cassidy →
Uncle Johns Band →
Cassidy →
Drums →
Space →
The Other One →
Wharf Rat →
Sugar Magnolia
Gloria
LIVE
Cal Expo Ampitheatre
Sacramento, CA
5/27/93 Set Two
DEAD
GENERATION 2nd
NOISE REDUCTION
SOUNDBOARD
✓ AUDIENCE
RADIO

Samson & Delihlah
Way to Go Home
Wave to the Wind
Terrapin>
Drumz
I NEED A MIRACLE
Space >
Dark Star>
Wheel >
Good Lovin'
- Encore -
Lucy in the Sky with Diamonds
GRATEFUL FRED
Noblesville In II
Deer Creek 6·23·93
SBD AUD FM GEN

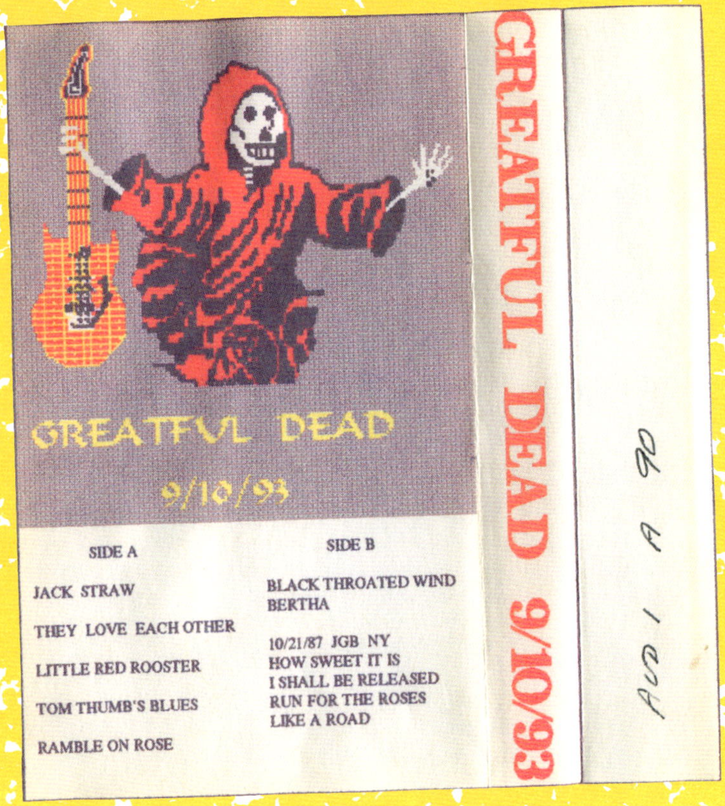
GREATFUL DEAD
9/10/93
SIDE A
JACK STRAW
THEY LOVE EACH OTHER
LITTLE RED ROOSTER
TOM THUMB'S BLUES
RAMBLE ON ROSE
SIDE B
BLACK THROATED WIND
BERTHA
10/21/87 JGB NY
HOW SWEET IT IS
I SHALL BE RELEASED
RUN FOR THE ROSES
LIKE A ROAD
GREATFUL DEAD 9/10/93
AUD I A 90

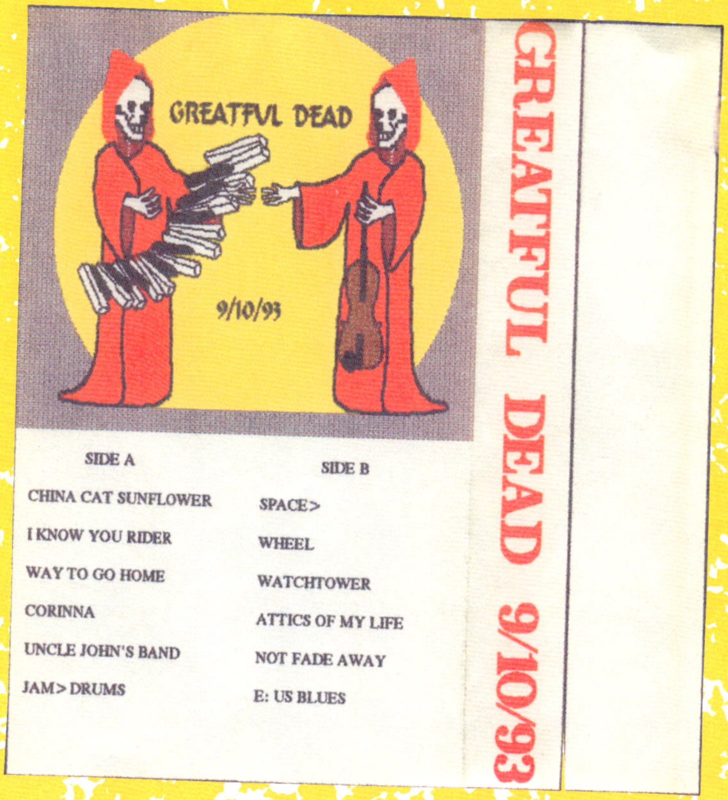
GREATFUL DEAD
9/10/93
SIDE A
CHINA CAT SUNFLOWER
I KNOW YOU RIDER
WAY TO GO HOME
CORINNA
UNCLE JOHN'S BAND
JAM> DRUMS
SIDE B
SPACE>
WHEEL
WATCHTOWER
ATTICS OF MY LIFE
NOT FADE AWAY
E: US BLUES
GREATFUL DEAD 9/10/93

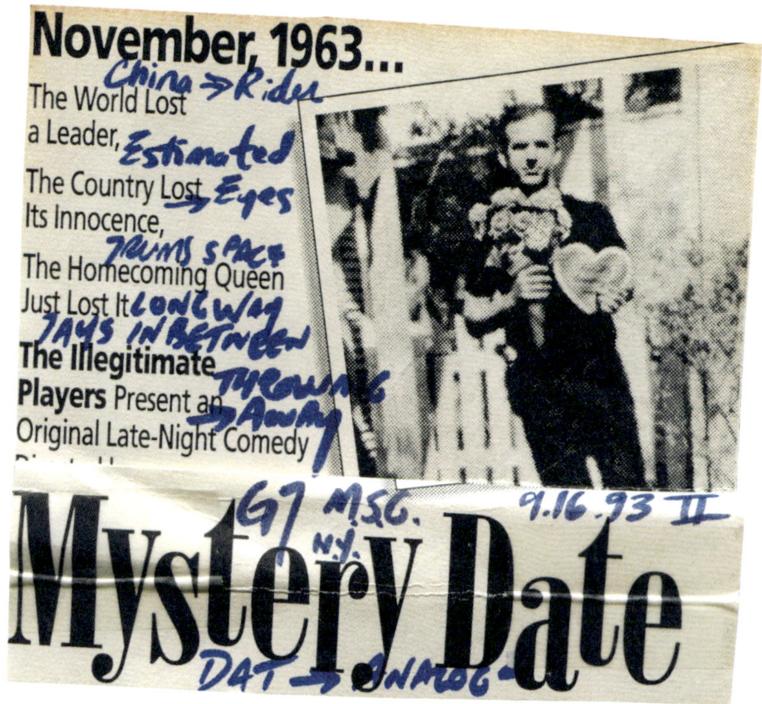
November, 1963...
The World Lost a Leader,
The Country Lost Its Innocence,
The Homecoming Queen Just Lost It
The Illegitimate Players Present an Original Late-Night Comedy
Mystery Date
China → Rider
Estimated → Eyes
Drums Space
Long Way
Days In Between
Throwing → Away
67 M.S.G. N.Y.
9.16.93 II
DAT → Analog

Stranger
Jack-A-Roe
Red Rooster
Queen Jane
Mountains of the Moon
Dark Star
Cryptical
Other One
Cryptical
Grateful Dead
audo fmo sbdo

Scarlet Begonias
Fire on the Mountain
Women are Smarter
Way To Go Home
He's Gone ...
... He's Gone
Drumz
Space
Last Time
Days Between
Around + Around
E: Liberty
grateful dead
9-24-93 Boston, Ma
Aud. Boston Garden
2
audo fmo sbdo
OUR LOVE WILL NOT FADE AWAY

Source: 5th Sgn
Audience X
Radio
Soundboard
Other
Noise Reduction: Yes No X
Dead - Boston Garden, MA 9/28/93 II
Boston Garden, Boston, MA 9/28/93 II
China Cat →
I Know You Rider
Samson
Uncle John's Band →
Playin' in the Band
Drums
Space
Attics of My Life
Throwing Stones
Good Lovin
Encore
U.S. Blues (cut)
THE KIDS THEY DANCE
AND SHAKE THEIR BONES
Aud / 5th gen

Looks Like Rain
Way To Go Home
Terrapin Station
Drumz
Space
Playin Reprise
Stella Blue
Sugar Magnolia
E: Liberty
2nd gen
Aud.
GRATEFUL DEAD
SBD
AUD
FM
GEN 2
OUR LOVE WILL NOT FADE AWAY

MARBLEIZED MIKE
3435 OAKTON DR.
HOPKINS MN 55305

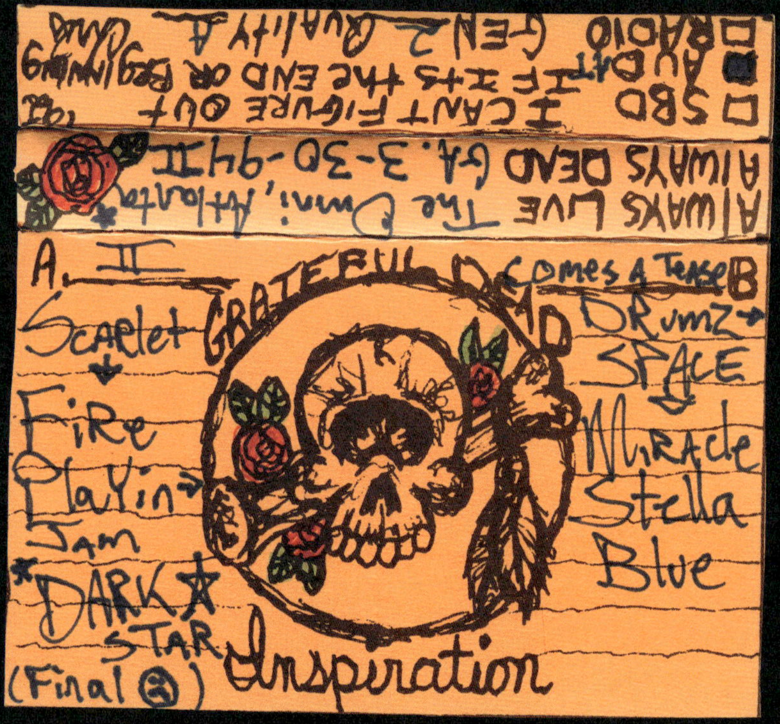
SBD I CANT FIGURE OUT
AUD IF ITS THE END OR BEGINNING
RADIO GEN 2 Quality A
ALWAYS LIVE The Omni, Atlanta
ALWAYS DEAD GA. 3-30-94 II
A. II
GRATEFUL DEAD
Comes A Time B
Scarlet
Fire
Playin
Jam
DARK STAR
(Final ②)
DRumz
SPACE
Miracle
Stella
Blue
Inspiration

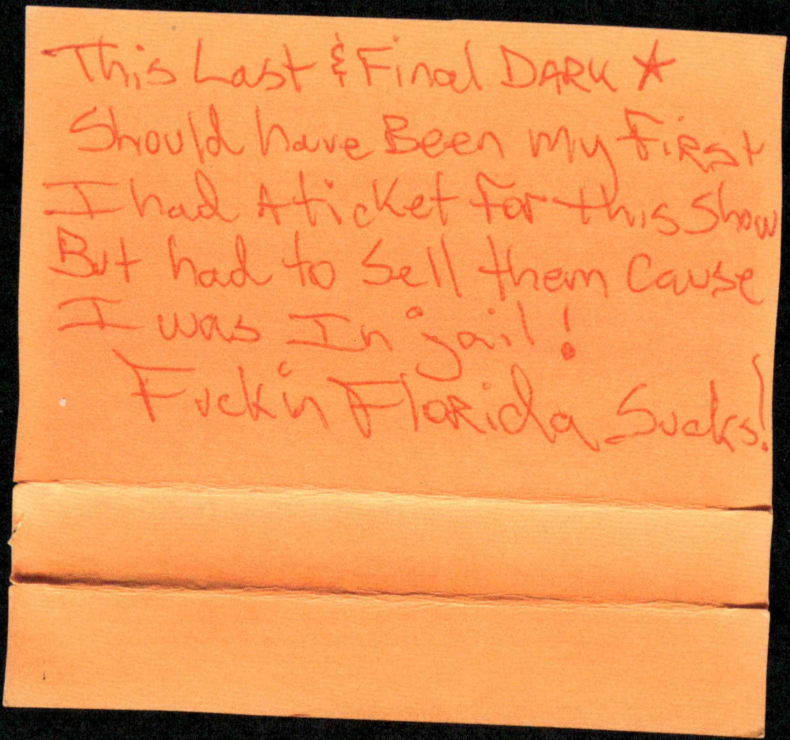
This Last & Final DARK ★
Should have Been my First
I had A ticket for this Show
But had to Sell them Cause
I was In jail!
Fuckin Florida Sucks!

Foolish Heart
Easy Answers
Samba In the Rain
Crazy Fingers
Corrina
Drumz
Space
Other One
Attics of My Life
Sugar Mags
E: Liberty
8-3-94 East Rutherford, NJ
Grateful Dead Giants Stadium
2
1st gen FOB
AUD
FM
SBD
Roger
MADE IN THE U.S.A.

Box of Rain
Jack Straw
Jack-A-Roe
Walkin Blues
So Many Roads
E: Brokedown Palace
Eternity
Childhoods End
Deal
Garcia, Crosby, Lesh
Kreutzman
Bertha
1st gen FOB
Roger
Grateful Dead 8-4-94 East Rutherford NJ 1
F.O.B. Giants Stadium
sbd
Aud FOB
FM

Picasso Moon
China Cat
I Know You Rider
Way To Go
Playin
UJB
Drumz
Space
Miracle
Days Between
Throwing Stones
Not Fade Away
1st gen FOB
Roger
GD 8-4-94 East Rutherford, NJ 2
FOB Giants Stadium
sbd
aud
fm
gen 1
FOB

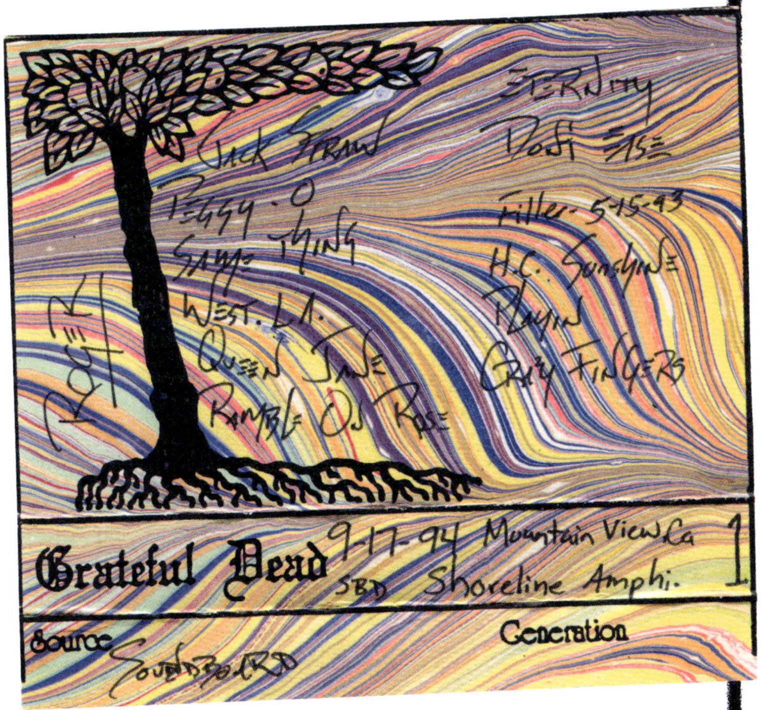
Jack Straw
Peggy-O
Same Thing
West. L.A.
Queen Jane
Ramble On Rose
Eternity
Don't Ease
Filler-5-15-93
H.C. Sunshine
Playin
Crazy Fingers
Grateful Dead 9-17-94 Mountain View Ca 1
SBD Shoreline Amphi.
Source
Soundboard
Generation

GRATEFUL DEAD

HELL IN A BUCKET
BERTHA
SPOONFUL
STAGGERLEE
BROKEN ARROW
ME + MY UNCLE
BIG RIVER

SO MANY ROADS
PROMISED LAND
II
HERE COMES SUNSHINE
SAMPSON

Grateful Dead
U.S. AIR ARENA
10·9·94
I

SOURCE: SOUNDBOARD ___ RADIO ___
AUDIENCE ___ LP ___

GRATEFUL DEAD

WAY TO GO HOME
SHIP O' FOOLS
ST. OF CIRCUM.
DRUMS
SPACE

SPACE
MIRACLE
COMES A TIME
THROWIN' STONES
LOVE LIGHT

(E) RAIN

Grateful Dead
U.S. AIR ARENA
10·9·94
II

SOURCE: SOUNDBOARD ___ RADIO ___
AUDIENCE ___ LP ___

GRATEFUL DEAD

HELL IN A BUCKET
COLD RAIN & SNOW
MINGLEWOOD
SO MANY ROADS
CHILDHOOD'S END

ETERNITY
DON'T EASE ME IN
II
SPACE
OTHER ONE
WHARF RAT
GOOD LOVIN'

w/B. MARSALIS

GRATEFUL DEAD
LA SPORTS ARENA
12·16·94
I

SOURCE: AUDIENCE X RADIO ___
SOUNDBOARD ___ OTHER ___

GRATEFUL DEAD

EYES O' WORLD
SAMBA IN RAIN
EST. PROPHET
JAM

w/ B. MARSALIS

HE'S GONE
DRUMS
SPACE

(E) LUCY IN THE SKY

GRATEFUL DEAD
LA SPORTS ARENA
12·16·94
II

SOURCE: AUDIENCE X RADIO ___
SOUNDBOARD ___ OTHER ___

Bertha
Greatest Story
Loser
Red Rooster
Rumble On Rose
El Paso
Ryan Howe
GRATEFUL DEAD
Lazy River Road
Cassidy
Filler- 2-21-95
Salt Lake City
11-11-85
Walkin' the Dog
Deal
Grateful Dead
2-20-95 Salt Lake City, UT
SBD Delta Center
Source
Sbd
Aud
FM
Generation

MA110
GRATEFUL DEAD
3-22-95 II
Charlotte NC
TDK

Victim or The Crime →
Foolish Heart →
Saint of Circumstance →
He's Gone →
DRUMS & SPACE
I Want To tell You →
Attics of My Life →
Lovelight
Mighty Quinn
MA110
TDK

SAW
IT
DEAD
The Omni I & II
Atlanta, GA. 3-26-95
1st Gen Aud DAT
4/1/95
A
B
BUCKET
CANDYMAN
TAKE ME 2
RIVER
LR ROOSTER
MASTERPIECE
CHILDHOOD'S
END
DEAL
ENCORE:
SAT NITE
Taped By Steve Fukawa w/ D5M / NAK100
LIVE
PYRAMID
MEMPHIS, TN
4/1/95 SET 1
GRATEFUL
DEAD
BOARD___RADIO___AUDIENCE X DAT___GEN 1
4/1/95
A
B
FOOLISH
WAY TO GO
HOME
SAINT
EYES
DRUMZ
SPACE
THE WHEEL
WATCHTOWER
SOTM
AUDI A
Taped By Steve Fukawa w/ D5M / NAK100
LIVE
PYRAMID
MEMPHIS, TN
4/1/95 SET 2
GRATEFUL
DEAD
BOARD___RADIO___AUDIENCE X DAT___ GEN 1
A

Grateful Dead
PicassoMoon
FOTD,WangDang
Althea
QueenJane
AUDdat A 90
Deal
10/20/78 I
WINTERLAND
Grateful Dead
5/19/95 A LAS VEGAS
TO MY FRIENDS
THAT LOVE AND RECORD LIVE GRATEFUL DEAD

Grateful Dead
HCSunshine
LongWay
Playin,UJB,Drumz
Space,EasyAnswers
SOTM,Around
E*LucyInTheSky
FILL SMITHERENE
AUDdat A 100
Grateful Dead
5/19/95 B LAS VEGAS
TO MY FRIENDS
THAT LOVE AND RECORD LIVE GRATEFUL DEAD

Grateful Dead
Memorial Stadium, Seattle

Feel Like a Stranger
Bertha
Good Morning, Little Schoolgirl
Peggy-O
El Paso
Tennessee Jed
Cassidy

- Set II -
Foolish Heart
Victim or the Crime
Samba in the Rain

GRATEFUL DEAD
Memorial Stadium, Seattle
5/25/95
Set 1

DSB2

Grateful Dead
Memorial Stadium, Seattle

He's Gone ->
drums ->

space ->
The Wheel ->
Throwing Stones ->
Not Fade Away

Quinn the Eskimo

GRATEFUL DEAD
Memorial Stadium, Seattle
5/25/95
Set 2

DSB2

Touch
Rooster
Lazy River Rd.
Masterpiece
Childhood's End
Cumberland
Promised Land
– Set II –
Shakedown
Samson
So Many Rds
Samba
Corrina →
Jam
Set ( )
Soldier Field
Chicago, IL
7-9-95 I : II
NOISE REDUCTION
IN
OUT
2nd Gen
SBD
AUD
RAD.
SOUND QUALITY
SBD
GOOD
AUD
FAIR
POOR
Touch of Grey
Red Rooster
Lazy River Road
Masterpiece
Childhood's End
Cumberland Blues
Promised Land
Jack Straw
Friend of the Devil
Minglewood Blues
So Many Roads
Tom Thumb's Blues
BIODTL
Soldiers Field – Chicago – Rosemont Horizon
7-9-95 (1) Grateful Dead 3-16-94 (1)
Shakedown Street
Samson + Delilah
So Many Roads
Samba in the Rain
Corrina
Space →
Unbroken Chain
Sugar Magnolia
Black Muddy River →
Box of Rain
Soldiers Field
7-9-95 Grateful Dead (2)

AUDIENCE
SOUNDBOARD
RADIO

TAPERS SECTION

How It All Went Down

11/29/72

Jon—

Enclosed are some letters regarding a group which calls itself the Free Underground Grateful Dead Tape Exchange.

1) a letter from Leslie Kippel to us inquiring about possible sales arrangements (10/24)

2) one from Jim Watson (11/8) in reply to an inquiry Eileen sent to him

3) one from G. Sargent, their "local rep." in Felton (nr. Santa Cruz) (11/14)

I believe we need to work out a policy on this sort of thing (— band's opinions?), i.e. should we a) stomp, b) license, c) tacitly tolerate, them? — or what?

If live tapes are that popular, should we look at this as an "alternative method"? We've got a lot of those tapes, (over)

of good quality, which cost plenty to produce.

DP

JERRY GARCIA INTERVIEWED BY STEVEN MARCUS
10/14/1986

Steven Marcus: Well, how do you feel about people taping Grateful Dead concerts and trading the tapes?

Jerry Garcia: Hey, when I'm done with it, it's theirs. If somebody can find a use for music after it's been performed, fine with me. I used to be a bluegrass music freak, and I spent a lot of time taping bands, and I loved being able to do it and I loved having the tapes afterwards. Being able to trade them around, I think that's healthy stuff. That's OK with me, as long as the people who are doing the taping aren't obnoxious about it. I have to view it from that point of view, because at worst, somebody will complain that there's too much hassling for the best spots and that kind of stuff. As far as I'm concerned, those matters don't really happen to me experientially, but I hear about them, and if I hear that somebody in the audience is unnecessarily rude or copping an attitude of some kind, I don't want to be authoritarian about it. I don't care, really, if everybody comes in packing high-tech gear. Everybody who's doing it should just be aware of everybody else who's there. That's all.

Steven Marcus: And respect their space.

Jerry Garcia: If possible. Sure.

Steven Marcus: Well, now we're in the video era. Why should the line be drawn at audio? Why not allow video also?

Jerry Garcia: I haven't drawn it. I think if the stuff is compact enough and it doesn't get in anybody's face and the people are clever enough at sneaking it in or whatever, hey, it's fine with me.

Steven Marcus: It's already being done. I've seen some pretty good videos.

Jerry Garcia: Yeah, I know. I'm aware of that.

Steven Marcus: Another question I have is: How about releasing the CDs of choice live Dead from the vault?

Jerry Garcia: I think it's a good possibility that that will happen sometime. But see, the thing is that I don't have the time to do this kind of stuff. I also don't have the inclination; every time I hear myself in the past, I'm basically embarrassed. It's like, "Why did I do that?" I have that kind of hang-up going with my own performances. Just like listening to your own voice on the tape recorder; you don't want to be confronted with it, really. You already did it. It's over. It's like anything that happened in the past. So, for me, I understand the value of it to people who really feel that they have to have these performances. And if they want them that badly, hey, that's just fine. The whole thing is farming this stuff out to people who are interested enough to do it. Because I don't want to have to deal with it.

Steven Marcus: Right. Yeah, I understand that.

Jerry Garcia: Yeah. You can dig that, can't you?

STEVE PARISH AND DICK LATVALA ON QVC
6/5/1998

Steve Parish: Dick, I'd like you to explain to everybody: we have a vault here at Novato, and that vault has thirty years of music in it. Dick gets the joyful pleasure of going into that vault and picking music to use for the Dick's Picks series. I'd like him to explain how he does that a little bit, talk about the whole taping phenomenon associated with the Grateful Dead.

Dick Latvala: The Grateful Dead is one of the only bands that ever had this thing of taping and allowed it. Some people didn't want it to go on. It was very controversial, and it managed to keep going because the people had a passion about it. They really wanted to make tapes of these shows.

Steve Parish: Now, what you're talking about is the way that the band allowed their audience to tape the show. This is unheard of. It was argued about and bantered about. It was something not done everywhere.

Dick Latvala: There was a bunch of people who didn't like it.

Steve Parish: A lot of meetings: record companies didn't like it, roadies didn't like it.

Dick Latvala: There [were people] cutting cords!

Steve Parish: There was protection that needed to be done. It needed control. Because Dick could tell you, there was so many people taping at the shows at times that they would get in the way of everything. It was like, "I'm taping here and I don't want dancing around me. Don't bump into my mic."

Dick Latvala: Yeah. "Be quiet!"

Steve Parish: But it was a live show and a party.

Dick Latvala: This whole thing is about a live experience. We understand this. This is a very important moment. It was a live phenomenon . . . I think [out of] sheer determination on the part of the tapers, they just kept doing it.

Steve Parish: These tapes were from our vault, or from our soundboard.

Dick Latvala: Yes, and they were not made with the idea that they're going to be released someday. I remember in the old days, they were made and you guys would listen to them in the hotel room or something like that.

Steve Parish: Exactly. On the road we'd take those tapes and at night, we'd all meet together in a room and play them and learn what was going on that night--relive the night. The band would learn their music. Great little fun times. They never would've thought about them going out.

Dick Latvala: No, no; they reflected what was coming through the PA. It's not "record perfect," but it reflects our passion for having the whole show, hearing each night as a special night. There's so many of them. See, this must be mystifying to some people--why we have so many of one band, so many tapes of what may seem like the same show over and over. But none of these shows are the same. Each one is different.

MINUTES OF THE MEETING WED 11 JULY 1984

Present: M. Hart, P. Lesh, J. Soto, B. Weir, E. Law, M. Greene, R. Taylor MJo Meinolf, H. Kant, S. Parish, Kidd, R. Hunter, S. Gottlieb, J. Cutler, D. McNally, B. Kreutzmann, B. Parker, D. Rifkin, S. Stephens, H. Popick, C. Brightman, D. Healy, W. Legate, B. Mydland, J. Garcia, P. Roehlk, J. Thomas, Ram Rod

Meeting was called to order at approximately 2:25 pm by P. Lesh. The minutes of the last meeting (18June) were read.

1. Red Rocks. B. Weir stated he was willing to do about anything to facilitate our playing there in the future. Although advance crew notified Feyline of our requirements prior to our last appearance, we didn't get satisfaction; general feeling is that problem is with Feyline rather than unwillingness on city's part. Changes have to be made, i.e., (JG): "take away dumb side panels and dumb roof." D. Healy suggested the Tolares be moved and put back on wheels, keep the physical structure of the roof, cover with wire cloth and hang weighted blue tarps on the sides; this modification would allow roof fabric to be rolled in matter of minutes. We will submit a proposal; and depending on cost (to be determined) possibly pay for a portion of these improvements.

2. Security. Policy, whenever possible, will be accountable security (ID# or name). We issue cautionary statements with all tickets we sell in particularly troublesome venues, Nassau, Wisconsin. Recent legislation regarding search and seizure may increase problems in cop/audience situation.

3. Philadelphia Mini Fest, 22 Sept. Offer: $200,000. Proposed ticket price: $20 GP at this price for 90,000=$1,800,000. Promoter says expenses are $800,000 including talent guarantee (for 4 groups).Note: we usually make about $5/ticket sold. We will counter with: $350,000 guarantee VS % of gross, whichever is greater. Hal suggested 50% of gross over breakeven point. (Note: $20 ticket price too high.) We're calling shots re staging and sound; D. Healy will submit proposal. If this gig is confirmed, we will play "warm-up" gigs starting around 14 Sept-- possibly Austin, New Orleans, Atlanta, Philly.... Oct tour starts on 5th.

4. Danny clarified his position re road managing--he doesn't <u>not</u> want to go on the road <u>ever</u> again. Replacement trial road manager will be responsible primarily for getting band from point A to B and settlements (assisted by Shelly Diamond.) John McIntire is available and will be offered this position for short tour, on trial basis.

4. GD Movie on video cassette; Hal is negotiating for sale in US and Europe.

- 1 -

5. *Merchandising:*

A. % to venues. Kidd has been working with Jack Lavine/Winterland Prod in lower % fee of merchandising we pay to halls. Now that we're selling out venues, we're more in a position to make deals.

B. Artwork. We need to draw up pay scale for 1)Idea/execution 2) execution only and set up some guide lines. We will dig through our files; proper agreements will be drawn up. It's very important that we own copyrights and trademarks, and have actual possession of separations. We will buy artwork andpay a % or royalty to artist. We copyright it, and own separations. (Note: T-shirts will not be imprinted with individuals' names.)

C. Dicken will be given severance pay: 4 checks @ $1,600 Gross (no w/h) minus O/A owing in exchange for execution of agreement relinquishing all rights to artwork, etc. and return of all equipment, merchandise, etc. to our satisfaction. These files will have to be updated as to issuing of agreements/contracts, payments to photographers, etc.

D. We will do a 1986 calander--too late for '85.

E. Winterland is preparing report on merchandising status. Hold on new fall merchandising. Evaluating present inventory.

Records and other merchandise can be sold through catalog/mailing at better price to consumer. Hal cited Mobile Fidelity deal (did American Beauty/ Mars Hotel) whereby we buy albums at wholesale, are paid a royalty, and sell retail). Must have sufficient stock on hand (and necessary processing equipment) if we expand our mail-order operation.

Note: We own trademark: Skull/Roses, Skull/Lightning Bolt, Dead Heads

Bob Thomas and Bear (Designers/Skull-Lightning Bolt) will be paid $2,000 each advance against %. Terms to be determined and agreement issued.

6. Betty Cantor is suing GDP for $25,800 and Brent for $45,000. Hal will confer with Bonnie, Janet, and Sue in representing GDP in this matter. GDP does not owe Betty any money; will consider settling for nominal sum paid to Betty in exchange for permanent release.

7. Hal, not having "much of a law office" at this time, will continue representing us in some areas, coming to meetings, etc, and can recommend good litigation and criminal counsel. We will have to hire someone to assist with day to day legal work, trademarks, copyrights, etc.

8. Individual/Warner Bros. is going thru archives for possible LP of previously unreleased material; Jerry will guide him ...at first... 56. take up to point of assembly

9. Press. Dennis distributed copies of recent press release.
Life is doing article re: '60's, in exchange for shot, will do free band PR photo ½ hour after Sun Greek show.
Jerry and Mickey/contributors: Video Tribute to Bill Graham (Mill Valley Film Festival on Sept. 29.
Schedule CBS TV interview w/Jerry, Grace Slick, Bill Graham to be aired at approx. 8:30 am on 17 July.
No People Magazine people backstage. Jim Marshall to receive no special consideration.
Dennis McNally's salary approved at $500/week.

10. Kidd mentioned a KPFA-type radio station that wants to play GD tapes. We will decide on terms in these situations with non-profit stations and drawn up informal agreement.

11. A special 'tapers' section w/higher priced ticket was suggested; proposal to follow. We must protect ourselves with special no recording disclaimer.

12. Special light show budget in the amount of $6,000 to $7,000 was approved for Friday 13 July--Dark Star, second set. (This amount includes rental of projector and screen.

13. Candace suggest possible tour bonus for Danny English. Will be tabled until D. Rifkin is present.

14. John Cutler is in road crew category (re: tour bonus). Brian Williams is approved on salary at $500.

15. B. Weir suggested selling of hackey sacks toys at Ventura. D. Healy would like the following added to our rider: no more green glow things.

16. Hal would like to call a Rex Foundation Board of Directors meeting.

Meeting was adjourned at 4:50 pm. Ice Nine Meeting followed.

Dave Lemieux

March 4, 2020

DL: I was an archivist. My background was in film archiving and I'd done a couple of undergraduate degrees, one in history and one in film studies and film production, and then a master's degree in film archiving. I'd worked in a couple of prominent Canadian film archives, the national archives in Ottawa and the British Columbia archives in Victoria, BC. About six months at each of those gigs, and then the Dead thing happened. I came in as a video archivist; I wouldn't really call it a videographer. Film archivist, I guess. Then those kinds of duties morphed into audio and video archivist once I got the position full-time and that almost immediately became producer, that then, a decade later, became all those things plus a legacy manager, with a title [Bob] Weir and I came up with.

I honestly had no plan. I had no designs on ever working for them. I had no designs on a contract. What happened was around May of '98, I wrote Dick Latvala an email. I got his email address from Susana Millman, that's Dennis McNally's wife, and she's a photographer and I was in touch with her about buying a photo of the Other Ones. Remember the Other Ones? They got together in '98 and she had a photo online, so I emailed her through the Dead's website. I didn't know she was Dennis's wife. It's just a great photo. I said, "I'd love to buy this photo." She goes, "Well, maybe I'll sell it." I said, "It's so cool. I'm really into collecting things. I'm just doing a masters of archiving." I didn't say anything about anything. And she goes, "Oh, you're an archivist. Well, my husband Dennis says that you should totally talk to Dick Latvala. Here's his email address."

So I sent Dick an email in May of '98 just saying, "Hey, Dick." I still have it somewhere. It's one paragraph. I say, "Hey, Dick. I'm a film archivist and just finished a master's degree. I'm finishing and now I'm writing my thesis. I worked in a film archive in Canada and I'm going to be in California at the end of July"—I didn't tell him I was coming to see the Other Ones at Shoreline, but I just said, "I'm going to be in California in July. If you have any time to show me your archive, I'd love to come see it." I sent the email off and then that's it. That's what we do in life, right? We press send. Maybe I'll get a chance to spend five minutes looking at the Dead's archive. It would be a thrill of a lifetime.

A couple of months went by and I didn't think anything about it. Then the Other Ones were on tour and about four days before the Shoreline shows, I was about to fly down from Canada to Shoreline and I get a call and it was Dick Latvala. He's got an unmistakable raspy voice and said, "Hey man, I'm sorry it took so long to get back to you. I got your letter," and he said, "It seems like an important one. So I wanted to know, are you still coming?" I said, "Shit man, I'm coming tomorrow." And he said, "Are you free the next day?" I said, "I am." He said, "Come to the vault, then." So he gave me the directions and I went up to the vault and I spent, oh, a good four hours with him in the vault. Then John Cutler, who is the Dead sound guy and studio producer, studio head of Grateful Dead Productions, he took me into the studio and showed me around and we spent, like I say, a good four hours and then, it was the thrill of a lifetime. End of the story. About two months later, I finished my master's degree, about September of '98, and I wrote Dick and John both a letter, not an email, but an actual paper letter. I printed it out and just put it in an envelope. Dick's was more like [to] a Deadhead dude. John's is more professional, just saying, "Hey John, it really meant a lot to me. I was able to use your archive and how you hold your film and video within your archive in my thesis, so it was really helpful. I just want to say thanks." And then I noticed when I was there, that Dick was extremely focused on the audio and he wasn't all that interested in the video, so the video collection wasn't quite as organized and cataloged the way the audio was. So I wrote in the letter to John, I'll never forget this, "PS, if you'd like somebody to come and catalog your video collection and film collection, let me know. I'd love to come and do it." And then I deleted it from the letter. I deleted it. I was about to print it and I said, "You know what, you only live once. I'm going to put it in there." So I put it back in: "PS, if you need somebody to come and catalog your video collection, let me know." And I printed the letter, I sent it to Dick and John and that was the end of it. A week later, John called me and he said, "Hey man, were you serious about coming to catalog the video collection?" I said, "Oh shit. I was dead serious. I was totally serious." And he goes, "OK, why don't you come down in the next couple of weeks and tell us what you'd envision doing?"

So I went down in November of '98. I told them I would use FileMaker Pro, a good database system. I had a meeting with John, a meeting with Dick, and a meeting with the Dead's CEO. And then John, before I even left the building, he said, "OK, let's make this happen. When do you want to start?" I said, "How about February first?" And he said, "It's my birthday. That's perfect." So, I went back to Canada. I told my job at the BC archives I'm going to leave for three months and I went down for that February, March, April contract. The point was to catalog the film and video, because at the time there was this brand-new format called DVDs and the Dead thought, "Hey, maybe we've got something here where we can put out more home videos." Because I think they had some good success with the *Downhill from Here* and *Ticket to New Year's*. And they figured, "Let's get a proper cataloging done." I also provided them with a preservation assessment, because there were some video tape formats that needed to be backed up. So I gave them a good preservation assessment of what I thought. I stayed three months. Then in August, the Dead were very keen on doing *The Grateful Dead Movie* as a DVD. So they needed to know what they had for outtakes of the 16-millimeter film, and that's when I came down in August, and Dick went into a coma and died a few days later. I mean, I kept having to work and then . . . [They] asked me to just stick around and get a place to live and do that. So that's what I did.

Mark A. Rodriguez: Was there any expectation at that time that Dick would be leaving, anything like that?

DL: No expectation. Dick was young; he was in his mid-fifties, and he was my mentor and hero. By no means did I have any designs on taking over the gig at any time, and it was just terrible: Dick got sick pretty [quickly]. It was early August, around August 1 or 2, and within about a week he had passed. So it was completely unexpected. I'd been working with him during the previous contracts, virtually every day. I don't know whether he was healthy or not, but he certainly was a vibrant, enthusiastic person when I was working with him and it all kind of happened very quickly.

So Dick was gone and they needed some help guiding the Dick's Picks series. So I helped with a lot of the Dick's Picks releases right up until the series ended with #36. But I remember, in typical Grateful Dead fashion, things happen because they need to happen. Dick's Picks just kind of kept going—it kept going for twenty-one picks after Dick died. It went from #15 through #36 while Dick was gone. We put out #36 with absolutely no design of it being the last one. We pulled that and the funny thing was it happened to be a show that Dick had pitched as Dick's Picks volume 1. So we ended the series with a show that Dick absolutely loved and [had] wanted to be the first-ever Dick's Picks and ended up going with the Tampa '73 show instead. So we put out Dick's Picks 36, which was actually supposed to be #35, but then the houseboat tapes arrived, all those tapes from Keith's parents, and then that became #35. So Philly '72 is #36, put that out and then we were about to start working on 37 and we were told, "Yeah, we're not doing this anymore," and so that was kind of the way it happened.

MAR: But you were a taper before right, correct?

DL: I was. I saw a bunch of Dead shows, as we all did, and I taped the Dead from '89. I think the Kaiser '89 shows were the first Dead shows I taped, and I taped right up through spring of '93. I didn't tape all the shows I saw in those four years but I did tape most of them for sure. Yeah, I probably taped sixty shows, maybe sixty or seventy from the tapers section. I think even more than that, going back even five years before I was taping, [I] was a tape trader. That was certainly a big part of what I did. I dedicated pretty much all my time to either trading tapes or going to see the Dead and then recording them.

I got my first couple of boxes of tapes. I got two boxes from a good friend's older brother, as many of us did. There was an older brother in the neighborhood who was a Deadhead, so I got twenty tapes that I remember. Then the local Ottawa DJ on the local classic rock station, somehow I got hooked up with him, and found out that he had live Grateful Dead tapes too, and he hooked me up with another box or two. Pretty

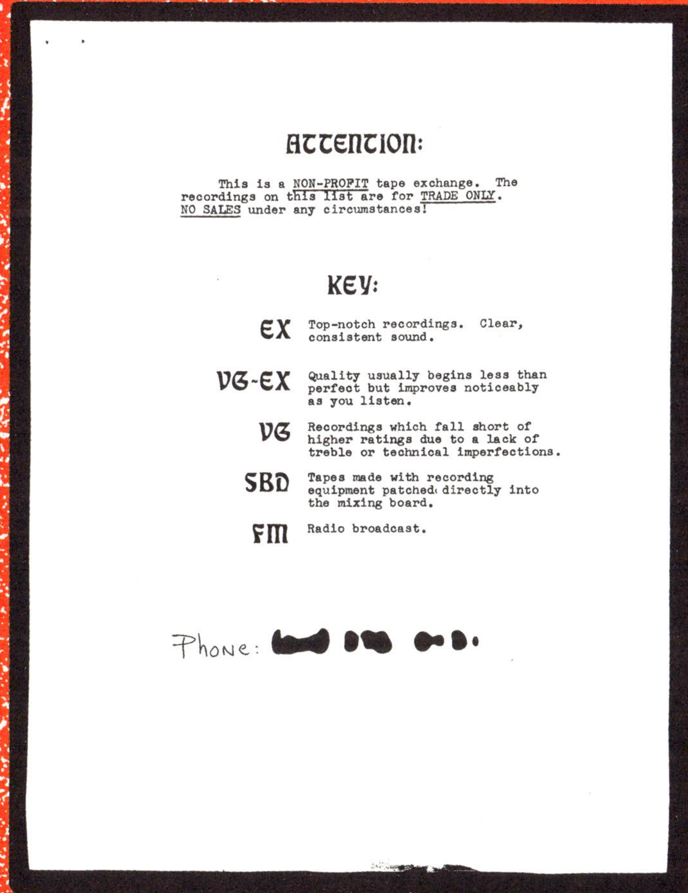

ATTENTION:

This is a NON-PROFIT tape exchange. The recordings on this list are for TRADE ONLY. NO SALES under any circumstances!

KEY:

EX	Top-notch recordings. Clear, consistent sound.
VG-EX	Quality usually begins less than perfect but improves noticeably as you listen.
VG	Recordings which fall short of higher ratings due to a lack of treble or technical imperfections.
SBD	Tapes made with recording equipment patched directly into the mixing board.
FM	Radio broadcast.

Phone:

grateful dead

November 79

All times listed are music or band jokes etc. The breaks between songs are cut out. I record shows with a Teac portable PC-10 and transfer them onto reels with a Pioneer RT-707. I trade cassette tapes only. I will not under any circumstances sell Grateful Dead music. I try to stay away from those who do because they will be the downfall of the trip.

I have found it necessary to save time and space by abbreviating a great deal on the song list found after the concert list. I've included a list of abbreviations in alphebetical order for those of you who will be totally confused. You will also come across other abbreviations that you might not understand, such as: w/(with), -(hyphen, which means that the songs are connected in some manner ex. cat-rider is China Cat into I know You Rider) acc(accoustic) el(electric) Ins (Instrumental) inc(song is incomplete) My rating system is simple and to the point. P(poor) F(fair) G(good) VG(very good) EX(excellent)

Cathy Santacroce
Box 373
Bridgehampton, NY
11932

STELLA BLUE CLUB
Box 51
Cedar Pines Park, California
92322

12-19-85

Greetings from The STELLA BLUE CLUB !

The Stella Blue Club collects, trades, and copies live concert tapes of the GRATEFUL DEAD and associated bands. These tapes are not for sale! Also, we collect, trade, and copy news articles, original artwork(by permission), songlists from shows, and in general help spread the Dead.

Stella Blue has at this date 228 hours of tape, from very old to very new, fair to excellent in sound quality, the majority being very good to excellent. Although we realize that quality is a subjective thing, we have rated most of the tapes on our list.

Anyone can get tapes from Stella Blue, either by trading or by the free copy service. Please follow these simple instructions to keep things flowing smoothly.

To Get The Stella Blue Tape List:

Send your tape list to us and we'll send ours. Or, send 5 stamps and we'll send our list with some news and art copies, and a SASE is helpful.

TRADES

Trades are very limited for us in the immediate future due to lack of funds for expansion. Therefore, all trades must be pre-arranged by letter or phone. We love to trade but please keep in mind that we don't have the money(blank tapes,postage) to trade with everyone that we connect with. Please trade only two 90 min. tapes at a time. We send only Maxell XL II high bias tapes out because they are the most reliable, and we prefer the same sent to us. Allow 4 weeks for return of tapes, but depending on the backlog it's usually less. Should you not receive them by 6 weeks, get in touch with us.

COPY SERVICE

Pick what you want from the list, and send two blank 90 min. tapes together with a pre-addressed stamped return mail envelope of the same size. Again I recommend Maxell XL II or II-S as the best overall tapes. At least get high quality, high bias tapes. Allow up to 6 weeks for their return, though usually it's less. Please remember to send only 2 tapes for copy service at a time, and wait till you receive them before sending any more.

FOOTNOTES ON- - -

Tapes: We only use Maxells, but when unavailable TDK SA or SA-X will do okay. Best prices on tapes come in buying by the case(10 or 12). Also look for sales ads from stereo-video stores(Pacific,Federated,etc.), as they sell tapes very low just to get you in the store. Record stores are usually higher. There are some very expensive high-tech tapes made, if you can afford them(Teac,Loran).

Mailing: Always use 1st class mail, and we mark ours as "audio cassettes" to keep them from being x-rayed by the Postal Service. Padded envelopes are nice, but you can also use regular ones and pack the tapes in air bubble plastic. Always print very clearly.

FIRST CLASS
AUDIO CASSETTES

immediately I ended up with about thirty or forty cassettes. This would be late '84 into the spring of '85. Then from there, a couple of again older, two years older, people in my community high school, they pointed me in the direction of a magazine called the *The Golden Road* and another called *Relix*. They all had huge amounts of ads in the back of them for tape traders. You just go through them and it would say, "Have a bunch of 1973 to '82, looking to trade," and then you send a list and they send a list, and before you know it, you've got a pretty prominent trading network.

It's pretty immediate for those tapes to go from forty, up to a couple of hundred, up to eight hundred, up to well over a thousand, and that's pretty quickly because you're trading ten or twenty at a time. There were times when I was getting two or three packets of tapes in the mail every week and there'd be anywhere from six to ten in a packet. Then I'd be, of course, dubbing six or ten per packet and trading back. Tape trading was a ton of fun. It was an all-consuming passion. It certainly was not what I'd call a hobby.

MAR: What was the final count of your tape collection?

DL: Probably about twelve or thirteen hundred. Well, yeah, about thirteen hundred hours maybe and at ninety-minute tapes, probably about nine hundred to one thousand tapes, closing in close to fifteen hundred hours. Which I think in the tape trading world of the people I was trading with, that was pretty calm and that was a pretty standard amount. That seems to me to be a pretty common number.

MAR: Were you familiar with kind of the older clan of tapers or the stuff that the pioneers were taping in the seventies?

DL: I think there was not all that much known about that early generation. I mean, no, actually there was—the ones that were advertising in *Relix* in the early seventies and doing the very early audience tapes going back to '70 and '71, and then the board tapes that would appear. I got into the Dead at a time when the Dead's popularity was really surging. I mean, there were a lot of people my age, and it just seemed that most of the people who were as enthusiastic about trading and as energetic and enthusiastic were my age, so it seemed. It wasn't so much that I wasn't aware of the older tape traders. I don't think they were the ones necessarily putting the ads in the back of a magazine. I think they had their networks and occasionally you get hooked up with someone who was somewhat legendary in the taping world and that was very cool. But for the most part, the people I was trading with were my age, or maybe slightly older, but that was I think because so many of us were getting into the Dead at around the same time. In my case, it was kind of that '85 to '87 [period] when a lot of people were getting really heavily into them. Those ads—I found the people that I would respond to and end up trading with, just by happenstance, would be people roughly my age. I was certainly aware of the history of tapers but not to the extent that I am now because a lot more has been written about them. But I remember the first time I saw Dick Latvala's name was around '88 or '89 and it was in a Dead-based magazine. Maybe it was '90. It was sometime around then. So I wasn't even aware of those first five years of Dick, both as a serious tape trader going back to the late seventies, but nor was I familiar with him as the Dead archivist until I saw his name referred to as the Grateful Dead's official archivist. Around 1990, it was in a Dead-based book that I got in Eugene, Oregon. It was an interesting world to learn about for sure.

[When recording shows] I was a novice and I had probably four microphones, which was such an important part of it. I probably had the [worst] microphones for that kind of recording. They were high-level microphones but there were much, much higher level microphones that I did not have—they were just too expensive. The ones I had were, I don't know, three or four hundred a pair maybe, and they were the best mics I could afford. I used them exclusively. Actually, the first three shows I recorded, I used some Shure microphones, but after that I got Nakamichi and then stuck with them. But there were much, much better microphones and therefore much better recordings. There were people who had certain ways to place their microphones, in a certain pattern. I didn't do that only because I didn't understand it. It wasn't that I didn't think what those people were doing was valuable to the recording, I just didn't understand what doing this pattern or that pattern of the microphones meant. I didn't want to chance getting a bad recording, and my tapes don't sound great. I pointed them at the two stacks of speakers, left and right. From the tapers section, that was all you could really do. It certainly wasn't . . . I didn't bring any EQ in or anything like that. It was a straight shot from the microphone, down the mic stand, through the cable, right into my recording device. It was pretty straightforward.

The last shows that I recorded were Albany '93, and I only saw one more show after that, in Buffalo '93, that was my last show, which I did not record. It was '93 and by then I'd been in university for two years and I realized . . . going back to something I said earlier, the Dead being an all-consuming passion. I didn't want to be . . . I didn't really have it in me to be a half-assed Deadhead. I really was getting serious about my studies. I'd taken a year off after high school to basically go see Dead shows. And in that year, I didn't particularly enjoy myself, short of the actual shows that I went to, which were substantial amounts. I didn't dig what I was doing, which is to say, kind of low-paying jobs, things like that, and no steady work or anything. I wanted to give 100 percent to the Dead, so it was either all or nothing. So I decided to focus on my studies and I basically took almost four years off of listening to the Dead, from '93 to '96. It was interesting because in late '96, my buddy Rory came to Montreal, where I was living, and he had a bunch of Dead tapes. I'd been out of the Dead for about three years. And he sent me a bunch of things—new board [recordings] that had started circulating. He hooked me up with a lot of really good new soundboards that I'd never heard before.

I got back into the Dead basically as hard as I ever was. But the nice thing, and I think this has been important for the job I have now, I came back with very critical ears—whereas before, everything was great. Everything was the best. It was all about accumulating quantity of tapes. When I got back into it [in] '96, I wanted to get back into tapes. I wanted to grow my DAT collection, but I wanted it to be quality of both performance and quality of sound. Whereas prior to that it had been almost entirely based on quantity of tapes and quality of sound. I think that's been extremely helpful with the job I have, because a second part of what I do is listen to the Dead and be very critical about it. Which is to say, when it's really good then maybe that's a show that comes out on CD, and when it's not, then OK, maybe we move on.

MAR: Would you say that your experience being a taper, in terms of accumulating sound, finding what you like about the sound, chasing the sound . . . did that inform an archival passion, or do you think that's just kind of part of your personality and you naturally gravitated towards that?

DL: I think it's both. I think it is part of my personality. Since I was very young, I was very aware of the importance of keeping things. I'm certainly not a hoarder or anything like that but I'm very aware of the importance of keeping things. As I was doing my first university degree, which was in history, that's when it really occurred to me that every bit of history . . . everything we know about the past is based on secondary sources, which are the books that people write about history. Those are written based on what they're finding from the primary sources, which is what's in the archives. So if you're not keeping those primary documents, you can't write the history properly. So I realized very early on—and this related to my academic side, and then as a taper—it was partly the same thing too. That was, to me, the thrill of taping a Grateful Dead show. It was listening to the show afterwards and reliving the memory of that concert an hour later, but it was also preserving that forever, and that was important to me. Then as a taper, it was very concerning to me to know that magnetic audio wasn't forever. So you have to do certain things to make sure it is—whether that's back it up every few years, or keep it in a climate-controlled setting, and keep it out of the sun and keep it out of warm temperatures and humidity. I was very aware of those things, going back to even before I saw the Grateful Dead, and then it was the reality as I got more into magnetic media and film in the nineties in university. The film archiving degree is what really solidified that; that pretty much everything we know through history and history books came from an archive. That's where a good historian goes in hard times.

So then when I started working with the Dead, I viewed those recordings as that master document that was in the room. Aside from the ten thousand people who were there and the band, these are some of the last items that are still in existence that were at that actual show. So I've always been fascinated with the original documents, I guess you could say. I viewed the Dead's archive as one of the most important cultural archives. Music, of course: I think it's one of the most important music archives in the world, which is to say, in history. Remember, recorded music has only been around for a hundred years and change. So it's not a great history, but I certainly do think that both in terms of [the Grateful Dead archive's] importance and size and scope, but also the length that it was recorded, thirty years of recordings, and it's virtually complete. There are certainly gaps in certain years, without a doubt in the early years. But from 1971 through 1995, I think there's only one Grateful Dead show for which there is no known recording, and that is unbelievable. It was actually quite late. It was the 1979 [Tulsa Pavilion, 2/6/79] concert. I think that's amazing, that in the last twenty-four years of Grateful Dead, there was only one show for which there is no known recording.

MAR: Yeah. It amazes me, it really does, that we have this archive and it is physically immense. It's imposing and it's impressive and . . . It has been kept in incredibly good condition going back fifty years, and consistently.

DL: It was really when the Dead got their own space around 1976 at the Club Front [the Dead's studio and rehearsal venue] in San Rafael, California, that's when it really got its proper home. Then when they moved into a new building in 1995, in Bel Marin Keys, it got its second proper home and its own climate control vault where it lived until 2006. It then went to LA, where it's now housed and safe and happy.

MAR: Archive.org was happening kind of in the midst of the seven years of your tenure in the Dead organization, unless I'm incorrect?

DL: Yeah, I think, as far as I remember, it just kind of appeared out of nowhere around 2004, 2005, and you know, one day there were ten Grateful Dead shows on this site and the next day there were a hundred, the next day there were five hundred, next day there were a thousand, and it all happened pretty darn quickly.

MAR: Were you consulted during the Terrapin Station Entertainment and Historical Center planning at all? Technically that would be before your time, right?

DL: Oh, the [proposed] museum? Before my time. That was something that was conceived around '96, '97, and by the time I got there, there were still meetings being held with architects, designers, real estate people to find the proper place. But it didn't end up happening. I remember they were talking about one of the components [that was] going to be like a little movie theater, and I would curate, maybe once every month, a show out of the vault on video that would be this month's feature, and we'd show it at the little theater.

MAR: Weren't they planning to have a whole thing where you could order the show you wanted, a CD of it, at your visit to the museum?

DL: That was always the hope. That was one of the things they talked about: digitizing everything, and then you'd pay your $20 and walk out with a CD of the show you wanted.

MAR: Was that, at that time, being new to the organization, were you like, "That's crazy"? Or was everyone kind of like, "Yeah, we can do this"?

DL: You know, I don't think anything in the data world is viewed as, "You're crazy." Honestly, I think that everything is good as a challenge. You look at the Wall of Sound, you look at when Jerry started playing the MIDI guitar. If they willed it and it was doable, they would generally be able to do it. Now, twenty-five years later, what you're describing is incredibly feasible and very doable. Then, it would have been much more of a challenge, but certainly they would have got the best people involved.

MAR: You had mentioned that the first time you went to visit the vault, you hung out with Dick and John for a few hours. And I was wondering if you could articulate any more of what that experience was like, or what actually got communicated when you were in the vault together.

DL: I'll tell you exactly what day it was too, it was July 23, 1998. Because the Other Ones played at Shoreline, and that's what I was doing in California primarily. And so, [Dick] was just really showing me, more than anything, cataloging and his organizational system. And to me it was fascinating, because the best way to describe it is that it was organized chronologically by format. And he was very, very diligent about it. And that's when we talked about the database, and I asked him, "Is there a database?" And he goes, "Well, there is, but . . ." He said [he] never turned it on because, even though there were many, many thousands of tapes, there was no need to turn it on because it was so well organized chronologically by format. So, if you were looking for a certain show that you knew was on ten-inch two-track reels, that's one section. And so, you just go there and you'll find it. So, when I started working there, I never needed to open up that database. And I do have a printout of that database—I have a very handy printed binder of it. But I never turned that FileMaker program on, because it was really well organized. And that's a testament to Dick. And I think prior to that, Willy [Legate].

MAR: I'm kind of curious if you ever got any history from Dick, in terms of what he had done to the archive, or how he had

Dan Healy interviewed by Toni A. Brown in *Relix* vol. 18, #5, October 1991

Relix: Garcia was quoted as saying, "We're starting to deal with the possibility of having a permanent venue of some kind." Can you speculate as to what that would be like?

Healy: Some variations go from someplace like Shoreline, for instance, that we would, say, do two or three months a year there, some long run, and the idea would be people would come like they go to Disneyland or something. That's one variation, but now there's some other new possibilities. We're now working on an exhibit of high definition TV, HDTV, and we will do that the next time we play at Shoreline in August. The program will originate there. It will be distributed there. And it will be distributed to theaters around the country.

High definition TV is just infinitely more of a higher resolution than regular TV as we know it. The screens will be 40-foot-wide screens, which is the width of our stage. So, the scale will be one to one, and the picture and color and texture will be absolutely pure, even better than 35 mm film. It'll rival 70 mm film, extremely good quality. And then each one of these places will have a custom-specified sound system by one of us that will go with it, so that each place will have an immensely beautiful picture and an immensely great sound system. This is a test, another one of the Grateful Dead's firsts that we're famous for, and this will be our first endeavor at high definition TV.

There's only six of these projectors that can project high definition TV in the country, and the idea is that from Shoreline we'll send a signal to the satellite, and then it will come down into these six cities that we have yet to pick but will pick. And then each one of these six systems will go into one of those theaters, and it'll be like a custom exhibit. So that's another possibility. I don't think that it's really known yet whether the place will be a place where people actually come to or will exist in the form of some electronic conveyance.

The thing is that it's difficult and expensive to tour, and I think that we might be getting to a place in our lives where being on the road all the time isn't that desirable. So, the object will be to get a place that's more consistent with the time that we have to spend on it and still enable our fans to see and hear the music. Those are just some suggestions and ideas, but I don't think that it's necessarily become a fixed reality yet, it's something that's still an exploratory.

Buckminster Fuller once designed for us, that I have the blueprints for, like a floating venue that looked like a spaceship and held about 10,000 people. The object was that we could go to different cities and have our permanent set-up, like the carnival shows, and that's another possibility. That happened about 15 years ago, before he died. He came up with a design that worked similar to a dirigible. You could take on or remove buoyancy, and you could float to a different city and then you could lower it down and tie down and everybody would come and see the show. That's a more space futuristic version of it, but it certainly is a good idea. I would like to see something like that happen. I don't know if it will happen in my lifetime, but it sure would be nice.

Relix: You folks are the forerunners in so many realms of musical technology. It might not happen in your lifetime, but who knows? ■

The vault, upstairs at Club Front, San Rafael, CA
Photos: David Gans

The vault, Novato
Photo: Susana Millman

historically wrangled all the tapes and chronologically ordered them, and kind of kept that—like, how he did his job.

DL: I did, yeah. The Dead's archive, the first archive, the first vault I started working at for the first four years, it was an incredible facility. It was a huge warehouse. And within that they built the vault, which was about a twenty-foot-by-forty-foot room, fire suppression, climate control—it was a state-of-the-art archive facility. And as a professional archivist . . . I'd seen a lot of archives and it really was a wonderful place. The way Dick had organized things was very straightforward and very easy to find. And then in the mid to late nineties, before I got there, they had cataloged everything in the database. And I remember Dick kind of laughingly said, "Man, the database is there," but you know, Dick never turned it on once because it was so easy to find anything that you didn't have to be a Deadhead, you didn't have to do anything like that. We're talking almost thirteen or fifteen thousand unique audio recordings, and they were so incredibly easy to find. They did have these little barcodes on them, like a library code. And again, I've never had to use them. It was so incredibly well physically organized.

MAR: Do you think that Dick listened to every case in the collection, or no?

DL: No. One of the things I did learn from Dick, amongst many things, was Dick would put a lot of work into finding shows for release by listening to all of the shows from, let's say, a given tour. And then, first of all, seeing if there was a show worthy of release from that tour, and if there was, finding the best one. And that's why something like the Hartford '83 show got picked. It's a great show. But Dick listened to every show from that tour and he wanted to get something out with a "Scarlet/Fire," and that fit the bill. So there were a lot of examples of that. Honestly, I couldn't tell you if he listened to everything. I know he listened to the Dead as much or more than anybody I've ever met.

MAR: What was the difference between the first and the second vault? Did you have any input in that?

DL: Yeah, I helped design it, for sure. Because what happened was we were in a huge building in Novato, California, and then the Grateful Dead sold that building, to Marin Mountain Bikes, of all companies, which is very cool. Then they leased back a portion of it, and the portion they leased back was the studio. And so, what we then did is we ended up building a vault within the studio that was much smaller, probably closer to twenty-by-thirty-feet, and that meant we had to get rid of the bulk of the solo material. And I don't mean "get rid of"—I mean the band members had to take responsibility for that and put it in their own archives. So Mickey built an archive on his property; Bobby's went to a storage facility; the Garcia estate [took his material]; Billy didn't have too much. [Then] in 2006, I went down to LA, and part of the deal with Rhino was that they would then take care of the tapes. And they have a magnificent facility, and the tapes ended up going to live in the greater Warner Music Group facility.

The vault, Novato
Photo: Susana Millman

The vault, San Rafael
Photo: Susana Millman

DEAD AIR: D. Healy proposes that we provide quality tapes of live material to NPR type radio stations for a weekly syndicated radio program. Will consult with Bruce and Hal re legal aspects. More at next meeting.

David Gans

March 13–14, 2020

MAR: OK, so in going to the archive last week, I went through some business minutes and, in October of 1984, basically Dan Healy starts to mention a desire to organize a syndicated radio program with Grateful Dead live concerts being the heart of it, and I was wondering if that correlated with the *Dead Hour* [radio show] that existed already?

DG: Wow. I have no idea. No, KFOG started doing *The Grateful Dead Hour*. In November of '84, KFOG started doing a strip of specialty shows at ten o'clock on weeknights. There was a jazz show, a new age show, a reggae show, and I forget what the fifth one was—but one of them was the KFOG *Deadhead Hour*. They started that in November, so if Healy was talking up—I don't know, I have no idea about any of that because I didn't know Dan Healy had been talking about doing a radio show. It's interesting that that's the case, because it might explain some of the behavior that took place down the line.

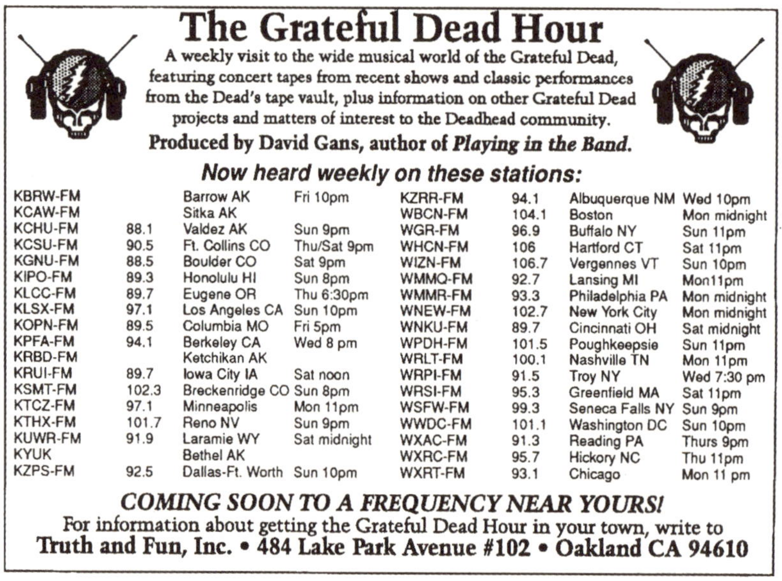

In February of '85, I went to KFOG and appeared as a guest on their show. My first book, *Playing in the Band*, was about to be published, so I went as a guest on the KFOG *Deadhead Hour* to talk about my book and talk about Grateful Dead music and stuff. And I had a really good time putting together some material for them, and the guy who was hosting the show was seriously overworked—he was the morning drive DJ and he had another show and stuff, and he was into the Dead, but he wasn't really into it the way I was. And so me and a couple of other local guys were providing him with tapes and stuff, but the program director of the station saw that I was putting out a book about the Dead and stuff, so he encouraged me to continue helping with the show. And sometime—I don't remember exactly when, but sometime after that—the station asked me to take responsibility for the program, which I was happy to do because I was really into it. I had a tape collection, and I was friendly with the band members and stuff, and they opened up the vault and let me in to get tapes out and stuff. So I became the host of that show sometime in '86 I guess, and started getting calls from other radio stations. WHCN asked if they could carry it, a classic rock station in San Diego, and then WNEW asked. So it became an opportunity without any real impulse from me; I just was doing it for the fun of it locally, and then the demand came into existence for the show. And so, the next thing I know, I'm hosting a nationally syndicated radio show where I had permission from the Dead. Somewhere in those [business] minutes is a visit that I made to the band under the auspices of manager Jon McIntire to secure permission to do this, and everybody said, "Fine. We trust you, go for it. Do it."

I started doing [the show] at KFOG in '85. It started going national sometime in '86, and I built my own network of sending tapes out to stations through 1988, and then started getting offers from syndicators to distribute the show. I talked to several of them, and got a really, really good offer from MJI Broadcasting, went to the Grateful Dead and said, "We could do this. What do you think?" And they said yes. They required me to incorporate in order to enter into this contract. I signed a contract and the Grateful Dead signed a contract with MJI for us to do a syndicated show. That's when the name of the show changed from *Deadhead Hour* to *Grateful Dead Hour*. I did a year of syndication with MJI, where

Dialing For Deadheads

One doesn't have to go to every Grateful Dead concert to keep up on the group and their music. For those who prefer to tape the group in the comfort of their own living rooms, there's a radio show to suit the occasion, and for those who want to keep in touch with each other via computer, there's a hackers' bulletin board set up for that purpose. Both are the handiwork of writer and editor David Gans, author of *Playing in the Band: An Oral and Visual Portrait of the Grateful Dead*.

The Deadhead Hour radio show, hosted by Gans, is an audio kaleidoscope of sorts, featuring a mixture of high-quality concert tapes, interviews with band members and associated figures, an eclectic sampling of The Dead's source music, up-to-date concert information and other news, and Gans' offbeat sound montages.

Originated by San Francisco's KFOG in 1984, the weekly program, not surprisingly, found a waiting audience on The Dead's home turf. Gans, music editor at *Mix* magazine and a 15-year veteran of Dead concerts, took the reins a year later. Today, in addition to its home station, the show can be found on WMMR in Philadelphia and WNEW in New York.

Though he has a vast and varied collection of concert tapes as well as permission to use material from The Dead's own vaults, Gans is not interested in trying to "fake" a Grateful Dead concert on the air. Rather, he uses the hour to offer a kind of community resource to Deadheads, aware that the Dead scene isn't just the music.

Like Dead concerts themselves, no two *Deadhead Hour* programs are ever alike. Shows in the past year have ranged from an evening with bassist Phil Lesh commenting on Charles Ives' Fourth Symphony, a piece he describes as having a major influence on The Dead's early musical philosophy, to *Prairie Home Companion*'s Garrison Keillor performing acoustic versions of Dead tunes with his band, The Wigglers, to a night of The Dead's versions of Bob Dylan songs. Ultimately, Gans hopes to deliver the program digitally via satellite.

In addition to his role as radio producer, Gans is the cofounder and online editor of the Grateful Dead Conference on a computer network called The WELL. Essentially a hackers' bulletin board, the Conference is a social forum where Deadheads, via computer modems, can wax lyrical, statistical, or otherwise about the band. In so doing, they conduct long-running conversations on a host of related topics and form friendships with people they've never seen.

Both *The Deadhead Hour* and the Grateful Dead Conference serve a uniquely interactive community, one not likely to fade away. *M.N.*

(*Editor's Note:* Radio stations and individuals interested in *The Deadhead Hour* can contact David Gans at 484 Lake Park Ave., Suite 102, Oakland, Cal. 94610. Those interested in the Grateful Dead Conference can call The WELL at 415-332-4335.)

Voice of KFOG's *Deadhead Hour*, David Gans has been going to Dead concerts for more than 15 years.

Audio vol. 72, #1, January 1988

they pressed it onto vinyl records with advertisements embedded, and sent it out to radio stations. That was from Labor Day '88 to Labor Day '89.

It was interesting who advertised on the show: Greyhound and the Army recruiting. Anyway, at the end of that year, the syndicator and I could not come to terms for a second year, so I took the show back from them and started distributing it myself. The Grateful Dead said, "That's fine." They allowed me to continue doing the show, and that's when I began the migration from commercial radio more toward public radio and community radio stations. And that's how it's been ever since. Starting in the fall of 1989, I've distributed the show myself, and have basically been a one-man operation ever since. Doing it, producing it, and handling all the distribution and stuff myself.

Well, I became a Deadhead in 1972. I went to my first show in March, then I went to four more in August, and I was up and running. I was born in Los Angeles and grew up in the San Francisco Bay Area since 1966, then I was living in San Jose, California, when I saw my first Dead show. I moved to Berkeley in 1973 and met up with a bunch of other Deadheads, and I started playing music with Deadheads and going to more shows and stuff. In '74, one of the guys I was in a band with, Al Feldstein, we went to see the Dead at Cow Palace in March—that show called the "Sound Test," where they debuted the Wall of Sound. And a couple weeks later, my buddy Al had a tape of the show, and we sat in his apartment and listened to the concert again, and it was like, "Wow. That's great. Let's do that again." So I started connecting with other people who had tapes and stuff. So I was off and running and started collecting Grateful Dead tapes. And I was a musician, so I was learning from this music, and I was writing my own music and I was playing music with people who loved that kind of music and stuff. I just sort of got deeply into it.

And then in '76, I started writing for a music magazine called *BAM* here in the Bay Area—it was a biweekly free music magazine, and I started freelancing for them and then joined the staff as a contributor, and I wrote about all kinds of music and I interviewed Leo Fender and the Doobie Brothers and Joe Walsh and people like that, but my favorite topic, of course, was the Dead. They had a regular feature called Dead Ahead, keeping track of what was going on in that world, and they put me in charge of that column. So that led me to go visit the Grateful Dead office, and start making friends with people over there and getting information directly from the source. And because I was writing for the magazine, I started doing interviews: I interviewed Bobby in LA in 1977, and then Robert Hunter in November of '77. So I started becoming friends with people in that world. I interviewed Phil Lesh in '81, and that led to having a friendship with him and becoming sort of a protégé of his. Bobby and Phil were both my advocates in the Grateful Dead organization and they supported my doing all this stuff.

When the radio thing came up, I had relationships already with people in the band, I had done a lot of journalism and published articles about them, so they knew that I was a musician and that I understood what they were doing in a way that could be useful to them—that I was a journalist who could help the world understand what they were doing and sort of bust the myths of "stupid hippies," or whatever. And so I became a colleague as well as a fan and had the support, somewhat—everything with the Grateful Dead was complicated, and whoever was supporting you, there was somebody else over there fucking with you; it was just always the way in that world. And, in fact, it's interesting that you say Dan Healy was proposing a radio show in November of '84, because it sort of helps me understand why he wasn't particularly supportive of my efforts.

Grateful Dead band meeting minutes

11/8/84

> DEAD AIR: D. Healy would like to proceed with plans for a taped syndicated radio program to start next year. It would be available to any radio station wanting to participate; stations would cover cost of tape, shipping, etc. P. Lesh and M. Hart would like to help work on this project. D. Rifkin feels we should not exclude audience tapes, but selection and all other details would have to be coordinated through us; perhaps D. McNally and D. Latvala could spend a few hours per week on this aspect of the project.

11/30/84

> DEAD AIR: D. Healy is preparing twelve radio shows that can be used in one or two hour formats; these programs will be high quality tapes available to radio stations for a nominal fee to cover costs of tape, shipping, etc. Healy will layout a brochure; proper release forms will have to drawn up and executed by stations wishing to subscribe to service; legalities will have to be carefully worked out. Hal mentioned that we could make use of these programs for our own commercial messages--info on dates, merchandising, etc. Inserts with TICKET MAILORDERS is another advertising media that could be better utilized.

2/1/85

> Re KFOG's use of audience tapes for Dead Head Hour, J. Cutler feels we should pull tapes because of poor quality. We should set up standards of quality control; perhaps Dick Latvala could be involved in this. The show is Dead Head hour, however, not Grateful Dead hour--so public is aware that these are amature audience tapes.

MAR: So on October 25, he mentions that. He mentions it again on November 8 and on November 30, and then on February 1, 1985, actually, John Cutler makes a comment about pulling the tapes from *Dead Hour* because of the poor quality of the recordings he's hearing. So I guess kind of a quality control.

DG: In fact, that was one of the things in my dealings with [John Cutler]—because I had good quality tapes, and one of the other guys that was providing material didn't, and I think they gave me the gig because I was a musician and I was curating it knowledgeably rather than just being a fan playing tapes and stuff. But again: they gave me access to the vault once I started doing the show in '85, but before that, I was just a regular freak, meeting people and collecting tapes. At *BAM* magazine, one of the staff photographers was Ed Perlstein, who you should look up. He's an amazing photographer.

MAR: I feel like Ed's also in the archives with a letter.

DG: I'm sure he is. He was involved with the Grateful Dead at that time. And I can put you in touch with Ed, he lives in Petaluma, California, and he's retired. He's a wonderful guy. Ed introduced me to tapers—Bob Menke in particular—but he also had a great collection of tapes himself, so he was happy to let me copy tapes from him. So I was collecting tapes in the mid-seventies, just like anybody else. I didn't really do much taping of shows myself, because I didn't have the gear. I wasn't obsessed with it on that level, and I didn't want to miss the show in order to get a recording of it. There was that thing . . . it took a special mentality. And in fact, when you listen to the interviews that I [did with tapers], Bob Wagner says one of the most wonderful things. I asked him about that, I said, "How is it that you could enjoy the show while you're having to hold perfectly still and all this stuff?" And there's just a great quote in there: he goes, "Well, I managed to dance anyway." And I just loved that. But he could somehow dance and hold the microphones at the same time.

2/26/8

> DEADHEAD HOUR: David Gans and Bonnie Simmons at KFOG have been putting together shows of old material combined with anecdotes; Mickey did one show. Also suggested for involvement were Michael Dung, Lou Timbakas, Dick Latvala. Dick will have access to the vault under J. Cutler's supervision. Need to determine vault policy and set up review committee of several band members.

MAR: So in terms of getting access to the vault eventually, could you tell me when that was, or what that conversation was like?

DG: It probably would've been some time in the spring of '85, and they just said, "Willy Legate will let you in." Willy was the sort of caretaker of Club Front, and he just opened the vault and let me in. Nobody was keeping an eye on me or anything—they just trusted me to get some stuff out and do something constructive with it. I think right around that time was when they hired Dick. The thing about letting Dick in was that Dick wanted to see that things were organized and preserved and cataloged and stuff. That all came about because Phil Lesh overheard Dick raving to Eileen Law in the office one day about Primal Dead [recordings], and Phil said, "What are you talking about?" And Dick said, "Well, let me play you some stuff. And I hope these things are being protected and taken care of." And that led to them hiring Dick to become the archivist and organize and catalog stuff. So it was really a beautiful case of a guy opening up a niche for himself because he cared so deeply about it, and they said, "OK, well, do it."

4/17/85

> Per W. Legate, Dick Latvala's services have been invaluable. Suggests that Dick keep track of his hours and be paid at a rate of $10/hour. Approved.

[Legate] wasn't an archivist or anything. He was a very interesting guy, he was both the resident philosopher and the janitor in that building. It was kind of a joke in a way, but he was known for writing these big, long, deep, complicated letters and stuff, and he went all the way back to the Palo Alto days with those guys. I didn't spend much time with him, didn't have a lot of conversations with him—he just let me into the vault and left me alone. Once Dick was hired, everything got easier, because he and I were friends and he supported me putting the stuff out. John Cutler was not in favor of letting random strangers in to get materials out of the vault, and he wasn't particularly in favor of giving music away for free on the radio. But the people in the organization and the band said, "Well, we want him to do this, so let him do it."

MAR: What did the vault look like when you first encountered it? Was it just random boxes?

DG: No, everything was on shelves in order. I don't know if *everything* was on shelves in order—it was upstairs at Club Front, in a not-particularly-secured room, and later they put it into really a proper vault with atmosphere control and fire protections and stuff, but originally it was just a room upstairs with a lot of shelves in it. And there was a lot of stuff organized on shelves in order, and there were a lot of boxes of stuff that weren't shelved, and I don't know anything about what was in the boxes.

MAR: Would you try to find recordings that weren't traded often to play on the radio?

DG: Yeah, of course. When I went into the vault, I was trying to get things out that weren't already available. But here's the thing: there was always the tension between the music and the collector bullshit. There were people that were like, "How dare you play something I've already heard?" And it's like, "Well, fuck you man, I'm playing the music, not fattening your tape collection." There was a certain amount of that kind of thing. But mostly, I just celebrated the music, and promoted the music, and tried to bring people stuff that they hadn't heard before. I did play things that were already available, because it was great music. I was happy to give people stuff they hadn't heard before, but I wasn't there to suit the needs and the desires of the tapers.

Every once in a while, I'd run into somebody who had something I wanted to play on the radio and they would demand that I trade them something, but it wasn't mine to give. So there was this certain amount of tension between the tapers who felt entitled to everything, and my relationship with the band, which was that I was protecting their interests as well as promoting them—but that I wasn't there to funnel tapes to collectors. And how ironic it was that after Dick Latvala died, many years later, it turned out he had been giving stuff away to people secretly, and essentially gave away the whole vault. Which was a profoundly lame thing for him to have done, despite the fact that it makes him a hero among thousands and thousands of people, right? He essentially destroyed the scarcity value of the Grateful Dead's vault, by giving it away to traders who later didn't respect the embargo.

MAR: Once Dick entered the organization by way of organizing the vault, were you doing more interacting with him than Willy Legate?

DG: Yeah. When Dick became the vault archivist, he became my primary contact. It was great. Because the road crew and everybody were such dicks about everything, we usually waited until the band went on the road. And I would bring all my equipment over, we would spend a day in the vault making copies of things—because it was hard to do, in the sense that various people didn't like what we were doing, so they intimidated Dick and gave him a hard time for helping me and all this other stupid bullshit. But when the band went on the road, Dick and I would set up our stuff in there, and we would get three or four different things copying, so I could collect a bunch of stuff in a short time, and then we would just get high and hang out and listen to music. We'd listen. We had conversations. We loved this music, and we talked about it together.

AN INTERVIEW WITH

DICK LATVALA

KEEPER OF THE VAULT

Interview by David Gans

The following is a transcript of an interview with Grateful Dead vault archivist Dick Latvala, which took place at my studio on October 5, 1993. Latvala is the man who chose the material for Dick's Picks Vol. 1, released late last year by Grateful Dead Mercantile in an experimental, CD-only, mail-order-only plan aimed at the most dedicated Grateful Dead fans. Portions of this conversation aired on the Grateful Dead Hour. - D.G.

Gans: I first heard from you in 1977. I was writing a Grateful Dead column for BAM magazine and you were living in Hawaii, and you sent me a letter.

Latvala: Yes. And it probably had to do with wanting information about the Grateful Dead, or wanting tapes or wanting contact because I lived over there for - well, I discovered that live tapes existed around 1974 when I was living in Hawaii, so once that happened, that's the only thing that became important to me: getting the tapes, finding people who made them, and collecting them, so that's all I did from '74 through the present time, really, is collect and listen to Grateful Dead tapes. So when we met in '77 - I can't remember the specifics but it must have been I wanted tapes.

Gans: How did you get turned on to taping?

Latvala: In late '74 I discovered that tapes existed and I started writing people from Hawaii, you know, collecting a few tapes and then writing someone else and getting to know a few more people and just trying to get to the real core, the hardcore tapers.

Gans: What was the value of having all those different tapes?

Latvala: I remember when some bootleg record came out around 1970, it had another version of Casey Jones, and I remember thinking, gosh, I want to hear them all. You never know when you're going to have an unreal version done of any song, so from the very beginning it became like I want to be at every show. Of course, that became very unrealistic the older I got. I didn't go on tour ever, but I wanted tapes of every show, so that's what I pursued.

Gans: It seems to me that in those days there would be concerts that you'd get on tape and you'd go "not much happening on that one," and maybe you'd record over that one. What do you suppose the Dead's batting average was in the early to mid-'70s?

Latvala: I kept them all. I wanted every one, and I saw value in each. I have books, you know, outlines of each date, with stars by each song and all that, but the more I got into it, I became a little more discriminating and realized that some shows weren't so good. I was, as I said, pretty naive. I just thought every show was the greatest thing I ever experienced for a very long time. It's only been in the last ten years or so I've not been screaming after a show with excitement. You know, I mean there are some terrible shows, and the more I've listened and the more I've educated myself -- through the help of some brilliant people I work with -- I mean educated myself sonically, being able to understand the music, not just the emotional message, but I've realized there aren't so many great shows. It's not as vast a quantity of great material as I thought. So what I have done is erase most of my tapes at home. I have my own collection, you know.

Dick Latvala interviewed by David Gans in *Unbroken Chain* #47, March 1994

Gans: Who was Kidd?

Latvala: Bill Candalario. He's one of the roadies and one of the prime players at Grateful Dead Merchandising. He offered me a backstage pass and I ended up taking him up on it. That's a real long story. I ended up on that rock behind there for my first time backstage and it was a powerful moment. It changed me forever, you know. From then on, I started meeting people. Gradually, over the next five years, I got to know a lot of people, was always able to go backstage and get passes or things like that, and then one day I was up in Eileen's office [Eileen Law, who is the head secretary of the Deadheads organization] and I was telling her I had these tapes. I called it "primal Dead." I was telling Eileen, "I want you to hear this" and I was explaining what primal Dead is, you know, and that's where it's as good as it gets. This is some great stuff. And I didn't know that Phil [Lesh] was standing behind me in the doorway listening to me tell Eileen this. He popped in, and I had the nerve -- I don't know how I summoned it up, but I said, "Hey, Phil, sit down here, I want you to listen to this stuff." I put on something like 10/12/68 Avalon Ballroom, just an incredible *Anthem* jam. He was so enthralled with it, he ended up listening to over three hours of the primal Dead tapes I had put together for someone else, you know. Even Eileen had to close the office and Phil sat there, and I kept telling Phil, I said, "Is someone taking care of these tapes? I mean, this is really important stuff. I just really hope someone's taking care of these tapes." I wasn't saying it as though I wanted a job doing it. I was just really concerned that someone was, you know. And the next day I found out I had a job. So I have always interpreted it that he felt that I really cared about the tapes and they needed someone that really cared about them to make sure that they stayed in their proper places and were organized and all that. So that's how I got hired, and that was in 1985. My first chore, or goal, or job, was to go through the tapes and write in logbooks what was actually on the tapes. A lot of the boxes weren't labeled properly, and in many cases even the years were wrong.

Gans: So your job was to listen to every tape in the Grateful Dead vault?

Latvala: Not listen to every tape, but to go through and see which ones had anything on the box and then also check the ones that didn't and find out what was on the boxes and label the boxes and put them in a logbooks. So it was in a sense to start going through them all, but, you know, that's a never-ending job so it was just something I was doing for many years at my leisure, besides doing other things at the studio.

Gans: And you had your own annotated list of what was on your own tapes as a great starting place for going into the main collection.

Latvala: Right, right. I assumed that the band members knew that I was a hard-core tape collector. I had like 900 reels at home that are all old audience tapes and hard to listen to... But I took it as I was to listen to the tapes and see what was on them and I was told not to listen to the whole tape because I'd be spending all my life in there, but just see what songs are on them. But of course, being a freak about it, I certainly perused shows as I had the inclination. It's like a kid in a candy store to the max.

Gans: This is obviously the highest moment of your calling.

Latvala: Yes, and it's very special because that's the material I really like the most - the stuff that's on two-track - because that was in the era from '69 through '78 or '79, you know, before digital, and I like that era the best. The way Dick's Picks started was, in the beginning of 1993, Kidd asked me to come up with the best three shows on two-track, in case he could float this idea by the band. And so that's how this started. It was Kidd's idea. I put together some shows, and then there was a long period of waiting. You can't be too impatient.

Gans: The first set on the CD is *Here Comes Sunshine*, *Big River*, *Mississippi Halfstep*, *Weather Report Suite*, *Big Railroad Blues*, and *Playing in the Band*. Is that the entire first set?

Latvala: No. These shows are always going to be edited. This is something we probably should talk about because I was of the feeling, always try to release the whole show. I'm a tape collector, too. But when it came to these two-track tapes, when it became a reality to actually sit down and listen, there are so many inherent problems dealing with two-tracks that you have to edit it. These shows weren't recorded for the purpose of someday releasing them. They were recorded so the band could hear them afterward and hear how they performed, and Kidd's job was to not only mix the recording, but to take care of Keith's equipment. So he'd have lots of responsibility on him to do both jobs, so he'd be busy with Keith, a reel would run out, and you'd miss 10 minutes or a couple songs. There were millions of technical problems in that era, so editing them becomes a necessity. Sorry, folks, but that's the way it's going to be. They're not going to release material that has glitches in it or doesn't have one of the mics turned up high enough or something. So we're going to have some shows that have a lot of really good things in them, but the recording might have been screwed up so we can't release them.

Gans: Among the missing items from the set list, according to Deadbase, is the song Sugar Shack.

Latvala: Yes, that is missing on the master itself. It is not there. I was looking for it. It's even written on the tape box, but it wasn't recorded. I have no idea what happened there.

Gans: So unless somebody's got an audience tape out there, we'll never know.

Latvala: Yes, we'd love to hear what that was like. I'm sure it was only a second or two. But anyway, this first set is edited. And it became apparent to me and John and Cutler and Jeffrey Norman, who were working on this, that each CD should have a life of its own. This isn't an attempt to recapture the total picture or the whole show. We tried to make disc one have the feel of a first set, but Weather Report is actually from the second set.

Gans: So you rearranged a few things to give it sort of the contour of a first set even though it's not, strictly speaking.

Latvala: Right. It's not going to ever be literal just like it happened in the show itself. You can check Deadbase or your audience tapes for those things.

Gans: Backstage in 1978 I saw Betty [Cantor] off to one side making a separate mix. She had a split from the stage microphones and she was making a separate mix just for tapes. And I assume that somewhere around 1979 she stopped doing that, and therefore the only tapes that were being made were being made out in the sound booth.

In my own poking around the vault, I've noticed that '79, '80 and '81 are pretty much only represented on cassette.
Latvala: That's right. I don't know what happened to those tapes, if they were recorded or not, or were lost, or what's happened to them. That period is missing, yes.

Gans: And then Dan Healy started recording everything on PCM digital in...
Latvala: '82. So from late '82 on, things are relatively intact.

Gans: Are you ever going to be looking at that stuff for possible release?
Latvala: I don't know. I think there is a problem with that in terms of the contract with Arista Records. We can't release anything after our contract started with them, which was in '77. That's another reason why we can't use stuff after that.

Gans: When the subject of vault releases is discussed out on the computer networks, there are of course a hundred thousand potential producers out there who have their own ideas of what ought to be released. There are people who [would choose] certain Red Rocks shows, Greek Theater shows and stuff. Eventually it would be nice to see a lot of stuff released.
Latvala: I think everyone's getting a lot of that stuff on your Grateful Dead Hour, aren't they?

Gans: Yeah, but I don't play whole shows. I manage to get 45 minutes of the best out there - I mean, I see the radio show as more of a magazine. It's certainly not a satisfactory downloading service for tapers, and Lord knows my irate mail proves that.
Latvala: Well, who knows what can happen? I just sort of incline towards the years '68 through '78, because I'm more familiar with that material, but who knows what's possible.

Gans: Well, they picked the right guy for the job.
Latvala: Well, thanks, David. I feel like I'm just the luckiest person on earth. I know there could be any number of you out there doing this just as well, but I happen to be the one doing it, so that's my goal: to get the great stuff out.

Illustration: Una Toibin-Hamilton

DG: Then he supported me and he helped me find good stuff, and together we would say, "Oh, what about this tour? We haven't heard much from this tour. Let's see what's on this tape." So he was just a wonderful companion for these things, because we shared this deep love of the music, and his primary interest was in getting it out into the world for more people to hear it and love it. He supported what I was doing because we both shared the same mission: we were trying to turn the world onto this music. He was great. He was wonderful to work with. He suffered a little bit from it, because the various interferers in that world always kind of wanted to make things difficult. But that's less important than the fact that we had a wonderful relationship, he was devoted to this music and to this community, and he made it possible for me to get lots and lots of great music out into the world.

MAR: Did you ever have any contact with any of the audio cassette companies like Maxell, TDK, Denon, etc?

DG: Through Terrapin Tapes in Connecticut. Terrapin Tapes became my sponsor, and I don't remember—I was sponsored by Maxell at some point, but I don't remember how it happened. There were lots of other radio shows, by the way; we were not the first one by any stretch. There was a radio show in Chicago already, Los Angeles, KPFK in Los Angeles had one which I think was first called *Thursday Lunch*, and then also WBAI had one called *Morning Dew* that had been going on since long before KFOG started theirs. So we were not the first people to do Grateful Dead on the radio by any stretch.

MAR: How do you think the radio show contributed to the rise of the taping phenomenon?

DG: The taping phenomenon was unrelated to the radio stuff that had been going on since the sixties and seventies. It had picked up steam in the eighties, when more and more people were doing it. Just tape trading, [the] tape collecting thing caught on on its own, and more and more people wanted to do it and the number of people doing it became problematic for the band and for other fans. Dan Healy talked about the tapers dicking around with other people at the show, where they'd, like, try and kick people out of their seats because they wanted to put their mics up in the optimum spot, and shushing people and all this other stuff. So [the organization] decided to acknowledge reality by officially allowing the tapers, but restricting them to a specific spot so they wouldn't bother the other customers. Now, of course, they didn't always put them in optimal spots, and very often the taping section was not in a great place to be recording [from]. So lots of the guys who really wanted great recordings snuck their stuff out, and did it in front of the board anyway.

[The creation of the tapers section] was one of those great things where the Grateful Dead gets credit for this visionary movement but it was just, like . . . nobody wanted to be a cop.

Jerry, and a lot of people on the band side, thought it was a good thing; Phil recognized that this was viral marketing before that term existed. This was a way of formalizing something that had been happening informally, and without authorization, for years.

MAR: Out of all the members of the band, do you think Phil took more of an interest in the documentation of the band itself and the subculture?

DG: I don't know. I didn't have a personal relationship with Jerry on the same level, but he was always very encouraging to me personally, and always recognized that I was doing something that served the music. Bobby was also very supportive of me because I was promoting him and writing articles about his bands and stuff like that. Mickey also was very friendly with the press and recognized that people like me were helping them, so he was pretty forthcoming. So I don't think Phil was necessarily more so than the others—he's just the one I had more of a personal connection with, and he was very specifically supportive of me in dealing with the bureaucracy over there.

Mickey always was very radio-friendly, and hired me to produce specials for him for Sirius XM over the last eight or ten years. And Mickey always had a project, so I went to his house or studio any number of times and did interviews with him and stuff. So he was constantly on the air. Bobby made his music available. Phil and Friends, for some reason, didn't want to broadcast their stuff, so I never got into the habit of broadcasting Phil's material, but I've always had access to Bob stuff and Grateful Dead stuff. So the radio show never ever ran out of material or came close to running out of material, because there was an immense archive of existing stuff, and new things coming in. And the other wonderful phenomenon in the last five or six years, maybe more, is that more and more musicians from elsewhere have begun to acknowledge that the Grateful Dead were influences. I would not have expected in 1995 that I would still be doing the radio show twenty-five years later, and that I would be facing a gigantic pile of cool new takes on Grateful Dead music.

A Conversation With Dan Healy

By Barry Barnes

The following interview with Grateful Dead Sound Engineer, Dan Healy, was conducted by Barry Barnes of Lanexa, Kansas. It took place on June 25, 1991, prior to the second night's Bonner Springs show. It was arranged by Ted Carleton for use in conjunction with the premiere of David Gan's Grateful Dead Hour on KKFI-FM, Kansas City Community Radio.

Dan Healy at RFK 6/14/91 *Eric Soble*

BB: The most recent question that comes to mind is Videotaping versus Audiotaping. Videotaping is not allowed -I mean that's the rules and that's fine with me, but I'm just curious as to why.

DH: I think that the main point is that people videotape with the intent to only get close-ups. You see the tapers and the rest of the audience usually clash because of all of the obvious reasons. So, I think that's the main reason. I don't really feel that anybody feels that's there's a basic philosophical difference between audiotaping and videotaping.

BB: So it's the same as in the old days when the tapers were always huddled down there in front?

DH: Well now they're huddled in the taper's section.

BB: I know, but at least they've been segregated.

DH: The thing is, too many times too many people became upset and disgruntled that they've been thrown out or physically molested by tapers who felt that they've deserved that space and stuff. It got to be real disgusting - you know the typical example would be a 14-year-old kid and his girlfriend would come to the booth in tears saying "Me and my girlfriend stood in line for three hours in the snow to get tickets and when we got to our seats these guys just threw us out saying that they needed that seat to tape." It's rude and inconsiderate. It's really too bad because the rules really resulted from, on the whole, the very things that are most Anti-Grateful Dead, which is violating other people's space, general rudeness and lack of consideration for fellow humans.

BB: This is an issue that a lot of us deal with every time we're at a show. For example, how do I ask this person not to yell, even though I want them to have a good time? I don't want them to yell in my ear or hit me as he's dancing wildly and crazily, which I like to do too.

DH: The main thing is that, and this probably sounds dumb, but you want to do unto as you'd have others do unto you. The general basic rules of consideration are where its at. Coming to a Grateful Dead show doesn't mean you're free from either the law of the state or the law of humanity. In fact, this is a good place to come and demonstrate consideration and stuff. Its a good place to practice and it's one of the few strong holds that tries as hard as it can to not mandate rules and form and protocol. As long as everybody can be cool, you can do anything you want.

BB: What's your feeling this summer tour, how's it shaping up in those terms?

DH: The message is finally beginning to get across. There weren't any large scenes or incidents anywhere on this tour. I think that the word is finally starting to get around... "Hey if you're a Deadhead, are you causing the world to not like Deadheads or are you doing your part to cause the world to like Deadheads?" And that's really what it comes down to. Each and every individual in the audience is solely responsible for the collective of all of us and whether or not we are welcome in communities. We all know who we are down inside, but we have to portray that picture outside as well as inside, so that others can see it too. And its not that hard! Get in a good mood and be a nice person. That's all you gotta do!

BB: It felt really good in the crowd last night.

DH: Yeah, that's where I live. I'm sort of the audience's representative to the band and the band's representative to the audience in a strange way. I love it. I wouldn't trade it for anything in the world. Its a dream come true for me, for anybody for that matter. I've also had an opportunity over the years to cultivate and develop the world's finest sound system. I have extreme undivided, unsplintered support from the band, in terms of budgets and stuff like that. I obviously haven't always been successful, there have been times when we've spent large amounts of money to try an idea and I've fallen right on my face. All they did was pick me up and "say go for it again."

Dan Healy interviewed by Barry Barnes in *Unbroken Chain* vol. 6, #3, August 1991

JERRY MOORE INTERVIEWED BY DAVID GANS
1/19/2008

David Gans: Now, taping wasn't allowed. In those days, you had to sneak your stuff in and you had to keep an eye out for the ushers and sometimes the road crew, right?

Jerry Moore: Yeah, you had to keep an eye out for everybody because even the environment itself, it's unpredictable. Random audience members could do some really erratic things, even without active opposition. There's this myth--and, I mean God bless them, it's not a total myth--that the Grateful Dead encouraged taping. This is a crock of hooey, because they didn't. They actually didn't. They totally did not encourage taping, at least not in the early days. They tried their best to stop it. They couldn't stop it. Basically, they lost the war. They struck a compromise deal somewhere down the line, and then like the party line--I guess it's embarrassing to say, "Oh, well. We tried to stop it, but we couldn't do it. We surrendered." The party line changed over the years to, "Yeah, we encouraged it. Yeah, yeah. We're all for it." It actually was a great deal for them; they should have been all for it earlier, because I think it's probably what made them what they were. I mean, definitely the music made them what they were and that whole other scene made them what they were. But what blew the thing into mammoth proportions was all the tapers.

David Gans: That's very true, very true. Because when I was a young Deadhead in the early seventies, I went and saw the Dead at the Cow Palace in March of 1974, and a week later, my buddy Feldstein had a reel of that show.

Jerry Moore: Those guys would send reels out, so I was hearing stuff from the summer of '74 tour before the tour was over. We formed this sort of network and it was very small at the beginning. There was me and about a half a dozen other people. There was a guy that predates me or you, Marty Weinberg--who, as it turned out, I knew his kid brother--but he was one of the first tapers. Not that that's why I got into taping, but there really weren't many of us. We were a brand-new thing. At first it was a couple of us. Suddenly, there were a dozen of us, then a couple hundred of us, and then there were a couple thousand of us. Then, forget it.

David Gans: But you started, what was it called? The Free Underground Tape Exchange? Weren't you one of those guys that had little business cards made up?

Jerry Moore: Yeah, yeah. The business cards weren't really my thing. I knew several people that were really hot on the business card idea, and I went along with it. It seemed a little silly to me, but yeah, my name was on some of those business cards.

David Gans: But the point of it was to build a trading network.

Jerry Moore: Absolutely, and I think it did. It worked very well. [It] was a great way of deepening everybody's relationship with the music and turning new people onto it.

David Gans: Tell me a couple of good stories about smuggling your gear.

Jerry Moore: Well, I used to do things like wrap it up. I'd package it, address it to myself. Usually, I went with the blatant, in-plain-sight thing. People look for things that people are trying to hide. Misdirection--you'd try and send people through and jam up the exit, jam up the aisles, and [you'd] look nonchalant while they were busy with other people. It usually worked out one way or another. There's a funny moment on one of my Miami tapes where an usher is coming along and showing people their seats and he asks, "What's that?" I said, "A tape recorder." He said, "A tape recorder?" He said, "You can do that?" I said, "Yeah." It's true. There's another funny moment on my Barton Hall tape: you can't hear it on the tape, but I remember it clearly. It's why I drew a picture of the Eiffel Tower [for] my cover art. Somebody came along, obviously somewhat the worse for chemicals, and said, "Wow. The Eiffel Tower. How'd you get that in here?"

David Gans: What was he looking at?

Jerry Moore: My tripod.

Phil Lesh interviewed by Blair Jackson in Dupree's Diamond News #28, Spring 1994

What's been your level of involvement with* Dick's Picks*?
None really, except that I had them cut a bass solo I didn't like. I think I played two bass solos during that period, and one was okay and the other wasn't, and this is the one that wasn't. It was *not* usable. There was absolutely nothing to it; nothing happened in it. It was just a bunch of strumming. The other I remember being much more interesting, though I haven't heard it in a long time.

How do you feel about the whole archival end of the Dead trip?
I love it. We're hoping to get some kind of idea of the response we can get on these releases by using only mail order. I don't have the latest figures, but I think *[Dick's Picks]* has done pretty well. It sold 20,000 in one month and I know the people in GD Merchandising were very happy about that. I assume that's a good rate for mail order.

Is it true that you were the one who essentially nixed the last pick for the* From the Vault *series [2/19/71, Capitol Theater, Port Chester, NY]?
Yes. I didn't care for the performance. Somebody else had chosen it; in fact Dick [Latvala] wasn't even that involved with that choice. It was a situation where it was desired that it be a multitrack, and it was one of the multitracks from that period we'd already mined for the *Skull & Roses* album. So aside from the fact that that performance wasn't that good, we had already been through it years ago and gotten what we could out of it then. I don't recall if we actually used anything from that performance on the record. But the bottom line was the performance wasn't up to my standards.

And everyone in the band has that power over releases?
Yes, exactly.

Is it fair to say so far you've shown the most interest in the archives?
It's fair to say that I'm the only one who's listened to a lot of it, I think. Actually I don't know what it's fair to say. [Laughs] I don't know that anyone else in the band has a particular interest in making a decision about these things, so it's sort of fallen to me. Since everyone can trust me to be pretty cold about it, I think they feel safe that I won't let a sloppy performance or a lousy performance or a meaningless performance get by.

Once you excised that hideous bass solo from* Dick's Picks*, what did you think of the rest of the show.
The rest of it is amazing. In fact, I can't imagine how I managed to play such a bad bass solo in the middle of it! [Laughs]

What does the '73-'74 Grateful Dead sound like to you today?
It sounds pretty good; pretty interesting.

Of course, the fans all want to know why you don't put out more CDs, and why you don't put them out faster. And of course, they all claim to know what's great, etc. How do you deal with that level of intensity?
I ignore it. [Laughs] We'll put it out at our own speed. I'm really glad there's a demand for it out there, because that's our old age insurance in a way. We're going to keep putting it out, and personally I'm always interested in having people tell me what they think are the great shows. That's one reason Dick is involved with this — he's so deeply steeped in the shows, he gets other people's input, and he has opinions of his own as well. That's invaluable in dealing with this, because nobody in the band wants to go through and listen to all of that.

Living through some of them was probably bad enough.
Yeah, that's true. [Laughs]

Sometimes I'll run into Dick and he'll ask me, "Did that show on Thursday night really suck, or is it just me?" I'll say, "No, Dick, it was really cool — check it out!"
[Laughs] Well, sometimes they do suck.

MAR: What are your thoughts on the state of what bootlegging has become? At least in the Dead scene, or maybe jam band scene, where you're able to just download the show that you just went to that is recorded by the band.

DG: We wanted that all along. We proposed that. Dan Healy in the nineties, I remember, proposed that they would literally bring a truck—there was an outfit in Petaluma called Kaba, that made massive rack-mounted CD duplication systems and [the Dead] owned a couple of them. They used them in the studio to make copies of shows after the tour, just for band members and crew members and staff. But Dan had proposed that they would do this on tour, that you could, like, line up after the show and get a cassette of the show you just heard. It didn't happen back then, but the technology to do that became cheaper and better, and over the years, it became feasible to do. And Bob Weir and RatDog had their guys: there was an outfit called Gnomes and Hobbits. They were a couple of fans, hippies, that built this system. They recorded the show, they had high-speed CD duplicators, and you could go before the show and buy the recording, and they'd give you a wristband. So during the show, they [knew], "OK, we got forty-five orders," they would burn forty-five CDs of the first set during the break, and immediately after the second set, they would burn forty-five CDs of the second set. And the people with the wristbands would line up to get their CDs, and they would go home with the CDs. This technology wasn't practical when the Grateful Dead were still extant, but it became practical in recent years. And now it's even more practical than that, because you can just get it for download. Nugs[.net] streams everything live, and then you can buy the show and download it directly to your phone or your computer the next day.

And they do that with video streams, as well. So the technology has made all of that stuff much easier to do and to monetize. It's been my observation that the taper culture has receded quite a bit, because I think the sort of fashion of doing it might've passed a little bit. There's still a lot of people that like to record, but not nearly as many, but it may also be that the scene has broken up so much. It used to be everybody would go to the Grateful Dead show. Now it's kind of like, you go to Phil or you go to Dead and Company or you go to Widespread Panic or you go to String Cheese [Incident], or whatever. There may be as many people taping, there just isn't the thing that brings all them to one place at the same time. But I think that for a great number of people that convenience—[of] being able to buy the damn thing—serves their needs. If you're not a recording hobbyist, or you're not obsessed with the music such that you have to make a recording of it yourself, then these other options are convenient if you can afford them. So in a way the technology has kind of made taping less of an exclusive thing, and more the domain of the people that really, really love it for its own sake. And then the audiophiles—I know these guys. Some of these guys, what they want to do is make the best possible recording. Have you listened to [my interview with] the Oade brothers yet?

I heard that you recently transferred the tape archives to compact disc...
No, that's not true — what we're doing is we're gradually transferring the stuff mostly to DAT (digital audio tape), not to compact disc. We're just getting into the digital domain, just so it'll last longer. But that's a project that could take a hundred years, you know? We're not doing it in any kind of methodical way. We certainly don't have the ability to say "Get it done" — we know we can't *assign* that kind of work. It's one of those things you have to do in real time...it's tedious and it's time-consuming and it's a total bummer. We may or may not do it. It may be that we'll just take certain stuff and convert it to DAT, I don't know. Again, it's one of those things. It's a resource that in a way we're not exactly sure what to do with. We've got it all. It's all sitting there, but none of us has the heart to go through and listen to it. I certainly don't. None of us has the time, either. We're all moving ahead, so the idea of going back and looking back — it's for somebody else to do. It's not for us to do.
Have you considered maybe someday putting out an extensive anthology?
Yeah, we may anthologize stuff by slowly activating the things and putting out limited edition versions of them through our own merchandising — CDs of various performances — and see just what happens, you know? We've tossed it around for a long time, but we haven't really figured out exactly quite how to deal with it. Ideally, the thing we would do is record the shows, and after the show is over you can get a cassette of the show you just went to. We wouldn't have the tapers. We'd cut all that loose, but we would still be able to provide the music to anybody who wanted it from any given show. That's kind of our ideal, but then implementing that kind of an idea is totally out of the question. It can't be done. That's one of the reasons why we still let the people tape and so forth. It's hard to figure out exactly how to approach this stuff when you're dealing with the reality of it. I mean, where do you start? What year, say, or what performance specifically?
Well, how far back do you have recorded?
It goes back to '66, '67 somewhere. There's some stuff that's really old. Certainly not all of it is good by any means — most of it is terrible. There are some things that are pretty interesting. But it does go back pretty far.
Do you ever go back and listen to any of that stuff?
Nah. I can't do it. I only hear it in terms of what I — although I'm so far removed from most of it now, I don't have the trouble with it that I used to have. I hear what's wrong with it. I don't hear what's good about it, I hear what's wrong with it, and I listen to it and say, "God, that's terrible! It's out of tune, and the tempo's all weird," and it's just horrible. For me, it's a kind of pain. It's not something I can enjoy.

Jerry Garcia interviewed by Steve Peters in *Relix* vol. 16, #6, December 1989

Relix: Where did the idea to go into the vaults come from?

Healy: Since day one, we've tried to record as much of our shows as we possibly could. In early days, like the '60s, the tape recorder technology was not as advanced. It was before the days of portable equipment and cassettes. If you were to record something with any kind of quality, it was a big ordeal. So the tapes are somewhat sketchy, but by 1969 we were able to maintain a good quality standard collection of shows.

Some of the old stuff has fallen out from sitting on the shelves because the earlier formulas that tapes were made of, it was before the days of plastics that don't ever go away, so while it's bad for the environment it's good for tapes. But at any rate, because the old tapes are starting to get flaky, we decided that it was time to go through our entire collection of tapes and convert them to digital tapes and restore them on modern format and modern media. At the same time, there's been requests for years from our audience, from fans wanting us to pull out favorite old shows and release them. We know that this has been coming for a long time, but it's also true that the technology up until recently was such that it would have been diminishing returns to try and master some of this older material.

We're now on a monumental project because there's 80-some-odd shows a year average for 25 years, so that gives you an idea of the wad of tapes we have. We've got three rooms, and each room is about 20 x 20, and it's full to the door with tapes. It's a really ambitious task to do it, but modern technology being the whole digital format provides us with the means of retrieving the old tapes and restoring them in a much longer lasting format in such a way that the audio quality will be enhanced or at least not [degraded]. As long as we're going through the tapes and we're going to update them all, we figured while we're there doing it we can also select various shows from the past and make them available to our audience through our own merchandising at a lower price than sort of the record company/record store version of studio releases and stuff like that. The object is to get the music to our fans, while at the same time we're developing a database, and we're going through and updating all of our old tapes.

Relix: Are your tapes chronologically by date?

Healy: Pretty much. We're in the mid-'80s now, so we've gotten that far. What we're doing is, we are developing a computer database that has all the shows and each tape listed individually, various comments about the tape and notes about what formats they're on and so on and so forth. We've recently constructed a new part of our studio rehearsal complex in so far as we've built a room that is strictly for listening, editing, and dubbing tapes. It has the computer in it that's doing the database of all the tapes, but it also has other computers in it that [are] converting the analog tapes to digital. Plus, it has all the format machines of the past years that can play the various formats of the tapes because our tapes exist on every known tape format, like cassettes, multi-tracks, two tracks, even some of them are old monaural tapes and stuff like that. So this little room is like the work center where we're going through the vault, noting what we've got and retrieving it and converting it to digital stuff.

Relix: Some Deadheads have actually been collecting reel-to-reel tapes over the years, which is almost an obsolete format at this point.

Healy: We've certainly got our share of those!

Relix: They've stocked away extra equipment because they know at some point they're not going to be able to get the machines anymore.

Healy: I still have a machine from 1967 that we did *Anthem of the Sun* on. It was a machine that was a radical format not compatible with any other machines, but we built it because we wanted to have a four-channel tape recorder, which in those days was big news, but it also needed to be portable. So it's a 1/4" four-track. The tape is really strange in the terms of its format, so I packed away the machine, and now I have it. I actually have a number of machines. There was a period of time when we had three-track tapes and I saved the old three-track tape machine, too. I'm glad I did now, because I go through hell trying to play back some of these old tapes.

Relix: How far back do the archives date?

Healy: They date back to the very beginning, clear back to the Warlocks days in sketchy forms. It's fairly sketchy until about '68-'69. First of all, you have to realize that in the early days none of us realized that the Grateful Dead was going to become what it has become.

Relix: What other shows do you have in mind for release?

Healy: Well, I haven't decided. Let me just say that I'm hoping to do maybe four releases a year, plus maybe at the end of the year do, like, a 10-CD set of bits and pieces of stuff that we can sell real cheap so the idea is a bonus that's virtually free at the end of the year. Later on, ultimately, it might get down to one release a month. But those are all sketches of ideas in the future. The main goal is to get the most significant shows out, to retain the honesty in audio quality and in performance, and to make it available packaged nicely, at a much lower price than the record industry would try to sell it at, and so those are the guidelines. It also has to be done interspersed with my other Grateful Dead activities, namely live shows and stuff like that. I don't have unlimited time to spend doing it. Because of that, even four years is a fairly ambitious project, because by the time you actually get it ready to be released, there's a surprising amount of time that goes into it and a lot of effort. It's not the type of thing you're going to say, "Oh yeah, here, let's release this tape," and tomorrow it's ready to go, because while in theory it seems like that, in reality it never seems to work like that.

Relix: Since it is impossible to release the entire back collection of tapes on CD, do you foresee a time when the band might make the archives available to Deadheads directly? Let's say they send in money for a specific show.

Healy: That idea has been kicked around a lot, and I'll tell you where that idea is right now. We've just recently, as I've described to you, put together a room that is solely for listening and digitizing and working with the tapes. I think later on, one of the considerations is to maybe have a mail-order basis or something, whereby if you have a specific show in mind, you can write in and then we'll make you a CD or a tape of it. It'll be along those kind of lines.

Relix: That would be interesting!

Healy: We've definitely thought about it, it's definitely in the dialogue. I think that [it is] the type of thing that if it happens at all it has to be consistent with the whole unfolding of the larger scale picture of it. But the answer is yes, there's a good chance that that could happen in the future.

Relix: It's an interesting perspective, really. So many tapes are available anyway, but such poor quality is in circulation. How's the tapers section been working out? Do you still feel in control of it?

Healy: Well, the tapers section has been a mixed blessing since day one. My own personal philosophy, since I'm an engineer and a recordist, I'm naturally sympathetic with it. The main friction is the tapers colliding with the rest of the audience that could care less about the tapes, but are there to enjoy the show. What happens is, the tapers tend to become abusive to the rest of the audience, as they push people out of the way and set up their equipment and force people to not talk in the vicinity of their microphones. Those are all things that are really anti-Grateful Dead, and so a few years ago, before I formed the tapers section, the mandate was laid on me by the band to do something about the tapers, and it was looking like there would be no more taping because it was the type of thing that was only being allowed to happen, but was by no means a right that anybody in the audience had. So, at the last minute, somebody came up with an idea. I think it was my wife that said, "Why don't you form a tapers section?" The idea being that if all the tapers will go and be in one section, in return for that we'll sell tapers tickets at the same price for that section, and you can buy it, and if you're in that section with your ticket, you actually have rights. And the idea of that is to get everyone together and to get them out of the general dispersion of the audience whereby they were trashing the rest of the audience around them.

It's unfortunate, but life has people who can't seem to enjoy a good thing, and always have to be pushing at it, and so there's been a number of people pushing up front, which is something I don't understand because it doesn't sound good up there, anyway. But I think it's a combination of getting away with something and thumbing your nose at authority, which is kind of ridiculous in our scene, because it's not like our scene is an authoritative kind of scene.

Dan Healy interviewed by Toni A. Brown in *Relix* vol. 18, #4, August 1991

DOUG AND JIM OADE INTERVIEWED BY DAVID GANS
10/24/2007

David Gans: And when you guys started recording, it wasn't technically allowed. They didn't create the tapers section until the fall of 1984. So you were sneaking your gear in?

Doug Oade: You had to sneak your gear in; you had to hide it. Before the show, as soon as the lights went down, that's when the mic stands went up, the gear came out. And you got good at hiding your mic stand, concealing it and camouflaging it in various ways. You got good at dropping the thing quickly at the end of the set before the lights came up, because [otherwise] we'd be hassled by venue security.

Jim Oade: I do remember times, before the tapers section was established, that it was OK to bring your gear. They had it established ahead of time you can bring your gear in. They did actually allow taping prior to the advent of the tapers section.

Doug Oade: Maybe the first year before it, some venues would let you bring the gear in. You still had to sneak it into a lot of venues on the East Coast. The Carrier Dome [at Syracuse University] was supposed to be open taping, and I brought a lot of extravagant gear in road cases, fully expecting to be able to carry it in. We were told, via the Grateful Dead flyers and the like, it was open taping. I called to confirm it was open taping, but the local security chief got it in his mind that this was something he wanted to squash down, to prevent. So I couldn't get in, initially, with this gear in road cases because it was so obvious. No way to sneak it in. Talked to the guy, tried to reason with him. Pointed out how many people were in there with their gear set up, [that the] band said it was OK. He just had a hair up his butt and wasn't going to let me in. I invested the entire first set getting the gear in. I got it in for the second set.

Jim Oade: Taping the gear under women's dresses was a common way to get it in there. It was probably the funnest way to get it in.

Doug Oade: It was often a group effort for PCM gear--eighty, ninety pounds worth of gear. Pretty large boxes that comprise the recorders, about two and a half inches thick by eight inches wide by fourteen inches deep. There were two of those plus the batteries, the tapes, and then of course the microphones, cables, and the like. Very rare that an individual could do it by themselves. I did it a number of times with just two people.

Jim Oade: I carried it in a backpack. Oftentimes, [you'd] just look at the crew that was taking tickets, look at the person that seemed to be the happiest, and just--the Jedi mind trick. Just walk right in. I do remember at one show, Sean Weber-Small and Don Crandall having to create a diversion as they went in. They acted like they were fighting while I cruised in with a backpack full of PCM gear.

Doug Oade: The "bringing a birthday present to a friend at the show" trick. [Or] bathrooms, for example, that had an open window to the outside--one person goes in, and you drop all the gear. I'm sure those things aren't as easy now as it used to be, given the paranoia of modern security teams. That was often a lot of the fun. Like at Red Rocks, I remember, after the third show in '83, security guards came up to us and go, "Please tell us--it's all over with now. We just want to know how you managed to get this much gear in." Of course we didn't tell them. That was before they realized that one of their bathroom windows was adjacent to the outside. It was pretty easy to get gear into Red Rocks.

Jim Oade: I've seen people get it in with a twenty-dollar bill too, for that matter.

Doug Oade: Or hundreds, in some cases.

Jim Oade: Oftentimes you could sort of intimidate the person there. I had a mic stand and I told him it was my tent poles. Didn't have a car, I was hitchhiking and I didn't want somebody to steal my stuff. If the person didn't want to be hassled, usually they'd let you slide in. We used a variety of techniques.

Doug Oade: And then there was those who you could tell by the look on their face, clearly knew what you were doing, but approved.

DG: [The Oade brothers] have this experience and became Deadheads, and they wanted to be able to save it and share it with other people. Their motivation for doing it combined a true sense of altruism with their technical knowledge. Doug Oade is an electronic technician and stuff, so he was designing modifications for the recording devices and stuff, and selling them to other tapers. They became the go-to tapers and enablers of other tapers for this wonderful, pure, openhearted reason, but there were other guys that got into it for competitive reasons, and thought their tapes were better than the other guys', and a bunch of other bullshit like that. So like everything in the world, it takes all kinds, and there's bunches of really, really neat people doing it, and there's a bunch of people doing it for lame reasons as well. For me, I wanted to hear the music, and I wanted to hear it as clearly as possible. So I liked any clear-sounding tape. And when I got into radio, I needed to prefer the soundboard tapes, because audience tapes mush up too much on FM radio, and they don't really work very well. Only the very best and clearest of audience tapes can withstand the depredations of the FM signal chain. So I use the soundboard tapes almost exclusively on the radio, for technical reasons, and for aesthetic reasons, because it's clearer and easier to hear.

MAR: In regards to CD duplication, and getting the show after you're done witnessing the show—did Dick ever think in that direction or dream in that direction?

DG: I don't know. He was a background character, or an inside guy. I don't think he would've considered it his purview to propose such a thing, because he was surrounded by people like John Cutler and Dan Healy, who had very strong ideas. Cutler was producing the albums with the band, mixing live albums, and Healy was the live sound engineer and [was] also involved with archiving and recording. So those were the guys that would make that kind of proposal. And I don't think Dick ever would have thought it was his place to propose such a thing, and if it were, he would have discussed it with Cutler, rather than going to the band himself to promote it.

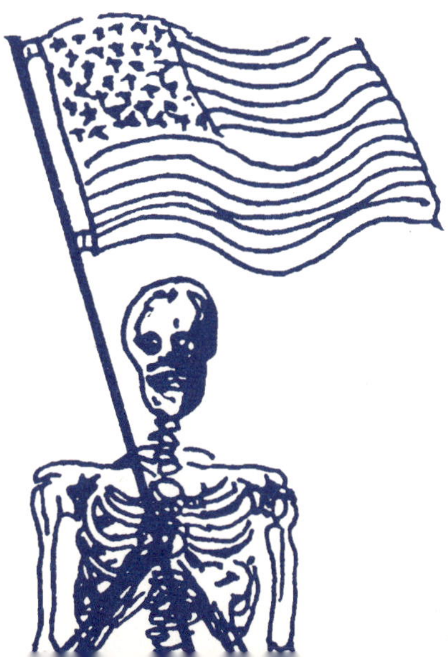

MAR: Did Dick ever mention anything about Dick's Picks to you before that conversation started?

DG: Yeah. Gary Lambert and Dick and I hatched that plot together. It sort of got hijacked from us by Kidd Candelario, who was the Grateful Dead crew guy who was running the merchandise operation. When he found out we were doing this, [Candelario] took a proposal to the band that cut me and Lambert out, and just put Dick and John Cutler in charge of it and named it after Dick. We wanted to call it Dick's Picks and it became Dick's Picks, but it became Dick's Picks without me and Lambert being part of the team, and that's all fine. Everything all worked out great in the end. All that matters, when all is said and done, is that they eventually got around to releasing stuff, and it was curated reasonably well by the combination of a fanatic but nonmusical Dick Latvala and a technically proficient John Cutler, with supervision from Phil Lesh, who I think reviewed the releases. Probably the other guys all got copies to review as well, but my memory is that Phil was the band member who most participated. So I would say that Dick's Picks was ultimately probably to be credited to those three guys: Dick, John, and Phil.

MAR: Right. I mean, going back to even 1972, with the free tape exchange, it's like [the fans] are trying to get the Dead to release their shows somehow, in some distribution system, and it took twenty years to make that a reality.

DG: Well, it was not practical to do it in the early seventies, and they also still had record deals in those days, and their record label would not have wanted them selling similar versions of the same music separately. And in those days they would have had to duplicate reels of tape, and people would've wanted to find them on vinyl. And to press and release on vinyl a concert recording, in those days, would have been prohibitively expensive. So it made no economic sense to do it in those days, regardless of what the Deadheads in *Relix* magazine are demanding. And they resolved the issue themselves by setting up the tape exchange. [The Free Underground Grateful Dead Tape Exchange] distributed the music themselves, in order to get it done in the only feasible way to do it—unofficially, illegally, and by other parties. Worked out great in the long run, didn't it?

AN INTERVIEW WITH DICK LATVALA

Since your last interview with us you've had quite a change take place as far as your ability to get Vault releases out. Why don't you tell us what happened.

A combination of factors came into play that created the circumstances. For example, "Dick's Picks" didn't get started because I thought of it. Believe me, I never would have thought of it. Kidd [Candelario] skated it past the band, and they went for it. Healy didn't care about the two-track tapes, so I had to submit any entry to a band member, Phil, who would then say yes or no — veto power. I'd give Phil things to listen to and he would try his best. He was the only band member that even wanted to put attention on it. I wasn't sure how other band members felt about the whole Vault program. In fact, I had feelings that maybe they didn't think it was a worthwhile thing, as if they were embarrassed by what their past efforts had been. After so many months of submitting things, Phil was giving me feedback that was not always based on careful analysis, like the rejection of Miami 6/23/74. Granted, it's not one of the greatest shows in Dead history, but it's one of the best in '74.

Have you gotten specific rejections or just grumblings?

It's not a matter of yes or no. It's a matter of timing. These shows will come out! I want it on record that everything everyone wants will be out there at some point when the time is right. The process has started, and it appears to be going okay. Everyone's happy with it. We've narrowed things down.

There was a board meeting, and Peter McQuaid (Head of Grateful Dead Merchandising and one of the few people ever hired outside the Family to do something) threw a bunch of bootleg [CD] boxed sets on the table. I was going to go to the meeting and say they're missing out on a wave; there are so many bootlegs out there and we gotta start competing. Peter did all that for me. I didn't have to say a word. Band members were finally looking at actual, real bootleg boxed sets, seeing the prices and the inferior quality. Weir turned to me and said, "Looks like it's time to put Dick to work." I just raised my hands up and said, "Yeah!"

It was like *let the gates open*. It was a huge thing. It meant no veto power from the band anymore. But that doesn't mean Dick and engineer Jeffrey Norman do it all. I do make the final decision on my own inspiration, and I do take responsibility for that part, but what goes into my database is a lot of input from all kinds of sources. (Thanks to all the people on The W.E.L.L. writing letters to me, giving me information I was unaware of.) That board meeting was really important. The operation was going to be trimmed down to bare essentials, so we could get things going. The logjam would be broken, to maybe get three or four out a year. I still skate my ideas past certain people before I go for it. There's politics. There's something behind the scenes that influences the release. It's important to mention that although it's called "Dick's Picks," I don't have any final say. I'm just a vehicle. Actually, that's a misnomer. I'm a gathering point of information that I try to pass on to others.

How will things work now?

That meeting simplified things, so Jeffrey and I will have primary control. Jeffrey is a brilliant engineer and producer. He isn't a Deadhead, but he is into music. We make a very good team, so if we agree on something, it must have merit. That goes into a whole other subject: what is a good show and what isn't. When you go to a live show, it could be the drugs, it could be you had an orgasm, or you didn't have a cheeseburger, and you miss out. Then you hear it on tape and think it was good. All of us have had that experience, thinking it was great and hearing it on tape to find out it wasn't. That ambiguity is a factor I'd like to address.

How do the band members feel about this? How did Jerry feel about this?

I only spoke to him a few times in my life, and he gave me solid answers to solid questions. When we moved the studio from Front Street to a new location, a new Vault was built with a very high degree of sophistication, even down to an Inergen fire extinguisher system instead of water, which would ruin the tapes. This was a huge expense. Finally, all the band members saw some value and made sure it was done right. I feel they've come to see that these tapes are valuable, at least to a certain group of people, like us.

Some of the more serious tapers don't understand why you're releasing partial shows instead of whole shows.

Everyone must understand that I came into this with the idea that the whole show should be released. I always advocated that through the years Healy was running the ship. When we were going to do a Europe '72 release, which became Frankfurt, Phil wanted to do a jam from one show and a jam from another show and put them on two CDs. The shows were 4/8, 4/14, and Frankfurt. I finally stood up and said, "Hey, I gotta speak for Deadheads because I'm probably the only one in this room with any degree of Deadheadness in him left. We want the whole Frankfurt, the whole Wembley, and the whole Copenhagen. *And we're not even getting into the month of May yet."* Phil turned a corner right there and went with my thought. He said, "Let Dick pick the filler tunes." We had to go with the long jam and the final third set. In Frankfurt they took a second break!

Photo by Susana Millman ©1996

Dick Latvala interviewed by Johnny Dwork in *Dupree's Diamond News* #34, Summer 1996

Have the members of the Grateful Dead actually sat down in the last decade and listened to 2/13/70 knowing that Deadheads love it so much?

There are a lot of people out there that can't understand this answer. I seriously doubt any of them have listened to the show. I don't know for sure. I doubt any of the band members currently alive have listened to the reissue of that show. I doubt for sure Phil has. I don't think they like to hear themselves. There should be a book written about that, at least a chapter about how creating the music has a different mindset than receiving it. Together they make the explosion we call the Grateful Dead Experience. The audience perceives it differently than the creators. That's the difficulty of dealing with this release thing.

Even when it's 30 years down the road, sometimes you're still too close to the art as an artist to have any objectivity to it.

To the extent you try, you get frustrated, because you are the creator, and you can't tell the client, Deadheads, who want to buy it, what they want to hear. Your conception is too esoteric or sublime. The people involved with this don't have the same awareness. They don't keep records of information of what happened the night before. They're on to the next thing.

There was a certain point where they were listening to the music.

That was '73 and '74, when Kidd was making tapes. They would go into the hotel room after the show or the next day and listen for purposes of doing a better job or something. It wasn't for the fun of it. I don't think any one of them went home after a show and listened to the Grateful Dead. What I'm trying to say, is that we Deadheads receiving it are looking for something different than what they would be willing to let go of. That's the problem I face, not having any of the people that created it determine what's releasable because they don't see it the same way. For example, the whole show concept. You know it's something every Deadhead wants. I came into this with that idea and then realized it was impossible. We would never be able to release anything with the censors I had at the time. Now we're moving closer, actually because of these surveys (thank you, Deadheads). Accepting the idea of releasing whole shows is pretty difficult for some people who are more directly involved in creating the music, like various band members. They're putting their names on it, you know? It's authentic. I can understand now when Garcia told me long ago that he'd never want to go through those tapes because it embarrassed him. Every time he heard anything it reminded him of what he was trying to do. What he was trying to do, we'll never know, but what came out was really pretty cool for us.

The best artists are rarely happy with their work.

That's what causes the difficulty of getting what some Deadheads want out there, like whole shows.

Only releasing part of a show brings up the semantical issue of how we should approach collecting the Dead's music in general. For many, collecting as much music as possible is more important than enjoying the music aesthetically. A lot of Deadheads are really into the pursuit and acquisition of music, more than the actual listening to it. There are people out there who pride themselves on having X amount of shows that are complete. Even if there's just one song missing from a show, they're not happy. They want to get the whole thing. That puts you in an odd position. It also calls to question the emphasis. I know your first love is the music, and you could be happy just listening to one tune if that's all you have that makes sense.

The act of acquisition has two sides. I got in touch with the best tapers, according to my ability to get contacts, some of the best: my buddies Eddie Claridge and Steve Rolfe, Barry Glassberg, Rob Bertrando, Pat Lee, Jerry Moore, Bob Wagner, Dave Weldner, and the king of the tapers, Bob Menke. These guys were the first wave of real intense tapers. There were even a few guys that preceded them, who made tapes in the '60s or '70s. A lot of those tapes weren't real good quality. This passion for acquisition was the same one I had. Soon I knew my goal was to expand my list, typing it up, and sending it to others. I soon faced the issue, do I keep padding my list, or do I want just what's good? How much money could I spend on this? So you become selective, and choose certain things. I know now that I missed out on a lot of other things during that same period. I can see that point of view, when you gotta have the whole show, but that's what tape trading is for. "Dick's Picks" is a product release by the Grateful Dead. That helps the band members do their thing. That's the difference. It's a product that occurs in your own environment. It isn't a live show. The live show is a phenomenon that only happens there. You aren't there when you're listening to it on the tape, no visuals, no people all around, just the bare bones. That's a different subject. It gets back to what I want to discuss: Choosing what is and what's not a good show. That is a very difficult and slippery thing.

At this point in the process, how much weight do you put on releasing shows that aren't in circulation, vs. releasing what is a must-have in our collections?

You must be talking about Harpur College. I can't run that one up the flagpole right away, because I've done it too many times. I don't want to irritate the powers that be who know I've been pushing that one. Once I got involved I tried to find stuff that I thought people didn't know about.

Dave Lemieux

May 13, 2020

MAR: I was curious more about your interactions with Dick Latvala and your opinions about his conduct as an archivist. I was wondering if that lax attitude that Dick had towards distributing tapes from the vault ever came back to bite the Grateful Dead organization in the butt.

DL: I don't know. I came in in February of '99, and was fortunate to work with Dick for about six months, I guess—he passed away in August—and I worked pretty closely with him for a good three or four of those months. And to say he was a mentor is an understatement. To say my respect for him was massive is an understatement. And he's one of these people who—literally every single interaction you have with them is memorable, because they are larger than life, and what they say means something. And Dick was one of those people. So I considered him a friend. In terms of him being, as you say, lax in terms of copying vault contents and distributing them to people—that was his thing. [When] I came in, I didn't know anything about that. I was hired specifically to catalog the video collection. It was a very different world. He was in charge of the audio, I was in charge of the video.

Dick was the one who gave the thumbs-up to hire me, but it was really John Cutler who was the head of the studio. He was front-of-house sound man from '94 onward for the Grateful Dead. He was Jerry Garcia's front-of-house sound guy. He produced a lot of Grateful Dead records. So, man, I'll never forget the very first day I worked there, very first day. [John] came in, they gave me a key to the vault, and he said, "We trust you, obviously, to come and catalog the videos every day for the next three or four months. And there's lots of rules, but the two things I'm going to tell you is don't take anything home with you, and don't copy anything." And that was literally all I needed to hear. I didn't take the job for the purpose of taking things home. Dick was hired, I think, in '85, so a good fifteen years before I was. And maybe he simply wasn't given that directive—I honestly don't know. But I was given that directive, and I've to this day followed it, where I do get people occasionally asking, "Oh, hey, there's this one show from whatever, that there's no good board tape. If you have it, is there any chance you could put it into circulation?" And, you know, I'm flattered that they'd ask that I would do that, but I just say no. It's part of my job to not do that. And that's kind of the end of it.

I'll say this too: another thing, shortly after Dick passed, when I was beginning to have more influence on the release decisions starting in late '99 onward, a big part of the criteria earlier on was—and I even, my philosophy was this too—to try to focus on things that didn't circulate, or at least not in very good quality. And when I realized that virtually everything—and if not everything, everything really good—circulated because it had been leaked from the vault, whatever you want to say, it really became no longer part of our criteria. It was always a goal—like, sure, if we had something that for some reason nobody's ever heard and it's excellent, it would always be an exciting thing to put that out.

MAR: Do you think that his distribution helped somehow in, I don't know, interest in the vault or interest in the music in some other kind of way?

DL: I don't. And the reason I say that is I think that we saw, back in '99, 2000, the floodgates open. I think it wasn't so much that these great shows were now out there. I think it was more a case of there was so much out there on BitTorrent, or CDs, or dubs, or whatever you were doing, and then along comes Grateful Dead Productions and we release a wonderful show on CD—no matter how good the show is, what's one more show when you just got thirty new ones? So, I think it was the quantity and the ease of getting virtually anything, but I don't think it helped us. Our sales certainly didn't go up when the floodgates opened, I'll say that.

JG: I actually think that bio was written by Willy Legate.

SW: Who is he?

JG: Willy Legate is this guy who's an old, old friend of me and Hunter's and Phil's and our whole scene, and he's a lot of things. And one of those things he is, is sort of a bible scholar. And he's a madman. We were exposed to him really a lot during a formative period of our intellectual life. And he's still around in our scene.

He's the guy who wrote "There's nothing like a Grateful Dead concert" and he wrote the little blurb inside the Europe '72 album about the bolos and the bozos. We also call on him to do various things. One time we asked the Deadheads to send us their thoughts, just to get some feedback from them. And they sent us lots and lots of letters and we gave 'em all to Willy. And he ended up with, like, a two page condensation of all the letters, with every viewpoint, that was just tremendously amazing to read. It was just so packed with information.

Willy is someone who has a lot of different kinds of gifts. He also even wrote some lyrics to some of our early songs before we started recording, but we've subsequently stopped doing the tunes. But he's another creative head in our scene that operates way back from the public.

Jerry Garcia interviewed by Steve Weitzman in *Relix* vol. 15, #4, August 1988

MAR: Was there ever any mention of Willy Legate and his participation in the maintenance or upkeep of the archive at all?

DL: No. I've heard the name, obviously, a lot. He wasn't there when I was working there, but he was a man who was spoken of in reverential tones around the studio and the vault. He was a person who I really do wish I had got to know, because I heard such wonderful things about him. A sage, that was the word I heard, "sage." Willy had a massive impact on the archiving, for sure, because he was in charge [and] had a responsibility to catalog, make sure everything was safe. He did have a huge impact on the, if not the preservation of the collection, the safekeeping of the collection. So, yeah, he was a really, really wonderful guy, by all accounts.

MAR: What magazines were available when you were starting to collect tapes and starting to get into the Dead? Were there any that you were paying attention to? And furthermore, how important were these things, these broadcasts of information, for you getting deeper into the scene and keeping in touch with people?

DL: They were hugely important. So, the two magazines that were a huge part of me being a Deadhead were *Relix* and, the one I preferred—like, the one that I still have all my old copies of—was *The Golden Road*. And that was the one that Blair Jackson put together, a magnificent Dead zine. And I think it wasn't monthly, it was every two months, six times a year. I loved *The Golden Road*, I loved *Relix*, and then later, a couple of years later, like '87, maybe, [was] *Dupree's Diamond News*. And I was a big fan of *Dupree's Diamond News* as well, but *The Golden Road* was the one for me. And then for books, it was really primarily three books: it was *The Official Book of the Deadheads*; it was Blair Jackson's book, *The Music Never Stopped*; and then it was David Gans and Peter Simon's book that came out, I think, in '85, *Playing in the Band*. Those three, and then shortly after that—probably about '88—was Jerilyn [Lee Brandelius]'s *Grateful Dead Family Album*. So, until the internet really started hitting, which for me wasn't until like mid-nineties, those magazines and those books were it. And then, otherwise, it was the community of Deadheads I met through those things, through tape trading out of those magazines, where I would get most of my tour information before anything—like, I was calling the Dead hotline every day, but oftentimes I would get a call from a tape-trading buddy in Maryland or California or wherever, saying, "Dude, they just announced the summer tour." And so news traveled quickly in the Dead world; not internet social media quickly, but quickly. I remember getting phone calls from concerts at 11:30 at night—and I lived with my parents, so, the phone would ring at 11:30 at night from a hotel lobby, [someone] saying, "Oh dude, they played [whatever song]." And I was like, "Wow." So news traveled much more quickly than you could imagine in the days before cell phones, but certainly nothing even remotely like today.

And you talk about webcasts, but I remember very well: September '88, I was seventeen years old, and I went to the four shows at the Cap Centre [in Landover, Maryland], September 2, 3, 5, and 6, and then I went home. I was finishing up high school, I had a year left. And then, I'll never forget this: About two weeks later, [the Dead] were doing their massive run at Madison Square Garden, and a buddy of mine somehow weaseled his way into a private box at Madison Square Garden. And he called me up on the phone, on the landline from the Madison Square Garden private box, and he left the phone receiver hanging out of the private box and I just sat there—I remember my mom's living room, I remember exactly where I was sitting. I can visualize it today—and I sat there listening to the second set through a telephone, and the crowd going nuts. And I remember it was the night that they played "Morning Dew." I think they played it a couple of times at that show. So, I got to hear "Morning Dew" live, over the phone, and that was the 1988 version of a webcast. I could barely hear what was going on, because it was so muffled and loud, and the crowd was going nuts. But I was like, "I was there!" You know, you take what you can get, when you're obsessed with something.

MAR: It does speak to how powerful the information is. And I'm doing music an injustice by calling it information, but just the desire to record it, convey it, and transmit it is so profound in the community. Also your friend was dialing up the phone long-distance, which must have cost the Madison Square Garden a pretty penny, I'm sure.

DL: I remember it was not a collect call. I remember specifically it wasn't collect. But that was the other thing: so many of the phone calls we'd get from hotel lobbies or payphones were collect. The number of times where I'd get a phone call at 11:30 at night at my mom's house, saying "Collect call from Chris, will you accept the charges?"—the answer was always yes, because you knew it was going to be Grateful Dead news.

MAR: It's so interesting just how much more of a process it was to communicate—whether it's through magazines, telephone, collect calls, mail through different media, audio cassettes, or reel-to-reel—and how this community just utilized all of it to transmit information.

DL: Yeah. And you go back to 1971, when the Grateful Dead [published their call to fans] "Who are you? Where are you? How are you?" That was exactly what we're talking about, going back fifty years ago when they started the mailing list. And that's how Deadheads got their information: they would [be sent] a mailing list with tour dates, and you'd be at home and you'd say, "Oh shit," you know, "the Dead are playing in Baltimore and Philly, next to me. I can go to those two shows, they're nearby."

MAR: How did your experiences with tapes change once CD-Rs became more normal?

DL: [In] '98 or early '99, I got my first CD burner. It was an HHB CD burner. And I'll never forget burning a cassette tape to a CD. It was 11/10/73 at Winterland, playing "Uncle John's Band." And I put it on in the car, and it worked. And I remember I leaned over to my buddy. I said, "Dude, the future is here." And I remember saying those exact words. The quality was good, and I knew that just like that, you could make many, many copies and the generations wouldn't be affected. I liked the ease of CDs, the portability of them. At the Dead, we use them in the studio all the time for reference. So if Jeffrey [Norman, engineer] was mixing a show, and he finished two songs that day, he made me a CD of those two songs at the end of the day, and I'd drive home with them, listen to them at home. And then the next morning, it would be easy for me to give them notes, because I listened to it a few times. So, yeah, we use them, but no different than we would have used cassettes. But the quality was certainly pretty good.

MAR: I see. Back when you first started using CD-Rs though, were you like, "Oh, tapes are totally irrelevant now, I'm not going to do that anymore"?

DL: I'll show you my collection. I've still got all my tapes—I have thousands of tapes still in boxes. So "irrelevant," I don't know. I had some masters, but everything else is certainly not a unique copy of something, and yet I still felt a need to keep it. I certainly wasn't tossing anything. To me, it was just a different format. We still do a lot of Dick's Picks from cassette sources quite often, so, to me, it's all about just formats changing, period. And that's just how it happens, just like VHS became DVD became Blu-ray became who knows what's next.

MAR: When you say cassettes were used for releases, are those actual, like, audio cassettes or are they bigger tapes?

DL: No, I mean, we use audio cassettes as our master source, all the time. All we have from like '80 until '87 is cassettes. And we also have Beta PCM digital, but they have a lot of digital problems. So, pretty much anything that we're releasing as a Dick's Picks or Dave's Picks from the eighties is from a cassette master, whereas from the seventies and sixties [it] would be from a reel-to-reel master. Eighty-seven is when the DAT [masters] started—New Year's '87 was the first run with that.

David Lemieux in the vault
Photo: Susana Millman

Ken Hays
July 10, 2020

KH: My first Dead show was November 11, 1985 at the Brendan Byrne Arena in New Jersey. But I was a big fan of the Grateful Dead, had always been. Since my first show, I pretty much went on tour and did about 355-plus Grateful Dead shows while Jerry was with us. With Terrapin Tapes, which I started on spring tour 1990—basically I set up a distributorship with Maxell and TDK and Sony and Panasonic. I went to school out in Boulder and paid ridiculously high prices for blank tapes out there, and then came back home to Connecticut and went into New York City and got unbelievably low prices on blank tape and figured there needed to be a way, nationwide, that everyone could get their tapes at a significantly less price point on blank cassette tapes than they could buy them for in the stores, in bulk. Went on tour, handed out flyers with Maxell and TDK tape prices, and immediately we were off and running, and had a bunch of friends at the office that were packing up boxes of fifty and a hundred cassette tapes and shipping them out and putting them on a credit card. And that just continued to thrive, and Deadheads loved to do business with like-minded people. I went out on tour, and pretty much financed it with selling *DeadBases*. We were one of the largest distributors of *DeadBase*, just by holding up the new [editions]. And it was just a blast. It was so much fun, and I traveled with all my friends and everything was going beautifully and, before we knew it—right around 1994 or so—we were doing almost $3 million in sales. Not only cassette tapes, but we were the largest distributor of DAT machines, where the bands and all the tapers could record on mostly Sony DAT machines and then on home and professional DAT recording equipment as well.

There were a bunch of forums. This was the early, early days of the internet—rec.music.gdead—and there'd be tape forums, where to get your tapes, and our name popped up quite a bit. We were all having fun doing it—it wasn't like people placing orders online. It was all, pick up the telephone, and talk with Heads about shows that we saw here and there, developing relationships with the client base. Which is something that, today, you really don't get that brand loyalty by placing an internet order. Picking up the phone and talking with a like-minded individual who was also into taping and into live shows was something that was really quite unique.

MAR: Where would you get your tapes from originally?

KH: Local record stores, or—this was before Best Buy, I think, so there were really very few options, other than regular retail outlets that were selling cassette tapes. There was certainly a need and our pricing was significantly less and most people, if you bought fifty tapes, we would ship them out for free. There really wasn't, at that time, a company that was servicing the individuals and bands that recorded their shows. And so we were able to fill a void. And then all the bands—everyone from Bruce Springsteen, Grateful Dead, Phish, Allman Brothers, Dave Matthews—all bought their DAT tapes and DAT machines from Terrapin. We really were the go-to, and for tech-support questions as well. It wasn't just the sale—it was really a development of the relationships with, again, like-minded individuals, and if they had any questions and problems with their

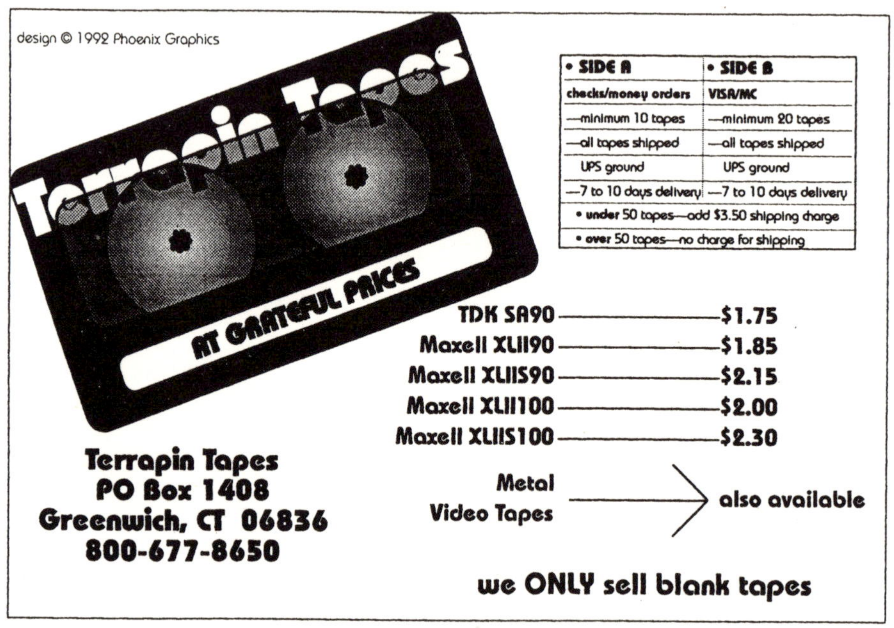

decks in terms of how to clean tape heads and stuff like that, we'd walk them through the process. It was very much a community-based company [where] we all loved what we were doing.

I started just myself, and then, within a month or so after I got home from spring tour, I mean, the phones were ringing off the hook. So I hired up a couple kids, a couple friends, and they were helping answering phones, packing up boxes, shipping out UPS. It really took off quite quickly. So, within a year, probably, we had four full-time employees.

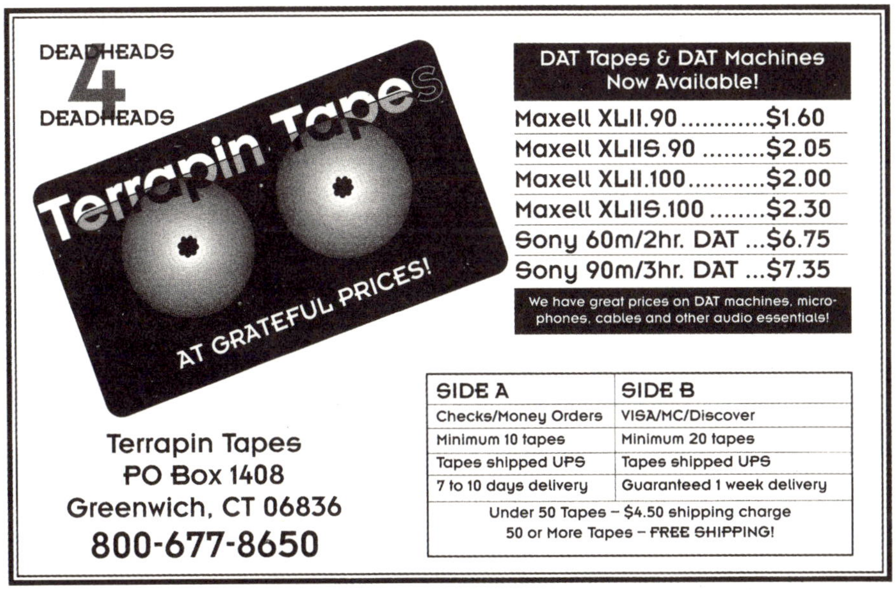

MAR: Can you maybe describe to me the relationship you had with *DeadBase*?

KH: It made sense, because the majority of our customers were Deadheads who were tapers or tape traders. It just made sense that we sold *DeadBases* as well. I think right at pretty much the beginning of my starting Terrapin Tapes, I spoke with the owner of *DeadBase* and said, "Hey, I'm Terrapin Tapes and want to sell your *DeadBases*," and did just that.

MAR: How did your relationship with Maxell start and how did you form those partnerships with those companies?

KH: They were skeptical. They really didn't know anything about the live-tape-trading space. They questioned how it was that record labels' signed bands would allow their fans to record their concerts and trade their tapes, and they were always fixated on, well, who's making money here? And they didn't understand that there was no money exchanged. That was totally against everything the tapers and the tape traders stood for. Taping and trading tapes was solely for personal enjoyment and they didn't have a clue as to what this was all about, so they were intrigued by the concept, and when they saw our sales numbers, they were more engaged.

MAR: Was there a particular person you had contact with?

KH: No, I made a cold call. I called Maxell corporate office and said, "Hey, I'm interested in starting up a distributorship with Maxell and I want to talk with someone." They put me in touch with their regional director and, again, no one within Maxell was hip to what was going on, and where tens of thousands of cassette tapes that were being sold were going. Within a year, they were very supportive. And then we moved into digital audio tape and digital audio recorders and a bunch of other hardware, and then we went through the blank CD-R phase, and then, obviously, where we are today is everything's recorded onto hard drives.

After Jerry's death in '95, in '96 I started a festival called Deadhead Heaven: A Gathering of the Tribe, and that was a beautiful event in Westchester, New York, at SUNY Purchase College. The following year, we changed the name to Gathering of the Vibes, and the attendance doubled, and we did that at Croton Point Park in Westchester. I really wanted to focus more on live musical events, and then people started contacting me saying, "Hey, I work with a charity and I want to get a band and have a stage and do a charity benefit concert. Is that something you can help me with?" So I got much more into the production of live music events and producing unique fundraising concerts in nontraditional-type venues. After Jerry passed, I mean, obviously, it was devastating to the Deadhead community. I knew that my world was going to radically change. All the friends all over the country that get together and we see each other at least a couple times a year and hang out—I knew that that had to immediately come to an end. It was devastating. But, at the same time as Jerry died, Phish was really coming on strong and a bunch of the Phishheads came on board and were buying their tape and their DAT machines and such from us. We didn't see a huge sell-off. And Dave Matthews also was raging at that point, and the Allman Brothers were continuing to do what they were doing and [there were] tons of tapers there, tape traders. Was there a decline in tape sales? Yeah, maybe. I don't really remember, to be perfectly honest with you, but nothing radical. Emotionally, it was devastating—Jerry's loss. It was just indescribable, the most significant loss that I had ever felt in my life.

MAR: As a result of running Terrapin Tapes, did you get access to tapers offering you really choice recordings or anything of that sort?

KH: Yeah, that was definitely one of the perks. Working with sound engineers, with the bands, that's just the nature of the space that we were in. I mean, when someone calls up Terrapin Tapes, it wasn't like, "Hey, I'd like fifty XLII 90s, here's my credit card." It was more like a fifteen, twenty minute conversation of, "Hey, you got anything new in? I just got this incredible recording from the Greek, and do you want to trade something that you got out at Alpine?" or whatever. It was friends talking with friends. It truly was a beautiful thing. Headquarters was more home office, which it was until, I think, '96. [We had] the ability to back up tractor trailers in residential areas, at which time one of the tractor trailers, backing in to drop off product, took out an electrical pole, brought down the electricity within the whole neighborhood. City of Stamford zoning commission said, "You can't be doing this." At that point, we had to go legit and actually get an office. Yeah, it was always nice to be able to go downstairs where all the tapes and the DAT recorders, all the equipment, was. And the office was downstairs, and then go upstairs and hang out and have a lot of fun with friends that were roommates and such.

MAR: Was the office basically then just a warehouse in a house, like boxes and boxes of tapes and a desk and a telephone and maybe a computer?

KH: We had probably four of the old Apple iMacs, the purple iMac. And we had probably about two thousand square feet of office space in the home office. So, large space with the ability to easily transport, getting tapes and machines and product into the office and then turn it around, box it up, and ship it out [via] UPS with relative ease.

MAR: How many tapes was your initial order with Maxell, if you can remember?

KH: My guess would have been in the neighborhood of twenty-five hundred XLIIs, twenty-five hundred XLII S's, a thousand MXS's—five thousand or so was the initial order, and that would last us, when we started up, for about three weeks. And then it doubled and tripled and all of the sudden we're doing right around a million dollars of sales with Maxell. Maxell was really the tape of choice. TDK had a quality tape, but Maxell was without question the tape of choice for tape traders and tapers at that point. Well, the MXS's, the metal tapes, were more for the live tapers. And then the XLIIs and XLII S's were for the tape traders.

MAR: For the first year you made a million in sales. How many tapes does that correlate to, roughly? How many were going out the door?

KH: We did about a million bucks the first year, the cassettes were about $1.75 each, so for the first year of business we did fifty-seven thousand cassette tapes.

MAR: Just by 1995, how many tapes were going out the door?

KH: In '95, it would probably be about fifty-fifty cassette tapes versus digital audio tapes, DAT tapes. And on top of that were all the decks that we were selling. It mutated from 100 percent analog cassette over to DAT. There was a short timeframe in there where CD-R was so inexpensive, but CD-R was just not a format that really took off in the live-tape-trading community. Yeah, I priced out a bunch of wholesalers, but when people were buying fifty tapes, the wholesalers were still significantly more expensive than what I could sell them to [customers] for, and I didn't have the overhead that required a huge margin. We were working on thin margins and we were lucky enough to have a lot of volume. I was pretty much winging it from the beginning all the way through. There was no business plan or nothing like that.

Towards the end, so, in '95, [tape prices] went down. It was a combination of the volume that we were doing—we were hitting numbers so that we were getting better pricing—and, additionally, there was a competitor that jumped into the marketplace. He was one of the largest distributors of Maxell tapes in the country and they took out an ad in I think *Relix*, with pricing that just blew ours away. Pricing that I couldn't come close to buying it for. And then I did some research on these guys and it turns out that they were a large corporation that owned an aircraft company, and this was a subsidiary of it. It was clear that what they were doing was predatory pricing: getting and selling product below value for the extent of the time until Terrapin Tapes would have to fold, because we just couldn't compete. It was totally unfair. They were selling tapes for less than what I could buy them for directly from Maxell, and I went to Maxell and said, "Hey, guys, what the hell? How can these guys be selling tapes and advertising pricing where it's below the pricing that I'm buying it for, directly from you guys?" I wrote up a letter to the Deadhead community and put it in I think *Dupree's* or *Relix*—and once I wrote the letter, people responded and it started getting circulated around the rec.music.gdead forum and on AOL forums and stuff like that. But basically, yeah, our business doubled. It was just a confirmation of how loyal and committed the Deadhead community was and confirmed that Deadheads want to work with like-minded people. It was quite remarkable.

In 2003, as I was focusing more and more on live festival production and music production, I sold Terrapin Tapes to two companies: one on the East Coast, so all of our customers on the East Coast, they got half of the client list; and all of my clients on the West Coast, they got the West Coast client base. It made sense that way, where these were two companies that had started up that were similar—they were Deadheads that actually had worked for me. They started up their own companies on the East and West Coasts. And so everyone could get their tapes or their DAT machines or whatever they needed much faster. When you ship out from Connecticut to the West Coast, it'd be five UPS working days, and now, with the East Coast/West Coast operations going, everyone could get their tapes within two business days. So it really worked out well.

Terrapin Tapes

8 0 0 - 6 7 7 - 8 6 5 0

PO Box 1408 • Greenwich, CT 06836

Dear Fellow Deadheads:

I've never written a letter like this before, but I think it's important to let you all know what's happening here at Terrapin Tapes. Some of you may have heard about the difficulties we are experiencing. In May, a large tape distributor started significantly undercutting our prices. You might ask why one of the country's largest tape distributors would go after Deadheads and Terrapin Tapes. Well, there's an easy answer.

The blank tape industry is extremely competitive and most companies are looking to expand into new markets. Growth and expansion of a company could be helpful to us all because it would promote greater competition, which in turn should lead to lower prices and better services. Unfortunately, that's not what's happening here. The most frequently used sales tactic deployed by this company is to engage smaller, more vulnerable companies in bitter, unwinnable price wars. THESE GUYS SELL TAPE AROUND COST JUST LONG ENOUGH TO DRIVE THE LITTLE GUY OUT OF BUSINESS. ONCE WE'RE GONE, THEY CRANK UP THEIR PRICES SO THEY CAN START TO MAKE MONEY. If they succeed, like they have with other small companies, we all lose. I lose a company that I love, and we all go back to paying too much for our blank tapes. I need your help, your continued support, to keep Terrapin Tapes alive.

Although this sounds like a difficult battle for us to win, I think we can do it. Here's the first step:

- **We've Lowered Our Prices:**
  We were able to renegotiate the price we're paying for Maxell XLII90 and XLIIS90's. This significant savings is passed directly on to you. So, effective immediately, our new price on the XLII90 is $1.60, and the XLIIS90 is $2.05. All of our other tape prices including our *kind* shipping policy (we pay all shipping charges for purchases of 50 or more tapes) will remain the same. The good news continues…

- **A Rapid Delivery Guarantee:**
  With the help of UPS's brand new select air service, all customers, nationwide will receive their tapes within 1 week of ordering — guaranteed! If you don't receive your tapes within 1 week, we'll give you $10 worth of blanks free! I'm serious about fast delivery and psyched to be able to offer this service to you at no additional charge.

So, that's the scoop. Truly killer prices, friendly service, and guaranteed lightening delivery. Let's send a loud message to this corporate giant that we won't be suckered by their short-term, mean-spirited sales tactics. I think you know my level of commitment and that my intentions are honorable.

I know there's "nothing you can hold for very long," but I really hope Terrapin Tapes can be here for you in the years to come.

Ken Hays

DDN 34

Dear Ron, April 26, 1974

Thankyou for replying to my letter. I hope we will be doing some work together in the future involving the tape exchange program.

As for your request for a sample tape showing you my definition of "almost soundboard quality", I am sending to you a cross-section of cuts taken from some of my best audience tapes and some of my best soundboard tapes. Please excuse the use of 3 3/4 i.p.s., but I thought it would be nice to have more listening time for yourself.

On Side 1 of the tape, you will find the cuts that were made from a cassette deck being taped from the audience. Big River, Truckin' → The Other One → Eyes of the World, and Here Comes Sunshine were from February 23, 1974 at Winterland;

-2-

and Candyman and Playing in the Band were from February 24, 1974 at Winterland.

If you listen to the jam during The Other One, you will find my definition of "almost soundboard quality". The quality excedes most of the usual audience tapes quality, and except for the usual drawbacks in audience noise and hiss, these particular cuts on Side 1 constitute a pretty good example of what I mean by "almost soundboard quality".

On Side 2, I have cuts from some of my best sound board tapes. These cuts include:

Fillmore East - 4/28/71

The Rub

Cumberland Blues

Fillmore East - 4/27/71

Some Dark Hollow

Too Hard To Handle

Ripple

Ed Perlstein

July 13, 2020

MAR: So the reason that I'm talking to you, I guess, is to try and figure out the mystery of this letter that you sent to, I believe, [then–Grateful Dead manager and label head] Ron Rakow. It's just addressed to "Ron," and I found it in the archive at Santa Cruz.

EP: Interesting. Well, it doesn't surprise me that I don't remember that, because my memory is not great anyway.

MAR: It's written on April 26, 1974. It basically thanks Ron for replying to a letter that you had sent previously—it seems like you also sent him live recordings and that you were trying to showcase the best audience tapes that you had that sounded like a soundboard recording, and also to give him examples of soundboard recordings that you had, and you sent him one Old & In the Way show from Sonoma State in '73. It seems, from the letter, that you're also talking about trying or petitioning for [the Dead] to work with certain types of tapes to distribute to a wider audience.

EP: OK. Was this actually from me, and signed by and all that stuff? I don't remember anything even remotely like that, what you're describing. I mean, yeah, I was involved in collecting tapes, but rarely did I collect or trade audience tapes. I was collecting since about '71. At that point, there weren't that many tapes, period, and so I'd take anything I can get. And I mean, back when I was living on the East Coast—which would be like '70, '71—I did meet up with Les Kippel and talk, and he was kind of like a Don Kippel. He would sit there and you'd almost have to kiss his ring to get anything.

-3-

New, New Minglewood Blues
Fillmore East - 4/26/71
Sugar Magnolia
It Hurts Me Too
Beat it on Down the Line
} w/ Duane Allman on guitar
Harpur College, Binghamton, N.Y. - 5/2/70
Morning Dew
Fillmore East - 9/20/70 (acoustic)
Cumberland Blues
Fillmore East - 4/27/71
Lovelight
Old and in The Way - Sonoma State - 11/4/73
Earl's Breakdown (Jerry's Breakdown)

I hope you enjoy the tape. The Old and in the Way cut was off a tape I recorded at Sonoma State last year. I just thought I'd put it in for the quality of it. If you want more, Jerry Garcia has the whole concert.

-4-

Probably my favorite cut on the tape is Lovelight, just for the sheer energy of it, especially during the finale. That energy is one reason why I want to try to get good quality tapes to the public. There's so much energy locked away in the vaults and I believe the people should be able to share in that energy.

I hope we can arrange a meeting where we can discuss some of these possibilities. If you wish to get in touch with me at any time, don't hesitate to try. My phone # is 848-2143. I hope to hear from you soon.

Sincerely,
Ed Perlstein

BOB WAGNER INTERVIEWED BY DAVID GANS 11/30/2007

David Gans: It was hard to make bargains with the tapers back in the day. I remember that, too. I didn't have anything to bring to the party at that time and I was fortunate to have a friend, Mike Dinhofer, great, great guy that I met through a New Orleans connection, who was just unbelievably generous: his whole mission in life was to spread the music around. But then I would run into these other guys for whom it seemed like it was gold doubloons, and they wanted something. If you didn't have anything for them, they wouldn't have anything for you. This was a time when analog tapes, every copy degraded the sound, so you needed to get it closer and closer to the master. What do you suppose is the deal with all that?

Bob Wagner: It's hard for me to understand. Obviously, it's a power trip of some sort that people feel, if they have a tape that you don't have, that they have some sort of power over you, over all the people that don't have the tape. I've never understood the philosophy. To me, it even works the other way. If you want power, you can get more power by doing good things to people than by hoarding and not spreading the music. But, there came a time, once I started taping, when I was the source of the music and people wanted to patch out of me, or people wanted to trade with me and to me, it was always obvious that the music would be spread. Barry Glassberg and I used to tape together, back starting in '79; we co-owned Nak 700 microphones. That was around the year when more and more people started showing up and wanted to tape shows. Many of these people wanted to patch out of us, and a decision had to be made: Do we let these people, who we don't even know, patch in and get the music, or do we not? Barry and I, I don't think we ever even discussed it. It was obvious to us that the music needed to go out and be shared with everyone. Certainly, we felt that's the way the Dead would want it. They wouldn't want us making tapes and then not letting other people hear them. I think that's an important legacy, really. I hope that many other people followed the lead and spread the music.

EP: But, at that point, that early, it was "Get anything you can just to get the music, just to listen to the stuff." And I was connecting with people that had recordings coming in from the West Coast as well. But I really never set up to record from the audience, except for maybe one time, and it was a disaster. I tried it once at the Academy of Music when Bo Diddley was backed by the Dead, and it was "Hell's Angels present the Grateful Dead." I brought a cassette deck in and it was terrible. I did it once on September 18, 1970, at the Fillmore East—I had a cassette deck and I was all the way in the back of the room, and we ran into Phil Lesh getting out of his limo in front of the hotel half a dozen blocks away from the Fillmore. And we stood around smoking a joint and chatting for an hour or so, and I took out the cassette deck and I played it for him and he goes, "What the hell is that?" It was basically my friend and I talking with some muffled music in the background. I was always more into the higher quality recordings. And you mentioned Old & In the Way at Sonoma State; I mean, the period around '74, '75, something like that, I was taking recording engineering classes, and my teacher happened to be doing the sound for all of Garcia's and all of the Dead offshoot bands: Old & In the Way, Garcia and Saunders, King Fish, stuff like that. And so he would let me plug my reel-to-reel deck into the soundboard, as long as I got the band's permission, and record some of these shows. The Old & In the Way Sonoma State [recording] is one. There's a King Fish show from Chateau Liberté in the Santa Cruz Mountains. There are at least three, maybe four Garcia and Saunders shows that I plugged into. And when I'd go to the next show, I'd hand Jerry a reel-to-reel copy of the last show I went to. [That was] pretty much my extent of direct taping; other than that, I was just into trading with people.

MAR: I see. And then I'm just curious because you were originally mentioned to me by David Gans, and I don't really remember the context for why he was like, "You should talk to Ed."

EP: Well, Dave has always said that I was one of the first people to turn him on to tapes. I opened up my collection to him, and he's always been very grateful for that. So I kind of started him on collecting. But I don't know, the only reason I say that is because he has said that publicly. That's the only reason that he may have mentioned my name, because I was there at the beginning. I grew up in New Jersey, and actually Englewood Cliffs, which is right across the George Washington Bridge from Manhattan. So it was really a hop, skip, and a jump to go into the city and go to the Fillmore, or even to go to Port Chester. So I mean, my first show was January 3, 1970. I was into the Dead in '69, but didn't make it to a show, even though I've been kicking myself because my friend tried to get me to go to one in the summer of '69. But after seeing them live, I was hooked and saw as many shows as I could on the East Coast in '70 and '71. And then went off to college on Long Island, one year of college, while seeing as many shows as I could—selling my record collection, doing whatever I could to get money to go to these shows. Went to the entire Academy of Music run in spring of '72 in New York. And basically, through different mind-expanding sessions, realized that San Francisco is the center of the universe and moved to the Bay Area in September '72. But I mean, at that point I was still a fan. In '73, '74, I became really good friends with a musician in the Bay Area who was a good friend of Mickey Hart's, and he brought me up to Mickey's ranch, and so Mickey and I became friends. And then I decided I was going to try to become a recording engineer.

I was into collecting tapes. But in the summer of '75, a friend of mine loaned me a 35mm camera, and that's when I went to my first Dead show with that in hand. And it was Golden Gate Park, September 28, 1975. The free Golden Gate Park show with the Starship. And I talked my way onto the stage—I actually got there early enough so they built the backstage fence around me. I talked my way up onto the stage and shot the whole show from the stage, and those photographs were pretty good. I must have given some of those pictures to the Dead, because when *BAM* magazine started out at the end of '75, they needed a picture of Bob Weir—so they called the Dead office, and the Dead said, "Here, talk to Ed." So they called me and I ended up being one of *BAM*'s first photographers, and being a photographer for a magazine gives you press credentials, and access, and things like that, so that helped in my photography career. I wasn't really going to have a photography career, but that sure compelled it. Then I started to do stuff with Bill Graham and shot a lot of Dead shows, and that pretty much is it.

But all that time, I was still collecting tapes, not just the Dead. I was trading cassettes with people all over the world: Japan, Germany, England, all across the US. I have all those tapes still, and I've slowly [started] digitizing them over the years, and I have two radio shows now where I play those recordings, so I've got people listening all over the world, which really comes around full circle for me, because I love sharing music. And back when I started this stuff, when it was only reel-to-reels, we used to get together with friends and plug a bunch of reel-to-reel decks in together. And to make copies, you had to do it in real time, and so you'd spend the entire day or weekend making copies, plugged in, listening to the music and all that stuff. And that doesn't happen anymore. Kind of miss that. But I wanted to be able to share all this music that I've accumulated over the years.

I wasn't a member of a tape exchange. My friend Harvey Lubar, he had the tape exchange, I forgot what it's called—Hell's Honkies, I think it was. And Les Kippel had one, and stuff like that. I was never part of it—it was always "a friend knew a friend." I found that a lot of ways you can get really good tapes is get to know the band members, or their sound people, or their crew, because I wasn't into collecting tapes from people who would tape from the audience, because back then it was crap. I would mostly—I don't think I placed ads, but I think I responded to ads in *Relix* or *Goldmine* magazine.

MAR: Was it easy to find people that were in tape exchange clubs then? It seems like it was quite prevalent on the East Coast, at least.

EP: Oh yeah. The East Coast was really just hungry for anything Grateful Dead. And I mean, I understand it because I grew up there, and they didn't get as much satisfaction, because the Dead lived on the West Coast. I mean, when I was living in Berkeley I was able to get my Dead fix any time Jerry played a club in Berkeley. But I really can't address the tape exchange stuff, because I wasn't really a part of it. I can't remember any time that I was involved in or communicated with people in the tape exchanges. It might've happened, but I don't remember it.

MAR: I see. So you said that you were one of the first photographers for *BAM*. Were there only a handful of photographers shooting the Dead at that time, or were you kind of it for a while?

EP: Because of my love of the Dead, I concentrated on the Dead. I mean, there are other photographers that would shoot—maybe they'd do a Dead session or something like that. Of course there was the original guys: Herb Greene, Jim Marshall, stuff like that. But as far as shooting live shows—and that was my favorite thing to do; I was not really into doing photo sessions with bands—I liked to shoot live shows and I did a lot of Dead live shows. So I don't really know, there were some other Dead photographers that were shooting around the time that I was, even before I was, like Larry Hulst and Bruce Polonsky, they both were shooting a few years before me. But they would shoot mostly from the audience. I got to know the band and would get the ability to shoot on stage. Or in the case of Mickey, would go up to his ranch to do some photography. Or working with *BAM* magazine, David Gans and I flew down to LA to photograph and interview Weir for *Heaven Help the Fool* while he was recording that. So I had a little bit more contact with the band because I had some close knowledge of the band members, friendships with the band members, and also the press pass.

MAR: Did you ever have one of your pictures showcased on a J-card or anything like that?

EP: I have no idea. My pictures are all over the place. I mean, they are some of the most famous live Dead shots ever. And so my stuff will pop up all the time. But I never really was concerned with J-cards. I mean, when I labeled my cassettes—and I still have all my hundreds and hundreds of Dead cassettes put away in storage, because they're not worth digitizing because everything's online now—what I did was, in my computer, I would type in a label, I'd print it out on regular paper, and I'd wrap it around the J-card. And so the J-card that actually comes with the cassette, I didn't do anything with—it's blank. I never colored them or anything like that, or did pictures. It was just a text, it was just informational.

DAN HEALY INTERVIEWED BY KATIE HARVEY
11/12/2008

Katie Harvey: I wanted to talk to you about the formation of the tapers section, why that was made.

Dan Healy: I'll give you the dissertation on the tapers section. There are people--and I'm not one of them, in fact I'm vehemently not one of them--there are people that believe that every nuance of every note should be recorded as though it were the holy grail. And I'm a proponent of "the one that got away." Like, what if we all just went and heard the concert and the only thing you had from that concert is your memory of hearing it, right? See, I'm that guy. That's the romantic guy in me, OK? For me, being able to play it back takes the romance out of it, takes the fun or the enjoyment or the excitement. I can't think of the right word to say but I think you get my drift. It's like Paul Simon's song, "Kodachrome": that's what that's about. It's about being there and seeing it, witnessing it. There doesn't need to be tape. There are people who for some reason absolutely object to that and believe that every nuance . . . I mean, they would record sound checks and everything if they could. And so, in the seventies when cassette machines came out, that's when it started happening. People would bring machines and microphones and record. Of course, record companies always hated that, because they believed it disrupted record sales. Actually, it turns out it's the other way around; it enhances [them], because people that love you so much that they come to record you, they are the first ones in line to buy your records when they come out. For some reason--because I was out in the audience where my mix board was--they became "Dan's tapers": and it was only because they were in the same part of the place. It had nothing to do with me; I didn't invite them there. I had nothing to do with it. But in the end, I went through years of grief with record companies, with some of the band members, with all kinds. It was an unending pain in the ass to me, OK?

So what happened was, people would just be randomly spaced around the room recording. But then, by the eighties, our concerts were so sold out that a lot of the places we played had assigned seating. So people would wait in line for hours to get tickets and stuff like that. And the record company was always saying, "Dan, you've got to stop this," and some of the band members who bought into that were like, "Dan, you've got to make this stop happening." And my answer was, "Why me? If you want it to stop, you make it stop." Because no one was going to stop it anyway; we tried for a while, so people just snuck teenier machines in, and that effect was that the tapes were shittier sounding, but there were still tapes out there. It was just one of those things you can't control.

But what happened was, this one night, this young boy and girl who were maybe fourteen years old came to me at the mix board crying. And they said, "We waited all day and all night in line to get tickets, and this guy came and told me that he wanted to put his microphone there, and if I didn't leave it he'd beat me up." That was the straw that broke the camel's back. I went nuts over that, and it's like, "OK, I am going to get involved now." So I threaded out to the tapers --I created the tapers section behind my mix board. Because I had tried a little bit to stop it, and I even had some heavies beat--not literally beat people, but get heavy with people. I confiscated people's machines and told them they were never going to get them back. I always gave them back. In the end I'm a softy, but they didn't know it at the time. I'd hold them for a few days and let them talk me into giving them back, and stuff like that. When I saw that it wasn't going to [stop], but I saw that it was also becoming a problem in assigned seating, that created the tapers sections.

The tapers section had two functions: One, if you were in the taper's section, you had taper rights. Two, if I caught you out of the tapers section, it was karmically clean for me to kick your ass, and throw your ass right out. At least having them in the tapers section took them away as a problem in the audience at large.

July 11, 1984

Dear Media:

This will introduce our new press representative and publicist, Dennis McNally.

The author of a leading biography on Jack Kerouac, "Desolate Angel," McNally first became associated with us as our house historian and biographer some years ago. He's now on board full time, and we ask that you direct press and interview inquiries to his attention.

Two years ago, after nearly 18 years of doing interviews, we realized that we hadn't said anything new in a while and were pretty sick of listening to our own voices -- so we decided on a no-interview policy, with the occasional (and inevitable) exception. Until we do find something new to talk about, this policy will stay in effect.

But if you have any creative or interesting ideas, please do be in touch with him.

Regards,

Jerry Garcia, for
Grateful Dead

JG/dsm

Grateful Dead

BOX 1073, SAN RAFAEL, CA 94915 • TELEPHONE (415) 457-2322

Dennis McNally

July 14, 2020

DM: OK, let's back up just a little. I wrote a book about Jack Kerouac and wanted to write a book about the Grateful Dead. Very long story short, I connected with Jerry during the [1980] Warfield run. The Warfield run was fifteen shows, and then they were going to do two in New Orleans, and then Radio City, ending it on Halloween. The last show, the Halloween show—this is pre-cable—was going to be a closed-circuit broadcast to movie theaters on the East Coast. And it was a celebration of the fifteenth anniversary, which they had botched because it had been printed on the ticket. The promoter had printed on the ticket that this would be a celebration of the anniversary, but nobody bothered to tell the band. Literally, they came off the stage the first night and, basically, they're looking at each other going, "What was wrong? I mean, we played OK." But they could feel the disappointment coming off the audience. And somebody said, "Yeah, because they were expecting something special. It's your fifteenth anniversary." Now, fifteen years is bupkis. Nothing. But then, it seemed like a long time. And then they started giving it some thought.

So the run at the Warfield was to acknowledge the anniversary. I met Jerry, and talked about the Kerouac book that I had published and sent to him. And because Kerouac was his role model as a kid, he got very excited, and eventually, a couple months later, he sent [the head of the Dead's music publisher] Alan Trist and [sometime manager] Rock Scully to me, and they said, "Jerry says, 'Why don't you do us?'" by which he meant do a biography of the Grateful Dead, which, of course, is what I'd been desperately wanting to do for seven years. And I went, "Well, gee, that sounds interesting. I'll give it some thought." And so I started working on it. I spent about three years researching. I had a part-time job, and I went and worked for Bill Graham as his first archivist for a year, and then, long story short, that was over.

So now, it's the spring of '84, and I had no money. At those band meetings, Mary Jo Meinolf, who was the receptionist, raised her hand and said, "What are we going to do about the media? They keep calling, and nobody calls them back." See, in theory, it was Rock's job, except that Rock had finally gone to rehab three months before. And Danny Rifkin was the manager and wanted nothing to do with the media, and was too busy in the first place. So Mary Jo raised this question, and Jerry said, "Eh, get McNally to do it. He knows that shit." I had done a book tour for my Kerouac book, so I had some idea what a publicist did, and other than that, I learned on the fly and became their publicist. And as a result, I attended the next meeting—they were called "band meetings," and that was all employees. When it was just the band, and their attorney, and their manager, and a representative from the crew, and the financial officer—those were "board meetings."

So somewhere in the band meeting, Healy brought up the fact that something had to be done about taping. And everyone understood that you couldn't prevent taping, unless you set up and ran everyone through a metal detector coming in, and set up X-ray eraser machines on the way out. Or to put it in a slightly less silly way: in order to end it, you would have to destroy the very ambience of the Grateful Dead. And none of them were cops, and none of them gave a shit. There was no reason to. Every show was different. It wasn't like Def Leppard, where if you recorded a show, you had their last album, and it would cut down on album sales. We didn't sell albums anyway, so nobody cared. This is four years into not having put out an album. And it would be another three years before they put one out. They didn't want to do albums; it wasn't the way they made their living, etc.

But anyway, so it had reached the point where people made the assumption, not unreasonably, that the best sound—the sweet spot in the building—was directly in front of the soundboard. They started setting up their mics right in front of the soundboard. Now, if you set up two or three mics, it really wouldn't matter, but it reached the point where Healy couldn't see the stage, or the stage couldn't see him. It was out of hand. So they came up with what I thought was a truly wise and Solomonic decision, which was, "Fine, put them behind the soundboard." [The tapers] don't care about seeing the show. I mean, they don't need to see what's going on on the stage, because there's nothing going on on the stage, except guys playing music. They know what they look like. So put them behind the soundboard, and that way they can crank up their mic stands, and you got nice, clean sound away from the audience.

Minutes of the Meeting Fri 3 August 1984

Present: J. Soto, H. Popick, J. Cutler, S. Gottlieb, W. Legate, El. Law, Patti Harris S. Marcus, M. Greene, MJo Meinolf, S. Stephens, M. Hart, S. Parish, P. Lesh, Kidd, B. Kreutzmann, Ram Rod, B. Parker, H. Kant, R. Taylor, Betsy Cohen, D. McNally, D. Healy, J. Garcia, J. Meyer, D. Steadman (portion), Bear

Absent: D. Rifkin, B.

Meeting was called to
Minutes of meeting of

1. **Security:** Dennis

2. **Merchandising:**
be three shirt designs
were approved. OK w
shirt and a photo or
Bob Thomas brought
portfolio.

Henceforth, all mercha
the difference between
the mark (c) i physic
If something i publish
obtains a trademark, w

The subject of bootle
with each item or pr
stantial and we ignore
tions, but it is expensi
step would be a warn
GD Olympics shirt.

Winterland Productions
deal in placing ads fo
ads or products.

Hal feels merchandisi

Merchandising office w

3. **Video GD Movie:**
is screening movie for
Mobile Fidelity Amer
product. Mars Hotel

4. Attorney **Bruce St**
duced. Bruce, and his
will be working with
ment. "Hal will cont

---

5. Kidd will chair our next meeting 28 August.

6. **Rock/Betty** what is the practical bottom line....
Sue Stephens mentioned an outstanding Sharon Bail Bonds bill in the amount of $4,000 incurred by Rock and Alan. Bonnie will see that it's paid.
In reference to a proposed nominal settlement amount ($1,500-$3,500) in exchange for permanent release, Sue also suggested that whatever our agreement with Betty, it stipulate her cooperation in the location of tapes, etc. Note, per Faust, Crow has some tapes he rescued from unpaid storage (probably BC's tapes/Europe72).

7. Zena, Sonny Heard's widow, will be sent a small contribution of approx. $1,000 to help out the family. Gold records will be sent to Sonny's mon.
Hal mentioned that after the Rex Foundation received proper classification from IRS, a % of the Foundation's grants may go to individuals.

Kidd reqested that Bill Graham be invited to Rex Foundation meetings.

8. Jerry briefly went over the Kevin Laffey project--it will be a random selection of stuff, previously recorded unreleased material during our tenure at Warner Bros.

MTV movie: In addition to old footage, producer would also like 1 minute of current stuff; we will check out the Radio City footage for this purpose.

Some thoughts were expressed re proposed **tapsters** section and feasibility: hot line service #, head high with microphone stands, no video clause, disclaimer. More at next meeting...

9. **Joe Kerr** was introduced at the meeting to be considered for the travel coordinator position, being vacated by Randy. If this job is done on a split commission basis with an agency, there would still be a savings to us of approx. $15k on annual travel commission. Other options such as computer hook up for flight information, etc. can also be explored; the travel agency would then just write the tickets.

10. Eileen needs storage room for press clippings and other archival material. Willie said the upper vault is overflowing, but he might have some room in the lower vault. Healy's room is being used. Room 8 has approximately 100 sq. feet. "Real estate committee" will check out the burned building on Lincoln.

11. Possibility of **Blue Cross medical coverage** for Bill Grillo and Candace is being researched.

12. High Tech Committee--consisting of P. Lesh, J. Garcia, M. Hart, B. Cohen, J. Meyer, J. Cutler. Kidd.

Non-exclusive **Hewlett Packard** promotional deal was discussed; copy of the plan and equipment to be received is attached.

John Meyer proposed a **joint-venture research project** whereby the room would be included in the total picture of the sound. Digitalizing the system would be very complicated and very expensive. Over $1 million could easily be spent; a realistic low-end figure for the budget is approx. $250k. Jerry feels we should move slowly, starting in ove area at a time: Phil's equipment...monitors... CCRMA (Stanford) and personnel would be involvedin the development of this project. Dan Healy will coordinate with J. Meyer in formation of an outline: Proposal for Step One: Budget and concise starting point will be presented at our meeting on 28 Aug.

2

MINUTES OF THE MEETING TUES 28 AUG

Present: B. Parker, J. Cutler, H. Popick, D. Healy , J. Soto, E. Law, C. Brightman, S. Marcus, M. Greene, W. Legate, S. Stephens, MJo Meinolf, Kidd, S. Parish, D. Rifkin, Ram Rod, B. Mydland, B. Stilson, H. Kant, S. Gottlieb, R. Taylor, D. McNally

Absent: J. Garcia, M. Hart, B. Kreutzmann, P. Lesh, P. Roehlk, J. Thomas, B. Weir, P. Harris

Meeting was called to order at 2:35 pm by B. Candelario. Minutes of the last meeting on Fri 3 August were read.

MOBILE FIDELITY: Patricia has been in contact with their office; we're ready to go. Contract with proposed revisions has been sent to them; we're received no answer yet (they've been out of town.

BETTY: Per Hal, Re Brent: Betty admitted that she was not to be paid--that it was a spec deal. However, she would like the right to sell it; she'll talk to Brent about that. Re GD: Hal told her that she's been paid, perhaps overpaid, but if she feels that she is due something, to detail it in writing. Claims she didn't see the letter that her attorney wrote. At this point, nothing is happening. Kidd will pick up the tapes.

Money has been sent to ZENA HEARD. Eileen will see that Gold Records are sent to Sonny's mom.

TAPESTER Section: They feel dead center 30 feet from stage center is ideal--the area in front of sound booth. "Now way are they going to move." We would like to set aside a section for them behind the booth, starting with local show. We're doing this not so much for the tapers, but for the others in the audience. How do we police this: (SP) special ticket to bring stuff in. What if they buy a whole row and bring in a 16-track. Policy needs to be developed and set forth in writing as to size of equipment, etc. Video will not be allowed. A Taper entrance was suggested. Re: confiscation of video tapes after the show, Hal cited a "self-help" point of law: we can take the tapes--but no hassels, if so, it could be serious.
Do we want to stop the taping. Do we want to enfore the clause in our contract rider. Danny feels that we should not stop the taping. Philosophical aspect of this issue is tabled until the next meeting.

TRAVEL: Per Danny, we have to do something; tour is only month away. We need someone NOW.
SP: has a friend/agent in Concord who is all set up.
Danny will meet with these people.
Randy would probably still write the tickets; just doesn't want to be the one on call anymore.
Joe Kerr....

1

knows someone.

d be on payroll
Hal recently
could find no
an independent
B. Grillo is
e can no longer
are no longer on

will coordinate
ime being will

has been reviewing
any re-lease

roached us with

playing.
at it be "kissed

be helping in

ong book.

an be present.
d
involve federal
court). We will urge Bob to come to next meeting. Ram Rod will call.

HK: our position has been so amorphous. We should start telling them no re TAPING and TRADING. Eileen says there are people out there trying to make records. Imports/bootleg LP's.

SUSAN REED--did not do a great deal of artwork for us. Mostly paste up, layout, and photo reduction for passes.
Since she will not sign a contract relinquishing her rights, we will inform her in that she was an employee for hire, that that she doesn't own the art work and dare not use it.

NEW BUSINESS

FRONT STREET: Our lease is up April 85. Per Ram Rod, the owner will not consider sell[...]e property--but he might consider a trade. Estimated value is $300k. We will consult with a real

MINUTES OF THE MEETING WED 5 SEPTEMBER

Present: C. Brightman, P. Roehlk, W. Legate, B. Kreutzmann, Janet Soto, D. McNally, J. Cutler, P. Harris, R. Taylor, S. Marcus, B. Parker, S. Gottlieb, S. Stephens, M. Greene, D. Rifkin, MJo Meinolf, E. Law, B. Candelario, S. Parish, B. Weir, B. Stilson, J. Thomas, Ram Rod, B. Mydland, B. Hunter.

Bob Nichols, Bob Thomas, Bill Graham

*

TAPESTER SECTION: Philosophical issue; sale of premium seats.
BK: has gotten out of hand, and can't be policed effectively.
SP: Sale of our own tapes. Is this contractually feasible?.
(Taper audience likely would object if we came up with tape.)
BW: flyer to obtain feedback.
Will try tapers section at home gig. Must be policed, especially reserved seating--to make sure tapers are not taking anyone's seat.
DMcN doesn't think we can stop. D6's ellude search.
[But the little ones aren't as bad as the big setups]; feels that most tapers come in through the back stage door.
Bruce Stilson: we've always allowed taping; if we said no more taping, they wouldn't bring in the big stuff.

RT has seen cataloges of tapes available--both audio and video.

What will be our policy:
1) Anything goes
2) Close it down completely
3) Taping only in this section
4) Make and sell our own tapes.

BK: suggests flyer--no taping; offer to sell our tapes.
Another flyer suggestion re nuisance aspect--handbill letter to audience: asking for their cooperation. In general we don't mind if public records our concerts--but not if it interferes with the audience s enjoyment; ask for their cooperation. If anyone in violation of our regulations, they will be escorted from building. Statement rather than questionaire. NO VIDEO will be allowed.
DR: They can tape it or leave it!
Dennis will draft couple of things for presentation at next meeting.

Cover Med & Dental $300. 1st 200. after

TRAVEL: DR was not impressed with Katy Short's (via SP's friend) qualifications; just recently out of travel agent school.
Travel Quest--impressed; Hewitt Jackson has been in both rock and travel business for many years. (Most recently took Prince on road, etc...)
Joe Kerr: Danny would like to re-introduce. Feels that Joe could help in other areas; has been in business for a long time.
BW: a good, experienced travel agent important.
We'll go with TravelQuest on a trial basis.

Per Greg Anton one more office will be opening up soon.
1016 Lincoln office worker meeting. (Thursday)
3:50 pm break until 4:00 pm

ICE NINE: Hunter will bring in sample book (re pending projects).
Along with JG has okayed use of "Truckin'" for Nissan Truck commercial: period of 1 year starting 9-15; Fee $5k

S. REED: matter done with.
FRONT/Real Estate property for trade: working on....

2

MAR: I'm just wondering if that conversation around tapers at the meetings was a little bit more nuanced? Or you remember it in a certain way, like a back-and-forth between people?

DM: The conversation didn't really take place at the board meeting. The conversation was an ongoing discussion that had gone back and forth, and probably really happened on some charter airplane flight, where Healy got with the band and said, "Look, fellas, it's getting ridiculous." And they would respond, "Yeah, you got a point. What do we do?" And either Healy, or I don't know who else, maybe Jerry, would say, "Why don't you just put them behind the soundboard? They won't mind, and that way it protects Healy"—and every time I said this, Jerry would immediately say, "And the rest of the audience"—their sightlines. I mean, the objection was not only that Healy couldn't see the stage, but that you want everyone to be able to enjoy the show in their own fashion. And it went beyond that. Tapers would get real psycho about people talking around them and stuff like that. Better they should be together, you know? It was as simple as that.

And as the minutes noted, this was fairly in parallel with the significant growth of the Grateful Dead ticket [office], which was Danny Rifkin's genius legacy with the Grateful Dead. I say that because it had reached the point where older people—that is to say people, say, over twenty-five who, like, had jobs—couldn't spend the night sleeping on the sidewalk in front of Ticketmaster, and had large sums of money. Because at the beginning, you could buy a whole tour, for instance. After a while, we realized, encouraging people to travel along is maybe not such a great idea—that it increased the traveling-circus aspect of things. So then people had to buy them one by one. So anyway, by '84, you have demographically a set of people who are still Deadheads [but] they've got jobs, they've got lives, and they can't do things like camp out all night to buy the ticket. So they can do it by mail-order. And the college kids and high school kids who can and gladly will camp out all night, they can buy tickets that way. So it diversified our audience. It accommodated more [types]—they might look the same as the high school kids, but they weren't. You had all these hairy people who were actually lawyers, and doctors, and teachers, and politicians, and you name it.

So this [mail-order ticketing] was coming along at the same time. So now, we add a second area of accommodation: taper tickets. And it worked like a charm. The tapers bought their tickets. They went into that section. Everybody's happy. The most interesting reaction to that was Page and Plant. Robert Plant and Jimmy Page came to a show, I want to say in the late eighties, though that's a most unreliable estimate. They, like, stuffed their hair in a hat or something, they tried to keep a reasonably low profile, and they walked around the show. What blew their mind was the tapers section. [Led Zeppelin] had never permitted that, and of course, they had a conventional record company. The record companies were the ones who [said], "It'll cost a sale." Not really; not in the case of Grateful Dead, anyway. That's what happened in '84. They finally made it official. They then sold taper tickets for the fall tour. It worked like a charm, as it did for the next eleven years. I mean, I don't ever recall a significant hassle about taper tickets. And that includes things like bootlegging. By bootlegging, I mean taking money for tapes. There was some of that in the Grateful Dead before we allowed [taping]. After we allowed it, I don't remember ever hearing about it.

I mean, what no one realized when they made that decision—and I might add, I was repeatedly, for no good reason, credited with the idea—[it was] the most brilliant promotional idea in the history of rock and roll. Not that anybody thought of it that way. What it demonstrated was the band's trust in the audience, and the audience rewarded that trust, honored that trust. It made the connection between the audience and the band all the more intimate and intense. And in a sort of anthropological sense, the tapes were artifacts. They were a way of introducing you to the culture of the Grateful Dead in a way that no other band had. It made it clear that this wasn't your average rock and roll concert. Among other things, a ninety-minute cassette was by far a better way, a better envelope for holding a Grateful Dead concert than a record, or even a CD.

MAR: In October, [according to] these minutes, a handbill was made for the tapers section. Do you have any memory of there being a major discussion on how to wax the language around that, at all?

DM: I vaguely remember Healy telling me what he wanted, and I drafted something. I don't recall it as being a big deal.

MAR: Was Dan Healy the person that was put in charge of making sure everything happened smoothly, in that sense, until you come about as publicist?

DM: Oh yeah. I mean, it was Dan's sort of department, as it were, simply because literally he was there and would occasionally give people board seats—when he felt like it, and his mood was right, and a friend popped up. But it was connected to him, so it became part of his job. And yeah, I would be involved with it, solely as a matter of language.

MINUTES OF THE MEETING MON 17 SEPTEMBER

Present: P. Lesh, W. Legate, J. Cutler, J. Soto, S. Stephens, B. Parker, S. Marcus, P. Harris, E. Law, M. Greene, MJo Meinolf, D. Rifkin, S. Gottlieb, S. Parish, Kidd, B. Weir, B. Mydland, B. Stilson, Ram Rod, J. Thomas, D. McNally, R. Taylor, M. Hart, B. Hunter, H. Popick, J. Garcia, B. Williams, C. Brightman, J. McIntire

Absent: B. Kreutzmann, D. Healy, H. Kant, P. Roehlk

Meeting was called to order at 2:50 pm by W. Legate.

BOB NICHOLS BOOK: Bruce has not received copy of book; it is forthcoming.
ZENA HEARD: Money was sent.
COLE: It was agreed that we would contribute $200/mo to Cole's care and maintenance while he lives with his grandparents in Oregon ($300 the first month to cover clothes and school supplies) and medical and dental expenses. (Medical and dental insurance is available for approx. $180 annually.) Any other needs can be brought up as they occur.

HANDBILL: Dennis is preparing text for handbill to be circulated at shows: 1) cautionary/common sense statement re recent legislation affecting search seizure laws; 2) statement re taping problem, our regulations, and what will happen to violators; 3) catalog/mail-order offerings of T-shirts, etc. 4) listing of Rex Foundation beneficiary recipients. Will bring to next meeting.
Tapers: Per S. Marcus, approximately 5 out of every 100 BCT ticket mail-orders to date are requesting tapers section.

S. REED: Has threatened suit if GDP does not pay by Sept 28; on hold until and if she serves us. GDP would counter--in Marin Muni Court.

Real Estate agent is coming to appraise Front Street.

SCHEDULE: LA Forum is out for 84.
Spring 85 tour (Mar-April): Hampton, Rochester, Nassau, Portland ME, Providence, Spectrum in Philly, followed by Irvine. Note: Rochester not available--will be replaced by Springfield.
Possibility of using Berkeley Community Theater (rather that Marin Civic) for March 85 benefit run was suggested; discussion to be re-opened after Oct/Nov gigs.

PUBLICITY/PRESS: Video segments are being edited for TV promo use.
Carrier Dome would like to show GD video spots during football games on in-house video setup.
S. Parish will talk to Burr Snider (who has written for Oui) about possible piece on crew.
Evening Magazine has approached us re possibility of 3-minute interview (with Parish) focusing on Dead Heads.
Blair Jackson has approached S. Marcus to do a story for Golden Road.
No on Sam Chu Lin's proposed piece on GD computer use (not mentioning HP specifically): we will be stingy with our endorsement.

John Warner: Discussion re possible assistance is tabled until a presentation is made in his behalf.

MINUTES OF THE MEETING MONDAY 1 OCTOBER

Present: B. Hunter, P. Lesh, M. Greene, W. Legate, C. Brightman, D. Rifkin, B. Candelario, S. Parish, J. Garcia, Ram Rod, E. Law, J. Cutler, B. Stilson, H. Kant J. McIntire, M. Hart, D. Healy, H. Popick, D. McNally, S. Gottlieb, MJo Meinolf, S. Stephens, B. Parker, S. Marcus, Bear, Mountain Girl. D. Pearson, Gary Leo, John Meyer, Helen Meyer

Absent: B. Kreutzmann, B. Mydland, P. Roehlk, R. Taylor, B. Weir

Meeting was called to order at approximately 2:40 p.m. by B. Hunter.

HANDBILL: Proposed handbill for audience distribution was approved as presented, with the exception of the paragraph soliciting artwork. Hall pointed out that we could be leaving ourselves open to possible legal hassles were we to accept artwork without the appropriate releases having been signed; this paragraph will be deleted.

FIRE ALARM/FRONT: Expenditure of $2371 was approved for installation of fire alarm a Front. The proper addendum to our lease or legal agreement with the owner will have to be drawn up to protect our ownership of this equipment.
FRONT STREET has been appraised at approx. $400k. Careful itemization will have to be made of all our equipment or improvements; the real estate agent will have to be made aware of this, so that in the event of our acquisition of the property, we will not be double-charged.

RECORDING STUDIO: Next meeting....

VIDEO CAMERA: C. Brightman requested increase in approved budget of $1500 to $2200 fo purchase of Panasonic portable video deck and camera with zoom lens. Approved.

NEXT MEETING: THURSDAY 25 OCTOBER

FALL 84 TOUR: Jimmy Cliff will not open at the Carrier Dome 20 Oct; venue is approximately half sold-out three weeks prior to show.

SUMMER TOUR SCHEDULE: D. Healy feels that Harrisburg venue needs to be improved reference to backstage area, delay towers, staging; will review with R. Taylor and make list of suggestions. Danny would like us to reconsider Toronto venue.

NEW YEAR'S: J. Cutler will book NPR satellite for RADIO BROADCAST; suggestions for professional-type host include: Robin Williams, Jane Dornacher, Bob and Ray, Red Blanchard (Dr. Dimento), Fred Willard (America Tonight).
TV BROADCAST: We will consider a 30 to 60 minutes show around midnight on a local public station. Hal mentioned that Ted Turner (with whom he is negotiating for a cable system in Costa Rica) is forming a cable music station (to compete with MTV) and may be looking for material; Hal will speak to him.
OPENING ACT: Suggestions included Clasmorum, The Bobs, Nylons.
Breakfast will not be served; there will be no in-house video setup.
GDP has approved $5000 for New Year's extravaganza production to be entered into final settlement.
Tickets will be mail-order, first come-first served; price is $15 for first two nights, $25 on New Year's Eve, plus $1 service charge.
Bart Bull/SanJose Mercury will run a GD feature story around New Year's.

MINUTES OF THE MEETING THURSDAY 25 OCTOBER

Present: B. Kreutzmann, W. Legate, D. Healy, H. Popick, B. Hunter, B. Parker, M. Greene, S. Gottlieb, MJo Meinolf, S. Stephens, A. Flowers, C. Brightman, J. Thomas, P. Lesh, D. Rifkin, S. Parish, M. Hart, J. McIntire, B. Weir, B. Stilson, J. Cutler, B. Williams, Ram Rod, R. Taylor, B. Mydland, P. Harris, D. McNally, P. Roehlk, J. Soto, J. Garcia

Absent: E. Law, Kidd, H. Kan

Meeting was called to order at

FIRE/BURGLAR ALARM: South
a Fire Alarm system at Fron
B. Grillo, W. Legate, J. Cutle
alarm systems are still being r

FRONT STREET: Property ow
and B. Stilson will meet wi
Bruce feels that purchase price

RECORDING STUDIO: M. Har
At present, early 1985 is open.

NEW YEAR'S: We will approa
host our radio broadcast; appro
be invited to our Berkeley sho
B. Graham) for Robin Williams
OPENING ACT: Still being con
TV BROADCAST: Ted Turner
did not consider unsolicited
personally. A MTV show i
preliminary contact did not fe
further discussions with station
EXTRAVAGANZA PRODUCTION
1985. Danny has verified $5k
will appear in our final settle

20TH ANNIVERSARY: Jerry
will present a menu of formats

B & K FREQUENCY ANALYZ
time a decision will be made r
we must consider the tax adva
with B. Parker and a committ
Kidd, J. Cutler, M. Hart for fu
ULTRA SOUND's fee for the f
pointed out that this figure wa
$1500/gig more than next best-
on East Coast to reduce cost
comparison. The above comn
will also address the John Meye

PRESS/PUBLICITY: Evening Magazine project is out. Time Magazine is considering a possible piece on Dead Heads; reps will attend BCT shows.

D. Healy requested 10 pair tickets/night for December shows as part of KERG promotion. Approved. Danny feels all employees should have access to extra tickets if necessary; individual requests will be considered as presented.

GD MOVIE/VIDEO CASSETTE: B. Stilson reported that one company is forwarding proposed contract offering $12K advance.

DEAD AIR: D. Healy proposes that we provide quality tapes of live material to NPR type radio stations for a weekly syndicated radio program. Will consult with Bruce and Hal re legal aspects. More at next meeting.

TAPERS SECTION/BCT: Handbill was moderately successful in regulating tapers. We will inform security and enforce our regulations all nights. "If you come in a wheelchair and don't need it, you will."

BROADCAST: J. Cutler will be production coordinator on the project. Radio stations will pay their own uplink charges, since GDP is incurring all other expenses.

Meeting was adjourned at 5:38 p.m.

-3-

The audience is always a part of the show. You, in our audience, customarily grant all those around you their space. Where we play is also a part of the show. Please remember that a community includes everyone, and policemen are working people who would rather enjoy the show than feel obliged to arrest conspicuous lawbreakers.

"One man gathers what another man spills"—So watch where and what you spill!

* * * *

We've always been loose about private, noncommercial Dead Head taping—*"When we're done with it, you can have it,"* Garcia once said. *"But lately,"* says Billy Kreutzmann, *"I look out in the audience and see hassles, not enjoyment."* The hassles are caused by a small group of tapers who are taking seats away from people with appropriate tickets in the *"taping pit"* 30 feet in front of the stage. In addition, a sizeable part of the audience, including our own Dan Healy, is losing stage visibility due to overly tall mikestands. Thirdly, people are beginning to videotape.

This is all creating a problem.

Basically, we figure that if we advise you of this problem, we can deal with it in a low-key, positive way. At our upcoming Berkeley Community Theater shows, we will be setting aside the area behind the soundboard for tapers—it will be OK to tape there, but nowhere else in the hall; get caught elsewhere and you are gone for the night. Videotaping is not OK at any time.

But on the current East Coast tour, the only reason you'll get a hassle is if you ask for one. Tapers (and, similarly, photographers) do *not* have special privileges. Deprive somebody of their seat and create a fuss and you'll have the option of checking your equipment or checking out the scene on the street. Put up a mikestand above 6' and the same thing will happen. Videotape and you'll be asked to leave.

We don't want to turn this into an issue, and it would be nice to see the problem simply vanish over the next few gigs. It's up to you. Let us know what you think at the address below—and please mark the outside of the envelope *"TAPER ISSUE."*

* * * *

In March the Dead played four nights of benefits for The Rex Foundation, named after the late Dead crew member Rex Jackson. Recipients so far this year have been:

Greenpeace
Meta Tantay
Camp Winnarainbow
Marin Wildlife Center
Bay Area Music Archives
San Francisco Blues Festival
Petaluma People Service Center
California Marine Mammal Center
International Indian Treaty Council
San Francisco Mayor's Fund for the Homeless
Southern Humboldt Retired Senior Volunteer Program

* * * *

Artists! Some of you do great work, and we'd like to see photos or samples of it, to consider buying the design for one of our regular issues. Please send this to Bill Candelario at the address below. We cannot promise to return them, but they'll definitely get an honest evaluation. **(This message is especially for the folks who did the 1) 1984 as stars and stripes on the outline of the U.S., 2) the *"Club Dead,"* and 3) the Olympic Rings designs of this summer.)**

* * * *

Finally, we're going through various changes with our merchandising trip, and want to start fresh. As a result, we're going to liquidate all the artwork in the catalogue at a 50% price cut, on a first-come, first-served basis. Send your order to Winterland Productions, P.O. Box 77505, San Francisco, CA 94107.

* * * *

Yours,

Grateful Dead

P.O. Box 1073, San Rafael, CA 94915

MAR: In terms of that relationship that you guys have, and the responsibilities you both were given in respect to this whole formation of the tapers section, would you say the band was fairly hands-off? They just, in typical Dead fashion, didn't really want to deal with that issue, at all?

DM: Well, that's not entirely true. They dealt with it as much as they needed to. They said yes. They said, "Yeah, let's at least try," and it turned out to be successful, so it never needed to change.

MAR: When was mail-order ticketing started? Was it started after you had become the publicist, or before?

DM: Slightly before. I want to say it was started in '83.

MAR: I have this *Unbroken Chain* from 1992, and you have an interview conducted by Tim Ashbridge, and in it—I'm just going to quote you—you said, "I spent '81, '82, and '83 researching, during which I started the research part of what later became *DeadBase*. I'm proud to say I kind of assembled that team." I'm just curious because I'm trying to contact all the people from that *DeadBase* team, but I was just curious what you meant by that, and what your role was in forming *DeadBase*, if that's the case.

DM: Before I'd even gotten Jerry's invitation to be the biographer, I was sort of slithering my foot—I use the word "slither" precisely, as in, faintly sleazy. I mean, I was up to something. I had met Jerry, and we had talked, and it was like a couple months later that he suddenly came up with this idea—the point being that it couldn't be my idea. It had to be his, and it all worked out that way. In that interval, I had run into Rock [Scully], and I had said to him, "It would be really neat to have a list of all the shows." And he said, "Well, we've got one at the office, at least. It starts in 1970 because the earlier files had been stolen by [previous Dead financial manager] Lenny Hart," at the time, or at least that was his rap. So I put together a list of all the contracts from 1970 on which they did have, plus all of the Bill Graham tickets, all of the Avalon tickets which I knew about, and various others. So there was a partial list, and then I had my two legwomen—two young women, Deadheads, who were very sweet, who went to school on Long Island—and I would send them to the Brooklyn College newspaper stacks; you know, references for shows. And I was doing that in other places besides Long Island. So I was working on this list of shows.

I wrote a piece about the Grateful Dead which appeared in the Sunday Magazine of the S.F. Chronicle during the 1980 15-night run at the Warfield. I had met Eileen Law, the queen of Deadheads and one of the best people on the planet, through Jan Simmons who was then Bill Graham's secretary and is now the Grateful Dead's tour secretary. Franken and Davis did a skit between sets and they were picking out a Deadhead to be <u>the</u> Deadhead for the skit. The whole spoof was on Jerry's kids, and I was invited by Eileen to audition to be a Jerry's kid. I was already too old and too straight and all that, but of course I seized the opportunity to meet Jerry and say to him, "Did you read my book?", to which I had the wonderful experience of having him literally jump out of his chair and say, "You wrote that book? It's the best biography I ever read!", to which I said, "Aw, shucks." That was in September, and in December, Jerry sent some people to me and said, "Why don't you do us?" To which I replied, "Fuck Yes!" So I spent '81, '82 and '83 researching it, during which I started the research part of what later became DeadBase. I'm proud to say I kind of assembled that team.

Dennis McNally interviewed by Tim Ashbridge in *Unbroken Chain* vol. 6, #6, March 1992

Healy and some of the folks in the tapers' section at the Berkeley Community Theatre shows. Photo: David Gans

Is there an ideal-size hall?

I think a place that seats about 6000 and doesn't have too horrible acoustics is about right.

Well, the second part of that eliminates Winterland . . .

Winterland was *awful* acoustically. I'm glad it was like that in a way, though, 'cause that's where we cut our teeth. I was raised in the worst tub going, so by the time I had to venture into bigger halls around the country I'd lived for so many years with that, the rest of it was a piece of cake.

You have a unique relationship with Deadheads. For one thing, there isn't another soundman alive who is so well known to the fans of the group. But also, you're very open with them, not cut-off like others are.

They're my pals, my buddies. See, I've always been out there right in the middle of 'em. God, over the years, so many people have been so nice to me. People bring me cookies and stickers and shirts, just *everything*. There's one guy who brings a new joke to me every gig. He writes it down, and when I step up to the console there's the joke of the day. There's a girl who keeps fresh flowers on my board every show. I don't ask for it; they just do it.

In a way, I guess I'm their representative. They make suggestions, tell me things. I only require that you not hurt anybody and not destroy any of the equipment. I show people the soundboard and they can't believe that I'll do that, because at other shows they've been to it's like this elitist trip — "*You* can't come up here!" How could I say I'm doing sound for the audience if I isolate myself from the audience? To be *with* them I have to be one of them. Obviously we can't let it get too crowded, but we try to let people check it out if they want to. There are a lot of young audio freaks out there, and it would be a shame if I weren't willing to share what I know with them. These people are the future of audio!

Is the state-of-the-art of audience taping pretty good right now?

Oh yeah. Shit, some of those tapes sound *grooood!*

I understand you make an audience tape of each show. What do you use?

I use an AKG stereo microphone — one of those two-mikes-in-one that was developed in Europe for recording classical concerts, a matrix box that I built for the figure-eight thing — MS — and then I have a Beta hi-fi PCM video deck that gets the board mix onto the video band, and then on the beta hi-fi track I put the audience MS mike. Then I can take that back to the studio and take this new analyzer we've got and it will compare the notes and the impulses of the music and regulate the delay so I can play back and mix the room mikes and the board mix. It's beautiful to hear.

Were you happy with the taping section at Berkeley?

I thought it was great, a real wise idea. In some of the places we play around the country, portions of the audience are very impolite and rude with their recording, and somehow these people have developed this self-importance and they tend to push people around and shove kids out of their seats. Well, there are a lot of people who buy tickets who just want to see the show, who don't give a damn about the recording part of it, and it's unfair for them to be abused by the recording people. So that's why we created the recording section. What we've really done by this is actually give these tapers real rights that they never formally had before. And as long as people don't abuse it, it can go on forever as far as I'm concerned.

You haven't worked much with the band in the studio the last few years . . .

I don't dig it anymore. The Grateful Dead kill a record in the studio. I can't stand it.

What could you do to prevent that?

Slap 'em! [Laughs] I don't know. I refuse to go in the studio with those guys. In the case of working in the studio, Weir is one of those guys who thinks that fame is predicated on fashion. His notion of how to make a record that's a million-seller is to hire some fashionable producer or something. And none of those fashionable slick producers have the energy to put up with those guys. You have no idea the energy it takes to keep up with all those creeps in a session! [Laughs] The producers try to use drum machines and stuff because Mickey and Billy won't perform Pavlovian stuff for them. Then Weir is so concerned with sucking up to those industry people that he winds up turning against his musician brothers and pulling out the drum machine. To me, it's just a convoluted can of worms.

I think the Dead should either concentrate on making good live albums, or at least try to play as live in the studio as they can. But having a hit record isn't important to me. Different things are important to different people. I don't give a fuck if we ever record again. Playing live is what's important to me, because that's where it all comes together. That's the real thing. *That's* the Grateful Dead. ☐

Dan Healy interviewed by Blair Jackson in *The Golden Road* #5, Winter 1985

MINUTES OF THE MEETING 8 NOVEMBER 1984

Present: B. Weir, Kidd, S. Parish, P. Roehlk, M. Nelson, B. Williams, J. Cutler, B. Mydland, B. Stilson, C. Brightman, R. Taylor, D. Rifkin, H. Popick, P. Lesh, D. McNally, W. Legate, S. Giottlieb, S. Marcus, D. Healy, P. Harris, MJo Meinolf, S. Stephens, B. Parker, M. Hart, J. Garcia, B. Hunter, Ram Rod, R. Scully, Bear

Absent: E. Law, B. Kreutzmann, J. Thomas, H. Kant, J. Soto

B & K ANALYZER/SOUND: D. Healy reported that a buy-out/lease-back of yr-old equipment is not tax advantaged due to prior depreciation. The possiblity of renting speakers and amps (this would not include snakes, however) on the East Coast to reduce sound costs is still being researched and to be discussed. At present, the B&K is being rented (with an option to purchase for $27k) at a $9k fee for a 90-day period. Bonnie feels that for tax reasons, it is best to purchase outright. Approved. Equipment will be kept at Front Street with possibility of renting it out (with experienced operator only) at $1k/per night.
John Meyer Proposal: Purchase of analyser is phase one. Healy feels that a customized version of phases two and three could be completed at an approximate cost of $50k-$60k (rather than the R & D proposal with budget of $300k-$500k).

RECORDING STUDIO: We will put a hold option on Fantasy Studios for January and February; (we are still awaiting news of record company negotiations).

REHEARSAL for December shows will start 15 Dec; band members will discuss stage configurations, etc.
P. Lesh would like it a matter of policy to have 5 working days of rehearsal time before the truck has to leave.

NEW YEAR'S: OPENING ACT: Still trying to reach or speaking with management of: Bobs, Nylons, Brass Band....
TV: KQED is interested and through the PBS network will try to raise the $10k to $15K for production and satellite hookup costs for a one-hour video cameo; KCET in LA is also willing to underwrite portion of these expenses. J. Garcia will coordinate direction.
RADIO BROADCAST: J. Cutler will order 900-area code phone lines for audience polling; cost is approximately $75. A "gag-writer" committee (Kidd, S. Parish, B. Hunter, W. Legate) was appointed to assist with polling questions, etc.
D. Healy has checked the facilities at SF Civic; there is plenty of room for the video equipment if that happens. J. Cutler reported that to date 30 stations will be broadcasting our show; approximately 20 more stations are expected to participate.

MERCHANDISING/VIDEO TAPES: J. Garcia suggested the following for us to think about for discussion later: video taping a few gigs/per tour and marketing a video cassette. Pre-recorded tapes sell for approx. $35. We would have to check copyright law, etc.

TAPERS SECTION worked out very well at BCT--avoided a lot of congestion and hassels. D. Healy motioned that we continue to do this. Approved. We should insert a clause in our contract rider concerning the taper's section; S. Marcus will have to be advised of the exact location of the sound board for all venues. Tapers section at SF Civic will be located in middle of balcony.

SPRING BENEFIT LOCATION: BCT was discussed; D. Healy said that the abnormal amount of bounce-back could be fixed with further prep. B. Weir feels that it's the ideal size for local gigs; P. Lesh liked it; S. Parish and Ram Rod had no problems. Danny will check BCT availability for Rex Foundation March benefit gigs; BGP will do production.

- 2 -

MAR: Just for your own personal use, at this point?

DM: Yep. And by now, Jerry has invited me to be the biographer. So I'm doing that and realizing that it's really demanding. It's fascinating, but also tedious and slow. You look and [see that] they played Boston, and then, three nights later, they played Philly. Well, obviously, they played somewhere on the East Coast in between, and you start filling in the gaps. So it was fun, but it was also slow work, and I had other things to be doing. And just at that time, John Scott got in touch. John Scott was a computer programmer at Dartmouth. He wanted to assemble a list of all the shows and all the songs of the shows, and what did I think about that? I said, "That's fine. You have to give 10 percent to Rex [the Dead's charity organization]," and he said, "Fine." And I had a buddy named Mike Dolgushkin, who works in the California State Library in Sacramento. He's extremely—he's a librarian. I mean, he's, like, detail-oriented. He was doing all this by hand, typing out lists. I don't even know if it was an electric typewriter, I swear. But anyway, it was really, really, kind of obsessive. So they were going to combine forces, and I said, "That's great."

MAR: Just to interrupt you, did John contact you through the Grateful Dead office? Or did you guys know each other from before?

DM: No. He called me at the office. So then Dolgushkin became part of it, so I suggested, "You guys need somebody to sort of bridge the gap." Mike was more Deadhead than you could be, and John was, I mean, clearly a Deadhead, but also just a classic computer nerd. I said, "What you need is my friend, Stu Nixon," who at the time was working for Genentech—so he was very sophisticated technologically and computer-wise—and was a Deadhead. So I stuck him in there and said, "Guys, go do it. I get three copies." That's how that worked. And it just got crazier. I mean, the depth of information and the depth of the cross-referencing, and all that. It was extremely handy when I was writing the book for things like the first date [a certain song was] played, and things like that. The same thing happened also at the same time, in the early eighties, when I conceived of a need to have, in one handy place, the original versions of songs that the band covered. I mentioned that, and within a month or two, I had like three ninety-minute cassettes full of original versions of Grateful Dead covers.

MAR: Was *DeadBase*, then, the first end-all-be-all compiling of that history of live shows for the Dead, before the internet?

DM: Yes, at the time, sure. It was the first substantial, well-researched effort, mostly because there were lots of like people who relied on tapes. A lot of the tapes in the interval—literally, labels would fall off, and they would get mislabeled, and you'd have wrong dates and so forth that had floated around the tape world for years. I had access to much more credible sources of information, like the contract lists. So I was a little more credible than somebody's stack of tapes.

MAR: So you would double-check the *DeadBase* team's research? Or did you supplement it?

DM: What I did was I gave them the nucleus of what they worked on. I said, "OK. Take it. Run." And I handed them the list that I had developed.

MAR: Can we talk about Dick Latvala and his participation in the tape scene?

DM: He started out as a gopher for the band's crew. And eventually Phil saw his notes, and although he had no academic training, he was nothing if not thorough, and careful, and meticulous, which is really what you need to be to do what he was doing. At that point, and to that point, Willy Legate had been the archivist. Willy had other interests—he sort of did the bare minimum, but it wasn't his primary interest—at which point Phil said [to Dick], "Hell, you should be the archivist." And I don't know what Dick said to that, but that was a very wise decision, maniacal as Dick was. And there were certain things he did that, I mean, making copies of board tapes and sharing them with everybody and his brothers, probably something we look back on and go, "Maybe not quite so generous." But there was no one on the planet—I mean, I dedicated the book to Jerry and him, OK? There was nobody on the planet that cared more about the Grateful Dead than Dick Latvala.

Interview with a Vault Archivist

by Steve Silberman

Dick Latvala interviewed by Steve Silberman in Unbroken Chain #52, September 1995

SS: A lot of Deadheads are curious about who Dick of *Dick's Picks* is.

DL: I'm Dick Latvala. My job has changed over the years. I was hired 10 years ago to keep the tapes organized in The Vault, though I ended up getting involved in a lot of other projects. I wanted to help participate in getting the music out to the people, because I'm a tape collector myself. I had hundreds and hundreds of tapes, and I thought I knew what was a good show and what wasn't. I got hired because I cared, and still, when I go in The Vault, I'm like a kid in Candyland. It takes my breath away.

When did you start collecting tapes?

In 1974. I'd taped a couple of New Year's shows from Winterland that were on the radio, but I didn't know there were tapes of other shows. Once I found that out, I spent 12 hours a day finding the people who were making the best tapes, communicating with them, and trading. I used to walk four or five miles to the post office in Hawaii when I thought tapes were coming. It's been a long trip, but I'm still just as thrilled by the music as I was in the beginning.

Do you remember what your first favorite tapes were?

Like everyone's: Harpur College 5/2/70, Fillmore East 2/13/70, 2/14/68, and 4/6/69. The reason I got so into it was that I wanted to hear tapes of shows that had so devastated me in '68 and '69. Believe me, it was the most incredible thing in the universe, and that's why I'm so compulsive - *things happened* that were in your bones. I got into tapes hoping to find those shows. And I did. What a thrill, when you find them.

Some people have an attitude. I remember people in '72 - "*Stella Blue*? Gimme a break! That ain't the Grateful Dead." But I still like them every year, and there are good shows in every year. I love tapes, and I can't think of anything more important than to sit and listen. That's all I want to do, and now, that's all I'm supposed to do, so I'm happy.

Are you going to try as often as possible to release complete shows?

Well, the first two *From the Vault* releases were complete. Some shows warrant it. I really am going to be pulling my best to get 2/28/69 out - that show is completely worthwhile.

The concept of putting out only whole shows - I came into this job as a proponent of that, thinking that way. I was really adamant about it. I've learned that that's unrealistic. That's what tape collecting is for, tape trading. We're lucky we're getting what we're getting.

How do you feel about David Gans' *Grateful Dead Hour*?

I think it's the greatest thing! I don't know why any Deadhead who cares isn't taping every broadcast. That's the greatest stuff you can get. I know, because he comes to me, and me and him deal with it. He chooses it, but I give him input, and he chooses great. He does the best job imaginable. I'm proud of him. I wish something like that was around when I started tape collecting!

What was the source tape for the Halloween '71 show?

A quarter-track, 7 1/2 inches per second, seven-inch reel, made on a Sony 770. This is one of the only quarter-track tapes in The Vault.

What process did you use to transfer it to CD?

The same as the first *Dick's Picks* - flat, no EQ's, straight into the Sonic Solutions digital editing system, which is a miracle making machine.

If you were on a desert island, what ten tapes would you want to have?

Oh God, what a terrible question. If I could think for awhile, maybe I could do it. Could I have a hundred?

[laughing] Is there any message you'd like to give to Deadheads?

I love you all. I think you're the most beautiful people in the history of the planet.

MAR: You mentioned Willy Legate, and I'm curious because I interviewed Dave Lemieux, and he came in in '99, so he would not have any dealings with Willy Legate, necessarily, although he was still alive. I'm just curious if you had any dealings with him, and any more input you could give to filling out who he was, and how he came to be the archivist before Dick.

DM: He came to be the archivist because he was the janitor, that is to say, he was the superintendent of Front Street. And the reason he was the superintendent of Front Street is that he was homeless and that he had known Jerry since 1961. Jerry had slept on his floor in '61. He had a room at the Palo Alto Peace Center. And if he had floor space, you had a place to crash. He was exceedingly eccentric, sort of on another planet, and had been around forever. But as I say, in the late seventies, he was borderline homeless, so in effect, it was his pension, to take care of certain things at Front Street. At that time, it was dawning on them that they really needed to protect the tapes—I don't know if they realized how significant it would be to their incomes in the future, but it was their heritage. They knew that, and they wanted to cherish it. So they built this very nice room at Front Street with temperature control, which was then rebuilt up in Novato, and then, now, it's all in some vault in Burbank, I think, with fire suppressant and blah, blah, blah, for maximum care. It's interesting because, of course, the archives contain almost, except for wire, almost the history of recording. Start with quarter-track tape, and then inch tape, and giant sixteen-track tape, and just endless—HDCD, or whatever the stuff was called, these little magnetic tape things—and then digital. You know? They've just got everything in there. Which meant you had to have endless playback machines, too, but that's another story.

So [Willy], sort of by default, became the archivist, and worked on it, but it wasn't his passion the way it was Dick's. So Dick was the perfect archivist. I think Willy recognized Dick's passion and said, "You're the right guy for this job," and just sort of handed it over, said, "Here. There it is."

MAR: Is there a reason why Willy was called "the sage"?

DM: He was kind of a Bible scholar and somewhat mystically inclined. If he was a sage, it was much more like . . . that he knew about stuff. He was, like, sending off to Sandoz for LSD in 1959, years before Jerry ever heard about LSD. He studied Zen. He was bizarrely but interestingly well-read about all manner of strange esoteric subjects, stuff like that. He was very smart, as I say, somewhat otherworldly, and people respected that.

MAR: I was just thinking of this in terms of mythmaking—or I guess we'd use the term "legacy" at this moment in time—but I'm wondering if taping was kind of part of that mythmaking, after many years of that occurring in the scene and it being kind of a presence?

DM: I don't know if that was actually a question. The point is, in terms of this making of legacy—any mythmaking of legacy had to do with the audience. They were the ones doing the taping, and they're the ones thinking in those terms. The band did not think in those terms. The band—as I think I've made clear—OK'd taping because they didn't want to be cops. They couldn't be cops; they'd be terrible cops.

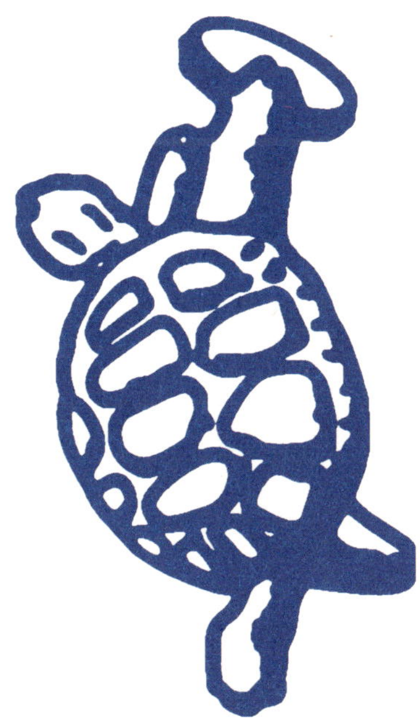

Stu Nixon

July 18, 2020

SN: I had a whole wall of tapes. I had many thousands of tapes, all color coded, and when we got to around 2010, I was no longer trading and [didn't know] what to do with them all. I remember giving away to two or three different Deadheads who I was friends with, who were beginning tapers. They just freaked out. "Hey, I'll give you three bankers boxes of tapes for nothing. I just don't need them anymore." That's a weird time to give up something you put your heart and soul into for decades, [for it] to just be over. But it was a small example of, when Jerry passed—look at what it did to all of our lives, at that point. The Dead were gone.

MAR: I wanted to interview you, and possibly Mike [Dolgushkin] and John [Scott] to kind of get the story of *DeadBase*, which I think is this very important record-keeping device.

SN: Oh, as a tool. Some people have called it "the taper's bible." Other people have said they keep it right on the side of the desk when they're doing their tape labels. Because a lot of times, if you're trading tapes, people often add in a couple of extra songs to fill the ninety minutes or whatever and it's not necessarily labeled correctly. *DeadBase* was often the reference to look stuff up and get the labels done right.

MAR: Right, and I use it in my process even to make sure that certain tapes are what they are, and a number of hiccups always happen while I'm doing my thing and I'm like, "Oh, time to bring out the *DeadBase*." It's amazing, all the info.

SN: Yeah, I am so happy that *DeadBase* has turned out to be such a tool, not only for Deadheads like you and me—I even use it myself—but Billy [Kreutzmann] and Phil [Lesh]. When they were writing their autobiographies, Billy asked me for a copy even though I'd sent him an edition of every single book we put out, but I guess he didn't keep them all. Phil said he had the whole collection on a whole row of his bookshelf right next to his desk. It was very cool to know that they fact-checked—and probably remembered a cool story at some location that they forgot what the date was exactly, or even what tour it was. So *DeadBase* was a reference for them to try and get a semblance of accuracy.

MAR: In those early shows that you saw, did you ever see the row of tapers?

SN: I saw them and didn't see them. I could tell what somebody was doing; it was sort of like passing a joint in the crowd, and you can't let anybody see you, because smoking wasn't even allowed back them. Yeah, I think when I first got to Syracuse, like in '78, I think I might have picked up one tape prior to that.

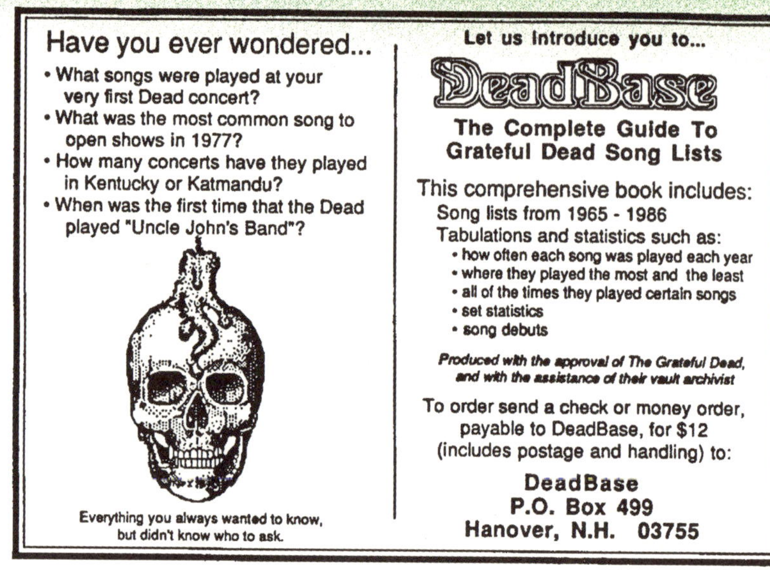

I don't remember where it was from, but I ran into a few heads that were tape trading, so that's where it all started. It just was exponential. In the two and a half years I was in Syracuse, I accumulated five hundred tapes at least, trading with people on campus, off campus, and then on tour in the northeast—because the band would constantly be touring, from Maine all the way down to Virginia. I would often go and do a mini ten-day road trip, because, as a graduate student there at Syracuse, timing was very flexible. So I was able to catch a lot of shows.

That's when I started taping, as well. A couple of my friends, like three guys from New Hampshire—I forget where I was, Worcester, Massachusetts, or something. And I went really early, like at midnight, to get in line just like everybody else, to buy tickets. And these guys were in line with me. So we just struck up a conversation, and they were some of these clandestine tapers. I was able to get first-gen copies of their masters. And then they were telling me about decks and things like that, so I popped and bought a Sony D6, later a D5, but I started small with the D6, and would plug into their decks. I didn't actually own stands or mics, but some of them spent big bucks on good Sennheiser mics and things like that. So I was a taper. I guess I had a small reputation at that time that came from being at the radio station or whatever, or maybe just the way I carried myself, but these guys—they were very happy to let me tape and then get the hell away, because it was crowded. Before there was the tapers section, people still went around the board—either in front-of-board, or behind the board, mostly—even before it became official.

In the early part of the seventies, I was not really aware of any taping going on. You know there was—because there are audience tapes from the sixties and seventies—but it was a very rare event. In the eighties, there were a number of different recordings of the same show, versus the seventies, [when] you'd maybe find one or two, the earlier you go. Then, afterwards, in the late seventies, that's when it seemed to be starting up. I can't give you an exact year, but certainly by '78, where I had good friends who were taping, then it was way more commonplace.

OK, so from '80 to '84, it gradually became more and more organized, but not approved yet. When they finally approved it, it was really a foregone conclusion. There were tall mic stands starting in maybe '82—that I remember. It was a rare event that somebody would get busted. I think it eventually just got [to be] more and more people doing it, so eventually, they approved it so that they could set rules. Because the tapers were setting up in the second row and all over the place. That was not good for other audience members or for the band. It was distracting. So they said, "OK, we know you guys have been taping a lot. We're cool with that."

I was a really poor grad student; it was a big investment for me just to get the D6. There's no way I could afford any stands or mics by myself. There were so many people, and the community was cool, [that] as long as you asked politely and made it a smooth part of your conversation to patch in with somebody, [you were] almost never told no. It was, "Oh, OK." Some of them, it was, "Sure!" Especially if it was somebody I knew. But other times, if I went to a show where I didn't know any of the tapers, I would just at random start hanging out, talking to the person, and then, if they seemed friendly enough, I'd say, "By the way, I have a deck in my backpack. Any chance I could patch in with you?" I'd say 90 percent of the time they said yes, even if they never knew me before. It was such a—I don't know if "brotherhood" is the right word, but it's such a great family. It was very cool.

From this point on, '81—because that's when I moved from the East Coast—a few very cool things happened in that first year. The first thing was that I got married: my wife Robin and I flew from New Hampshire to Seattle for our honeymoon, drove down the coast catching shows in Seattle, Portland, Eugene and Berkeley, and never went back. Another thing was I got my first real job at a company called Genentech, which was one of the founding companies of genetic engineering, and I sort of got in at the ground level and stayed there for like twenty years, and moved up, and did very successfully in my biotech career. At the same time, I started seeing lots of shows (my first show was in 1969 in New York, but it wasn't until the late seventies that things got real serious), and I ended up bumping into people that were very close to the band, just by chance. We were all over at one family's house after one of the Greek shows, and [Dennis McNally] happened to be there from San Francisco, and he needed a ride home, and we were crashing at my wife's sister's place in the Haight, so I said, "Yeah, we can drop you off." He was in Polk Gulch, which is not too far from the Haight, so we took him home. Soon after that, he got hired by Bill Graham Presents, and was part of their archiving, and he brought me along to help go through a lot of Bill Graham's vault of tapes and posters and handbills and everything, and then later, he got to be the publicist for the Dead. He got married in San Francisco and Jerry gave the bride away. Half the band was there, [Robert] Hunter, TC [keyboardist Tom Constanten], and I was there, so I just hung out and played it cool and was a nice person to talk to, and just got in further and further. I was working with Dick Latvala in the vault, and working with Eileen Law in the office, and then *DeadBase* happened in '87.

MAR: What was the nature of your work, you working with Dick Latvala and Eileen Law and that sort of thing?

SN: We had a real early version of *DeadBase*, back maybe ten years earlier. I hadn't met him yet, but Mike Dolgushkin was compiling setlists off of either people's notes or off of tapes, and I got a copy of Mike's master list. And so, many times Dick got an unlabeled tape box, reel-to-reel. He would ask me from time to time, "Hey, can you check the master list"—he was already calling Mike's list the master list—"to see what this show could be?" Or, "There's a problem with this date. It puts them [as playing] this particular song way before they ever really did." So I was sort of his fact-checker off of that early version. And with Eileen, it was just a friendship kind of thing; it wasn't actually doing anything for them. I forgot how I got introduced to her, but early on, she was just my contact person to give me tickets and backstage passes. I think, probably, it was Dennis and Dick that introduced me to her, and she assumed that, if they approved of me, then I was good to go. So I basically didn't buy tickets from '84 until '95—anytime I wanted to go, I'd get those stick-on passes. There's two kinds of backstage passes: there's the laminate plastic ones, which are basically only for the crew and the band and the friends of same; but then they were very, very generous to friends of friends, so backstage at some of the major shows, like at Oakland Coliseum, or the Bill Graham Center in

San Francisco, there could be three or four hundred people backstage with these stick-on passes.

MAR: I'm just curious, you were working at Genentech, right, and then you meet Dennis and he brings you in on the Bill Graham archive. Is there a reason why he specifically brought you in?

SN: Well, I think I was in the right place at the right time, number one. He didn't necessarily know a lot of people that had time on their hands. I had my nine-to-five job, but I also had time on my hands. Maybe I wasn't your typical Deadhead—I was your professional person who was also into the Dead. I didn't have to wear ties and stuff to work, but at least I had a nine-to-five job. We had worked together on Grateful Dead minutiae, and he saw that I was as compulsive as he was. He would often give me little assignments. One time he was interviewing Pigpen's mother, and she, in answering some of his questions, relayed to him, "I think there was a time when the boys went to Stanford, down in Palo Alto, and they played an afternoon show at the student union." Nobody had ever heard of that. That was not on the master list. Dennis had never heard of it. Nobody had ever heard of it, but we had an idea of approximately when it was. We knew the year, we knew it was summertime. So I went down to the Stanford library one day and pulled out all the student newspaper on microfilm, and looked through it and found an ad for the show. It had a picture of the boys standing, and it said, "Grateful Dead, Tresidder Union, two hours," or something like that. So we now had the exact date. That was one of many examples—most I got from Dick, but then from Dennis as well—of things that were not in the overall body of knowledge yet.

What was happening at that time was Dennis sort of researching the Grateful Dead in general to write their official biography—because they picked him to be the person to chronicle their whole existence, and he got permission to interview anybody and everybody. He was doing tons of research, and he couldn't do the legwork on a lot of those. As a matter of fact, if you look in his book, *A Long Strange Trip*, he thanks me, and I think he calls me his "legman" or something. Because he would put me to work on all the things that are time-consuming or a little ill-defined, and knew that I would be creative in searching things out. A little detective work.

MAR: Getting back to kind of your relationship with Dennis: Can you describe either how everything came together for *DeadBase*, or your relationship to Mike and John W. Scott?

SN: Oh good, I thought you'd never ask. This is a story that I've had practice with. This was '86, maybe? A year or so prior to the first *DeadBase* book, which came out in '87. Maybe it was '85. Eighty-five was a good year. I probably didn't have a lot of time to work on a project like this, because in 1985 I went to every one of the Grateful Dead shows that they had.

MAR: And you were still working, yeah?

SN: I was working at Genentech, and I was hiring a new department. Rather than have these candidates fly to San Francisco from God knows where, I told my manager, "Hey, I could save you a bundle of money if you just fly me to the East Coast, and I'll take a hotel room in Boston for two or three days and interview the candidates who live around there, and then go to New York and interview candidates there, and then go to Philly and interview the candidates there, and then fly home, and then we bring just the second-round choices to San Francisco." Needless to say, I also caught all the Boston Garden, Madison Square Garden, and Spectrum shows. Great tour of '85—for me, not just because I saw them all, but I think they had some of the best energy ever. Wish I could go back.

So Dennis, right. Dennis, by this point in whatever I said, '84, '85, I was really developing a good friendship with him. Because, by that point, he had already been picked as the biographer, and he was also hired as their publicist, so he was on the road, as I was. I was going to all the shows and he was going to all the shows, so we had a lot of time under sometimes challenging, sometimes euphoric situations. When you're on the road, you've got cool things going on, you've got challenging things going on. When you've got a common opportunity or a common enemy, then two people get to being closer. So him and those three or four other folks in our extended family—my wife, Robin, our friends Barbara and Lou, and their friends—it was a nice camaraderie.

So I'd been working with him now for a couple of years, and Mike, whose list we worked on, but we didn't know who it was from, reached out to Dennis. I don't remember exactly why. If you go interview him, he'll tell you probably a slightly different variation of this story. But, in the beginning, basically, this whole *DeadBase* project is Dennis's fault. I often like to say it that way. It's all Dennis's fault, because he didn't want to work on the book hands-on himself. Mike had come to him and said, "Look at all this stuff!" He had this big binder of loose-leaf, three-hole-punch, typewritten-with-a-manual-typewriter setlists. He said, "I'm amassing the master list." Dennis said, "Oh, that's cool. Let me introduce you to my friend Stu. Stu and I have been going through the archives. We have a similar master list, although it doesn't have all these setlists and everything. At some point, maybe we should pool our resources." But we didn't do anything with it right away.

Then, soon after, John called Dennis and said, "Hey, I've got this database and I want to put out this book. I want to call it *DeadBase*, but I'm wondering if we need permission." Dennis said, "Yes, sounds like a good idea, but there's two conditions. One is you've got to do it right. You've got to work with my two friends Stu and Mike"—who, it turns out, was the basis of John's database. [Mike's] master list had gotten all the way to the East Coast, and John got a copy of it, or somebody else did, and eventually he put all the data into a Honeywell computer at Dartmouth, and that's how he published the first mini *DeadBase* books. But he didn't want to just do it without permission, so he asked Dennis, and Dennis said, "Yeah, work with my friends Stu and Mike. They've got sources you probably don't have, so you'll make the best version possible if all three of you put your effort together." So that's why there's three authors. The second thing, the second condition that Dennis told John, he said, "Besides working with these guys, if you ever do get to get it published, I'm going to bring it by the band meeting and get them to approve it, if I can, but you have to agree to give 10 percent of the profits to the Dead's charity organization, the Rex Foundation." So John agreed to that. We pretty much did that for the first many years, and then we took it a little bit off-track. We still gave it to charity, so we were in the spirit of giving it to Rex Foundation, but we gave directly—like Rex does—to worthy organizations. Rather than going through them as the clearinghouse of the money and their deciding who gets it, John took that over. So basically, the introduction is made. Dennis puts Mike and I and John together, and then he goes to a meeting. But it wasn't him. I went and talked to Dick. I'd been seeing Dick a lot in the vault, and I told him about the book coming out.

MAR: Were you talking with Dick a lot, or what did that relationship look like?

SN: Dick and my's relationship was a junior version of Dennis and my's relationship. We ran into each other at shows, we got introduced somewhere along the line. We ended up showing up at the same people's houses after shows. Whenever we had an opportunity to talk about tapes, we did. He invited me over to his house a few times. Actually, when I moved back to the Bay Area and was looking for a house, I crashed at his house for a couple of weeks. So we were just friends, but he had a very cool job. Whenever I would say, "Can I come up [to the archive]?" he would say, "Yeah, I'm going through '81 today," or whatever.

How much music is in the Vault from the Acid Tests and from the 1965-66 period? Have you ever thought of releasing any music from that period?
There's basically not anything in the '65-'67 period. Bear showed me a box that had a bunch of Acid Test stuff on ten-inch reels from early or mid-July 1966. It's hard to tell what's what because the dates aren't accurate or even listed. I'm just sorting through that stuff now to see if there's any usable stuff. I think there's gotta be something worthwhile, at least a CD or two of craziness, that everyone would love down the road, but I wouldn't start off with that stuff right now.

Is the most challenging part of your detective work making sense of mis- or unlabeled tapes?
The hardest part is trying to figure out what happened when none of it's labeled, just the month and day but not the year, or just the year, or just the location. It's next to impossible to find old shows because reels are missing all the time. In the

'68 period a lot of the shows went into "Anthem of the Sun." Parts are missing or jams are cut. Finding a reel that had three separate concert endings on it was a big find. That's the fun of detecting, sleuthing in the Vault, because you have all these information sources and you think you can match things up by looking at the handwriting, comparing it to the handwriting that went before, and asking everyone whose handwriting it is. All these things go into play.

What's your greatest detective story?
I don't know if this is a detective story, maybe a finding. There are lots of tapes that are great shows, but we're missing reel four of six or five of six, which is in the middle of a jam. This makes the show unusable. 10/25/73 Madison, WI was a show I really thought was worth putting out, but we were missing 45 minutes of it, parts of *Eyes of the World*. A friend of mine said he had 45 minutes that he found at a flea market or something. I was able to pass that 45 minutes into the whole show. There are rough edits, but they could be fixed if we ever wanted to use it. Finding the missing reel from a great show is an incredible find. Lately the one that blew my mind was finding the complete 3/23/74. We were missing reel five and when we found the whole set in Bear's collection, it was really a shocker. Then a couple of weeks ago, he pulled out another series of six tapes from 7/17/76, those six Orpheum Theatre shows. I've been looking for those for centuries. They was considered some of the best.

frustrated. Then I was looking through the tapes and realized there had been two sets of tapes made that night. In one of the sets the box was mislabeled, and I listened to the tape and realized it was the missing reel. Now the whole show's there. Things like that are really rewarding, especially when it's a good show.

Tell me what people need to know to really understand what you're doing.
I think my fundamental goal is to hear the goods for myself. I'm an archivist. I keep in my mind what's good, and I want to get that out to Deadheads. I'm a hippie fundamentally, and my thing is the Grateful Dead live. It took me ten years to get to the point where I'm in control to a degree. The only thing I can say is buy them. If this organization knew we could put ten CDs out each month and people would buy them, we *still* wouldn't take advantage of this opportunity. The Grateful Dead moves at glacier speed. I am in a real fortunate circumstance. I'm not saying there aren't 100 other people that could do the job just as well, if not better, but now I'm working on credibility from the Office to Deadheads. I want Deadheads to know they have one of their own on the inside. I see my purpose as doing this task that's set out before me. I used to pray that a semi would run me over given the level of frustration I had to deal with. Only Kidd saved me on this "Dick's Picks" deal. I gave up so many times, and then he brought it back. Now it seems like they're serious about the Vault release program, and they'll open the door so more and more will come out. No one that's a Deadhead will ever get this far again in the history of the Grateful Dead. Let's just hope it goes all the way. ◊

Dick Latvala interviewed by Johnny Dwork in *Dupree's Diamond News* #34, Summer 1996

I would often just hang out while he was listening to stuff, and then he would shove the headphones in my direction and say, "Here, listen to this jam." He even made me copies of special ones. He would often—he knew that the board tapes were going to be the ones used for any CD releases, but if he got a really good audience tape, he would say, "You've got to hear this. It's a shame I can't release this one." They generally didn't do too much audience stuff in their official publications, unfortunately. Couple of matrix [recordings].

MAR: Do they have audience recordings in the vault, then?

SN: Yeah, they did. And Dick had a lot. He was a taper himself. Although I didn't actually see him. I think he may have graduated, sort of like I did. I had friends who he had taped with in the beginning, and then they gave him first gens or whatever. He was big in the taper scene, and who better to get hired to do the archives after Willy had gone away than Dick? Phil picked him out, pretty much. Said, "Hey, you have a good ear." Because Dick would hear something in the vault, and then he'd go to Phil and say, "Hey, man, remember this show? This is such a great jam, you've got bass up on full." Phil said, "Mm-hmm, good. I don't remember it, but good. Whatever you say." Ninety percent of the time, he was just listening to stuff. He had to listen to everything. If you ever see pictures of him with headphones, that's my main memory of him. Unless we were focusing on a particular tour—and before he was actually listening, he was making sure that he had the setlist right. That's where I could help. By this time, it was probably about '87, '88. We had the first [*DeadBase*] book, or at least a draft version. It would be a symbiosis. We would look at a problem tape box and find it in the master list—pre-*DeadBase*—and if we were missing something, we'd copy from the tape box into paper, and if there was stuff in the paper that was missing from the box, he would write it down in pencil, and then he would go and listen. "Yep, sure enough, that's this song, not that song." I think, when they were labeling stuff, back in the day when they were live, they were distracted and doing a lot of other stuff, besides being pretty high. So the accuracy is a little bit less than 100 percent. But over the years they got checked out.

MAR: Would you be the only one double-checking and cross-referencing for the *DeadBase* crew, or were Mike and John also there with you? What was that like?

SN: Yeah. I was really, really fortunate to be in that group of three, because John was in charge of the database and the publication of the book. Mike was sort of the historical reference, and he still is, to this day. Any time I've got a question, he has this photographic memory, and he can rattle off almost any show and all that stuff. He was the accuracy guy, but I was sort of the glue. I was the interface of the book project to the band and the archives and the office, so I was just so lucky. I could talk to Garcia about the book, I could talk to Dick, I could talk to [Steve] Parish [the Dead's roadie and equipment manager], and I was OK, because I was doing it for *DeadBase*, and they were in favor of it. They approved it.

I was starting to get to the point of telling you how Dennis got it approved, but it wasn't him. One day, I was in the vault with Dick, and I said, "Hey Dick, there's this other guy that put all the setlists that we were marking off all in a book, and he wants to go and get it published, and he checked it out with Dennis and Dennis said something about giving money to Rex and then getting it approved. How do you think we should go about getting it approved?" He said, "Oh, no problem. Let me go and take it to the next band meeting." So Dick was going down the hall with this big binder under his arm, heading into the band meeting, and Phil was in the hallway, coming out of the bathroom or someplace, and said, "Hey, Dick, what you got there?" "Oh, it's this idea, these guys want to publish all the setlists. It's called *DeadBase*. It's got all of our shows and setlists and special guests." He said, "Oh yeah? Really? Who is it?" And Dick mentioned my name, and he said, "Oh, Stu Nixon, really? I know him. Give me that. Let me present it." So it was really Phil presenting it to the band that got everybody saying yes, and then the yes filtered back down through Dick or Dennis. Phil didn't reach out to me, but he doesn't usually.

MAR: I had a question there somewhere. Is that '85 or is that '86, when it got approved?

SN: Oh boy. I don't even know how I would check to find that out, because the book came out in '87. It would have been the last entry, [which] was about when we cut off and went to press.

MAR: December 31, 1986.

SN: So I imagine it was sometime early in '86, rather than '85, especially given the fact that I was still a bit busy in '85. Let me tell you this other little story that I did for the band. It was a *DeadBase* spin-off. One of the things that we did each year, from '88 to '94, is we did the annual book. You have *DeadBase*, and then *DeadBase II, III, IV*, up to *XI* every year, but, at the same time, we put out an annual edition. A little bit smaller. A lot of the stuff in that ultimately came from the Grateful Dead conference on [the online message board] the Well. Have you heard of the Well? That's where I first really got down and dirty with David Gans, because he and Mary Eisenhart, the other name I mentioned, and a third guy [Bennett Falk], formed the Well. I was very active back then. That's where you'd get access to the setlists. People who were at a show could now, for the first time—well, they usually would call a friend who was in front of a computer, and they would put the setlist on the Well. We all were, with baited breath, waiting to see what they were playing in Des Moines.

What I did, from, I can't give you the exact dates, but I can go home and find it. I've got one bankers box full of these binders. About four times a year, like every quarter, I would put out Grateful Dead tour notes. I did maybe twenty editions of this, from somewhere around '88 to '91 or something, in parallel to what went into *DeadBase* '88, '89, '90. In '89, for example, there was one *DeadBase* book, the *DeadBase* '89, but then there were four tour notes. Basically, the Dead would do a spring tour and then summer tour and then fall tour and then New Year's run or whatever, and so, as part of the *DeadBase* stuff, I would go into the office and meet with Eileen Law. Besides thanking her for the tickets she gave me the week before, she would give me all the newspaper clippings that they got. They subscribed to a news service that would find any article, any magazine or newspaper article, that involved the Grateful Dead, and they would send that to her. She had these big manila folders bulging with stuff. So I did two things. For the *DeadBase* book—if you have one handy, you can flip to the back, and you'll see all the bibliographic references. That would be the newspapers, title of the article, the name of the newspaper, the author, the date, that kind of reference. [With] the yearly one—this is an anal-retentive, way-too-close-up collection of data on one year—it had the timings. John would get out his stopwatch, and he would get every tape, and he would time every song. So you could figure out, in a given year, they played twenty-seven-and-a-half hours of "Sugar Magnolia," or whatever. That's an example I often give of how crazy Deadheads can be, and the kind of details they go after. The statistical side is crazy, and my contribution to that part was all the crazy academic references to the articles and press.

That decision, along with the actual data mining and corrections, was all communicated on marathon phone calls. We would talk about what statistics [to include], and, as it turned out, we didn't have room for everything. We had so many good ideas that, by around *DeadBase IX* or *X* or something, we couldn't fit the "every time played" and Garcia's base and Weir base [logs]. Because of the printing costs, we just kept it within a certain amount. When we did *DeadBase 50*, we said, "Fuck it, we don't care about the cost of pages or anything. Our one and only goal is to print everything that exists at that point." We went up to 992 pages. It was gargantuan, and it cost a lot to print, except we did not have a publisher. So I had to get a loan and go to a very cool printer, a guy that used to be the chairman of the Rex Foundation. He was a printer in San Francisco. He helped us out.

But, for the tour notes—and there were two or three or four that I put out each year, to correspond with *DeadBase* '88, '89, '90, etc.—I [had] very limited distribution. I made twenty-five copies, so I gave it to close people, like Dick, and Dennis, and Lou, and crew members, and band members. That was pretty much it. It was about fifty pages, more or less, that had each show's setlist, and then it had—and I got this from the Well; Well people just couldn't hold back giving their comments or stories. People that were out at the actual show, they would tell the story of either them going into the show or their experience around it, how they played certain songs or sets. A little bit like reviews that are in the main *DeadBase* book. I would include a lot of that stuff, and, in going through all the stuff from Eileen, I'd have all the newspaper articles. I would photocopy the whole article, so they could read the whole story from the newspaper or magazine. There was stuff they had, that I picked and chose from, that each band member and maybe crew member got at the beginning of the tour. Our friend Jan [Simmons] worked for them at that point, and she was making these itineraries. They were very small, maybe four or five page, condensed things, that would show, "9:00, up for breakfast," "9:30, get on this bus or that bus." It was tailored to the individual person, like Jerry or Bobby or whatever. It had a lot of their day-to-day schedule. I didn't offer every single day or every single show. My sources were limited and random, but it was cute to throw them in, because I would give them to band members, and they would read through it and say, "Oh well, we've got to remember not to stop at that place anymore. That was a shitty lunch," or dinner, or whatever. So that was a fun project, and one full set of that made it into the Santa Cruz archives as well.

Electronic Village Forming: The Grateful Dead Conference on The WELL

The WELL (Whole Earth 'Lectronic Link) is a computer conferencing system/experiment in community-building, operated by Whole Earth in Sausalito. The Grateful Dead conference on The WELL is a place for Deadheads from far and near to exchange ideas, make plans, trade tapes, discuss issues, and hang out with kindred spirits. Current hot topics include get-well messages to Jerry, feedback to the band, songs you wish the Dead would play, what it all means, etc.

The conference is hosted by us--David Gans, Bennett Falk and Mary Eisenhart. Aside from free computer time, pleasure of the conversations, and the opportunity to discuss things we're interested in with like-minded souls, we don't get paid for this. The WELL does get paid for this. There's a monthly charge of $8, plus $3 per hour for connect time. (If you live outside the Bay Area, call Uninet 800/821-5340 for information on low-cost phone access.)

To access The WELL, you need a computer and a modem. Call (415)332-6106, follow the instructions to become a WELL user, then type "go gd" at the OK prompt. For further information, call The WELL at (415)332-4335.

Mike Dolgushkin

July 25, 2020

MD: I'd heard "Golden Road" on the radio in 1967 and I thought, "These guys are pretty good," but then, in the summer of 1970, *Workingman's Dead* came out and I heard "Uncle John's Band." I really liked that song so I bought the album. I liked the entire record. The Grateful Dead immediately became my favorite band. But then, in September of 1970 as I was starting my senior year in high school, the Asian Studies class I was in took a field trip to Memorial Park, which was kind of in the mountains down the San Francisco Peninsula there. And somebody had brought a cassette machine that had a tape of *Live/Dead*. I heard that and thought, "Well, wow! This is the greatest music I've ever heard in my life." So, it just kind of went on from that. I saw my first show at Berkeley Community Theater on August 22, 1972. And then, I think I made it to—not every show in the run at first, but I at least tried to make it to one show of every run from then on in the Bay Area.

[My first setlist] was after the November 1973 run at Winterland. We went to the Saturday show, and afterwards, I could still remember what songs they played, so I wrote the songs down and I made a list. I had a tape of the New Year's '72/'73 show, so I made a list of that. And I started showing it off to people. It's like, "Look. Look what you can do. You can compare what the Dead played at different shows. Isn't that cool?" In just these two lists, right? But then at the February '74 Winterland run—once again, only went to the Saturday show, but a friend of mine went to all three nights. So he wrote down what they played at all of them. So I got that, and it just went on from there. I started to know people with large tape collections, so I copied down all the songs that were on their tapes, and people who had gone to shows I didn't go to who wrote the songs down, I got that. That's how my typewritten list started and how it developed.

MAR: In that time period, what was your relationship to taping or tape collecting?

MD: In '74, there was a friend of ours, in my circle of friends who I went to shows with, who got a portable Sony deck and started recording West Coast shows with that. He recorded the Reno show, he recorded the Santa Barbara show, and then he recorded the Oakland show. Those are the three shows I know that he did on-site, but then he started getting tapes from other people, too—some of what was circulating at the time, like the last night at the Lyceum in London, from '72. He got the December 2, '73, show from Boston. He got the September 23, 1972, show from Waterbury. Stuff like that started trickling in at the time. But back then, people had these kind of minuscule tape collections and the shows weren't necessarily complete. They didn't necessarily sound good, but at the same time, you'd listen to them over and over again because they were so great. And then every now and then, you'd run into someone else who had tapes and you'd trade for whatever bits and pieces they had. It didn't really proliferate until after the hiatus [in 1975].

MAR: Did you ever see people getting chased around by roadies or that sort of thing?

MD: Not back then, no. But at the October 10, '76, show at Oakland, at the second day of the Who and the Dead, my friend had a little boombox kind of thing. Actually, it wasn't even that big. It was a little portable tape recorder. He had it on his shoulder and he was taping the show. We were next to someone who had a more elaborate setup, but he was still being discreet about it. But then, during the break, his friend showed up with this big kind of wooden cross thing, said, "I want separation on this baby," and hung the mics off the ends of the cross. Of course, that attracted attention from the stage and, yeah, we all got popped during "Brown-Eyed Women," I think it was.

MAR: And could you describe how that went? Was it the Who's people or was it the Dead's people that popped you?

MD: It was an Oakland Coliseum cop. Security. He was very nasty about it. He was yelling at us. "We told you before you can't do this stuff," blah, blah, blah. My friend was still recording. I was trying to grab his attention. "Put that down." But I wasn't able to. And so, one of the people with this cop was like, "Oh, what about this guy?" They took him back under the stage, because my friend was claiming, "Oh, I'm not taping the band. I don't like the Grateful Dead. I'm just listening to Pink Floyd until the Who comes on." So, "Oh, really? Well, why don't you come with me?" And then, "OK. Where's the tape?" "Oh! I left it back there." "Why don't you go back and get it and bring it back?" They let him take the machine with him to go back and get the supposed Pink Floyd tape. So, not being a complete idiot, he just left and didn't go back.

MAR: Back to your list. When was it so substantial that you started distributing it to other people?

MD: Early eighties, I used to make copies of it and give it out to people. And I think I had started doing that before I met Dennis [McNally]. I mean, I had my own copy of it. I met Dennis backstage at the Halloween '83 show. Dennis, of course, was working on his biography of the Grateful Dead. So I showed it to him. He said, "Well, you have to come over to my house." So, I came over to his house and I met his research assistant, who was Stu [Nixon]. And then, Dennis had compiled lists of his own, because that was kind of like the backbone of his research of the shows, right? That's how I met those guys.

MAR: I see. And how did you find yourself backstage in 1983?

MD: My friend Ruth. She was Phil's girlfriend back when the Dead first started. Anyway, she got me backstage access.

MAR: I think in someone's relaying of events, John had access to your list somehow before he even knew who you were.

MD: No. That's not my understanding of it. What I remember is that John had compiled a list of his own and he had made a project out of it at Dartmouth College. He did a database of this stuff. Then, he wanted to put it out as a book. So, he met Dennis at one of the shows back east, in the spring '86 tour. And Dennis said, "Well, I know these two guys you should get together with." So, he did. He contacted us. I don't think he had my list before that.

MAR: OK. So, basically your list was distributed locally then, or on the West Coast?

MD: It was distributed to people I knew. I mean, once I met Stu, and we started to work on this project more, Dennis handed that part of it over to us, you might say. So the setlists became our project, and Stu and I started making copies of the list as we added on to it and developed it further. We started making copies of it and giving it out to people.

MAR: Were you basically completing years' worth of setlists at that point, like '80, '81, '82?

MD: Yeah, because that was easy to get then. I mean, in '82, I was actually getting lists right after the shows happened, pretty much. I mean, sometimes there'd be some [excitement], "Oh, they played a new song," or I remember when "Wang Dang Doodle" came up, that was a big thing. Oh, and then, when they brought back "Help on the Way" earlier that year, in '83. I heard about that pretty much right away. I mean, people I knew were at least going to the West Coast shows, and I was finding out what was happening back east, too. That kind of communication had gotten a little better. I would say, [as to] how complete was the list by '83—it was probably most of what was circulated at the time. I don't know if I can say it was all of it, but most of what circulated at the time. I mean, nothing had come out of the vault yet. The first complete year I had was '77. Right after the California tour in '78, somebody came up, who had compiled every setlist for '77 and into the California tour, except May 5. They didn't have that, but everything else was there. So that was the first almost complete year I had. Stuff like '78 and '79, I started finding out about that around '81, '82 maybe. People start coming up with those lists. And some of it was just tape lists, more complete tape lists started getting made at that time.

THE BOOK OF THE DEAD

COMPUTER PROGRAM DESIGNED AND IMPLEMENTED BY MARC S. SOKOL

Phil Lesh
I hope you enjoy this.
Billy

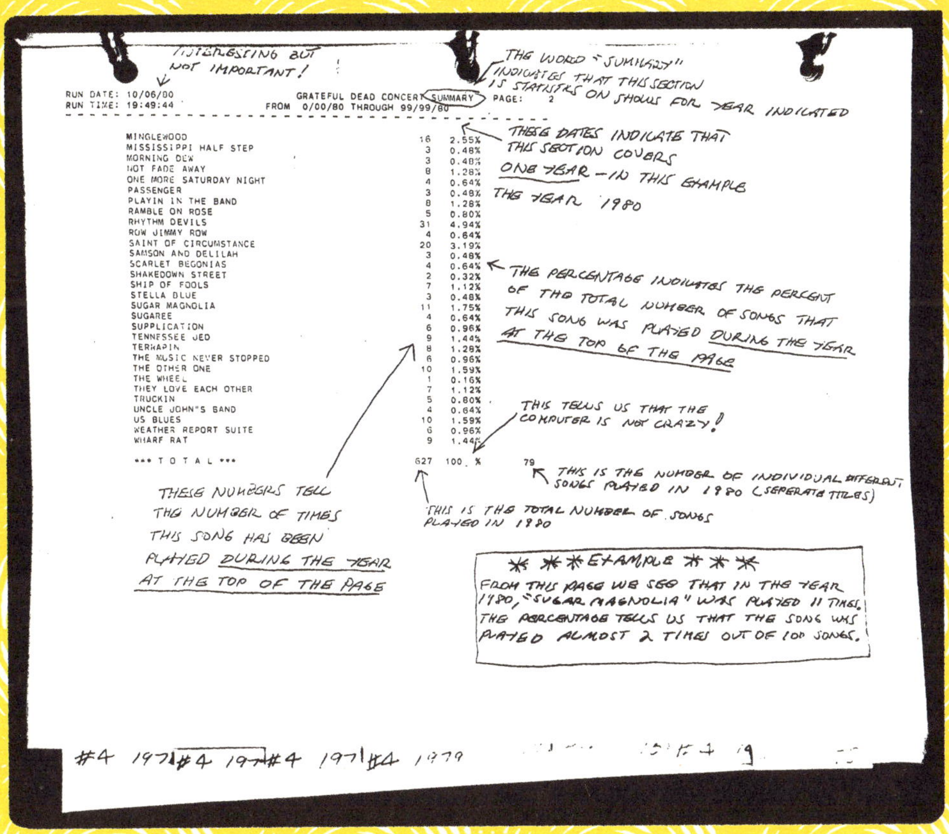

INTERESTING BUT NOT IMPORTANT!

THE WORD "SUMMARY" INDICATES THAT THIS SECTION IS STATISTICS ON SHOWS FOR YEAR INDICATED

RUN DATE: 10/06/80 GRATEFUL DEAD CONCERT SUMMARY PAGE: 2
RUN TIME: 19:49:44 FROM 0/00/80 THROUGH 99/99/80

MINGLEWOOD	16	2.55%
MISSISSIPPI HALF STEP	3	0.48%
MORNING DEW	3	0.48%
NOT FADE AWAY	8	1.28%
ONE MORE SATURDAY NIGHT	4	0.64%
PASSENGER	3	0.48%
PLAYIN IN THE BAND	8	1.28%
RAMBLE ON ROSE	5	0.80%
RHYTHM DEVILS	31	4.94%
ROW JIMMY ROW	4	0.64%
SAINT OF CIRCUMSTANCE	20	3.19%
SAMSON AND DELILAH	3	0.48%
SCARLET BEGONIAS	4	0.64%
SHAKEDOWN STREET	2	0.32%
SHIP OF FOOLS	7	1.12%
STELLA BLUE	3	0.48%
SUGAR MAGNOLIA	11	1.75%
SUGAREE	4	0.64%
SUPPLICATION	6	0.96%
TENNESSEE JED	9	1.44%
TERRAPIN	8	1.28%
THE MUSIC NEVER STOPPED	6	0.96%
THE OTHER ONE	10	1.59%
THE WHEEL	1	0.16%
THEY LOVE EACH OTHER	7	1.12%
TRUCKIN	5	0.80%
UNCLE JOHN'S BAND	4	0.64%
US BLUES	10	1.59%
WEATHER REPORT SUITE	6	0.96%
WHARF RAT	9	1.44%
*** T O T A L ***	627	100. %

79

THESE DATES INDICATE THAT THIS SECTION COVERS ONE YEAR—IN THIS EXAMPLE THE YEAR 1980

THE PERCENTAGE INDICATES THE PERCENT OF THE TOTAL NUMBER OF SONGS THAT THIS SONG WAS PLAYED DURING THE YEAR AT THE TOP OF THE PAGE

THIS TELLS US THAT THE COMPUTER IS NOT CRAZY!

THESE NUMBERS TELL THE NUMBER OF TIMES THIS SONG HAS BEEN PLAYED DURING THE YEAR AT THE TOP OF THE PAGE

THIS IS THE TOTAL NUMBER OF SONGS PLAYED IN 1980

THIS IS THE NUMBER OF INDIVIDUAL DIFFERENT SONGS PLAYED IN 1980 (SEPERATE TITLES)

*** EXAMPLE ***
FROM THIS PAGE WE SEE THAT IN THE YEAR 1980, "SUGAR MAGNOLIA" WAS PLAYED 11 TIMES. THE PERCENTAGE TELLS US THAT THE SONG WAS PLAYED ALMOST 2 TIMES OUT OF 100 SONGS.

#4 1979 #4 1979 #4 1979 #4 1979

MAR: I see. And did you run into anyone else, during these years before '83, that was generating a list as expansive as yours?

MD: No. And I figured that there must have been. There must have been somebody. People sometimes will tell me, "Oh, you've done the best job of this." And I thought, "No. That couldn't be. There must be somebody else that's doing a better job of it." I figured that I couldn't have been the only one doing it.

MAR: Right. Did you ever run into someone named Marc Sokol, by chance?

MD: Yes. I think I did. The name sounds familiar.

MAR: There's a huge binder in the archive at Santa Cruz, I think in Dick's papers, that was a computer-generated listing of shows [created by Sokol]. Kind of a proposal, I guess, sent to the Dead. It's like, "This is how you can generate a computer program to file it." Basically probably what John was up to in Dartmouth, but I'm just curious because I don't really know. I'm just curious if that name rings a bell and you might have some more to say about him.

MD: The name rings a bell. I might have met him, but I don't remember for sure. Now, I used to hear stories that there was a computer printout of setlists going back real early, but I never saw it. I heard stories about it. I knew someone who claimed to have it, but I never saw it.

MAR: Right, the holy grail of sorts at that point in time.

MD: Right. I mean, for some reason, there were people who knew that they didn't play "Alligator" until June of '67. There's stuff like that. I was doing it just for the fun of it. For me, it was just a really fulfilling thing to go back and get an idea of when the Dead introduced certain songs, and look at the way they structured their set and how it changed over the years. I mean, that was the whole reason I was doing it. And we shared the information with people. That's what it was.

MAR: I have the first *DeadBase*, and even from this outset, you guys have all these extras at the end of the book.

MD: Right. Having it in computer form, in a database, that's what facilitates that.

MAR: So was that a decision that you all came to, or is it something that one or the other was more interested in?

MD: I think John pointed out, "Hey, we can do this, this, this, and that with it." It's like, "Yeah. That's great. That's wonderful. Let's go for it." A lot of it's pretty obvious: I mean, how many times each song was done, how many times it was done during a certain year, and then, first set opener or second set opener or that sort of thing. That's all pretty obvious. I did like the whole "every time played" list for each song, where you could list which set it was in, what position of the set it was in, what came before and after. I thought that was really important, because if you came up with a tape that you didn't know what it was, you could identify it through that.

MAR: And when it came time to print the first *DeadBase*, do you remember any kind of conversation about how many copies you would be printing and how you were going to distribute it?

MD: Yeah. I mean, we had conversations about that. To this day, I don't remember how many we've done of any of them. I mean, the editions went up, and of course, the book got bigger and bigger and bigger as we went. I think we were always going to do a mail-order and of course, we sold them to stores, too. So, we did do that.

MAR: Right. And, at that point, you were just an independent outfit separate from the Grateful Dead, but with the Grateful Dead's blessing?

MD: That's what we always were, yes. And, I mean, the story of how we got, I mean, I think you've heard the story about how we got the Grateful Dead's blessing. Stu was the one of us who had the most, he had the connections with the actual, the Grateful Dead organization, with them. So, I think he asked Dick Latvala if he could present the project at a band meeting. Dick said that he would. Dick went to, I think he ran into Phil and he said, "I'd like to present this project at a band meeting." Phil looked it over and said, "Oh, this looks really good. I think I'll present it." So, that's how that happened.

I was friends with Dick; I met him backstage. One of the nicest people you'd ever meet. For our project, he was always very forthcoming and always willing to give us information that we didn't have. I drove over to his house sometimes. I was in San Francisco, and he lived across the Bay over in Albany, you know, those big apartments that overlook the freeway that you see up there. So, I'd go up there and hang out with him. I remember one time we drove around Berkeley—he was showing me where all the good rib joints were. He grew up over there, so he knew all that stuff. Sometimes, he'd come over to my house and we'd talk about stuff and then we would go out for pizza or something. That's how that was.

MAR: And did you ever go to the archive at all?

MD: Never. Well—you mean the vault? Stu did. He went there. I never did.

MAR: I see. So, your relationship with Dick was more of a friendship relationship more than just you checking, doing your due diligence as far as nurturing your list?

MD: Well, it was both, and he was very happy to answer whatever questions I had. Because I did sometimes ask him specific things about specific shows.

MAR: Did you have any relationship with David Gans, at this same time when he is doing *Dead Hour*?

MD: Yeah, sure, I mean, David's been a friend of mine since those days and I was on [his show]. One time, Stu and I were both on. Another time, Stu couldn't make it, so I went by myself and did it.

MAR: As far as distribution and that stuff, did that seem to be more of John's thing or Stu's thing?

MD: Early on, it was John's thing.

MAR: Where did you distribute? I'm assuming nationally, but are there maybe any particulars you may remember about where?

MD: Not really. I mean, a lot of people just direct-ordered from us, you know?

MAR: Yeah. And then, I know you advertised in *Relix*, and *Golden Road*, and *Unbroken Chain*, and those sorts of things. Was that kind of your main method of kind of getting the word out about *DeadBase*?

MD: Yeah. That was big, I would say so. I'm trying to remember if there were any other ways we got the word out. We had mailers, too—we sent out mailers to people who'd ordered from us before, when a new book was coming out.

MAR: Did you ever sell it before a show or anything like that?

MD: I never did, no. I think friends of ours did. I think we had friends of ours do that, but I don't know the particulars of that because I wasn't involved in it. I know there were unscrupulous individuals who took it upon themselves to reprint the book and sell it themselves. People bootlegged it.

MAR: How did you know that it was bootlegged?

MD: It was reported to me that that was going on. I don't think it wound up being a big problem.

DeadBase IV The Complete Guide To Grateful Dead Songlists

We are pleased to announce two new editions of The Complete Guide To Grateful Dead Song Lists. DeadBase '89, our year in review, provides the sort of detailed analysis of a year of Grateful Dead performances that would be impossible for the complete DeadBase. Exclusive features include song timings and reviews for every Dead concert in 1989 and a bibliography of articles on the Grateful Dead. Since DeadBase '88, we have added 64 pages in order to include FeedBack '89 results (our readers' opinions on the past year) and set list comparisons (which help determine the uniqueness of a given set list). Additional features include attendance and gross figures, and photos and ticket stubs from most of the venues played, making this the most comprehensive coverage available on an exceptional year of Grateful Dead concerts. DeadBase IV has finally returned from the printers after many delays. Features include: song lists (1965-1989), Songs Played (authors, first played, etc.), Yearly Table, Statistics, Every Time Played, Places Played, Arena Survey, Questionnaire Results, Reviews and commentary on over 250 shows, a comprehensive discography, and a cross-reference of lyrical images and ideas. (In order to make room for new lists and features GarciaBase will be removed from this book and will be published separately.) Sometimes called the taper's bible, DeadBase is an invaluable resource for any Deadhead.

	Book Rate	Priority
DeadBase '88	$10.00	$12.00
DeadBase '89	$12.00	$14.00
DeadBase IV	$24.00	$27.00

Send check or money order to:
DeadBase Orders
P.O. Box 499
Hanover, NH 03755

DeadBase V

- Do you schedule your vacation time around Dead tours?
- Is Phil's birthday the only religious holiday you still observe?
- Do you have nightmares about missing the next Dark Star?

If you answered yes to any of the above questions, you may already be a Deadhead. While there is no cure, there is a product to help improve this happy affliction: DeadBase. *The Complete Guide To Grateful Dead Song Lists* is the ultimate Deadhead's reference book. Do you remember what songs they played at your first show? Which do tapers consider to be the ten best concerts on tape? When *is* Phil's birthday, anyway? Discover the answers to these questions and countless others in *DeadBase V* — 512 pages of fascinating information and opinion on the Grateful Dead. Our latest edition features information on 1,964 Dead concerts (1965-1990), listing a total of 29,063 songs, extensive statistics, complete cross-references by song and venue to help place those mislabeled tapes, Feedback (opinion from our readers including the best concerts, versions of songs, and albums by the Grateful Dead), reviews and commentary on over 280 concerts, a discography, and lists of Jerry Garcia's and Bob Weir's solo performances. Sometimes called "The Taper's Bible," *DeadBase V* is an indispensible resource for any Deadhead.

Book Rate	$26
Priority	$29
Canada	$33
Europe	$38

Send check or money order to:
DeadBase Orders - R
P.O. Box 499
Hanover, NH 03755

(wholesale inquiries welcome)

MIKE DOLGUSHKIN AND STU NIXON INTERVIEWED BY DAVID GANS

3/26/1987

David Gans: Now some of you may know I'm the coauthor of a book called *Playing in the Band*. During the time I was writing that book, I called a big-time taper, a friend of mine, to ask him if he could help me figure out how many different songs "Dark Star" has gone into and come out of. And much to my surprise, he called me back in about half an hour with a very complete list, which I put in the book. And I said, "How did you do that?" He said, "I have a book here." And it turned out he had a complete book of Grateful Dead song lists--a very nearly complete book that had been put together by this crazy chap in San Francisco named Mike Dolgushkin. And now we can all have a copy of that book. It's called *DeadBase*. And Mike and a couple of other fellows got together and produced this. And here they are in the studio. Now this was done on a computer, I know, but the first version of it that I saw and Xeroxed was all done on a typewriter. Whatever possessed you, Mike, to mount such a gigantic research project?

Mike Dolgushkin: I didn't have a computer so I had to use a typewriter. Actually, I started it about a year after I first had seen the band. I've always been a list freak, and I started to notice how the Dead's concerts really lend themselves well to that--just different ways that each show is structured. So about the end of '73, I started to keep lists of all the shows I was seeing, and I started to look through people's tape collections and gather more lists, and it went through different forms until finally it just wound up as a three-hundred-page, typed, Xerox book.

David Gans: You still haven't answered the question of "why?"

Mike Dolgushkin: Why? Well, like I told you, I've always been into lists and I just thought that the Dead's show structure really lent itself well to that. And you could look through and compare things very easily.

David Gans: OK. Well, of course, as soon as I got hold of this thing, I found it pretty fascinating too. And when I started working on this radio show, it turned out to be a very valuable thing also. From time to time, I would want to collect a bunch of the first performances of songs, things like that, and now it turns out that you guys have taken care of some of my homework by compiling those sorts of pieces of information and putting them in the back. Let's bring Stu Nixon into the conversation now, because Stu is a computer-type worker. How did you guys meet, and how did you get involved in this, Stu?

Stu Nixon: Mike and I met about three years ago, I guess it was now. Two or three years ago. I was working with a mutual friend of ours, Dennis McNally. At my work, I do statistics and computer programming and things. And with Dennis, we were compiling lists and Mike contacted Dennis and Dennis introduced us.

David Gans: Now, were you working on the master gig list with Dennis?

Stu Nixon: Yes. It wasn't a song list to the extent of Mike's collection, but it was more the master show list of all the dates and places.

David Gans: Now, what were you using for resource material there? Where were you gathering your data from?

Stu Nixon: Anything and everything. We were going to the library and digging up clippings from the newspapers and interviewing people and a lot of tapes and a lot of personal contacts as well. So Mike and I put our heads together and added to Mike's collection and started to fill it out a bit.

David Gans: When did you decide you would publish this thing?

Stu Nixon: We never did. That wasn't our idea. That was our third author, John W. Scott. He's not here today. But he really had the idea of a publication. I think he got ahold of an earlier version of Mike's book and he put that on a computer. God knows how many hours that he spent doing data entry, but he typed it all in.

Mike Dolgushkin: He got a copy of the same Xerox typewritten thing that I had and put it into a computer.

David Gans: You people are nuts. I am really glad you did it though. I mean, I have a professional use for this stuff. Well, all right, I'm sorry, we have to backtrack here. How did John find you guys?

Mike Dolgushkin: Through Dennis McNally, actually.

David Gans: He had your book first?

Stu Nixon: And he met Dennis on some East Coast tour and Dennis thought that he'd be a good person for us to work with. So we got in contact.

David Gans: I should explain that Dennis McNally is the Grateful Dead's publicist and is also working on the authorized and complete history of the band. And as such, he too has desperate need for this information. OK, so how did you get the idea to publish this thing and how did you go about doing it?

Stu Nixon: Well, it was John's motivation to actually put something out that a lot of people could get their hands on and use, and it's his computer work that forms the basis of not only the typesetting here, but the appendices that follow the list. Some of the things in there are quite creative, and besides being nice statistics to look at, some of them are quite amusing. He does anagrams based upon song titles and band members' names.

David Gans: What's very interesting is that in the early years, the list of songs is pretty... well, actually there's not as much data available.

Mike Dolgushkin: Yeah, the early years and some of the middle years, we could still use a little help.

David Gans: OK, that's something important that we should talk about. This is an open-ended project in a way, at least, isn't it?

Mike Dolgushkin: Oh, yeah. We're talking about the second edition already. Because in addition to including all the shows from the year, we want to make corrections, make additions, and even add new chapters and sections.

David Gans: So you're open to suggestions from out there as to what to do with your statistics and stuff?

Mike Dolgushkin: That, as well as specifics in the way [of] missing song lists and corrections that you might run across.

David Gans: Where would people send their information if they want to make corrections to this book? I have a few right now, by the way.

Mike Dolgushkin: Probably people should send all communication to the same address for ordering.

David Gans: OK, so once you've got your book and gone through it and realized that you have that one tape that is not covered in here, please send the list to these guys at that address.

Stu Nixon: Yeah. Actually tape lists are some of the worst sources of primary data that we've run across, because we've run across so many tapes that have been mislabeled, misdated--

Mike Dolgushkin: Particularly from the early years, where you'll have not only mislabeling, but three different tapes put together and labeled as one, things like that.

Stu Nixon: I hate when that happens.

Mike Dolgushkin: Me too.

Stu Nixon: That's another reason I started doing this, because I hate when that happens.

David Gans: So you wanted to just try and create a definitive database for this thing?

Mike Dolgushkin: Yeah. So brand-new show lists are one thing, but if anybody thinks they were at a show or have a tape of a show that's not on here at all, a brand-new date or location, that one is going to require a little closer scrutiny. You need documentation like a library clipping or a ticket stub--

David Gans: Or a college newspaper announcement or something like that?

Mike Dolgushkin: Yeah. Any advertisement--

Stu Nixon: More importantly, follow-up publications would be better.

David Gans: You don't think the memories of the psychedelic generation are reliable, gentlemen?

Stu Nixon: No comment.

David Gans: You guys made some decisions here; you've named some jams and stuff. There's something in here called "Alhambra," and there's something that you referred to as "Heaven Jam" in here. I was curious as to where you got those names.

Mike Dolgushkin: Well, how we chose to use some song titles was a bit subjective. We tried to be as objective as possible [with] all of this quantitative data, but sometimes we had to take some artistic judgment into account and do some naming that we didn't have any basis for. And there are some jams that just sound like certain songs, and they started playing them before the songs came out on an album. "Heaven Jam," in particular, we believe is the melody for "Heaven Help a Fool."

Stu Nixon: Do we want to mention the band was aware of this project?

David Gans: Oh yeah. There are, I've heard, other Grateful Dead list books available. In fact, I got one that was on big, wide, old-fashioned computer printout paper from Chicago a few years ago. That was not as accurate as this for sure. What's the story: How did you guys manage to get approval from the Grateful Dead to do this?

Mike Dolgushkin: Well--

David Gans: The answer's obvious. McNally, he works there; the guy's got pull right?

Mike Dolgushkin: Well, actually Dennis was not involved at this point. He was instrumental in introducing us to other folks at the office. Phil was our spokesperson on this one. Our good friend Dick Latvala, who works for the Dead and works in their tape vault, was using this book quite a bit to help out in his job, and we had asked him if he would present it to the band. We didn't want to go and publish anything, charge anybody money for anything, until we had the band's approval. So what we did, we asked Dick if he would present it in front of a band meeting sometime and see what they thought. So one day he saw Phil and showed it to him and Phil said, "Oh, OK, let's go for it." And lo and behold, they approved it.

MAR: Was John working remotely on the East Coast then, while you and Stu were working on the West Coast?

MD: Yeah. All the way through it, he never came out. He never came out to the West Coast while this was all going on. I did meet him in person, in 1990. I went to the Madison Square Garden show—in fact, he got me my ticket. So, I went out there and hung out with him. Stu never met him face to face, but I did.

MAR: Stu's never met John in person?

MD: No, he hasn't.

MAR: So, how are you guys also transferring information, then? Just by mail?

MD: By mail, by phone. By mail, mostly. We'd talk on the phone, and that's sometimes when we'd discuss things: "This person is claiming that this happened [at a show]. How do we deal with it?" Depending on what kind of proof the person had [we'd add it to the database].

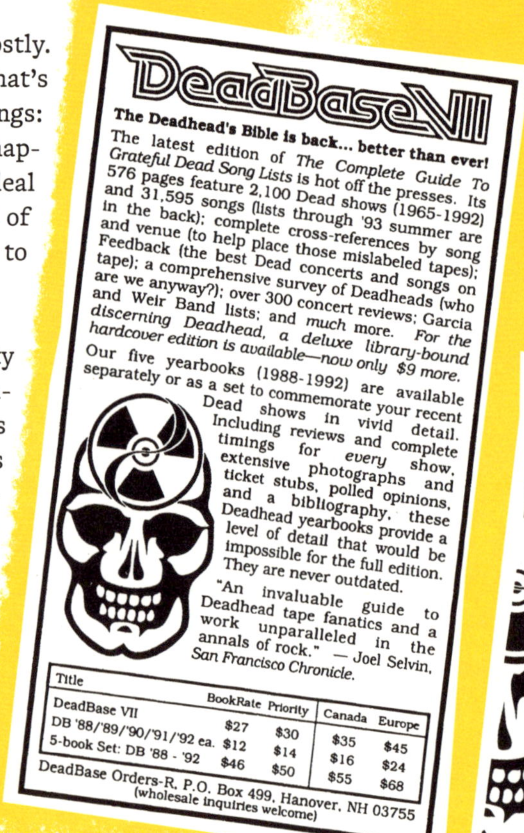

MAR: I see. And then, when the Betty Boards [collection of previously unknown board tapes] popped up, was that kind of a big to-do in terms of you kind of redoing a lot of information or validating certain information?

MD: To a certain extent. I mean, a lot of that stuff we had the list for already, but some stuff—like the 1972 Academy of Music shows, that was in the second batch [of Betty Boards]—we didn't have accurate lists for those until then. The first batch was '86, I believe, but like I said, I don't know that that changed a whole lot, because a lot of those shows had already circulated.

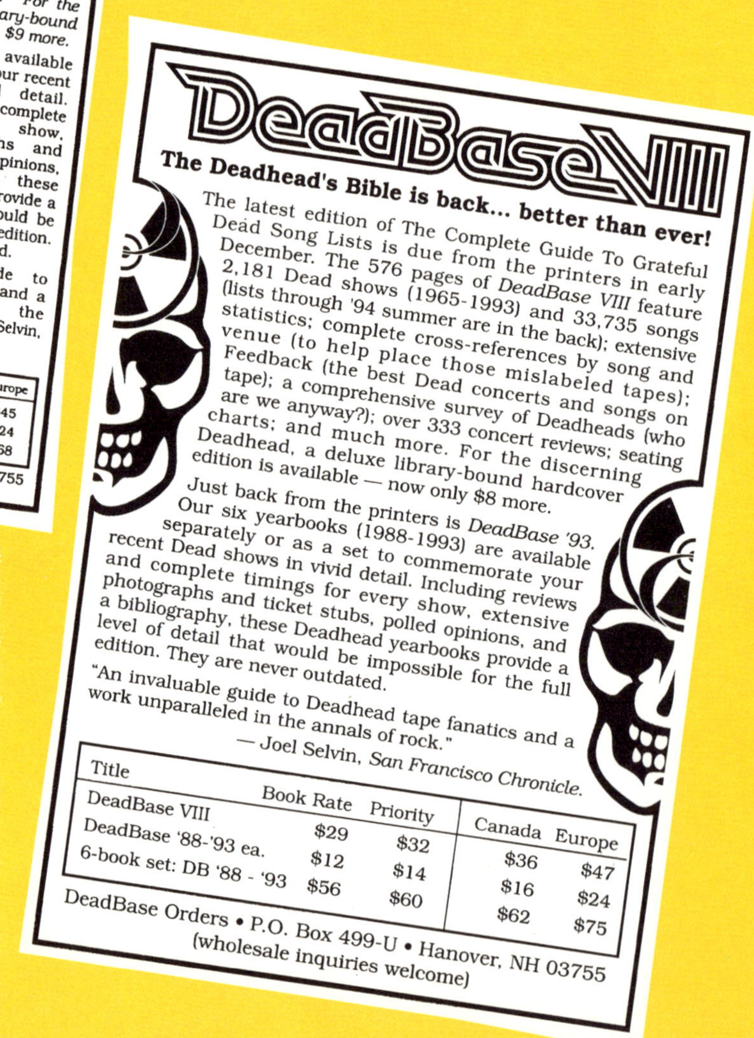

MAR: I see. Can you speak to your impression of the effect that *DeadBase*s had on the Dead community from the very beginning? Have you witnessed any kind of reaction to it?

MD: It was a big help, because here was all the information in one place, instead of being scattered around here and there and everywhere before that. We centralized it. It wasn't perfect in the beginning, but it was a great start and then it built from there. It enabled people to see what they really had. There were misconceptions before that—I mean, I knew someone who had the

’72 Veneta show under three different days. Stuff like that. It cleared up misconceptions. So, we were able to clear up misconceptions, and do a better job at it the more we found out about these things—the more the fragments of things turned into full setlists after they got leaked out of the vault, right?

MAR: Ultimately, the prime thing to cross-reference against was the vault, correct? So, you were ultimately using the vault to kind of validate these setlists?

MD: Ultimately, yeah. When that information became available to us.

MAR: I see. And then, before that, it was just like people’s history, in terms of you having generated your list before, and then just about having a system in place to kind of make sure all the information is correct?

MD: Yeah. We’re the setlist source, whether there’s a circulating recording of it or not.

MAR: On a personal thought, I just was wondering what your thoughts were on that missing show—I think from 1979, from Oklahoma.

MD: Oh, that. I’m almost positive it was out there at some point. I mean, I’ve known people who swear they had everything from that time period. That’s a tough one there. And then the next night—which we do have, partially—that’s screwed up as well. The seventh. We don’t know what order that really goes in, either.

MAR: How much time have you spent on kind of trying to dig into that particular date?

MD: Oh, well, not an extraordinary amount of time, but I mean, we have a list for it. We have a list, but there’s no recording out there of that.

MAR: Is that the only show that hasn’t, kind of, resurfaced? Or do you think there’s other shows that you might not even know about that exist?

MD: Since March ’71, it’s the only one. And then, like I said: the night after, whether that’s the correct sequence, I don’t know. Before ’71, there’s plenty of missing shows there. Plenty of missing shows.

MAR: Right, and the vault really also reinforces that because it’s not complete, either.

MD: The vault’s not complete, no. Some of our setlists early on came from a woman who had contacted Dennis at some point—during ’69, ’70, she and her sister used to go to shows and they wrote down the songs. So, we got some of those setlists, right? And it turned out, when recordings surfaced, of a lot of those, those lists turned out to be almost 100 percent accurate. That was ’69 and ’70, [and] there was a ’72 show they went to. I mean, but it was the shows they went to; it wasn’t anything really comprehensive. But it was stuff that was unknown at the time. When we put out the *DeadBase 50*, the last [edition], like I said, we tried to be very thorough, really thorough this time, and I checked all possible sources of information, just to make sure that we weren’t missing anything.

MAR: How long does that take, to just cross-reference that with the amount of information that you’d already compiled, which is already massive?

MD: I would say about a year.

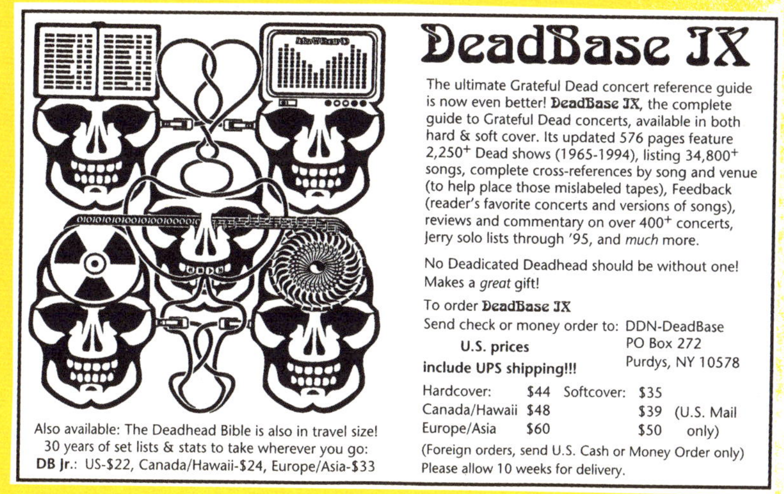

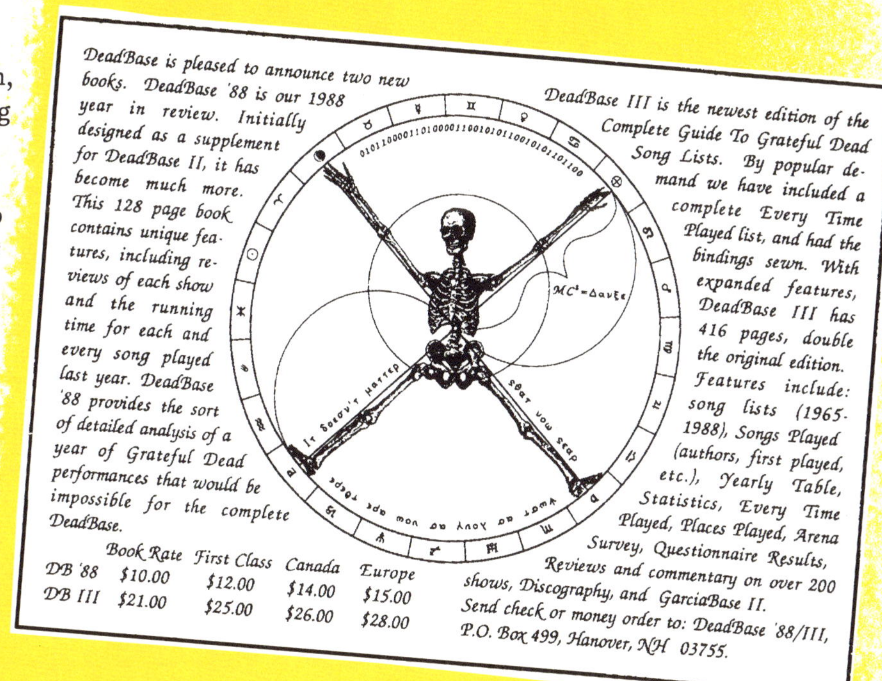

Dennis McNally

July 24, 2020

MAR: We were talking about mail-order tickets.

DM: The newsletter—which was actually printed and mailed to people—was a creature of the record company. They had a budget for it and it was quite costly; it needed a source of support that had, in the record company era, long gone away. By the early eighties, the newsletter had been replaced by, I think, five phone lines, each with their own answering machine, so that Eileen [Law] would record the upcoming show [dates] and when mail-order would start, and give instructions as to how to do mail-order.

MAR: That was literally what the hotline was used for, then?

DM: That was the hotline—to give information in general. Obviously the information most Deadheads wanted was: "When's the next show? Where? How can I buy a ticket?"

MAR: There's one more follow-up. I had forgotten to ask you about David Gans. I think you had mentioned that you were in the GD office around 1980. I'm wondering, is that because you were working for Bill Graham and that got you access to the Dead office? How exactly did you find yourself there, aside from the Warfield shows and that thing?

DM: As part of my fiendish plot to introduce myself to the Grateful Dead, I decided I would write a piece for the *San Francisco Chronicle* about the New Year's Eve ritual which, by the late seventies, had become quite a thing. On December 31, 1979—with a 103-degree fever; work called first, and I was sick for weeks after, I might add—I went to the show and took a lot of notes. Then, because I could not reach out to the Grateful Dead—I didn't have a phone number, [and] it's the only band in the world with a completely unlisted number. But of course, Bill Graham was in the phone book, so I called up Bill, and Bill was always willing to talk about the Grateful Dead. Late in January, I interviewed Bill. Easiest interview ever. You have to turn on the tape recorder. As I left his office, his assistant—who later became a Grateful Dead assistant tour manager—Jan Simmons said, "Have you talked with Eileen Law?" and I said, "No." And she said, "Well, if you're going to do something about Deadheads, you have to talk to Eileen. Here's her phone number," and I said, "Gee, thank you." So now I have the Grateful Dead office number. In February, I suppose, of 1980, I called Eileen and said, "I'm doing this piece for the *Chronicle* and blah, blah, blah. Could I talk to you?" She said, "Sure," and I said, "I work a regular job, could it be nights or weekends?" And God bless her—this is just so typical of Eileen: she met me and we ended up talking for three hours

In 1971, the Dead, obviously intrigued by the quick growth of their following, established an official Dead Heads organization for the first time, urging fans to write them at a post office box in San Rafael. The initial plea ("Dead Heads Unite!") appeared on the inside gatefold of the Dead's enormously popular double LP called simply *Grateful Dead*. (It was initially supposed to be called *Skullfuck* but Warner Bros. nixed that idea. Most people call it the "skull and roses" album, after its cover graphic of a skeleton crowned with a halo of roses.)

The response from Dead Heads was quick and tremendous. Maryann Mayer of the Dead organization was initially in charge of assembling the mailing list, but by early '72, the volume of mail pouring into the Dead's small downtown San Rafael offices was so heavy that a second person was brought in to help—Eileen Law, who took over the Dead Heads job completely soon after, and remains the Head Dead Head to this day.

"I've never really considered Dead Heads a fan club," she comments, "because we don't send out the standard promo pack with glossy pictures and the offers to buy all sorts of merchandise. Also, we've never charged any money to be in Dead Heads, because if we did we'd feel obligated to put out a newsletter often, and we just don't work that way."

The infamous Dead Heads newsletter was started in the fall of '71 but came of age in '72 and '73 when Garcia and his songwriting partner Robert Hunter would design elaborate four- and eight-page flyers littered with poems; bizarre, post-psychedelic doodles that made the drawings of the French surrealist Bresson look normal by comparison; utterly undecipherable smatterings of a pseudo-philosophy called "Hypnocracy," the teachings of a fictional sage named St. Dilbert (who was sort of a combination of Henny Youngman and the Buddha); and, oh yes, tour information and hot scoops on all the latest doings within the band. The newsletter came out sporadically up through 1974, after which the organization was temporarily shut down when the band went into a one year "retirement." At that point, Eileen had about 40,000 names in her files. Today, the Dead Heads list contains more than 85,000 names and it's still free . . . for everyone but the Dead. To mail a four-page circular today costs the Dead nearly $15,000, and they are not (and have never been) a wealthy organization. In addition to the newsletter, which just started again after a three-year absence while Eileen updated her files and caught up on back correspondence, the Grateful Dead organization has also set up two telephone hot-lines Dead Heads can phone to get tour information—one in San Rafael, and one in New Jersey—that one for the insatiable hordes of Dead Heads on the East Coast (which remains the band's strongest area).

The Dead have saved practically every letter they've received since the days of the original Grateful Dead Fan Club ('67–'68). Boxes of letters, cards, and original poems and drawings sent in by Dead Heads fill much of Eileen's office, and she says there are thousands more stashed away in some mysterious hiding place. One box of what looked to be about 1,000 pieces of mail, consisted entirely of get-well cards sent to Garcia when he was hospitalized with throat problems a year ago.

A perusal of a few hundred random letters from Eileen's boxes reveals Dead Heads to be a far more literate lot than many people have given them credit for. Instead of the expected litany of "far-outs" couched in stoned prose, most of the letters are quite well-written and cover a broad range of topics. Many are sincere testimonials to the power of the Dead's music ("your music speaks from the soul, not from the pocketbook"), with lengthy explanations of why the Dead moved them. Others offer suggestions of where to play and where *not* to play in various cities ("the band really pays attention to those," Eileen comments), and suggestions of what songs they'd like to hear. And believe it or not, there are even a few complaints—"Please change your repertoire. It's become rather boring in the last few years hearing the same songs all the time," wrote one. "They've gone from a dismal three nights of material to an almost unforgiveable *two* nights worth of material: a never ending nightmare of 'Mama Tried'/ 'Mexicali Blues'/ 'Estimated Prophet'/ 'Eyes of the World,'" wrote another. And a third: "I'd much rather just hang out with Dead Heads than see the current Dead."

Most interesting though, is the incredible artwork and handicrafts that are sent in, and occasionally even given to the band out on the road. Most offer unique graphic interpretations of the traditional Grateful Dead symbols. There are skeletons on horseback, skeletons with wings, infinite variations on the skull-and-roses motif, and the "white lightning man," (the famous skull with a lightning bolt through it, a variation of which appears on the cover of this magazine). No other group has been the inspiration for folk art to the degree that the Dead has. There are literally thousands of hand-painted, -drawn, -sewn, -crayoned, -appliqued Grateful Dead T-shirts, jackets, patches, hats and other clothing in Dead Head closets and on Dead Head bodies. At a given Grateful Dead show, you can probably spot upwards of 100 different Dead shirts, some homemade, others officially licensed by the Dead, or by Kelley & Mouse, the two brilliant Marin County artists responsible for the bulk of the Dead's album covers and, by extension, most of the Grateful Dead iconography.

"Dead Heads: A Strange Tale of Love, Devotion and Surrender" by Blair Jackson in *BAM* #76, April 1980

on a Sunday afternoon. That was in February. I turned in the article, and it was substantial. The editor said, "Look, I don't want to cut this. This is good stuff, but it's going to take a much larger ad book to support it. It's going to have to be a fat magazine to include this, so we have to wait." That was in March. In August, the ad for the Warfield run appeared. So first-thing Monday morning, I called the editor and I said, "They're about to do thirteen shows in September. I think it's time to run the article." She said, "You're absolutely right." So the shows began on a Friday, and that Sunday, it appeared in the paper, which was ultimately perfect timing. I went to all the shows, and on Tuesday, I came into the Warfield and the article had been framed, and was on the wall of the lobby already. That's Bill Graham Presents for you. I was watching people read my article. It's not often a writer gets to see somebody actually absorb what they're saying.

MAR: Did you work for Bill Graham after that?

DM: Yes. That was in 1980. In December, Jerry invited me to be the biographer. I started at BGP late in '82. In the interval, I had gotten to know Jan Simmons as a friend—she lived not far from me. We got to be pals and Deadheads together, and she said, "You ought to be Bill's archivist." He didn't have one at that time. To that point, I had been working in an office that had nothing to do with anything, and so I said, "Yeah, sure," and so I spent 1983 as Bill's first archivist. At the end of the year, I was fired by his CEO, Nick Clainos, because as far as I could ever tell, Nick hadn't participated in my hiring. He felt he'd been end-arounded, [which] was kind of true. Long story short, Eileen started having me work part-time for her, sorting clippings and things. I got laid off in December '83 and started working for the Grateful Dead in an hourly capacity in, like, January. Then in May, I got hired as the publicist on a regular paycheck.

MAR: Going back to the *DeadBase* question, performing that historical research. You said you had some gals in New York that were helping you out?

DM: They were helping me with the biography. It probably extended after I became publicist, but I only tried to be publicist and biographer simultaneously for about six months, from May until January of '85. Both in terms of the point of view and also the energy required, the time required—not to whine, I have no complaints, but I was getting seventy phone calls a day. Being the Grateful Dead publicist was a very full-time job. As a consequence, in January of '85, I finally looked myself in the face and said, "You can't do both." Plus, I was an honest historian. I was trying to be fair. I was not necessarily trying to cover up anything or represent the Grateful Dead; I wanted to write a straight history.

MAR: I also see that David Gans pops up in these meeting minutes, just as a name, not as a participant. In relation to *Dead Hour*: I'm wondering if you have any comment on [the approval for the radio show] happening at the same time—are there any other conversations that would have happened between the archiving that's starting to become more solidified and Dave getting tapes for broadcast?

DM: All of these things are examples of the maturation of the phenomenon of the Grateful Dead. The ticket office, again, was Rifkin wanting to diversify the audience, and who had access to tickets. Hiring me was another step in developing a more reliable interface between the band and the media, because I at least answered phone calls. Gans was another example. He wanted to develop it, and he did, with the band's blessing.

MAR: Was there any impression that you got during these meetings that Dan Healy or Kidd Candelario were trying to do the same thing, but without Dave Gans?

DM: Not that I'm aware of. Kidd came up with the idea of those various size stealies—*Steal Your Face* logos. The first ones were about the size of a quarter. They were some very light metal, a little more soft and with quite a sticky back, and you could stick them on anything. It was a nice piece of merch. As a result of that idea—which the band approved—[Kidd] eventually became the head of merch. Because, quite frankly, to that point, merchandising had never—and never did, in fact—become a major priority with the Grateful Dead. It was very funny when we banned merchandising, that is to say sales, the Shakedown Street in the parking lot, there were many Deadheads who were muttering about, "The band wants to make all the money and blah, blah, blah. It's greed." Which is just such bullshit. The fact is, the Shakedown Street was something that attracted—what they call, in city planning circles, an "attractive nuisance." It gave a focus to people who didn't have a ticket to go hang out. As far as the money: For starters, most of the really clever T-shirts would not only bootleg the Grateful Dead, but bootleg some other thing. There was one called "Deadopoly, the Game of Dance." I don't know if you ever saw it, but it was a take on Monopoly. The point being that merchandising was never really a priority until after Jerry died. Then, the sales were not so much T-shirts as CDs. That became important.

MAR: That's interesting, because then at that point Dick's job got more pronounced, because he would have already been in the groove. Can you speak to any change in that or not really, because you'd just do the publicizing?

DM: I was publicizing the work. As far as how it changed for him, you'd have to review the timing of the releases. I think there were at least one or two or three before Jerry died, or more. I can't remember. It wasn't important enough to me, but after he died, obviously, it became a significant source of income for the company.

Francine Accardi-Peri

July 30, 2020

MAR: How did you come to be in the Grateful Dead scene? Were you a fan beforehand?

FA-P: I was definitely a fan long beforehand. My friend Carrie Rifkin was married to the Grateful Dead's manager, Danny. It was Danny who created the GD ticket office. I worked on a seasonal ambulance at the time, and when the season was over, I needed a job. And Carrie said, "I'm going to get you a job!" And Danny gave me the job at the Grateful Dead ticket office. That was February 2, 1984. For the first seven or eight months, I was a ticketing person. I would process mail-order ticket orders. Then, in November, Danny asked me to co-manage the office. So, I co-managed the office with Steven Marcus until 1995.

MAR: Eighty-four. So then the mail-order tickets had already begun the year prior, is that correct?

FA-P: Yes, but, the whole form was still being developed: how we ticketed, who we hired, how we balanced, everything. It was all just in its very early stages. Tickets were just put on the desk—and we had tour tickets then too, which made it a little bit more complicated—and we would fill them, and check each other's work. There were no actual checks and balances. We worked on that, and developed it to where we matched all of our tickets with our money every step of the way. At first it was all very new, but the process actually worked all the way from 1984 through 2015. For the Grateful Dead reunion shows in Chicago, we received $90 million via mail order in the mail and were only $35 off for the whole ticketing process. So, I'm pretty proud of that.

MAR: Do you have any history to share about the beginning of the mail-order tickets in general?

FA-P: Well, I believe it started with Ticketron wanting to charge the band as well as the fans. They were charging the fans a fee, then they wanted to charge the band five cents a ticket. Danny Rifkin, the band's manager, said, "No, let's sell our own tickets," hence mail-order ticketing was developed.

MAR: I see. And is that PO box number the same throughout the history of mail-in?

FA-P: It was the same throughout the history of Jerry being alive. When GDTS TOO [the second iteration of Grateful Dead Ticket Sales] took over, we kept it for several years. But when Ruby retired, I brought it all out here to Stinson Beach, because it was just crazy for me to go over to San Rafael every day to pick up mail.

MAR: I see. And who is Ruby?

FA-P: Ruby was Ruby; everybody knows Ruby. She's gone now. Her name was Calico van der Mei, and she was the one that came up with the term "pesky tapers." Because she was the main ticketer.

MAR: So Ruby worked under you and Steve, then?

FA-P: Yes. She was actually there longer than I was, but she had little kids at the time, so she was not able to be there as much as I was.

MAR: How many people were working when you started, and how many people did that turn into eventually?

FA-P: When I started, there were probably four or five people at the most, and that turned into about thirty people as Grateful Dead Ticket Sales. For the 2015 fiftieth anniversary reunion, GDTS TOO had to hire sixty people, although there were many people that went in and out; I mean, we had well over a hundred people that were workers at some time or another.

MAR: In busy moments when a tour was about to hit?

FA-P: Well, we had seven supervisors that would be there full-time. And then, when the tours were announced, the crew would go up to about thirty. Ticketers would be issued a certain number of tickets, and they would fill orders equal to that number of tickets. That certain amount of tickets had to match their deposit totals. There were several steps involved.

MAR: And were you ever in charge of the look of the tickets, or how they were printed?

FA-P: Steve Marcus and I shared that, yes. And then, when GDTS TOO took over, I designed / helped develop the New Year's Eve commemorative tickets. But yes, I would choose the color of the tickets by whatever the moon sign was going to be in that night. That made it easier for me. Also, the ticket companies had several designs on file that we would pick and choose from. And we changed things throughout the years.

MAR: Was there any rhyme or reason to choosing those particular graphics, or did that change over time?

FA-P: No, it would just be what we felt was right for the time or circumstances. Every single one of our shows had counterfeit tickets, so we always tried to mix them up. We really were on the avant-garde edge of recognizing counterfeit ticketing, having the ticket companies come up with more designs to make our tickets safe, which included tri-colored stock, raised lettering, and glitter. The foil was the best. We had two different companies that we worked with: Weldon, Williams and Lick, and QuickTix. And each one of them offered different features. Together, we stayed one step ahead of counterfeits.

MAR: So, I guess you actually came on board right when the official tapers section started.

FA-P: I don't remember the exact dates, but yes, the official tapers section happened very early on, and that was because of the band's attitude. The tapers would come in with these six-foot mic poles and recording gear, sitting everywhere, and blocking other patrons' views. So the band decided to put them in their own section, behind the soundboard. And then, once they did have their section, the tapers section, boy, that was their section. You weren't allowed to talk in that section. They would scowl at you if you made any noise in that section. Then they got a little bit carried away, where they'd order four tickets and have four different tape machines all over the four different seats. That just wasn't fair, when people were out front trying to get in. We always tried to be fair with everything that we did, all the way up until it was over in 2015. We tried to give people different sections—they'd have a good night one night, and then a medium night, and a not-so-good last night. It was always well thought of, because we were all Deadheads, too.

MAR: I know that the official tapers section started in October of 1984.

FA-P: Yes, that's when I started comanaging the office.

MAR: So you would have been kind of in the heat of the discussions about how to actually tackle this?

FA-P: We used to use stamps for tapers. We would stamp the tickets, but then somebody started duplicating our stamps. So, we actually had to put it on the ticket text. Ruby coined the phrase "pesky tapers" and that's what we thought of them, the whole way through until Jerry passed. But then, we were like, "Thank God for those tapers."

New Year's Eve was always a difficult show to choose which ticket requests to fill, because we had to turn so many people away. That was the worst part of the job, not being able to give tickets to everyone. All the other stuff—the employees, the bank, the lawyers—that was all easy breezy compared to not being able to give tickets to someone. The promoters limited us to the number of tickets that we were allotted because they had contracts with the venues that we were working with. So, we were limited to 25 percent of the stadiums, 35 percent of the sheds, and 50 percent of the arenas. Which was fine, because that's all we were filling anyway. And, the promoters and Ticketmaster actually abided by that all the way through 2010, when Live Nation and Ticketmaster merged, and then they no longer honored our agreement.

MAR: So when the tapers section started, if it's different than just the fans mailing in, can you just walk me through that process a little bit? Obviously, they would label their requests for tapers' tickets and mail them to you, and then would you just separate them into a separate pile and do another lottery for tapers?

FA-P: Yep. That's what it would be. They'd be separated out and then picked in their own lottery.

MAR: And did the requests for tapers' tickets ever rise significantly or was it always kind of steady?

FA-P: It was pretty much the same group of people that tried to get taper tickets. After Jerry died, the different manifestations of the band decided they weren't going to issue seat locations to tapers any longer. There was just going to be a general admission section. So there were no reserved seat locations given to them in their lottery.

MAR: So it was very specific, to the seat, actually, before Jerry's passing?

FA-P: Unless it was an arena or general-admission show. Towards the end, it was all general admission for them.

MAR: You said that the same group of people would request tapers' tickets. Was there any familiarity that you could speak to with those particular individuals over time, just through their mail?

FA-P: Some of them were sweet and kind. Some of them were scorchy. I'm not going to give names.

MAR: Can you maybe give a description of the difference between those two personalities?

FA-P: Well, being very grateful for what they got. "Thank you. Thank you so much," or demanding: "I should've gotten this or that."

MAR: Right. You can't make them all happy, I guess.

FA-P: Everybody that got a ticket was happy. And the ones that didn't weren't happy at all. But down the line we made sure that everyone got tickets somewhere along the way.

MIKE DOLGUSHKIN, STU NIXON, AND JOHN W. SCOTT
INTERVIEWED BY DAVID GANS
8/5/1992

David Gans: Tonight, we're going to have some long-distance guests: these are the authors of *DeadBase*, the unbelievable statistical resource for Deadheads. As most of you out there in the audience probably know, these guys ultimately got around to publishing this thing as a book and it's been updated several times. *DeadBase VI* is about to come out. They've started publishing individual-year books too, after each year, sort of a wrap-up, and *DeadBase '91* has just recently hit the mailbox. The annual edition of "The Complete Guide to Grateful Dead Song Lists." Let's bring [these] guys in. Stu, how did you get into the *DeadBase* picture?

Stu Nixon: Well, I'm a statistician by trade, and a longtime Deadhead. The two naturally went together--in my head, anyway. I met Mike in the early years, maybe about '83. And we compared some notes, and got some lists from various friends and then we were sort of palling around in the weird world of list collection, and then a mutual friend put us in touch with John Scott. And then it's been a threesome ever since.

Mike Dolgushkin: I think this is a historic moment here. This is the first time the three of us have talked together all at once.

David Gans: Really? You guys have never all been in the room together?

Stu Nixon: No, and John and I have never met, ever.

Mike Dolgushkin: I'm the only one who's met everybody face to face.

Stu Nixon: Michael's the middleman.

David Gans: Well, what do you have to say for yourselves? There's an awful lot of work that goes into this thing. The *DeadBase '91*, the lists of the shows, there's what? Eighty-something shows from 1991, and it doesn't take very many pages to print these out, but then you go and develop all sorts of alarming statistics. Why don't you guys run down a little bit of what you're thinking and what you're doing here with this book?

John W. Scott: Well, the original idea for the book was to provide just an update, so people wouldn't have to buy a big fat one every single year. And I guess I started obsessing with making it bigger and bigger, and started timing every song, from every show, and looking at all the different permutations and so on. And it just grew a little bit out of control. [The update] probably takes significantly more work per page than the big one does these days.

David Gans: Well, for my purposes, it's kind of great, because you have the running times of every song on here, and I need to time these things to put together a radio show. So, in a sense, you guys are helping me do my job in a major way. I will say that there is a collection of tickets, nice photographs of all sorts of different things, people on stage, and some of the venues and stuff. It's kind of a nice yearbook for people who've spent their lives on tour in any given year. Let's talk about the surveys. There's a tremendous amount of consumer feedback involved. What are you guys driving at when you do that?

John W. Scott: I don't know what we're driving at. I guess we don't feel that we're the be-all and end-all, as far as what the best shows are. And so it's only fair to ask everyone else what the best shows are.

Stu Nixon: Yeah. We get feedback from people and it even molds the product. If people say "This particular section is very useful to me," then we'll put energy in that direction. If they say, "Forget these graphics," we don't waste any time on that one anymore.

David Gans: I thought you were going to say that it molded the Grateful Dead's product and that the guys in the band went and looked.

Stu Nixon: Well, we have gotten some feedback from some band members: that they look at it from time to time, and some of them even take note as to which ones they overplay. Another thing related to the feedback we get from our readers is actually the reviews: in addition to timing, for every show we also have a review--a written description of the concert and maybe some colorful events surrounding the concert. And the three of us don't write all of them, by any means: we have maybe ten or twenty or more coauthors on this project. A real community effort.

David Gans: Who thinks up these strange statistical charts, pie graphs, and distribution maps and stuff like that?

Mike Dolgushkin: John does.

David Gans: Do you have anything to say for yourself about that, John?

John W. Scott: I have no defense.

Mike Dolgushkin: Give a man a computer and see what he can do.

David Gans: What do you do for a living?

John W. Scott: Well, I started out as a starving artist and I wrote computer software for a while, and I decided that being a starving artist wasn't that great. And found that I was pretty creative, so that was OK. And then, I now do *DeadBase* for a living.

David Gans: Is it an OK living?

John W. Scott: Yeah. It doesn't put much money in the bank, but my family doesn't starve.

David Gans: How do you guys get your old information? You must do a lot of digging around in people's tape collections to get these lists, and correct them, and all.

Mike Dolgushkin: I see it as being like musical archeology, in a way.

Stu Nixon: Things keep popping up all the time. Somebody that saw shows in the early days will have all of a sudden cleaned out their attic and be getting ready to move and they'll discover all these tapes or notes or something, and then they'll show it to somebody else. And then somebody will say, "Hey, the *DeadBase* people would like to see that."

David Gans: Yeah. I remember, I think I upset your applecart last time, John, because I was exploring in the vault and found something from 1969 that turned out to have Stephen Stills on it. And you had to hold the presses to get that in, right?

John W. Scott: Well, what's a week or two delay, in the name of historical accuracy?

David Gans: "What's a week or two delay?"

Mike Dolgushkin: You heard him, America.

Stu Nixon

August 16, 2020

MAR: As far as news coverage of *DeadBase* and you guys making it—there's interviews with David Gans, right? There's one with you and one with Mike [Dolgushkin], I think?

SN: No, actually Gans did several, including one on KPFA which had all three of us. That was an interesting thing, because having all of us on a phone call together is certainly unique and only happened one time. It's an interesting example of how diverse people who are in very different places can collaborate.

MAR: I think what's even more interesting about [your collaboration] is it's in a time before the internet, and you guys are dealing with plethoras of information.

SN: Yeah, but we did have the phone, as well as sending files. Email existed, I think. And we were definitely sending each other spreadsheets or lists or whatever. The visits were such a long time ago now that I forget, even. There are these memory images of us having these marathon phone calls and looking at paper and reading stuff off to each other. It was very manually intensive. Quite crude, by today's standards.

MAR: So, you never met John. Can you maybe describe, when you did jump on the phone for epic amounts of time, what that was? Was it just literally going over data?

SN: It was super boring. It was ridiculously super boring. He was the keeper of the database. I would have preferred if I had remote access, just to make updates myself. That would be a lot more efficient, but back in those days, he was the keeper of the keys. I had long lists, multiple pages, each with single line entries of corrections or additions, so I would say, "OK, on this day, this song came before that song." We were very, very anal and very detail-oriented, such that [to determine] whether or not a song flowed into the next song, we had to come to an agreement as to how many seconds of silence was permissible to count it being a gazinta. The greater-than sign: we fondly called it the "gazinta." So I'd say, "Oh yeah, clearly 'China Cat' had a gazinta before 'Rider,' 99 percent of the time when they're played back to back." But some songs, [the silence] would be longer than the two-second rule, in which case we had to change a number of those, because a lot of times we would get setlists from Deadheads or a variety of sources. And over time we got tapes and we'd be able to fine-tune.

MAR: And what was it, two seconds was the actual rule for the addition of the gazinta?

SN: Yeah. Like, when you hear the last note of a song, you count one, two, and then they went right in—you count as a gazinta. One, two, three, four, and then they go in—no good. That's a problem.

MAR: So when you talked on the phone, that would be a major discussion point. Were there any other kind of major particulars that you guys would go over that necessitated a phone call?

SN: Often the phone call would be three or four items of interest. That would be one. Others would be sharing any communication we had with other people outside the trio, the three of us—because sometimes John would reach out to Dennis or somebody. Mike would probably reach out to [renowned taper] Charlie Miller or some other of his taper friends in California and elsewhere. And I could reach out to a number of people, Eileen or Dick or David [Gans]. David came later, but yeah—we would just share people outside and the communications we had with those people, any business matters that came up, like with printing or coordinating the two books that were coming out [at any given time]. Because they would also be putting out two books at the end of the year.

MAR: You said there's four things you guys usually talked about? So that was the third, what is the fourth?

SN: Might be finances. But the interesting thing on finances, though—just to answer my own question—was we really didn't talk much about that. John basically ran the whole business side of it: both in paying any expenses like the printer, which was by far the biggest expense of anything, and then the disbursement of our proceeds. We never knew specifically when the check would be coming or how much it would be. And we never asked to speak about his books. We even got copies of a K-1 which, as a partner, we would have to have for financial purposes, but we never looked at the full partners' income tax filing. I'd only look at the K-1 enough to know how much I've got to put down on my tax return. So John really was turnkey in terms of the business manager. And he kept the lion's share of the profits, accordingly. It was not a clean one-third, one-third, one-third. He was doing so much of the work; Mike and I were just having fun. Mike was glorifying in setlists, which was his historical and continuing joy. And I was just tickled pink to have the excuse to go up to the Novato office or the San Rafael office and hobnob with office people and crew members and band members once in a while. It was like, "Oh, my gosh. What did I do to deserve this?" It was a lot of fun. But then there was a lot of boring work. Dick would pull out twenty-five boxes of reels, and say, "We've gotta [check these]." Usually, we would hope to have a few corrections for our *DeadBase* list from the stuff, but in fact, it turned out that more often we were updating the tape boxes, because they often didn't label all the songs. But we were really, really glad to get any new shows or any new corrections from him. That was a really great relationship.

MAR: He would call you in when he found another box? Or he was just organizing another box and then, basically, used *DeadBase* as a way to actually locate what was on tape because it was unlabeled?

SN: Sort of, yeah. Sort of like the tapers do themselves, more commonly. They would pull out the book to see—what am I missing, or what was the setlist? Yeah, I did that to a small degree, but it wasn't really on any real regular basis. We didn't have a regular time to get together, nor was it specifically due to any backlog or tape boxes needing correction. It was just sort of, it seemed, whenever he felt like it. More often than not I think I reached out to him, because he was happy to keep going on his merry way. He was detail-oriented—you couldn't have that job without being so—but, as Phil has pointed out, the reason he got that job was due to his great ear. He would listen to a version of the song and could describe it to you, or describe it to the band, and convince them or you how great it was, and why it should be released as an official release.

MAR: I was curious, because I did end up asking Mike this, but I neglected to with you. But February 6, 1979—it's the one show that exists after '72 that there's no audio record of, so we can't really know what exactly was played. Can you speak to that in any way?

SN: I'm surprised there's not more occurrences like that. If you count from whatever the starting point in '72 was to the end—how many shows that was—one out of that, that's like 99.999 percent accurate from that point on. So that seems pretty amazing, that there wasn't many more than that. Whoever was there may have spaced out, not remembered any setlists or [are] just people that are not communicating currently with a larger group of people who would want to know that.

MAR: Was there a moment in time where you realized that that was the only nondocumented show?

SN: No. I never went back year by year saying, "Hey, are we missing any here? Are we missing any here?" Not something that ever crossed my mind until somewhat recently.

MAR: How did distribution of the *DeadBase* books themselves work, early on?

SN: It was predominantly mail-order. John would get them printed, and luckily, he lived in a place in New Hampshire where there was a large barn. So he was able to get five or whatever thousand copies printed, UPS would truck them all to his barn, and then people would send him checks and he would faithfully ship individual copies to people, one at a time. He would also sign a number of them. I don't know if you were able to get your hands on any of the numbered copies, but especially in early years, for some of them, he wrote the person's name and then number 12 or number 50 or whatever it is. So you'd get a numbered copy as well. He also sold them through at least one store, probably more. Have you heard of the Psychedelic Shop [head shop in Haight-Ashbury]? Mike worked there, and we sold it there as well.

Dick Latvala in the vault. Photo: Susana Millman

MAR: How did you get the addresses, though, in the first place?

SN: I think it was the Well again. The Well had a couple of hundred users of the Grateful Dead conference. The Well was really big—[it] had sports, music, music generally but the Grateful Dead specifically, all sorts of sociological topics, government topics, everything you can think of. There was a "conference," as they called it. Within the conference there were topics, and then you could just put in your comments, or load announcements or graphics or whatever up there. I had a presence there a couple of years before '87, before *DeadBase*. I can't remember, specifically, any big horn-blowing banner-raising announcement about it. Probably it was just an average post saying that the book was coming out and the address to mail to, or to send your address to.

MAR: Mike also mentioned that, at one point, someone was counterfeiting *DeadBase*. I was wondering if you had anything to say about that.

SN: Yeah, that goes back to the very beginning, with *DeadBase I*. I never saw a copy; I heard about it and talked to Dick about it, and we just threw our hands up and said, "Well, it's Deadheads. There's nothing you can do about it." We didn't even know who to contact, either, about who's doing it. How do you stop such a thing? But that was very short-lived, and I think had almost no impact on our sales.

Steven Marcus

July 31, 2020

SM: Well, my history is I worked for BASS Tickets in northern California from late '75 to late 1980. BASS was like a precursor to Ticketmaster, and it was started by Jerry Seltzer, whose father, Leo Seltzer, invented Roller Derby. Jerry Seltzer had controlling interest in the San Francisco Bay Bombers Roller Derby team, and he sold them and used the proceeds to start BASS Tickets. I had known Jerry as a family friend since I was a little kid; I used to go to the temple with his children. Anyway, so I worked at BASS Tickets, in the main office in Oakland, and when the Grateful Dead played fifteen nights at the Warfield Theatre in 1980, the Grateful Dead wanted the shows to be mail-order only. So, I was put in charge of overseeing the mail-order and that was my last actual job for BASS; then, fast-forward to October of 1982 at Frost Amphitheater, and I had tickets to the first show on October 9, but I couldn't get tickets to October 10, so I sat outside and listened. In early February of '83, I had been unemployed since October, and had run out of unemployment; I had no idea what I was doing next. And I got a phone call from a cousin by marriage, Eddie Washington. He produced *The Grateful Dead Movie*. He called me out of the blue and said, "Do you want a part-time job for six weeks?" And I said, "Shit, yeah. What is it?" And he told me it was to help him set up a mail-order ticket office for the Grateful Dead. That six-week job lasted thirteen years. And I went from not being able to get a ticket to a Grateful Dead show to never having to worry about a ticket to a Grateful Dead show ever again.

MAR: Can I rewind a little bit back to the BASS time period, just for clarification: When you were working with the Warfield shows, was BASS then contracted through Grateful Dead to do mail-order at that time?

SM: No, it was contracted through Bill Graham Presents. I wasn't working for the Grateful Dead in any way, shape, or form, and if you had called me up a minute before I got the phone call asking me to work for them and said, "You're going to be working for the Grateful Dead soon," I would have told you to go to hell. The thought of that—it was a dream of mine since I was seventeen, but actually doing it? That was never going to happen.

MAR: I saw that the Dead offered mail-in tickets in May of 1976 and then October of 1978, and I'm wondering if you had any knowledge of that or that was referenced—

SM: Well, '76 was the year of their comeback after their hiatus. And I believe that the promoters were the ones that did the ticketing. It wasn't the Grateful Dead. The promoter John Scher had the Capitol Theatre in Passaic, New Jersey. The Capitol Theatre was the one that actually did the mail-order. My first experience with mail-order was actually mailing for Beatles tickets in 1965, and then the next time was 1974 for Bob Dylan and the Band. And I used every scam I could think of to get tickets: I used a metered mail and I predated the meter—because the orders couldn't be dated before x date—and so, I would actually predate them and then take them to the post office the night before, and all my orders got filled. And that was also one of the reasons why we didn't accept metered mail in the mail-orders, because I knew you could scam them.

MAR: The 1980 version of mail-order, then, doesn't seem like it was too nuanced. Like, it was just kind of Bill Graham requesting that BASS Tickets kind of just handle it, right?

SM: Right. And BASS did. The advertisement for the fifteen-night run was a full-page ad in the section of the *Chronicle* called "Datebook," where all the major concerts were advertised. The ad had a picture of the Warfield or drawing of the Warfield with two skeletons and the marquee with [the line] "They're not the best at what they do, they're the only ones that do what they do." But the ad never mentioned the Grateful Dead once. Actually, I had worked for Bill Graham Presents from 1976 to 1979 as a bluecoat—security guard and stagehand. The guy that was in charge of booking all the bluecoats knew I was a Deadhead, so when I started working, he said, "I assume that you want to work all the Grateful Dead shows." And I said, "No, I want to work all the shows that you really need me to work. If they're Grateful Dead, great. If they're not, that's OK, too. But I want you to promise that when the 'Closing of Winterland' happens"—which we knew was going to happen sometime—"I want to be booked for that gig." I worked all the shit shows: heavy metal, AC/DC, all that crap. And when it came to New Year's Eve 1978 at Winterland, Mark Lewis, who was in charge of the bluecoats, stationed me at the camera that was fifty feet away from the stage and the front, in the center. So, that's where I was all night, wearing rabbit ears and a Groucho Marx nose, glasses, and mustache.

Actually, Eddie Washington had been in a band meeting when Danny Rifkin had brought up the fact that he knew that Bill Graham was ripping them off, and that they decided that they would do these upcoming Warfield shows by mail-order only to try to keep tabs exactly on what Bill Graham was doing. So, they actually had announced those three benefits at the Warfield before I was involved, and Eddie had set it up, and they already had orders in for that one. We worked out of a one-bedroom apartment next door to Front Street, where the band rehearsed and recorded sometimes. It was a really sketchy part of town and here

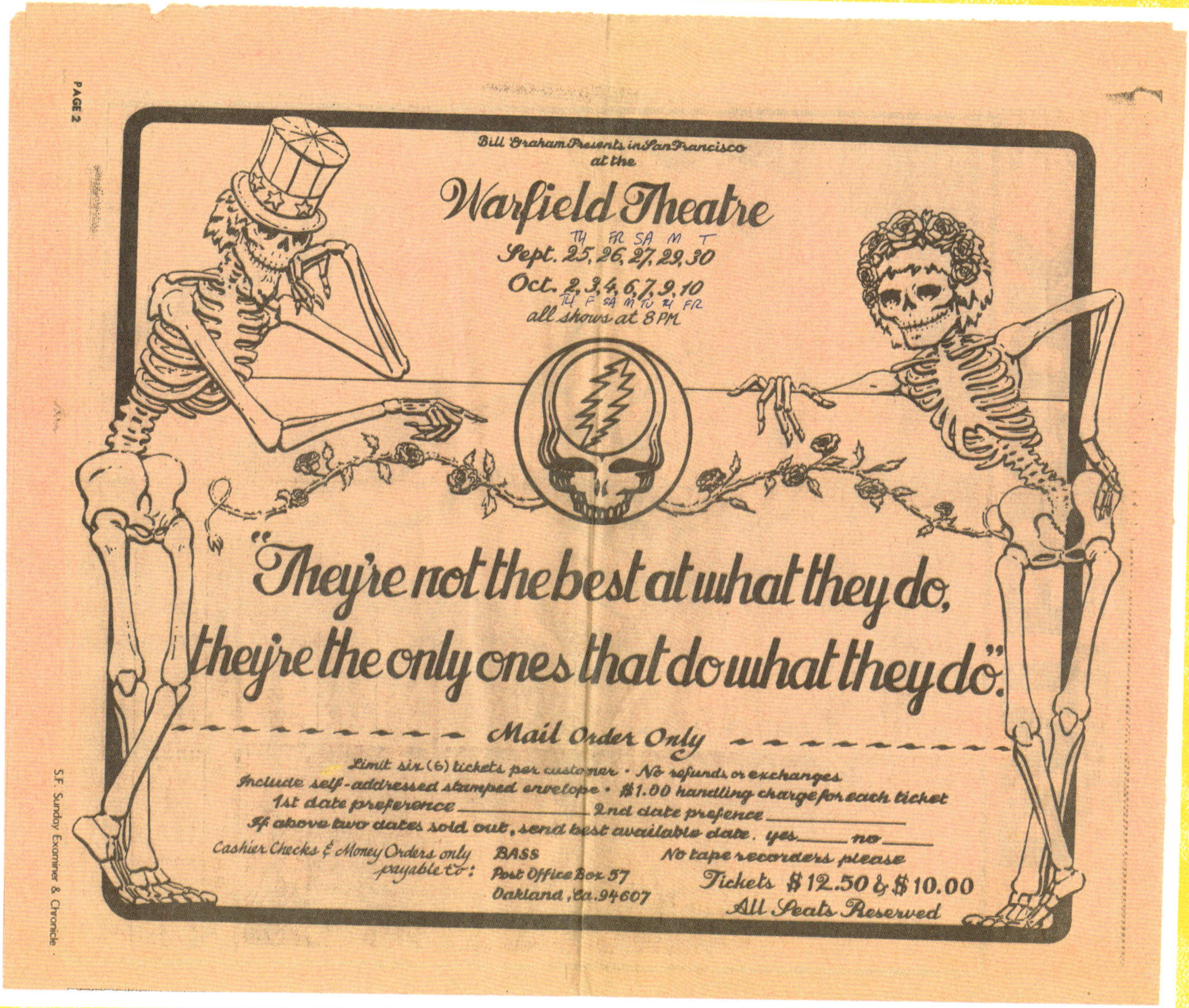

we were, with hundreds of thousands of dollars of tickets and money orders. The police were constantly going in and out of this apartment complex, busting people for drugs and prostitution. And the back window from this apartment was about twenty feet away from Front Street. We could hear them rehearsing all day long. And then we would be done at the end of the evening, and I would take all the tickets and the money and everything and put it in the Grateful Dead's tape vault, which was the most secure place they had. So I got to go in the vault a lot; I spent more time in there than I probably should have, because it was fucking amazing.

So anyway, I got the call; Eddie asked me to come in. He said that the managers at that time—Danny Rifkin, Rock Scully, and Alan Trist—wanted to talk to me. I went in, and I said, "I think you should know that I was fired from Bill Graham Presents because I complained about them overselling Grateful Dead shows." And all three of them looked at me and said, "You're hired." That was my interview. And then Danny Rifkin said, "We know that Bill Graham is ripping us off. We don't know how. You've worked for BASS, and you worked for Bill Graham. Can you go over our settlements for the last year, and tell us how we got ripped off?" So, I spent a day going through their settlements, and just for 1982 alone, I found over $300,000 of bogus charges—the main one being that Bill Graham submitted a bill from BASS Tickets, charging [Bill Graham Presents] 5 percent of the total gross of tickets sold as their fee for using BASS. And it was printed on BASS Tickets letterhead. Well, I knew that BASS never did settlements on their letterhead. I also knew that the way that BASS started was that Jerry Seltzer had a deal with Bill Graham Presents, that BASS would pay Bill Graham Presents nine and a half cents a ticket under the table. Instead of charging Bill Graham Presents, they actually paid Bill Graham. Plus, they paid Bill Graham Presents four and a half cents a ticket for everything, other than baseball, that BASS sold tickets to. So in essence, Bill Graham Presents was like a silent partner.

The very first bill that I looked at was this BASS Tickets letterhead bill and it was for, I don't know, thousands of dollars. And I said to Danny, "Well, that's fake." And he was floored, absolutely floored. This is for five shows at what became the Oakland Auditorium. Bill Graham Presents [claimed that they] paid 10 percent of the gross as a rental for the building. Well, I had actually been promoting shows myself, and the Oakland Auditorium manager had told me that the rent was $1500, a flat fee, and that was it. I said, "You don't want a percentage?" He said, "No, that's not the way we're set up." So, that was another charge for thousands of dollars that Bill Graham not only never paid, but it was bullshit. I mean, they would just add it up and add it up.

The funny thing is, our closest relationship was with Bill Graham, and Bill Graham's people did everything in their power to sabotage Grateful Dead's ticket sales when it first started. One example is when the Grateful Dead had two shows in '83 at Madison Square Garden. We would ask for half the tickets to the shows, and Madison Square Garden gave us the worst half of the tickets in the building. And Danny Rifkin called up John Scher and said, "The concerts are canceled until you can get Madison Square Garden to divide the building in half, right down the middle starting in the front row, and we get one side, and they get the other side." Madison Square Garden was the most corrupt box office of all of them. That was like pulling teeth from a baby. We got all those tickets, but they weren't happy about it.

Actually, many months after I was hired, Danny Rifkin approached Bill Graham, and actually said to him, "I need to talk to you about some of these charges. It's my understanding that not only does BASS not charge you anything, they pay you nine and a half cents a ticket." According to Danny Rifkin, Bill Graham slapped his own face and was rubbing his chin and said, "Well, I'll have to look into that." Which basically was, he got caught. And then in 1986, when Jerry went into his coma—at that point the Grateful Dead was not very good about their business, and when Jerry went into the coma, they were broke. They had no money whatsoever. Bill Graham showed up at a band meeting with a very large Halliburton suitcase, and slammed the suitcase on the table at the meeting and opened it up and there was, according to everyone there, a million dollars in cash. And what I heard, from three different sources that were at the meeting, was that they took that million dollars and divided it among all the people at the meeting, which was the six band members, and the crew, and the management, and a few office workers. I was not at that meeting. I said to Danny, "Where's my share?" And he said, "You weren't there." And I said, "I wasn't invited." He said, "Tough."

The thing is, Bill Graham's second lieutenants and stuff, they knew me because I worked as a bluecoat, and they knew that I had complained about them overselling Grateful Dead shows. They realized that I was giving the Grateful Dead all the information about the scams. They weren't happy. And they set me up twice by giving me verbal amounts of tickets I could sell [for] the shows. An example is the 1983 New Year's Eve show. It was 100 percent mail-order, but the two nights before were not—they were 50 percent mail-order. Bill Graham's lieutenant, Bob Barsotti, had verbally given me, out of ten thousand tickets, five thousand [of them]. Well, the capacity, which I didn't know, was actually ninety-five hundred. So, I ended up selling five hundred tickets over capacity and the fire marshal wanted to shut the place down. And what ended up happening, of course, was he was invited into the box office and left a few minutes later with a big smile, meaning they gave him a couple of thousand bucks, cash. Bob Barsotti approached me in the box office itself, and physically chest-butted me, knocking my glasses off my face, yelling at me for doing this, and that I was fucked and was going to be fired. And then, maybe twenty minutes to a half hour later, Bill Graham approached me in the hall while the band was playing, and starts yelling at me. But he's yelling at me and saying, "I'm not yelling at you. I'm trying to be heard over the music, but I'm not yelling at you." And I said to him, "Is this one of these conversations where I listen and you talk?" And he said, "Yes." And I said, "No, thank you." Turned around and walked away. Nobody walks away from Bill Graham. So, the first set is coming to an end, I went backstage, and Phil Lesh comes off the stage, walks over to me, puts his arm around me and says, "Don't worry, you're not getting fired." And I said, "You know what's going on?" He said, "We know everything that's going on." And that was their way of saying, "We know that you're getting fucked. And we're telling them to stop it." That was because of the stuff I was telling them. It really opened [the company's] eyes. And Danny Rifkin was friends with a lot of managers of other bands. And basically what he said to Bill Graham was, "You're going to start paying us what we deserve, or I'm going to start calling these managers and telling them how you're ripping them off."

The first shows at the Warfield were at the end of March; after those shows, theoretically, I no longer had a job. What I did was something that I found out, later, most people who got permanent jobs with the Grateful Dead did, and that was that I kept coming to the office every day without being paid, just doing busy work, until Danny Rifkin said, "Hey, we want to do mail-order for the Greek Theatre, and we want to do mail-order for Frost Amphitheater," and blah, blah, blah. That's how I made a six-week job last thirteen years.

We started with the Greek Theatre and then we started doing a couple hundred tickets here and there to shows, a few thousand to their local shows. In 1983, we sold twenty-four thousand tickets by mail-order. The Grateful Dead were famous for starting fly-by-night businesses that never made money—in fact, lost lots of money. They had a travel agency called Fly by Night. They had a clothing store that wives of road crew and band members and stuff ran. And then they had their record label, which famously lost them shitloads of money. So, my rules were: number one, the mail-order had to be word-of-mouth only, through the Grateful Dead's hotline—which, in fact, was an unlisted phone number. The hotline number was word-of-mouth, [but] I believe that they had actually put it in a couple of ads. Also, on *Live/Dead*, there was a [printed message on the back cover] about, "We want your information, and here's the address." Then, when things [like] the newsletter got sent out, the Grateful Dead hotline was listed on that newsletter. And then I was told to set up a separate phone number just for mail-order, because at that time, the mail-order information was on recorder phones, which had three-minute tapes. So we had to somehow get all the information for all the shows on a three-minute tape. We had ten recorder phones with the same message on all ten. It was a clusterfuck, but Deadheads got through.

But what I was going to say is, we did 24,000 tickets the first year. The next year—again, strictly word-of-mouth—we sold 115,000 tickets. And then the next year, we sold 300,000 tickets. By the time Jerry died, we were doing 600,000 tickets a year out of a million and a half of the tickets being sold. No other band has ever done that. The largest fan clubs [had] maybe two or three hundred tickets to shows, and here we were selling half of Madison Square Garden, which was unheard of. We just built it up. Oh, and when I got hired, Danny Rifkin gave me a list—a handwritten list of names and phone numbers of people that I should consider hiring. And I don't know if you've ever heard of Calico, but she was the first person on the list. He wrote next to her name, "She's a hard worker, but you two will butt heads." And he was right. But she was the heart and soul of the office.

MAR: That's Ruby then, right?

SM: Right, Ruby Begonias. She's one of the original Hog Farmers [commune member] and traveled all over the world with them.

MAR: The main thing that I'm really interested in is 1984 rolling around, when you guys started to plan the official tapers section.

SM: Dan Healy, the sound guy, complained about not seeing the stage. And in the discussions, they were throwing everything out like, "Let's let them tape, but we're going to charge them $5 extra a ticket." That's when I said, "No, just sell them the obstructed view tickets that we never sell, and that's found income for us." I said, "If you charge them extra, they're going to think that they have the right to sell the tapes." They were not diligent about tapers, except for the ones that would go up front at reserved-seat shows and steal seats and not let the people that had the tickets sit there.

MAR: And you said that Dan Healy was very adamant?

SM: He was upset because he couldn't see the stage. There were these ten- and fifteen-foot microphone stands, and Candace Brightman, who did the lights, couldn't see the stage, so she was pissed off. My suggestion to put the tapers behind the soundboard was not only accepted immediately, but the whole idea that the Grateful Dead would make an extra six hundred bucks or a thousand bucks a night from tickets that they normally wouldn't have sold—I know it sounds like not a lot of money, but it was for the Grateful Dead.

MAR: Right. You're saying that it was your idea to put them behind the sound booth.

DOUG AND JIM OADE INTERVIEWED BY DAVID GANS
10/24/2007

David Gans: I remember Dan Healy had a good relationship with a lot of tapers, and I think he was learning stuff from what you guys were giving him, right?

Jim Oade: Yeah, he was an interesting, amusing character for sure, and he was always very friendly to me and very friendly to the tapers, as long as you weren't arrogant and creating a problem. Always respected him. And I'll never forget: after '86, when they were going to move the taper section to the rear of the building where there's no possible way to get a good recording, I just went up to him after the show and asked him if we could run a rig on the soundboard and then share all the tapes. He said, "I don't care what you do with the tapes; yeah, you can run a rig on the soundboard." So he actually let us set up our rig on the soundboard to at least get one good recording out of the building. I think Doug went backstage that night with him, and he was even offering to loan some of his gear out to do the recording.

Doug Oade: Yeah. We rented a motel room the next day, handed out flyers that night, and had a bunch of tapers show up to do various daisy chains to go ahead and immediately distribute the audio. It was quite an affair--and a serious disappointment to management, who rented us the room without really realizing what was going to be happening. It was a fun time. I remember a number of times when we were pushed away from directly behind the board, a number of friends took pictures of that spot, and where the tapers section was, was largely empty and not used by anybody. Brilliant on Dan Healy's part to utilize the space that was normally dead space for "Dead space."

SM: They were in killed seats. Every concert in every building, the seats behind the soundboard were always "obstructed view" and not sold. So, at big stadium shows, we would have up to 250 "tapers' tickets."

What happened with the first three Warfield shows was: Eileen Law—who was the voice of the hotline, and was in charge of Deadheads—she had told me that when it came to Bill Graham holding tickets for the band to use, their tickets were always upstairs in the balcony. They never got any good seats on the floor. Since I had all the tickets to all three shows, I was the one that distributed who got what holds. So I put Bill Graham's tickets all up in the balcony—where they usually put our tickets—and I put the Grateful Dead tickets downstairs, and not in the first ten rows. My rule was small shows under the size of arenas, under fifteen thousand, I never put any holds in the first ten rows, because I felt they should go to fans. And then for bigger shows, like arenas, the first fifteen rows were held for fans. And then for stadiums, the first twenty rows. Anyway, I got a phone call from Bob Barsotti, really angry about the seats they got for their holds. And I said, "These are the same seats you held for the Grateful Dead. If they're good enough for the band, they're good enough for you." And of course, I had actually held extra seats on the floor for them, because I knew they would get pissed off. But the end result was from that point on when it was a reserved-seat show, I picked all the holds, not the promoter. And I did that for every show, starting around 1986. That was when I started really taking control of the tickets.

I was given more attack power, and slowly but surely, the buildings and the promoters realized that in many ways this was saving them a lot of money, because we would have mail-orders that would go on sale for weeks before tickets would go on sale to the general public. So we had four weeks to fill the orders and send them out, depending on how many tickets we would sell. Sometimes we would sell 50 percent of the tickets by mail-order, and the promoters knew that they didn't have to spend a penny on advertising. And the other thing was that while I had the money from the tickets being sold, I didn't keep the money. The night of every show, I gave the promoter a check for all the tickets we sold, and then they paid the band. It made it clean. Because otherwise, I would have to use Federal Express to turn in all the unsold tickets before the show, and [the promoter] checked the ones that we had sold, and then the unsold mail-order tickets would be sold at the door or whatever. But then towards the end, we sold 99 percent of our mailer allotment.

MAR: I'm going to go back to '83 when you're starting. Was counterfeiting a big issue, or is that just something that kind of creeps up?

SM: It creeped up. I mean, we learned a lot: like, we accepted money orders, bank money orders and postal money orders, etc. Well, I found out that bank money orders are actually considered single-item checking accounts, which meant that whoever got the money order from the bank could actually take the receipt and cancel the money order after they sent it in. So we were having a few incidences of sending out tickets and then having a money order bounce. And then I found out that you couldn't do that with Western Union money orders or postal money orders, and in fact, if you did that with postal money orders, it was a federal offense. So we changed it so that you could only use Western Union or postal money orders.

We figured it out by the end of '83. And then when it came to New Year's Eve, we had so many orders for tickets, and I would say 70 percent of the orders were from the East Coast. Well, there's no way in hell that Bill Graham was going to allow 70 percent of New Year's Eve tickets to go to the East Coast, so, while we did it randomly, we, in fact, made sure that at least 70 percent of the tickets went to the West Coast. And then we found that scalpers were sending in money orders and mail-orders and stuff, and in the classified sections in the newspapers under "tickets for sale," there were hundreds. So, we had to figure out a way to make sure that our tickets went directly to fans and not scalpers, which took a while. Then when it came to counterfeits, we had a few crappy ones that were handmade. The big thrust for counterfeits was in '77 while I was working at BASS. We started getting lots of counterfeit tickets to all the general admission Bill Graham concerts, and I became an expert in finding them. But when it came to the mail-order tickets, that's where I had to really sit down with the ticket printing companies and come up with new ideas to make the tickets counterfeit-proof. As soon as we came up with an idea, the counterfeiters would come up with a way to make them.

The FBI got involved in '91, because we were using tickets by Weldon, Williams and Lick which had colored threads in them, that were very similar to money, which at that time had colored threads. I figured if people were counterfeiting these Grateful Dead tickets, they may be counterfeiting money. So, I was put in touch with a woman who was the FBI agent in charge of all this stuff, and she was based out of New York City. I found out later that the character Clarice Starling in *Silence of the Lambs* was based on her; that was interesting, but she refused to talk about it. What ended up happening was the FBI got involved, and they busted a printing place in New Jersey that was, in fact, creating thousands of Grateful Dead mail-order tickets. They figured out it was a mob front. That stopped counterfeits for about an hour.

MAR: And the Nixon stamp you made, can you describe that?

SM: It was a rubber stamp of Tricky Dick. I said, "Well, this guy is the king of the tapers," because of Watergate. "Let's put him on the back of every paper ticket." That was my decision. I got one rubber stamp, and that's what I used.

MAR: And you called it Inky Dink?

SM: No, that's the company that made it. Tricky Dick was just the face. Also, Eileen Law used to end every hotline message with, "Thank you and stay in touch." [Once] I was at the Exploratorium in San Francisco—which was a great place at the Palace of Fine Arts—with a couple of friends, very high on acid, and in the gift shop they had a rubber stamper where you could stamp three different colors at a time and it said—two fingers like the picture in the Sistine Chapel of God touching [Adam's] hand—it had that picture image engraved in it, and it said, "Stay in touch." So, I used that rubber stamp for most of my correspondence with people from that point on. I still have that rubber stamp somewhere, or I gave it to [the archive at UC] Santa Cruz, I'm not sure.

MAR: And where is the Nixon stamp? Is that with you?

SM: It's on a shelf in my house. I'm probably going to give that to the archives. But that rubber stamp was the one that we used [to mark taper tickets]. There was a period where a lot of the buildings would not let us print our own mail-order tickets; the tickets had to be sent from the building, the box office. And for those, we'd rubber stamp on the front of the taper ticket. That made it easier for the security and the ticket takers to figure out what was what.

I would [also] sit at a table and check for counterfeit tickets in the parking lot before the shows—that way, if I found any, I could give them to the ticket taker so they knew what to look for. But I always had comp tickets in my pocket, and in case somebody would come up with a counterfeit, I would give them a real ticket and keep the counterfeit. But I also would go around [to the] people walking around the parking lot with their finger up in the air—"looking for a miracle." I'd sneak up behind them and slip a ticket in their hand and walk away. And I would do this to sometimes twenty people, sometimes a hundred people, and that's why they called it "the miracle," because they had no idea where these tickets were coming from. They just knew that all of a sudden there was a ticket in their hand, and they couldn't figure out where they came from. Then the word got around that I was doing it. A friend of mine gave me a shirt that said, "No, I don't have an extra ticket." I wore that shirt just to see if anybody had the guts to approach me. And I always had free tickets in my pocket.

MAR: Could you speak to just the numbers of taper tickets alone?

SM: For reserved-seat shows, it was whatever was obstructed, behind the soundboard, so we would have anywhere from one hundred to two hundred tickets. Word of mouth about taping got around, and we sold out immediately. The first tapers sections at the Berkeley Community Theater were at least a hundred tickets.

MAR: I see. And then by the time of Jerry's passing, how many tapers' tickets were you selling?

SM: It was still basically whatever was obstructed behind the soundboard, so it might be two hundred tickets for the fifteen-thousand-seat arenas.

MAR: Did you ever collect tapes?

SM: I had three tapes when I started working for the Grateful Dead. I walked into the Grateful Dead office one morning, which was a two-story Victorian house in downtown San Rafael. And everybody went up the back steps—you knew that somebody didn't belong there if they went through the front door. I went up the back steps into the kitchen, and Phil Lesh was sitting at a table with Bobby Petersen, who was a poet friend of his, who wrote the words to "Unbroken Chain." Anyway, this was at a period when Phil was a drunk. They were sitting at this table at ten o'clock in the morning with a stack of cases of Heineken behind the curtain—they had each already gone through a six pack. Anyway, Phil got up and put his arm around me and said, "I want to welcome you to the Grateful Dead. We're really thrilled to have you here." He gave me his phone number and he said, "If there's anything I can do for you, just call me and ask me." And I said, "I do have a question." And he said, "Well, what is it?" And I said, "About tapes in the vault." And he laughed and said, "What do you want?" And I said, "Well, the show that I got it at was June 9, 1977, at Winterland." I said, "I'd love to get that tape." I said, "David Gans gave me a really shitty audience tape." And he said, "As long as you don't go crazy, I'm happy to have tapes made for you." About a week later, in my mail slot, was a box with all three shows from that weekend and a note from Phil saying, "I forgot which night you wanted, so here's all three nights." Well, those were Betty Boards. I'd never heard those before, and I was flabbergasted. So from that point on, I was spoiled. By the time Jerry died, I had over a thousand tapes. One hundred of them were soundboard masters, and probably four to five hundred of them were first or second generation of the vault masters. I was spoiled.

MAR: Did you have a lot of interaction with Dick at all?

SM: Yeah. He was the one that made all the tapes. I actually saw Dick, driving to the Grateful Dead office, the day that he slipped into a coma. I honked my horn and waved at him, but he looked horrible. He looked really horrible. And then, I learned later he went home and told everyone he was going to take a nap and he never woke up. He was a raving drunk at one point, and he went sober a few years before he died; I mean, except for pot. And Dick was very funny: he lived next to his ex-wife, Carol Latvala, who worked at the ticket office. Their friends had a gate inbuilt so they could go back and forth, and people would come over to his house and sit around, and Dick would play music. And if he got to the point where he wanted you to leave, he would turn the volume up really loud, painfully loud, and leave the room and go to his bedroom. And that was his way of saying goodbye. The other thing was, he had a family of skunks living underneath his back porch. And he left his sliding glass door to the living room open all the time, so his cats could go in and out and eat their food. And the skunks would come in and eat the cat food too. And they never sprayed; you just left them alone.

The first official tapers section,
Berkeley Community Theater, October 1984
Photos: David Gans

Alan Trist

July 31–August 3, 2020

MAR: The initial reason I wanted to contact you were the documents I found in the UCSC archive. Within a folder that contains letters and documents from Les Kippel and the Free Underground Grateful Dead Tape Exchange there is a letter, dated August 27, 1973, from a "Muskrat Miller" that's part of a series of letters between Les Kippel and Jon McIntire, Sam Cutler, and Ron Rakow. Les seems to be trying to establish a relationship with the GD organization and trying to make a legitimized business distributing and selling mass-produced bootleg tapes to Deadheads—I think he called it the Connoisseur's Club. I was wondering, since you are named in the document quoted above, if you remember any of these discussions at all from this time period?

AT: My recollection is that 1972 to 1974 was a fertile period for the Grateful Dead's internal philosophizing about its outlier position in the music business. The file you have seems to reflect that, and that the band's ultimate decision-making went in the direction of a hands-off approach to taping shows and tape-trading, encapsulated in Garcia's comment about the fate of their concert music, "We're done with it, you can have it." This was the opposite direction from Les Kippel's, which seems to have been to commercialize the tapes. I remember having some correspondence with Les at that time, or maybe later, about print publishing in regard to his magazine, at that time entirely devoted to the GD, where what he wanted to do as an outside businessman was not approved by the GD, but I don't remember exactly what that was about. The other direction the GD embraced in the early to mid-seventies was forming their own record company(s) with Rakow at the helm (GD Records and Round Records) and leaving Warner Bros. This venture was successful, until it wasn't. It was a lot of fun. The clear implication of these two business decisions is that they were self-contradictory from a traditional sales standpoint; how can you sell stuff to people who already have it; record companies are famously tight about this sort of thing. Nevertheless, several decades later when the GD were well-known for their unusual practices, economics Nobel laureate and *New York Times* columnist Paul Krugman wrote a column saying that "Everything I know about business I learned from the Grateful Dead"! The band has proved to this day that if you give it away, Deadheads will buy the official releases, even as Archive.com has it all. Some have claimed that the GD invented a new way of marketing, but they eschew such an interpretation. But there is probably more to it than simple brand loyalty and dedicated fans . . . After the hiatus, in 1976 the band went in another direction with Richard Loren, assigning all recording, publicity, and marketing at first to United Artists and then to Arista, these functions having previously been internal, keeping only touring and publishing under their own wing. Further evolutions and changes in business practices and relationships have occurred right up to now, but taping goes on forever!

MAR: I recently talked to Steve Marcus about GD tickets and the beginning of the tapers section. He told a story of being hired by Danny Rifkin, Rock Scully, and yourself. It seems at the time the managers were trying to figure out if Bill Graham was ripping off the band, and Steve seemed to have a lot of key knowledge in this regard deriving from his experience working for BASS Ticketing and as a "bluecoat" for Bill Graham Presents. Do you have any memory of that meeting or any corroboration of that event or events, and how all that was going down within the scene?

AT: I have a vague recollection of that meeting, at the time the ticket office was being set up. But this was much later, late seventies/early eighties; the tape-trading issue was long settled by then, though maybe the tapers section was not formally set up till later. Steve probably has as much info as I do about what was going down with Bill. Selling our own tickets? This certainly was an issue for Bill, but we went our own way anyway. In the end, though, I don't think figuring out the ins and outs of our financial relationship with Bill ever resolved anything—he had multiple reasons for evading the bottom line, some of them good, some questionable. We just had to keep hammering out good relationships, on both sides, and holding his heels to the fire as far as that was possible.

MAR: I also was wondering if I could also ask you about [the Dead's music publishing company] Ice Nine. I was just curious what you did as the director and if taping/tape trading made your position more interesting/challenging? I ask because usually the recording and distributing of music from a rock band would be something that would make a typical band and corresponding music publisher adversarial towards whichever entity was distributing unofficial merchandise.

AT: Strictly, my job was copyrighting and registering with the performance rights societies the new songs as they were recorded, and administering the licensing of those copyrights, which involved correspondence with all kinds of folks about all kinds of ideas, great and crazy, publishing songbooks, and generally looking out for "publishing matters" of all sorts. So I was involved in the management discussion of tape trading as discussed earlier. If the GD had been regular music-biz people, the publishing company, owners of the copyrights, might have objected to the band's turning a blind eye to the taping, but since Ice Nine was "in house" this never came up. So, no, the tape trading did not impact Ice Nine. Nowadays, we all live with the apparent paradox that Rhino's very successful official legacy releases from the band's thirty years of concert recordings in the vault provide good income to the songwriters through Ice Nine, despite that Deadheads and Archive.org have it all anyway!

MAR: I think what is incredible about what you have said and about the research I am conducting in general is the interconnectivity of it all. I like to think that everyone I have talked to was working together in a hive, and of a hive mind of sorts.

AT: That's a pretty good description. Interconnectivity—certainly our minds were connected by daily working interactions about issues, working as a team(s), often elevated to conjunction by the psychoactive properties of marijuana. Likely we took cues from the band, who clearly functioned as a unit, famously through the listening/conversational powers of improvisation. At business "band meetings" in the seventies, typically everyone would turn up, secretaries, crew, engineers, band, managers, maybe thirty folks, but we managed to get through agendas in a few hours with some discipline . . . In later decades, parliamentary rules were instituted and meetings became more "committee" like.

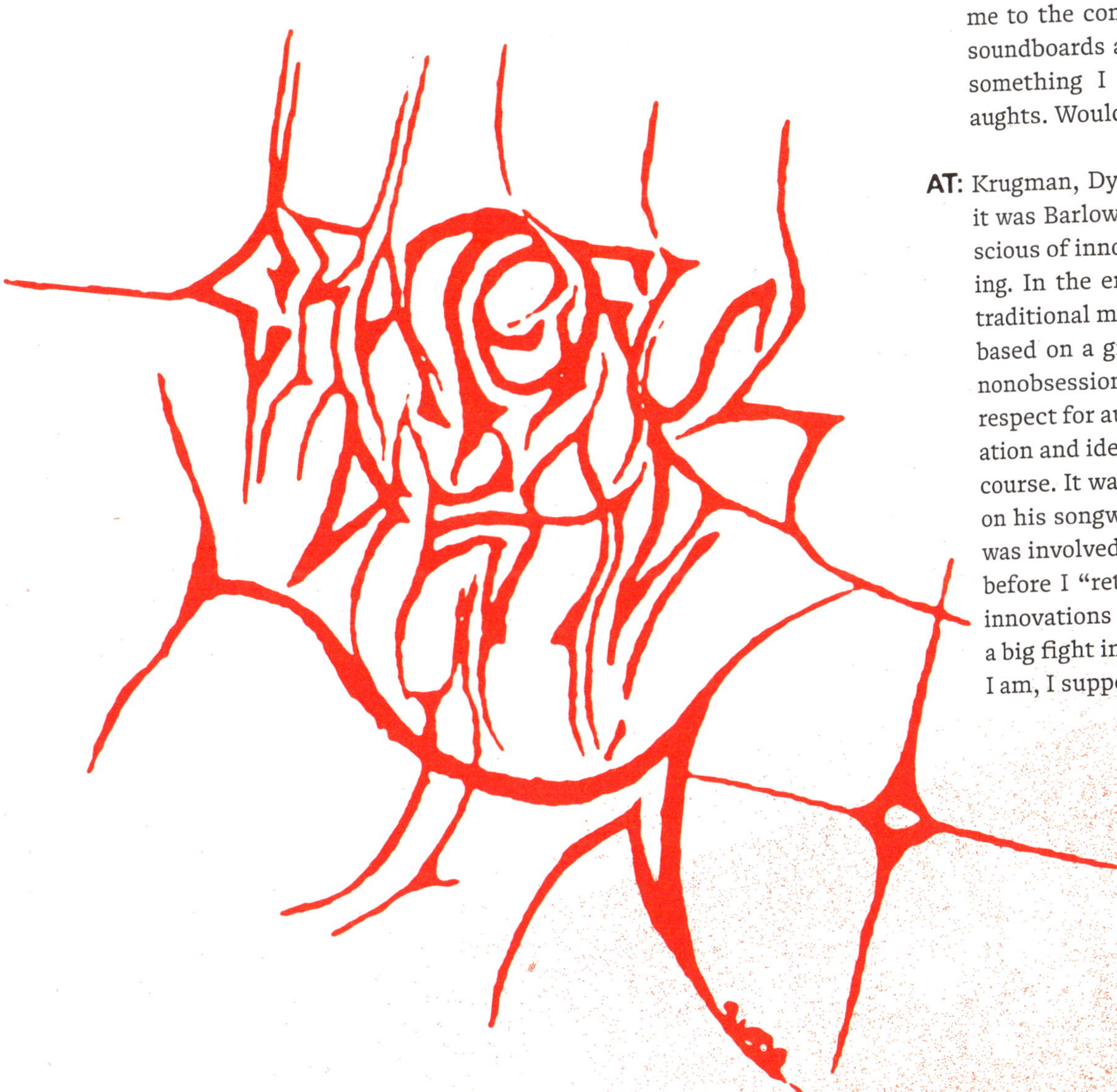

MAR: You had mentioned Paul Krugman, who wrote a short *New York Times* snack of an article which led me to remember [Deadhead and business scholar] Barry Barnes's book *Everything I Know About Business I Learned from the Grateful Dead*, which is the quote you attributed to Krugman. Reading Krugman's article led me to trace back the source of his rumination to [investor and commentator] Esther Dyson, who was actually riffing off of [Dead lyricist] John Perry Barlow's 1994 essay "The Economy of Ideas." It's very interesting to me that the trading of tapes within the Grateful Dead community served as a building block and inspiration to both Barlow's and Dyson's expanded theories on intellectual property and the spreading of information in the nascent digital age, forming new economies. Dyson especially is fascinating in that she applies this network to what would eventually become viral marketing and the proposition of a business surviving off of what we could now call an "influencer," or influencers. It always amazes me that all of these cultural developments can be traced back in some way and form to the Grateful Dead's allowance of tapers taping and distributing their shows. Furthermore this led me to the controversy over the allowance of the plethora of soundboards and audience recordings found on Archive.org—something I had forgotten about happening in the early aughts. Would you have any comment on this phenomena?

AT: Krugman, Dyson, Barlow—a fascinating crew indeed. I think it was Barlow in his foreword who said the GD were not conscious of innovating any marketing techniques, e.g. tape trading. In the end, I would attribute the "contradictions" with traditional marketing to the obvious magic: additional factors based on a ground of love such as high intent, high quality, nonobsession with commercial and self-serving "values" and respect for audience interests, all of which reciprocal appreciation and identification translate into sales just as a matter of course. It was always interesting to me that Barlow depended on his songwriting royalties, which I oversaw at Ice Nine, yet was involved in publicly proclaiming an end to copyright. Just before I "retired" in 2015, the digital file-sharing and other innovations in payment for music making was ramping up to a big fight in the music biz, which I mostly missed (phew!!) so I am, I suppose, old school!

Computer Wizard Dreams Up A Database for Deadheads

United Press International

Hanover, N.H.

A Dartmouth College computer expert is bridging the gap between the age of Aquarius and the computer age for die-hard rock and roll fans of the Grateful Dead.

John Scott, a computer programmer at the Ivy League college, is creator and editor of "Deadbase," a profit-making, 300-page printed document. Soon to be made available as a software package, the book lists all known Grateful Dead concerts and songs dating back to the band's inception in 1965.

"This started out as actual course work when I was a student in computer science at Dartmouth in 1984," says Scott, a veteran of more than 100 Dead concerts.

"I began collecting lists of songs the Dead played in concert in 1980 or so. A lot of that was by looking through people's Dead tape collections. I have some friends who have a thousand tapes plus," Scott said. "I myself now have somewhere over a 1,000 Dead tapes, which is somewhere near 1,500 hours of music."

After graduating from Dartmouth, Scott, 29, began adding to the information he had stored on the college's computer. He has since purchased his own Macintosh personal computer, which he used to produce the books Deadbase, Deadbase II and Deadbase III (due out this summer).

The band allows its fans, known as Deadheads, to legally tape nearly all the band's concerts, making the live music available second- or third-hand to anyone willing to track down the cassettes.

"Almost everyone thinks Deadbase is a taper's bible because of the song and show lists," Scott said. "They use Deadbase as a reference and then look for the tapes."

There are other sources, where Deadheads find song lists from the most recent tours, including the Oakland-based Dead fan magazine The Golden Road, which helped finance Deadbase's first printing.

"One thing about being a Deadhead, is that it's not just what songs the band is doing now, but a lot of it is uncovering some of the things they did way back then," Scott said. "Being a Deadhead could be a legitimate field of study for sociologists or ethno-musicologists."

BY UNITED PRESS INTERNATIONAL

Dartmouth computer programmer John Scott used his home Macintosh to write 'Deadbase,' all about the Grateful Dead

And that is just fine with the Grateful Dead.

"Deadbase makes perfect sense," says band publicist Dennis McNally. "The Grateful Dead have long moved into the world of the computer, particularly the Macintosh, which we use in our office."

Scott struck an informal deal with the Dead to donate some of the profits to charities supported by the band, particularly several organizations working to keep South American rain forests intact.

A big step for getting Deadbase off the ground came when McNally introduced Scott to San Franciscans Mike Dolgushkin and Stu Nixon, who became co-authors of "Deadbase." Dolgushkin works at the famous repository of '60s art, the Postermat in North Beach, and Nixon is a manager of biomedical data at Genentech in South San Francisco.

In addition to song lists, Deadbase has information on how many seats there are in arenas across the country, how often a particular song has been played, how many times the Dead have performed in the 50 states and the proper titles and writers of all the songs in the band's repertoire.

Scott says everything in Deadbase is much different than the college-level educational and research programs he writes for various social science departments at Dartmouth College.

"Deadbase was just something fun and it began to get real interesting and it's taken off," Scott said. "I imagine about 99 percent of America thinks it's silly, but I take it very seriously."

San Francisco Chronicle, March 1, 1989

John W. Scott

January 24, 2021

JWS: I started listening to Grateful Dead in high school, around 1973—only albums to start. At that time I was mostly into Pink Floyd and Bob Dylan, having been raised on Beatles, Bob Dylan, and Elton John.

MAR: Can you describe any relationship you had to taping and tapers early on?

JWS: Although I owned a D6 and a portable DAT, I did not own my own mics. I did patch out sometimes. I had two good friends who were serious tapers: Rich Senicola and Jeff Silberman, and would often help them and/or patch out.

MAR: Were there other lists or early computer programs that you were aware of before you started *DeadBase*?

JWS: I am not aware of any Dead software or computerized lists in circulation before *DeadBase*. *DeadBase* started as a computer-science project in 1983 for a database course. It appealed to me as a nontraditional sort of data, giving me the opportunity to find my own patterns and relationships in the information and thus new ways to organize and visualize it. I had been collecting setlists both to catalog the tapes I had (sometimes they were mislabeled) and to figure out which shows I wanted to find. There were other lists of tapes/shows circulating, but not much in the way of setlists. I still managed to collate a huge number of songs for those lists from tape collections and such, when Rich Senicola gave me a photocopy of a huge (two-plus-inch thick) list with one setlist or show per page. This list was unattributed, and though I already had a large majority of the songs incorporated there were many new song lists (two hundred?) and many (one hundred?) new shows of which I had been previously unaware. Many of these lists were from important shows I had been seeking for a while. I was unable to track down where the list had come from.

In 1986 I contacted the Dead's office seeking permission to publish a book of setlists. Dennis invited me to meet him at a show in Portland, Maine, to discuss the project. At our meeting (my first time backstage) he suggested that I might collaborate with Stu and Mike. That suggestion was very fortuitous as it soon turned out that they had produced the unattributed list which had been so useful.

MAR: How did your appreciation for computer graphics factor into *DeadBase*? Can you name any influences?

JWS: I don't remember there being much in the way of computer graphics back then. The Mac had just been released two years prior, and black-and-white MacPaint was the "state-of-the-art." Again, it was mostly a matter of finding out what worked for me, what I could do, and that suited me well. Most of my art inside those early editions was produced more traditionally on paper then photographed. I was a former/failed struggling artist, and getting to do art for the books was very important to me. The computer art was mostly done in MacPaint and perhaps MacDraw to start. When color graphics became a reality through various programs such as FreeHand, Photoshop, and Illustrator, I was smitten. Doing cover art became an obsession for me and I would spend countless hours researching then executing the various themes I used for those covers. I would put lots of "hidden" "meanings" into them.

The layouts and the features were entirely what seemed to make sense to me at the time. Again, there was nothing (that I was aware of) to base it on. I designed the setlists first. I wanted it to be space efficient which is one reason I did not go with the vertical layout Mike and Stu had used, but more important was that I wanted the lists to read like a sentence, expressing the progression of the show more directly. After I had those done, I wanted to find other views of the data.

MAR: Can you describe the process of creating the skull faces that are a very prominent part of the design of *DeadBase*?

JWS: I think I found a small skull icon somewhere and started with that, blowing it up, and editing it. I also worked with clip-art books such as *Harter's Picture Archive*, which in retrospect is similar to how many of the old-school poster artists worked with found engravings and other art.

MAR: Would you say you shared the same objectives with Stu and Mike as far as your participation in *DeadBase*, or did each person contribute something unique?

JWS: Mike and Stu mostly provided data from the original setlist pages described above to updates, and then collecting information for the origins of the songs (who wrote them, albums, etc.) for the "Songs Played" section. They continued to provide updates and corrections to the setlists. Stu also collated the comprehensive article indices for the annual editions, working directly with the Dead's office. Stu may have also been instrumental in getting approval from the band. Stu had direct connections to the Dead's office, which were very useful throughout.

Mostly they provided research and I took it from there. Their research was indeed paramount and it would have taken years, after an even more meager first edition, to have caught up from readers' additions without their work. Our collaboration often boiled down to sorting out conflicting corrections, coming to agreement on what to call a given song, how long a pause between songs and still use an arrow rather than a comma between them (we settled on three seconds or less was not paused). Thirty-five years is a long time ago, and I only have fuzzy memories of the conversations. But there was definite give-and-take on song titles, and some of them took a while to resolve. I moved "Themes" and "Tunings" to the comments below the list. The three-second rule described above still seems a little long to me, as there is no direct transition, but that was our consensus. Perhaps in retrospect, I might have used a different delimiter for transitions, such as a double arrow.

I took free reign in designing the books, the features and layout, the typesetting, finding printers, publishing, and the distribution. I added features in subsequent editions to try and capture a more rounded appreciation of the data. The first edition had the most obvious stats, such as how often each song and each venue had been played, and an early version of the "Every Time Played" list. Already I started to look at how the shows were "formatted" with set openers/closers, into / out of drums, etc. I later conceived of, designed, distributed all the feedback surveys and entered and collated all that data. I also personally timed every show from 1986 to 1995, and then many older "classic" tapes.

I was very driven to find new ways to approach the experience and resulting data that were the Grateful Dead—not just numerically, but descriptively. The "Every Time Played" list, for example, was my solution for someone trying to figure out which show an unlabeled list came from. I devised and included those four-character abbreviations for the song before and after, which meant that you could pick a less common song from that list and very quickly narrow it down (and usually figure it out) very quickly.

MAR: How many copies of *DeadBase* number one were printed? Can you recollect why you went with that number or how much that number increased over time?

JWS: Not sure. The first edition was either 1K or 2K; the next one was double. After that I started doing reprints. I think the most we ever sold was 8K.

MAR: How did distribution work in the early days?

JWS: The books were delivered to my home, and I shipped them from my tiny local post office. While the postmaster appreciated the revenue, I don't think her clerk liked my business as my packages would fill the already claustrophobic space.

Steven Marcus

August 12, 2021

MAR: I wanted to figure out if Steve [Parish, Dead roadie] and Kidd [Candelario] have any memory of actually trying to cut tapers off from taping or that sort of thing.

SM: I don't know about that. I know that I did, at one point, in the Kaiser Auditorium. I went out and stopped some tapers in front of the sound booth because they were just being obnoxious. One taper accused me of cutting the cords, which of course I did not do. And I almost got fired because of that, by the way. Danny Rifkin called me into his office and said, "This is really serious. You can't be doing this." And I said I didn't do it, and then I put the word out to some tapers that I knew who were there and I said, "Just tell them the truth—exactly what I did." And he got a bunch of calls including from Dick Latvala who said, "Steven didn't do that." I remember one taper, Bob Menke, said to me years later: "You didn't stop me from taping." And I said, "I guess I didn't see you."

MAR: Yeah. I mean I think that's kind of what it boils down to: in this instance, they're saying that you cut the cord. It's this classic tale of the roadies cutting the cord to the tape decks, and I'm wondering if that's actually legit or not.

SM: I have heard that rumor over the years. Including when I was working for the Dead, but I never witnessed anything like that. In fact, after we started the tapers section, Dan Healy would—rarely, but he did do it—leave a cable from the soundboard out to the taping section for anybody to plug into, so they could actually get fresh master soundboard tapes.

MAR: Wasn't he also running FM signal, so that anyone in the proximity of the show could also tune and record [via] shortwave, if they wanted to?

SM: Yeah, it wasn't shortwave, it was just one of those frequencies that very rarely has any radio stations on it, and it's usually a weak signal anyway. But yeah, he did that a lot. And then there was the other thing that was happening, which was when they got the in-ear monitors. In '93 is when they actually got the teleprompters, so it had to be earlier than that when they got in-ear monitors, which were wireless—and so, people who were sometimes just right outside the building could actually get the feed. There are a bunch of recordings from the in-ear monitors, where you can hear them talking to each other during songs or before songs and things like that.

Relix: Well, go for it, because this is a good one. On another note, have you seen changes in audience taping with the new standards of equipment available now?

Healy: Yeah, the audience has very sophisticated equipment. And it's of course largely digital and stuff like that these days, and they use good microphones. And our sound system has really gone through a number of significant changes. I mean, the sound in the audience is just outrageously good these days, and so that, plus the better quality equipment that the tapers have, and I think the tapers, particularly the older ones, begin to learn more and more about the ways of doing it. I've heard recent audience tapes that are quite nice sounding. I applaud all those people, basically, I'm on their side, I'm a taper at heart. So I'm glad to see them doing well.

Relix: At one point you had been experimenting with an FM broadcast method during one tour. Was that working out?

Healy: Yes, but what happened is that the FCC was about to come down on me, so I had to stop doing it. In order to do it with good quality, I had to use more power than they allow you to have. The amount of legal power the FCC will give you without a licence is about enough power to go about 20 feet. So it doesn't really work. I was directly in violation. And people like the FCC would love to come down on people like us, so it started getting hot, and I got a few indications that they were about to make an issue out of me, so I backed off for a while. That's not to say I won't ever do it again, but what I've done is, I've decided to let it rest for a while, and I'm gonna do it on more of a hit-and-miss basis. And so I would say that the answer to the tapers is that if you were to bring a tuner, bring a little Walkman radio that you can plug into your tape deck or something, because you never know when I might be doing it again. But officially speaking, I've never done it. ■

Dan Healy interviewed by Toni A. Brown in *Relix* vol. 18, #4, August 1991

BB: **How do you and everybody else maintain your energy level on the tour? It wears me out.**

DH: Make sure and rest. Don't party ever. I never party after the show. Well I wouldn't say never. The point is that you've got to be conservative. You gotta mind your rest, mind your food, mind your eating, mind all that stuff. Work out, I try to swim and work out. All the hotels we stay in, usually have some kind of facility for that.

BB: **What happens after the show? Does everybody go home or to the hotel room?**

DH: Well yeah, I just go back to my hotel room. Go to sleep-get up the next morning. I get up in the morning and go out. Today I went out all over Kansas City. There's a form of energy there for me, it wakes me up it gives me a feeling an affinity to the community and so that's my own personal way.

BB: **How do sound board tapes get into the circulation?**

DH: Dear God, a thousand different ways. Generally one of us leaks them out. We never officially give away a tape, but since they're out there obviously someone does. I make tapes for everybody every night and so you can con one of us into loaning you a tape. I do it too. There are people that I know around the country that I loan my tape to and they take it home, copy it and mail the tape back to me. That's one way they get out. It's not a real big thing. If I let somebody borrow a tape, I usually don't put any restrictions on it, I sort of leave it up to their discretion. They might want to let one of their friends borrow it, I'm sure it works sometimes like chain letters.

BB: **I'm sure it does. Yes, I admit I do it too.**

DH: That's okay. There's an adage in the record industry that if you let anybody record your concerts you'll never sell a record, but I've never believed that from day one. My rebuttal to that had always been that the first record company exec to cough up one shred of evidence that letting people record your concerts has in any way related to your records sales then I'll stop doing it. But no one ever has... it's one of those things. The unique thing is that I believe it works the other way around. I think it creates enthusiasm and it creates fraternity and that in the end sells more records.

BB: **I believe you're absolutely right that it does facilitate the whole community spirit and family.**

DH: I think so. Its just one of those things that's pure bullshit. It's ok to let the audience have tapes, I flashed that right from day one! And it turns out that it's true. I mean now I've had 26 years to think about it and for other people to shoot it down, and no one has. Now I know it's never gonna change. There's a whole lot of stuff like that - the entertainment business is so strange about that - like another one that gets me is that you finish an album, and they have this time of year that they want to release it, like, right around Christmas, or back to school. When school's out they don't want to release stuff because they feel that people aren't in their normal paths and so they tend to not buy stuff. I'm sure that statistically, that's all borne out. But it's also true when someone releases a killer album, everyone gets it no matter when it comes out. There's another example of record company mythology, if you will. There's a lot of stuff like that. Years ago, when I was first starting out in the record business, an old guy used to say, "Dan, after all is said and done, it's in the grooves. It's either good stuff or it isn't, and after all is said and done, you can't force anybody to love something they don't, and yet anything that is really truly happening, people pick up on, and you don't have to push it." And it's really true. The thing that makes it hard to realize that is that the other thing the record company does is, they have...well there's this famous old adage, "In a town that only has a Ford Dealer, people all drive Fords." Well, if you apply that to the record company, if you con every radio station into playing the crap out of some song, you make it everywhere. They are forcing it down our throats, and unfortunately there are so many people in our country who are uneducated, that don't really think, so that these things at least wash partially. The sad thing is that it creates a cloud over the real truth and so it takes young people much longer to figure out what the real truth is because of so much subterfuge. That's a sad thing. People buy what they're sold, and if you jam it down their throat, they'll buy it. It's too bad, because, as I say, it really is in the grooves, and you don't have to do that, but if you don't know that, and people are using that other tactic...Anyway, let's move on. I'm a very opinionated person I want to warn you.

Dan Healy interviewed by Barry Barnes in *Unbroken Chain* vol. 6, #3, August 1991

MAR: And then when the teleprompter came in, did they just start doing sets via teleprompter?

SM: No. It was actually Steve Parish who ran the teleprompting. And he had to fly by the seat of his pants; basically, they'd start a song and he'd have to sync it. I remember when they did an encore of "Lucy in the Sky with Diamonds" [most probably March 17, 1995, at the Spectrum]. And when they left the stage before the encore, he had started taking the teleprompter down—because usually they do an encore that they all know. And they started doing "Lucy in the Sky with Diamonds," and if you listen to that version, you can hear that they play the beginning over and over and over. Because Parish has to reconnect the teleprompter.

MAR: Then Rifkin, McIntire, and Trist hired you, right? Or were in your initial interview?

SM: No, it was Rifkin, Rock Scully, and Alan Trist. After Danny left, he rarely came back. He left right when Jerry was really getting into heroin bad, in '85. I think he just really didn't want to be there.

MAR: I also wanted to revisit Calico.

SM: She really had a handle on a lot of Deadheads. When it came to Deadheads and their addresses, we used to go through and if there was multiple mail from one address, we would usually cancel everything but one. But she started giving me her heads-up of addresses that were actually full of real Deadheads—that we should accept all of the orders for those houses. There were some houses in Berkeley that had twenty people living in them. She had a really good handle on it all and she was just, like, an Earth Mother to a lot of people.

Calico was the first person that I hired, and we would just sit on the floor. We had a map of the seating chart of the Warfield, and we would go by and mark each seat, when we sold them or whatever. There would be a different color. I just remember us being on the floor filling ticket orders, and she was very, very concerned to make sure that Deadheads got tickets. And I didn't know this, I sort of knew it, but when it came to allotting the tickets to the various ticket sellers, she would always keep the absolute best seats to every show for herself. So she would make sure that real Deadheads were in the front rows.

John Ammons

September 4, 2020

JA: I was an audiophile before I was a Deadhead. I actually got a degree in audio production at San Francisco State. So I'm professionally involved in audio, I worked for a company that's on its last legs, but we grew out of Skywalker Ranch in the early nineties, and we facilitated the movement of real-time audio over digital phone lines for film and TV postproduction and advertising. So I was into audio before I got into the Dead, and I got into taping shortly after I got into the Dead, and I was one of those guys. I think everyone starts with a pair of shotgun mics and a tapers section [ticket].

MAR: And what year was this?

JA: This was 1987, when I began taping. I started seeing the Dead in '84. I saw them in Syracuse, October 20, 1984, because I was in a previous educational life. I was an engineering major at Cornell University and I met some guys on the dorm room floor, who were big Deadheads from one of these prestigious northeastern prep schools. That was like a serious place where the Dead got audiences—in the Boston area and all over New England and New York. These guys had [gone to] Choate Rosemary Hall, and they'd seen the Dead a bunch in high school. And they were like, "You're going to Syracuse with us." So I went to the show, we did mushrooms, and I had a little fun, but I wouldn't get into it. And one of the things I remember most about the show is they played "Revolution" in the encore, and Jerry didn't really know the words so well, because that was a song he didn't really play all the time. And Jerry wasn't above forgetting the words to songs he did play all the time. I was like, "Why is this guy playing this great Beatles song and fucking up all the lyrics? What the fuck?"

But I guess some seed was planted at that show, because during '85, without going to shows, I kind of asked these same guys for a couple tapes and dubbed a few cassette tapes from them. Mediocre at best audience recordings, I'm sure, and then it just kind of like blossomed and bloomed. And I came out to California in the summer of '86 and saw some shows here, right before Jerry went into his coma—had a bunch of tickets for shows that didn't happen, so that was brutal, and I'm like, "Wait, now it might be all over." But of course it wasn't all over, and Jerry got another lease on life. So I was kind of going on tours from Ithaca as a home base while still going to Cornell. But that didn't work out for me as far as education, and I ended up failing out at Cornell, because I was going on tours, and pretty much got into the taping concept then. I moved to California in '88, because I had been out here and I loved the weather and well, this is where the Dead were. You didn't have to kill yourself going up and down the East Coast: you could see twenty-five shows a year going no further than Sacramento or Mountain View.

So at that point, I had my pair of shotgun mics and portable cassette deck, and I was in the tapers section. And then I met someone out there, and he knew a guy who was taping with this PCM and beta digital recording, with the super-nice German microphones. And they were not in the tapers section, because the sound was much more high energy and better in front of the soundboard. So I realized there was this whole cult of people doing that. And then the concept of digital was like, "Well, wait a second. Now I don't have to be the guy making the master. If I'm helping the guy make the master, that's just as important as making the master," because all that matters is that the best-possible master gets made, because you can digitally clone it so everyone gets the master. So I bought a DAT player—a very early DAT player, Panasonic, hand-built, it was $2,500. And by virtue that I had this thing and these guys didn't want to kill the heads on their portable DAT players by cloning a bunch of tapes, I was able to kind of get in the club, and I'd go up front. I wouldn't be making the tape myself; I'd just be helping these other guys. That kind of led to me making the tapes myself, to some degree, but then I realized that these DAT tapes are ten bucks each, so if you want the show on DAT, that's twenty bucks just for your blank-tape cost for the show. And then you realize, "Wait, these guys have these crazy digital collections with shows from the seventies and all this, but they're all on these beta tapes"—and the beta tape was three hours. So one beta tape was a whole show and I could get those for, like, $4.50. So now, wait, whatever I spend on the equipment for the PCM and the two betas as a cloning system, I'm going to make that up with my first hundred shows, and then it's all going to be gravy from then forward.

MAR: Before, though—before the PCM, before the DAT, the tapers are generally just using either the D5, or in the early part of the seventies, were they just maybe using reel-to-reel that was snuck in and maybe just rudimentary Dictaphone crap recorders?

JA: Exactly. They might be using a portable consumer reel-to-reel recorder. Certainly some of them were, guys like Bob Menke, I think, did that. But they were also using cassette—because, of course, cassette was much easier to deal with at a Dead show than reels, and Sony put out a portable cassette player around 1970. I think it was called the TC-158, and then there was a few variants of Sony TC-158. They were bigger and more cumbersome and not as high quality as the D5, so that's what a lot of these early to mid-seventies tapers were using and at some point toward the late seventies the D5 came out and if you were a serious taper, you immediately got rid of that big old clunky TC-158 and bought a D5. That was just a great device.

The next new recording medium would be the PCM. PCM stands for pulse code modulation. That's basically a technical term for digital audio, as you know it from a compact disc—a compact disc also uses PCM to encode its audio. When you had PCM, you had a processor that was able to take an analog signal from your microphones and convert that to a PCM linear digital signal, and then output that digital signal on a video jack, and then you input that to the video input of your VHS or beta tape. So you were encoding the left and right stereo audio onto the video track of your video deck, which is kind of difficult to wrap your head around if you haven't thought about that. It's on the video track—it's not on the audio track, so it has nothing to do with whether it's mono or stereo. If you were to play that tape back on the TV set, there would just be weird snow coming down and some stripes of the video, like the channel didn't come in properly. But when you output that to the PCM processor, it knows that those are digital ones and zeros and reconstitutes it as audio. So you'd need a beta player and then you'd also need the processor to get the data out into audio.

I think a guy named Dave Kramer recorded Tempe, Arizona, March 25, '83. That was the first-known audience digital Dead recording. And that was the way that these guys made their recordings until 1989, when digital audio tape came out.

The next [recording format] was DAT. Because the DAT machine is about the same size as a Sony D5 [portable recorder], if you can picture that—you're walking into the show with a Sony D5, except you're making a digital tape. The beta stuff, those guys were just heroic, because if you can imagine, [they had] a portable video cassette player, a power supply, drive it with batteries, a portable PCM player, a power supply to drive *that* with batteries . . . All of a sudden, you've got a thirty-pound backpack stuffed with stuff, and that's before you deal with your microphones, and whatever else. That's what these guys were hauling around, before DAT came along.

MAR: So it kind of was almost alternating between huge amounts of labor to get these things into the concert going into miniature, then going back to huge amounts of equipment.

JA: Yeah, that's kind of an interesting way to think of it. This big huge portable cassette player, this cute little beautiful cassette player, this massive four-chassis digital system, this cute little digital box. And then that's where we ended up. Of course, if we were doing it today, people would have little hard-disk recorders or computers.

MAR: Were the FOB [front-of-board] kind of dudes that you met initially doing recordings with the PCM, or were they doing DAT?

JA: They had just transitioned to DAT. I was taking the PCMs they already had and cloning them.

MAR: I see. So you were kind of doing what I did with tapes—basically, you're like, "Oh yeah, this is like old technology in a way, but it's cheaper, but it's also just as good in a way."

JA: It's just as good. It's cheaper, it's bulkier, but it's old technology. I realized that I needed that to collect all of the historic shows that people had, and I also needed the DAT to get the shows that hadn't happened yet. So it was like a two-pronged thing. Then one of the guys I became close friends with, he had been involved in the original Betty Board transfers. Stuart [Nixon] came into my life through a friend of his. So all of a sudden, this guy has absolute blue-chip gold as far as trading material, because these front-of-board guys making the reference tapes that were better than anyone had ever heard—all of a sudden, he was their best friend, because they wanted all these Betty tapes, [and] he needed all their tapes that they were making of contemporary shows that he was seeing. So, I kind of got involved with both him and these other guys who were making the front-of-board tapes, and [it] was sort of the best of all digital worlds. And then some other friends of mine and I started getting our own microphones and making our own recordings. How it went with these serious tapers—and this is sort of the case from the beginning—a dude might've been hardcore for a year or two, or maybe five years, but you just didn't keep it up. You didn't just keep going on tour, year in and year out; you burned [out], or your life intervened and you sowed your wild oats on tour and then you settled down. But a lot of the people I met at that time did a year or two worth of touring where they were front-of-board, mostly, and recording everything.

Most of the people that were in that initial circle I met had some sort of trust fund or something going on for them, because the so-called "taping rig" that you wanted to walk into a show with was somewhere in the order of maybe $8,000. And this is late eighties money; it's a lot now, but in the late eighties, it was a tremendous amount of money. Not only did you need the money to do this, you also needed the time and resources to get to the shows and be able to not do anything else but be on the tour.

For example, I have a friend who I met in the late eighties, Jeff Silberman. And he got into surround sound and actually made recordings of the Dead with what's known as a sound field microphone—an AMS, Advance Music Group, ST250—which has a complex array of pickup patterns that can capture the 360-degree sound field. And you needed four tracks to do it; you couldn't do it on stereo. You needed four tracks, minimum. So he had this four-track open reel Nagra digital tape deck, which cost $35,000 in the early nineties. It's a concept called Ambisonics; it's this surround-sound format that's very little known. I heard some of his recordings played back in his special listening room with the Ambisonic playback system, and when you listened to those . . . It was like, of course, the band's only in front of you, so how important is stuff behind you? Well, let me tell you, really important, because the walls in the room just went away. You felt like you were in this huge space, not confined by speakers or a room. It's like beta versus VHS. Beta was a better video format than VHS, but it lost out due to marketing and consumer wars, not due to anything technical. Ambisonics was never really adopted [in a] mainstream way, but on a technical basis, there's nothing more lifelike in surround sound. Just amazing. But think about a

$35,000 tape deck, and then think about that in 1990 money. It's just outrageous. He actually rented his deck to Skywalker Sound for some recording projects back in the day. So if you're a Grateful Dead taper and Skywalker Sound is renting your gear, you know something strange is going on.

Part of the great thing about making the recordings here in the Bay Area was everything was general admission, so you kind of knew the people putting their blankets down around you. You certainly knew the people right around the microphones. So [on the recordings] you can totally hear you're in an audience: you're going to hear a dude whoop here and there, but the guy's not going to be whooping right next to one of your microphones. He's going to be whooping a few blankets over. So you kind of get the best of all those worlds. Whereas these poor guys up in front of the soundboard, on tour on the East Coast—well, it's impressive enough to get that perfect seat to record, but how can you control the seats directly in front of you and directly to the sides of you? You can't. That was the beauty of the West Coast, where there was a lot of like-minded folks coming together to make a few reference recordings.

MAR: You're saying that the East Coast, in the eighties at least, was not general admission, it was mainly tapers section?

JA: Not only tapers section, but reserved seating. So if you didn't have that proper reserved seat, you probably weren't going to make as good a recording. One of the ironies of the tapers section is that it made more tapers tape from further away, because they were allowed to be there—which is great, but it doesn't mean that you got a good recording, and certainly not if the tapers section wasn't right behind the soundboard. Whereas out here, we could just make sure someone was in early enough and put their blanket down, dead center, right where we wanted to be—which was typically about two-thirds of the way between the stage and the soundboard. Other tapers liked to be more in the way up there: "Let's just get all PA sound." It was a delicate balancing act and you never quite knew until you came home. And for example, if you see B&K microphones on a recording, then those are probably the best microphones anyone used on tour, but they are completely flat. They are scientific tools, and if there was anything wrong with the sound—if it was booming, crusty, whatever was going on, well, that's your tape. If the sound was pristine and glorious, well, that's your tape too. So when you see the Schoeps microphones—which you see a lot of in the later days, especially the digital guys—then they had a little boost in the frequency response around the vocal presence. They were a little more forgiving.

MAR: What's your opinion about Nakamichi mics being this weird thing that people gripped on to, even though I feel like they're not that great, actually?

JA: It's a monkey see, monkey do phenomenon. "Oh look, there's how the people are taping." How it came to be, who knows? The Nakamichi 700 was a pretty good microphone, so I think that's where it came from. People were using these Nak 700s with the cardioid capsule—those were pretty good, and I think you'll find good recordings even in the late seventies and the early eighties with those. They were more high quality, more like the German [mics]: the Schoeps, the Neumanns, the B&Ks. But they stopped making those and they replaced them with lesser quality microphones, either the Nak 300 or the Nak 100. But the biggest deal was the whole shotgun [mic] phenomenon. Everyone seemed to want to use shotguns and that was not what they were intended for. A Nak shotgun would be a great mic to capture dialogue in a movie or television set—which is what they were made for. It has some weird phase-cancellation patterns, so it cancels the sound coming from the sides and just gives you the sound coming from straight ahead. It just kind of beams what's coming straight at it. So those recordings sound crystal clear, but they don't sound like an event that occurred, because they don't really have the ambience of the hall, and they're not made to capture low bass, they're made to capture speech. Maybe Jerry's vocals might sound pretty good, if you got lucky, but the entire gestalt wouldn't be there.

And then, the other monkey see, monkey do that you'll see in the eighties, before Jim and Doug Oade introduced the Schoeps to the community, [were] the Sennheiser microphones. You'll see 441s and 421s a lot in the mid/early eighties. A Sennheiser 441 is a great microphone in a recording studio, but it's made to close-mic a drum. It's not made to be thirty yards away from a PA system. You're never going to get a great recording; the drums might sound pretty good, but you won't get good bass, you won't get proper highs; it just won't all come into focus. Microphones like the Schoeps and the B&Ks and the Neumanns, well, those are something someone would hang in a symphony hall to record a symphony from far away; they were made to do that.

Author Michael Nash (center) enjoying himself with friends at a concert last summer. A typical pair of microphones (opposite page) wears flowers and a Dead sticker.

GRATEFUL TAPERS

An Informal History Of Recording The Dead

MICHAEL NASH

Photography by Philip Gould

"Hey, you down there with the mike," Grateful Dead guitarist Bob Weir calls from the stage. A reprimand in the making? "If you want to get a decent recording, you gotta move back about 40 feet."

"It sounds a lot better back there," chimes in bassist Phil Lesh.

It is August 1971, about the time that live taping of The Grateful Dead began to take root. The Dead are playing the second of two nights at the Hollywood Palladium. And yes, these are words of encouragement—musicians advising their audience where best to record their concert. How do we know it happened? Why, it's all on tape, of course.

In the 16 years since that Hollywood date, tapers have evolved into an officially recognized and sanctioned group among the fans of The Grateful Dead; they've even got their own designated area from which to make recordings. Their concert habitat—the tapers' section—is a hi-tech sea of sundry microphones; of foam, Plexiglas, and other sound-baffling materials, and of analog and digital recording equipment. All for the purpose of capturing The Dead, and all for free. "Once we're done with it, they can have it" is Jerry Garcia's oft-quoted remark on the subject.

Grateful Dead sound mixer and audio wizard Dan Healy, with the band since their Fillmore Auditorium days in 1965, puts it this way: "Philosophically, we come from a place where the music belongs to everybody. Only the machinations of financial motivation work against that. And it's just not enough. It wasn't what got me here, it hasn't been what's sustained me, and it won't be what will dissuade me."

As for the industry claim that allowing recording results in fewer record sales, The Dead would simply chuckle. "There's never been one shred of proof—none whatsoever—that live recording hurts anything," says Healy. "If anything, it makes it better," he adds, noting that concert tapes have brought the band's music to a wider audience.

The Dead have notched nearly 2,000 concerts on their collective fretboards, probably more than any other touring band in history. And their appeal just continues to increase, especially in the wake of 1987's platinum-selling *In the Dark*, the group's biggest commercial success ever.

Audio vol. 72, #1, January 1988

THE DEAD...THE DEAD

There may be nothing like a Grateful Dead concert, but a dedicated taper would say that a good recording comes close. And from one good tape, literally thousands may be bred, disseminated through a social network that has spread The Dead's music near and far. Whether one's interest lies in studying the music and its evolution, archiving it for posterity, or reliving those moments when "the music played the band," the tapes are there to fill the role.

Just as the music of The Dead has continually moved forward, so too has the state of tapers' tech. But even before the multitude of high-end microphones appeared, before the days of dbx noise reduction and PCM digital processors, before there even was such a thing as the tapers' section, a lot of field work was being done.

One of the first to record The Dead on tape was Steve Brown, who first saw the group (then known as The Warlocks) in their old Palo Alto stomping grounds back in 1965, an experience he describes as "love at first sound." Working in both local radio and record promotion at the time, Brown continued to see the band over the next couple of years.

Later, Brown found himself in the Navy, where his job was to make tapes for the on-board entertainment systems of Navy ships stationed in the Pacific. On his free weekends, he would regularly head north from San Diego to catch the shows at San Francisco's Fillmore Auditorium and Avalon Ballroom, including performances by The Grateful Dead. One weekend in early 1968, Brown trotted his Navy reel-to-reel—a Uher 440—up the coast and sneaked it into Winterland, where Cream was playing. He discreetly recorded the show dead center from the first row of the balcony, over which his Uher condenser mike hung in all its monophonic glory.

The next morning, Brown heard that The Grateful Dead was going to play a free concert on Haight Street that day. His deck conveniently at hand, though pretty well depleted of battery power from the Cream show, Brown hit the street; sure enough, the band appeared and began playing. Holding the microphone with alternating hands, Brown was able to record the first four tunes—"Viola Lee Blues," "Smokestack Lightning," "(Turn on Your) Lovelight," and "It Hurts Me Too"—before the battery gave its last gasp.

Within a week, a large number of unassuming sailors throughout the Pacific were listening to a wild and psychedelic version of "Viola Lee Blues" blaring from channel 4 of the Navy's entertainment system. "It's why we lost the war," Brown laughingly surmises.

It turns out that Brown was probably the *only* person to make a tape of the Haight Street show (recorded, for the record, at 3¾ ips on a 5-inch reel, and sounding remarkably good after two decades). So, for anyone who has a dub of those four songs, this is probably where they came from.

A homemade yet effective attempt at improved directionality.

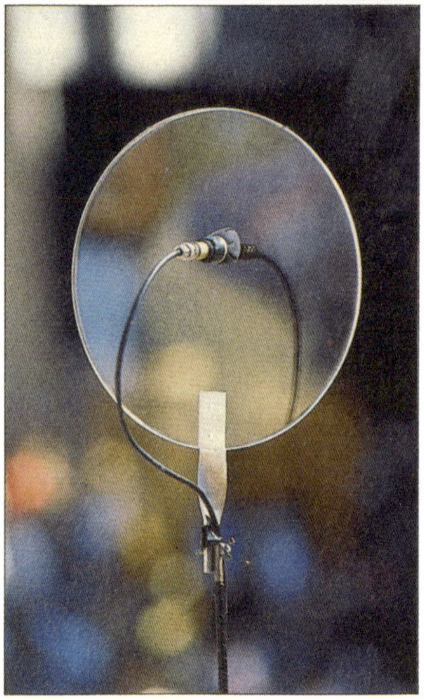

That concert, on March 3, 1968, was the first and last Grateful Dead show that Brown taped, although he did go on to help form Round Records, The Grateful Dead's own recording label, back in the early '70s. During his tenure there, he says, never did the idea of people having live tapes become a negative concern.

A year after Brown made his Dead recording, Bob Menke went to a Blind Faith concert with his older brother. His brother brought along a Craig 5-inch reel-to-reel deck to record the show. They did the same thing at a Crosby, Stills, Nash and Young concert the following summer.

"I kind of liked the idea," Menke remembers. Within a year, he bought a Sony TC-40 portable cassette deck and taped his first show. A few months later, in July of 1971, a radio broadcast of The Grateful Dead closing Bill Graham's fabled Fillmore West brought him his first exposure to the band. He taped the show off the radio and decided the next logical step was to go to a Dead concert, Sony in hand.

In August, Menke taped the first of nearly 200 Grateful Dead concerts he would record over the next 16 years. The result was certainly listenable, though hardly state-of-the-art. But just making a tape in those days was no small feat: The practice was essentially prohibited, as it worried Warner Bros., with whom The Dead had a recording contract. Still, if one was able to sneak his gear in and keep a low profile, there was a good chance of success.

Having graduated to a stereo portable Sony 124 by August 1972, Menke tried out his new unit up front at the Berkeley Community Theater, only to get busted during the first song. Disheartening, but not enough to end his new hobby.

At the time, Menke says, the handful of tapers on the East and West Coasts were using essentially the same equipment, generally Sony portables. As taping bans became more closely enforced over the next couple of years, tapers turned to ingenious means of sneaking in their recording gear. Tales abound of tape decks strapped to womens' legs or hidden beneath sleeping babies in their carriages, microphones stuffed through bathroom fan vents from the street (to be retrieved inside), and a host of other diversionary tricks to fool security guards. Menke himself would wrap his deck in towels, stuff it into a Boy Scout backpack, and cover it with packaged food. "You always had to keep one step ahead," he recalls.

In 1974, Menke began using a Sony 152 recorder; suddenly, he says, "taping became more serious." The 152, equipped with a one-point stereo mike, adjustable input levels, Dolby noise reduction, and equalization that could be switched to match the tape type in use, was a major boon to tapers. Though it was hardly a small deck and definitely more difficult to conceal, soon everyone was buying it, simply because it meant better sound.

And by 1974, better sound was certainly what the Dead audience was hearing, as Dan Healy and sound designer/engineer Ron Wickersham had completed their massive Wall of Sound, an awesome sound-reproduction system involving 641 speakers. Very likely the most ambitious project of its kind (and ultimately too large to continue using), the Wall of Sound represented an exponential leap forward in the quality of concert sound, much to the delight of Deadheads and tapers alike. Practicality and expense aside, the system sounded magnificent.

From late 1974 to early 1976, while The Dead took a break from live touring and pursued various recording and solo projects, Menke and his pals honed their skills by taping the club shows of Jerry Garcia's band and of Kingfish, a group featuring Bob Weir. Victories, such as laying their mikes next to Garcia's stage monitors, were balanced by upsets, such as having their mike cables snipped by a diligent roadie. Menke remembers one particularly good experience during a surprise free show in Golden Gate Park in September 1975. Someone had turned a vocal monitor out from one corner of the stage. Using a mismatched pair of Sony condenser mikes, Menke pointed one at the monitor and the other at the instruments. The result, he says,

Getting the axis of each mike pointed at just the right angle is important in live concert recording because sources are usually fairly far away.

A small forest of expensive high-tech microphones sprouts from the tapers' section at virtually all Dead concerts.

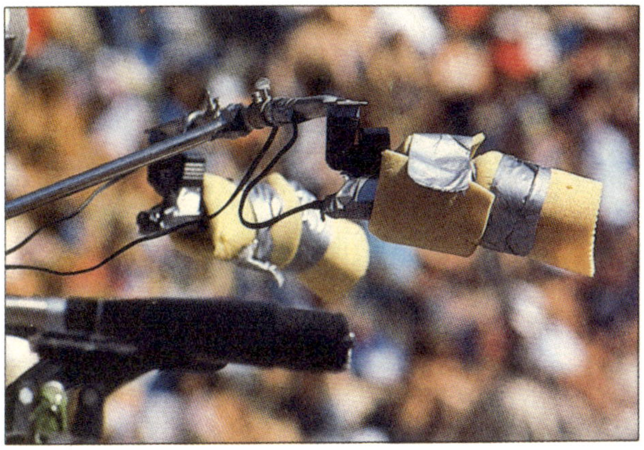

Foam and gaffer tape are regularly used to extend the reach of even directional mikes.

Three Sony TC-D5M portable cassette recorders atop a Nakamichi 450, which has its pot taped to avoid changes in level. Despite the rigors of outdoor use, fairly large sums have been invested in this equipment.

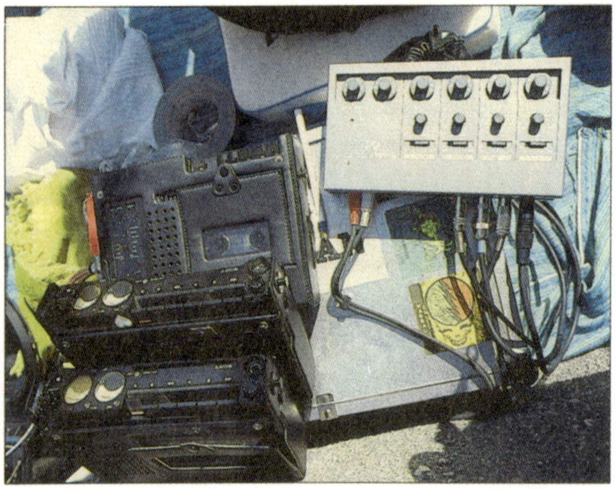

Heavy-duty cabling connects three Sony TC-D5Ms and their mixer, a Yamaha MM-10. Crowd noise takes on a new meaning when you're taping a Dead concert.

"sounds like a board tape, no ambience whatsoever."

When The Dead returned in 1976, the taping population slowly increased. The procession of Sonys moved on from the 152 to the 153 and then the 158, which Menke bought in 1977. He had also acquired improved mikes, Sony ECM-270s and 280s. In addition, he was using high-bias chromium cassettes, which had first appeared in 1971. By degrees, the recorded sound was improving.

In March 1977, while taping a show at Winterland, Menke and his friends happily discovered an a.c. power outlet conveniently located on the first-row balcony floor. Wasting no time, at The Dead's next Winterland appearance in June, they carted in two 10-inch reel-to-reel decks—a Tandberg 10X and a Revox A77—and plugged in. Adding a new pair of AKG D-224E dynamic microphones, which they fastened to a stick and hung over the balcony, resulted in yet another small step forward in good sound. They continued using the reel-to-reels on and off for the next year, with the best results, according to Menke, coming from a friend's December 1978 combination of a Nagra deck and Neumann mikes with external power supplies.

In 1979, Sony introduced the TC-D5, the first cassette unit truly designed for serious field-recording enthusiasts. Far more portable than its predecessor, the 158, the new deck proved to be a boon to the entire Grateful Dead taping scene, and the number of tapers grew even larger. Initially listing at $700, the TC-D5 was no small investment, but it soon became the norm. Menke bought one immediately, replacing it about a year later (as did many others) with a TC-D5M, a newer version with metal-particle tape capability.

Also in 1979, Menke began using a pair of Nakamichi 700 microphones. Condenser mikes outfitted with both cardioid and omni capsules, the 700s, according to Menke, had improved presence in the high end and a better sound from farther back than the AKGs he'd been using. The Nakamichis have remained his choice ever since. Menke also built a passive preamp to add a 6-dB bass boost to the mix, later dropping the unit when The Dead's sound system began to deliver more bass.

THE DEAD...THE DEAD

As the number of tapers continued to grow, so did the difficulty of getting equipment into The Dead's concerts. Of greater import was the growing number of problems regarding certain tapers infringing on the rights of nontaping concertgoers. Early tapers were always careful to maintain a low profile, to get their spots legitimately, and to respect those who didn't care about taping. Unfortunately, as more tapers joined the ranks, not everyone was so courteous. Menke says that the appearance of tripods on the East Coast started to spell trouble. Things were slowly beginning to get out of hand. Meanwhile, he settled in with his Sony/Nakamichi combination.

Jaime Poris, a taping acquaintance of Menke's, was using a similar system but felt there was room for improvement. Poris, an electrical engineer at National Semiconductor, first saw The Dead on the East Coast in 1971 and taped a few shows in '73 on what he calls "lousy portables." In 1979, he moved to California and began taping seriously. Ever since then, he has been experimenting with a broad range of means and methods.

Early on, Poris realized that the best way to decide what equipment to use and how to use it was to just go out and experiment. He began playing with phase and amplitude differences, alternating pickup patterns, and angling his microphones, all in various combinations.

One experiment that caught on for a while was blending three mikes into two channels with a homemade passive mixer while varying the capsules, e.g., two cardioids and one omni. The results, Poris says, compromised the signal-to-noise ratio but still sounded better than the results from two mikes.

In 1981, Poris decided that he and his new taping partner, Jim Olness, were getting too much indirect sound, particularly at indoor shows, where reflection presented a problem. A more directional mike, such as a cardioid, seemed to be a solution, but Poris preferred the sound of an omni. The problem with cardioids, he felt, was that they weren't the same at every frequency; their response pattern changed as they were angled away from the sound source, leading to some coloration. The partners opted to alternate omnis and cardioids and compare results.

Hoping to increase the ratio of direct to reflected sound, they started shaping foam in various forms around the mikes. Anything more than 90° off the mike's axis became attenuated significantly; thus, the crowd noise was muffled and the music was made more prominent. While not sounding completely natural, the results were better than they had been. "Good," Poris says, "but not the solution."

By the following year, Poris and Olness had made further changes in their system. Attempting to improve their Nakamichi 700 mikes, Poris replaced capacitors with better ones, got rid of the transformers altogether, and made separate power supplies, which he hooked up to the capsules via BNC connectors. In the process, the mikes were reduced in size from 9 inches to about 4 inches. The resulting "mini-Naks," Poris and Olness attest, are quieter and definitely better sounding than their precursors.

In addition, Poris also built a new mike preamp, using some high-quality op-amp chips, to replace what he felt was a relatively low-quality preamp in the Sony TC-D5M.

Another step was to improve the tape's signal-to-noise ratio by turning to dbx noise reduction. Poris and Olness purchased a dbx 224, a home unit; then they replaced several capacitors and op-amps and inserted a portable power supply of eight 9-V batteries in the transformer's place. Adding a patch bay, they were able to split the signal into a dbx side and a Dolby side. Adding more patch bays down the line allowed up to 15 additional tapers to plug in.

The microphone modifications, new preamp, and addition of dbx resulted in tapes that sounded appreciably better than previous efforts. Though carting around a dbx unit designed for home use was certainly no fun, it was worth the hassle to get an improved sound. At the same time, Olness and Poris continued to experiment with shaping ordinary foam, and later Sonex, trying to reproduce the music as best they could.

While the serious tapers were developing their craft, the rude behavior of some of the newer tapers became increasingly felt. More poles began to appear, interfering with people's sight lines and their ability to enjoy the show. Some tapers showed up late and moved in on spaces that others had stood in line for hours to get. People were asked not to talk or sing along, so as not to "ruin" the tapes. Although those causing problems were a minority, they were numerous enough to make a difference. More and more complaints were voiced.

By 1984, Healy and the generally tolerant Grateful Dead organization had had enough. The choice they faced was to enforce a total prohibition on taping or find a way to prevent ongoing trouble. The Dead opted for a creative solution and established the tapers' section—a designated area at each show where those so inclined could record the music without having to be surreptitious about it. Suddenly, tapers had rights.

In October 1984, The Dead, via their telephone ticket hotline, began instructing those who wanted to tape to specify that on their mail-order ticket requests. In return, they were sent tickets marked appropriately. This process has been used ever since for facilities with reserved seating; at general-admission shows, a designated section is filled on a first-come basis. Almost invariably, there's been enough space in that section for everyone who wants to tape.

Some old-school tapers were upset at losing their sweet spots in front of the sound board, but overall the tapers' section made things much easier for everyone. Suddenly free from

the need to act covertly, tapers were able to pursue their audio experiments with a new-found sense of legitimacy.

Jaime Poris had been reading articles about Pressure Zone Microphones (PZMs) and decided to give the technique a shot. Though it appeared, Poris says, more apropos to string quartets, he and Jim Olness figured they had nothing to lose.

Their idea involved using a Plexiglas plate to create a hemispherical pickup pattern for the microphones. The mikes were mounted on the plate, facing the flat surface, and sound was reflected back into them. The main advantage was that almost nothing behind the plate got into the mix. The disadvantage was that the bass rolled off depending on the size of the plate.

Starting with a plate of reasonable size, the partners changed the size of the capacitors in the mike power supplies for both the cardioids and the omnis to acquire more control over the bass. Ultimately, they preferred the bass response of the omni capsules and opted for those. The Plexiglas plate, meanwhile, was built with a hinge and operated like a book. In this way, Poris and Olness could adjust the relative angles of the mikes. The resulting tapes, Poris says, "had no coloration, relatively flat frequency response, good bass, and good directionality."

Experimenting further, the two split the mikes 20 feet apart, using two separate Plexiglas plates. The effect, they decided, was significant; the split mikes seemed better suited to the panned signal and resulted in appreciably better imaging. Later, they built larger plates and began alternating the Nakamichi 700s with some capsules made by Knowles—tiny electret condenser mikes often used in telemetry, hearing aids, and surveillance. For their price (all of $25), the Knowles sounded quite good but had some slight coloration in the upper midrange.

At around the same time, Poris also built a peak meter and linked it to the system, allowing Olness to easily read the peaks on his Sony recorder in 3-dB steps instead of settling for the average offered by the deck's VU meters. Poris is currently working on a new microphone preamplifier, with built-in mike power supplies, which will allow him to tailor the bass response in four steps.

While always striving for better results, the two make sure they enjoy themselves in the process. "It's still a lot of fun," a friend observes, "but they take their fun seriously."

If tapers like Poris and Olness are serious about their pursuits, certainly the same must be said of those who have converted to the digital faith, incurring serious costs as they use PCM processors to put digital signals onto portable videotape decks. "The standard joke," says one digital taper, Ross Lipton, "is that when you go digital, you sell your TC-D5 to buy the batteries." Indeed, the four 12-V rechargeable cells that Lipton and his taping partner Chris Hecht use in their phantom power supply go for about $100 a pop.

A thin blanket provides precious little padding beneath recording gear that has been tweaked in every possible fashion.

Three Sony PCM-F1 digital processors and several video recorders, including two Sony SL-2000s.

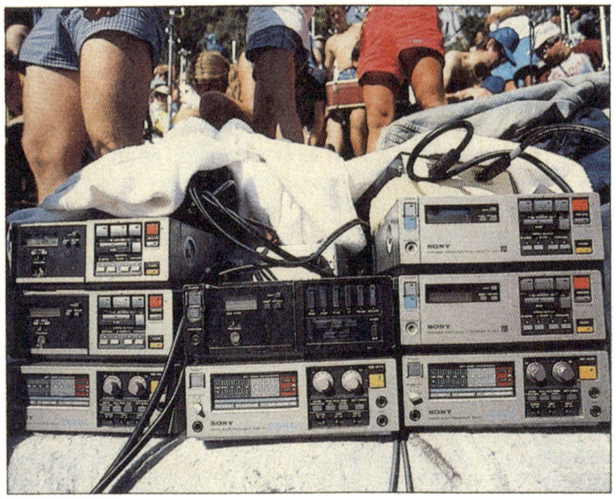

Digital's first appearance on the Grateful Dead taping scene came in the spring of 1983. Dave Cramer had been taping since 1979, using the standard cassette format and collaborating with Jaime Poris on three-mike blends. Convinced that no other band offered the same incredibly high fidelity in concert as did The Dead, he figured it was worth giving digital a whirl. He rented a Sony PCM-F1 digital processor and a portable Betamax video recorder, powered them with heavyweight ni-cad batteries, and put them to work at a show in Tempe, Ariz.

The difference was huge, Cramer recalls, with a complete absence of tape noise which was most noticeable in the pauses between musical numbers. With great dynamic range, no wow or flutter, and no harmonic distortion from 20 Hz to 20 kHz, it became unquestionably clear to Cramer that digital was *it*.

He soon bought his own equipment even though PCM processors were rather hard to come by at the time. Eventually he sold his Sony processor and bought a Nakamichi DMP 1000, which offered what he felt was a warmer sound. He also exchanged his Beta machine for a top-of-the-line VHS, as that tape format was more readily available out on the road.

With a background in studio engineering, Cramer had tried out virtually every microphone in the book. Ultimately he decided on three Sennheiser 421s—cardioid dynamic mikes—two of which he places in an X-Y configuration with the third slightly behind them and out of phase. Aside from a slight rise in response at 30 Hz, he says the result sounds great.

With a $12,000 investment and 120 pounds of equipment, Cramer's efforts have not been minimal, but he feels they have been worth the results. His sentiments are shared by Hecht and Lipton, who estimate that, between the two of them, they could be driving a BMW for all they've poured into their system. The two began taping together on and off in 1982 after often seeing one another in airport baggage areas in transit to and from Dead shows. In 1985, Lipton bought a digital system. Today they use a PCM-F1, a Sony SL-2000 portable Betamax video recorder, and a variety of high-end micro-

phones which are traded among the members of a taping co-op to which they belong.

Hecht and Lipton feel the tapes they make offer a vastly improved dynamic range, better signal-to-noise ratio, and far more presence in the bass. They also like the fact that video decks have a much faster writing speed than audio decks. Their tape of choice is the Sony Pro-X 500, thicker than the standard Beta tape, and they record at the fastest speed available. Further, unlike audio cassettes, the process of digital transfer ensures that successive copies suffer no generational loss of sound quality or increase in noise.

Last summer at Berkeley's Greek Theater, an outdoor amphitheater considered by many to be the best place to hear The Dead, Hecht and Lipton's group conducted a microphone comparison test. Controlling all variables, they set up three separate pairs of top-quality mikes: Neumann TLM170s, Schoeps CMC 341s, and newly re-engineered AKG 414s. On each of three successive days, they matched the pickup patterns in the respective mikes, using the switchable pattern capability of the Neumanns and AKGs and manually replacing the capsules of the Schoeps. Each pair was placed within a 7-foot range and run into similar units to allow A/B/C comparison.

After listening to the tapes on a reference system, all members of the taping co-op concurred that the Schoeps mikes with the omni capsules sounded best. Hecht felt that the Neumanns still had lots of potential, noting that they had been underpowered. (It turns out that they're not truly compatible with the power supply which had been used for the test.) As a result, Chris built a separate power supply for the

170s. As well, he's working on a new, all-purpose preamp with an active circuit using the SSM chip recommended by Jaime Poris. Eventually he plans to build a series of dedicated preamps, each specifically optimized for a particular set of microphones. He is also planning to field-test a pair of B & K microphones to see how they perform in Grateful Dead concert conditions.

Poris, meanwhile, talks about getting into Ambisonics. Theoretically, Poris says, the idea should result in better imaging. "We've gone as far as we can go with two mikes," he says, but adds that in any thought of a new endeavor, he always considers "the pain-in-the-ass factor. If it's too complicated, forget it."

One next step that everyone in these circles seems to look forward to is the arrival of DAT recorders, if and when they become available and affordable, let alone portable.

"I think a digital cassette is where it's at," Dan Healy says unequivocally. Tapers seem to agree, and eventually DAT may make as deep an impression on the Grateful Dead taping scene as did Sony TC-D5 recorders almost a decade ago. Whatever they use, however, all tapers are quick to attribute their high-quality tapes to one primary source.

"All this would be meaningless without the incredibly high-quality sound we have to work with, the raw sound," Hecht says. "An audio purist, an engineer, would start laughing if you told him that we actually record the sound at a rock 'n' roll concert. It's like, 'Why would you bother?' And most of the time, they'd be right. But at a Dead concert, it's different. This is the best sound system in music today."

The soundman for The Grateful Dead, Dan Healy, plays on his instrument, the mixing board, during a concert.

Veteran Dead taper Bob Menke, in his Bay Area home, has been recording concerts since 1971.

And then you have omnidirectional microphones—the so-called "spaced omni," where you have each one eight feet apart—that's a whole 'nother conversation we probably don't have time for. It's just a different scientific pattern that you use to pick up the sound, and it's omnidirectional, so you're picking up sound from everywhere rather than sound coming from one pinpoint location in space. So when you spaced those two microphones, you had this big huge enveloping soundstage and great low bass, because the omni microphones actually had a frequency response that was better than the cardioid microphones. I think they went down to 15 hertz, that area where you can't even hear it, you can just feel it. If you listen to some of those mid to late eighties, early nineties recordings with the omnis, then you can hurt yourself if your woofers aren't up to the task. There's always a trade-off—you wouldn't get quite as good a center image with the omni, but that would be compensated for by this big huge space and amazingly powerful low frequencies. In a professional recording situation—like say you're recording an orchestra from the far field—an engineer might use a pair of omnis and, in addition, a pair of cardioids on a T-bar with a pickup pattern that he or she saw fit, and then mix them together so you'd get the best of both worlds.

MAR: Did omnis come after cardioid, or were all these technologies kind of available right at the same time?

JA: They were available. I think it just came to where tapers just got more advanced in their use of the technology. Once you'd recorded at a venue a bunch of times, you could start sensing where, what kind of pickup pattern to use and where to be. [You'd be] walking around in the venue, and maybe the dead-center image wasn't dead center between the speakers; maybe you went over eight feet to one direction and then all of a sudden that stereo image came into focus for you. And that's all well and good, but who can walk around a venue and decide where to put their taping equipment? You're lucky to have any quality space in a venue to have your taping equipment. You kind of pick that space in advance.

MAR: You also just never know what the sound's actually going to be like until the concert starts. It's not like you're in the studio. Do you think there were ever any tapers that you know of or heard of who used, like in the symphony situation, a little bit of omnidirectional and a cardioid just to bring a whole picture both of atmosphere and direct sound?

JA: No. I think the Oades tried that a little bit, but not really. Especially [because] when you're up front, you've got to hide your equipment. You've got to carry your equipment in there. To have all that extra stuff and then to mix it together you would almost have to have a multitrack deck, and there really wasn't postproduction happening per se. You either got it right or you didn't. There's [also] the Nak 550. Have you ever encountered that? That's a tape deck. It's much bigger than a D5 or a D6, and they discontinued it in the early eighties. But people had them, and it was a big thing, hard to get in, and it had a third mic jack that it called "blend mic." If you look at lineage on a lot of early to mid-eighties recordings, you see three microphones were used into a Nak 550. You had your left and right stereo mics, and then they just put a third mic in that blend mic, and there's a dial you turn up as to how loud you want that blend mic. But that made absolutely no sense in the arena of making a far-field recording. That blend mic was [for if] I'm recording a trio of musicians and one instrument is a little quieter than the others—so I've got my stereo mics way away from them, and then the blend mic is what I put on the flute, because the flute wouldn't be loud enough otherwise. Something like that. Completely irrelevant to recording a Dead show forty yards away from the PA. But [people thought], "Oh, there's another mic jack. I can put another mic in this thing. Let's do it."

In fact, a recording you might want to seek out is April 21, 1984, at Philadelphia Civic Center. A guy named Rob Eaton—you may know his name—worked in a New York City recording studio in the early eighties, and he showed up at that Philly show with a pair of huge diaphragm Neumann omnis, which were very expensive mics. You really don't see a lot of Neumanns, certainly not Neumann omnis, used to record the Dead. He basically borrowed them from the studio so he didn't have to go buy them, and he hooked up with Jeff Silberman who had just bought one of those digital rigs—the old PCM beta, pre-digital-audio tape, digital rig. It's the things the Oades were using. So Silberman had this digital rig. Eaton shows up with these Neumann omnis and they're like, "Hey, let's combine this stuff and do something." And they spaced those Neumann omnis, like, way further than eight feet: front of the board, really wide spacing. And that recording is just amazing. Silberman went out and bought a pair of Neumann omnis, so if you see Neumann omnis as lineage later on in the eighties, that's because Silberman was so blown away by how good that tape sounded.

By the nineties, you're seeing a small group of dedicated tapers who kind of were heirs to the Oades' mentality with these European microphones: the Schoeps were German and the B&Ks, Brüel & Kjær, are [Danish]. You'll see a lot of B&K 4011s, and those were incredible-sounding microphones.

MAR: Did you know all this information in the eighties, or did you come to learn it later?

JA: No, I was learning it, and a lot of it came clear later on, where you see the body of recordings and you hear more recordings. Back then we were just kind of feeling like we were making the reference recording—like we're leaving this show with the best recording to come out of the show.

MAR: Are there any ridiculous stories you have from taping?

DOUG AND JIM OADE INTERVIEWED BY DAVID GANS
10/24/2007

David Gans: You started out with cassettes, and the D5M was like the sine qua non of cassette decks. When did you switch to digital?

Jim Oade: We switched to digital in late '84. I tried to convince Doug to do it earlier, but digital had its problems, and being a perfectionist, he didn't want to start using the PCM rig. But we did go to PCM. I think he'd heard some 14-bit recordings and we ended up buying the Sony--which was 16-bit--sometime in '84. One of the beauties of it was, it was a continuous two hours of music, so no more having to be worried about when to flip your tape.

Doug Oade: But the most important part about digital recording was not that it was so good as a mastering medium: what was so powerful about it was that everybody could have a recording of the same level of quality. No longer would separation from the source limit the quality of the experience for the person receiving the recording; they could have a recording as good as the master. And that drove me to a new level of passion in rebuilding the PCM-F1, so it would at least be as good as the cassette deck. And in time, I managed to surpass that. But for the first year, we ran both. I do remember one amusing incident at Hershey Park, 1985, a phenomenal show. I was using the PCM recorder and all of a sudden somebody was hitting me [saying] that they weren't getting a signal anymore. So I looked at the PCM--in the middle of "Morning Dew," it shut down. It was flashing "DEW, DEW, DEW." And I later found out that it was the dew sensor coming on. It was too wet at the venue for the machine to operate.

Jim Oade: Then, in '89, the DAT recorders came out. We started using DAT. That was a wonderful experience going from carrying this big humongous rig into one small DAT recorder. As Doug mentioned, it was great because it got the ego out of the live recording. Everybody was getting the same recording; no longer was the guy who mastered it getting the best recording. And we were very open to allow people to patch in, to get a digital patch. In fact, when DAT came out, if it hadn't have been for Doug, it'd have been a mess in the taper section. He invented a cable that would allow you to take the Sony portable DAT and daisy-chain up to fourteen of them together. Sony never produced a cable that would allow you to do that in the field.

Doug Oade: They were paranoid about digital transmission of data, thinking that what they were releasing commercially was actually worth having, and that if they offered that level of functionality, they would lose control of their product. Well, in my world, their product had zero value. What I was interested in doing was distributing that wonderful experience, unadulterated, to as many people as possible. So I engineered a solution to allow for daisy-chaining of digital data without any restrictions.

Jim Oade: Plus it really reduced the mass in the taper section, and that reduced the number of microphones that had to go up. People could patch into a $10,000 rig, and get the exact same recording, as opposed to putting their microphone stand up.

Doug Oade: And more importantly, in the way that the experience of the Grateful Dead peaked when there was an epiphany, a moment during which both the musicians and the audience transcend time and space and meet in this connective area where we share a common consciousness, a common joy, a common experience of the beauty--that connectivity was key to the Grateful Dead experience. It's the same thing that was mirrored in that digital distribution of data. It allowed people to connect to that epiphany in a way that was unadulterated. So they were synergistic. They were harmonious.

JA: After Dan Healy left the band and John Cutler was the mixing engineer, the shows didn't sound as good anymore—the PA system didn't sound as good and the band wasn't as good. This is getting into '93, '94, '95, and Garcia was on his last legs. You still went, because you knew the magic still could be had. It just wasn't had on a song-by-song basis anymore. I actually have recordings from the same spot at the Oakland Coliseum: one is like January '93 and one is January '94, same equipment, same everything, and you listen to those two recordings and you're like, "What happened?" The one in '93 sounds great; the one in '94 sounds awful. That's just because the PA wasn't as good anymore. I think the story was they weren't going for a sweet spot. They didn't even try to get a sweet spot. They said, "OK, let's get everybody sounding OK everywhere, at the expense of it really sounding good anywhere."

MAR: You're saying that Dan Healy tried to make a sweet spot intentionally? And was that usually the sweet spot for the tapers themselves or just for him to mix?

JA: For him to mix, exactly, yes. And he figured anyone who cared about the sweet spot would work on getting in the middle. People who didn't really care would be up in the rafters, tripping or dancing or doing whatever they do, and they'd be happy with it. Some people are happy listening to a boom box. Other people need tweaky audio equipment.

As all that was happening, they were cracking down harder and harder on the front-of-board tapers. At this point, we weren't putting the mics on a mic stand anymore, or a T-bar—which would have the microphones professionally arrayed, as you would if you were actually recording, say, a symphony. You were putting the mics in a hat: just the tip of the capsule, and then the active cable would come from just the tip of the capsule—something smaller than your thumb—down into your recording device in your backpack, fanny pack, or whatever. Eventually, it got to the point where they would send security up there, and if you were wearing a hat and not moving they would hassle you, assuming maybe you had mics in your hat.

Why, all of a sudden, were they just swarming with security up there? Let's say I have a DAT player in a fanny pack at my stomach and I have mics in my hat: Who cares? Who am I bothering? I'm not taking up any more space. I'm not stopping anyone from having a view of the band. Nothing. Anyway, the point of the story is, this guy had this kind of mane of hair and he just didn't wear a hat. He put the capsules in his hair and he ran the cables down his back, down his pants, and then he took an old pair of high-tops and drilled a hole in the sole of them, so the cable was coming out of the middle of his foot. And then, if you can imagine your foot—you just put your foot where two blankets come together so then the cable can go under those blankets and across to the back of the blanket where there's a little pile of people's belongings and coats and stuff, and that's where you're running the recording. So the security would just see a dude with long hair standing there, look down at his feet, and not hassle him. Just the fact that anyone would go to that extreme, much less have to go to that extreme. This is a band where, decades ago, people would put mic stands up as high as they wanted anywhere they wanted to. You almost were wondering: maybe they know that the music isn't very good anymore and it sounds like shit up here, so they don't want anyone to capture it. That's where my mind was going, weird places like that.

MAR: Also, in my experience looking through the archive and particular files, it seemed like towards the end of the nineties, CD replication and distribution seemed to be more prevalent, and people were raided.

JA: Ah, maybe it was bootleg CDs they were freaking out about.

MAR: Did you know this man, the guy who was recording without a hat, or did you just observe that?

JA: Yeah, he was a taper buddy for a little while there. He was an engineer at Apple Computer, actually, so he had some money to buy equipment and whatnot.

MAR: And waste some shoes.

JA: Yeah. No, he was a good guy. Some of these guys are good guys. Some of them were shady characters, I guess, as with any other walk of life, right? You do have to be somehow driven to be that hardcore. That's not to say the tapers section people couldn't be just as hardcore and driven; they just maybe weren't audio snobs.

Blair Jackson

October 23, 2020

BJ: My first show was March 20, 1970, at the Capitol Theatre in Port Chester. I was sixteen when I first saw [the Dead]. I'm originally from the suburbs of New York, Pelham. I was at Northwestern for a year and a half—just one academic year and one quarter, I guess, then I transferred to Tufts in Massachusetts for one semester, and then in the fall of '73 moved out to the Bay Area to go to UC Berkeley, and I've stayed here the rest of the time.

MAR: I see. Did you partly move because of the Dead or was it mostly for academic reasons, or a little bit of both?

BJ: It was more for California reasons than academic reasons, actually. But that summer before I transferred to Berkeley from Tufts, I did see the Garcia Band a couple of times at the Keystone Berkeley and Old & In the Way in Cotati, and that certainly had an impact on me.

Beginning in 1976, while I was finishing graduate school at UC Berkeley in journalism, I got involved with a magazine called *BAM*. We had a column called "Dead Ahead," which covered the Dead closely, written by David Gans, who became a good friend. Today, we live four doors from each other, as fate would have it. My first interviews with Garcia were done with David—actually, I was the one who got the interview and I invited David along, because he was so knowledgeable about the Dead, to do it. So we did a giant two-part interview with Garcia in '81 for *BAM*. Earlier, I had interviewed Mickey for what ended up being really the first major piece on Deadheads, for a 1980 *BAM* cover story.

So that's how I got into "the Dead scene," per se. I mean, I got to know Eileen Law, who was the band's link with the Deadheads, and she was super-helpful opening doors for me, all that stuff. My involvement with *BAM* is how I got my first book contract to write *The Music Never Stopped*, which came out in 1983, and that book is what led directly to my starting *The Golden Road* in 1984.

I never really liked [the New York–based Dead magazine] *Relix* particularly. They did some good stuff, too. I'm not going to totally drag on them, but I thought I could do better. I thought the Grateful Dead were kind of magical and mystical and strange and interesting and I didn't think that *Relix* really captured any of that. Some of it was sort of West Coast versus East Coast a little bit, and because through *BAM* I had sort of been in the scene, as it were, and knew folks in it, I thought I could do this. And then, just being the kind of person I am, and the researcher I am, I thought I could fill a magazine with all the stuff that interests me, and it turned out it interested other people too, so we kind of lucked out in that sense. I mean, it's not like it was a huge deal ever—I think the most copies we ever printed of one issue was around twelve thousand, which was smaller than *Relix*. It was more West Coast than East Coast, but we definitely had subscribers all over and even overseas. My wife, Regan, who did the magazine with me, she worked at the *San Francisco Chronicle* as copy editor, so she was good at that, and she and I both did the rather unsophisticated layouts. It was a labor of love done nights and weekends.

MAR: I think Stu told me that you guys used to have parties to put the addresses on your magazines before you sent them out. Is that correct?

BJ: Yes. Our famous stuffing parties. We'd get all the issues back from the printer, and we had the envelopes pre-stamped with postage and we'd get eight or ten of our friends together and put on the labels, stuff the issues. Then, the next day, a friend who had a pickup truck and I would take the boxes down to the main Oakland post office. We always sent them first class, which was cool. But we didn't really have a distribution network. Tower Records, which was national, carried it, so we always sold a couple of thousand through them. So we didn't really have a distribution network at all. We also had the Psychedelic Shop in San Francisco, and we had some friends who I had met through the Deadhead network who were in Geneseo, New York, at Sundance Books. So there were a couple of little spotty head-shop type places who would always get a bunch of copies. But mostly, it was just done by mail subscriptions. And it was just "send us your address."

MAR: In terms of the lifespan of the magazine, did the number of subscribers escalate during the time that you were running it?

BJ: Oh, yeah, it escalated, but it started out really small. Basically, when we started, we had some East Coast friends do some leafleting for us. These were people that I had met by mail after they had liked my book, *The Music Never Stopped*. They said, "Hey, I love your book." I said, "Hey, well, I'm putting out a magazine. Do you guys want to do some leafleting?" So I did one leaflet and had these guys give out a couple of thousand at Syracuse or wherever the hell they were going. And we had said, "Well, if we get enough subscriptions to pay for the first issue, we'll do it," and we did. And it kept growing from there. I don't know what the first issue was: a couple of thousand, three thousand, I don't know. And like I said, eventually it got up to ten or twelve or thirteen thousand, something. It was a word-of-mouth phenomenon, and it was really fun. It was quarterly at the beginning, then we went to three a year, just because it was too burdensome. And then when we had our first kid in 1990, we announced that we were going to stop regular publication at the end of 1991, or I guess issue 25, which came out in mid-1991 and was our so-called "last issue."

We never did that much touring; there were so many shows in California during the eighties, we were completely spoiled. We'd get shows at the beginning of the year at Kaiser or then later at the Oakland Coliseum, then there would be the Greek, Frost, Ventura, Cal Expo—it just went on and on. It was fantastic. It was easy to see twenty-five or thirty shows a year, just in California.

MAR: Yeah. I've been thinking about that a lot. In talking with Stu [Nixon] and Mike [Dolgushkin] and you and David [Gans], and all these people who have contributed quite immensely to the culture of the Grateful Dead and the history that a person like me can trace back really far, it seems like the supposed paradigm of being a Deadhead and traveling with the band and going on whole tours was almost not actually something that a lot of people did. I mean, maybe there were a lot of people that did, but people such as yourself actually stayed in California, because there were just as many shows that you could see there, and that was enough.

BJ: Yeah, there were definitely many thousands of people who did travel with the Grateful Dead, and it increased as the years went on. But it wasn't practical for Regan and me to go on tour for weeks at a time. We both had full-time jobs. And we took our vacations going to Europe and Hawaii and visiting our parents. But we went to plenty of shows. I didn't feel like I was under-showed.

MAR: Do you think that became more of a pronounced paradigm of sorts in the nineties—the push for the people to follow the band?

BJ: Oh yeah, definitely. It was starting during the eighties for sure; I mean, I know people who were doing it a little bit in the seventies, even, and then it kind of steadily increased all through the eighties. The whole thing about the professional Deadheads like us—and when I say "professional," I mean Deadheads who were professionals—it was a pretty new phenomenon in the eighties. People like us would stay in luxury hotels when we went to Red Rocks. As we got older and became more "successful," our lifestyle following the band reflected that. But there was also always an element of people that some later called the "Grateful Dead homeless," which were people who really had no place to live, and lived on buses and would camp out wherever the Dead were playing. So there they are trying to camp in a parking lot in the middle of downtown Hartford, so that's how you get all these problems around the Dead scene in the late eighties. But yeah, it's *always* been a mixed bag of people, which is part of what's so exciting and fun about it. We knew people in every one of those situations—from being semi-homeless and following the Grateful Dead to guys who were incredibly successful doctors and lawyers and all that kind of stuff.

MAR: I'm curious about Eileen Law and the way that she preserved a lot of Deadhead-focused material. Do you think that that was a mission she had made for herself from the outset based off of her involvement with the early days of the Deadhead newsletter and setting up that kind of loose framework for Deadheads?

BJ: Yeah, absolutely. She took on the mantle of being both the archivist of Grateful Dead stuff—so, clippings from newspapers and all of that—and she was also the liaison for the Deadheads. Not that she sat around and talked to Deadheads all day, although there were enough local Deadheads that were in with the band, so she would talk to them, and they were her friends, too. She made that her mission, and she is the reason that the entire UC Santa Cruz Grateful Dead Archive exists, because it's all the stuff she saved and kept pretty organized. She was something; to be working for a hippie band, and to be as organized as she was, was pretty amazing. And she was also, you might have heard, the "voice" of the Grateful Dead on the band's ticket hotline. You would hear there's a new hotline message, and you'd call it up and it would be Eileen saying, "On April 3 we're going to be in Portland, Maine. On April 5 in Boston. . . To get tickets, send in an index card and money order to. . ." All that clerical stuff that involved the Deadheads, was her doing. And she was just such a lovely, wonderful person. She's so nice, just the greatest person, and it was nice to have somebody like that in that position.

MAR: The main reason I wanted to talk to you was because there was this article in the *San Francisco Chronicle*, which I'm wondering if Regan had something to do with. It's from March 1, 1989, and it's profiling John Scott and *DeadBase*.

BJ: I don't think we had anything to do with that.

MAR: Something I didn't know before is that it mentions *The Golden Road* as an entity that helped finance the first *DeadBase*. So I was just curious if there was anything more to that, or if you could explain how that came about?

EILEEN LAW

The Dead's Link with the Heads

As many a Deadhead can testify, the Grateful Dead organization is very difficult to communicate with effectively. The fan in search of information or eager to get a message to the group encounters an interesting paradox: the band establishes an uncommonly close bond with its followers onstage, yet they are all but unapproachable once the final notes of "Day Job" have echoed through the hall and the show is over. There is that post office box in San Rafael, of course, and the Hot Line to disperse the vital facts about tours, but beyond that, most Deadheads have little idea of whether their letters are read, their ideas listened to, the sincerity of their devotion to the group appreciated.

To their credit, the Dead have tried to bridge the performer-audience gap in various ways through the years, and at the heart of that quest for better communication has been Eileen Law, who for the past 12 years has ostensibly been in charge of Dead Heads, the loose "fan club" the Dead formed following the release of the 1971 "Skull & Roses" album. In addition, for the past year, Eileen has been heavily involved in the Dead's song publishing company, Ice Nine Music, as well as worried endlessly about guest lists and keeping the Western U.S. Hotline up to date. (On the East Coast Monarch Entertainment handles the Hotline tapes.)

In the abstract, most Deadheads probably think of the Dead organization as a rambling hippie collective that stumbles from project to project with little planning and less efficiency. Nothing could be further from the truth. This isn't IBM with a punch-clock and a dress code, but neither is it an anarchic "do your own thing" setting. Eileen and the others in the Dead office work fairly normal business hours at fairly normal business tasks. There is a lot of drudgery and paperwork involved, and no, they don't hang out and rap with Jerry all day. (In fact, Garcia rarely appears at the office.)

Eileen's office, on the second floor of the San Rafael headquarters of the Dead (the location of which is not publicized for obvious reasons), is piled high with boxes containing correspondence from Deadheads, thick binders stuffed with 20 years of newspaper and magazine clippings about the Dead, computer printouts of the huge Deadhead mailing list (which currently contains about 90,000 names), the code-a-phones that ceaselessly spit out the Hotline information, and sundry items mailed to her from Deadheads all over the world. (On the day I formally interviewed her, one table in her office held a beautiful antique mirror that someone sent her to give to Garcia.) It looks like a lot to keep track of, and it is — as we sit down to chat in a porch adjoining manager Danny Rifkin's office, she laments that she's just getting to her 1983 letters from Europe, and that she has several boxes of domestic mail to answer. It's been four years since the last Dead Heads newsletter went out, and there are a lot of people out there who write wondering when they'll hear anything from the organization again.

"I really miss the newsletters," she says in her warm California accent of the mailings that went to Deadheads in the mid- and late '70s. "People really liked them and I loved sending them out. We're just getting our lists organized for

Eileen in her office with code-a-phones. Photo by Blair Jackson

Eileen Law interviewed by Blair Jackson in *The Golden Road* #4, Fall 1984 the computer, so maybe sometime soon we can get back to doing some regular mailings. Phil came in here last week and said, 'Since we're getting our computer thing together, we can put our 10,000 names on it!' Ten thousand?" she laughs. "That's how many we had in 1972! I said, 'Where have you been?!'

"I feel a little guilty about it because I think people assume that we do put something out on a regular basis. The last thing that went out was the Dead Art catalog, but that caused some problems because we couldn't send one to everyone so a lot of people thought they'd missed out on something. Plus, it was a little weird for the first thing to go out in a few years to be something asking people to spend money. We probably could have done something differently on that one."

The Dead also found that when they did the last newsletter mailout at a cost of nearly $18,000 they had more than 10,000 address changes. "If we mailed things more regularly," she comments, "we could keep up with everyone better."

I tell her that on that very morning someone supporting Walter Mondale asked me if I thought the Dead would let them use their list for a mailing. "That doesn't surprise me," she says. "We get a lot of that. Someone from the Gary Hart campaign called up and wondered if they could use names from New Jersey awhile back. But we don't let the list out. We've had friends ask us to use it because they're starting a business or something, but we don't even let them use it. I'm really against letting those names out because I respect the privacy of these people who have joined Dead Heads. They didn't join it to get mail from politicians."

That sort of integrity runs deep in the Dead organization and is unquestionably a by-product of the era in which the Dead scene was spawned. The group was wary of exploitation by profit mongers in the '60s, and today they carry their hip business ethic into every aspect of the operation that they can, maintaining a distance from the straight business world philosophically while attempting to use their business savvy to meet their own ends.

Eileen has been involved with the Dead on some level — personal or professional — since the group's beginnings. She grew up in Guerneville, a rustic old resort community on the Russian River a couple of hours north of San Francisco. "I've always loved music," she says. "I have a brother five years old than me, and he had what must have been one of the only stereos in town. He was also the type who would sit down and try to build a guitar. I used to play air guitar for *hours*, listening to Little Richard and Chuck Berry and all those others." Guerneville wasn't exactly a hotbed of activity in the late '50s and early '60s (though it was frequently visited by Hell's Angels), but Eileen kept up with both rock and folk trends and was an active partier.

"Like a lot of girls, I spent a lot of time dancing with the door frame in my bedroom," she says with a laugh, "but as I got older I'd go with friends to Rio Nido and hang out there at the dances. A lot of times they had a band called Dick Crest & His Orchestra — Phil actually took lessons from him or something — and we'd go there or just hang out in the parking lot outside. To move from that to San Francisco was like being at a continuous party."

She moved south into the City after graduating from high school in 1964, and took a secretarial job at AAA insurance, where her uncle worked. "On weekends we'd just party like crazy," she remembers. "This was before the Fillmore and the Avalon and all, so what my friends and I would do is store up the addresses of parties we heard about all week and

'I deal with a lot of people in the outside world and I find that we're really not so bad after all. They space out, too.'

then just crash them all. Eventually there was a garage party where I smelled something a bit odd, and that was my first joint. That experience sort of changed the type of people I wanted to hang out with. I was living with a family at the time, and I noticed I wanted my own place, my own phone.

"Then, all of a sudden, The Warlocks and the Jefferson Airplane and all these other groups started playing all these neat places like the Matrix and the Longshoremen's Hall, and the whole scene started to grow really fast. After a couple of years at AAA, it got very hard to stay interested in work, and my party life sort of took over."

Needless to say, this was happening to a lot of people in San Francisco, and Eileen found the community very supportive. "People really would help each other, and everyone seemed very open then. When the dances started happening, *everyone* danced. It was so easy to meet people. A band like Quicksilver or the Airplane might play a set, and then you'd see all the players out on the dance floor mingling with everyone else. Eventually, after meeting a lot of people, I started hanging out in the back area more. By the time Winterland got going, it seemed like everyone I knew was hanging out backstage."

Eileen got to know various members of the Dead scene, particularly Danny Rifkin, Pigpen's girlfriend, Veronica, and various members of the road crew. She got to know the band after they moved into Haight-Ashbury in the fall of 1966, and in 1969 she lived briefly at Mickey Hart's Marin ranch.

"I don't know *how many* people were living there," she says. "People were in every room and out in the barn. You had to have seniority to reach bedroom. I'd sleep in haystacks sometimes, with the horses and all these other animals."

Eventually, Mickey decided he wanted his ranch back and asked most of those living there to leave, so Eileen moved in with Bob Weir and his lady friend, Frankie, in a small house in the tiny West Marin town of Nicasio.

"That's where Cassidy was born," she says of her daughter, whose father was Rex Jackson, a Grateful Dead crew member until his death in a car crash in 1977. "Weir wrote the song at the house during that period. I lived in a tent behind Weir's and I'd go out there and practice my breathing exercises. I'd hear Weir playing these beautiful riffs in the house. Later I think he asked Hunter to write some words for the tune, and he was going to write something about a card game, and I said, 'No, no, that's not what that tune is about.' Around that time, John Barlow came out here on his motorcycle, and the next thing I knew, he and Weir had this song, which was about my daughter, Cassidy, and had parts about Neal Cassady, too." Ironically, Cassidy wasn't named after Cowboy Neal at all, but after the character in the popular film of that year, *Butch Cassidy & the Sundance Kid*. "I decided on it before Cassidy was even born because I thought it sounded good for either a boy or a girl. I don't think she's ever really liked the name, though."

Cassidy, who is now 14, began going to Dead shows from birth. "I took her as a newborn," Eileen says. "Like the other kids, she sometimes would sleep wrapped in blankets in equipment crates during the shows. Other times I'd hold her all night and then not be able to move my arms the next day."

Eileen first started working for the Dead in early 1972, shortly after the Dead Heads organization was formed. At that point, it was headed by Mary Ann Mayer and staffed by various women in the office who spent their time taking down the names of people who wrote in and sending off the first of what became a long series of entertaining and scintillating newsletters. These mailings, for those who have never seen one, contained tour information, little pieces on the band, their equipment, the organization, poetry, artwork and the now famous "Hypnocracy Papers," post-psychedelic doodles by Robert Hunter that teased readers with the improbable adventures of a Zen prankster named St. Dilbert. Garcia, too, was heavily involved with the newsletters, which continued for several years at unpredictable intervals. Eileen and Mary Ann were in charge of the newsletter for most of its existence, with Mary Ann also contributing some splendid art work.

Eileen was laid off by the Dead during the year they retired from performing to concentrate on solo projects and launch their ill-fated record label. "To be honest, I never understood why they let some of us go," she admits, "because it all seemed to be peaking then. The mail got really voluminous around the time of *Mars Hotel* and *Wake of the Flood*. I could understand why *the band* wanted time off, but we were swamped." She didn't have to go far to get a job, however — she started working at the nearby offices of the New Riders of the Purple Sage.

She came back to work for the Dead when they returned to performing in mid-1976, and has been a steady employee ever since. She has served in a number of different capacities, primarily as a link with the Deadheads and also on the publishing end of things.

"I find that aspect of my work very complicated," she says. "There's unfinished business that dates all the way back to the record company days, though we're getting caught up. We've even copyrighted the new songs finally. Now that we've got the computer [a Hewlett-Packard 9121] things will get even more efficient, though I'm not good at machines *at all*. Back when the band played in Egypt, there was this emergency where all their equipment was sent to Pakistan by mistake after the gigs and I was supposed to send messages over there on the Telex. I just couldn't work it and had to call up someone in the middle of the night to help me with it!"

Eileen says that between ten and 40 letters come to the band every day, with the mail ranging from inquiries about tour dates and merchandising information to personal letters for the band. "I make sure they get their mail," she says, "though I do look at most of it. Some people will write to Weir or somebody for tour information, so I intercept those. Then there are the ones like, 'Hey Jerry, I really want to jam with you sometime.' We get a lot of those. One guy sent us his whole life history, all his scrapbooks and everything; they arrived in these boxes one day. I got a letter a couple of days later saying, 'Hey, I'm sorry, but I flipped out and didn't mean to send all that stuff. Can I have it back?' People have sent backpacks and clothing through UPS thinking they want to travel light and that we'll hold it for them until they get to California. It gets pretty strange now and then, but most of them are real nice letters about the band or suggestions of places to play or not to play. The band gets those, and I know they try to read them."

Though the Dead office number is technically a secret, Eileen still gets a lot of calls from Deadheads in search of information. "It's funny," she says, "I can sometimes hear people taping the conversation on the other end. I guess they want to get it right for their friends." It's doubtful that there are many tapers who count the "Eileen Law, 12-18-83 Conversation Tape" among their collections, but there is no question that she is well respected and liked by Deadheads, most of whom have never met her. Deadheads regularly send her set lists, photos and memorabilia, all of which she keeps.

"I've collected some great stuff over the years, especially since the *Book of the Deadheads* came out. Lots of beautiful artwork has come in because of that. Someday I'd love to have a Grateful Dead museum," she says, sounding almost a little embarrassed at the revelation of her private ambition. "I don't know if I've ever even talked to a band member about it, but I think it would be a lot of fun to put some of this stuff on display in a place that would be open all year 'round for the Deadheads who come through town. I was really blown away by the big King Tut exhibit that came through San Francisco a few years ago. We had our own night there — with our own guest list and everything — and I was so impressed with how simple and beautiful it was. I thought, 'This is what I'd love to do with the Dead.'"

That dream is still a long way off, though. There are more immediate concerns on this late summer afternoon, like recording the Hotline tape that will give information about the fall East Coast tour. In the absence of regular newsletters, the Hotline has become the primary means of disseminating information. "These machines are running every second, 24 hours a day," she says of the code-a-phones. "I come in at the end of a weekend and the tapes are just covered with black soot from playing so much."

With the addition of a part-time worker to help her out, Eileen feels like she's close to finally catching up with her work. "I feel bad that I'm not quicker responding to people," she says, "but I try not to let it get me down. I deal with a lot of people in the outside world and I find that we're not really so bad after all. They space out, too. They don't follow through on things. We're getting better."

One example of the trend towards genuine organization has been the inception of regular meetings involving the band, roadies and office workers. "Frankly, I'd rather stay here and work because I've got so much to do, but the meetings have been a good way to get everyone together to talk about whatever needs to be talked about."

She says that the best part of her job is still Deadheads. "I really love Deadheads, and I only wish I could give them the attention I'd like to. That's the one thing I'm working on the most. They need to know that there really is someone here." □

BJ: Well, I was friends with Stu. Stu was somebody I met through other friends pretty early on, in the early eighties or maybe even late seventies. Stu and Robin. So I don't know, when they say we helped finance *DeadBase*, that's very kind of them, but I have no memory of how much we gave them. Or what we gave them. I can't imagine we gave them very much, because we didn't have money to be financing things. I'm sure we gave them advertising space for free in *The Golden Road*, which helped them a lot. We were supportive of them for sure, but I would not want to overstate it. Those guys really did it themselves.

It was amazing. I mean, *DeadBase* changed everything. The first time I was really conscious of what shows I had gone to was when *The [Official] Book of the Deadheads* came out, which had a sort of very rough list of shows in the back. It didn't have setlists or any of that kind of stuff, but it was the first time that I could sort of sit down and say, "Oh, yeah. I was at two shows in that run," and, "Oh, that's right, they played at the Fillmore East in September and I went to that show, and I went to *these* two shows at Manhattan Center in '71." I hadn't been keeping lists after 1970 and '71—I kept lists of the shows I went to [then], but after that, it never occurred to me. I never kept a setlist. I didn't even know that setlists were "a thing" until much, much later. So I was never in that headspace that I got into later—actually once I started *The Golden Road*—of saying, "Well, they played 'Scarlet-Fire' two nights ago in Long Beach, so they probably won't do it until the end of the run or when they get to the next city." *The Golden Road* is really what got me into setlists in a hardcore way.

And I was also not that into tapes until later. I had an OK tape collection, but nothing heavy. David Gans was the guy that really got me into collecting tapes, and then once I started *The Golden Road* it became a lot more obsessive, because I felt like I had to hear all the shows that happened to do the magazine. I had people on the East Coast who would call me up, friends of mine on tour who would call us up with the show report. The phone would ring, and we'd say, "It's the call!" And they'd say, "Oh, it was incredible! So are you sitting down? Set one, they opened with . . ." That was really fun because those guys were always high, of course; they're calling from the road from a phone booth. "Oh yeah, we're on the Massachusetts Turnpike going south to the show in Providence," or whatever.

MAR: So you were putting the setlists in *The Golden Road*, am I correct? And was there a reason why you decided to print that? Was that something that was lacking in other publications of the same time period?

BJ: I don't think *Relix* was doing setlists. In fact, I'm sure they weren't doing setlists.

MAR: I don't think they did. I think *Unbroken Chain* is probably the only other magazine I've seen setlists in.

BJ: In our first issue, I think we reprinted the complete setlists for 1983. Our first issue was Winter '84, so we had the complete setlists from '83, complete with errors from the person who did it for me—which would be true all the way to the end. All the way to the end, we'd get notes saying, "Oh, you forgot 'Minglewood' between 'Brown-Eyed Women' and 'Bird Song.'" It was always hard to get everything exactly perfect in that pre-internet era, but it was still cool. The first few years, maybe through '85, we didn't have reports on every show, and then we started doing that obsessively, too: either I would do them from tapes, or better yet was when we had somebody that I could count on who could do that show in Richmond or whatever, Miami, and try to find people who were actually at the shows. But otherwise, I would do them from tapes.

MAR: So you knew Stu at that point in time. Did you know that Stu was working with Mike . . . Or I guess that wouldn't be until '85 or '86, right, that they started working on *DeadBase* with John Scott? Did you ever discuss with Stu or did he ever say, "Hey, I'm working on this thing," or maybe express working on setlists with you? Or was that a totally other project?

BJ: They were their own thing. They certainly didn't rely on us for setlists! They were super well connected and had the archives. There were actually a bunch of people who were sort of working on *DeadBase*-type things at the same time, who were trying to just keep complete lists, and all that. So I think once their project became concrete, they sort of became the de facto clearinghouse for accurate information, or what was then accurate information. Like I said, Stu was definitely a friend, and we'd see him around. Mike Dolgushkin I did not know before this, but he became a friend. I got to know him through the Psychedelic Shop where he worked, and then he was also working on *DeadBase*, and he was a regular at our stuffing parties. It was the only place I'd see him, there and at shows.

MAR: In terms of tapes, you said you weren't really originally collecting, but it kind of grew on you. And I remember—this is years ago, but I know you posted a story about your tape collection on Dead.net.

BJ: Oh, that's right. I guess that was the blog I wrote about how I should probably get rid of my tapes now that everything was digital. My son now owns some of them, the rest are in boxes in my garage. Originally, I organized them by color for my tape walls, which were in the back room of my garage: like '65 to '70 had red, and then '70 to '75 was a dark blue, and then '76 until Brent joins the band was another color, and then the eighties were green, until—you know, whatever. A whole bunch of different color coding just as a way to keep them semi-organized. But I was not obsessive about keeping them organized within the colors, so they weren't *that* organized. I don't know. I'm pretty lazy basically, and it's hard for me to be too organized about anything.

Oct. 24, 1972

The Grateful Dead,
San Rafael, Calif 94901
Dear Dead and Family,

The Free Underground Grateful Dead Tape Exchange (FUGDTE) is interested in developing a business around the idea of making and/or distributing recordings of Dead Concerts.

As of this time FUGDTE is obtaining copies of concerts recorded from the audience by various Dead Freaks. Our collection spans from 1966 through the current concert series INCLUDING tapes from Europe.

Thru our efforts in obtaining tapes we have cemented solid ties with many people in numerous states. All these people agree with one feeling....there is a fantastic desire by people everywhere to own a tape of a concert.

There are serious collectors of Dead tapes everywhere. It is not unusual to find notices on bullitin boards or ads in newspapers like the Village Voice in New York placed by people seeking to further the scope of their collections.

As FUGDTE we have even gotten calls from people willing to trade pictures, bikes and even their sisters for concert tapes.

The potential is enormous, people want concert tapes. We get calls constantly asking us to sell copies of our tapes, but we are at the present refusing to .

We would like to know if you feel it is possible to work out some type of arrangement thru royalties or purchase, in which we can put our ideas to the test.

Greatfully yours,

Leslie D. Kippel
of FUGDTE

Les Kippel
November 19, 2020

LK: I'm not the first person in history to record the Grateful Dead. The first person was this guy that we would call "Legendary Marty," from the Bronx. He would take a Uher [reel-to-reel] machine to concerts and record the shows, and he would do a commentary while he was doing the shows: he would say, "Oh, they're going into that boring drum solo crap again, so I'm going to turn off the tape machine. That saves the battery." The first time I went to see the Grateful Dead, I believe, was February of 1970 at the Fillmore East, and my dear good friend, Steve Kraye, bought tickets for us. We were sitting in the upper balcony, and going down into the lobby during intermission, I bumped into about eighteen people that I knew from Pace College, which is now Pace University. And we were all laughing, out of our minds that no one knew that the other person was going to be there. They smuggled me into the eighteenth row, and here I am in the eighteenth row enjoying this stuff beyond compare. I started thinking, "My God, I have to be part of this. I mean, this stuff is absolutely amazing. How can I be involved in this?" I started thinking, "Well, after the show is over, how about I record the next show?" And I went to RadioShack and I bought a tape machine for $19.95. I used the microphone that came with it, and I brought it with me to the very next show. I was in, like, the eighteenth row, and I had a bunch of friends in the first row, and I said, "If I give them the tape machine in the first row, I should be able to get the best recording possible." So I gave them the tape machine and man, oh my God. What a great show. I couldn't believe I was getting this on tape. I was so thrilled. And then, during intermission, I got the tape machine back and I asked the guy where he put the microphone. "Oh, we put it on the seat." And all I heard was, "Hey man, pass the joint. Hey man, pass the wine." The music was horrendous. I realized that from that point on, I had to record the shows myself, and started to improve my quality. I think one show after that, I used this little microphone, and then Sony came out with this little cassette deck, and they'd use the ECM-99 microphones. I started to record shows like crazy. And it was just me. No one else taping, period, at that time. No matter what anyone else will tell you, that's bullshit and they're lying. The reason I know that is because of what I went through to make this shit happen—the fights that we had with the road crew until the band realized what was happening.

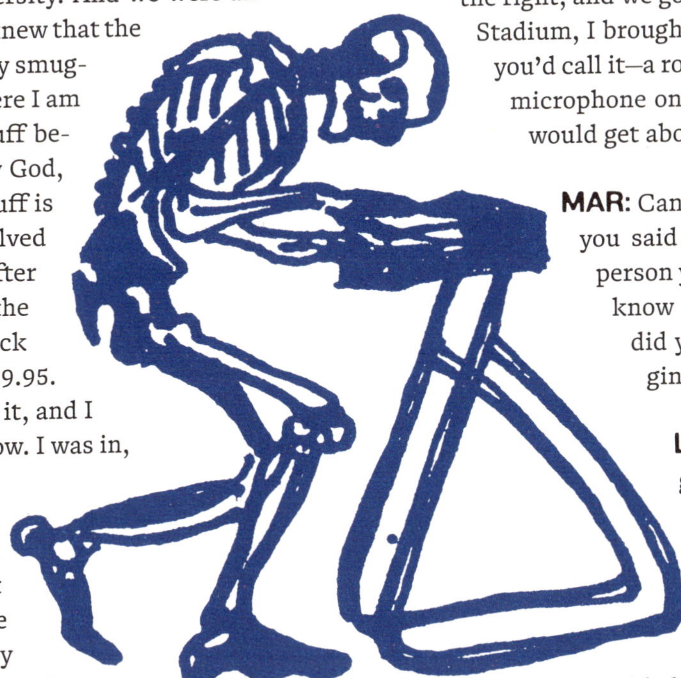

But anyway, to continue, we formed the First Free Underground Grateful Dead Tape Exchange. And even though I was the main person recording the shows, I had three friends of mine. That was the original tape exchange. That was the beginning. And it all was going along where I would be letting people copy my tapes. *Dead Relix* magazine actually came out of the tape-trading scene, because at one time I had twelve people in my house lined up with tape machines: "OK, ready? One, two, three, press record!" And at that point I said, there had to be a better way of doing this, and the better way turned out to be a magazine dedicated to tape trading, which was *Dead Relix*. So, at the Academy of Music shows, what we did, which is very interesting: We got three sets of tickets in the first row in the loge. And I was sitting in the middle with the tape machine, and we had thirty-foot cables. We took the microphones, and one person was sitting last seat all the way to the left, and one person was sitting last seat all the way to the right, and we got beautiful stereo tapes. Roosevelt Stadium, I brought a six-foot wooden dowel, I guess you'd call it—a round piece of wood—and I taped the microphone on top of the piece of wood so that I would get above all the noise.

MAR: Can I stop you? You'd mentioned that, you said that Marty was kind of the first person you knew that made a tape. Did you know Marty before you started taping or did you run into Marty as you were beginning to tape?

LK: Actually, Jerry Moore got together with me, because he was part of this group called Hell's Honkies, which developed after I started the first Underground Grateful Dead Tape Exchange. Since they were from the Bronx, what they decided to do was to find this Legendary Marty, because he was in the Bronx, and they found him. But at that time, I believe Jerry Moore had moved to Brooklyn—it might've been like eleven o'clock at night or something crazy like that, and we packed up our car with a reel-to-reel tape machine and went up and hung out with Legendary Marty for probably two, three hours in the middle of the night, copied a tape or two from him, and came home. So literally, I met him once. But if I had to call anyone, I hate to use the word "God"—Marty was, again, the Legendary Marty. He was the first person, bar none, to record a Grateful Dead show. And no matter what anyone might say, I was number two. I'm the guy who made it into a reality. Jerry Moore and the Hell's Honkies were always separate from *Relix*. Jerry was part of the Hell's Honkies, which—again—came after the first Grateful Dead Tape Exchange was created.

JERRY MOORE INTERVIEWED
BY DAVID GANS
1/19/2008

David Gans: You did start *Relix* with Les Kippel?

Jerry Moore: Oh, yeah. I could tell you the story if you really want to hear it. I have a good memory for words and these words are verbatim. A phone rang one day and it's Les--and I had known Les for about a year or two by this point. He says, "Hey, we've been doing this tape thing for a long time now, right?" I said, "Yeah." He said, "Well, it's time we made some money at it." I said, "Les, how are we going to do that? That's illegal." He said, "We're going to start a magazine." I said, "That sounds like fun." That's what happened with that. We did start a magazine, and I had fun, and Les made money. It's the truth.

David Gans: What was the content of *Relix* at that time, aside from tape trading, want ads, and stuff? What did you write?

Jerry Moore: Everything. The first year and a half or so, we didn't have anybody but me that could write, basically. If I didn't write something myself under a false name, I heavily rewrote what other people wrote, which is a bad thing to do. I mean, that's not how you edit things. I learned better, but it was a wonderful experience. I learned how to write. I met a lot of people for certain.

David Gans: It was entirely devoted to the Grateful Dead culture?

Jerry Moore: Basically. Yeah. Les wanted to make it *Disco Relix* at one point. I vetoed that one.

MAR: In regards to the original tapers' club, how are you deciding on the complete group of people, just out of curiosity? Did you guys cap it at some point where you're like, "That's it"?

LK: At a certain point, we didn't need business cards anymore. It just started getting out of hand. Too many freaking people doing it—when you go from twenty-four tape exchanges, to a tapers *section*.

MAR: When did you start getting trouble from the road crew, and can you remember any of those situations at all?

LK: It would have to be '70 to '71. I really don't know the specifics, but I'll tell you something. We had the best ways of getting equipment. This one guy, Barry Glassberg, he was so fucking smart. What he would do is, he would keep his tape machine and all of his equipment in a box and put postage stamps on it. He would walk into the concert and they would look at the box and he would say, "Oh, this is from work. I gotta mail this out. No, you can't open this up; I'll get fired." "Oh, OK, go ahead. Take it in." This is some of the stuff that we did, and it worked.

The first year to two years, through 1972, I don't know how many other people were recording. All I know is in 1972, that's where it started picking up, the 1972 shows. I think after Waterbury [the Palace Theater shows in September], maybe other people were starting to record. And that's when things started to take off. I would give people a tape and I would say, "Here's a tape. This is your beginning. Go out, get yourself a tape machine and record." And that's what they would do; they would go get themselves a tape machine, and all you need is one tape. They would get their tape and they would start going on from there.

LESLIE D. KIPPEL
951-6430
990-1100
NEIL (MUSKRAT) MILLER
252-2830
Dead Relics
Grateful Dead Tape Exchange
JIMMY — DAVE
FREE UNDERGROUND
Grateful Dead
(CONCERT)
TAPE EXCHANGE
501 COTTAGE STREET
PAWTUCKET, R. I. 02860
(401) 722-4546
724 0136
IN DENVER:
GLENN (303) 277-0850
IN DENVER:
REET (303) 759-9245
FREE UNDERGROUND
Grateful Dead
TAPE EXCHANGE
IN BROOKLYN:
LES (212) 951-6430
TECHNICAL ADVISOR:
CAL BROMFIELD
IN BROOKLYN:
LES (212) 951-6430
IN BROOKLYN:
ART (212) 253-7923
FREE UNDERGROUND
Grateful Dead
TAPE EXCHANGE
IN NORTH JERSEY:
JIM (201) 768-3264
IN SOUTH JERSEY:
HARRIS (609) 429-7060
JOHN MITCH JAIME
FREE UNDERGROUND
Grateful Dead
TAPE EXCHANGE
108 E. YATES ST.
ITHACA, N. Y. 14850
(607) 273-7619
GRATEFUL DEAD TAPE EXCHANGE
LIVE CONCERTS
HAVE TAPES, WILL TRADE
SANTA BARBARA, CA.
PHONE (805) 966-7648
BROOKLYN
LES 951-6430
BROOKLYN
FREE UNDERGROUND
Grateful Dead
TAPE EXCHANGE
QUEENS
QUEENS
FREE UNDERGROUND
New Riders
TAPE EXCHANGE
DENNIS 773-7556
FREE UNDERGROUND
GRATEFUL DEAD
TAPE EXCHANGE
PORTLAND, MAINE
NEIL (617) 682-8908
PAT (206) 866-0473
FREE UNDERGROUND
GRATEFUL DEAD
TAPE EXCHANGE
LES (212) 998-1100
DENNIS (207) 773-7556
(206) 322-5483
FREE
GRATEFUL DEAD
TAPE EXCHANGE
MATT WILLIAMS
620 MALDEN AVE. E. APT. 4
SEATTLE, WASHINGTON 98112
FREE UNDERGROUND
GRATEFUL DEAD
TAPE EXCHANGE
KENT, RANDY, SUE
austin, texas

Mr. 'Tapes' of Brooklyn: He Rules the Grateful Dead Tape Empire

BY CHARLEY ROSEN

BROOKLYN—Don't let anybody tell you differently, Brooklyn is the Grateful Dead center of the world. For one thing, Mickey Hart's grandparents live in Bayridge. Bill Kreutzman's niece goes to school on Coney Island. And on East 18th Street, cleverly disguised as a mild-mannered inspector for the New York City Housing Authority, lives the man Jerry Garcia calls "Mr. Tapes."

Les Kippel pointed to his collection. "Over 500 hours of Grateful Dead tapes," he beamed. "More than 100 concerts from early 1968 right up to Watkins Glen. The Dead by themselves, the Dead with the New Riders, with Duane Allman, with the Beach Boys, the Airplane—there's even a tape with Janis Joplin." Les closed his eyes for a beat. "Let's see . . . that one was from the Fillmore East, January 3rd, 1970.

"The first concert I personally recorded was on May 25th, 1971. I had a borrowed cassette machine and a 45¢ microphone—now I use a Sony TC1-10A and an Uhr mike. It's a real pain in the ass doing an audience tape. It takes a lot of preparation—you have to attach the mike to a long pole to get above the crowd noise. You also have to know the concert hall very well—in some places, for example, the best sound is in the first row balcony. You also need a partner to help with the equipment and a lot of dope to keep you mellow."

Les moved out of the apprentice class last year while he was waiting in a Ticketron line at Macy's. "There were some 200 people screaming to get tickets to see the Dead at Roosevelt Stadium," he said. "And three or four of them were screaming, 'We have tapes. We have tapes.' One of them was a cat named John Alberts—and we wound up exchanging collections. That brought me up to about 200 hours."

It wasn't until a Dead concert at Waterbury, Connecticut, last year that Les became a Grand Master. "John and I were hanging around the backstage area before the concert. We needed a super-good 'Box Of Rain' for our collection." So they made up a little gift in a small box and attached one of their cards. "We managed to get it to Bill Kreutzman. Ten minutes later he comes running outside with Phil Lesh, looking for us. . . . They gave us stage passes. We handed out over a hundred of our cards backstage, and the tapes really started coming in after that."

Approximately two-thirds of Les's tapes are audience tapes, the remainder being either radio-simulcasts or soundboard tapes which have been borrowed, copied and (sometimes) returned. There are also a couple of tapes from Warner Bros.—but Les never involves himself in the shadier aspects of tape procurement. "All I want to know," he said, "is how good the sound is and what concert it's from."

With Les as source, free Grateful Dead tape exchanges have been set up in Oregon, Arizona, Colorado, Florida, California, Maryland, Massachusetts . . . there have even been inquiries from Australia.

"A lot of people want to set up exchanges. I tell them to get cards made up with their telephone numbers on it, but I also insist it says 'free' on them. Then they come over here. If they can make me like them, I'll start them out with 15-20 hours of tape—they can trade their own way from there. If they're assholes, I'll charge them outrageous prices for a couple of tapes and tell them not to come back."

* * *

John Orlando got his tapes for nothing. He lives in Brooklyn, of course, and he is a member of one of the nine Dead tape exchanges which Les has spawned in New York City.

"Mr. Tapes is a bitch," John said. "He set up me and two of my friends with tapes, right? Man, I was doing wall-to-wall taping 18 hours a day, four machines going at the same time. I had to quit my job—it was very intense. I had to stay high all day or I'd go nuts. After a week, my chick comes over and says, 'John, is it me or the Dead?' 'Take a walk,' I says. I'm a Grateful Dead hermit—but I have an understanding with them, so it's cool. But Mr. Tapes, man, he can fuck your head good."

* * *

Back on 18th Street, Les talked about the future. "I'd like to go legit," he said. "Sam Cutler told me we can make some money working with the Dead. It seems that they have a lot of holes in their archives—somebody ripped off some tapes while they were in Oregon. There's certainly a demand for old stuff, and the Dead are cut loose from Warner Bros. now, so the next move is theirs."

Mick Stevens

Les Kippel, however, is the Tape Master only because the old one is in addled retirement. Somewhere, walking the streets of Flatbush, is a man known only as "The Legendary Marty." Clasped in his hand is a suitcase—full of Dead tapes, the best and the most exotic. The leaders are split and tangled, and there are no labels on the tiny five-inch reels, but the very thought of them is enough to give Les cardiac arrest.

"I haven't seen the Legendary Marty in over a year," said Les. "Nobody knows where he is. What I would love to do is close my eyes, stick my hand into the suitcase and record whatever I pull out. Who knows what goodies he has in there?"

As he talked, Les poured out three glasses of wine. He sipped at one and handed me another—the third he put on the table.

"What's that for?" I asked.

Les answered in a reverent tone, "It's for Marty. Just in case."

Rolling Stone #143, October 1973
Illustration: Mick Stevens

MAR: So then in 1973, this [*Rolling Stone*] article comes out, "Mr. Tapes of Brooklyn." How did that come about? I understand that you're one of a few people making tapes at that point, but was that just the curiosity of the audience from the magazine or the reporter?

LK: This reporter found me, or maybe it's *Rolling Stone* who was looking—I don't know. I don't remember, it's a long time ago. And, PS: I was working at the New York City Housing Authority when that article came out, and I don't know how long I existed after that at the New York City Housing Authority, but I would get more phone calls at work—there were five lines coming into the switchboard, and this one time all five phone calls were for me. It was time to pay full attention to the tape scene and to this little fledgling magazine, and my father and brother, they said to me, "Well, leave your options open." And one year later, I left the New York City Housing Authority.

MAR: When I was at the UCSC archive, I found some interesting documents, including a very long and in-depth proposal to mass produce and distribute Grateful Dead live shows with the band's blessing.

LK: I'm glad you found those documents, because there was maybe two or three sets of those made. I remember the first part of it was nicely typed, and then the second part—which I believe is all in my handwriting—were numbers of costs and potential earnings.

MAR: In these documents, in 1972, there's the letter from Jim Watson from New Jersey. Did you know Jim?

LK: Yeah, Jim is one of the founders of the tape exchange.

MAR: He must've sent a letter to Dead Freaks [the PO box advertised on the back of the *Skull and Roses* LP] after that newsletter popped up, I'm guessing, announcing the tape exchange. Did the crew members already kind of know about the tape exchange at that point, by October 15, 1972?

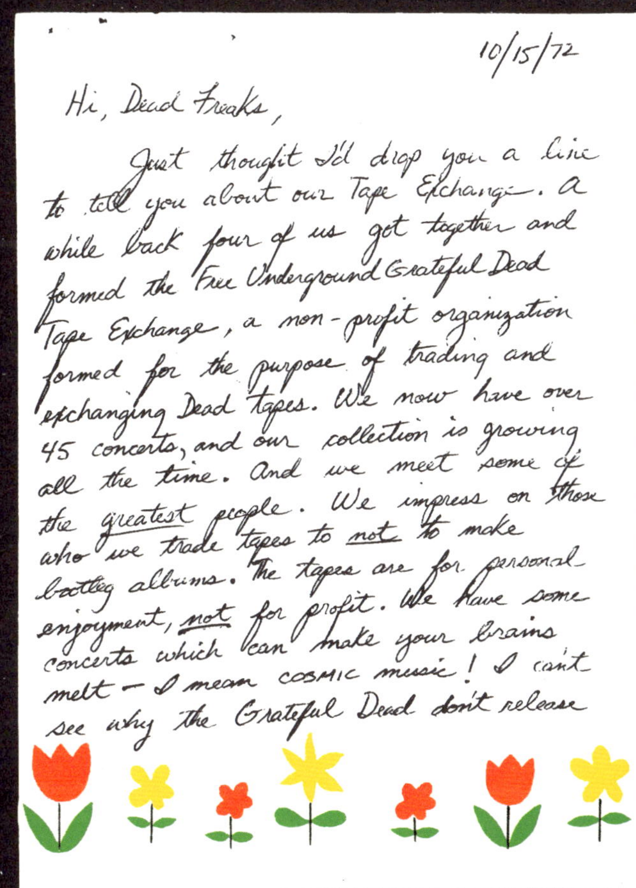

10/15/72

Hi, Dead Freaks,

Just thought I'd drop you a line to tell you about our Tape Exchange. A while back four of us got together and formed the Free Underground Grateful Dead Tape Exchange, a non-profit organization formed for the purpose of trading and exchanging Dead tapes. We now have over 45 concerts, and our collection is growing all the time. And we meet some of the greatest people. We impress on those who we trade tapes to not to make bootleg albums. The tapes are for personal enjoyment, not for profit. We have some concerts which can make your brains melt – I mean COSMIC music! I can't see why the Grateful Dead don't release

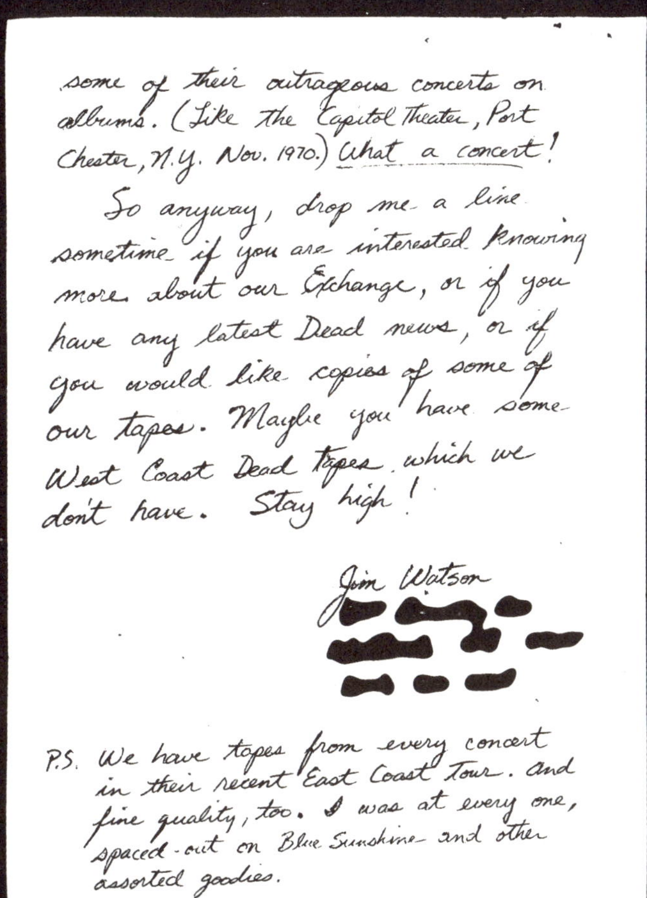

some of their outrageous concerts on albums. (Like the Capitol Theater, Port Chester, N.Y. Nov. 1970.) What a concert!

So anyway, drop me a line sometime if you are interested knowing more about our Exchange, or if you have any latest Dead news, or if you would like copies of some of our tapes. Maybe you have some West Coast Dead tapes which we don't have. Stay high!

Jim Watson

P.S. We have tapes from every concert in their recent East Coast Tour. And fine quality, too. I was at every one, spaced-out on Blue Sunshine and other assorted goodies.

LK: Oh, yeah. And by the way, just another little stupid piece of information: Grandma Tessel, Mickey Hart's grandmother who lived on Nostrand Avenue in Brooklyn, I used to go over to their house. We used to hang out, and Grandma and Grandpa Tessel—when I would tell them about the tapes and everything else like that—they were very, very supportive. When I told them that I was going to create this magazine, they pushed me and guided me. So I am quite sure that Mickey Hart might have been one of the first people to know about the magazine.

MAR: It seems like you were also writing the band to announce the exchange. But I have this document, and it's interesting because someone whose initials I can't make out is writing to Jon McIntire in November of '72, and they said, "I believe we need to work out a policy on [the tapers]. Should we A) stop, B) license, C) tactically tolerate them, or what?" So within the stack of documents, there's that kind of memo, I guess.

LK: That's exactly the point that I was talking about before, where the decision is out there: What do we do with these people? So that's probably where, as I said, it went from the crew to the band.

note Date →
Pre-
Relix May.

April 25, 1973

Mickey Hart

Dear Mickey,

I am writing to you out of the insistance of your grandparents to explain an idea that I have been working on that they feel you might want to help make a reality and be part of.

One night, while at their apartment, they were going to call you and have me speak to you. I felt that it would be improper for me to impose on you in such a manner, and I suggested that it might be better if I wrote to you .

I am part of the "Free Underground Grateful Dead Tape Exchange" and we have a large collection of tapes of the Dead that we use for trading. A lot of our material is of extremely good quality.

Recently the pressure on us to increase our output of copies of tapes has been tremendous. People are always calling asking for tapes.

On the current East Coast Dead tour, Jerry Garcia and Ron Racouw expressed interest in arranging some type of a deal with us concerning tapes.

On April 12, 1973 I sent letters to John McIntyre, Jerry Garcia and Ron Racouw requesting an appointment to discuss mass production and distribution of Dead Tapes. The letters were sent per the instructions of Jerry Garcia during a talk we were having in Buffalo, N.Y.

I would like to know if you feel you can help us in making the exchange an official means of distribution of Dead Tapes, and whether or not you would like to be part of it.

Sincerely yours,
Leslie D. Kippel
Leslie D. Kippel

P.S. I have a nice copy of the Pavillion concert in Queens if you'd like it!!

MAR: I'm curious if you can recollect any kind of bit of what that initial conversation was like. Did you approach [the band] and you're like, "I have these tapes"?

LK: Yeah, probably I approached them. If they were approaching me, it would have been more of a legal thing. I think the crew were trying to protect themselves, and trying to protect the band, until a consensus opinion was made. I think that [the band] embraced it—because you can't stop it, so you control it. How do you control it? You have a taping section. Grateful Dead concerts was a family, a family tradition. Every show was a Thanksgiving dinner: you would meet people who you haven't seen in six months; you'd meet your girlfriend there; you would get married there; you'd bring your children there. You just embrace. And the taping scene was something that was part of the scene—embrace it. It was absolutely 100 percent the right thing to do. You and I would not be talking if it wasn't for what happened in 1971 and '72 and '73. We wouldn't be here today. We're now family. I would be surprised if anyone else you speak to talked negative about the taping scene; I will tell you, it was a lot of fun, meeting new people, creating new brothers and sisters.

In '73, when the magazine became a thought in my mind, it took nine months to pull it together and create the first issue. There were so many people who just loved the concept: remember, it was *Dead Relix*, the tapers magazine, the first issue dedicated to the trickiest tape collector of all time, the president of the United States, Tricky Dicky. And people came together: I had a person in a high school who was teaching printing, and he printed the first few issues of *Relix* magazine. I had a person who got postage from where he worked. People would come to edit and put it together for free. This was the vibe—it was a brotherhood.

MAR: I guess the question that came up while I was looking at these documents is, I know that Eileen Law was making the Dead Head newsletters, I think, starting in 1972. Were you in contact with her at all?

LK: I spoke to her, wrote to her, and I think the Dead Head newsletter might've actually been semi-competition for our concept of *Dead Relix*—cost them a lot of money to put out their newsletters, cost them a lot of money.

MAR: So on June 27, 1973, you're explaining expenses as well as "professional bootleggers," which was a dumb term. But—for the sake of this conversation—you mentioned these bootleggers selling your own concert tapes.

Free Underground
Tape Exchange

June 27, 1973

Dear Ron,

I was glad to receive your letter, but sad to read what it said. Perhaps I could outline some of our ideas and maybe you can use the ideas to formulate a use for our fine organization.

Tape manufacture and distribution....We have monies and labor. Using the Infonics system 200 we could produce 15,000 C-90 cassettes a day with distribution through mail. The cost would be so low its amazing. Perhaps a corporation owned bt the Dead and the Exchange, or totally owned by the Dead who would salary us to produce and mail tapes.

Maybe we could work on a one tape deal to see if it would work??

Sales of limited produced records or tapes called "Concert Records"or "Concert Tapes" to be sold outside of concerts. The aim of this would be to eliminate the sale of poor quality bootlegs that are sold at every Dead concert I have ever seen.

Perhaps using a past concert by the same location; for example, make a record of a previous Roosevelt Stadium concert to be sold at a future Roosevelt Stadium concert. We could use a Dead soundboard tape or one of our great quality tapes.

This method would totally eliminate the sale of poor quality bootlegs, which I am sure you would consider important.

Make the Tape Exchange an official branch of the "Dead Heads" which would be controlled and funded by the parent organization.

This method would help increase the reach of the exchange and help to spread the music to more people then it now does. Also, this would help us now by reducing the financial burden we are experiencing in running the Exchange.

continued.......

Perhaps keeping the Exchange as a free organization, but affiliating it with Dead Heads and funding it so that it can continue in operation as it now is.

My purpose in all this is to keep the Exchange going, to keep the costs from burying the Exchange, and to eliminate the possibility of bootlegging of our tapes. Our Waterbury tape was finally bootlegged in Conn. It is our first tape to be bootlegged, and it wasn't even us (I don't know which gets me more, the fact that it was bootlegged, or the fact that we didn't do it ourselves!)

Something should be done so that we can make or change the Exchange to meet the demands of the people in a good manner. People want us to use our tapes to bootleg, to wipe out the proffessional shit bootleggers who are now operating (especially in New York). I myself, as well as many other people in the Exchange want a nice legal way of doing this. Isn't there some way that we can work on this? Isn't there some way we can either keep the Exchange going or change it into something bigger and better???

I would even come to California to discuss this further if it might help.

Sincerely yours,

Leslie D. Kippel

P.S. Any possibility to obtain passes (3or 4) for the Watkins Glenn and Roosevlet Stadium Concerts??

LK: People would take the concert tapes and make vinyl. *Relix* actually had to go after a few people, because they were using our artwork and we always were worried that the Grateful Dead would think it was us. They took the *Box of Rain* artwork off the cover of *Relix* magazine and they put it onto a vinyl, and that pissed the fuck out of us.

MAR: How major of a problem was that, the phenomenon of a bootlegger that was more commercial? Was that in opposition with what you were trying to do with the exchange, or was it just an annoyance?

LK: No, it's not an annoyance. You were not supposed to be making profits on trading of tapes, and if someone is going to steal the tape and put it out on vinyl, that's wrong. That's not what you're supposed to be doing, and that's not the nature of the game. So if someone is ripping off—and it's weird because I guess as strange as it sounds, if you make the tape, do you own a copyright in the creation? Even though you don't own music, do you own a piece of the creation? It's always an interesting thought in itself. And in the Disney realm of things, I've had conversations with legal people about that—because Disney owns Mickey Mouse, but if you take Mickey Mouse fucking Minnie Mouse, do they own the copyright to the creation of that design?

[We and the band], as I said, did have conversations. We tried. They didn't want to do business. I mean, maybe their lawyers turned to them and said, "You can't sue them. They're not making money out of it." And that's reality: Damages. You're suing someone because they did something wrong to you. OK, right. How much did they financially hurt you? "Well, I can't figure that out." "All right. You're right. Do you want a penny?" And this is what happened with the Grateful Dead. You can't sue [the tapers] because they're not hurting you. You're not losing anything. If anything, they're making you more famous. Proposals were made. They never responded, but [they said], "Go ahead: Here's the tapers section, enjoy yourselves." That's it.

MAR: I see. That business plan in the archives—I think it's eighty pages long, which I think is amazing, how thorough it is. I was wondering if you can remember any part of doing this extensive research about how to build the organization between two business entities, one being what you're calling *Dead Relix* and the other being the "Connoisseur's Club" of tape collectors [with whom the band would share recordings from the vaults for a small fee]?

LK: I remember creating it. I remember handwriting the numbers—either I typed it all out or my mother typed it all out. It was just something that was created, an attempt to move it into a business format. The business format ended up being *Dead Relix* magazine, which is still alive as *Relix* magazine, with distribution of a hundred thousand, and three or four venues and festivals.

TABLE OF CONTENTS

Page

NEWSLETTER

We would like to try to issue a monthly newsletter to the Connoisseur Club Members.

The Newsletter will be programmed for a three month cycle. The first month the newsletter will go out with current information, concert happenings, offerings for posters or other items, and a selection list from which members can choose what concerts they would like to see offered in the coming months. There will also be allowances made for suggestions by the Members.

The second month we will tabulate the results and pick the concerts that the Membership would like. We will then arrange to secure copies of that concert for distribution. The newsletter, the second month, will include more news and a summary of how the tabulation is going.

The third month the offer for tapes and the prices will go out to the Membership via the Newsletter. The members can order their tapes which will be produced and bulk-mailed in the third month of the first quarter, and first month of the second quarter.

If we find that in the second month we do not have enough information to fill a newsletter we can either eliminate it or just out a small postcard with a message stating that we are tabulating the results of the first Newsletter and we will let them know the results soon.

The current Newsletter that I am sending out is being put together by volunteer help. These same people have expressed the desire to work for the Dead Relics to make it a reality sans pay.

DEAD RELICS
Grateful Dead Tape Exchange

Dear Friend,

I have just returned from a trip to California. While there I had meetings with representatives of The Dead and Dead Records.

We decided that the proposed Club would be operated by mail only and would not be advertised. The membership list would be comprised of club members and friends who send us thier names. We will not use any other mailing list.

One problem that we discussed was the availability of tapes to the Club. It seems that the Dead had an air-tight contract with Warner Brothers that gave Warner Brothers complete ownership of all rights to all music that the Dead performed between Mid-67 and 1973. Some type of arrangement has to be worked out with Warner Brothers for these tapes. If it isimpossible for the Dead and the Club to work out an agreement, we will not be able to listen to soundboard copies of concerts from that period. Luckily, The Acid Tests are before the Warner Brothers contract.

I would like to know what concerts you would like to obtain tapes of; either specific concerts, or periods. Please send me your preferences as well as any additional names and addresses of friends interested in belonging to the Connoisseurs Club of Dead Relics.

In Addition, I might be able to obtain posters of early Dead concerts. Would you like to see these posters offered to the membership?

Gratefully,
Les
Les Kippel

MAR: Along those lines, in these papers, you do mention in the proposal that there would be a newsletter. I'm curious if at that point, was *Relix*—or what you called *Dead Relix*—did that begin at that point, or were you already thinking of that before? This proposal is March 1974, and I think you started *Dead Relix* in September.

LK: As I said to you, we started promoting it in 1973. I do have an original flyer. The flyers were handed out in concerts all over the United States, and the first issue—even though it is dated, I believe November or December—the first issue was actually created in September of '74. So [when] we were telling them in March that there would be a newsletter, that was already in the works.

MAR: I'm also wondering, because you also propose distribution to radio stations, do you think that informed the Grateful Dead organization at all? Or do you think that was just kind of something that everyone was interested in in general?

LK: That's one of the things that I was personally interested in, was getting tapes to radio stations, which also would have been helpful in promoting the entire taping thing. Now, Jerry Moore and I used to go up to WQIV in New York—which doesn't exist anymore—and I believe it was every Saturday night, eleven o'clock or midnight, and we would go up there and we would bring our Tandberg tape machine, our seven-inch reels, and we would play a concert. We would play music. One time, we were doing the New Riders [of the Purple Sage] and the Grateful Dead, and all of a sudden, we get a phone call in the studio. It was John Dawson, from the New Riders. He says, "Hey man, we're coming back into town and we find this radio station, and oh my God, it's us. We had to call you up and thank you." You've gotta love it.

MAR: There is a mention in the documents that states that Warner Bros. have a contract over all the Dead's live music. I'm wondering if you remember that being the nail in the coffin for the Connoisseur's Club not being able to go any further?

LK: It probably was Warner Bros. that stopped it. Because the Grateful Dead did have a deal with Warner Bros., and Warner Bros. probably felt that [the Connoisseur's Club] would hurt vinyl sales. And gosh, we're in 2020, and for the first time in fifty years, vinyl sales have outsold CDs. I guess tapes are going to hurt your sales Warner Bros., but I don't know . . .

MAR: What were your feelings when the official tapers section happened in 1984?

LK: I honestly don't know. I don't know the actual dates because, honestly, between you, me, and the brick wall, when I started the magazine, the whole concept was this would be my method to assist tapers to get out there and start trading tapes. Now, I don't know if you've seen any of the early issues of *Relix*, [but if] anyone subscribed, they got a free ad. If you wanted to do an ad to trade tapes, it was free. If you were in jail, and you wanted an ad to meet people, it was free. The whole concept was a magical formatted word, "free." We always tried, as much as we could, to keep things free, just to keep it moving.

MAR: I was going to ask about when Dick's Picks came out. Were you ever consulted? Or when they came out, were you like, "Hey, this seems familiar from like twenty years ago"?

LK: It's funny. Dick used to live in Hawaii; he used to be a farmer in Hawaii. And we used to trade, and he would send us some of his product, and in exchange we would send him tapes. And he used what he did with *Relix* [writing and trading with it] to get his ass out to San Francisco and meet the Grateful Dead. No, Dick was a very fine person. He was there at the beginning, and he had a goal to be the vault keeper, and he got there. This is a man who lived his dream. I was tickled pink with the stuff that he did. We all were.

MAR: It seems like you weren't bummed that this big business plan didn't work out. Am I correct in assuming that?

LK: No, I wasn't bummed that anything didn't work out because you know what, it did work. As I said, *Relix* is thriving. And it all started with a Tandy RadioShack tape machine and cheap cassettes at the Fillmore East. And look at where it is today. It started out with thirty dollars' worth of tape and a bunch of hippies, and now it's this monster publication. The first issue of *Relix* magazine? I think we printed 200 or 250, and it just went up from there. But if you go back fifty years and ask me . . . who was it? The president of the United States, the guy who was an actor. What was his name?

MAR: Ronald Reagan?

LK: Yeah. I remember one thing he said. It was during the Iran-Contra [hearings], and they asked him a question, and he said, "If you are going to ask me what I ate for breakfast on November 16"—whatever year it was—"I'd have to say to you, 'I don't remember, because it was so long ago.'" And that's it. How much of this stuff can you remember?

In terms of setting up the corporate structure of Dead Relics we have considered the possibilites of incorporating in as many ways aspossible.

Below are the Block Diagrams of the different possibilities with an explanation afterwards:

(A)

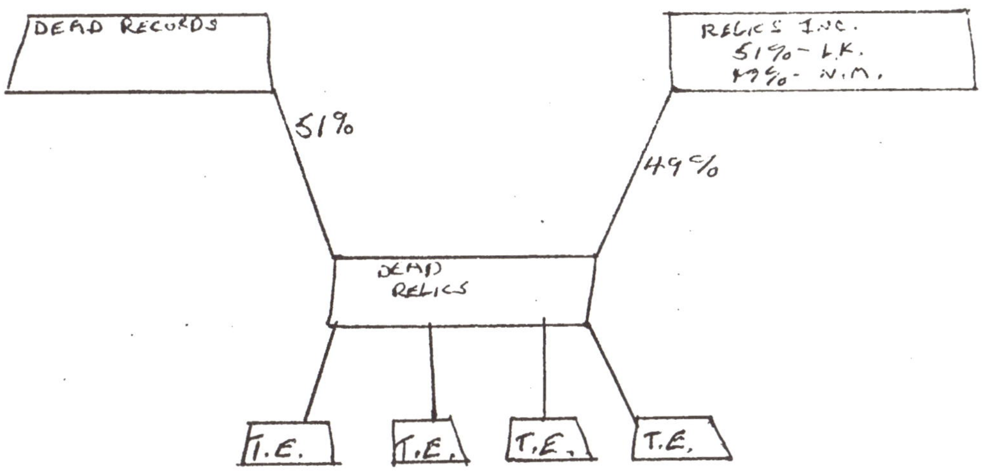

This first idea is to split ownership of Dead Relics between Dead Records and a Corporation called Relics Inc. In turn Dead Relics will maintain Tape Exchanges in every state for distribution. Each Tape Exchange would have to be incorporated.

We feel that this idea , even though it might be workable, will be too costly. To incorporate 50 tape exchanges might cost upwards of 30 to 40 thousand dollars.

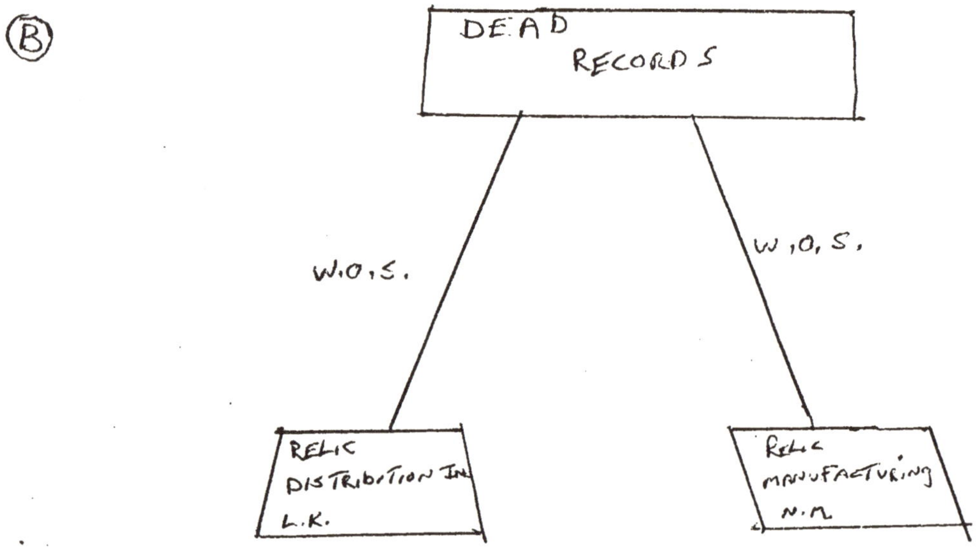

In this corporate structure Dead Records will Wholly Own Subsidiaries that will Distribute, and Manufacture. The individuals in charge of the Subsidiaries will be covered by Management Contracts running the life of the Subsidiaries.

In this structure the Dead Record Company will pay all expenses involved in set up and other costs. For a tax loss set up this would be the best because the Dead Record Company would be using all their own cash.

(C)

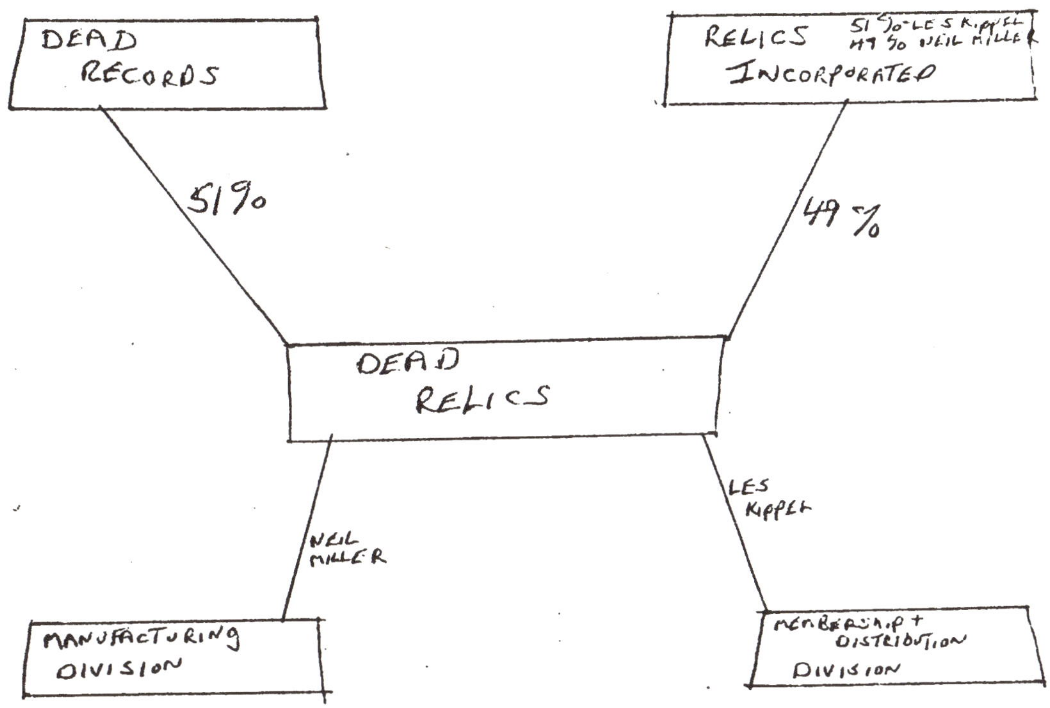

This Corporate structure would involve splitting the ownership between Dead Records and Relics Incorporated, which would be 51% owned by Dead Reocords and 49% by Relics Incorporated.

Relics Incorporated will be owned by Neil Miller and Les Kippel. 51% by Les Kippel and 49% by Neil Miller.

We will derive no income from Dead Relics through Relics Inc. Dead Relics will be divided into two Divisions, Manufacturing to be controlled by Neil Miller, and Membership and Distribution to be controlled by Les Kippel.

Monies for Dead Relics will come from Dead Records (51%), and Relics Inc. (49%).

This structure will permit Dead Records to control Dead Relics while still giving working control to Relics Inc.

Relics Incorporated will still be free for other entiprises such as posters of Dead concerts, photes, and other cooector items.

Steve Brown

December 28, 2020

SB: I'd been with a band out of San Francisco, Haight-Ashbury, that I managed [called Friendly Stranger]—we were doing California Hall and all the places, and playing with the local bands at the time. So I got to run into the Warlocks when they were playing, and got to know them. So I had a familiar connection in that regard, having liked the band, and been a big Deadhead fan early on—as a matter of fact, I think I got called a "proto-Deadhead" way back when. Then, later on, I was the head buyer for a chain of record stores and our own wholesale outlet, the guys that I worked with at Warner Brothers, gave me the information that there was in fact some talk by the Dead that they were going to be looking at doing their own record company. In fact, I went and found out also that Ron Rakow had put together a proposal [the So What Distribution Company, to distribute records via the Dead organization's own means]. So I thought, "Well, what the hell? It would be fun to work for them with their own record company," being a big, big fan, and having been outside of the gigs with them getting high and stuff, I knew these guys. It seemed to me that I would propose a similar kind of thing. It was a kind of thing that I put together with my experience—having been in radio and having a band and being in the record business and all that. It was pretty close to everything that they might want as far as experience. So I took that up to the building up in San Rafael, and dropped it off, and crossed my fingers to see what would happen. Towards the end of '72, I had a callback from Rakow saying, "You've got an appointment. Come on up." Went up there, and went into the conference room. It was Rakow and Garcia, just the only two people on this huge table right there in their conference room. Then, at some point, Rakow had to go out to do something or other, and he left me with Jerry. I'm a native San Franciscan, and Jerry also had all these stories about where he lived in the city and stuff, so the whole damn thing, as far as business, dissolved into being guys that grew up in San Francisco . . . it just turned into a whole different kind of a procedure of finding out who I was, and him getting a sense of who I could be for them, I guess. We left the room and Jerry got Rakow from another room and said, "He's hired." That's how that started, and then from there it was a matter of putting together all the pieces for making a record company.

MAR: Were the So What papers available then, or that was just something that came afterward?

SB: They weren't available. Just the concept was available of what they were talking about. I didn't have the details that he had written it as such. Not till later in life did I know about that, when I actually was working with them. Yeah.

Steve Brown manning the "Free Stuf" booth made by Alton Kelley and Stanley Mouse, U.C. Santa Barbara, 5/20/73

MAR: So you were probably familiar with the taping going on. Did you have tapes of live shows or anything like that? Were you aware of the bootlegging of concerts and that sort of phenomena popping up?

SB: Of people recording the concerts? Yes. As a matter of fact, I was one of them. I had been using—courtesy of the US Navy and our tax dollars—a German tape recorder, which was a portable, battery-operated tape recorder with five-inch reels only. I'd gone up to San Francisco, to Winterland, and recorded Cream at Winterland. Then I was told by somebody that the Dead were going to do a pre-concert on Haight Street the next day—this was, like, March 3, 1968. Took what was left of the battery power and tape on my recorder and got up close to the stage and recorded the band doing a live concert on Haight Street. Turned out it was the only recording ever made that day. That was my introduction to being a taper of the Grateful Dead, from that point on. Actually, what was interesting is I then took it down to the radio station where I was moonlighting and doing a midnight show, and played it back that night. It was almost like a delayed live broadcast.

MAR: Did you continue taping after that?

SB: No. I just had done that one for fun. Everybody else was doing the taping later on—because really, there weren't that many people. This was, again, a reel-to-reel recorder. Not a lot of people had portable reel-to-reel recorders that they'd go out with in 1968, and really up to the seventies. Whoever was doing it illegally were getting them into the concerts. Matter of fact, because I was a head buyer for a record retail chain, I found stores that were selling bootleg albums from recordings being done in the concerts in the late sixties, early seventies. This one company called Trade Mark of Quality, with a pig on [the label]—they were releasing full LP albums of live concerts all the time. That was kind of interesting, because this is even before the whole taper thing started. Somebody was going in and getting them into these stores. There was a store on Geary Street in San Francisco that featured bootleg albums.

MAR: Were you tape trading in the early seventies?

SB: Oh, yeah. There was tape trading going on when the whole cassette thing started happening and people were able to start doing more of that. That's what kicked it in. Because reel-to-reels were one thing, but with cassettes, everybody could make copies.

MAR: And were you participating in that then, actively trading tapes, or that was just something that was happening at the time?

SB: Well, when I was working for the band, I didn't need to, because I was recording the stuff in the studio onto cassettes, so I could give Jerry a copy when he would leave every night, or every day, whichever our recording was. It was really unnecessary because I would get two copies, one for me and then one for them. That was studio stuff—then the stuff that was out in the concert scene, I had friends that were getting all of that, and they would give me copies; oh my God, I got huge amounts of copies. People would send them to me at the office sometimes and stuff too. It got to be more than I could even deal with, at a certain point in time, to listen back to them all. Because I was at the concerts, for one thing.

MAR: I'm curious, going back to the initial interview with Rakow and Garcia: Did they ever mention at that time, or early on when you were starting to forge ahead with Grateful Dead Records, about live concert recordings and what to do with their archive of recordings or anything like that?

SB: Well, the only thing I remember was [band financial manager] David Parker. After the meeting, I guess it was Alan Trist who was mentioning that it was an issue with the copyrights and such. I remember hearing talk about that. I think David Parker and his wife, Bonnie, were also concerned about [what might happen] if this stuff started going out. I heard some talk about that. It didn't come up when I went in just to apply for the job, but afterwards I started hearing about it.

MAR: Can I get a little more context about who David Parker was and what he did?

SB: Yeah. He was an old friend; he played with Jerry back in the days when they played bluegrass down at the [Top of the] Tangent, down in Palo Alto. Then he and his wife, Bonnie, became part of the scene for the Grateful Dead and were the bookkeepers for them early on. Bonnie stayed on, doing that for a long time. I think they were concerned about the money issues that had to do with what the band was getting and what they were having to spend, and stuff like that. So I think he was a little more grounded than a lot of the other people that were in that scene at the time. It sounded like when that idea again came up for the [So What] papers and such, he was more concerned than others at the time.

MAR: I see. Do you feel like that memo, signed by "D.P.," that I found in the archive and sent to you, might be just more erring on the side of caution?

SB: Yes, because this is just when taping was starting to happen. I mean, that's what I figure—they didn't have a lot of people bringing in reel-to-reel recorders at the time. And the cassette thing didn't happen till a little bit after.

MAR: I mean, I know it's probably hard to recollect any specificity about the discussions after you were hired, but could you maybe try and recollect what the general feeling was around that taping stuff developing?

SB: One of the things I remember everybody was getting problems with was the fact that people were complaining about the tapers becoming kind of pushy and getting in the way of people after concerts and such. Then by later on, they actually had, I remember, a meeting where they had to decide what they were going to do about this, and they wound up getting a section going.

MAR: So that meeting you're talking about is the '84 meeting to establish the tapers section?

SB: Yeah, because I was working with [filmmaker] Len Dell'Amico around that time. That's why I knew about it—we were working on the videos at that time. Yeah, it was making a decision on no taping or allowing the fact that when people did tape, they shared them with other people. But the bootleg albums that were coming out before sort of disappeared after that too.

MAR: In terms of them realizing that the distribution of the live tapes was somehow a happy accident in terms of developing a wider audience, was that discussed in the seventies?

SB: That was going into the eighties, where they decided that, I think. It was kind of off and on: "Yes," "no," "allowed here," "not allowed there." It seemed off and on deciding what the hell to do during the seventies, then we took a [hiatus] in '75, and the [*Grateful Dead Movie*] took up a lot of our consciousness as far as not being concerned about the taping thing.

MAR: Did you ever get the impression that maybe the band didn't really care either way and it was more so the personnel surrounding the band that was trying to make a decision about the taping?

SB: Yeah. There were different attitudes about it. Obviously, Garcia was pretty much laissez-faire, and he didn't seem to consider it really a bad thing. I think Phil had an issue with it at one point. I remember hearing him complain about it in some fashion. This was in the seventies.

MAR: Can you recollect any of the specificity of Phil's griping, or do you know anything to that effect?

SB: Yeah, I'm trying to think; I don't want to be wrong here, but... I mean, I'm seventy-six years old. There's not as many of those cells left in the back storage of my brain here. Let me think. I think Phil's thing, also, was the behavior factor that really made it an issue for him, and not even so much on the people capitalizing on it. It was just the attitude of some of the tapers. I wish I could give you a line of what he might've said. Phil was the only one I can think of that had something [negative to say]. It had to do with the whole copyright thing.

MAR: What about the business plan by Les Kippel of *Relix* fame, the eighty-page document describing what recording equipment they would use, how they would have a Connoisseur's Club for tapers—distribute, gather clientele, etc.? I'm wondering if that was a conversation amongst you or amongst Ron Rakow, Jon McIntire, Alan Trist, and how that's kind of laying the groundwork for what happened in the nineties, when Dick's Picks started.

SB: Yeah, I think I have the introduction to the proposal letter, and then I took that initially and showed it to Rakow. That was something that seemed a little out of balance at that moment in time, anyway, for what we would consider doing. But [Les Kippel] went on with getting all these tapes and getting them out to people, I remember. But just being a native San Franciscan or a West Coast person, [the proposal] just sounded like a pushy East Coast guy, you know, who wanted to make something more important than we needed to consider at the moment. Luckily, it evolved into a good thing.

MAR: So in general, could you maybe generalize that most of your colleagues, at this point, probably thought the same of Les's kind of vibe with this proposal?

SB: Yeah, I would say that. I think, even Hal Kant, our lawyer, was concerned about that.

MAR: Can you recollect Hal's position on the proposal? What would be the pitfall of it that would make him opposed to the idea?

SB: That it would be illegal, first of all, I guess, in the lawyer sense—because [the tapers] don't have rights to [the recordings], if they were in fact selling it. But I think there was a small amount of people, out in those parking lots or whatever, actually trying to sell tapes at one time or another. The majority was all the sharing of these great concerts that turned out to be a bonus to building a bigger fan base. I think people as smart as Hal Kant realized that, too. Later on, and even to this day, stuff that comes up on their merchandising and stuff has all these different live concert [recordings]—whether they were from Bob [Matthews] and Betty [Cantor-Jackson, of the Betty Boards] or whether they were from Dan Healy or whoever provided them at the time, or Owsley [Stanley, engineer and chemist], if you go way back. We had them on tapes, and then they got transferred and stuff. I made the whole original archive list. It goes from '69 all the way through '75, I think, is what I finished off with at the time. I did all their archive listing.

MAR: You actually had access to the tape archive of live recordings?

SB: Yeah. I was the first one to actually write it all down. I had a person help me as I read them off, and we wrote them all down. There's pages and pages and pages. We just needed to know what we had. And Jerry said, "Go in there and get them all, so we know what we have at this point in time."

MAR: Was Willy Legate working then?

SB: Yeah, Willy Legate was there. He came in also, I think, at another time. I don't know if he finished up on it after '75 himself; the ones I wrote down were from '69 to '75.

MAR: So, to recap the sequence of events: The initial Grateful Dead newsletter brought about people like Les Kippel and other tapers, who then wrote to Dead Freaks and told them that they had tapes. But then that turned into the conversation and business proposition of Kippel to the organization—which was then obviously not negated, but there was only mild interest at the time for something like that, sort of a curiosity about what he had to pitch, but it didn't come to pass. And then the record company was made?

SB: Yeah. I guess he was just a little too early on for this whole thing to gel the way he wanted it to. By the time everything else started rolling, [the proposed business] was already under water because of all the regular tapers that were doing it for themselves already.

MAR: If there was a problem with the tapers, it was really about their pushiness and attitude and them taking up space. So could we logically assume then that Parish and Kidd acted on their own accord [in trying to stop the tapers], or were they pressured by someone higher up within the Dead organization to actually act upon these tapers that were making a ruckus?

SB: Well, Jon [McIntire] was involved with the talk at the band meetings and such, but I wasn't in the band meetings, per se. I heard responses after, oftentimes, and attitudes going into it. It seemed like the band had to get "yes" or "no" out of this whole situation.

MAR: I see. So really, it fell on Jon McIntire in terms of making a decision to enact certain protocols via the roadies and maybe Dan Healy?

SB: Right.

SBD AUD FM DAT GEN
P.O. BOX No. 2151
Baltimore, MD 21203-2151

Michael P. Cohen

March 14, 2021

MAR: How did you come into contact with the Grateful Dead universe? What was the catalyst that brought you to create your first J-card set?

MPC: I got into the Grateful Dead back in the early eighties and then saw my first show in Worcester, MA, on October 21, 1983, a phenomenal show with a memorable "Scarlet Begonias/Fire on the Mountain" to open the second set. Back in those days, none of my friends were interested in the band, and it was tougher to connect with like-minded people. One friend told me of his older brother who was into the band for a while and made his way selling tape covers at concerts. I didn't think much of it at the time but the idea must have stuck. About six years later, when I got out of school and wanted to go on tour to see the band play, the thought came back. I worked with a friend to design the first set and we considered it a joint venture.

MAR: What kind of technology if any were you using to create the designs/graphics, or was this traditional drafting into early computer tooling?

MPC: At the time we were not using computers for the work; it was a standard art-board photography process. We used graphic-design aids to add grayscale halftones that gave people the impression we used a computer, but they were all done by hand. We chose a heavy cardstock and a two-color print scheme. Distributing them as a single sheet helped offset the cost of the cardstock and inks, while allowing people to interact with it a little more by cutting them out and folding them themselves. They were very well received on the summer tour of 1989. After a year or so my friend and I went different ways, and I kept producing more covers and selling them to retailers and individuals and on tour. As I sold more to music shops and other places around the country, I developed the "Smoking Gun Tape Covers" name to use in advertising and business.

MAR: Where does the name Smoking Gun come from? Was it a Nixon/Watergate reference?

MPC: Yeah, it's a reference to the famous smoking-gun tapes, but there's no deeper meaning beyond the wordplay.

MAR: Were your tape covers specifically made for the Grateful Dead community, or for other audio cassette subcultures as well?

MPC: I've always approached tape covers as a unique art form with its own particular sensibilities. Initially they were designed for the Dead, and we used elements from their lyrics for inspiration. The band's music is so full of colorful imagery, it's a treasure trove of ideas to play with. Because you asked, the only person I recall regularly trading tape covers with was Marbleized Mike, whose covers are on some of my favorite shows.

MAR: Do you have any reaction or comment on how large a distribution your tape covers became? Every GD tape collection I come in contact with usually has at least one Smoking Gun cover, which to me means the distribution of the tape covers became quite substantial.

MPC: I'm proud of the impact my covers had within the trading scene; it helped that I distributed them in retail outlets and shops around the country. They were the only tape covers that were a product, not a craft.

MAR: When did you decide to stop making covers?

MPC: When Jerry passed away, it really seemed like a turning point, and the tape card business dropped off. I never needed to purchase any more stock, since demand fell. In a few more years things started moving online, people were getting into mp3s and then it was like "What's a tape?" The only people using tapes were tapers, and they were never interested in tape covers, because of the volume and overhead. I made DAT tape covers for a while, but for that reason they had a limited appeal. It really was the end of an era. Tapes and the tape-trading culture was a unique part of the Grateful Dead experience, but at its best was barely enough to sustain a business.

Dennis McNally

March 18, 2021

MAR: Do you recall any conversation you had specifically with [lawyer] Hal Kant about the litigious aspects of allowing tapers to tape? Along the lines of whether it was legally possible at that point in time—in respect to the law—to record an artist?

DM: This is me putting words in Hal's mouth, so I really wouldn't listen to me. That's the artist's right. That's the artist's decision, and God knows, the only people that really cared about that stuff at that time were the record companies because they felt it threatened their sales. Our sales were not overwhelming, and in that era, you know, the practice was that you recorded an album, and you went out and you performed it to sell it. And since we never ever repeated a show, the strictures about recording just didn't apply to us. The people who recorded and collected tapes collected the albums too, because they felt obligated. So it just wasn't an issue.

MAR: To put a nail in the coffin on that line of questioning, did you have to defend the band in a litigious way to the record companies in a way that allowed you guys to kind of open that up?

DM: In a litigious way? No, you think Arista was going to sue us because we allowed taping? At any rate, no, they didn't, they pissed and moaned and had to give in. And on that level, that was a decision the band made and the record company just—they had no leverage. Were they going to remove us from the label because we allowed taping? Clive Davis had been at Columbia, had been unceremoniously dumped there because of internal politics, and resurfaced at Arista. And fairly early on in his Arista experience, the Grateful Dead signed with him because they knew him, and knowing a person in the world of the Grateful Dead, having some kind of personal feeling for whoever it is [you're] doing business with, it was very important. So they knew him and he made a play for them when they finally folded Grateful Dead Records and sort of started over. And he was there, and he was eager and they went, "Fine." And then, you have to understand, we have the band meeting in which it's officially decided that taping is going to be sort of consciously permitted, and we started selling the tapers tickets. Undoubtedly at some point the record company called management and said, "How could you do this?" And they said, again, "It's not going to hurt you."

But the point is they did that, they made that decision in 1984. They had not recorded a studio album in three years, four years. And they wouldn't for another three years. So what was the leverage there? Obviously they decided that if they made a big fuss about it, we'd just go somewhere else. And Clive Davis, for reasons—not just about sales, because until *In the Dark*, we never sold big for them—but for reasons of history and ego and legend, Clive clearly wanted to keep the Grateful Dead on the list. So they were not in a position to give us a hard time. They probably moaned, and then went, "What can we do?" If I were the manager, I would have said, "Listen, in addition to the fact that it won't hurt you, in order to prevent taping, we would have to do things that would ruin our live show. That would damage our relationship with our audience. And I don't think you want us to do that, do you?" And they probably [would have gone], "Probably not."

And then Hal laid waste to Ticketmaster [over their refusal to allot the Dead 50 percent of tickets for their shows]. He was brilliant that day; it was one of his really good days. He really just started asking the guy questions and eventually the guy said, "Why are you asking me all of these questions?" And Hal replied, "I want to see how you're going to do on the stand when I cross-examine you." The point was, "Our relationships with these venues long precede yours, so you can't argue that we're interfering with your relationships—you're interfering with our relationships." That was Hal. And I'm sure if [Arista] called Hal, they got an equal, "This is the band's decision. It's not a matter of contract; it's not in our contract that we can't permit taping." If there were legal requirements, then he took care of them after the band made that decision.

EXCERPT FROM BAND MEETING RECORDING
11/30/1984

Speaker 1: OK, I guess we'll start just by going down through the minutes of the last meeting. The Bear situation, is that clear to everyone?

Speaker 2: Not to me.

Speaker 1: I don't . . . Has [he] been paid full payment on this amount?

Speaker 4: Yes.

Speaker 2: Well, I was under the impression that me as well as Scully were to sign releases after we finally went for this--

Speaker 3: We own the logo, so he can't sell us the logo. We own it already, and so we sort of like kicked it around and--

Speaker 9: We basically said it's a gift.

Speaker 1: Yeah. I understand that.

Speaker 3: OK. Which means that we were even willing to pay the taxes on it, if it came to that.

Speaker 1: We have to.

Speaker 3: That doesn't mean we have to keep giving him a gift every time he asks for one.

Speaker 1: No. Bonnie says he wouldn't have signed--

Speaker 3: OK, well, that was the understanding that I believe we had around the table, that he would sign a release.

Speaker 1: I think that was really foolish, to give a check out, to make payment without--

Speaker 8: I think originally . . . We do own the logo. We have it somewhere on paperwork. I'm not, yeah.

Speaker 3: We better own that fucking logo.

Speaker 2: The logo is trademarked in our names. You're talking about the skull and--

Speaker 8: --As far as that goes.

Speaker 2: I've got to go back to an earlier point because--not just for this meeting, but for all future meetings. I think we're recording this meeting. We also have minutes of meetings. And the minutes of your last meeting indicates that you're handling this transaction in a particular fashion. And I would say that if you had these minutes and an IRS agent looking at them, there might be very, very substantial problems.

Speaker 1: We'd have to pay the taxes.

Speaker 2: You might have much more substantial problems. Then you'd pay the piper.

Speaker 1: Yeah.

Speaker 3: Why are we recording meetings anyway?

Speaker 1: In fact, are you suggesting that our proposal here is in fact approaching, let's say, "not acceptable business practice"?

Speaker 2: Let's be very clear, then. If you're making a loan to somebody, knowing that it's going to become a bad loan in the first place--

Speaker 3: Just pull it.

Speaker 6: OK.

[Audio cassette recording cuts]

MINUTES OF THE MEETING 30 NOVEMBER 1984

Present: H. Kant, P. Lesh, RamRcd, J. Soto, H. Popick, J. Thomas, S. Gottlieb, D. Healy, B. Parker, MJo Meinolf, S. Stephens, S. Marcus, M. Nelson, E. Law, P. Harris, D. Rifkin, Kidd, B. Kreutzmann, J. Cutler, S. Parish, R. Taylor, B. Williams, M. Hart, D. McNalley, W. Legate, C. Brightman, B. Mydland, J. Garcia

Absent: P. Roehlk, B. Weir, A. Flowers, B. Hunter.

Meeting was called to order at 2:49 p.m. by D. Healy.

BEAR has received $30k; he has not been cooperative in preparation of necessary documentation. There is some difficulty in how this disbursement is to be declared. Bear has been unable to obtain resident status; Hal pointed out that the law as to tax residence is different than legal residence. There is some question as to whether the Australian $70k income tax exemption would apply to Bear; if Bear were to sign a release in exchange for payment, the transaction would be considered income. Minutes of the last meeting are revised as follows: GDP will be responsible for any tax liability if, after attempting all possible options, it is determined that taxes are due.

ROCK received six months severence pay; he is responsible for the taxes on this income.

FRONT: An offer of $450k will be made next week; the transaction would involve a trade, but the owner will find suitable property. (Our lease expires end of April 85) There was some discussion re obtaining a different piece of property in lieu of Front (e.g., in Ignacio) but Front Street is so centrally located and the cost of constructing a new shell of the same size would be considerably more than our offer. If we are looking for studio space, perhaps it's best if it is separate from our warehouse. Phil montioned that we proceed with the offer for Front, and that the real estate committee pursue other alternatives and bring to the attention of the table. None opposed.

RECORDING OF MINUTES: Hal advised against the recording of minutes for legal reasons. It will be up to the chairman to assure that an accurate vote count is obtained on all decisions.

PENSION PLAN has been set up; a few details remain. This is a highly tax-advantaged corporate investment. Trust representative, Dave Dominic, will explain entire plan at future date TBA and then consult with individuals re their options. Basically, a certain amount of money will be deposited annually into this profit or retirement trust fund; each employee's share is relative to salary amount. These funds accumulate tax free and are payable to employees at age 55; even if withdrawn early, funds are taxed over a five or six year period separately and not counting other income. B. Kreutzmann asked to see a copy of the documents.

ON ACCOUNTS: P. Lesh proposed that on-accounts be wiped out and that we start over again. Brief discussion followed re possibility and advantage of forming a credit union. Hal pointed out--in view of both new and stricter enforcement of tax laws, the IRS would be extremely likely to scrutinize o/a's in the $70k and above bracket. We are audited annually. Bonnie stated that for the past 15 years, there have been no problems regarding IRS; and that all proper documentation and adjustments were made and declared. Hal stated that IRS is cracking down on enforcement of witholding regulations on what is or may be considered compensation; at which point does an o/a become compensation--from IRS's view point; GDP could be liable for interest and penalties if IRS decides that proper withholding was not made. Amounts of $1k-$3K aren't a problem, but the larger bracket definitely could be. Laws have also changed with reference to liability of signator, accountant, or tax preparer. Hal reports calls from accountants and IRS questioning this situation. Bonnie cited the instance of R. Pimintel responding on the basis of misinformation; he thought o/a's totaled $600k rather than the correct figure of $240k. Per Hal, most accountants are not versed in the intracacies of tax law; tax attorneys, or attorneys doing considerable tax work or tax accountants (e.g., Laventhol, et al) are most qualified. Danny said that we hire professionals to advise us re potential problem situations, and should heed their advice. Hal feels that a current list of all o/a's should be distributed monthly. Hal, Bonnie, Fred Wolinsky, Phil and Bill K. will meet for further discussion on this subject....

NEXT MEETING: Thursday 13 December; D. Healy will chair.

B & K ANALYZER: D. Healy feels that $50k-$70k budget is a realistic figure for the completion of customized phases two and three of J. Meyer proposal (purchase of analyzer completing phase one). Dan will present final picture of the plan at our next meeting.

RECORDING STUDIO: We have a second hold on Fantasy Studios for January and February. P. Lesh and B. Kreutzmann stated that they would rather not record at that time. Let's see what happens with Arista....

REHEARSAL is scheduled beginning Sat 15 Dec through Sat 22 Dec, times TBA. Set up is Fri 14 Dec. J. Cutler will schedule some pre-production work with Guido Sarducci one day during this period.

NEW YEAR'S EVE: The Bobs and The Brass Band have been confirmed as opening acts. Danny is still hopeful that the VIDEO will happen, though at this point is not optimistic since the total production budget of approx. $15k has not been raised. About 50 RADIO STATIONS in 26 states will carry our broadcast (including an Alaska station which can be heard in Siberia).

MERCHANDISING/VIDEO TAPES: Per D. Rifkin, J. Garcia feels that we should consider the possibility of merchandising our own video cassettes not re our New Year's show, but as part of our 20th year celebration. Kidd is collecting ideas anyone may have re artwork/merchandising for our 20th year.

TAPERS SECTION was a success at BCT; this section will become a permanent part of our concerts until we decide otherwise. At SF Civic the tapers section will be located in the balcony opposite the stage. Per S. Marcus, we are restricting tapers to one deck per person and "for personal use only."

SPRING BENEFIT will be held at BCT March 9-10, 12-13, ending one week before departure for Spring 85 tour. D. Healy feels that he may want to drape the ceiling and the back wall; we'll get a cost estimate.

SAW IT

AUDIENCE · SOUNDBOARD · RADIO

This book is dedicated to Sarah, Ume, Mr. Fantasy (RIP), and Jerry J. Stone.

ACKNOWLEDGMENTS

First and foremost, a colossal and galaxial thank you to the Grateful Dead, the Family, and to Deadheads and Dead Freaks everywhere.

A very sincere and mega thank you to David Jacob Kramer for introducing me to Anthology Editions.

A major thank you to the Anthology crew—what a great team to work with! Thank you to Jesse Pollock for continuing to pursue this project over six years of discussions, brick walls, potential pitfalls, successful contacts, and surprise wins. Many thanks to Andres Santo Domingo and Keith Abrahamsson for believing in the potential for this book and keeping the door open through the years. Bailey Elder, thank you for hunkering down for a weekend in the frosty New Mexico cold to create the art direction blueprint with me, and thank you to Mark Iosifescu for having the patience and enthusiasm to work with the hefty amount of data and information I was trying to load into this text. Thank you to Bryan Cipolla for putting in the crazy amount of work needed to make the design really stand out, and thank you all for having the patience to walk along with me as I wavered back and forth between realistic and unrealistic requests, fantasies, and expectations while trying to bring a nascent book with no precursor into the world.

Thank you to Mark Pinkus and Bernie Cahill for opening the gates for the little guy.

I am so thankful for the Grateful Dead Archive at the University of California, Santa Cruz, and send the utmost respect and gratitude to Eileen Law for saving all of the documents that ended up there, which proved so useful in anchoring my research and interviews. Thank you to Alix Norton and Luisa Haddad for being there during a student strike right before the 2020 lockdown to provide me with the material that made a substantial part of this book possible.

Thank you to all of my interviewees: Dave Lemieux, David Gans, Ken Hays, Ed Perlstein, Dennis McNally, Stu Nixon, Mike Dolgushkin, Francine Accardi-Peri, Steven Marcus, Alan Trist, John W. Scott, John Ammons, Blair Jackson, Les Kippel, Steve Brown, and Michael P. Cohen. Thank you all for setting aside a lot of time to consider my questions and to entertain my funny thought processes. A very special thanks to Dennis M. for being there for the most nitpicky questioning, and a big appreciation to David G. and Stu N. for being so generous with their wealth of information and documentation.

Thank you to Jeff McLane for making the tape racks consistently look good, and thank you to Gillian Garcia for taking the time with loving care to document the multifaceted process of this sculptural endeavor.

Thank you to my tour and tape-trading roots: Micah Pollock, Bill Cromie, Abe Cater, and the elusive Bad Larry.

Thank you to Matt Siegle for helping to bring about the crystalline spark that brought the initial artistic concept of this project to the surface during our conversations as closeted Heads in the art world, back when being a Deadhead wasn't that cool.

Thank you to Trixie Garcia for accepting my project through her curiosity and interest, and reaching out to help with guidance along the path to the revelation that the tape racks could exist as fine art. I am extremely thankful to her for the time she took to write such kind words for the foreword to this book!

So much thanks to the tape mules who have aided and abetted in some comical and astounding logistics: Eric Heineman, Kathryn Carr, Chris Lamas, Cindy Holloway, Cass McCombs, Darryl Norsen, Dave Keady (who also moonlighted as legal counsel), and the United States Postal Service. Thank you to the tape collectors who were always inquisitive and supportive of the project: Grinchie, David Endris, Tom Stack, Bryan, Donald Rumsfeld, Florida Jon, Bill from SF, Rick Young, Bill Marshall, Sherri Longyear, Paul Bailey, Chris Larson, Mark Piersante via Ed Jurgen, John Salazar Jr., Patrick Pataky, Dick Driscoll, Larry Lawson, Matthew Vidmar, Bill Early, Mitch, Eric Axelrod, Pat Conroy, Thomas Behrendt, Kirsten Jensen, Marc Zappa, Eric Kaiser, Sherri Cobaugh, Bob Trudeau, Rich from Reseda, Anthony Katsaris, Bob Hunt, Michelle Terman, Jonathan Harris, Nick Santora, Ruby Fitch, Mike Axlerod, Ian Kennedy, Steve Gould, Daniel Greenberg, Jim Siteman, Liz Weil, Michael Johann, Bob DeLorme, Jon Huck, Keith Turner, Scott St. Germain, Michael Zipkin, Joe Nattress, Marc Bernicker, Jason Malone, Thomas "Bo" Fritts, Ross Hannan via Michael Fell, Jeff Hoyt, Eric Cassady, Scott Davenport, Richard Bell, Drew Davis, Ian Scott, Grady, Michael Phillips, Barry Barnes, Paul Vercoe c/o Christopher Hunt, Matthew Freedman, Alex Reppen, Mark Schecter, Weston B. Loucks, Tadd Miller, Gregg Knapp, George Sturiale, Ferguson Tapes from Speck's Records, Michael Oreskovich, Christopher Hull via Kristin Flock, Robert Nyberg, James Brickman, Janet Simonowicz, Scott Schillo, Jimmy Kaprow, Brian Caraway, Ryan Bradie, John Renken, John Sipple, Pitterger, Eric J. Hastert, John Sendelbach, Colleen Carroll, Dennis M. Farias, Ryan Gunther, Chad Jenkins, Brad Darr, Taylor Van Zile, Laurel, David Hirt, Elizabeth Elliott, Maria Nucci, Matt Siegle, Chris via Blake, St. Mary, Rhyne Elliot Cannon, David Skye, Timothy Buller, James Adams, Rob via Casey Block, Mike Wood, and last but not least Stuart Krimko, who also moonlighted as a brilliant writer capable of describing my very detailed artistic process in such eloquent and profound words.

Thank you to the art collectors and enthusiasts whose support and interest have sustained this project thus far: David Kordansky, Alex Blavatnick, Beth DeWoody, John Mayer, Nicholas Pritzker Jr., Mark Dowley, Eric Greenspan, and Dave and Carol Aronowitz.

Thank you to all those who provided assistance with sculptural fabrication and finalization: James Anderson, Ahrum Hong, Chloe Maratta, Corynne Pless, Josh Culberson, and Shay Myerson.

Thank you to Stephon Lew, Diane Lew, and Jesus Castro at Solutions—without you, my tape decks would all be dead, and then what?

Thank you to *DeadBase*, Setlists.net, and Deadlists.com for always being there to set the metadata and chronology straight.

Finally, a thank you is also due to all of the consultants and connectors with whom it was always a joy to discuss possibilities, and whose contacts were vital for the life of this book project: Elizabeth Cline, Tom Stack, Jason Scheuner, Steven Baker, Ricky Swallow, Paul Soto, and David Serrins.

PHOTOGRAPHY AND ARTWORK
Collection of Mark A. Rodriguez

ADDITIONAL MATERIALS
Audio: 167, 185, 267–274 (interview by Michael Nash, photos © Philip Gould)
BAM: 242 (© 1980 *BAM* magazine, used by permission)
Steve Brown Collection: 302
Toni Brown, former publisher, *Relix* magazine: 181, 194, 262
Michael P. Cohen: 306 (© 2022 Michael P. Cohen)
Johnny Dwork, editor, *Dupree's Diamond News*: 192, 197–198, 231
David Gans: 170, 181, 184 middle and bottom, 223, 256–257
Gillian Garcia: viii, ix
Burt Glinn / Magnum Photos: xiv
The Grateful Dead Archive at the UCSC Special Collections and Archives: 169, 173–175, 177–178, 184 top, 186, 206–207 (letter by Ed Perlstein), 212, 214–216, 218–221, 224, 235, 245, 284 (letter by Les Kippel), 289 (letter by Jim Watson), 290 (letter by Les Kippel), 292–293 (letter by Les Kippel), 295–297 (letter by Les Kippel), 299–301 (letter by Les Kippel), 308, 310–311
Katie Harvey: 211
Ken Hays: 202–203, 205
Blair Jackson: 184 bottom, 223 (photo by David Gans), 280–282
Stephen Kaltenbach: xv, xvi
Les Kippel: 193 (© 1989 *Relix* magazine), 199 (© 1988 *Relix* magazine), 286 ("Breakfast in Bed with the Dead" © 1980 Relix International, Inc.)
Steven Marcus: 255
Jeff McLane: vi, xi, xii
Susana Millman Photography: 182–183, 197, 201, 249
Bob Minkin: iv, 3 (© Bob Minkin)
Rolling Stone / Charley Rosen: 288 (illustration by Mick Stevens)
San Francisco Chronicle / UPI: 260
John W. Scott, Stu Nixon, Mike Dolgushkin: 208, 228–229, 233, 237, 240–241 (© 2022 John W. Scott, Mike Dolgushkin, and Stu Nixon)
David Serrins: 226
Laura Smith: 187–189 (illustration by Una Toibin-Hamilton), 190 (photo by Eric Soble), 222, 263